THE AGE OF WARS

OF RELIGION,

1000-1650

THE AGE OF WARS

OF RELIGION,

1000-1650

AN ENCYCLOPEDIA OF
GLOBAL WARFARE AND CIVILIZATION

Volume 2, L–Z

Cathal J. Nolan

Greenwood Encyclopedias of
Modern World Wars

GREENWOOD PRESS
Westport, Connecticut • London

Library of Congress Cataloging-in-Publication Data

Nolan, Cathal J.
    The age of wars of religion, 1000–1650 : an encyclopedia of global warfare and
civilization / Cathal J. Nolan.
        p.   cm.—(Greenwood encyclopedias of modern world wars)
    Includes bibliographical references and index.
    ISBN 0–313–33045–X (set)—ISBN 0–313–33733–0 (vol. 1)—
ISBN 0–313–33734–9 (vol. 2)
    1. Middle Ages—History—Encyclopedias.   2. History, Modern—17th century—
Encyclopedias.   3. Military history, Medieval—Encyclopedias.   4. Military history,
Modern—17th century—Encyclopedias.   5. Biography—Middle Ages, 500–1500—
Encyclopedias.   6. Biography—17th century—Encyclopedias.   I. Title.
    D114.N66   2006
    909.0703—dc22   2005031626

British Library Cataloguing in Publication Data is available.

Library of Congress Catalog Card Number: 2005031626

ISBN: 0–313–33045–X (set)
        0–313–33733–0 (vol. I)
        0–313–33734–9 (vol. II)

First published in 2006

Greenwood Press, 88 Post Road West, Westport, CT 06881
An imprint of Greenwood Publishing Group, Inc.
www.greenwood.com

Printed in the United States of America

The paper used in this book complies with the
Permanent Paper Standard issued by the National
Information Standards Organization (Z39.48–1984).

10 9 8 7 6 5 4 3 2 1

Covenants without swords are but words.

—Thomas Hobbes, *Leviathan* (1651)

You are engaged in God's service and in mine—which is the same thing.

—Philip II, of Spain

[The terms are] null and void, invalid, iniquitous, unjust, condemned, rejected, frivolous, without force or effect, and no one is to observe them, even when they be ratified by oath.

—Pope Innocent X,
On the articles of religious toleration in the *Peace of Westphalia* (1648)

Who brings famine? The army.
Who brings the plague? The army.
Who the sword? The army.
Who hinders trade? The army.
Who confounds all? The army.

—Hugh Peter,
A Word for the Army and Two Words to the Kingdome (1647)

CONTENTS

List of Entries

List of Entries

List of Entries

List of Entries

List of Entries

List of Entries

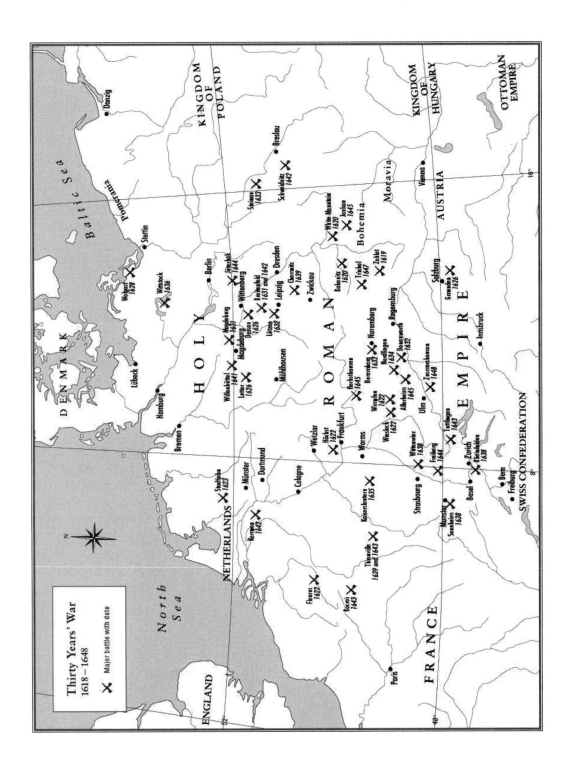

Thirty Years' War
1618 – 1648

✗ Major battle with date

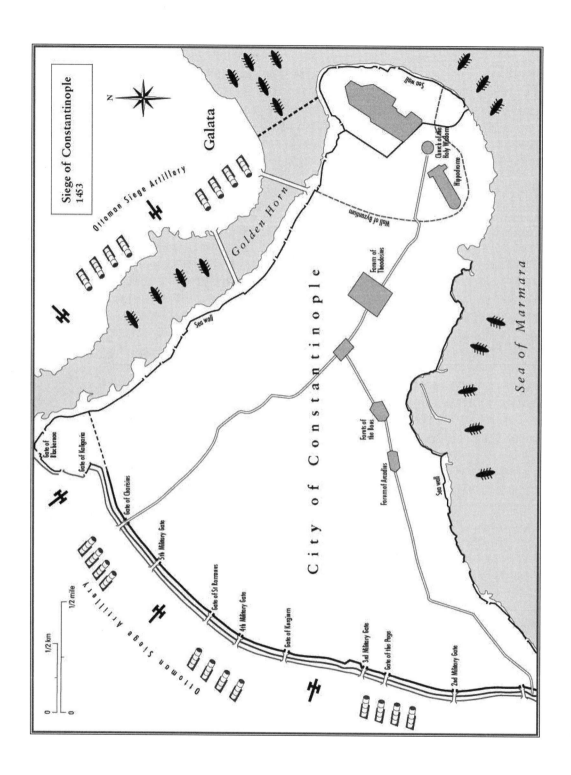

Siege of Constantinople
1453

Galata

Ottoman Siege Artillery

Golden Horn

Sea wall

City of Constantinople

Sea of Marmara

Wall of Byzantium

Forum of Theodosius

Forum of the Bous

Forum of Arcadius

Church of the Holy Wisdom

Hippodrome

Sea wall

Sea wall

Gate of Xylokercos

Gate of Kaligaria

Gate of Charisius

5th Military Gate

Gate of St Romanus

4th Military Gate

Gate of Rhegium

3rd Military Gate

Gate of the Pege

2nd Military Gate

Ottoman Siege Artillery

1/2 mile

1/2 km

0

0

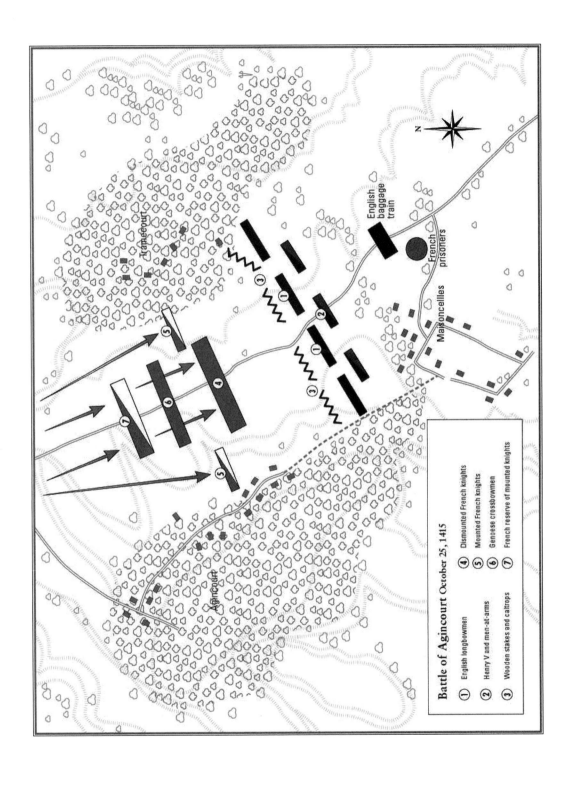

Battle of Agincourt October 25, 1415

(1) English longbowmen
(2) Henry V and men-at-arms
(3) Wooden stakes and caltrops
(4) Dismounted French knights
(5) Mounted French knights
(6) Genoese crossbowmen
(7) French reserve of mounted knights

Tramecourt

English baggage train

French prisoners

Maisoncelles

Agincourt

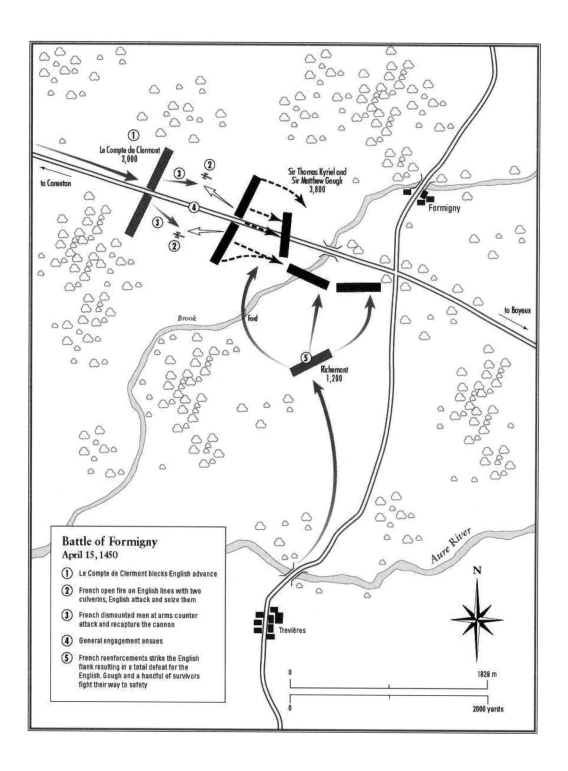

to Carenton

Le Compte de Clermont
3,000

Sir Thomas Kyriel and
Sir Matthew Gough
3,800

Formigny

Brook

Ford

to Bayeux

Richemont
1,200

Aure River

Battle of Formigny
April 15, 1450

① Le Compte de Clermont blocks English advance

② French open fire on English lines with two
culverins, English attack and seize them

③ French dismounted men at arms counter
attack and recapture the cannon

④ General engagement ensues

⑤ French reenforcements strike the English
flank resulting in a total defeat for the
English. Gough and a handful of survivors
fight their way to safety

Trevières

N

0   1828 m

0   2000 yards

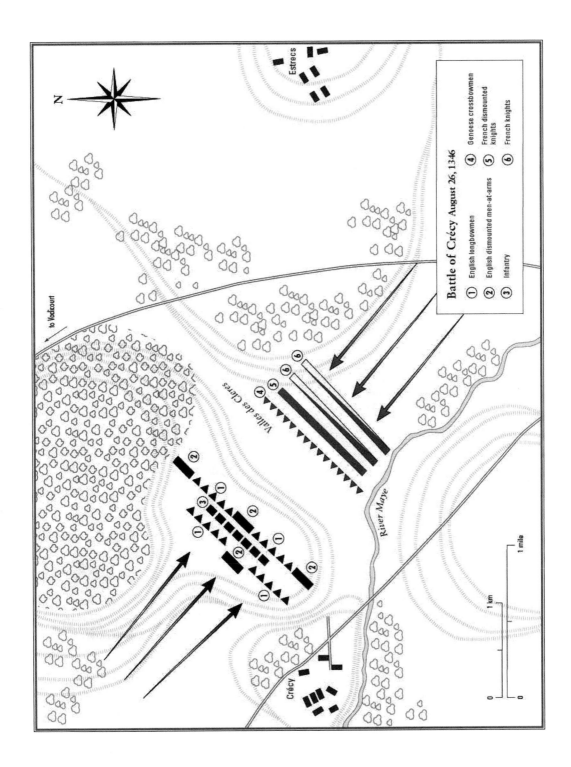

Battle of Crécy August 26, 1346

① English longbowmen
② English dismounted men-at-arms
③ Infantry
④ Genoese crossbowmen
⑤ French dismounted knights
⑥ French knights

N

to Vadicourt

Estrecs

Vallée des Clercs

River Maye

Crécy

1 km

1 mile

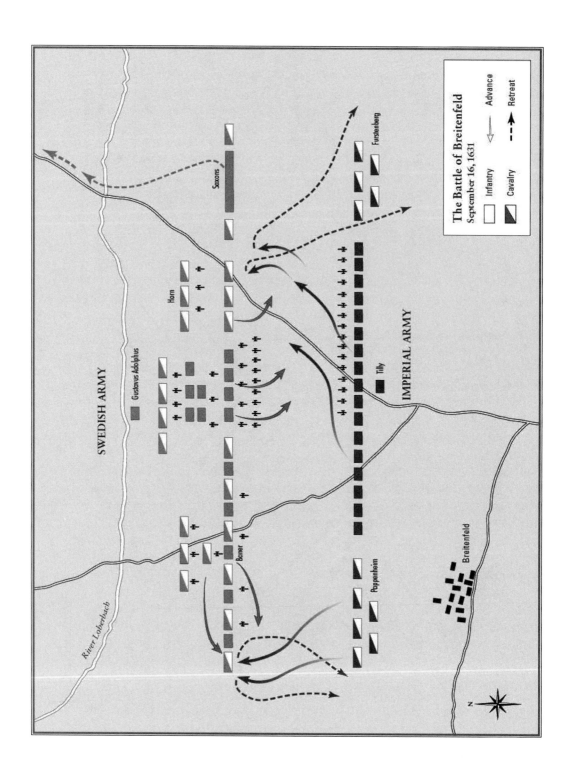

The Battle of Breitenfeld
September 16, 1631

Infantry
Cavalry

Advance
Retreat

SWEDISH ARMY

River Loberbacb

Gustavus Adolphus

Horn

Saxons

Baner

Pappenheim

IMPERIAL ARMY

Tilly

Furstenberg

Breitenfeld

N

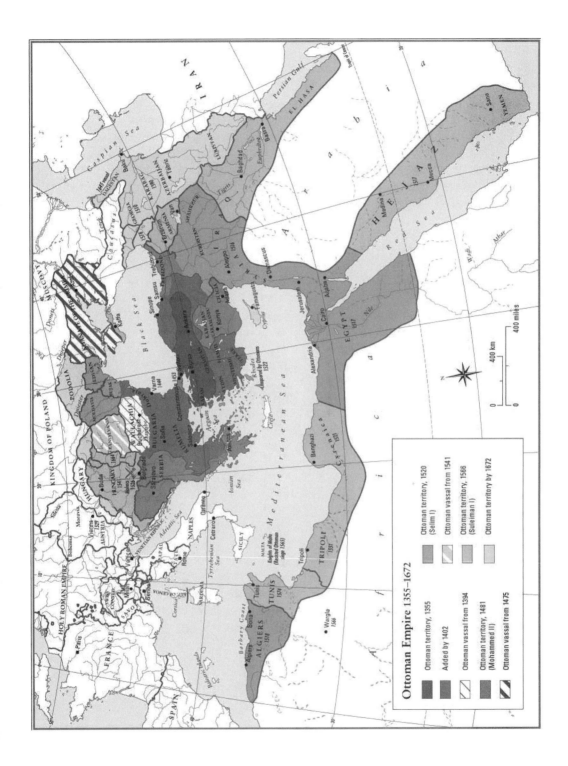

Ottoman Empire 1355–1672

Ottoman territory, 1355	Ottoman territory, 1520 (Selim I)
Added by 1402	Ottoman vassal from 1541
Ottoman vassal from 1394	Ottoman territory, 1566 (Suleiman I)
Ottoman territory, 1481 (Mohammed II)	Ottoman territory by 1672
Ottoman vassal from 1475	

Europe 1648

Spanish–Habsburg land

Austrian–Habsburg land

'Spanish Road'; main supply routes to Habsburg possessions

N

0   200 km
0   200 miles

SWEDEN

NORWAY

SCOTLAND
Edinburgh

North Sea

Baltic Sea

DENMARK

IRELAND
Dublin
York

ENGLAND

Lübeck
Hamburg
Stettin

Brandenburg
Berlin

POLAND

Bristol

London

Calais

Amsterdam
The Hague
Antwerp
Brussels
SOUTH
NETHERLANDS
Luxembourg

UNITED
PROVINCES

HOLY ROMAN

EMPIRE

Mainz
Bamberg

Saxony

Breslau
Silesia

Bohemia
Moravia

ATLANTIC
OCEAN

Brest

Paris

Lorraine

Orléans

Nantes

Franche
Comté
Charolais

FRANCE

Bordeaux

Toulouse

Geneva

Basel
Swiss
Confederation

Der Sund

Bavaria
Augsburg
Munich

Tirol

Milan

Albano

Vienna
Archd. of
Austria

Pressburg

Buda

Mohács

KINGDOM OF HUNGARY

Danube

OTTOMAN
EMPIRE

REP. OF VENICE
Venice
Parma
Mantua

Carniola

Marseille

Genoa

Lucca
REP. OF
GENOA

REP. OF
FLORENCE

PAPAL
STATES

Adriatic Sea

PORTUGAL

León
Burgos

CASTILLE

San Sebastián
Pamplona

Saragossa

ARAGON

Corsica

Rome

KINGDOM
OF NAPLES
Naples

Madrid
Toledo

Barcelona

Roussillon

Sardinia

Lisbon

Valencia

Córdova
Seville
Cádiz

Jaén
Granada

Murcia
Cartagena

Palma
KINGDOM OF MAJORCA
(1521–24)

Palermo

Sicily

Mediterranean

Algiers
Bugia

Tunis

Sea

l

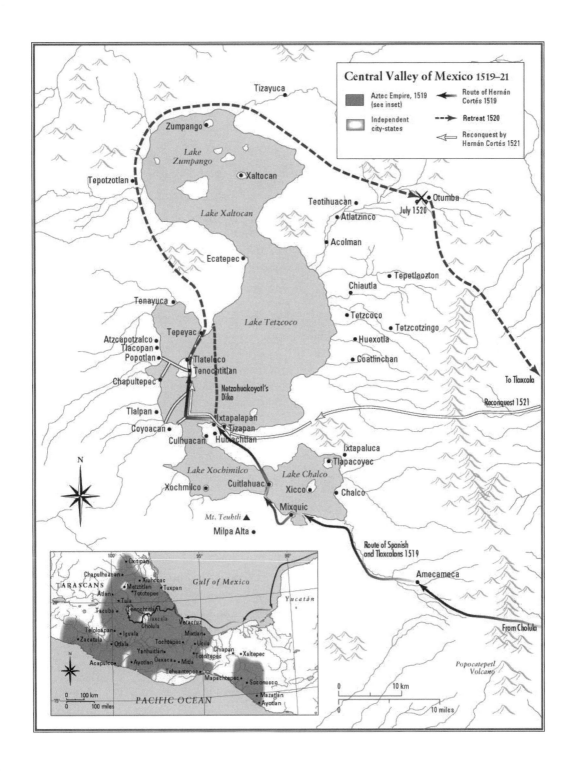

Central Valley of Mexico 1519–21

▨ Aztec Empire, 1519 (see inset)	← Route of Hernán Cortés 1519	
▢ Independent city-states	⤑ Retreat 1520	
	⇐ Reconquest by Hernán Cortés 1521	

Tizayuca

Zumpango

Lake Zumpango

Xaltocan

Tepotzotlan

Lake Xaltocan

Teotihuacan
Atlatzinco

Otumba
July 1520

Acolman

Ecatepec

Tepetlaozton

Chiautla

Tenayuca

Lake Tetzcoco

Tepeyac

Atzcapotzalco
Tlacopan
Popotlan

Tlatelolco
Tenochtitlan

Chapultepec

Netzahualcoyotl's Dike

Tlalpan

Ixtapalapan
Tizapan
Coyoacan
Culhuacan
Huaachtlan

Tetzcoco
Tetzcotzingo

Huexotla

Coatlinchan

To Tlaxcala

Reconquest 1521

Ixtapaluca
Tlapacoyac

Lake Xochimilco
Xochmilco
Cuitlahuac

Lake Chalco
Xicco
Chalco

Mixquic

Mt. Teubtli ▲
Milpa Alta

Route of Spanish and Tlaxcalans 1519

Amecameca

From Cholula

Popocatepetl Volcano

N

0   10 km

0   10 miles

Inset map:

100°   95°   90°

Oxitipan

Chapulhuacan

TARASCANS

Xiuhcoac
Metztitlan
Tototepec   Tuxpan
Atlan

Gulf of Mexico

Tula
Tacuba
Tenochtitlan

Yucatán

Telolospan
Zacatula
Iguala
Oztla
Tlaxcala
Cholula
Veracruz
Moxtlan

Yanhuitlan
Tochtepec
Ucila
Chiapan   Xaltepec
Acapulco
Ayotlan Oaxaca   Mitla
Tototepec
Tehuantepec
Mapachtepec   Soconusco

Mazatlan
Ayotlan

15°

0   100 km
0   100 miles

PACIFIC OCEAN

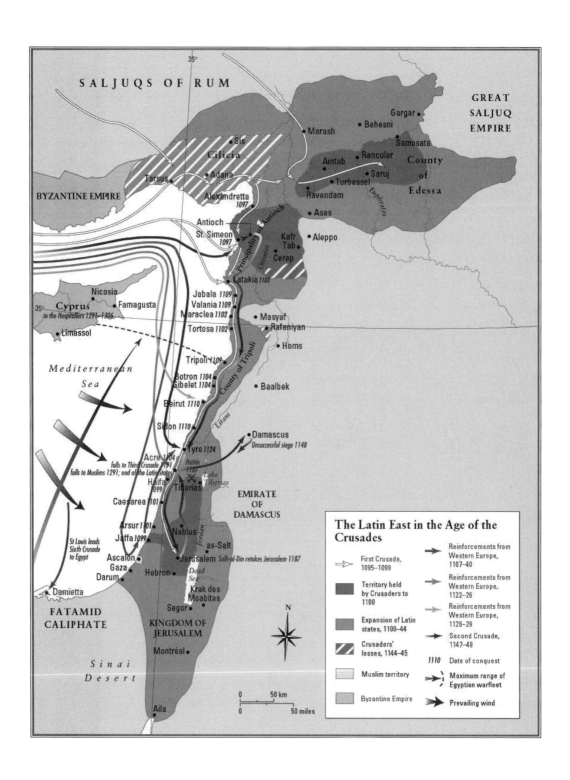

The Latin East in the Age of the Crusades

First Crusade, 1095–1099

Territory held by Crusaders to 1100

Expansion of Latin states, 1100–44

Crusaders' losses, 1144–45

Muslim territory

Byzantine Empire

Reinforcements from Western Europe, 1107–40

Reinforcements from Western Europe, 1122–26

Reinforcements from Western Europe, 1128–29

Second Crusade, 1147–49

1110 Date of conquest

Maximum range of Egyptian warfleet

Prevailing wind

0 50 km
0 50 miles

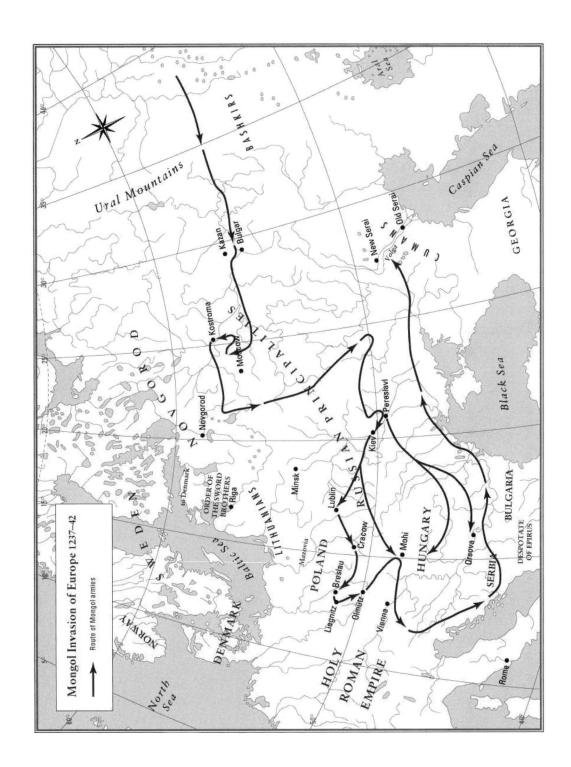

Mongol Invasion of Europe 1237–42

Route of Mongol armies

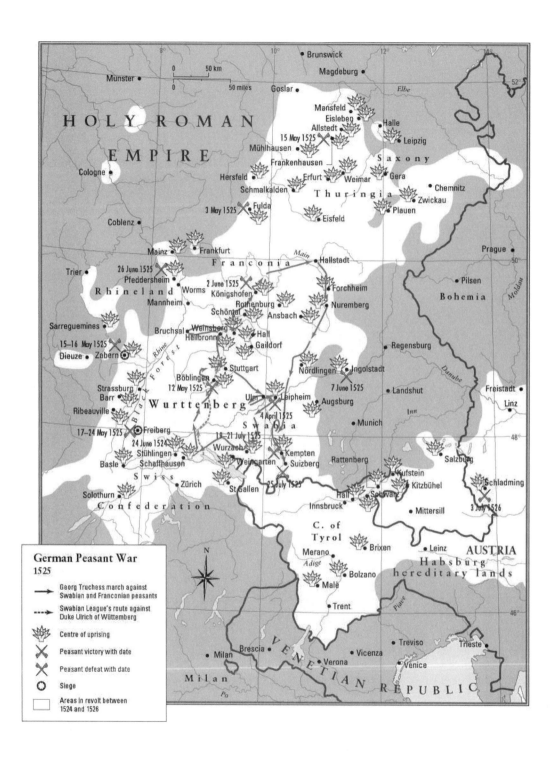

German Peasant War 1525 (map)

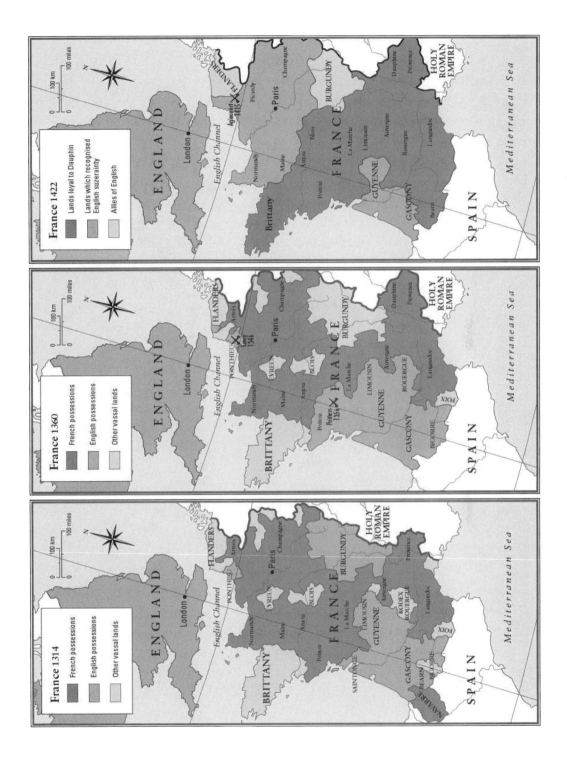

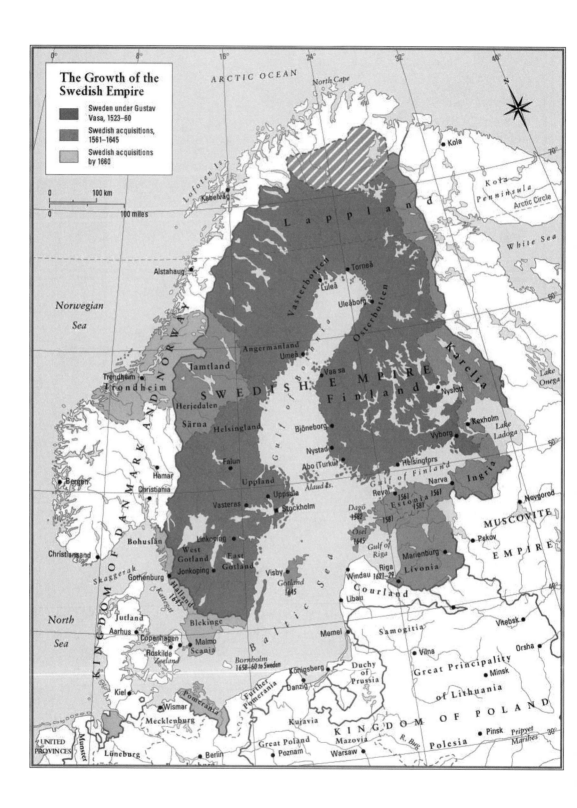

The Growth of the
Swedish Empire

■ Sweden under Gustav
Vasa, 1523–60

■ Swedish acquisitions,
1561–1645

□ Swedish acquisitions
by 1660

0   100 km

0   100 miles

ARCTIC OCEAN

North Cape

Kola

Kola
Penninsula

Arctic Circle

Lofoten Is.

Kabelvåg

L a p p l a n d

White Sea

Norwegian

Sea

Alstahaug

Vasterbotten

Torneå

Luleå

Osterbotten

Uleåborg

Karelia

Lake
Onega

Trondheim
Trondheim

Angermanland

Umeå

Jamtland

S W E D I S H   E M P I R E

Vaasa

Finland

Nyslott

Herjedalen

Särna

Helsingland

Björneborg

Kexholm

Lake
Ladoga

Gulf of Bothnia

Vyborg

Bergen

Falun

Nystad

Helsingfors

Hamar

Uppland

Åbo (Turku)

Åland Is.

Ingria

Christiania

Uppsala

Gulf of Finland

Narva

Novgorod

Vasteras

Stockholm

Reval

1561

Estonia 1561

MUSCOVITE

Dagö
1582

1581

1581

Linköping

West
Gotland

East
Gotland

Osel
1645

Gulf of
Riga

Marienburg

Pskov

EMPIRE

Bohuslän

Jonkoping

Visby

Gotland
1645

Windau 1621–29

Livonia

Riga

Christiansand

Skagerrak

Gothenburg

Halland
1645

Libau

Courland

Vitebsk

Kattegat

North

Sea

Jutland

Blekinge

Baltic Sea

Memel

Samogitia

Orsha

Aarhus

Copenhagen

Malmo

Scania

Vilna

Great Principality

Minsk

Roskilde

Zeeland

Bornholm
1658–60 to Sweden

Königsberg

Duchy
of
Prussia

of Lithuania

Kiel

Danzig

Pinsk

Pripyet
Marshes

Wismar

Pomerania

Further
Pomerania

Kujavia

K I N G D O M   O F   P O L A N D

Mecklenburg

Great Poland

Mazovia

R. Bug

Polesia

UNITED
PROVINCES

Munster

Lüneburg

Berlin

Poznam

Warsaw

KINGDOM OF DANMARK AND NORWAY

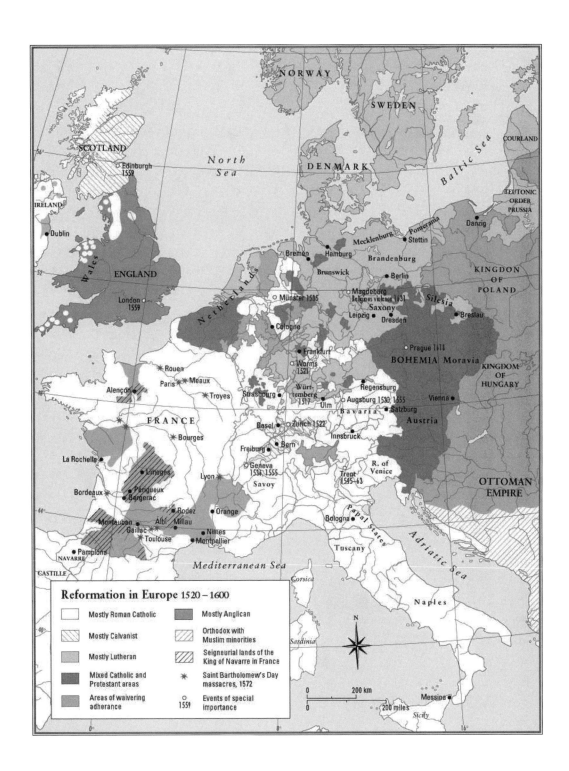

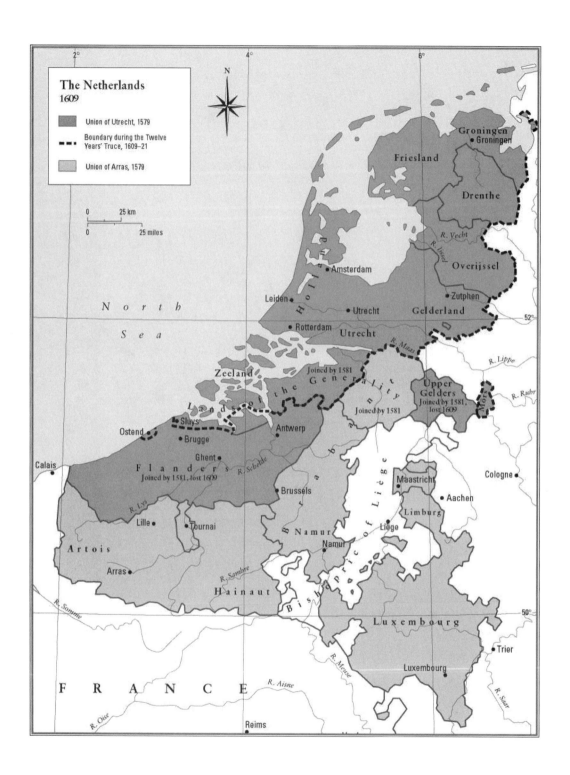

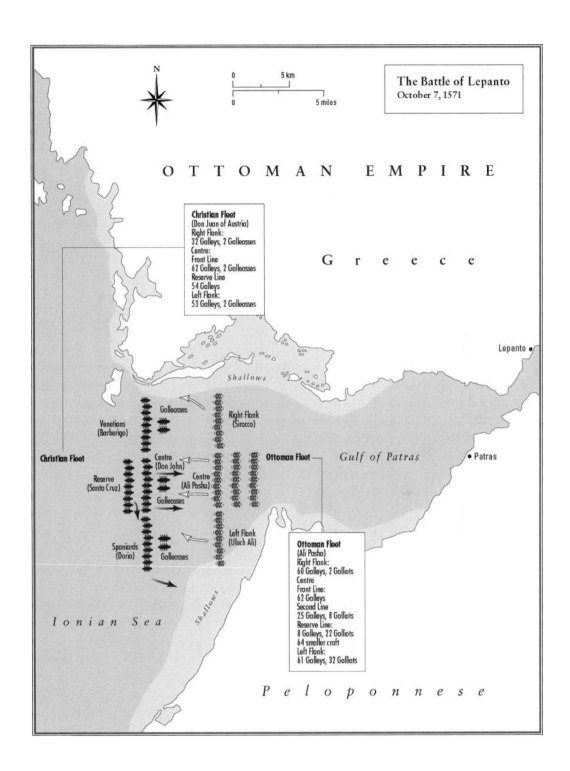

The Battle of Lepanto
October 7, 1571

N

0   5 km

0   5 miles

OTTOMAN EMPIRE

Greece

Christian Fleet
(Don Juan of Austria)
Right Flank:
32 Galleys, 2 Galleasses
Centre:
Front Line
62 Galleys, 2 Galleasses
Reserve Line
54 Galleys
Left Flank:
53 Galleys, 2 Galleasses

Lepanto •

Shallows

Galleasses

Right Flank
(Sirocco)

Venetians
(Barberigo)

Centre
(Don John)

Ottoman Fleet

Gulf of Patras

• Patras

Christian Fleet

Centre
(Ali Pasha)

Reserve
(Santa Cruz)

Galleasses

Left Flank
(Uluch Ali)

Spaniards
(Doria)

Galleasses

Ottoman Fleet
(Ali Pasha)
Right Flank:
60 Galleys, 2 Galliots
Centre
Front Line:
62 Galleys
Second Line
25 Galleys, 8 Galliots
Reserve Line:
8 Galleys, 22 Galliots
64 smaller craft
Left Flank:
61 Galleys, 32 Galliots

Ionian Sea

Shallows

Peloponnese

Invincible Armada
May – September 1588

Route of the Armada

Individual or small
groups of ships
blown off course

Site of battle

Spanish Empire

United Provinces in
revolt against Spain

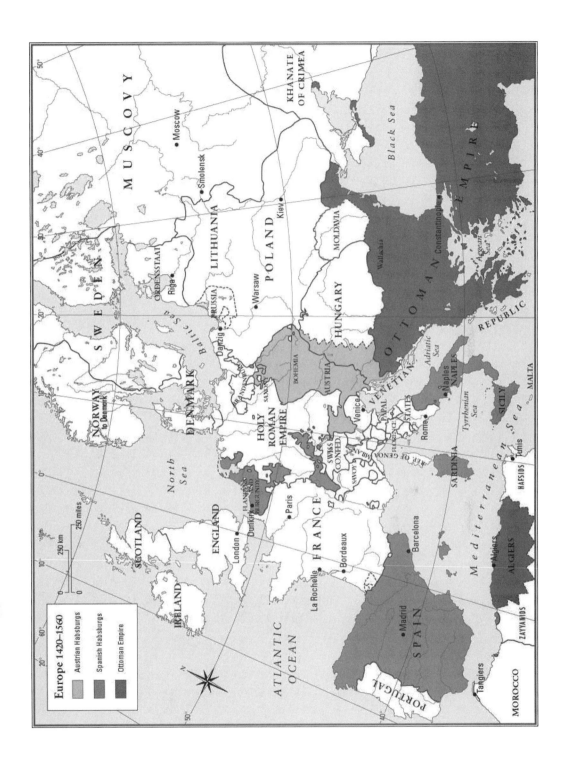

Europe 1420–1560

Austrian Habsburgs
Spanish Habsburgs
Ottoman Empire

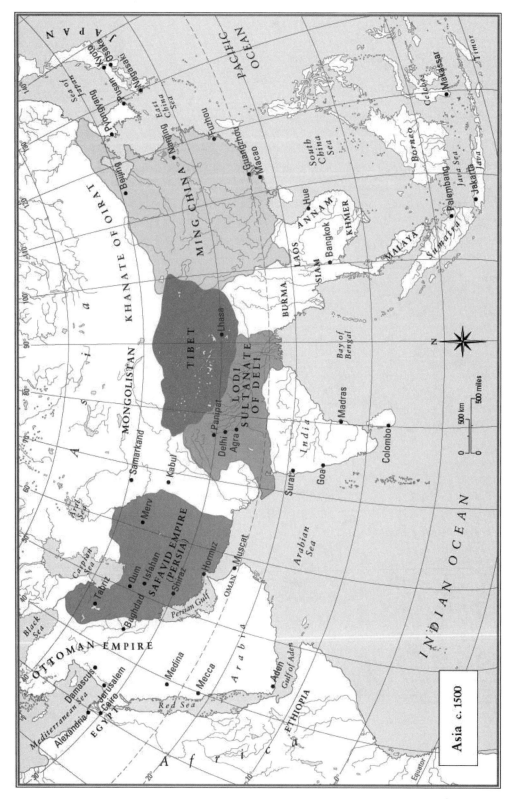

Asia c. 1500

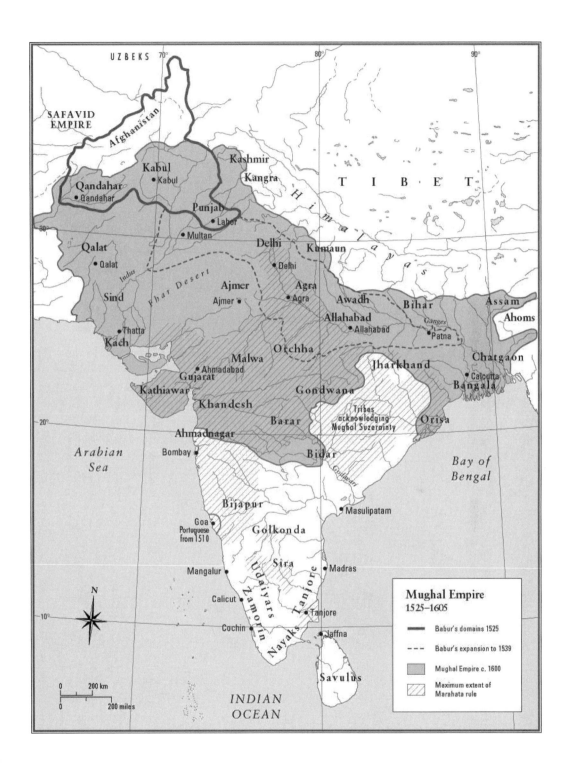

Map legend:

Mughal Empire
1525–1605

━━━ Babur's domains 1525

╌╌╌ Babur's expansion to 1539

▨ Mughal Empire c. 1600

▨ Maximum extent of
Marahata rule

Map labels:

UZBEKS

SAFAVID
EMPIRE

Afghanistan

Kabul
• Kabul

Qandahar
• Qandahar

Kashmir

Kangra

T I B E T

Punjab
• Lahor

• Multan

Qalat
• Qalat

Sind

Indus

Thar Desert

Delhi
• Delhi

Kumaun

Himalayas

Ajmer
Ajmer •

Agra
• Agra

Awadh

Bihar

Ganges
Patna •

Assam

Ahoms

Allahabad
• Allahabad

Thatta •
Kach

Otchha

Malwa
• Ahmadabad

Gujarat

Kathiawar

Khandesh

Barar

Gondwana

Jharkhand

Tribes
acknowledging
Mughal Suzerainty

Chatgaon

• Calcutta
Bangala

Orisa

Ahmadnagar

Bombay •

Bidar

Godavari

Arabian
Sea

Bijapur

Goa
Portuguese
from 1510

Golkonda

• Masulipatam

Bay of
Bengal

Sira

Mangalur •

Udaiyars

Zamorin

Nayaks

Tanjore

• Madras

Calicut •

• Tanjore

Cochin •

• Jaffna

Savulus

N

INDIAN
OCEAN

0   200 km
0   200 miles

70°   80°   90°

30°

20°

10°

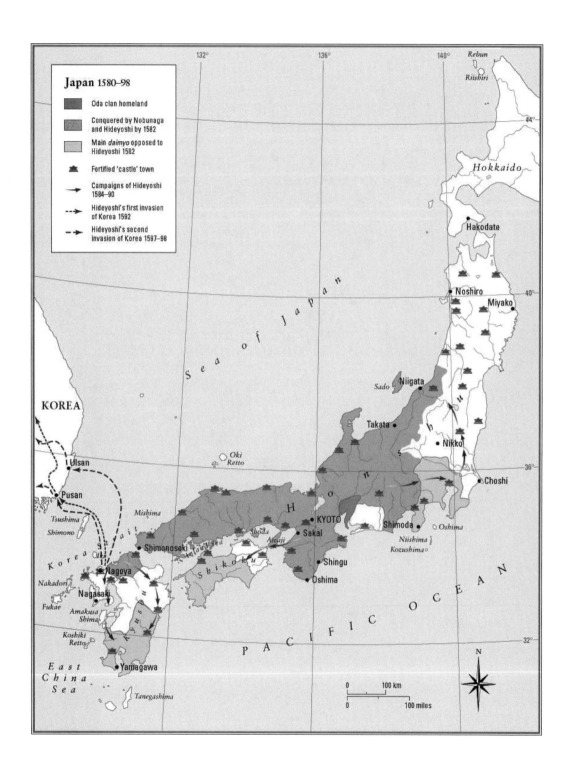

Japan 1580–98

Oda clan homeland

Conquered by Nobunaga and Hideyoshi by 1582

Main *daimyo* opposed to Hideyoshi 1582

Fortified 'castle' town

Campaigns of Hideyoshi 1584–90

Hideyoshi's first invasion of Korea 1592

Hideyoshi's second invasion of Korea 1597–98

132°   136°   140°   *Rebun*

Riishiri

44°

Hokkaido

Hakodate

Sea of Japan

Noshiro

Miyako   40°

KOREA

Sado   Niigata

Takata

Ulsan

Nikko

Oki Retto

Pusan

Tsushima

Shimono

36°

Choshi

Mishima

H   O   n

Korea Strait

KYOTO

Shimoda

Oshima

Shimonoseki   *Shoda*

Sakai

Niishima

Kozushima

Nagoya

Shikoku   Shingu

Nakadori

Nagasaki

Oshima

Fukae

Amakusa Shima

Kyushu

Koshiki Retto

Yamagawa

32°

East China Sea

Tanegashima

N

P   A   C   I   F   I   C   O   C   E   A   N

0   100 km

0   100 miles

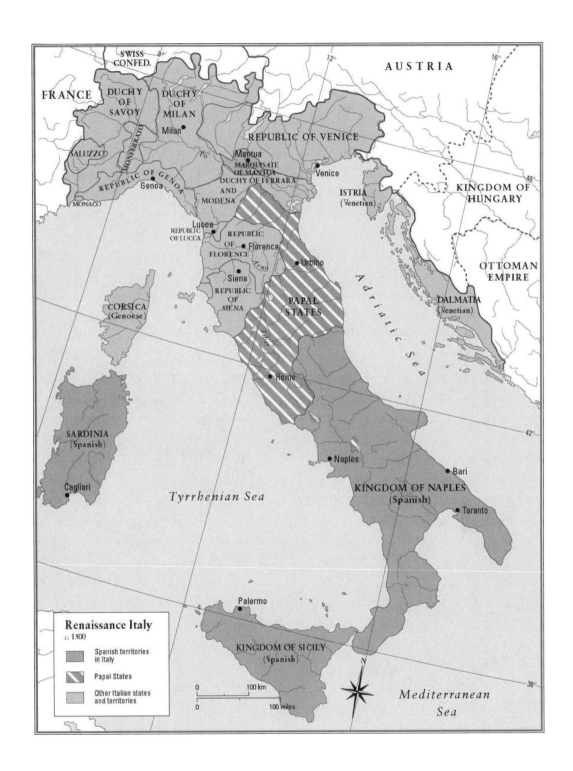

Renaissance Italy
c. 1500

Spanish territories in Italy

Papal States

Other Italian states and territories

SWISS CONFED.

AUSTRIA

FRANCE

DUCHY OF SAVOY

DUCHY OF MILAN

Milan

REPUBLIC OF VENICE

SALUZZO

MONFERRATO

REPUBLIC OF GENOA

Genoa

MONACO

Mantua

MARQUISATE OF MANTUA

DUCHY OF FERRARA AND MODENA

Venice

ISTRIA (Venetian)

KINGDOM OF HUNGARY

Lucca

REPUBLIC OF LUCCA

REPUBLIC OF FLORENCE

Florence

Siena

REPUBLIC OF SIENA

Urbino

Arno

PAPAL STATES

Adriatic Sea

OTTOMAN EMPIRE

DALMATIA (Venetian)

CORSICA (Genoese)

Tiber

Rome

SARDINIA (Spanish)

Cagliari

Tyrrhenian Sea

Naples

Bari

KINGDOM OF NAPLES (Spanish)

Taranto

Palermo

KINGDOM OF SICILY (Spanish)

N

Mediterranean Sea

0   100 km

0   100 miles

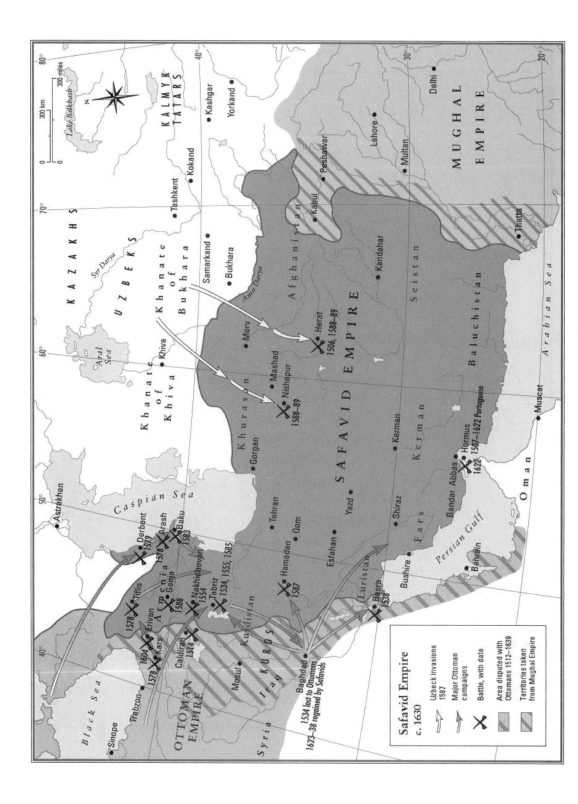

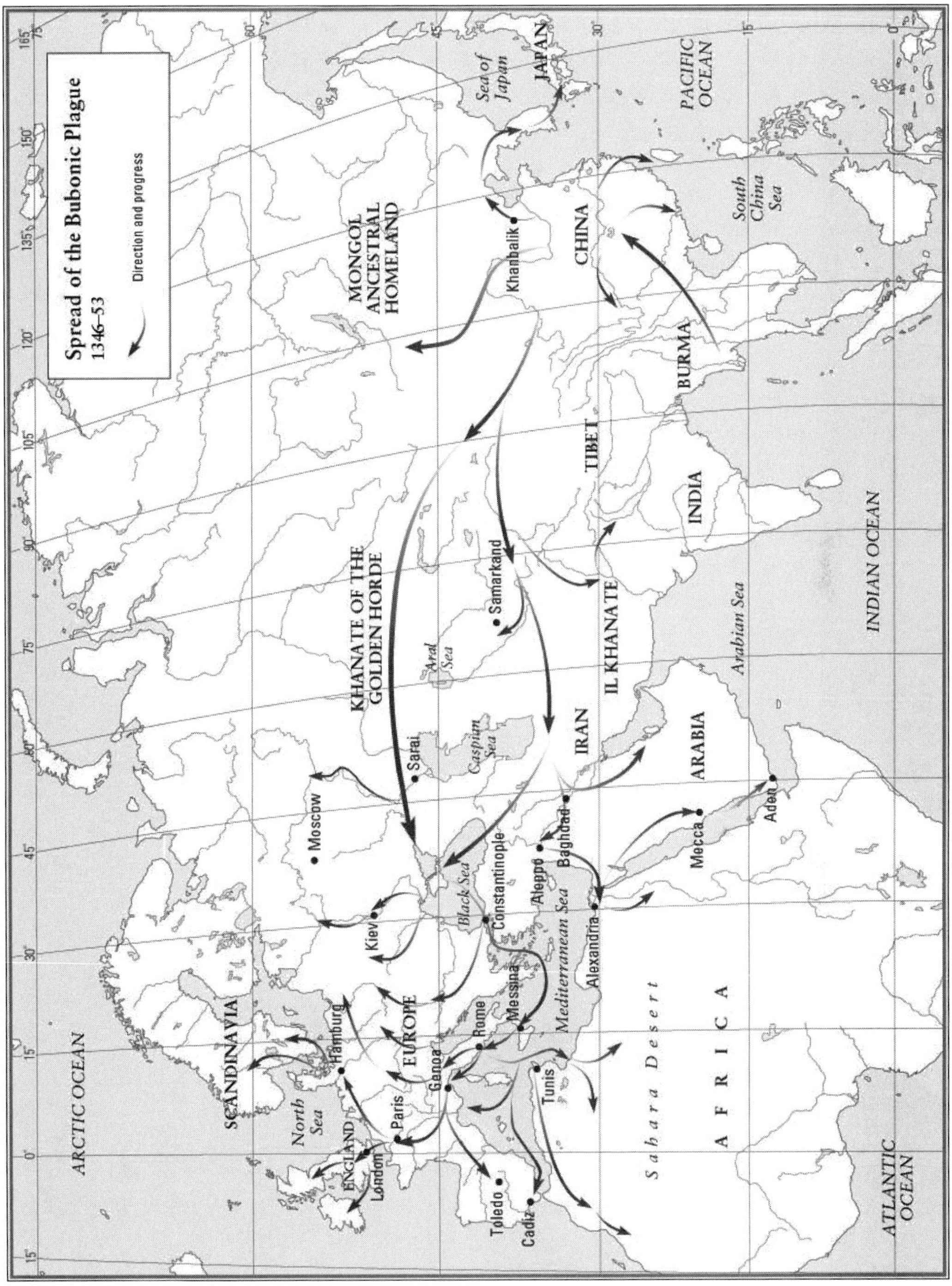

Spread of the Bubonic Plague
1346–53

Direction and progress

ARCTIC OCEAN

SCANDINAVIA

North Sea

ENGLAND
London
Paris
Hamburg

EUROPE
Rome
Genoa
Messina

Toledo
Cadiz
Tunis

Mediterranean Sea
Alexandria

Sahara Desert

AFRICA

ATLANTIC OCEAN

Kiev

Moscow

Black Sea
Constantinople
Aleppo
Baghdad

Sarai

Caspian Sea
Aral Sea

KHANATE OF THE GOLDEN HORDE

Samarkand

IL KHANATE

IRAN

ARABIA
Mecca

Aden

Arabian Sea

INDIA

TIBET

BURMA

INDIAN OCEAN

MONGOL ANCESTRAL HOMELAND

Khanbalik

CHINA

Sea of Japan

JAPAN

South China Sea

PACIFIC OCEAN

L

La Bicocca, Battle of (April 27, 1522). During the *Italian Wars* (1494–1559) *Francis I* assembled an army of 25,000, including thousands of Swiss mercenaries, and marched to take back Milan which he had earlier lost to *Charles V*. Waiting to meet him with 20,000 Spanish and Italian troops, supported by German mercenaries, was *Marchese di Pescara*. The Habsburgs were positioned behind a sunken road and were well dug in. Their musketeers stood in four ranks partially concealed by heavy hedges and unusually, with pikemen to the rear. The Swiss in French employ charged with their usual ferocious abandon only to see a third of their number fall to the massed Habsburg gunmen. Each rank fired in turn, then retired, a *countermarch* tactic developed to maximize the fire effect of the new "Spanish musket." That heavier weapon had been used in a siege at Parma in 1521 but this was its first test in a field battle. It was devastating: 3,000 Swiss fell dead or wounded inside 30 minutes. No more would the Swiss used outdated pike and halberd tactics in the face of opposing firearms. Henceforth, the Spanish *tercio* was admired as the best infantry formation in Europe, ahead of the suddenly outdated *Swiss square*. Francis withdrew toward Venice, his ally. See also *Pavia, Battle of*.

La Forbie, Battle of (1244). See *Knights Templar*.

laǧimci. Ottoman *engineers* who specialized in sapping and mining. See also *beldar*.

Lake Boyang, Battle of (1363). Zhu Yuanzhang (*Hongwu*), former leader of the *Red Turbans*, sent his Ming fleet to do battle with the Han fleet on this hundred-mile-long lake. His men fired off their early firearms, then switched to crossbows and bows. The battle waxed and waned over four days, with heavy casualties. In the end, Ming use of *fireships* turned the battle in their favor.

lamellar armor. Armor made from scales rather than mail *rings* or *plate*. See also *armor*; *waist-lames*.

lance (I). A long cavalry spear used for thrusting at the enemy. It was not a javelin, which it replaced among the Franks in the late 9th century. Early medieval lances were 8 to 10 feet long, usually carved from a sturdy wood such as ash or apple. Reliance on the lance by medieval cavalry began under Charlemagne (r.768–814), who ordered all knights to use lances in his 792–793 edict "Capitulare missorum." Frankish armies continued to use the lance as a thrusting weapon, and did not yet unite weight of warrior and warhorse in combined mounted *shock* combat. That development only arrived with the *couched lance*, probably around 1100 (the date of introduction remains controversial). It established battlefield dominance by 1150. The heavy lance thereafter served as the principal weapon of cavalry in the Middle Ages, and the main weapon of specialized units of lancers into the gunpowder era.

Since shock and not thrusting was the new method of attack, cavalry lances became heavier, sturdier, and longer: up to four meters of hardened wood with a solid iron tip (usually leaf-shaped to cut deeply into mail and flesh), and a *pennon* to prevent its passing right through an enemy soldier. When full plate armor became common for rider and warhorse in the 15th century the "*arrêt de cuirasse*" was used to bracket the lance against the breastplate. This allowed a still heavier lance to be used. However, this change came just as heavy lancers were being shuffled off the battlefield by gunpowder weapons, which led to abandonment of the lance in favor of alternate cavalry weapons and tactics such as the *pistol* and *caracole*, and a reduced assault combat role for cavalry in favor of large infantry formations. It has been argued by Claude Gaier and other French military historians that what finally drove the heavy lance from the battlefield, or at least from French battlefields, was "not infantry but mounted pistoleers." That is not the dominant view in more general military histories.

lance (2). A late medieval cavalry formation first set up in the mid-14th century. It consisted of a single heavily armed and armored *knight* on a heavy *warhorse*, surrounded by horse archers on spry mounts. Lances required many horses to operate: two or more *rounceys* to carry the knight to and from battle; a *destrier* to carry him in battle; and various *sumpters* for attendants, as carters of armor and weapons, and to haul away any captured armor or other plunder he might secure. This basic unit of heavy cavalry later varied in size according to country, with a tendency toward increased numbers and specialization during the 15th century when the man-at-arms was suppoted at the center of the lance by several mounted specialists, sometimes called "equitatores."

lance (3). The core organizational element of the Burgundian army set up by *Charles the Rash*. In 1470 he created a force of 1,250 lances subdivided into 100 lance units. Each lance included a man-at-arms and three infantrymen: a crossbowman, an arquebusier, and a pikeman. In his ordinance of 1473, Charles set up "compagnies de l'ordonnance" of four uniformed squads each comprised of five lances. He added innovations in drill, officering, and equipment. The French Army also used lances as its basic unit into the 16th century. A lance at the start of the *French Civil Wars* (1562–1629) consisted of a man-at-arms and four mounts, two archers with two horses each, and two pages. French lances were in companies that varied from 40 to 100 men, with about 50 arquebusiers added by c.1550. Introduction of the *wheel lock* permitted cavalry to fire pistols while mounted, so that lances were discarded as the principal weapon of Western European cavalry by the end of the 16th century. See also *Cossacks*; *lancers*; *poczet*; *tournaments*.

lance-rest. A bracket in the center of an armor breastplate that supported a *couched lance*.

lanceri. Italian infantry of the late 15th century, armed with either long or short lances.

lancers. During the Middle Ages most European *heavy cavalry* used the *couched lance* as their primary weapon. Later, medium cavalry using lances as their principal weapon also arose. Uhlan light cavalry lancers may have originated in Hungary, but the style was also adopted by the Poles and from there it spread throughout northeastern Europe and Muscovy via contact with Polish armies. Uhlans may have spread to Western Europe via Poland's close military contacts with France. *Stradiots* from the Balkans hired out as mercenaries to Venice were also light cavalry lancers. They doubled as mounted infantry, dismounting to use crossbows. Similarly, English *hobelars* could fight with lances or dismount and fight on foot with bows. Lancers survived in Eastern Europe and Russia as a cavalry mainstay into the 18th century. They were still an important part of Western European cavalry in the 19th century and appeared in battle as late as World War I and even World War II. See also *demi-lancers*; *hussars*; *knights*; *Mamlūks*.

Landesabwehr. "Territorial defense." The army of the *Holy Roman Empire* in the feudal period. See *Imperial Army*.

Landesaufgebot. "Territorial recruitment." See *Imperial Army*.

Landsdown Hill, Battle of (1643). See *English Civil Wars*; *Hopton, Ralph*.

Landsknechte. "Companions of the country." French: "lansquenets." Mercenary infantry originally formed in the late 15th century from petty war bands ("Knabenschaften") of wild youths. These were unemployed older apprentices overflowing from the highly restrictive Guilds, or other surplus young males produced by a time of demographic expansion. Such "lads" ("Knechte") waged private wars that usually amounted to little more than rural banditry against unarmed peasants; or they sometimes banded together to threaten extreme violence to extort money from vulnerable towns. In the 1470s all Europe was deeply impressed by the stunning defeat of the "rational" and "modern" army of *Charles the Rash* by the lowly Swiss during the *Burgundian-Swiss War* (1474–1477). Desire to emulate the Swiss fighting for France led to creation of Landsknechte infantry that drew in the "Knechte" of the country and trained them in service to the *Holy Roman Empire*. These "lads" were supplemented, and eventually replaced by, veteran mercenaries from Alsace and the Rhineland, the Low Countries and Scotland. Landsknechte were trained (initially, by Swiss *renegade* instructors) in the tactics of the *Swiss square*. Hence, they were mainly pikemen and halberdiers, though most also carried short swords (*Katzbalger*). Like the Swiss, many Landsknechte fighting behind the front ranks of the square wore little body armor so that they could better wield 18-foot pikes, swing their halberds, and fire crossbows and muskets. This origin in imitation contributed to an intense hatred the Landsknechte had for the Swiss, an animosity that was wholly reciprocated and which lasted many decades.

The first Landsknechte unit was formed in Bruges in 1487. The next year, the "Black Guard" was formed in Friesland by Emperor *Maximilian I*, who gave them special license and exemptions from civil law that the Landsknechte exploited to the hilts of their swords. For over a decade his "Black Guard" fought a savage frontier war around the North Sea, until it was wiped out by a large peasant army at Hemmingstedt (February 17, 1500). Other Landsknechte units fought in Hungary, but they mutinied and abandoned the campaign once they collected sufficient booty. To counter this tendency to indiscipline Maximilian seeded Landsknechte companies with noble officers (the Emperor himself set an example by marching like a common foot soldier, pike on shoulder) and imposed strict *military discipline*. Rather than replacing the old service nobility, later German emperors persuaded or compelled nobles to join Landsknechte units, thereby reinforcing aristocratic control of the new infantry. Finally, although many Landsknechte were northern Protestants they remained loyal to Catholic emperors because the latter did not try to catholicize the troops, even permitting them Protestant chaplains. Also, they paid well. As for the emperors, they tolerated religious dissent in the very armies that they used to fight prolonged wars to repress *confessionalism* in German and European society.

The Landsknechte first encountered the hated Swiss in battle during the *Swabian War*, at *Dornach* (1499). They fought hard but were defeated and then massacred by the ferocious Swiss. About 9,000 Landsknechte under *Francis I* fought and helped defeat the Swiss at *Marignano* (1515). Landsknechte fought for *Charles V* against Francis I at *Pavia* in 1525. Afterward, many returned to Germany to fight for the *Swabian League* in the *German Peasant War* (1525), against peasant bands sometimes led and stiffened by other Landsknechte in their ranks. It was Landsknechte mercenaries who sacked Rome in 1527. However, at *Dreux* (1562), they fared so badly in comparison to Swiss mercenaries that the French crown never again hired Landsknechte. See also *Bestallungbrief*; *Doppelgänger*; *Doppelsöldner*; *ensign*;

Feldarzt; *Feldobrist*; *Feldweibel*; *Generalfeldobrist*; *Generalobrist*; *Gevierthaufen*; *Hurenweibel*; *locumentems*; *martial music*; *Moncontour, Battle of*; *Nachrichter*; *Northern War, First*; *oberster Feldhauptmann*; *oberster Feldweibel*; *Obrist*; *Pfenningmeister*; *Pluderhosen*; *Provost*; *Reisläufer*; *Rottmeister*; *Schultheiss*; *Sold*; *Trabanten*; *uniforms*; *Vienna, Siege of*; *Wachmeister*; *wounds*.

Landstrum. See *Swiss Army*.

Landwehr. See *Swiss Army*.

Landwere. German militia. Although they were primary used in local defense and so were ill-equipped and poorly trained, they were sometimes mustered by the Holy Roman Emperor for major offensive campaigns.

Langport, Battle of (1645). See *English Civil Wars*.

Langside, Battle of (1568). See *Mary Stuart, Queen of Scots*.

"Lanowa" infantry. See *Polish Army*.

Lansdowne, Battle of (1643). See *English Civil Wars*.

lansquenets. The French term for *Landsknechte*.

Lanze. See *lance* (3); *men-at-arms*.

lanze spezzate. Rudimentary *standing armies* (permanent forces) maintained by several of the major Italian city states, including Milan, Naples, and Venice, from the mid-15th century. They were mainly militia but included mercenaries under long-term contract. This reserve greatly reduced reliance on more seasonal *condottieri*, some of whom were tamed by accepting the new form of salaried service.

La Rochelle. This French port was a key locale of fortified land power, as well as of marauding sea power, from the 13th to 17th centuries. In the 13th century it was a historic rival of Gascony, whose army did heavy damage to the town in 1293 and killed many of its inhabitants. La Rochelle was long a base for pirates preying on the Baltic–Mediterranean trade. Castilian *galleys* allied to France also operated from La Rochelle during the *Hundred Years' War*. In 1372 their ships intercepted and overpowered a passing fleet of armed English merchants. In other years they ravaged English shipping and raided southern England's seaports, adding to damage done by French pirates. During the *French Civil Wars*, La Rochelle was the main base of the *Huguenots*, servicing privateers and pirates and withstanding several Catholic-Royalist sieges. The siege of February–June 1573, was the single largest military effort of the entire civil wars. It was begun by 25,000 Royalist troops who received many thousands more reinforcements as the fight continued, along with royal ships prowling the outer harbor. It saw multiple assaults and miles of mining and countermining, but was decided by a steady diminution of the Royalists by desertion and disease. The king's army suffered at least 12,000 dead and perhaps as many as 22,000 total casualties, leaving just 7,500 survivors still outside the walls. Among the dead were 73 percent of royal captains. The effect of these losses was to significantly prolong the civil wars. La Rochelle's quasi-independence was guaranteed in the settlement brokered by Henri IV and affirmed in the *Edict of Nantes*.

The king's army suffered at least 12,000 dead and perhaps as many as 22,000 total casualties, leaving just 7,500 survivors . . .

As Huguenot numbers and military power declined, La Rochelle became a final refuge for hardliners, then an isolated military anomaly that could no longer be tolerated by France. It was besieged by an army sent by *Louis XIII* and *Richelieu* in 1627. It surrendered on October 28, 1628, after repeated failures by English fleets to raise the siege and once *Charles I* abandoned the city by signing the Peace of Susa (April 1629) with France. See also *Buckingham*; *Castillon, Battle of*; *Edict of Alès*; *Henri III*; *Île de Ré, Siege of*.

Suggested Reading: David Parker, *La Rochelle and the French Monarchy* (1980).

Las Navas de Tolosa, Battle of (1212). See *Knights of Calatrava*; *Reconquista*.

last. A measure of gunpowder on an English warship: 2,400 pounds divided among 24 barrels.

lateen sails. Large triangular canvases hoisted to mastheads by long yards secured to the deck with rope and tackle. Originating in the Mediterranean, they were adopted by Atlantic and Baltic shipbuilders during the 15th century and made already "weatherly" northern ships handle even better. Lateen sails were integral in development of the great hybrid ships of sail. See also *caravel*; *carrack*; *galleon*; *galley*; *masts*; *rigging*; *sails*; *sternpost rudder*; *zabra*.

launciers. See *demi-lancers*.

Laupen, Battle of (1339). Here, rather than at *Morgarten* (1315), Europe first witnessed the unfolding superiority of the *Swiss square* as it routed a numerically superior army of mounted knights on ground favorable to cavalry, and thus presaged the eventual demise of *heavy cavalry* in European warfare. The tactics used grew mainly from Swiss experience but may also have owed something to the lessons of the famous Flemish victory at *Courtrai* (1302). The battle resulted from the struggle of the plains city of Berne to break away from the growing menace of Burgundy, then allied with Fribourg. Berne struck preemptively by attacking and occupying the fortified city of Laupen. Its enemies responded with an allied army of some 12,000, which laid siege to Laupen. Berne appealed to the *Forest Cantons* for aid, and was sent about 500 men. Other cantons sent another 500 for a total of 6,500 Swiss. For the first time the troops of the cantons wore the white cross on their weapons or clothing that became the signature of the *Swiss Confederation*.

Outside Laupen the Swiss formed two columns with their backs to a nearby forest. The Forest Cantons and other allied contingents formed a van that faced the Burgundian heavy cavalry, while the Bernese militia faced mainly infantry from Fribourg. The Bernese immediately suffered desertions from rear ranks into the nearby woods, but front ranks held on both sides. Soon, Bernese skill with *halberds* began to tell: deep and bloody defiles were cut into the Fribourg ranks and the Fribourg infantry broke and ran. Instead of pursuing, the Bernese wheeled to attack across the flank of the badly outnumbered Forest Cantons. The Swiss were still mainly armed with halberds (the *pike* had not yet become a main weapon). Even so, they pinned the Burgundian knights between the Forest men and the Bernese. The Burgundian line was broken and scattered by a sudden onslaught: ferocious axe men and halberdiers pierced the enemy's warhorses with the iron spikes of their weapons, while others opened up a gut or hacked off the legs of horses, turtling riders to the ground. Still others went for the riders, using their hooked halberds to pull bewildered and frightened knights from their saddles to finish them off on the ground with axes and daggers. The battle ended in a swirl of spraying blood and screaming horses, shattered and splintered lances, the metallic clang of axe meeting helmet and breastplate, and the curses and screams of terror from men who knew there was no escape from great pain and death.

Laws of Olèron. A code of Atlantic maritime law promulgated c.1150–1339. The code was probably devised to govern the rich wine trade that flowed between Gascony and England, on which passage merchant ships passed the Ile d'Olèron. The laws forbade a ship's master from directly punishing a member of his crew for a major infraction of ship's rules. Instead, they granted the accused a right to trial by an admiral (in those days, often a land-based official in overall charge of naval affairs). The Laws of Olèron further specified that if ship's master struck one blow against a sailor this should be suffered without retaliation, but that if the master struck further blows the sailor had a right to physically defend himself without fear of punishment or accusation of mutiny.

laws of war. See *Articles of War*; *bellum hostile*; *chivalry*; *civilians*; *guerre couverte*; *guerre mortelle*; *"holy war"*; *Laws of Olèron*; *prisoners of war*; *prohibited weapons*; *requerimiento*; *siege warfare*; *"skulking way of war."*

league. Generally, three miles (of varying national lengths) on land. At sea, a league was one-twentieth of a degree of longitude, an inexact measure subject to disagreement among medieval and early modern navigators.

League of Public Weal. An anti-French noble alliance headed by *Charles the Rash*. It joined the ducs de Alençon, Berry, Bourbon, Burgundy, and Lorraine against *Louis XI* of France. At Montihéry, just south of Paris, the ducs beat Louis, forcing him to agree to major concessions (Treaty of Conflans). However, Louis mostly ignored the terms because he knew that the conflicting ambitions of each great duc militated against continuing alliance.

"leather guns." An experiment to reform the Swedish artillery undertaken by *Gustavus Adolphus* early in his reign led to these unique field guns. They were cast from iron but lined with brass or copper and reinforced with alloy. The barrel was bound with wire and rope splints, wrapped in canvas secured by wooden rings, and hard leather was nailed to the exterior. They weighed about 600 pounds and could be pulled by two horses (or just one, in a pinch). All-metal castings ultimately proved far more successful, especially the 3-pounder Swedish "regimental gun." In 1640, Scots mercenaries home from the German war, usually from service with the Swedish Army, used a version of "leather guns" to effect to cover their crossing of the River Tyne. However, by the 1640s leather guns were long discarded in Sweden in favor of cast iron cannon. Some Irish armies also tried to deploy leather guns, mostly to disastrous effect.

Lech, Battle of (1632). See *Rain, Battle of*.

legharnesses. Leg armor. See also *cuisses*; *poleyns*.

Lehnsaufgebot. See *Imperial Army*.

Leicester, Earl of (c.1530–1588). Né Robert Dudley. Arrested in the aftermath of *Wyatt's Rebellion* in 1554, Dudley was tried for treason but pardoned by *Philip II*; his father was not so fortunate. Dudley joined Philip in his war with France but returned to England when *Mary Tudor* died. Tactless and vain about his aristocratic breeding, he was nevertheless a favorite of *Elizabeth I*. Many at court thought that he was her lover. In 1563 she made him an earl and he remained a close advisor. A well-known patron of English Calvinists, in 1585 he was sent to the Netherlands to lead English troops dispatched there under the *Treaty of Nonsuch*. Nominally, he was also head of the *Raad*. In April 1586, Leicester instituted a blockade of the Flemish coast and other Spanish occupied areas, extending this as far south as the Somme in August. He also fought at *Zutphen*. In 1586, Leicester backed the most radical Calvinist factions in Dutch internal political wars. He earned the ire of Holland by plotting a failed coup against its regents in September 1587. He returned to England a failure and disgrace and soon died of a fever.

Leiden, Siege of (May 26–October 3, 1574). Leiden was first besieged by the *Duke of Alba* in 1573. Ultimately, it was under siege for 20 months, one of the longest and hardest sieges of the *Eighty Years' War* (1568–1648). It was defended by *schutterijen* (militia) who held out until the Spanish withdrew in March 1574, to fight *William the Silent* who had invaded from Germany. The

Spanish came back in May and surrounded Leiden with 8,000 men. In a act of desperation (Leiden was key to survival of the revolt), William ordered *Oldenbaarneveldt* to cut the dikes along the Maas south of the city on August 3, and sent a *Sea Beggar* relief fleet on flat-bottomed boats over the flooded plain. The waters did not rise high enough, however, and for weeks the Dutch ships could not reach the city. After a heavy rain the waters rose and finally lifted the Beggar boats, which fought off Spanish infantry who came out on barges to attack the relief fleet as it moved. The Dutch ships had taken two months to work up to the city walls, but they finally broke the Spanish lines at a dash to deliver food and supplies to Leiden's skeletal defenders. This was a crucial event in the Dutch Revolt as after the failure of its siege at Leiden the *Army of Flanders* evacuated Holland and Zeeland.

Leipheim, Battle of (1525). See *German Peasant War*.

Leipziger Bund **(1631).** A defensive alliance of the Protestant princes of north Germany who opposed *Ferdinand II*'s radical confessional and imperial policies but were reluctant to see *Gustavus Adolphus* intervene in the *Thirty Years' War*. It was formed on April 12, 1631, to resist further recatholicization and warn off the Swedes. On paper it created an army of 40,000 to be raised by the *Reichskreis* to advance these ends. However, *Johann Tilly*'s sack of *Magdeburg* in May 1631, and the strength of the Swedish Army in Germany, forced the princes to side with Gustavus. Its Catholic counterpart was created by the *Treaty of Fontainebleau* (1631).

Lens, Battle of (August 2, 1648). The last battle of the *Thirty Years' War*. As peace negotiations dragged on in Westphalia a Habsburg army of 15,000 men under Leopold Wilhelm, younger brother of *Ferdinand III*, attacked toward Arras in France. *Condé* feigned retreat, then doubled back on the Austro-Spanish force. He caught it strung out in line of march and annihilated it. The Spanish lost 8,000 dead and 30 field guns. This final defeat helped persuade Ferdinand to sign the peace accords, ending the great and terrible war in Germany.

Leonardo da Vinci (1452–1519). Florentine inventor, painter, scientist, sculptor and gun maker. He moved to Milan in 1482 under commission to the *Sforza* dukes, first Ludovico, then Maximilian. He pursued mostly the peaceful arts in Milan for some 16 years, achieving unparalleled brilliance in multiple fields, most especially the fine arts. He also turned his unmatched genius to designing machines of war. He built various siege weapons for the dukes and drafted more fanciful, yet brilliant designs for what centuries later would become tanks, submersible warships, and even a helicopter. In the early 1490s he published *Codex Madrid II*, a highly influential and reliable guide to gun types and gunpowder recipes. He was forced to leave Milan upon the overthrow of the Sforzas in 1499 at the start of the *Italian Wars* (1494–1559). In 1502 he accepted service under Cesar Borgia as a military engineer and spent a year in the field with the army. In 1506 he returned to Milan in the service of its French conqueror, Louis XII, whom da Vinci served as architect as well as military engineer. He closed out his remarkable life in the service of the French King *Francis I*, who allowed him to live and work undisturbed in the royal chateau at Amboise. Leonardo da Vinci knew *Niccolò Machiavelli*, but while enigmatic his varied and superficially mercenary career had far more to do with the turbulence of Italian finance and politics than any personal bent for Machiavellian intrigue.

Lepanto, Battle of (July 28, 1499). A climactic fight in the long naval struggle for supremacy in the eastern Mediterranean between Venice and the Ottoman Empire. *Bayezid II*'s large, new galley fleet won handily over the smaller Venetian fleet. As a result, Venice gave up some Greek island bases and came to an understanding on trade with the Ottomans, who henceforth controlled the eastern Mediterranean.

Lepanto, Battle of (October 7, 1571). In the eighth decade of the 16th century some 500 war *galleys* operated in the Mediterranean. Of these, 450 met in the last great galley fight in history, off the coast of Greece in the Gulf of Lepanto. On one side was an allied fleet of Spanish and Venetian galleys, supported by a few more ships sent by the pope, Malta, Genoa, and other minor powers. On the other was the Ottoman galley navy and the *galliots* of the Barbary corsairs. The Christian fleet was commanded by *Don Juan* of Austria, a cocky 24-year-old and half-brother of *Philip II* of Spain. It numbered 220 galleys and six Venetian *galleasses* and was crewed by 50,000 men; it carried another 30,000 marines on its decks. Sultan *Selim II* put 230 galleys and 70 Barbary galliots into the water, carrying 90,000 men, including thousands of

Also present was a young Spaniard who would later famously mock Spain's tired crusade . . .

marines and 6,000 of the sultan's crack *Janissary Corps*. The Muslim fleet was commanded by Ali Pasha. This staggering commitment of men and resources gathered to fight for the usual reasons of territory, trade, and the vanity of sovereigns. But they were also there to decide on whose side God truly fought in a long war of civilizations by then into its eighth baleful century. Thus, both sides indulged the usual rhetoric of "*holy war*": the Christians fought as the "Holy League" and sailed to war with the pope's blessing; the Ottomans rowed to battle confident that theirs was the superior civilization and that the green flag of Islam would soon fly over Venice and Rome, and once more over Córdoba, Granada, and Madrid. There were also men on each side of more worldly views, however. Among the Ottomans the normal cynicism of sultans nestled easily alongside ascendant imperial power, while sailing with the Christians were hard-headed Venetian merchant captains. Also present was a young Spaniard who would later famously mock Spain's tired crusade in the greatest novel of his age and culture: Miguel Cervantes, future author of *Don Quixote*.

The majority of the Muslim galleys were lighter and lay lower in the water than Western ships, especially the oversize Spanish galleys. To counter this, Don Juan ordered ships to cut off their spurs so that the centerline guns were not blocked from firing down into the lower Muslim ships. With the enemy spotted, he anchored his left near the north shore of Lepanto Bay, putting his fastest ships (the Venetian galleys) there out of fear that Muslim advantages in speed and shallow draft might lead to his left being flanked and becoming disordered. He put the heavy Spanish galleys at the center, with galleasses in front to disorder the Muslim line. His right was supposed to hold the Muslim left while the heaviest action was fought at the center. It was a straight-ahead, no nonsense plan. The Christian line of battle was: Right, 38 galleys and 2 galleasses; Center, a front line of 62 galleys and 2 galleasses, with a Reserve of 54 galleys; Left, 53 galleys and 2 galleasses.

The problem for Don Juan, and the opportunity for Ali Pasha, was along the north shore where shallow-draft Muslim galleys might outflank the Christian line and force a general mêlée. This was indeed the essence of Ali Pasha's plan—to get his faster ships in among the heavier Christian galleys and wreak havoc on them with his more numerous and highly skilled marines. Ali Pasha lined up his galleys in a near-mirror image of the Christian line of battle: standard formation on the right, heavy in the center, and standard on the left. His reserve was pre-committed behind his center. Each battle plan correctly assumed the main action would take place at the center. The difference was that the Muslims hoped for, while the Christians feared, a secondary flanking action along the north shore. The Muslim line of battle was: Right, 60 galleys, 2 galliots; Center, front line of 62 galleys and a second line of 25 galleys and 8 galliots, with a Reserve line of 8 galleys, 22 galliots, and 64 smaller *fustas*; Left, 61 galleys, 32 galliots.

The fleets spotted one another just after dawn. Over the next few hours they formed parallel *lines ahead and astern* and slowly approached, prow facing prow, each ship waiting for a signal from the commander at the center for the whole line to break into battle speed. This was crucial, because once it was given a signal to engage could not be rescinded: commanders committed the fleet to all-out battle or backed away from the fight, iron teeth bared to the front. There was no middle choice. The opening shots were fired around 11:30 a.m. on the north flank where a squadron of fast Muslim galleys broke into the shallows to outflank the Venetians. The Muslims, under Mehemet Suluk, were partially successful: five ships got around the north flank, sinking eight Venetian galleys in the process. The Venetians skillfully pivoted their line by backing water in unison, avoiding disaster by presenting a new front to the Muslims. All other ships on the north flank then closed at battle speed, firing all guns when prows touched, or even after, into the faces of the enemy crew. Survivors of the crashing cannon volley shifted to crossbows, muskets, swivel guns, and fought hand-to-hand with sword, knife, and pistol. The five Muslim ships free on the Venetian flank poured musketry into the unprotected sides of several enemy galleys, as all around a hundred galleys collided in a frenzy of intimate murder and bloody mayhem. The two galleasses played a crucial role, turning the fight with unmatched firepower from deck-mounted broadside cannon and their reloadable bow guns (galleasses could reload on high, protected decks while low-lying galleys could not). The whole northern wing of the battle now disappeared from view by both commanders at the center, concealed beneath rolls of cannon and musket smoke and darker clouds rising from burning ships and men. The fight on the north flank ended when surviving Muslim galleys were deliberately grounded so that their marines and officers could run away. Thousands of Christian slaves were rescued from the abandoned ships, which were then burned. More drowned as broken galleys went to the bottom, or died screaming chained to their oar and unable to escape the flames.

Don Juan and Ali Pasha remained calm throughout the fury and confusion on the north flank. The fight in the center started at mid-day, 30 minutes after firing broke out to the north. The thunder of heavy cannon at the center was immense, as the main battle fleets closed and loosed thousands of big guns at point-blank range along four heavy lines of over 200 galleys charging head-long and together. The cannon spent, the fleets locked and sent marines at each other. Fighting was ferocious around the two flagships, Don Juan's "Real" and Ali Pasha's "Sultana." The commanders locked prows, blasted raw holes in each other's crew with bow guns, and sent streams of men forward to have at each other with pistols, axes, knives, and swords. Twice, boarding parties from the "Real" pushed forward to the mast of the "Sultana," but twice they were pushed back by Muslim reinforcements fed in from the stern by ships of the reserve. The Christians reinforced the same way, so that the piles of bodies clustered around the masts of the "Sultana" grew by the minute. Meanwhile, other galleys closed in from the sides. Again, Muslim ships proved more maneuverable but also more vulnerable to action by the galleasses. The greater weight of firepower, including from better model pistols and muskets, lay with the Spanish. As the fight continued superior volume of hot metal from the Christian side carried the hour and began to win the battle at the center. Height advantage of the Christian galleys and galleasses allowed the tough veterans of Spain's *tercios* to fire down into the Janissaries and other Ottoman marines. The Muslims could not win this battle of crude attrition. Still, the outcome remained in doubt during more than an hour of hand-to-hand combat. Dozens of damaged and burning galleys drifted together, locked at the prow or grappled from the side, as their crews fought to the last man. Some men dived over board to flounder and drown in their armor or were shot in the water as they swam for their lives.

At first, things went better for the Ottomans on the southern flank where the Christian galleys stretched away from the Center. Their commander, *Gian Andrea Doria*, was either duplicitous or, more likely, feared another flanking maneuver like the one that nearly succeeded on the northern flank. His line kept stretching toward the south shore of Lepanto Bay to prevent flanking. But this opened a wide gap from the Christian center. The Muslim wing commander, Uluj Ali, ordered his galleys into the open water to fall on Don Juan's now exposed inner flank. Fifteen galleys broke ranks with Andrea

Doria to try to reinforce the Christian center. Before they arrived the situation was recovered by the *marques de Santa Cruz* in command of the Christian reserve, already positioned at the center. He moved forward and trapped Uluj Ali's squadrons between two lines of more powerful Christian ships.

Back on the "Sultana" a musket ball passed into Ali Pasha's eye, killing him instantly. A third boarding party, this time led by Don Juan himself, rushed the deck of the Muslim flagship under cover of volleys of musketry and killed its last defenders. With the Muslim commander dead and the Sultana taken, panic visibly rippled through the Muslim battle line. It suddenly burst apart as individual galleys broke formation and tried to run for shore. Only a few escaped a vigorous Christian pursuit and the immense slaughter that followed. Men were killed and ships burned without mercy. When it was over, Lepanto saw more death than any battle would for another 350 years: more died in the Gulf of Lepanto in two hours than died at Lützen, Blenheim, or Waterloo; more than at the Nile or Trafalgar; more than any battle on land or at sea anywhere prior to the failed British attack on the German trenches at Loos in 1915. The list of dead at Lepanto numbered no fewer than 50,000 fathers, brothers, and sons, all gone in an afternoon. The Christian side had lost dozens of galleys and about 10,000 men. Muslim losses were 40,000 dead and over 200 galleys sunk, burned, or captured. Thousands of heavy guns were forever lost to the sultans.

Selim II did not fully appreciate his loss. He said: "The infidels only singed my beard; it will grow back again." He was right in that the Ottoman Empire quickly replaced all galleys lost. Longer-term, he was wrong: among the dead were nearly all the Janissaries and *sipahis* who put to sea and more important, thousands of irreplaceable Ottoman pilots and sailors. Thousands more taken prisoner would never see home or family again. Most were sold into slavery, but some were murdered: the next year the Council of Ten in Venice polled its prisoners from Lepanto to identify galley pilots among them, pulled them out and put them to death. The Council secretly advised Philip II to do the same; he replied that he already had. This loss of skilled seamen, more than the loss of the ships and guns, crippled the Ottoman navy for decades. It did not recover for a generation, and when it did it found that galleys were obsolete, overtaken by great *galleons* that only Atlantic Europe built and which launched the "Age of Fighting Sail." Within just 17 years of the last great battle among galleys the first great battle of the Age of Sail was fought in the English Channel when the *Invincible Armada* sailed north from Lisbon in the summer of 1588.

Suggested Reading: J.F.C. Fuller, *Military History of the Western World*, vol. 1 (1954); John Guilmartin, *Gunpowder and Galleys* (2003).

Lerma, Duke of (1553–1625). Né Francisco Gómez de Sandoval y Rojas. First minister to *Philip III*, 1598–1618. He sought to maintain Spain's dominant position in Europe by shoring up through dynastic marriages what was being lost in battle with too many enemies. He negotiated peace with England in 1604 and agreed to the *Twelve Years' Truce* (1609–1621) with the Netherlands. Lerma was a strong supporter of *expulsion of the Moors*, which he oversaw during the Truce. He focused on war in the Mediterranean but tried to stay out of all conflicts brewing north of the Alps, and in the mind of *Ferdinand II*. This policy was reversed over his objections in the secret *Treaty of Oñate* (1617). Sensing the end was near Lerma obtained a cardinal's hat from Pope Paul V in March 1618. In October he was stripped of all offices by Philip and forced to retire. He is not to be confused with *Olivares*, also Duke of Lerma.

Les Espagnols sur Mer, Battle of (1350). See *Hundred Years' War*.

Leslie, Alexander. See *Leven, Earl of*.

Leslie, David (1601–1682). Scots general in the *English Civil Wars*. He fought under *Gustavus Adolphus* in the *Thirty Years' War* (1618–1648) and as lieutenant-general to the *Earl of Leven* early in the *English Civil Wars* (1639–1651). He fought alongside *Oliver Cromwell* at *Marston Moor*, and beat *Montrose* at *Philiphaugh* (1645); he took the surrender of *Charles V* at Newark on May 5, 1646. He joined the *Whiggamore Rising* in 1648. He took over command of the *Covenanter* army from his uncle, the Earl of Leven, and led it to disaster at *Dunbar* against Cromwell in 1650. He was beaten again by Cromwell at Worcester in 1651, where he was taken prisoner. He was imprisoned in the Tower of London until the end of the Commonwealth.

Leslie, Walter (1606–1667). Scots mercenary in Austrian service. He ingratiated himself with *Ferdinand II* by participating in the assassination of *Albrecht von Wallenstein*, whom he served under for years. He later secured the release of *Prince Rupert*, though it seems he wanted him to fight in the Palatinate rather than venture to serve *Charles I* in England. In reward for his years of service to the Habsburgs, Leslie accumulated titles, huge estates, and a vast fortune. He was promoted to Field Marshal, named an Imperial Count, and later appointed ambassador to the Sublime Porte. He died one of the most richly successful mercenaries of a mercenary age.

Le Tellier, Michel (1603–1685). Appointed Intendant to the Army of Italy (September 6, 1640), Le Tellier developed a system of standardized supply that ultimately included extensive use of *magazines*. This innovation was further advanced and completed by his son and successor, the marquis de Louvois (François Le Tellier). The idea of maintaining reserves of food, cloth, fodder for the transport and cavalry horses, dry powder and shot, and so forth was an old one. But the primitive levels of bureaucracy in the early modern state meant that most armies through the end of the *Thirty Years' War* relied on an admixture of plunder, and its handmaiden *contribution*, to supply field armies. No European army had its own transport corps. Instead, all leased civilian wagons and teamsters, or requisitioned wagons on the march (with or without compensation). Starting with the French Army in Italy, Le Tellier imposed tight contracts on merchants, insisting that they actually maintain at the ready all wagons and draft animals leased, even during the winter when little to no campaigning was undertaken. Appointed Secretary of War by *Louis XIII* in April 1643, Le Tellier set about fundamental reform of the French military supply and transportation system. For the first time a study of the matériel requirements of the French Army was made. This reduced corruption by contracted *sutlers* and royal officials long used to padding bills. It also led to standardization of food, armaments, uniforms, and equipment provided to the troops. Le Tellier even regulated the number of carts and teams allowed officers, strictly according to rank, of course.

Once the basic list of requirements was established, Le Tellier drafted standardized contracts through which he better controlled expenses. To further reduce corruption, all contracted goods were delivered not as before to commanders or regimental officers, but to central depots where they were checked by royal agents ("général de vivres"). Transport was arranged through major sutlers given special powers to draft wagons and teams, laborers, millwrights, cooks, and bakers. Le Tellier set aside a reserve of government owned wagons and horses which carried the first few days of supplies whenever an army moved into the field. In 1643 he set up a series of magazines along the usual routes used by the army when it moved out of its base area toward the Rhine; that is, at Metz, Nancy, and Pònt-à-Mousson. The next year he built a fodder magazine for the cavalry during the siege of Dunkirk, and in 1648 he set up more magazines at Arras and Dunkirk while a French army was besieging Ypres. In short, Le Tellier created the first true Ministry of War to set standards and protect merchants who cooperated with the royal system (including exempting their convoys from local road and river tolls). Most of all, he ensured that soldiers received good working equipment and regular pay, food, clothing, and shelter. Le Tellier further advanced this early magazine system during *Turenne*'s 1658 campaign of successive sieges against Dunkirk, Brégues, Oudenaarde, and Ypres. Le Tellier's system ultimately altered the conduct of logistics for the next 150 years. Yet, in his lifetime the changes made had only a modest effect on specific campaigns. Real progress toward a permanent magazine system was made by his son during the wars of Louis XIV.

> *Le Tellier created the first true Ministry of War to set standards and protect merchants who cooperated with the royal system . . .*

Suggested Reading: Louis André, *Michel le Tellier et l'organisation de l'armée monarchique* (1906; 1980).

letters of marque. A license given by a state or monarch to a *privateer* designating the captain and ship as a warship of the realm. This permitted private warships to capture or destroy enemy shipping in time of war. Captures were adjudicated by a *prize court*, and the monarch always took a share. See also *Sea Beggars*.

letters of reprisal. A license given by a state or monarch to a *privateer* permitting capture of enemy shipping from a foreign power, an act justified by some insult or injury whether real or imagined. The high margins and profits of privateering often led to deliberate misreading of innocent remarks or gestures as slights requiring a campaign of reprisal. And reprisals often far outstripped the original insult or injury in numbers of prizes captured or the time covered by the letter, which rendered otherwise piratical acts by the privateer permitted and legal. Such authority might be granted generally against the shipping of a foreign power or be given as a commission to a single ship.

lettres de retenue. See *French Army.*

Letzinen. Earth and log palisades and earthworks employed by the Swiss in defense. They were used to great effect at *Morgarten* (1315), *Näfels* (1388), *Vögelisegg* (1403), and *Stoss* (1405). See also *Mordax.*

Levellers. Democratic agitators and proponents of radical social reform in England. Their concentration in the *New Model Army* in 1646–1647 meant the political balance at a crucial moment in the *English Civil Wars* (1639–1651) teetered on Leveller demands. Their program called for a secular republic with universal male suffrage, abolition of the Lords, free speech, and religious toleration. This alarmed the Lords and Commons, the gentry and episcopacy, Presbyterians in England, Covenanters in Scotland, and the Army high command of *Fairfax, Cromwell,* and *Ireton.* In March 1647, the generals sat with the rank and file to discuss political change, and did so again in December 1648. What kept the movement alive were issues of arrears of pay, impressment, and veterans' relief. Renewal of the war in Ireland undercut Leveller influence. When some mutinied at Corkbush Field in November 1648, Fairfax and Cromwell had three ringleaders draw lots and one shot. Then they demobilized several regiments suspected of Leveller, Presbyterian, or Royalist infection, ending the threat to their own leadership of the Army and the Army's command over the country. See also *Fifth Monarchists.*

Leven, Earl of (c.1580–1661). Né Alexander Leslie. Protestant field marshal. A Scot by birth, he fought for the Netherlands at *Straslund* in 1628, and under *Gustavus Adolphus* in Germany. In 1630 he went to Moscow as a military adviser. Leslie saw action at *Lützen* (1632) and continued fighting in Germany to 1636. He then brought his skills home to Scotland in 1638 and led the *Covenanter* army in both *Bishops' Wars,* after which Charles elevated him to Earl of Leven. He fought with brutal cruelty against Catholics in Ireland from 1642 to 1644. Recalled to Scotland, he led the Covenanters in the difficult struggle against *Montrose* in the Highlands, then commanded the large Scots army that intervened in the *English Civil Wars.* He took Charles' surrender at Newark in 1646 and was the king's jailor to 1647. He joined the *Whiggamore Rising* in 1648. He later resigned his command to his nephew, *David Leslie.*

levend/levendat. "levents." The term, originally meaning "landless ones," applied to temporary Ottoman recruits used as irregular infantry and provincial troops from the 14th century. Some also served as marines. They were recruited at first among the bandits of Anatolia, but later from the wider *Raya* (general population). By the 16th century levendat auxiliary infantry expanded in numbers as the Ottomans looked for inexpensive musketeers to supplement the well-paid, professional *Janissary Corps*. Unlike the latter, a levend unit was demobilized at the end of a campaign. This made them less reliable.

Lewes, Battle of (1264). See *England*.

Liegnitz, Battle of (1241). See *Mongols*; *Teutonic Knights, Order of*.

lieutenant. On land: A junior officer who assisted the commanding officer of a body of troops. At sea: In the 16th century, an army officer in command of soldiers aboard a warship. In the 17th century, a new rank for younger naval officers who assisted the *captain*.

Lieutenant-General (Germany). A general officer in the Imperial Army, second in rank; above a Field Marshal but below Generallissimus.

Lieutenant-général du royaume **("of the kingdom").** The second in command of royal armies, after the Constable of France. During the *French Civil Wars* (1562–1629) the title was held by *François, duc de Guise* (1557); *Antoine de Bourbon* (1561); *Henri, duc de Guise* (1588); and the *duc de Mayenne* (1589).

Liga. See *Catholic League (Germany)*.

light cavalry. Cavalry wearing less than full armor and mounted on small, swift ponies, not the *destriers* of medieval *heavy cavalry*. Their primary roles were to escort land convoys, set ambushes, scout ahead of the main body, forage, and raid. They could also serve as auxiliary cavalry in battle. They went by many names: *genitors* in Spain; *chevaux-légers* in France; *demi-lancers* in Medieval England, and "prickers" and "scourers" during the *Wars of the Roses*. See also *Bedouin*; *cavalry*; *chevauchées*; *hobelars*; *jinetes*; *lancers*; *Mongols*; *samurai*; *stradiots*; *Turcopoles*.

limacon. See *caracole*.

line abreast. A naval formation in which all ships in a line sailed parallel to each other as they approached the enemy's line. This offered the narrowest profile (the bow) to the enemy's guns while allowing the attacker to turn all ships in his line at once, either ahead or astern, to engage with broadside cannon as each ship sailed along the enemy line. It is important to appreciate that while these orders and formations were used late in the period they were not fully mature until the late 17th or even early 18th century. See also *galley*; *Lepanto, Battle of (October 7, 1571)*.

line ahead. A key naval tactic of the later Age of Sail used primarily by *ships-of-the-line* of the Atlantic nations, it had loose origins in the Elizabethan era. In line ahead a fleet of warships sailed not in the Spanish crescent or Ottoman scimitar-like broad front, but in single-file columns ahead of the flagship or designated captains, with all following ships mimicking maneuvers of the lead ship. This avoided an inconclusive but potentially damaging and unpredictable mêlée in which individual ship-to-ship actions took place, while maximizing the power of broadside fire of the whole fleet. See also *line astern*.

line ahead and astern. A naval formation in which the flagship occupied the center of the line so that all other ships were either ahead or astern of it.

line astern. A naval formation in which all ships in line of battle followed the flagship. See also *line ahead*.

line of battle. Any fighting formation in which warships formed a line and imitated the movements of the lead ship or carried out uniform orders from the flagship. See also *line abreast*; *line ahead*; *line ahead and astern*; *line astern*; *ship-of-the-line*.

Line of Demarcation (May 4, 1493). With breathtaking arrogance, Pope Alexander VI issued a papal bull ("Intervention cetera divina") on May 4, 1493, dividing the non-Christian, non-European world between the empires of Spain and Portugal. (There was minor precedent for this in a 1479 papal mediation of a dispute over the Canary Islands.) The division ran along a nautical line 100 leagues west of Cape Verde and the Azores. Spain received the Western Hemisphere containing the newly discovered Americas; Portugal was granted the Eastern Hemisphere, including most of Africa where the Portuguese were already established. The Treaty of Tordesillas (June 1494) moved the line to 370 leagues west, securing West Africa for Portugal and giving the whole Caribbean to Spain. But the move meant that the great bulge of Brazil (then unknown to Castile, but probably known in secret in Lisbon) would fall within Portugal's sphere. Pedro Cabral landed on the Brazilian coast in 1500, securing the claim. With the Spanish discovery of the Pacific on the other side of the Panamanian isthmus in 1512, the line was extended into the new ocean. In 1514 the pope granted Portugal the right to any new lands discovered while sailing east from Africa. This spurred Spain to sail west across the Pacific from its base in the Americas, as both powers raced to reach and claim the *Spice Islands*. The Philippines thus went to Spain despite lying inside Lisbon's sphere because that archipelago was discovered by Ferdinand Magellan while he was in service to *Charles V*, King of Spain. In 1529 the Treaty of Zaragoza finalized the Tordesillas settlement by extending it into the Pacific at 145° East. All these "lines of demarcation" were ignored by other maritime powers from the start, and still more with the *Protestant Reformation*. As early as 1497 the Genoese explorer John Cabot claimed Newfoundland and Nova Scotia for England. In later decades explorers from

Protestant England and the Netherlands and from anti-Habsburg Catholic France mapped and settled much of eastern North America without regard for Spain's claims to the entire hemisphere. In addition, French, English, and Dutch *privateers* not only ignored Iberian claims, they preyed regularly on Spanish and Portuguese merchants, fishing, and treasure ships.

line of march. See *chevauchée*; *Le Tellier, Michel*; *lines of supply*; *logistics*; *magazines*.

line of metal. A gunner's line of sight, looking straight from the base down the muzzle.

lines of circumvallation. Making an entrenchment around an enemy position was a preliminary move in *siege warfare*. The parapet and accompanying ditch thus formed around the besieged place, or around the besieging army, was called the line (or lines, as plural trenches were often dug) of circumvallation.

lines of communication. Since *lines of supply* were weak to nonexistent in this era, lines of communication were similarly unimportant: movement of armies was determined far more by the requirements of foraging for basic supplies than by strategic direction or concern for communications. A rare exception was *Gustavus Adolphus* in Germany during the *Thirty Years' War* (1618–1648).

lines of contravallation. An entrenchment comprised of redoubts, earthworks, and a ditch—with or without a connecting *parapet*—engineered by a besieging force to protect their base camp against sallies by the besieged garrison.

lines of investment. Siege trenches dug toward the defending walls, until the terminus of the trench was close enough to serve as a sally point for *storming*.

lines of operations. There were two kinds of environmental lines along which any military operation was conducted and by which it was constrained in this period: "natural" markers such as mountains, rivers, plains, or oceans; and artificial barriers raised by fortifications, trenches, roads, or canals. Political barriers were far more pliable than in later eras. "Interior lines" (of operations) were created when a military force found itself between enemy armies, which happened rarely in this period. For some theorists, this created an advantage of shorter lines of reinforcement and supply, which derived from occupying the "interior" position. Many modern military theorists dismiss the idea of lines of operations as narrowly technical. The idea survives, however, as a familiar term of art among military historians.

lines of supply. Roads and wagon transport used by 16th- and 17th-century armies were rudimentary at best. Transport by river or along the sea coast was more efficient and did not require fodder (the most bulky item among all essential supplies) since horse-drawn transport was left on the bank or shore. However, rivers limited military maneuver to lines paralleling their course, while ocean transport was subject to interception by *pirates* or enemy warships. These facts meant that field armies simply could not be adequately supplied and therefore had to resort to plunder or some version of *contributions*.

In turn, that meant armies tended to move constantly, eating out each area before moving on. While this freed armies from any sort of base of supply and made it next to impossible to isolate them strategically, it limited their usefulness since most time, energy, and motivation was devoted to endless foraging rather than strategic maneuver or battle. Armies of this era thus did not march on their stomach, as Napoleon later famously said his did, so much as march to fill their stomachs and the bellies of their horses. See also *Gustavus II Adolphus*; *logistics*; *magazines*; *Maurits of Nassau*; *Wallenstein, Albrecht von*.

> *Armies of this era thus did not march on their stomach, ... so much as march to fill their stomachs ...*

Linköping, Battle of (1598). See *Karl IX*; *Sigismund III*.

linstock. A gunners' tool formed of a long pole with curved arms at the top end. These held the *slow match* which gunners used to light their *quick matches*, which in turn were used to touch off charges in nearby loaded cannon. Usually, one linstock was placed between two guns and used by both crews. At sea shorter linstocks were used, often with a carved hand grip and sometimes with the head also carved to resemble a dragon or other mythical beast. The slow match was wound around the handle while the jaws gripped the burning end. Otherwise, the basic actions of firing guns were the same as on land.

Lipany, Battle of (1434). See *Český-Brod, Battle of*.

Lipsius, Justus (1547–1606). Neostoic Dutch philosopher at the University of Leiden. He was a great admirer of *Machiavelli*, on whose work he based his own contribution to the *art of war*, "De Militia Romana" (1596). He was a key mentor to *Maurits of Nassau* from 1583 to 1584. Lipsius argued for a rational understanding of war as an instrument of state policy, not merely as feral violence. This led him to embrace *just war* notions of right authority and limited force correlated to limited goals. Drawing on the *Italian Renaissance* and Machiavelli's rediscovery of Graeco-Roman virtues and military systems, Lipsius promoted *drill*, unit cohesion, *military discipline*, and a new professional ethic among officers that tied their loyalties to the state rather than the old reliance on lordship, client systems, or personal gain. Responding to the confessional divisions of the *Eighty Years' War* (1568–1648), he tried to develop a universal ethics based on secular principles. In this he lost out in his homeland to Catholic reactionaries in the south and Calvinist fanatics in the north. He was a poor judge of more practical and political men: he was bitterly disappointed by the *duc d'Anjou*, then by the *Earl of Leicester*, eventually returning to a vaguely pro-Habsburg romanticism.

Lisowczyks. "Lisowczycy Cossacks." Polish cavalry named for their commander, Aleksander Lisowski (d.1617). This unit was formed into a single *pulk* for service in Muscovy during the *"Time of Troubles"* (1604–1613). As an unofficial adjunct to the *Polish Army*, it conducted a sustained border war against Muscovy. The Lisowczyks were unpaid but were given license to plunder freely. This backfired on Poland whenever they returned from campaigning, as they did not cease their habit of brigandage on the Polish side of the border. Although no longer led by their founder and first commander after 1617, they still fought under his name in the *Thirty Years' War* (1618–1648), to which they were sent as a secret contribution from the Polish king to the Catholic emperors of the Holy Roman Empire. They saw action in France, Germany, Hungary, Italy, and the Netherlands, earning everywhere a reputation for ferocity and pillage unusual even in an age of merciless confessional warfare.

Lithuania, Grand Duchy of. Early medieval Lithuania was a pagan land that consolidated politically in response to *crusades* launched against its Slavic population by several German *Military Orders*. Once the knights of the *Livonian Order* and the *Teutonic Knights* merged in 1237, they sought to follow the earlier conquest of Prussia (1230) with new crusades into the Slav lands. A protracted war thus broke out between the *Ordensstaat* and pagan Lithuania. Medieval Lithuania remained a major regional power in Central and Eastern Europe and parts of modern Belarus and Ukraine. It even competed for dominance in the region while Muscovy still labored under the "Mongol Yoke." Lithuania expanded into what is today western Russia, beyond Smolensk, reaching toward Moscow in the east, south to Starodub and north to Courland and Livonia. As Muscovy threw out the Golden Horde and as *Cossack* raiders attacked from the Ukraine, thinly populated Lithuania required military assistance to hold onto its far-flung lands. The solution was a dynastic marriage of the *Jagiellon* to link Lithuania with Poland in a 14th-century "union of crowns." Most Lithuanian nobles thereafter spoke Polish and converted to Catholicism, which distanced them from Ruthenian-speaking peasants who remained Orthodox. In 1410 a combined Polish-Lithuanian army defeated the Teutonic Knights at *Tannenberg*, finally ending that threat from the west. Over the next century Lithuania expanded into Ukraine, where the end of Kievan Rus left a fragmented, militarily weak state. In 1452, Volhynia was incorporated as a province of Lithuania; Kiev was annexed in 1471. The next existential danger to Lithuania came from the east with the rise of Muscovy. Poland-Lithuania faced an aggressive and expansionist Muscovite empire led by the brutal tyrant *Ivan IV* during the *First Northern War* (1558–1583). Unable to defend itself, Lithuania fused fully with Poland in the *Union of Lublin* (1569).

By the middle of the 17th century the sprawling Union of Poland-Lithuania occupied nearly one million square kilometers, making it larger than Muscovy or the Holy Roman Empire and twice as big as France. Its population stretched thinly over a vast plain that presented no natural frontiers before the Carpathian Mountains to the south. It was, therefore, easily invaded and difficult to defend. Moreover, following annual spring rains Poland and Lithuania were divided from each other by vast flooded marshlands and swollen rivers. This reserved military action to the winter season when frozen rivers were crossed easily by the great cavalry armies that dominated Eastern European warfare. This was the obverse of the Western European experience where winter brought campaigning to an abrupt halt. The Lithuanian army was about one-half the size of Poland's. It contained a high proportion of Tatars, and thus fought with less tactical discipline and in looser cavalry formations than their partners in Poland. The army was raised in "grand" and "small" levies, with the former reserved for national emergencies. In most other military matters, such as organization and terminology, the Lithuanians followed Polish practice. The quality and morale of this army was extremely poor due to its combination of overly proud nobles and peasant conscripts who were nearly worthless in battle. Tactical indiscipline led it to panic more easily than most armies, as happened most spectacularly at Pilawice in 1648 when the entire Lithuanian army scattered in face of a mere rumor that a Cossack host was approaching. See also *Livonia*; *Poland*; *Ukraine*.

living off the land. See *bellum se ipse alet*; *contributions*; *logistics*.

Livonia. Between 1198 and 1263 this Baltic region north of Prussia was attacked by smaller German *Military Orders* then conquered by the *Livonian Order* or "Knights of the Sword." After 1237 further conquest was carried out in tandem with the *Teutonic Knights* who absorbed the Livonian Order and ruled Livonia into the 16th century. From Livonia the Teutonic Knights crusaded against pagans of Prussia and Slavs in Poland. They built stone castles to mark and hold territorial conquests, notably at Königsberg (1254) and Ragnit (1275), as they expanded their *Ordensstaat*. Native tribes rebelled against the Teutonic Knights in 1240 and 1269. By 1340 the Brethren had completed the conquest of Prussia, but in 1525 they lost the long struggle with Poland-Lithuania. In the "Peace of Cracow" the Brethren surrendered much of territorial Prussia while a new "Duchy of Prussia" was created, becoming one of the first Lutheran states in Europe. That caused the Catholic knights of the old Livonian Order to break their association with the Teutonic Knights and return to Livonia. They arrived in time to face a Muscovite invasion that year, which they helped fight off. Given Muscovy's expansion and annexationist intentions, the Livonian Brethren sought and received Polish protection in 1557. A Muscovite invasion led by *Ivan IV* ensued from 1558 to 1561, marked by the opening atrocity of the *Dorpat massacre* that launched the "Livonian War," or *First Northern War* (1558–1583). The Livonians received assistance from Denmark, Poland, Sweden, and what remained of the Teutonic Knights. After four years of fighting Livonia agreed to become a Polish protectorate. The few Teutonic Knights left disbanded and Livonia was divided between Poland-Lithuania and a new "Duchy of Courland." Muscovy continued to covet Livonia and Poles and Swedes also fought over it from 1600 to 1611.

Livonian Order. "Brothers of the Knighthood of Christ in Livonia," or "Knights of the Sword," or "Sword Brothers." An ethnically German *Military Order* founded in 1202 at Riga by the Bishop of Livonia. Intensely zealous initially, the Livonian Brethren launched a crusade to Christianize the Baltic region. They enjoyed spectacular success in forcibly converting local pagans (Livs and Prussians), not least by killing those who refused. The territory the Order carved out in the east included what came to be called Livonia and Courland. In 1236 the Brethren were defeated by a pagan Lithuanian army, and in 1242 they were checked in their advance into western Russia by Alexander Nevsky (1220–1263), Prince of Novgorod. That also prevented further penetration of Kievan Rus. The Livonian Order merged with the *Teutonic Knights* in 1237. By the 15th century recruits were scarce as the Sword Brothers came under intense Muscovite assault by troops led by *Ivan III*, 1501–1503. Still, they bested an army of 40,000 Muscovites with just 12,000 Brethren and auxiliaries at the Seritsa River (January 1501). Three months later, 100,000 Russians and 30,000 allied Tatars annihilated the Livonian Knights at Dorpat. The Order did not become independent of the Teutonic Knights until a split between Catholic and Protestant Brethren in 1525. In 1558 the last territorial holdings of the Livonian Order were overrun by the Muscovite armies of *Ivan IV*. The last battle of the last crusade came on August 2, 1560, at *Ermes*, where the Order was utterly broken and humiliated. It was disbanded the next year. Its collapse destabilized northeastern Europe, contributing to prolongation of the *First Northern War* (1558–1583).

Livonian War (1558–1583). See *Northern War, First*.

Lobsters. A loosely contemptuous term for *Roundhead* cavalry in the *English Civil Wars*. It originally referred to a unit of London cuirassiers who wore full armor. It was later transposed to British redcoats.

lochaber axe. A Scottish infantry weapon falling some way between a *halberd* and a *bill*.

locks (on firearms). See *flintlock*; *matchlock*; *miquelet*; *wheel lock*.

locumentems. "Lieutenant-colonel." An officer second in command of a *Landsknechte* or comparable mid-16th-century regiment numbering about 3,000 men.

Lodewijk, Willem (1560–1620). English: William Louis of Nassau. Dutch military reformer. See also *Maurits of Nassau*; *New Model Army*; *volley fire*.

lodgement. In *siege warfare*, when the attacking force secured a position on the *covered way* and used part of the broken defensive structure to set up a temporary fortified position of their own.

Lodi, Peace of (1454). This treaty settled a round of war between Venice and Milan and for a time stabilized the political and military situation in Italy. This was possible because a balance of power had in fact been established by the mid-15th century. Lodi was followed by the founding of an "Italic League," a sophisticated security arrangement which helped keep peace among the main city-states (Florence, Milan, Naples, the Papal States, and Venice) for 40 years. This system gave early modern Europe, and later the world, a great part of the daily machinery and terminology of modern diplomacy. Also contributing to temporary stability, many *condottieri* had been bought out or otherwise tamed by salaried positions, or by taking power as in Milan. The city-states were financially exhausted by a half-century of inconclusive warfare and the Ottomans had taken Constantinople the year before, gravely threatening papal and Venetian interests in the eastern Mediterranean. With the once contested buffer spaces separating the five major city-states absorbed and annexed by one or another, a real and durable balance of power came into being. The peace lasted, with exceptions, until the French invasion of 1494 ignited the *Italian Wars* that lasted to 1559.

Suggested Reading: Garrett Mattingly, *Renaissance Diplomacy* (1955).

logistics. The problem of logistics, or supply of armies on the move, had an enormous impact on the strategy of medieval and early modern warfare and the makeup of armies. The problem was greatly exacerbated by a tremendous expansion in the size of armies brought about by the so-called "infantry revolution," which saw a shift from *heavy cavalry* to far larger armies of peasant foot soldiers and town militia armed with missile weapons, from bows to firearms. Also straining military supply was erosion of feudal military service systems in favor of mercenary and other professional soldiery. Whatever its form, no army in this period solved the core logistics problem by carrying all its needed supplies with it. Primitive transport, poor conditions of what few roads there were, and reliance on draught animals whose fodder needs made up a large share of whatever load they pulled or carried, all militated against a solution. The basic method of supplying an army on the move thus was to steal the food needed along the line of march, preferably through enemy lands that could be "eaten out" as a means of damaging his interests far beyond battle. This dictated that most wars were fought in densely populated areas sufficient to produce the food and fodder that all armies needed to steal to survive.

Not even the Ottomans, with their advanced system of internal supply depots (*menzil-hane*), could overcome the harsh limits imposed by fodder and food requirements. These forced all campaigns onto strict timetables that seldom exceeded 180 days. Thus, the traditional Ottoman campaign start date was May 3 with an end date usually in late October and no later than November 5 (New Style), on pain of risking destruction of the entire army. Troops were called up 40 days in advance of the departure date so that horses could fatten on rich spring grasses; there was no such leeway at the other end. By the mid-16th century the frontiers of the Ottoman Empire were, not wholly coincidentally, at the outer logistical reach of a single season's campaign march from Constantinople, or some other major assembly point within the Empire. In eastern and northern Europe winter campaigns were more common, even preferable. There, winter froze rivers that were unfordable in summer and allowed the vast and fast-moving cavalry armies maintained by all steppe powers to traverse frozen fields that in warmer weather were impassable bogs. Muscovy even deployed ski troops by the 1560s. This region was the exception, however, as everywhere else winter placed sharp limits on military operations.

Limits of Burden

Certain core logistic facts remained the same for all early modern armies. They were: (1) An average soldier consumed 3 pounds of food per day but could only carry about 65–80 pounds of equipment, weapons, and supplies. That irreducible fact limited soldiers to about 10 days' food supply (30 pounds) at the beginning of a march, and less if any food spoiled. (2) A normal packhorse ate 10 pounds of hay and another 10 of grain per day. Mongol ponies were grass fed, which gave them much greater range and utility. Most Chinese and European packhorses ate only grain. Each horse could carry about 250 pounds burden of which 100 pounds were devoted to its fodder. If a man rode the horse, even with additional packhorses in tow cavalry could move only 10 or 12 days before exhausting its portable food supply, which meant it had a return range of just five to six days without foraging. Camels were hardier than horses and carried a greater burden at about 400 pounds. Still, as many as 50,000 were needed to support a modest Ottoman field army for just three months. And even camels had to carry fodder along with their load of human food. Supply wagons improved these ratios but also reached a maximum dictated by fodder demands. The heavier a wagon, the greater the number of draught animals needed to pull it, which meant devoting still more space in the wagon to fodder. Oxen and water buffalo pulled much heavier wagon loads or heavy guns but were limited to certain climates and terrain and had high replacement costs. In any case, there were few passable roads in most of Europe. There were better road systems within China, and the Ottoman Empire was able to use excellent roads dating to the Roman and Byzantine Empires, but everywhere there were places of military interest carefully sited on hard terrain that were inaccessible by wheeled transport. Barges were the most efficient means of transport of bulk food and fodder, but using them limited lines of march to the route taken by a river for reasons of its own.

The need to carry potable water posed even greater problems of weight and range. Essential to man and beast but a terrible dead weight, fresh water was a major logistical worry. There was really no solution other than to drink from streams, ponds, and wells that one passed, all of which exposed troops to water-borne diseases. The problem was aggravated if an enemy poisoned wells as he retreated. Most non-Muslim soldiers preferred to drink small beer (a watery brew) or wine, which was far more healthy than taking a chance with an unknown water source. Nomads did much better at water rationing than armies of more settled peoples. Bedouin camels were famously capable of longer voyages in the desert. The small steppe ponies of the Mongols and Turkic peoples of Central Asia drew moisture from the grass they ate and certainly needed less water than a *destrier*. Chinese and European cavalry, on the other hand, faced a nearly absolute water barrier when they reached the edge of the steppe, which lacked both grain and potable water required by their mounts. The *Yongle Emperor* discovered this harsh reality on five campaigns he launched across the Gobi Desert into Mongolia. Each time the Mongols avoided battle until the Chinese were forced to turn back by a logistical wall, then they attacked. The key geographical determinant of Asian logistics in this period was thus proximity to the steppe: steppe nomads could survive and fight on the great ocean of grass because to their enemies it was closer to a desert.

Similarly, in Arabia and other desiccated regions nomad armies had a huge logistical advantage over neighboring populations of settled peoples. If the Bedouin chose not to fight a numerically or technologically superior foe they retreated to the desert and waited until their enemy's supply system failed. Then they pursued demoralized forces or stayed safely home in tent and oasis cities. Either way, the choice was invariably theirs. In the Americas, despite the absence of wheeled vehicles or large domesticated pack animals (with the partial exception of the llama), the *Aztec* and *Inca* created huge territorial empires. Still, it must be asked whether they had in fact reached the outer limits of logistically sustainable expansion before the arrival of Europeans. Great civil wars within, and unrepressed opposition at the edges of, each empire well before the first Spanish boot touched their land suggests that they may well have been near realistic territorial limits.

> *Each time the Mongols avoided battle until the Chinese were forced to turn back by a logistical wall . . .*

Plunder

Given fundamental transportation problems compounded by weak state finances, the basic rule for all armies was essentially to steal ("requisition," "forage for") food and fodder along the line of march, even if this left civilians on farms or in towns stripped bare of the necessities of life to starve to death, as it frequently did. In Europe logistical systems adopted by expanding infantry armies amounted to little more than organized plunder of the countryside—preferably, though not always, of provinces belonging to an enemy prince. Commanders relied on, and thus were tied to, a huge "logistical tail" comprised of an extended *baggage train* and large numbers of sundry *camp followers*. In good times and friendly territory local merchants might join a military column for a short time as it passed through their area, bringing goods for sale to what amounted to a traveling market place equivalent in population to a good-sized city. Wealthier and well-supplied *sutlers* would be engaged by a commanding general to supply bread and other basic necessities to the troops. As large as some sutler land convoys were, under the primitive road and vehicle restrictions of the day they could not support the swelling ranks of the new armies. This left armies no choice but to live off the land they passed through. Seizing field supplies from local peasants or markets was often disguised as legal requisition: promissory notes were dutifully passed out but almost always proved irredeemable later.

A mass of soldiers, along with their women and children in the baggage train, quickly consumed all there was in any area no matter how rich the fruits of its vines and fields. That often left the local population in such dire straits that many abandoned their homes to join the passing army, to eat out the next lush valley or province in turn. Without new sources of supply mutiny and chaos was a pressing danger to any army, but especially to one comprised of mercenaries. In short order, the impulse to move mustered troops out of one's home country and into enemy territory became a logistical imperative, and an alternative way of war to offering risky battle. Beyond the first days or weeks of the campaign season, which usually began after the spring rains, plunder of the peasantry and of small and mid-sized towns (walled and well-defended cites were less readily extorted) remained the mainstay of supply in early modern warfare. In truly hard times and always in enemy territory, armies and camp followers had the character and effect of a swarm of locust, eating out whole regions then moving on to consume the next.

The basic fact of 16th- and 17th-century logistics of European land warfare—that no army could bring with it on the march supplies sufficient to its needs beyond a few days—framed all strategy. Monarchs and commanders naturally sought to feed their unruly hordes at enemy expense by eating out his lands and billeting troops on his territory. The smartest converted this logistical necessity into an offensive strategy in which the main purpose of an invasion was economic dislocation rather than victory in battle. Large armies made up mostly of battle-shy mercenaries avoided combat in favor of destruction of an enemy's economic base by physical consumption of wealth in food and fodder, and by burning and plunder of portable goods. When enough damage was done the prince whose lands hosted the swarm would sue for peace to bring about removal of enemy troops. This suited the invading monarch as much as his troops, who went contentedly fat into winter quarters.

Plunder of basic supplies was an ancient solution to an age-old problem, but it no longer worked as a reliable system by the mid-16th century. What changed was the sheer size of the forces involved. Where an army of 10,000 was an impressive host in 1500, a century later armies were quadruple or quintuple that size: by 1600 European armies numbering many tens of thousands of men were on the move, a several fold-increase over the prior century. By the middle of the *Thirty Years' War* just three decades later, the Habsburgs and their enemies put armies into the field that exceeded 100,000 men. In the last years of the war, however, the armies shrank to less than half or even a quarter that size, and only resumed their secular growth trend during the reign of Louis XIV. Why? Because the destruction, depopulation, and length of the Thirty Years' War meant that in its closing decade most of Germany was already eaten out several times over, and could no longer supply either the military manpower or the food and fodder needed by large armies. In addition, plunder as a system of supply led to a loss of command and control by generals. Even the best generals had to bend to the sheer physical demands of foraging, which meant that their armies frequently deteriorated into little more than marauding bands of armed, hungry, and vicious men. Rape, murder, and pillage thus became the order of the day. These horrors so impressed themselves upon the German and European mind that, worse horrors and 350 years later, the dark years of the Thirty Years' War are still widely recalled and lamented.

Innovation

In trying to overcome this appalling situation commanders began to adjust the basic relationship between an army and its men. Instead of relying on soldiers who were themselves reliant on plunder more than on battle to make their living, far-sighted generals began to provide for the basic needs of the troops. In this they mostly followed the example of the mercenary general *Albrecht von Wallenstein*, who first introduced *contributions*. As should be expected, reform came about first in the two major powers of the Age: Spain and France. (China and the Ottoman Empire already had sophisticated internal magazine systems; the real changes came in European warfare, which shifted rapidly from primitive to modern.) Arms, food, fodder, and cloth were provided to the troops by a central cashier. The costs of items were deducted from a soldier's pay, but at least he no longer had to wander far from camp pillaging peasants just to keep body and soul together. And that meant the commander controlled an army which was increasingly professional rather than an armed rabble.

Even so, with the exception of the capital-rich Dutch Republic, states in early modern Europe were usually unable to pay their men as promised (arrears was a chronic problem) or supply expanding armies. Deficit financing of war leading to royal or state bankruptcy and to mutiny in the field was almost the standard of the day. This had a major impact on strategy, as it meant that other than garrisons attached to towns, in order to keep an army together it had to be kept constantly on the move. Strategic forays into enemy territory by bloated but mostly ineffective field armies resulted in economic catastrophe for peasants and towns along the line of march. Martin Van Creveld summed up the situation: "The fundamental logistic facts of life upon which seventeenth-century commanders based their strategy were ... First, in order to live, it was indispensable to keep moving. Second, when deciding the directions of one's movements, it was not necessary to worry overmuch about maintaining communications with base. Third, it was important to follow the rivers and, as far as possible, dominate their courses." All that made it impossible for armies to fix defensive lines and reduced most warfare to extended raids into enemy territory that could not bring about strategic victory but which were indulged in, year after year, to the dismay and destruction of the population, towns, and countryside. This situation was only slightly relieved by the development of an early and fairly primitive magazine system by France toward the end of the Thirty Years' War. Outside the interior lines of the Ottoman Empire and China, a true logistical revolution awaited the wars of the 18th century. See also *artillery*; *artillery train (1)*; *bellum se ipse alet*; *bedel-i nüzul*; *chevauchée*; *Edward I*; *Gustavus II Adolphus*; *Le Tellier, Michel*; *lines of supply*; *maneuvers*; *Maurits of Nassau*; *Ottoman warfare*; *prize*; *purveyance*; *raiding*; *Scottish Wars*; *siege warfare*; *Spanish Road*; *trebuchet*; *warhorses*.

Suggested Reading: John Childs, *Warfare in the Seventeenth Century* (2004); Martin Van Creveld, *Supplying War* (1977).

Loja, Battle of (1486). See *Reconquista*.

Lollard Knights. English nobles who initially endorsed the teachings of John Wycliffe and the *Lollards*, but later abandoned the movement.

Lollards. Middle English, from the Dutch "Lollaerd" or "mutterer." A Christian sect with a distinct pacifist tendency that grew out of the teachings of the Oxford teacher (Master of Balliol College) and reformer John Wycliffe (1320–1384). He made sharp criticism of widespread scandals of the clergy and of mechanical substitution of public ritual in the Church for true inner piety. He upheld the right of the secular arm to control the clergy, an idea later called *Erastian*. That attracted elements of the nobility ("Lollard Knights") but alienated the episcopacy and papacy. The Church hierarchy mobilized to condemn the Lollards as "heretics." In 1377, Pope Gregory XI issued a papal bull calling for Wycliffe's arrest. But when Gregory died in 1378 a papal succession crisis led instead to the *Great Schism* that produced two, then three rival popes and deeply undermined Church authority. Wycliffe and the Lollards used the respite to assault the constitution of the Church as well as the clergy's moral failures. He called for an end to the papacy and all episcopalian structures. He was one of the first reformers to publish in English, including a translation of the Bible. He sent out "poor priests" to spread the Lollard message. Doctrinally, in 1380 he rejected the central Catholic doctrine of transubstantiation during the Mass and rejected the claimed right and ability of priests to absolve sin. The theological faculty of the University of Oxford condemned Lollardism, as did the English Church in 1382. The Lollards were thereafter hunted, arrested, and forced to recant by torture and threat of execution, so that Lollardism was driven underground. Its influence remained dormant in England until a reform spirit broke out again during the *Protestant Reformation*. In Bohemia, *Hussites* were inspired by Wycliffe's teachings and rode out to do physical as well as spiritual battle with Catholic kings and popes.

Suggested Reading: G. M. Trevelyan, *England in the Age of Wycliffe* (1904; 1975).

lombarda. See *bombardetta*; *port piece*.

longboat. The largest of a ship's boats, useful for towing the mother ship on a becalmed sea, landing shore parties to gather supplies, and communicating with other ships in a fleet.

longbow. A six- to seven-foot ("two ells") yew bow with a plump "belly" and heavy draw. It took a strong man to "knock" the bow—pull the 36-inch "cloth yard" arrow on the drawstring and fit it into precut notches. The yew was critical: after it was boiled, bent, and sanded smooth with the scales of a dogfish, it presented a hard front yet a supple underside that imparted firing characteristics comparable to a composite bow made from different woods. Loosing three-foot arrows fitted with "bodkins" (metal-tips), the longbow could penetrate plate when shot directly from 20 paces, punch through chain mail at 100 paces when fired at the level, and could kill or maim an unarmored man or horse at 200–300 paces with plunging fire. At longer ranges longbows fired parabolic flocks of arrows ("arrow storms"). These took just a few seconds to reach the target, usually a mass of milling armored horse or a block of infantry arrayed beyond the range of their own cutting or thrusting weapons or of *crossbows*. A skilled longbowman kept two or even three arrows in the air simultaneously and could fire 10 or more per minute before fatigue set in.

> *...the longbow...could kill or maim an unarmored man or horse at 200–300 paces with plunging fire.*

This exceptional weapon probably originated with the Welsh (some historians disagree), who used it to such great effect against English armies in the 13th century that the traditional English short bow was discarded in favor of longbows. Edward I ("Longshanks") buttressed his armies in Scotland and France with over 10,000 Welsh and English archers. They helped him win at *Falkirk* (1298). His son, the military incompetent Edward II, lost at *Bannockburn* in 1314 despite deploying longbowmen. Major victories over French *heavy cavalry* that were greatly aided by longbows came under *Edward III* and his bastard son, the *Black Prince*, during the opening decades of the *Hundred Years' War* (1337–1453). The first of these was fought at sea. At *Sluys* (1340) longbowmen won the greatest naval victory of the 14th century, slaughtering the crews of enemy ships at long range before they could close and board. On land the longbow destroyed French armies at *Crécy* (1346), *Poitiers* (1356), and *Agincourt* (1415).

The longbow had an effective killing range of between 250 and 400 yards (or meters). This greatly exceeded that of mercenary crossbowmen, usually Genoese, found in the French ranks as an adjunct to the standard French reliance on men-at-arms and heavy horse. Yet, range was not the real secret of the longbow. It was the fact that under Edward III the English began to use such large numbers of archers with a superior rate of fire (starting at 8–10 arrows each per minute, declining thereafter with rising muscle fatigue) that they created an "arrow storm" on the field of battle that devastated enemy formations, especially the large and relatively unprotected *warhorses* of the French knights. Recent research suggests that the direct killing power of the longbow was not what proved decisive in these battles. Instead, it was the ability of longbowmen to harass and break up enemy formations at extreme ranges that forced disordered French charges into waiting lines of English men-at-arms, where they were also exposed to level flanking fire from archers on each wing. So important were longbowmen to English fortunes in the Hundred Years' War that fletchers and bow-makers were impressed into the army, and football and golf were forbidden as common holiday pastimes in favor of compulsory archery practice.

The demonstrated ability of longbowmen to devastate ranks of French knights as late as Agincourt made the English smug about their putative weapon superiority and overconfident that it would last. But defeat—the greatest teacher in military affairs—forced the French to change tactics. They incorporated more numerous and powerful hand guns and artillery into their armies and these proved a more than effective counter to longbowmen. Now it was the turn of long-range French cannon to break up longbow concentrations before the arrow storms could be launched, so that the French horse could then drive into the bleeding English infantry, ruining them with charges of lance and sword. The first such battlefield defeat of English archery by the new French tactics and weapons took place at *Formigny* (1450). A more definitive display of the mastery of gunpowder over the bow came at *Castillon* (1453), which ended the battlefield dominance of the longbow and closed out the Hundred Years' War all at once. Only in England's small wars in Ireland and during the *Wars of the Roses* (1455–1485) were longbows still used. And even in England's little wars a shift was underway to firearms and cannon. Still, English armies did not finally and completely replace the longbow with guns until 1595, and then only after a comical experiment in fitting longbows to pikes. See also *uniforms*.

Suggested Reading: R. Hardy, *Longbow: A Social and Military History* (1976); T. McGuffe, "The Longbow as a Decisive Weapon," *History Today*, 5 (1955); Clifford Rogers, "The Efficacy of the Medieval Longbow," *War in History*, 5/2 (1998).

longship. A sleek, northern *galley* pioneered by the Vikings, with descending versions used in Irish and Scottish waters for centuries thereafter. "Longship" was a generic term for all northern warships from the 9th to 13th centuries. Some were capable of oceanic travel, though at great risk to the crew. They were called snacca ("snake" or "serpent") by victims of the fierce raiders they bore. The reference was to their unusually elongated frames, and to the fear inspired when these ships appeared out of the fog along some quiet seashore, disgorging barbarian raiders intent on rapine and plunder; or when they worked hundreds of miles inland along a river way to appear suddenly outside the walls of Paris or a dozen other towns.

Long War (1593–1606). See *Thirteen Years' War*.

Lord High Admiral. See *admiral*.

Lordship. See *Ireland*.

Lorraine. See *Burgundian-French War*; *Burgundian-Swiss War*; *Catholic League (France)*; *Guise family*; *Jeanne d'Arc*; *League of Pubic Weal*; *Morat, Battle of*; *Nancy, Battle of*; *Richelieu, Cardinal Armand Jean du Plessis de*; *Spanish Road*; *Thirty Years' War*.

Lorraine, Charles, Cardinal of (1524–1574). See *Guise, Charles, Cardinal de Lorraine*.

Lorraine, Charles, duc de Mayenne (1554–1611). See *Mayenne, duc de*.

Lose-coat Field, Battle of (1470). See *Wars of the Roses*.

Lostwithiel, Battle of (1644). See *English Civil Wars*.

Loudon Hill, Battle of (1307). See *Scottish Wars*.

Louis de Bourbon. See *Condé, Louis de Bourbon*.

Louis of Nassau (1538–1574). Dutch rebel. Brother of *William the Silent*. He won a lonely rebel victory at the onset of the *Eighty Years' War* (1568–1648) at Heiligerlee, on May 23, 1568, but was defeated two months later by *Alba* at *Jemmingen* (July 21, 1568). Once the *Sea Beggars* took *Brill* (April 1572), Louis followed by taking Flushing, then invaded the southern Netherlands with an army of Dutch Calvinists, French Huguenots, and hired Germans. He was killed in battle at *Mookerheyde* (April 14, 1574).

Louis XI (1423–1483). King of France. He benefitted greatly from the military reforms of his father, *Charles VII*, who established a standing army under terms of the *compagnies de l'ordonnance*. Under Louis XI France emerged as the first early modern state in Europe. Its great feudatories had been beaten into submission, politically and militarily, during the final phase of the *Hundred Years' War* (1337–1453). This required Louis to replace the old feudal levies commanded by barons and other liege lords and *knights* with a new army built around trained *artillery* and *heavy cavalry*, a formation designed to deal with England's infantry archers and men-at-arms. In all this he gained from a burst of commercial prosperity in France that constituted a national "peace dividend" after 150 years of war, and royal protection given to commercial centers such as Bordeaux, Lyons, and Rouen, and the higher bourgeois families in general. In 1465 he was defeated by the *League of Public Weal* at Montihéry. *Charles the Rash* of Burgundy had him arrested and imprisoned in the middle of negotiations in 1468. But Louis had the final word: four years after the crushing defeat of Burgundy by Swiss mercenaries at *Nancy* (1477) Louis hired 6,000 Swiss for his own army. By the end of his reign he stretched the borders of France to the Pyrenees and annexed the original Duchy of Burgundy.

Louis XII (1462–1515). King of France. See also *Agnadello, Battle of*; *Blois, Treaties of*; *Cambrai, League of*; *Counter-Reformation*; *Flodden Field, Battle of*; *Foix, Gaston de, duc de Nemours*; *Francis I*; *Garigliano River, Battle of*; *Italian Wars*; *Leonardo da Vinci*.

Louis XIII (1601–1643). "The Just." He succeeded to the throne upon the assassination of his father, *Henri IV*, in 1610. When his mother, Queen Marie de Medici, betrothed him in 1614 to Anne of Austria, daughter of *Philip III* of Spain, the Court split with each Catholic faction seeking military aid from the *Huguenots*. Louis seized power from his mother in 1617, at age 16, after he had her favorite adviser assassinated. He reaffirmed the *Edict of Nantes* while also vowing to reduce the Huguenots. Then he called into session the "États généreaux" (*Estates*) for the last time in 160 years. Louis was at first sympathetic toward *Ferdinand II* concerning the revolt of Protestant subjects in Bohemia and the Palatinate, not for confessional reasons but as a sovereign dealing with comparable rebellion by a religious minority. He issued an Edict of Restitution for Béarn in June 1617, rolling back church property transfers since 1569, and intervened militarily in 1620 to restore Catholic worship in Béarn and Navarre. He was more concerned with Huguenot military and political infringements on his royal prerogatives than with their conversion, which he said was best left to God.

Louis thus reacted to a Huguenot assembly called in La Rochelle in November 1620 with a pronouncement not that those involved were heretics but that they were rebels and traitors. He led a military campaign against them the next spring which petered out when most of his soldiers fell ill. Confessional pressure on Louis came from the *dévots* in 1622. To placate the Catholic majority he adopted a more confessional stance in public. But his displays of piety gained little support from the more fanatic dévots. So he turned to *Cardinal Richelieu*, whom he appointed chief minister in 1624, to eliminate autonomous Huguenot military power within France without sweeping the monarchy or the country into the religious conflagration in neighboring Germany or succumbing to Spanish and papal influence. To Richelieu the king surrendered some royal will and much power, in return for which the "eminence rouge" expanded and deepened the powers of the French monarchy vis-à-vis French society. Richelieu also led an anti-Huguenot military campaign that culminated in the fall of *La Rochelle* in 1628, completing the military defeat of French Protestantism. This victory was capped by a return to religious and social toleration with the *Edict of Alès* (1629), a settlement that contrasted hugely with the *Edict of Restitution* in Germany that same year. With the home front secured, Richelieu and Louis embarked on the *War of the Mantuan Succession* in Italy, and war with Spain in alliance with the Netherlands. But they only actively entered the *Thirty Years' War* in 1635.

Suggested Reading: Lloyd Moote, *Louis XIII* (1989).

Lübeck, Peace of (July 7, 1629). This settlement between the Holy Roman Empire and Denmark, that is, between *Ferdinand II* and *Christian IV*, ended the "Danish phase" of the *Thirty Years' War* (1618–1648). It followed four years of repeated military failure by the Danes and *Hague Alliance*, culminating in occupation of Jutland by the Imperials. Christian IV was allowed to keep possessions outside the Empire and north of the Elbe, namely Holstein, Jutland, and Schleswig. In return, he foreswore all engagement in Imperial affairs by direct military action or in the *"Reichskreis"* (Lower Saxon Circle).

Lublin, Union of (1569). See *Union of Lublin*.

Ludford, Bridge, Battle of (1459). See *Wars of the Roses*.

Luther, Martin (1483–1546). Religious reformer. A Saxon by birth, he was schooled at Erfurt before joining an Augustinian monastery in 1505. He lectured in moral philosophy and theology at Wittenberg, 1513–1515. Luther was scornful of all with whom he disagreed, including the gentle Erasmus, and angrily intolerant of any who valued religious tranquility over doctrinal principle and conformity. He thus grew evermore outraged by the crass sale of "indulgences" (promissory notes of time off in Purgatory, a realm he denied existed, in exchange for giving money to the Catholic Church in this life) and other fiscal and moral corruptions of the clergy. In 1517, at age 34, he nailed to a church door in Wittenberg a statement of 95 theses protesting sales of indulgences and taking reform positions on salient moral and doctrinal issues then roiling the Church. Moving him to protest was his new theology of "justification by faith," a broad critique of scholastic theology (especially that of Thomas Aquinas), and total rejection of Aristotelian ethics as the "worst enemy of grace." Drawing instead from the writing of Duns Scotus and William of Ockham, Luther defined the central promise of theology as the certainty of salvation. He denied as unimportant Thomistic proofs of doctrinal positions, substituting for scholastic rationalism a theology of covenant with the word of God.

As for Church practices, Luther rejected the authority of clergy, mere men, to forgive sin in the name of God in exchange for donations; denounced clerical concubinage; railed against petty clerical fees; and raged against toleration of folk superstitions. Catholic authorities responded by publicly burning Luther's scroll. Reciprocal burning of competing lists of theses carried the argument into 1518. Then Luther was summoned to Rome by the Medici Pope Leo X (1475–1521), to answer to his critics. However, the Elector of Saxony and his University intervened to block the subpoena. In 1519, Luther expanded his protest into an all-out assault on papal power and doctrinal authority. In 1520 he published "The Babylonian Captivity of the Church," repeating to the German nobility his earlier protests but also denouncing the papacy as the "whore of Babylon." Rome answered with a papal bull condemning Luther's ideas and threatening excommunication should he not recant. With studied impudence he burned the papal bull in public on December 10, 1520, to the delight of his growing and increasingly fervent following. Luther was excommunicated and declared "heretic" by the pope on January 3, 1521.

Habsburg Emperor, and devout Catholic, *Charles V*, convened the Diet of Worms in 1521 to contend with the religious revolt in Germany. Although a condemned heretic under papal ban, Luther attended the Diet under safe conduct (which had not protected *Jan Hus* a century earlier). He defended his propositions and departed, closing with the famous statement: "I cannot do otherwise, here I stand, may God help me, Amen." The Diet banned all Luther's writings and ordered his books burned, declaring war on what was beginning to be called "Lutheranism." As always when one burns books to stop the spread of ideas, before long people were also burned, denounced as heretics by one side or the other. The Catholic Church reintroduced and ramped up the powers of the *Inquisition* and turned to the mighty Habsburgs to enforce doctrinal orthodoxy in Germany. Lutherans looked to the swords of secular princes in Germany and northern Europe to protect and defend reform communities and preachers from Catholic armies and courts.

Luther was in grave danger after Worms but was taken into protective custody by the Elector of Saxony. During a year of pleasant castellan living, he translated the Bible into German and advanced and deepened his critique of Church practices and dogma. Most famously, he emphatically defended "justification by faith," the idea of a "priesthood of all believers," and the primacy of scripture over papal and episcopal authority. The hardest divide from Rome came in his proclamation on justification by faith: salvation depended on God's grace alone, he argued, unsupported by the Medieval Church's encouragement of good works and charity. Luther denied the existence of Purgatory and hence the need to sell "indulgences." For good measure he denounced Catholic devotion to the Virgin Mary and intercession by the "community of saints." In 1525, Luther broke openly with Erasmus, the great Christian humanist scholar who advocated reform from within the Catholic fold. Schisms of a different sort broke out within the reform movement as well, notably when Luther split with *Zwingli* over the question of the sacramental nature of the Mass (which Luther declared "an evil thing that must be abolished"). Also in 1525, Luther abandoned clerical celibacy and married a former nun. The German Reformation, and the permanent Lutheran split from Rome, took a giant step forward in 1530 with promulgation of the *Augsburg Confession* of basic principles of reformed belief.

In more mundane affairs, Luther was a political and social conservative with no desire to shake kings from their thrones, not even Catholic ones. For him religion was about faith: it had nothing to do with ethics or social justice, however great the good one sought. Instead, Luther looked to the German princes to act as bulwarks to preserve virtue against the assaults of wickedness and the Devil. At no time was this more clear than in his reaction to the *German Peasant War*, which he denounced in a tract published on May 5,

1525, enjoining rebellious peasants to suffer and endure evil and injustice just as Christ had done. This calculated distancing from social radicalism probably ensured the survival of Lutheranism in Germany, which partly explains why Luther took the position. More tellingly, his opposition to revolution and regicide simply reflected the majority opinion of his class and of his day: like Thomas Hobbes a century later, and like most educated men of the 16th century, Luther much preferred tyranny to anarchy. Nevertheless, the ferment his ideas caused revived old debates about the power of episcopal appointments and the relative authority of secular princes versus the Church that had so troubled Medieval Christendom. Where Luther denied the just use of force to foment radical social change, he had fewer objections to secular magistrates using swords to defend religious truth. And so, for much of the rest of his life, Luther and Germany plunged into deepening confessional conflict that ultimately led to open religious warfare. See also *Augsburg, Peace of*; *Henry VIII, of England*; *Maximilian I*; *printing*.

> ...*like Thomas Hobbes a century later, ...Luther much preferred tyranny to anarchy.*

Suggested Reading: Richard Marius, *Martin Luther* (1999); Heiko Oberman, *Luther* (1989); Stephen Ozment, *The Age of Reform* (1980).

Lutheranism. See *Augsburg, Peace of*; *Augsburg Confession*; *Calvinism*; *Charles V, Holy Roman Emperor*; *confessionalism*; *Corpus Evangelicorum*; *Counter-Reformation*; *Declaratio Ferdinandei*; *Denmark*; *Ecumenical Councils*; *Formula of Concord*; *German Peasant War*; *Gustavus II Adolphus*; *Holy Roman Empire*; *Inquisition*; *Luther, Martin*; *Maximilian II*; *Netherlands*; *printing*; *Protestant Reformation*; *reservatum ecclesiaticum*; *Sweden*; *Teutonic Knights, Order of*; *Thirty Years' War*; *Utraquists*; *Westphalia, Peace of*.

Lutter-am-Barenberg, Battle of (August 17/27, 1626). The 18,000-man army of the *Catholic League* under *Johann Tilly*, reinforced by 8,000 Imperial troops, pursued a Danish-German Protestant army of 15,000 commanded by *Christian IV*. Tilly caught Christian at Lutter-am-Barenberg, just 20 miles shy of the Danish safe haven at Wolfenbüttel. The Danes faced about, blocking the main road, and the fight commenced. Tilly attacked the center with his infantry, who overran the main Danish battery of 20 field guns after hard fighting. With that the Danish flanks broke and ran. Some 6,000 Danes were killed and 2,500 were captives, accounting for half of Christian's army. The Lower Saxon Circle (*Reichskreis*) collapsed and Denmark was opened to Catholic and Imperial invasion.

Lützen, Battle of (November 6, 1632). As the campaign season began in 1632, *Gustavus Adolphus* was in Bavaria at the head of a Swedish and Protestant army, threatening to move into the core Habsburg lands. Perhaps he might even capture Vienna itself. *Johann Tilly*, who had commanded the combined army of the *Catholic League* and the *Imperial Army*, had been killed in April trying to prevent Gustavus from crossing the River Lech. That left Emperor *Ferdinand II* with no choice but to recall the great mercenary entrepreneur he had dismissed from command in 1630, *Albrecht von Wallenstein*. No one else could save Vienna. Wallenstein dictated extraordinary terms to Ferdinand even as he raised an army of 70,000 men. Soldiers of fortune from across Europe—Croats, Czechs, English, Germans, Irish, Italians, Scots, Swiss, and men like Wallenstein himself, of no faith or nation—rallied to the Great Captain and the prospect of wages of war and opportunity for plunder. Inside a month an army took form in Moravia.

Wallenstein marched north in a set of brilliant maneuvers designed to draw Gustavus away from Austria. He resisted calls to turn east and relieve the beleaguered Elector of Bavaria, *Maximilian I*, who was frantic over the Protestant horde eating out his country. Instead, Wallenstein moved into Bohemia where he attacked and defeated the weak Saxon Army which was reluctantly allied to Gustavus. Wallenstein next threatened Saxony, cutting Gustavus' lines of supply and blocking the Swedes from their base area of recruitment in north Germany. Joined by a small Bavarian force, Wallenstein was capable of directly threatening the Swedes, who therefore prudently withdrew to Nuremberg. When Wallenstein arrived he did not attack a force he knew to be superior in training and firepower, though inferior in numbers, to his own. Instead he dug in, as did the Swedes across from the Imperial lines. The two armies formed a series of parallel fortified trenches where they remained for the next several weeks. Wallenstein used light horse to harass Swedish foraging parties while the Swedes probed the Imperial lines, provoking minor skirmishes. Finally, moved by the hunger of his men, warlord hubris, and desire for decisive battle, and provoked by Wallenstein's *hussars*, Gustavus attacked. For the first time he was repulsed. While the action was not militarily significant, this first check to the great Swede's advance in Germany cracked his reputation for invincibility.

The effect reverberated through the strategic calculations of Europe. Because this made the Swedish position less secure politically, and therefore ultimately also militarily, Gustavus felt compelled to draw Wallenstein out of his trenches and defeat him in an open battle between the main armies. He thought he could entice Wallenstein from his fortified earthworks by moving south into Bavaria to once more ravage territory allied to the Habsburgs and threaten a dash toward Vienna. This was the moment when Wallenstein showed superior strategical ability. He declined the bait Gustavus dangled in the south and instead struck out northward, into Saxony. This move recreated the dilemma faced earlier by the Protestant alliance: Gustavus was again halted by a brilliant campaign of maneuver that avoided battle yet twice pulled his army back north by threatening its strategic rear. Next, it was the turn of the "Lion of the North" to display advanced command skills. Making use of the markedly superior training and maneuverability of his Swedish regiments, joined now by thousands of mercenaries and allies he had trained to make war in the Swedish way, Gustavus moved north to intercept Wallenstein. He did so with far greater speed than any contemporary army could achieve or commander imagine. The two forces thus met at Lützen on November 6, 1632.

Wallenstein had partly adopted Swedish tactics, marginally increased the flexibility of his *tercios*, and significantly increased their firepower by multiplying the number of musketeers within them. While the Swedes retained a clear qualitative edge, they were a reduced force in numbers and quality from the crisp professional army that crossed the Baltic two years before. In fact, Gustavus' army was no longer really "Swedish." Two years of fighting and Sweden's limited reserves and small population meant Gustavus now commanded an army close to 80 percent foreign mercenary. It had been trained to make war in the Swedish style, however, and the critical field artillery was still Swedish by nationality and command, and fiercely Lutheran by confessional temperament. The odds were also evened by a heavy fog that shrouded the battlefield during the most critical hours of combat, reducing the ability of Gustavus to take full advantage of his army's greater maneuverability and increasing the comparative fighting value of fixed Imperial heavy infantry. Still, Gustavus remained a master of tactical thrust and parry, and much to be feared.

The morning of the battle broke with the armies concealed from one another by a thick fog. Wallenstein chose the ground, placing his 35,000 troops in a broken line protected by a natural double ditch which he had deepened into full trenches. These he lined with ranks of musketeers. He thought this obstacle would blunt Gustavus' cavalry, obviate the superior training of Swedish troops, and deliver victory. Gustavus breakfasted, then led the troops in singing a Lutheran hymn. Next, he set in motion an attack plan that rested on superior maneuvers to dislodge the Imperials from their trench line. He sent a small cavalry force to attack Wallenstein's right, which was anchored on the small village of Lützen. He led the overweight Swedish cavalry on the right in a long ride right around the Imperial extreme left. This cut Wallenstein's lines of resupply and retreat. The main Swedish infantry was positioned at the center, deployed in their usual six ranks per line, two lines deep. As usual, the field artillery was placed before the mass of infantry at the center of the Swedish line. As the Swedish cavalry enveloped each Imperial flank, the infantry moved toward the tight ranks of Imperial musketeers awaiting them in the line of double ditches. The heavy fog concealed the movement of the Swedish infantry until they reached close quarters. As their formations broke through the fog and came into view of the Imperial musketeers both sides opened at close range. Then they slid into a heavy, prolonged small arms fight.

The Swedish regimental field guns were maneuvered into an enfilade position, to support the capture of the immobile Imperial artillery train by the cavalry. Under this threat many Imperial guns were *spiked*. Overrunning the Imperial artillery exposed large blocks of pikemen standing in rigid tercio formation, but with little of their usual firearms support because most musketeers were already lost to artillery fire or tied down by the fight over control of the line of double ditches. In the face of deadly fire, the overmatched pikemen retreated, pressed by ferocious charges by Swedish and Finnish cavalry on either flank of the Imperial line. In addition, the Swedish rate of musket and cannon fire was likely three times that of the Imperial side. Volley after volley tore into the static tercios. On the right, Gustavus led from the front, crashing into and through Croat light cavalry at the head of a Swedish charge with *arme blanche*. That brought him barging into Austrian cuirassiers, with whom a close fight ensued as the wider battle dissolved into a desperate struggle among clusters of men oblivious to all else but the enemy in front of them.

Wallenstein counterattacked with his surviving tercios, rolling up the Swedish left and retaking part of the ditch line. Meanwhile, *Pappenheim* led 8,000 Imperial horse in a successful attack against the Swedish cavalry which had become strung out and entangled with the Imperial baggage. Unprepared to receive this counterattack, the Swedish horse took heavy casualties. It was *Bernhard von Sachsen-Weimar* who saved the hour. He marshaled the rapid-firing Swedish artillery and cut down Imperial troopers and horses with volleys of canister, turning survivors away in disorderly retreat and killing Pappenheim. Bernhard then broke the Imperial line by rallying a Swedish charge that carried the main Imperial battery and captured the whole artillery train. Triumphant shouts quickly caught in Protestant throats as word went out that Gustavus was being carried bloody and dead from the field. He had been pistoled off his horse, then holed with three musket balls by the Austrian cuirassiers; one shot took off part of his skull. The reserve line of Swedish infantry now showed its mettle: it swept forward, retook the part of the ditch line Wallenstein had recovered, firing musket volleys and fighting furiously hand-to-hand. Wallenstein's last tercios wobbled and broke under this assault, then turned and fled. At least one-third of the Swedish Army, about 10,000 men, were dead or wounded. They lay intermingled with 12,000–15,000 Imperial dead.

Lützen was a sharp defeat for the Catholic cause. It shattered the Imperial military system built up by Wallenstein and ensured the survival of the major Protestant states of Germany. It was in that sense a decisive battle, the only one of the Thirty Years' War. Yet, even Lützen was determinative only in the immediate sense, for it did not directly shape the final settlement. The death of its warlord did not force Sweden out of the war, but it robbed the Protestant cause of its most dynamic champion. Never again would a Protestant prince alone decide the strategy of the anti-Habsburg coalition. After Lützen, Sweden remained in the German war, but it was *Cardinal Richelieu* of France, Prince of the Catholic Church, who henceforth took the lead in setting alliance policy, controlled the larger course of the war, and shaped its final outcome. The victory for Swedish arms at Lützen was most important for making it probable that a military stalemate would be the final result in the long confessional contest between Catholic and Protestant in Germany. That is what was agreed at the negotiating tables in Westphalia, though not until many more years of bloody murder and mayhem drove the point home to both sides. Lützen marked the high tide of the Protestant cause. Another 13 years of fighting lay ahead, and three more after that of desultory skirmishing while peace talks dragged on in the Rhineland. With the historian's privilege of hindsight it can be seen that Lützen was probably the last chance to unify Germany prior to the mid-19th century. For over 200 years afterward unification lay beyond the imagination or capability of Germans to realize and outside the will of an ascendant France to permit, but within the ability of Paris to prevent.

Suggested Reading: J.F.C. Fuller, *Military History of the Western World*, vol. 2 (1954); Golo Mann, *Wallenstein* (1976); Michael Roberts, *Gustavus Adolphus* (1992).

lymphad. A small oared warship descended from the Viking *longship* and in use for over 1,000 years, into the 17th century. Their main role was in lightning coastal raids and amphibious assaults in the isolated West Highlands and outer islands of Scotland.

Lyon, League of (February 1623). An alliance of France, Venice, and Savoy that aimed to expel the Habsburg garrisons from *The Grisons* and attach Genoa and Montferrat to Savoy as a buffer against Spain. See also *Spanish Road*; *Valtelline*.

Lyon, Treaty of (1601). See *Henri IV, of France*; *Spanish Road*.

M

Maastricht, Siege of (1579). The *Duke of Parma* began his new command in the Netherlands by besieging Maastricht. The city was defended by just 2,000 militia, against whom Parma hurled 20,000 veteran Spanish troops. The townsfolk flooded the surrounding plain and put up a stiff resistance that killed over 4,000 of Parma's men but only delayed the final assault. After four months of siege the Spanish stormed Maastricht's gates and wall. Once inside the city they slaughtered nearly 10,000. See also *Eighty Years' War*.

Maastricht, Siege of (June–August 1632). *Frederik Hendrik* invaded Flanders with 30,000 Dutch troops. On June 8 he invested the fortress city of Maastricht. The Spanish panicked, fearing another in a series of major humiliations inflicted by Hendrik. They recalled an army from the Palatinate and sent another under *Pappenheim*. Both assaults were beaten off by the Dutch. Meanwhile, Hendrik mercilessly bombarded the city while his engineers dug siege trenches and prepared a mine. On August 20 the mine was set off, blowing apart a segment of city wall. Three days later the surviving defenders surrendered. See also *Eighty Years' War*.

Macao. A Portuguese colony on the south China coast established as a trading outpost by Portuguese merchants in 1557. The Kangxi Emperor ordered all Chinese to leave Macao during the 1660s, then blockaded it to prevent their return. He tried to ban the Portuguese from Macao, but local officials connived at their continuing presence so that it remained their main base in China.

mace. Any of a variety of flails or spiked clubs, either made entirely of metal or with a metal head attached to a wooden shaft directly or by a chain. Their principal use was to defeat shields and armor by breaking bones with crushing concussive blows, rather than by penetration with a sharpened point. Some had flanges or spikes which permitted heavy blows and penetration, especially of the *helm*. Multi-headed maces were called "mace of arms" (from the Middle French "masse d'armes"). Lighter, nonlethal maces were widely used in *tournaments*. They carried great symbolic importance and may have been precursors to the scepter as symbol of royal authority. The popular idea that maces were the preferred weapon of clerics appears to be apocryphal. See also *Holy Water Sprinkler*; *knight*; *masse*; *military flail*; *Morgenstern*.

Machiavelli, Niccolò di Bernardo (1469–1527). Florentine political thinker. Like Jonathan Swift he was more often misinterpreted and vilified for his brutal honesty rather than understood or appreciated for his shrewd insight. Machiavelli's is surely the only name of a mere mortal used by Christians as an adjective to depict the moral character of Satan, often qualified as a great demon of "Machiavellian" cunning, duplicity, and low morality. Machiavelli lived in turbulent and violent times. Italy was torn by clashing armies of the city-states and then overrun by foreign armies, first from France, followed by Spain and the Swiss. Diplomacy was an instrument of statecraft in a battle for survival "red in tooth and claw," to paraphrase Tennyson. When the Medici, the ruling family of Florence, fled in 1493, the path of opportunity opened to Machiavelli. He was appointed secretary of the *Council of Ten*, the governing council of the Florentine Republic. He held that position until 1512, time he spent organizing the Florentine militia. He paid a great deal of attention to the problem of citizen militia versus mercenary forces and military problems in general. He undertook lesser diplomatic missions, including one to Caesar Borgia in 1502. Upon the restoration of the Medici he was arrested, imprisoned and tortured (1513). Machiavelli spent the remainder of his adult life seeking public office and longing to return to the practical exercise of power, but was not trusted by the Medici and was given only minor historiographical and diplomatic missions after 1519. Machiavelli's thinking reflected those realities. His most famous, and still widely read, works were: *De Principatibus* (*The Prince*, published after his death and later condemned by Pope Clement VIII and other clerics), the *Art of War*, and *Discourses on Livy*. These were among the first works to rediscover classical military virtues and recommend their revival for early modern states. Machiavelli thus emphasized *drill* and *military discipline*, the importance of a professional officer corps and a strict chain of command, all of which he gleaned from study of the ancient Roman legion.

Machiavelli lived in a transitional time between the agrarian-based *feudal* structures and armies of Europe and newly professional formations. This involved incorporation of *"condottieri"* into the armies of the Italian states. Machiavelli held condottieri in a deep contempt he did not extend to Swiss mercenaries, but he recognized that military reform of this sort was made possible (and then necessary) by the expansion of money economies—the "commercial revolution" in Italy and the Mediterranean. Fundamental transformation of the social and economic basis of military power lay at the heart of his conception of the emerging state, and thus of his political thinking as well. As a military theorist and organizer Machiavelli was determined to displace the unsteady and untrustworthy condottieri, whose uselessness he seriously exaggerated. He hoped to replace foreign mercenaries with a civic militia whose greater military virtues (which he simply assumed, based on classical models) and political reliability would permit Florence more independence in the conduct of its diplomacy and further stabilize its polity. He tried out his theories in a drawn-out siege of rival Pisa, with only mixed success. Empirically, he was wrong about militia versus mercenaries. Or at least, he was centuries ahead of the times: in his lifetime and for another 300 years after that, mercenaries dominated European battlefields, not the conscript militia armies he envisioned and proposed which only arrived in fact with the wars of the French Revolution.

Machiavelli's frank writing about the nature of early modern warfare—he disassociated thinking about war from ethics or high religious purpose, concentrating instead on its factual bases in economics and politics—startled and shocked his contemporaries. Most were not aware, as he was, that an end had already come to the old moral order of the *res publica Christiana*, so they were not prepared for his brutally honest disregard for abstract military and political ideals which had long only covered baser interests of princes and popes. Machiavelli did not waste praise defining the ideal condition of peace, that assumed universal good of the ancien régime of Medieval Europe, or on ritual incantations of old doctrines about *just war*. He wrote instead of more pagan, that is of Roman, qualities in war: courage, ferocity, duty, and love of country. Machiavelli thus moved European discourse about armed conflict away from medieval preoccupation with the idea of the Christian way of war, combat as the instrument and revelation of God's purposes on Earth as divined by the Church or at least the good conscience of a Christian knight. He advanced it toward the modern idea of republican or secular war, of war for and by the sovereign state ("prince") rather than for high ideals, of wars fought for what *Cardinal Richelieu* would later call "raisons d'état" ("reasons of state").

Antedating Thomas Hobbes, Machiavelli laid out an understanding of politics rooted in profound fear of anarchy. He upheld expedience by rulers in choice of means as a regrettable but unavoidable requirement of successful political action, dictated by the underlying wickedness and venality of the governed. He accepted the equivocal nature of public as opposed to personal moral judgment, maintaining what Max Weber would later call an "ethic of consequences" as the true political ethic, much to be preferred and indeed admired. What Weber called an "ethic of intentions," or right regard, Machiavelli thought weak and foolish (imprudent). He wrote: "Since love and fear can hardly coexist . . . it is far safer to be feared than loved." This emergent nature of the modern state as based fundamentally on its capacity to make war first became apparent in Renaissance Italy in his lifetime, and he was the first to apprehend it. Less widely recognized, Machiavelli wished for the successful exercise of power not for its own sake or in a vacuum of values. Instead, he yearned to see princely power advance specific causes he regarded as having inherent moral content, ruthlessly if need be, including republicanism and the liberation of Florence—and even all Italy—from foreign control. He is justly famous for his depiction of the workings of power in the real world: his understanding of the balance of power, and his intuitive recognition of how the lust for power curls naked and expectant beneath the covers of the most silken idealism, was instinctive, instructive, and brilliant. See also *Grotius, Hugo*; *Italian Renaissance*; *Leonardo da Vinci*; *Lipsius, Justus*; *Swiss Army*.

Suggested Reading: John R. Hale, *Machiavelli and Renaissance Italy* (1960) and *War and Society in Renaissance Europe, 1450–1620* (1986); Peter Paret, *The Makers of Modern Strategy* (1986).

machicolation. An opening (covered with a trap door or not) in a *barbican* or other projecting structure on a castle or town wall, through which stones could be dropped and burning oils or boiling water poured onto the heads of attackers below.

Madrid, Treaty of (1526). See *Italian Wars*.

madu. A small left-hand shield in wide use in Medieval India. It had two exterior horns or spikes that allowed it to be used offensively in close action.

magazines. For most of this period the idea of magazines prepositioned along the line of march of armies was widely contemplated, but the limited bureaucratic capabilities of medieval or even early modern states in Europe, Central Asia, and India, militated against it in practice. In Europe, the French army was perhaps the most advanced. It took along field ovens and bakers. Similarly, in 1620, Maximilian of Bavaria set up several supply depots. But bakers still needed supplies of flour and the Bavarian depots were only local in effect. The Habsburgs set up the *étapes* system along the *Spanish Road* that presaged the eventual development of full magazines. The first explicit effort to set up magazines in Europe came under *Michel Le Tellier* in the last years of the *Thirty Years' War*, but real progress was only achieved under his son during the wars of Louis XIV. In contrast, Ming China's sophisticated bureaucracy built forward magazines to address the logistics problem Chinese armies faced every time they struck at the Mongols across the Gobi Desert, into the also unforgiving Inner Asian steppe. In the early 15th century the Ming built a base at Kaiping 150 miles north of Beijing, to which they sent many hundreds of supply wagons in advance of northern campaigns into Mongolia in 1410 and 1414. They also set up supply depots, armories, and granaries within their borders more generally, and experimented less successfully with self-sustaining agricultural garrisons along the frontiers.

The Ottoman Empire also far surpassed European logistics in this era. The Ottomans built food depots filled with dried biscuit and grain, preset ammunition dumps, and prepositioned pontoon bridges along their invasion route into Hungary up the valley of the Danube River. Comparable magazines and dumps lined traditional routes of march to the east and south. The Ottomans maintained a sophisticated internal supply depot system ("nüzul") with food, fodder, and firewood for the sultan's household troops and horses (*Kapikulu Askerleri*), using the superb road system they inherited in Anatolia and Iraq from the Romans, Byzantines, and Seljuks. This "menzil-hane" (depot) network was supplied by pack horse and bullock in the temperate west and dromedary in the parched east. Depots had well-stocked granaries, military bakeries, and fodder barns along the regular routes of march leading to the frontiers. In addition, the Ottomans supported field armies with riparian supply systems linked by barge to centralized imperial granaries. This system was a unique military accomplishment for the age. Still, it did not extend past the frontiers, where the hard rules of 16th–17th century logistics applied also to Ottoman armies. Moreover, large numbers of seasonal troops such as *timariots* and *sipahis*, all peasant levies, and tens of thousands of Tatars were excluded and had to forage and fend for themselves.

Magdeburg, Sack of (May 20, 1631). The city of Magdeburg was a key fortress on the Elbe, and one of the few towns to resist the armies of *Charles V* in the religious wars in Germany in the mid-16th century. In 1631, Magdeburg again defied the Empire by refusing to restore its Catholic bishop. It was therefore besieged by a Catholic and Imperial army 22,000 strong, starting in April 1631. *Johann Tilly* arrived on May 18 just as the Imperial sappers reached the city's walls. He demanded that Magdeburg submit to restoration of its bishop, invoking both the despised *Edict of Restitution* of 1629 and the older *reservatum ecclesiaticum*. To the north, *Gustavus Adolphus* was still negotiating with *Georg Wilhelm* for access to key riverine routes through Saxony which he needed to transport his artillery train if he was to relieve the city and fight in the south. Tilly sent in negotiators while Imperial cavalry general *Graf zu Pappenheim* sent in troops to breach the defenses. They succeeded in undermining a section of wall and stormed the city. Magdeburg was then sacked in the single greatest atrocity of the *Thirty Years' War* (1618–1648). Perhaps 20,000 of its 30,000 townsfolk were butchered or burned—man, woman, and child, without distinction—and the city was razed to the ground. Only the cathedral still stood, aspirational spires rising over the smoking ruin of "Christian mercy," giving silent mock to the ideals of *just war* upheld by Fathers of the Church and paid impious lip service by the armies of wrath that waged this awful confessional war. The atrocity forced the hand of the *Leipziger Bund*, pushing those German princes who had sought a middle way into the Swedish camp, and hardening Protestants across Europe with thoughts of bloody revenge. Protestant propagandists made much of the event and Protestant soldiers remembered it in their *battle cries* and when they gave "Magdeburg quarter!" to Catholics, meaning none at all. Historian Geoffrey Parker agrees with contemporary Catholic apologists,

> *Perhaps 20,000 of its 30,000 townsfolk were butchered or burned— man, woman, and child, without distinction . . .*

defending the sack as in accord with "the Laws of War reinforced by strategic necessity" and accepted practice in which a city that refused surrender could be, and usually was, denied quarter. Yet, even by contemporaries the treatment of Magdeburg was seen as beyond the pale and failing to temper law with mercy.

Maghreb. "al-Maghrib" ("The West"). The western half of North Africa, populated mainly by *Berber* peoples. It included Algiers, Mauritania, Morocco, Tripoli, and Tunis, as well as Ceuta and Melilla. Its life revolved around major coastal cities supported by interior hinterlands which sustained nomadic tribes. In the 12th century it was united under the Almohad Caliphate, which also ruled Muslim Spain. However, it subsequently broke into three parts under rival Berber dynasties: the Hafsids, Wadids, and Marinds. The city-states of the Maghreb were termini of the trans-Saharan slave trade and buyers of sudanese military slaves well into the mid-19th century. See also *Barbary corsairs*; *Ifriqiya*; *Tripoli*.

maghribis. See *mangonel*.

magnus equus. See *destrier*; *warhorses*.

mahdi. "Divinely Guided One." A title taken by numerous historical figures claiming to be the embodied fulfillment of the messianic tradition in *Islam*, especially but not solely within the *shī'a* branch. The tradition looked to a temporal—but divinely anointed—ruler, a foreordained leader who would bring a final reign of righteousness to the world through revelation of the "hidden imam" and a final social transformation. This eschatological vision of history kept the Faithful constantly on the lookout for a sign of the arrival of the mahdi and the beginning of the transformation to a more just and godly society.

mail. Armor originally made from thick cloth or leather onto which were sewn strips or scales of metal, and later interlinked rings of metal. It was worn from the earliest days of European *knighthood*. By the 11th century this earliest form of mail was displaced by the *hauberk* of all-ring construction, under which a padded garment, or "*gambeson*," was worn. In the late 12th century "mail mittens" were added to the knight's kit, and "mailed fist" became a synonym for power and authority reliant on force majeure. "*Chausses*," or mail leggings, were worn to protect this dangerously exposed extremity when a mounted man faced a foot soldier wielding a slashing weapon. Mail was effective against slashing weapons such as swords and bills. It could not stop thrusting weapons such as lances, arrows, quarrels, or roundshot, all of which drove links of mail and cloth into the wound that often led to deadly infection even if the wound was not itself fatal. To defend against improving missile weapons mail was supplemented by plate. Over time it was displaced altogether by fully articulated suits of armor for wealthy knights, but was still worn by poorer knights and infantry. See also *aventail*; *bascinet*; *brayette*; *crossbow*; *lamellar armor*; *longbow*; *mail-tippet*; *miles*; *shields/shielding*; *sipahis*; *swords*.

mail-tippet. A medieval infantry helmet, often a simple *kettle-hat*, with a mail coif attached to it. See also *aventail*; *bascinet*.

main-gauche. A left-handed dagger used as a secondary weapon in close combat, particularly in naval boarding actions.

maître de camp. A French camp master whose main task was to communicate the colonel's orders to the ranks. Not the same as a German *mestres de camp*.

Majapahit. A syncretic Hindu-Muslim kingdom established on Java during the 14th and 15th centuries. It maintained extensive claims on several of the larger islands, including Kalimantan and Sumatra, and was a substantial regional naval power. It was the major state in the Indonesian archipelago encountered by European traders.

make sail. A command on a sailing ship to hoist and spread canvas to catch the wind.

Malacca. A small Muslim state founded in the 14th century. It was captured for Portugal in 1511 by *Alfonso de d'Albuquerque*, after which it became a center of the world *spice trade*. When the Portuguese arrived they discovered over 3,000 firearms of non-European origin, probably from Pegu or Siam. Malacca came under Spanish control with *Philip II*'s assumption of rule over the Portuguese Empire in 1580. *Aceh* made a supreme effort to take it in 1629, but lost its whole army and its fleet in the attempt. Malacca was captured by the Dutch in 1641.

Málaga, Siege of (1487). See *Granada*; *Reconquista*.

Malaya. The Malay peninsula was dominated by Hindu kingdoms in the second half of the first millennium, including the Kingdom of Langkasuka centered on Kedeh. The Sri Vijaya state dominated much of the peninsula, in rivalry with Kedeh, from the 8th to 13th centuries. For the next several centuries Malaya was a locale of divers minor states, a crossroads of Hindu, Muslim, and Chinese cultures, and a battleground for more powerful foreign invaders from Java, Aceh, and Siam, and from the mid-17th century from the Netherlands' colony at Batavia (Jakarta). See also *Malacca*.

Malcontents (Flanders). Catholic nobles in Flanders and Brabant who rebelled against *Philip II* and the States General starting in 1578. They later reconciled with the king. See also *Edict of Beaulieu*.

Malcontents (France). French nobles organized on nonconfessional lines during the fifth of the *French Civil Wars* (1562–1629), intent on reform of the monarchy and an end to social discord. They were angry over the huge loss of noble lives at the siege of *La Rochelle*, the resumption of a lead role of clergy in the civil service, and the presence of too many Italian fops and other "mignons" at the Court of *Henri III*.

Mali Empire. This great inland Muslim empire ruled a huge swath of West Africa for centuries. It was founded by Mande peoples who expanded all through the 13th century, conquering non-Mande peoples. It reached to the termini of the trans-Saharan trade route at Timbuktu and Gao. Mali's Islamicized ruling class relied on a large army of perhaps 100,000 infantry and 10,000 cavalry. Mali exacted slaves and tribute from *Songhay*, which it cut off from access to the main trans-Saharan trade routes, and from the Wolof of Senegal and other neighboring areas and peoples. Mali's capital, Timbuktu, hosted a great Muslim "university" (madrassa). After 1360 the Keita dynasty which governed Mali fell prey to internal rivalry and a resurgence of Songhay power, and Songhay and the Wolof alike stopped paying tribute. Timbuktu fell to the *Tuareg* in 1433, while Songhay pushed Mali's frontiers back to the Gambia. Mali survived, but in truncated form and as a much poorer and less powerful state. In the late 16th century Moroccan power was ascendant. Morocco utilized early access to firearms to expand deep into the desert and seized control of the ancient caravan (salt, gold, and slave) trades. A major expedition, 1590–1591, conquered Songhay, including portions of the old Mali empire. Thereafter, the *arma* governed a vast desert and tributary and slave-raiding empire stretching to Timbuktu and Jenne. Mali was thus ruled from far-off Morocco until the 19th century.

Suggested Reading: J.F.A. Ajayi and Michael Crowder, eds., *History of West Africa*, 2 vols. (1974); N. Levtzion, *Ancient Ghana and Mali* (1973).

Malinche, La (c.1505–1529). A young Tabascan girl called Malintzin, later baptized as "Doña Marina" and known to the Spanish as "La Malinche." She was one of 20 young women given as slaves in tribute to the *conquistadores* who landed with *Cortés* and quickly bested the coastal Tabascans in battle. Cortés took her as his interpreter; she later became his confidante and mistress and bore him a son, Don Martin. She was gifted in languages, including the Nahuatl of the Central Valley spoken by the Aztecs, a distant tyranny feared and hated among her people. She also spoke a Mayan tongue understood by one of the Spanish, who had been shipwrecked on the Yucatan peninsula two years earlier. And she quickly learned Spanish. La Malinche's judgement and abilities were a key to early efforts at diplomacy between Cortés and *Moctezuma* and between the Spanish and the Tlaxcalans and other enemies of the Aztecs. Even more important, she helped Cortés develop the acute insight into Aztec and tributary Indian politics and strategy which allowed him to bring down the *Aztec Empire*. Her memory is reviled by some Mexican nationalists, who employ the epithet "malinchista" to mean "a lover of foreigners, a traitor."

Despite the genuine horrors of the conquest such disparagement neglects how hated the Aztecs were by other Mesoamericans.

Malta. This island state is strategically located in the middle of the Mediterranean. As such, it was successively part of several ancient Mediterranean empires, including the Phoenician, Greek (ancient and Byzantine), Carthaginian, Roman, and Arab. The *Normans* conquered Malta in the late 11th century. It was a base for Christian armies and pilgrims heading for the "Holy Land" during the *Crusades*. When the Crusaders lost Jerusalem, and then Acre, the defeated *Hospitallers* retreated to Cyprus, then Rhodes. Eight years after Rhodes fell to the Ottomans (1522), *Charles V* resettled the Hospitallers on Malta, where they were known as the "Knights of Malta." From 1564 to 1565, some 9,000 knights and retainers resisted a siege by 20,000 of *Suleiman I*'s assault troops, later doubled to 40,000. The fortress of St. Elmo fell but Valletta held out until disease and hunger wore down the Ottomans. Most of the defenders were also killed, with just 500 or so knights surviving. In later decades the Maltese Knights lived as pirates operating slave galleys. Styling themselves "Armies of the Religion on the Sea" they preyed on Muslim trade and cut Muslim throats under banners of the Virgin Mary and John the Baptist, and the famous red cross of their Order. They even acquired three island colonies in the Caribbean (Tortuga, St. Barthélemy, and St. Croix). The Grand Master was made a prince of the Empire in 1607 and in 1630 he gained rank in Rome equivalent to a Cardinal Deacon. The Knights remained in Malta until expelled by Napoleon in 1798 as he stopped off on the way to Alexandria. See also *Johannitterorden*; *Osnabrück, Treaty of*.

Mamlūks. "Mamlūk" meant "owned," or "slave," with the special connotation of "Caucasian military slave." This was because most early Mamlūks were Central Asian-Turkic or Caucasus slaves who were imported to Syria and Egypt by the Abbasid *caliphs* of Baghdad to reinforce Arab tribal levies which were losing their military edge, and reputation, within the Arab empire. By convention, "Mamlūk" refers to the dynasty and military elites while "mamlūk" is used for ordinary slave soldiers. By the 9th century the Abbasids accepted annual shipments of mamlūks as tribute. A major expansion of mamlūk service followed as Turks displaced Arabs and Iranians from military service within the caliphate. As the Muslim states became increasingly military rather than civilian-religious empires, Turkic-speakers and soldiers became the predominant political class—a position they retained in the Middle East for a thousand years. In 868 a Mamlūk dynasty was founded in Egypt, the first breakaway state from the unified empire of the caliphs. In Iran, too, Turkic-speaking slave soldiers dominated, culminating in the military slave dynasty of the Ghaznavids (962–1186). The Umayyad Caliphate in al-Andalus, with its capital at Córdoba until the early 11th century, employed northern and western European slaves captured as boys, castrated, and trained as mamlūks. A Mamlūk dynasty ruled large parts of northern India for a time after 1206, but it was always weaker than its Middle Eastern counterparts as it lacked a ready source of new recruits. Training fell by the wayside and the Indian Mamlūks were compelled to share power with local civilians. A new bevy of mamlūks were brought to Egypt by *Salāh al-Dīn* (Saladin, 1137–1193), who pushed aside the last Berber Fatamid caliph to rule in his name, then put his family on the sultan's throne as the Ayyubid dynasty. He relied heavily on loyal mamlūk soldiers. After crushing a *Crusader* army under Louis IX, a rebellion led by the Mamlūk general Baybārs overthrew and murdered the Ayyubid sultan, Turan Shah. The Ayyubids tried to elevate a female sultan—Shajar al-Durr—as a replacement but this garnered wider support for the rebels from Muslims who could not conceive of being ruled by a woman. Mamlūk-governed Egypt is conventionally periodized as the Bahri (River) Mamlūk era, 1250–1382, and the Burji (Citadel) Mamlūk period, 1382–1517.

In 1260 the Mamlūks defeated the Mongols in Galilee at *Ayn Jālut*. The next year the remnant of the Abbasid caliphate moved to Cairo (from Baghdad, which succumbed to the Mongols in 1258). This did not alter the fact of rule by Mamlūk sultans over Egypt and Syria. The Mamlūks actually benefitted from Mongol disruption of northern trade routes, which diverted goods into mamlūk ships plying the Indian Ocean and Red Sea. The Mamlūks crushed the last Crusader state, besieging and storming Acre (including with suicide squads) in 1291. After that defeat, the Latins surrendered Tyre and all other strongholds without further fighting. To the south, the Mamlūks expanded into *Alwa* in southern *Nubia*, pushing that Christian state to relocate deeper south after 1316. Having tamed the last of the Crusaders, the Mamlūks governed Palestine and Syria until 1400, when they were beaten at Aleppo by *Timur* and Syria was lost to them. It was not recovered until Timur's unstable empire fell apart after his death.

> *...heavier mamlūk armor and weapons and superior discipline and training meant they usually prevailed.*

Since the children of mamlūks were originally forbidden to become knights, the Mamlūk dynasty continually drew fresh supplies of Turkish-Russian slaves to renew military formations. This meant that the language of the Mamlūk ruling class was Turkic, with many slave soldiers also unable to speak Arabic. The later Mamlūk system was semi-feudal: an officer was granted land from which he drew revenue (he still lived in barracks in Cairo) to sustain himself and perhaps some soldiers, too. By this time recruitment had changed, so that Mongols, Circassians, Greeks, Turks, and Kurds were also to be found in mamlūk barracks. After 1383 the Mamlūk sultans were usually also the main commanders. Although they sometimes trained as lancers and could fight as medium-to-heavy cavalry, the mamlūk military specialty was mounted archery. They were trained to hit a small circular target at 75 yards' range, five shots out of five, and to loose arrows at a pace of 6 to 8 per minute. They were originally formed to fight nomadic light cavalry and trained to equal or best the *Bedouin* in the skills of mounted archery. When fighting was hand-to-hand, heavier mamlūk armor and weapons and superior discipline and training meant they usually prevailed. This militarily conservative system was superb and effective against the normal threats faced by Egypt: Bedouin from the desert, North African nomadic warriors, and distant Nubians. It remained to be tested against more modern forces gathering to the north in the Ottoman Empire.

Mamlūks are often cited as having failed to adapt fully to the "gunpowder revolution," viewing muskets—as did the *Safavids* of Iran before the reign of *Abbas I*—with distaste, as dishonorable and disruptive of their settled social order. While generally true, this was almost certainly more a product of their lack of need for firearms than any rooted "cultural" rejection of guns. Like other Muslim armies, mamlūks had been so dominant in field battles for so long they did not feel a strong need for the new weapons, which were still inefficient as field artillery in any case. David Ayalon has documented that "horsemanship and all it stood for were the pivot round which the whole way of life of the Mamlūk upper class revolved." Since early guns required one to dismount to fire and reload they were disdained and left to black slave soldiers, a pattern common to European heavy cavalry, which also declined early guns. Finally, mamlūks did not abstain from using cannon or muskets (the latter in the hands of Syrian and other auxiliaries) when they conducted sieges or fought enemies more attuned to the new weapons than they were. In their first war with the Ottomans in 1485–1486, a mamlūk army took Aleppo, paused there to cast a number of cannon to supplement their traditional catapults, then marched on to besiege Ramadan. They bombarded the city with artillery of both kinds, then turned to defeat an Ottoman relief army. The Mamlūks again recruited Syrian musketeers as auxiliaries and re-took Ramadan in 1488, defeating a second Ottoman relief force. That led to a temporary peace with the Ottomans in 1491. Sultan al-Nasir tried to use the pause to supplement his mounted archers with a regular body of firearms infantry, to which end he trained a regiment of black slaves to use muskets. However, this breaking of the mamlūk military monopoly provoked the average mamlūk to a murderous rage: in 1498 the black musketeers were attacked and slaughtered in a running battle in the streets of Cairo. Survivors were dispatched by the sultan to fight far away from the capital in the empire's Indian Ocean territories.

The Mamlūks lost Syria after their defeat at *Marj Dabiq* (1516), where the sultan died among his troops (possibly of natural causes). Now that the conflict was a life-and-death struggle, no "cultural aversion" to guns was evident. Instead, a crash effort was made to build a firearms army that could stand against the *Janissaries*, including musketeers semi-protected by wagon forts or wooden shields that were borne to the field of battle by camels. Some light cannon were even mounted on camels. But this virgin force faced a superior Ottoman army of experienced firearms troops who fought exceptionally well from behind sturdy wagon-forts. From within their mobile fortresses Janissaries fired superior muskets and bronze cannons and destroyed the hastily raised Mamlūk army, not once but twice, at al-Raydaniyya in January and at Giza in April 1516. Egypt was lost.

Surviving Mamlūks proved useful to the pragmatic Ottomans and were kept in place in Cairo as sworn vassals, governing Egypt in the name of distant sultans. The lingering claims of the old Abbasid caliphate, reigning but not ruling in Cairo since the fall of Baghdad to the Mongols, also came to an end (1517). Though numbering just 10,000 to 12,000 at their peak, and despite their military conservatism, the mamlūks remained one of the feared militaries of the Middle East for another two centuries. Moreover, as Ottoman power declined Mamlūk rule revived in fact if not in name. Cut off from their supply of Turkic and Circassian slaves Egyptian mamlūks evolved into a hereditary military caste that remained in power until 1798, when their last cavalry charge was blown away inside an hour at the "Battle of the Pyramids" by French muskets and artillery directed by Napoleon Bonaparte. See also *itqa*; *naphtha*; *taifa states*.

Suggested Reading: David Ayalon, *The Mamluks and Naval Power* (1965) and *Islam and the Abode of War* (1994); Thomas Phillip and Ulrich Haarmaan, eds., *The Mamluks in Egyptian Politics and Society* (1998).

Manchester, Earl of (1602–1671). Né Edward Montagu. English general. He was one of a few nobles to back Parliament in his war with *Charles I*. The first *English Civil War* was sparked when the king sent troops to arrest Manchester and four others sitting in Parliament in 1642. Manchester commanded a foot regiment and saw early action at *Winceby* (1643). He then besieged and took Lincoln. However, his ultimate loyalties and his martial energy were alike suspect: he remained an amateur in an emerging age of professional soldiers and a Parliamentarian who could see no way around the king. While in nominal command of the army, in practice he lost battlefield control to more aggressive officers. He fared badly at *Marston Moor* (1644) and did no better at Second Newbury (October 27, 1644), after which *Oliver Cromwell* brought charges against Manchester that forced him to resign. He opposed execution of the king and hence was spared execution by the Restoration (1660).

Manchuria. The historic homeland of the *Manchus*, and three northeastern provinces of Imperial China—Liaoning, Heilongjiang, and Jilin. Manchuria was home to semi-nomadic Jürchen peoples who repeatedly invaded China. Part of Manchuria was briefly occupied by the Han Empire. From 1122 to 1234, Jürchen warriors ruled northern China ("Jin empire"). After their retreat they took subsidies from Ming China and remained mostly quiet inside Manchuria. Bridging the 16th–17th centuries, *Nurgaci* laid the foundation for an explosion of Manchu aggression and for the Manchu conquest of China as he consolidated Manchuria and reorganized it as a martial state. His descendants, the Qing emperors, forbade ethnic Chinese settlement in Manchuria, marking the forbidden zone with a willow ditch that ran the length of the border.

Manchus. An Inner Asian people originally known as Jürchen ("Jin Empire") when they ruled north China in the 12th century, but renamed "Manchu" by *Nurgaci*. They numbered fewer than two million at the mid-17th-century mark but had learned advanced bureaucratic skills from the Chinese of Liaodong, and had a superior military organization (the *banner system*) that channeled the ferocity of their clan society into external aggression. Nurgaci organized the tribes in the first quarter of the 17th century into a mass army and powerful empire. His son, Hung Taiji, renamed the state "Qing" ("Pure") in 1636. Under that name, a Manchu dynasty governed China until 1911. See also *mutiny*; *Sarhu, Battle of*.

mandate of heaven. The central Chinese Imperial governing doctrine, probably originating during the Zhou dynasty (1040–256 B.C.E.), arguing from *Confucian* principles that even an autocrat is bound by moral forces and the social compact that guides an entire community. In turn, that idea sustained the core myth of Chinese political theory (that is, of autocracy); to wit, that notwithstanding the absence of representative institutions in China the emperors governed from a mandate given by the people which demanded personal virtue and benevolent administration from rulers. Dynasties maintained the mandate by having the emperor ("Son of Heaven") ritually observe an imperial cult of ancestor worship and undertake other complex rituals on a daily basis, erecting temples, maintaining an effective and established state religion, keeping domestic order and upholding the laws, and by securing the frontier from barbarian invasions. The mandate was claimed by each new dynasty and even later secular regimes. Each claim was contested, but also usually accepted once "confirmed" by the fact that overt resistance was finally crushed.

mandrel. See *hoop-and-stave method*.

maneuvers. Much warfare in the 16th–17th centuries in Europe involved complicated maneuvers and strategic positioning rather than pitched battles of encounter. This was partly a consequence of primitive *logistics*, which forced armies to remain on the move eating out whole regions of the enemy's territory before moving on to winter in some as yet unravaged area. Maneuvering also reflected the interests of *mercenaries* on all sides in avoiding combat as long as possible. See also *chevauchée*; *condottieri*; *Gustavus II Adolphus*; *Lützen, Battle of*; *Mansfeld, Count Ernst Graf von*; *Thirty Years' War*; *Wallenstein, Albrecht von*.

mangonel. Any of several mid-sized medieval siege engines that hurled stones to break castle walls or smash siege or town fortifications. They could also throw heavy darts or body parts or offal. In India and Iran they were called "manjaniq maghribis" ("western mangonel"). Mangonel was essentially another name for *catapult*. See also *siege warfare*.

Mannschaftsrodel. See *Swiss Army*.

man-of-war. In this period, a generic term for whatever was the largest fighting sail (not a *galley*). First used about modified, multi-masted *carracks* built by the Portuguese, it later applied to *galleons*. From the late 17th century it referred to a separate class of very large fighting sail, a mobile artillery platform that brought to bear multiple decks of cannon in a devastating broadside. See also *Great Ships*.

mansabdari. The *Mughal* imperial and military system which employed extensive symbolism about traditional ideals of warrior honor while actually professionalizing the military by setting up complex ranks and salaries. See also *fitna*.

Mansfeld, Count Ernst Graf von (1580–1626). Mercenary general. Although a Catholic he fought for pay on the Protestant side throughout the *Thirty Years' War*. He was commissioned by *Friedrich V* to raise an army of 20,000 to intervene in Bohemia, alongside local forces under *Matthias Thurn* and *Christian of Anhalt*. Manstein took Pilsen (November 1, 1618) after a day's fighting. He was surprised and beaten badly at *Sablat* (June 10, 1619). His army was destroyed in less than an hour by *Johann Tilly* and *Bucquoy* at the *White Mountain* (November 8, 1620). He made a long retreat north where he raised a new army of 40,000 men in Alsace to defend the Palatinate. He fought Tilly twice more in the spring of 1622, at *Wiesloch* (April 22) and *Wimpfen* (May 6), campaigned in the Netherlands and fought a third battle at *Fleurus* (August 29). In these early years his reputation rose as a contractor who could recruit large mercenary armies at a low price and in great haste. However, his reputation as a field commander soon sank. Even though he never offered battle where he could avoid it, fearing wastage of his precious regiments, desertion rates among his recruits exceeded even the extraordinary levels of the age. Mansfeld's armies were also prone to scatter on first contact with the enemy. He was dismissed by Friedrich after the fiasco at *Höchst* (June 20, 1622) and retreated into the Netherlands. Despite his ineffectiveness, Mansfeld was considered the best at raising large, cheap, mercenary armies— at least until *Albrecht von Wallenstein* was hired by Ferdinand. From 1625 to 1626, Mansfeld was paid by the Dutch to raise an army to support intervention in Germany by *Christian IV*. As Wallenstein moved north to meet the Danes Mansfeld tried to intercept him on the Elbe, but was completely fooled and decisively defeated at *Dessau Bridge* (April 25, 1626), losing three-fourths of his 20,000 men. With the remnant, he fled into Saxony. From there he was driven to Moravia by Wallenstein's hot pursuit. Mansfeld hoped to link with the Transylvanian general Gabriel Bethlen, but when that rebel agreed to terms with Ferdinand in December, Mansfeld's rump army was stranded. The old man fled, but died before reaching Sarajevo. What was left of his abandoned army surrendered the next year. See also *flags*.

manteletes. Lightly and quickly built, mobile, roofed, wooden forts generally used for approaching fortifications during a siege. They could house up to 25 men, usually arquebusiers and crossbowmen who fired from gun ports in the sides. *Cortés* used them in reverse to try to break out of a city during the *first siege of Tenochtitlán* (1520).

Manzikert, Battle of (1071). See *Byzantine Empire*; *Seljuk Turks*.

maps. Chinese mapmaking skills far exceeded those in Europe in this period. In China land maps were reasonably accurate as well as numerous. Even coastal maps were detailed and accurate, a fact that helped *Zheng He* make his extraordinary long-distance voyages while the Portuguese still clung tight to coastal Africa and English and Dutch ships fearfully hugged the Channel and North Sea coastlines. European sailors had only rudimentary coastal maps before *Enrique "the Navigator"* began to chart the African coastline. After 1500, Iberian, French, and English sailors surpassed the Chinese in map accuracy and charted the coasts of the Americas, eastern Africa, India, the South Sea islands, and China itself, which had abandoned oceanic navigation. Military maps for land use in Europe were minimal to nonexistent during the Middle Ages, greatly restricting strategy and even hampering tactics. Commanders

> *Commanders were forced to rely on spies, scouts, and paid guides, or locals terrified into cooperation.*

were forced to rely on spies, scouts, and paid guides, or locals terrified into cooperation. Only in the late 14th century were decent land maps drawn up on anything like a systematic basis, and even then this was mostly done by private commercial interests. Most early modern governments classified maps, and often also destroyed them, out of security fears. Nor was this unreasonable: stealing or copying accurate maps that might prove of military or commercial value was a major goal of spies of the day.

In the 16th century the Spanish Habsburgs sought to systematize military cartography, and to control it. *Philip II* commissioned a major map for his own use in 1555 and had a more extensive atlas made based on a national survey in the 1580s, including 21 maps of the Iberian peninsula. A good map of Portugal was made in 1560, and in 1570 an atlas of Italy (an early center of mapmaking) and Spain was published in Flanders. Far more numerous and more detailed maps were produced by the protracted fighting in Flanders, including an atlas of the Holy Roman Empire and numerous maps of military roads and fortifications. Publication of these was highly restricted under orders of the *Duke of Alba*. Gerard Mercator published a map of England in 1570 which the Spanish used to plan their proposed invasion in 1588, but Mercator found few maps of Iberia to include in his atlases published serially but intermittently after 1585. By the early 17th century most mapmakers had migrated north of the rivers to the rebel Netherlands, so that Spain had to import foreign made maps of territory it claimed and spent blood and treasure to retain. See also *astrolabe*; *compass*; *dead reckoning*; *Exploration, Age of*; *portolan chart*; *technology and war*.

Suggested Reading: David Buisseret, ed., *Monarchs, Ministers, and Maps* (1992).

marabout. A Muslim holy man—often, a former hermit or sharif—of the *Maghreb* and Sahara. In the 16th–19th centuries marabouts preached jihads (*holy wars*) to purify the religious life of coastal cities such as Algiers, and to plunder their wealth. In Morocco divisions among holy men fed into a sustained succession struggle and civil war which invited a Portuguese invasion and led to the "Battle of the Three Kings," or *Alcazarquivir*, in 1578. See also *Fulbe*.

Marathas. The term most often used about a new military elite that arose in Maharashtra in the Deccan, outside *Mughal* control. Many were armed migrants from more marginal areas who had settled in Maharashtra in earlier centuries, exchanging contracted military services for protected status and rights, and acquired lands. They secured their territory with much new fort construction from the 15th century. In battle the Marathas deployed Hindu cavalry using the long *pata* sword-spear, among other weapons. Their position in the Deccan assisted Hindu resistance to southward expansion by Muslim powers. See also *Portuguese India*; *Rajputs*.

March. A frontier defense zone lying between two larger powers with discrete local militaries providing defense and engaging in chronic small wars. For instance, Charlemagne established a March in northern Spain, based in Barcelona (801). The early Holy Roman Empire had eight Marches along its Slavic frontier: Billungs, Nordmark, Lusatia, Misnia, Ostmark (Austria), Styria, Carinthia, and Carniola. Marches separated Christian and Muslim forces in Iberia (the comparable Muslim term was "thughur"). The *Teutonic Knights* fought and slaughtered pagans in the March of Livonia. England had two Marches on its home island, on its Scots and Welsh borders, and others along its continental holdings within France and in Ireland (*The Pale*). France had a March in Brittany, another at the Calais Pale, and a third in the Rhineland. In a sense, China's entire frontier with Inner Asia was a vast March, or series of marches, even though the *Great Wall* and Qing willow ditch on the Manchurian border meant that China's borders were more defined than most. Medieval and early modern India's states had very few fixed frontiers, and therefore wide marches. These tended to be in regions where climatic zones shifted, separating peasant farming societies from nomadic pastoralists in more arid regions. See also *Cossacks*; *Hungary*; *Ireland*; *Marathas*; *Militargrenze*; *Rajputs*; *Scottish Wars*.

maréchal de camp. A senior officer in the French Army who assigned men a place in camp.

maréchal de logis. The *quartermaster* in a French Army.

Mared, Battle of (1564). See *Nordic Seven Years' War*.

Margaret of Parma (1522–1586). Illegitimate daughter of *Charles V*; half-sister of *Philip II*. Regent of the Netherlands, 1559–1567. Although in fact broadly tolerant, she fed the mood of rebellion with impolitic remarks, including calling the Dutch nobles who presented a petition of grievances "Beggars" ("Gueux"), a name that stuck. She warned Philip against the savage repression later carried out by *Alba*. Her son was Allesandro Farnesse, *duque di Parma*.

Margate, Battle of (1387). See *Hundred Years' War*.

Marienburg (Malbork), Fortress of. The capital and central fortress of the *Teutonic Knights* in Prussia. It held out against the Poles during the "Great War" of 1409–1411. During the *"War of the Cities"* (1454–1466), it was besieged by Prussian conscripts and Bohemian mercenaries. In 1456 its Bohemian garrison sold the fortress to the Poles after the Brethren failed to meet their payroll.

Marignano, Battle of (September 13–14, 1515). "Melegnano." One of the largest and bloodiest battles of the age. It was fought over a day and a night about 10 miles southeast of Milan between an army of the Swiss Confederation on one side, and the French Army and supporting Venetian cavalry on the other. Although the main antagonists of the *Italian Wars* (1494–1559) were France and Spain, in 1512 the Duchy of Milan was occupied by the Swiss in the name of a "restored" Duke *Maximilian Sforza*. With the Swiss blocking the Alpine passes into Italy the 20-year old French king, *Francis I*, divided his army into three columns and sent them through the Alps along unmarked shepherd trails. He ordered an advance party of sappers to blast a wider trail for his cannon and ammunition carts to pass over. Five days later the columns emerged and descended to the north Italian plain to take a small Swiss force by surprise. Due to superior training and by virtue of its greater firepower from *arquebusiers*, the French Army was more up-to-date than the *Swiss squares*. Even so, Francis did not command a truly modern army so much as a traditional force armed with many more cannon (perhaps as many as 140) and handguns and arquebuses than was then usual. However, its mainstay was still armored *heavy cavalry*, the principal military legacy of *feudalism*. The knights were supported by ranks of lesser nobles and poorer men-at-arms. These were more lightly armed and armored mounted heavy infantry. They were organized around great dukes and barons of the French feudatory system. There were also poor knights of small title and no land, fighting to make their fortune in war. Francis also controlled a royal bodyguard comprised of Scottish "archers" (a misleading term, as most members of the long-serving Scots regiment in France had discarded bows in favor of pistols and other firearms). The French artillery was the best in Europe, but it suffered from the normal restrictions of the age: it was extremely heavy and could not be repositioned once emplaced for battle. The French infantry was actually about half German by origin: some 9,000 *Landsknechte* filled in the center of the line, alongside 10,000 French. Some of the latter sported crossbows, a weapon still nearly as deadly as an arquebus.

For several weeks the French Army encamped outside Milan, eating out the country, while Francis tried to bribe the Swiss to leave peacefully. On September 8 captains from three cantons signed an accord with Francis, accepted his gold, and led some 12,000 men home. Still, about 20,000 tough, veteran Swiss remained in the city and prepared for an all-out fight.

Five days later the Swiss marched out the old Roman Gate of Milan to offer battle. They fell first on the French vanguard breakfasting at Marignano and isolated from the main body of French encamped several miles away with the king. The Swiss—among them, a young *Zwingli*, who would later shape the *Protestant Reformation* in the Swiss Confederation—formed as usual into three squares, at Marignano numbering some 6,000 to 7,000 men apiece. Famous and terrifying all at once, the Swiss front ranks leveled pikes, the halberdiers and crossbowmen fell in behind, and the squares moved into a trot-in-unison toward the French position. The French horse scattered before onrushing groves of Swiss pikemen, impelled forward by the sheer weight of their numbers and momentum, and with the inner ranks blind to anything but the backs of their comrades to the front, on which they pushed hard and close. But the well-practiced Swiss cadence was suddenly slowed and their famous tactical discipline and battle order partly broken by a stumble into a shallow ditch the French had dug across the expected Swiss line of advance. The squares recovered, but the stagger disrupted formation, reduced their speed, and thus lessened the shock of collision. Still, with "push of pike" they slammed into the Landsknechte.

The Germans stood their ground in the center of the line, stabbing into the front ranks of the Swiss with pikes of their own while men on both sides swung halberds or shot quarrel, bolt, or bullet into the dense pack of humanity opposite. Men fell in droves on both sides, piked or clubbed or axed or slashed to death, or into terrible agony at the feet of their fellows. The forward thrust of the Swiss pikes—still propelled by the great mass of men pushing from the rear of the three leading ranks of each square—pushed the Germans back. A number of French cannon were overrun in their fixed positions as the Landsknechte slowly gave up bloody ground. Then the main body of French cavalry arrived, led by the king. Knights in full armor and lesser men-at-arms slammed into the Swiss flank. A mêlée ensued in which little quarter was asked or given by either side. Around the tangled mass of bloody infantry the French cavalry pranced in *caracole*, firing pistols at point-blank range into the mass of Swiss or thrusting lances into the mass of flesh. Swiss halberdiers stabbed and hacked ferociously at their tormentors while crossbowmen fired at point-blank ranges with more than their usual skill and accuracy. The French guns could not move, but whenever a line of fire cleared they opened up, tearing gaping holes in the Swiss ranks and files. And so the carnage went. Men locked in close combat and neither side gave ground nor quarter. The fight lasted into the night, until exhaustion cloaked with darkness forced a pause. Men clustered in small islands of comradeship and protection, surrounded by the dying, alert with fear and kept awake by screams and groans from severely wounded men and horses.

As dawn broke on September 14 exhausted infantry on both sides rose in place. The Swiss blew their famous "Harsthörner" ("Great War Horn"), their captains gathered survivors into shortened lines and the fighting resumed. French cannon and arquebusiers tore more holes in the lightly armored Swiss. The few arquebusiers deployed by the Cantons did little damage by comparison. So the Swiss formed a square and charged, pikes at the level. The French center held but the right gave way before the push of another square. The battle was nearly lost for Francis when, just after 8:00 A.M., 10,000 allied Venetian cavalry arrived. These fresh troopers fell on the exhausted Swiss, forcing them to disengage from the main body of French and Germans. About 400 men of Zurich formed a sacrificial rearguard, behind which the remaining Cantons withdrew to Milan, harried by French cavalry all the way. As many as 5,000 French and Landsknechte lay dead or dying, and some Venetians, but more than twice that number of Swiss never rose from the field of Marignano. This sharp defeat of what

> *As many as 5,000 French and Landsknechte lay dead or dying...*

was until then regarded as the most lethal infantry in Europe stunned the political world. France's military reputation rose to unfamiliar heights, that of the Swiss fell precipitously, never to recover. While dominance of the battlefield by gunpowder weapons was not yet indisputable and the ascendancy of the pike was not quite over, Spanish *tercios* nevertheless soon displaced the Swiss as the most feared infantry. Recognizing the import of what had happened the Swiss surrendered Milan and Lombardy to Francis and a year later signed the *Perpetual Peace*. After Marignano the French and Swiss did not fight again for 300 years. And while individuals and smaller groups of Swiss still hired out as mercenaries, the Swiss national army never fought again outside the home cantons. See also *Fähnlein*.

Suggested Reading: Douglas Miller and Gerry Embleton, *The Swiss at War, 1300–1500* (1979); Desmond Seward, *Prince of the Renaissance* (1973).

Marind dynasty. See *caliph*; *Maghreb*; *Morocco*; *Tangier*; *Tunis*.

marines. Naval troops as opposed to regular land infantry. However, in this period there was little distinction made between infantry serving on land or on ships. Most marines were regular troops posted to ships to serve as snipers or boarders. See also *Azaps*; *galley*; *Invincible Armada*; *Janissary Corps*; *Lepanto, Battle of (October 7, 1571)*; *levend/levendat*; *sipahis*.

Maritza River, Battle of (September 26, 1371). A large Serbian army invaded Ottoman territory and was met by an Ottoman force under *Murad I*, at the Maritza River. The Sultan crushed the feudal Serb levies with his *Janissary* infantry and *sipahis* heavy cavalry. Serb historians lament the Ottoman victory at *Kosovo* 18 years later as a catastrophic national defeat that ended Serbian independence. Ottoman and modern Turkish historians point

575

instead to the fight at the Maritza River, which they term "Serb Sindin" ("Serbian Defeat"), as the decisive victory.

Marj Dabiq, Battle of (August 24, 1516). A *mamlūk* army led by the Mamlūk Sultan, al-Ghawri, and supplemented by Syrian infantry auxiliaries, was met at this site near Aleppo by an Ottoman army led by *Selim I*. Sultan al-Ghawri was either killed or had a heart attack during the battle, in which his troops were soundly beaten by Selim's firearms-bearing *Janissaries*. As a result, Syria and Palestine as far south as Gaza were annexed by Selim, with Aleppo and Damascus serving as capitals of his new Arab provinces.

maroons. See *cimarónes*.

marshal. In most armies, the top ranking officer. However, in France a "maréchal" ranked below the *Constable of France*. Under *Henri II* there were three officers of maréchal rank. In Germany the rank was usually associated with *provost* duties. In some countries the title was hereditary in the medieval period and covered political as well as military rights and duties. The "Marshal of Ireland," for instance, governed from *The Pale* and commanded the English army in Ireland. In the 16th century a distinct military office of "marshal of the king's army in Ireland" was revived by the Tudors. The Navy Royal also used the title, as in "Marshal of the Admiralty."

Marston Moor, Battle of (July 2, 1644). *Prince Rupert*, who had never yet lost a battle, marched to relieve the Anglo-Scottish siege of York with 18,000 men, his infantry and guns moving behind a cavalry screen. He ran into the allied cavalry rearguard at Marston Moor and deployed for battle behind a long ditch. Seeing this, *Fairfax, Manchester*, and *Oliver Cromwell* agreed to send word to the *Earl of Leven* to return with the allied infantry. Both sides were set by mid-afternoon, each in the new style of deployment: infantry in discrete blocks two or three lines deep at the center, with cavalry on either wing. The Royalist cavalry was lightly sprinkled with dragoons, while Cromwell on the Parliamentary left concentrated his two regiments of *dragoons*. The fight opened at long distance with a three-hour mutual cannonade. At 7:00 P.M., Rupert and other Royalist captains retired for dinner, thinking the Parliamentarians would not fight that day and planning themselves to attack in the morning. Leven seized the moment and ordered an attack.

Cromwell's dragoons advanced on the left, deploying as skirmishers to clear out Royalist musketeers. Then Cromwell attacked with his Ironside horse, taking a wound and losing his mount during the charge. Rupert, roused by the noise, immediately counterattacked with a single regiment into Cromwell's strung-out horsemen. *David Leslie* led three full regiments of Scots in an attack on Rupert's flank, which had become exposed in turn. Cromwell and Leslie sent some troopers in pursuit of the broken and fleeing Cavalier horse, but turned their main force back toward the fighting underway at the center. There, allied infantry had crossed the ditch and pushed the Royalists back, capturing some of Rupert's cannon then turning to link with Cromwell's Ironsides. On the right, Fairfax's did badly. His cavalry was beaten and fled in disorder, and while his Scots infantry stood fast his English units were mauled by the Royalists. Fairfax was personally cut off, discarded his command sash, and rode behind the Cavalier lines to join Leslie and Cromwell on the left flank. Now Leslie and Cromwell attacked with foot and horse into the Royalist infantry occupying the center-right position taken earlier from Fairfax. Many Royalists refused quarter and were killed. Rupert had lost his first battle, along with 4,000 dead and 1,500 captured. He escaped with just 6,000 horse and no artillery. The king lost the north and center of England and his best army. Royalist morale and prestige plunged. See also *English Civil Wars*.

martial music. Music and war are ancient companions, on the march, in camp, or on rig lines when hoisting sail on a wooden warship. The *Janissaries* marched to the constant beat of drums and fought with the sounds of "Mehterhane" bands playing all during a battle. This made the Ottomans the first to incorporate military bands into their permanent ranks and the model that European armies imitated in the 18th century. In addition to large bands that played for the sultan and another for the *Yeniçeri Ağasi*, each Janissary regiment (Orta) had its own small war drum and pipe band. The instruments included large and small kettle drums (with the largest played while slung from a camel). Polish Catholics went into battle singing religious hymns, especially "O Gloriosa Domina!" The *Hussites* made a bloodthirsty hymn their main *battle cry* when killing Catholics. Lutheran Swedes sang Protestant hymns as they marched through Germany with *Gustavus Adolphus*. In France, *flagellant* fanatics of the *Catholic League* sang and whipped themselves bloody to accompaniment of chants and hymns. Beating drums and playing fifes was a common recruiting device in England, and among German *Landsknechte* companies. The latter were also accompanied by a "Speil," a small fife-and-drum band that took position near the *Fähnlein* in the middle of a square battle formation. Japanese armies marched to the beat of drummers ("taiko yaku") and used conch shell trumpeters ("kai yaku") to send battle signals, but did not travel with musicians per se. The *Mughal* emperors, in contrast, went on *mulkgiri* attended by their full court, including many artists, dancers, and musicians. See also *Harsthörner*.

martinet. See *trebuchet*.

Martinique. The Spanish discovered and chartered this West Indies island but disdained settlement in order to concentrate on their more profitable possessions. It was occupied and settled by France in 1635.

Martolos. Byzantine irregulars who later served the Ottoman Empire, mainly fighting mountain bandits and otherwise preserving public order in the wilder areas of Greece. In the 16th century they adapted to firearms and expanded their role as frontier troops into other parts of the Balkans and southern Hungary.

Mary I (of England). See *Mary Tudor*.

maryol taifesi. Emergency troops forcibly recruited from the Ottoman peasantry. They were employed in the Balkans during the *Thirteen Years' War* (1593–1606) and other conflicts.

Mary Stuart, Queen of Scots (1542–1587). Daughter of James V of Scotland who died within days of her birth, and Mary of *Guise*, the most powerful Catholic family in France. There is still no consensus about the meaning of Mary's life. Modern historians are nearly as divided by confessional opinion about Mary as were her contemporaries. Then as now, most Catholics see her as a heroine-martyr while many Protestants view her as treasonous and a frustrated regicide. At least all agree that she was impetuous and deeply flawed in her political and marital judgments as she tossed on religious and dynastic waters far more troubled and treacherous than she, or perhaps anyone, could control. The core problem of Mary's life was that her blood lines and marriages connected too many crowns: she was Queen of Scotland by birth; Catholics everywhere saw her as the rightful heir of an English throne usurped by a Protestant bastard, *Elizabeth I*, after the death of *Mary Tudor*; and she was Queen Consort of France by virtue of betrothal at age 6 to the 5-year-old future François II, followed by their marriage in 1558. Through Mary Stuart the ruthlessly ambitious Guise sought to create a Catholic empire in the British Isles, a plot opposed for 30 years by Elizabeth's chief minister, *William Cecil*. When François died in 1560, leaving Mary a 19-year-old widow and all power in France in the hands of the regent, *Catherine de Medici*, she returned to Scotland (August 19, 1561). She ruled for just six years before falling prey to what her finest modern biographer, John Guy, aptly calls Scotland's rough tribal politics "based on organized revenge and the blood feud." All that was further complicated by the growing hatreds of confessional division.

In Scotland, as a Catholic queen of an aspiring and increasingly Protestant people, Mary at first navigated confessional waters quite well. It was her choice of husbands that triggered tribal warfare and political chaos and gave *John Knox* and his ilk the opportunity to turn her out of office. Her politically fatal deed was a 1565 marriage to a descendant of Henry VII, Lord Darnley (né Henry Stuart), a feckless bisexual and, what was far worse from the point of view of the Lairds and the Scottish Kirk, a Catholic. This soon provoked a minor uprising known as "Moray's Rebellion" that was easily quashed. Darnley's debauchery disgusted Mary and they quickly grew apart. His ambition to be king in more than name was revealed, along with his cruelty, when he arranged the murder of her close friend and adviser, the Italian David Rizzio. The deed was done before her eyes with Darnley holding her rigid to see. He then took Mary prisoner and tried to rule in her name. She escaped and pretended a reconciliation, but Darnley had too many enemies due to his impolitic betrayal of nearly all sides in Scotland's struggle over the throne. That led a clutch of Lairds to conspire to blow him up in his sickroom (he had smallpox) at Kirk o'Field, just outside the walls of Edinburgh on February 9, 1567.

Mary's third unsuccessful marriage was to Lord Bothwell, the principal behind Darnley's murder. She probably was not involved in the plot but nevertheless was heavily suspected at the time. Innocence did not matter: marrying her husband's murderer three months after weeping at the burial was just too much for Scotland's nobles, even her erstwhile backers. It did not help Mary's cause or reputation that the wedding was preceded by a preposterous faked kidnaping, then a royal pardon granted to the kidnapper, Bothwell. A serious rebellion broke out. Mary sent an army to put down the uprising but it deserted early in the so-called "Battle of Carberry Hill" (June 15, 1567). She was taken prisoner and forced by the Lairds to dismiss Bothwell, who was then executed. She abdicated on July 24, 1567. Her infant son was crowned *James VI* at Stirling five days later. Mary was imprisoned by the rebels but escaped on May 2, 1568. A new army of 6,000 rallied to her at Langside, outside Glasgow. A larger rebel army met it there on May 13, 1568. Mary's defenders were quickly blown from the field by a cavalry charge and she fled, this time across the Solway to England.

Instead of receiving asylum Mary was imprisoned by Cecil and Elizabeth, first at Carlyle then in a long series of isolated castles, to end her days at Fotheringhay. During 18 years of arrest she engaged in numerous plots with Catholic ambassadors and monarchs, including *Philip II* of Spain, to kill the "Virgin Queen" and claim the English throne in her stead. As there was a large Catholic minority in England still, this posed a real threat to Elizabeth, who yet abjured approving juridical regicide of her less sensitive rival. However, one of Mary's plots was uncovered by the ever-watchful Cecil and *Francis Walsingham*, whose spies intercepted Mary's secret "casket letters." She went on trial for her life in September 1586. She was convicted of treason and plotting regicide on October 25. Still, Elizabeth would not sign the death warrant. Finally, Cecil persuaded her to do so for reasons of state and the great queen reluctantly signed on February 1, 1587. Mary's ascent to the block on February 8, resplendent in martyr's red, may have been her finest hour: she made an extraordinary speech of calculated religiosity that entranced Catholics ever after. As soon as Philip II heard the news he declared war on Elizabeth, took down dusty old invasion plans called his "Enterprise of England," and ordered forth his *Invincible Armada* to strike in the name of righteousness and restored legitimacy. In 1612, Mary's reputation was rehabilitated and her body re-interred in Westminster Abbey by her son, who had been crowned James I of England upon the death in 1603 of the barren Elizabeth.

Suggested Reading: John Guy, *Queen of Scots* (2004).

Mary Tudor (1516–1558). Mary I, Queen of England, 1553–1558. Daughter of *Henry VIII* by Catherine of Aragon. When her father divorced her mother he made Mary sign a statement affirming that she was illegitimate, which gave the throne to a boy-king, Edward VI, upon Henry's death. A devout Catholic from an early age, Mary sat out her sickly brother's short reign in apolitical quietude, only refusing to assent to his reforms and further establishment of the Reformed Faith. When her brother died Mary ascended the throne in place of her half-sister, *Elizabeth*, with full consent of Parliament and in accord with her father's last testament. She set out quietly, but with real determination, to re-establish Catholicism in England. She reinstated dismissed bishops and arrested firebrand reformers, but drew back from public affirmation of papal ascendancy as more radical Catholics in her Court wanted. The crisis of her reign, as it was of her father's, concerned the royal marriage and succession. Mary stunned Protestants by choosing *Philip II* of Spain, son of *Charles V* and the most powerful Catholic prince in Europe. This provoked *Wyatt's Rebellion*, which Mary cooly put down, she then married Philip (July 1544). Now she moved to fully restore Catholic supremacy, received a papal legate (Pole, who became Archbishop of Canterbury), and formally reconciled the realm with the pope. Her political vengeance for the rebellion and her religious persecutions took some 300 lives, including prominent reformers. For this Protestant subjects called her "Bloody Mary." They deeply resented her taking England into Philip's war with France, which cost it *Calais*. After suffering two hysterical pregnancies Mary was left in misery and depression by Philip, who sailed away from Dover. She died childless, abandoned and unloved, at age 42. Her death and the succession of her half-sister Elizabeth, along with the death of *Henri II* of France in a freak accident, were twinned chance events that greatly shaped the confessional wars that shortly thereafter broke out in France and the Netherlands. See also *Gravelines, Battle of.*

Masaniello. See *Naples revolt.*

masnada. A company of *condottieri.*

masse. A Turkic club (*mace*). It was also carried by Christian knights, along with a dagger, as an auxiliary weapon to supplement their primary weapons of sword and lance.

masse d'armes. See *mace.*

master. In the 16th–19th centuries, the commanding officer in charge of piloting and navigation of a warship, but not necessarily the officer in charge of fighting the ship. He was assisted in handling the ship by a petty officer, the *quartermaster.* Under the *Laws of Olèron* an English master was more a partner of his crew than their overlord, expected to make peace and resolve disputes rather than punish.

master carpenter. On a wooden warship, a highly skilled and experienced craftsman whose position by the 17th century was at the rank of *warrant officer.* He had carpenters and carpenter's mates and other crew assigned to aid in his key tasks of keeping the ship weatherly and ready for action and effecting repairs during and after combat.

master gunner. The "officer" mainly responsible for maintenance, loading, and firing of a ship's guns.

master's mate. On a warship in the 15th–17th centuries, a petty officer who assisted the *master*.

masts. Any vertical *spar* on a ship whose purpose was to support *yards*, *rigging*, *tackle*, *sails*, and smaller vertical or horizontal spars. A 14th-century *cog* might have a "made mast" (built from sections, not a single piece of wood) some 3–4 feet in diameter at the base and 100 feet high. The *Grace Dieu* built for *Henry V* in 1418 had a mast seven feet in diameter and 200 feet high. To hoist sail on such monsters was beyond simple human muscle power. Instead, it was done with help from a mechanical device: a ship's windlass. Until the 15th century even the largest ships were single-masted. After experimentation with double-masted ships a standard three-masted rig was settled on by most shipwrights. Square sails were set on the two forward masts with the spars of the main mast holding aloft most of the ship's canvas. A lateen sail was usually rigged on the mizzen mast. This rigging system permitted easier tacking and more rapid course changes. With the addition of foot-ropes divided sails became feasible. That led in turn to divided masts that were lighter and cheaper than the huge single masts they replaced. Multiple light composite masts and spars made ships faster and more stable, which meant they performed even better as big gun platforms.

> *Multiple light composite masts and spars made ships faster and more stable, . . . they performed even better as big gun platforms.*

During the 16th and 17th centuries the customary English terms for the main rig of a standard three- or four-masted warship were: "bonaventure," or the aftermost mast (aft even of the mizzen) on a four-master; "foremast," or foremost vertical spar; "main mast," the tallest and thickest mast on any two-, three-, or four-masted ship; and "mizzen," or the aftermost mast on a three-masted ship but the next to last (rigged to the fore of the bonaventure) on a four-masted ship. In addition, a "topmast" was a small mast used to extend vertical reach and add canvass. It was fitted to any of the lower masts, thereby earning the prosaic appellations "foretop," "maintop," and "mizzentop." A "topgallant" was a yet smaller vertical mast fitted to, and extending upward from, any of the afore cited topmasts. See also *top*.

match. See *linstock*; *quick match*; *slow match*.

matchcord. See *slow match*.

matchlock. A firing mechanism for early *muskets* and *pistols* invented sometime before 1411, but with the first reliable versions appearing between 1450 and 1470. It was the first major improvement in firearms from early "hand cannon" that were little more than metal tubes fixed to boards with a drilled touch hole. The matchlock permitted the gunman to fire while steadying the stock and barrel with both hands, instead of using a forked rest or a second man to apply *slow match* or a heated wire to the touch hole. The matchlock gripped several feet of slow match in a lock that descended into a pan of priming powder when a *serpentine* was lowered, at first by hand but later when a trigger released a spring-and-tumbler that moved the serpentine and match to the pan. The powder in the priming pan set off the main charge in the barrel, providing the signature two-step ignition of early firearms. The matchlock was one of three essential parts—"lock, stock, and barrel"—that turned primitive "hand cannons" into recognizable guns that could be aimed and fired while holding them against the chest or shoulder.

The term "matchlock musket" attained common usage even though the first matchlock firearms were actually *arquebuses*, a term itself subsumed under *"musket"* during the 16th century. Matchlock firearms were not practical for use by cavalry because of the tendency of the match to go out. Modern estimates are that a good matchlock musketeer could fire one shot every two minutes, though in the expectation that 50 percent of his shots would be misfires. Most musketeers retained matchlocks after invention of the overly delicate *wheel lock*, preferring a more robust mechanism. Other improvements were made that kept pace with the wheel lock by forming "snap matchlocks" in which the cock was fitted separately from the serpentine to better ensure ignition of the powder in the firing pan, with the entire mechanism attached to a metal plate that was recessed into the stock. It was this type of advanced matchlock musket that the Portuguese brought to Japan in 1543. The improved matchlock served throughout the 17th century and was only displaced in more advanced armies beginning in the 1680s by a clearly superior *flintlock* musket. Some matchlocks were used into the 18th century by poorer states and armies, and in less advanced frontier and border war zones. See also *Indian Wars (North America)*.

mate. See *boatswain's mate*; *master's mate*; *mattross*; *quartermaster's mate*.

Matthias (1458–1490). King of Hungary. See also *Hungary*; *standing army*.

Matthias (1557–1619). Holy Roman Emperor, 1612–1619. See also *"Defenestration of Prague" (1618)*; *Ferdinand II, Holy Roman Emperor*; *Habsburgs*; *Jülich-Kleve, Crisis over*; *Rudolf II*; *Thirty Years' War*.

mattross. A gunner's mate, or second to the master gunner in a gun crew.

Maurice of Nassau. See *Maurits of Nassau*.

Maurits of Nassau (1567–1625). Dutch military reformer and commander, eldest son of *William the Silent*. He lived on the Nassau lands in Germany until 1577. He was greatly influenced by the thought of *Machiavelli*, as channeled through Maurits' mentor, *Justus Lipsius*. At age 21, already preening and self-conscious about his status as Stadholder of Holland and Zeeland, he was elevated to Admiral-General of the Netherlands (*Generality*) and Captain-General of Brabant and Flanders. Vengeful and lusty, but also calculating and pragmatic, he maneuvered with cautious skill through the maze of Dutch political and religious disputes. With Willem Lodewijk, Maurits was entrusted by the States General with organizing a "new model army," a professional force to go beyond the *schutterijen* (town militia) and end reliance on foreign mercenaries. This army was to contest against the veteran Spanish *tercios* on land the way *Sea Beggar* ships already did on water. Drawing on study of classical infantry models, Maurits broke up large units into smaller, more flexible formations. He reduced infantry ranks to just 10, which meant lines rather than squares were his preferred tactical formation and that musketeer firepower replaced pike and shock as the main means to victory. These new formations were capable of quick battlefield maneuvers. They could fight separately or join to present a solid wall of muskets, while leaving measured spaces between infantry blocks. Maurits filled these spaces with cavalry and field artillery.

Maurits drew directly on Roman manuals to develop new methods of *drill* and introduce a system of effective *countermarch*. Even foreign troops accepted his hard but just *military discipline*, not least because they were paid well and on time. Maurits trained his "new model army" relentlessly in small unit battlefield maneuver, musketry, and the countermarch. This did not just practice new tactics, it instilled unit cohesion. He and Lodewijk also re-introduced *volley fire* by missile troops, which they recovered from descriptions of Roman javelin and archer tactics. To accommodate firing by volley Maurits standardized bores and patterns of muskets: his new "Dutch musket" was soon widely copied and adopted. Maurits also standardized artillery, eliminating excess and odd bores in favor of four calibers, each matched to standardized ammunition. This significantly improved rates-of-fire and assured that big guns hauled on campaign would actually have powder and shot measured and ready to use. And he limited the design and type of *gun carriages* that hauled his artillery. Among his most notable reforms was enhanced use of river barges to supply field armies and move siege guns, an area of logistical skill in which he excelled beyond any contemporary commander. He normally moved his massive artillery train along the great interior routes carved out by the Lek, Mass, Rhine, and Waal Rivers. This enabled him to bring big guns to a siege or battle site that was unreachable by road and to do so with a speed that surprised Spanish garrisons who thought him occupied elsewhere. Still, the basic limitations of early 17th-century logistics imposed sharp restrictions on his campaigns. Where Maurits made his most influential contributions was siege warfare. Besides expanding the siege train he gave a permanent role to military engineers and logistics officers. And he made his troops dig, even issuing entrenching spades as a regular part of their kit. By providing extra pay he overcame traditional mercenary prejudice against such military labor, thereby setting a new standard of troop behavior and enabling his armies to throw up good field works whenever necessary and in record time.

With a highly proficient and tactically disciplined force of 10,000 foot and 2,000 horse and a set of superb siege guns, in 1590 Maurits retook Breda in a rapid assault that stunned the Spanish and surprised all military thinkers and observers. The next year he captured Zutphen after seven days, took Deventer in eleven days, and received the surrender of Nijmegen in just six, all by quick sieges won as much by offering generous terms to the garrisons as by clever or novel tactics. In 1592–1593 he had more field successes but ran into real political restraints. He retook Geertruidenberg after a celebrated four-month siege that ended in June 1593. In 1594 he cleared the Spanish from Groningen. In 1597 he took the garrison towns of Oldenzaal, Enschede, and Grol. After a forced march of 20 miles in under nine hours, a remarkable speed for the time, he stunned the Spanish in a rare field battle at *Turnhout* (1597), inflicting 3,000 casualties. In his only other battle, at the privateer port of *Nieuwpoort* (1600), Maurits drove the Spanish from among the dunes with heavy casualties. During the *Siege of Ostend* (1601–1604) Maurits kept the city supplied from the sea for three years but failed to lift *Spínola's* siege. In 1602, Maurits took an army of 19,000 foot and 5,400 horse on a campaign he planned as a sweeping strategic maneuver to liberate Brabant and Flanders. He loaded 700 wagons with flour, mill stones, and ovens to bake bread for his men, and arranged for more flour to follow by barge. His artillery train was comprised of 13 massive cannon, 17 half-cannon, and five smaller field pieces, most of which he also transported by canal and river. His advance, typical of the period, consisted of several periods of five or more days march broken by periods of three or four days in camp baking bread. He failed to force the Spanish to battle and was forced to retreat to the Maas by exhaustion of his food supply and unusually hot weather. He resupplied by river, but the Generality grew tired of his maneuvers without a battle of encounter and forbade him an invasion of Flanders. He besieged Grave instead, which did little to advance either his original strategy or victory in the war.

Maurits opposed the *Twelve Years' Truce* (1609–1621). Then, as the United Provinces descended into factionalism and neared civil war, Maurits led the "war party" in opposition to a "peace party" led by *Oldenbaarneveldt* and *Grotius* that wanted to extend the Truce. Maurits launched a coup d'état in August 1618, arresting Oldenbaarneveldt and disbanding the *waardgelders* (militia) of Holland and Utrecht. He had Oldenbaarneveldt executed in 1619 for treason, ostensibly for trying to reduce the influence of the army by raising waardgelder units. (Grotius was jailed, escaped in 1621, and went into exile.) That left Maurits the most powerful man in the Netherlands since the death of his father. Alone at the helm, he goaded *Friedrich V* to claim the throne of Bohemia in 1618, sending him money and 5,000 Dutch troops. He led the United Provinces back into war with Spain upon expiration of the Truce in 1621, but already regretted the decision by 1624. Thereafter, the Dutch war merged with the great war in Germany, the *Thirty Years' War* (1618–1648). Maurits backed the Protestant princes with subsidies and troops, but with little success before his death. Sickly from 1623, Maurits died of a fever while trying to relieve the siege of Breda in 1625. See also *baggage train*; *brigade*;

Gustavus II Adolphus; *revolution in military affairs*; *Torstensson, Lennart*; *Turenne, Henri de*.

Maximilian I (1459–1519). Holy Roman Emperor, 1493–1519. He married Mary of Burgundy after her father, *Charles the Rash*, was killed at *Nancy* (1477). This brought most Burgundian lands under Habsburg control. Their son, *Charles V*, united even more of Europe in his person, under many crowns. Maximilian reorganized the army after witnessing repeated defeats inflicted on the Burgundians by the Swiss. He organized *Landsknechte* units in imitation of the *Swiss square*. He sometimes shouldered a pike himself and served in the front ranks. Then he made nobles serve with the infantry, providing the Landsknechte with officers. At the Diet of Worms (1495) he tried to impose a new land tax on the *Holy Roman Empire* to finance an expanded Imperial Army. The Swiss baulked at this and launched the *Swabian War* (1499) when Maximilian seized a border monastery from the Swiss Confederation. He set up territorial defense institutions within the Empire (*Reichskreis*) in 1500. He banned the *wheel lock* by edict in 1517, probably because he loathed its effect on knights and chivalric warfare, of which he was one of the last champions. His death may have saved *Martin Luther* by drawing attention to the Imperial succession just as the powers of the Catholic world were preparing to crush the German monk and his followers. See also *Agnadello, Battle of*; *Imperial Army*.

Maximilian I, of Bavaria (1573–1651). Bavaria was in an odd position within the *Holy Roman Empire*: it was rich and powerful in its own right but overshadowed by the Habsburgs in southern Germany. To enhance his power and prestige Maximilian adopted a radical Catholic policy that drew in other princes to his *Catholic League* and made Bavaria the most important ally of the emperor other than Spain. He contributed troops to the Imperial cause that lifted a Protestant siege of Vienna and later drove *Friedrich V* from Bohemia following defeat at the *While Mountain* (1620). After dissolution of the *Protestant Union* in 1621, Maximilian intervened in Bohemia and Moravia to damp down potential social revolution and peasant unrest in the wake of three years of war. Once Friedrich V was outlawed by *Ferdinand II* and the Palatinate overrun by *Johann Tilly*, in 1623, Maximilian was invested with the title "Elector" taken from Friedrich and the Palatinate. Despite long alliance with the emperor, some of Ferdinand's advisers considered Maximilian a secret enemy of the Habsburgs. There was some evidence of this, or at least of his independence of mind and desire to leave the German war at different points. In 1630 he led opposition among German princes to Ferdinand's plan to send 50,000 men to intervene in the *War of the Mantuan Succession*; he also opposed the *Edict of Restitution* and compelled Ferdinand to sack *Albrecht von Wallenstein* and reduce the size of the Imperial Army. In May 1631, Maximilian signed a defensive alliance (Treaty of Fontainebleau) with France to counterbalance Habsburg power in Germany. Maximilian took on a military role after Tilly's death, in command of the army of the *Catholic League* at *Alte Feste* and *Lützen* in 1632. Like other German princes he hoped the war would end with the *Peace of Prague* (1635) but was forced to keep fighting for another 13 years by the French intervention. He withdrew from the war early in 1647 under a separate peace, then re-engaged the fight in the autumn. This brought an immediate Franco-Swedish invasion of Bavaria and a crushing and final defeat at *Zusmarshausen* (May 17, 1648).

Maximilian II (1527–1576). Holy Roman Emperor, 1564–1576. He was so sympathetic to Lutheranism that his rigidly Catholic brother, *Charles V*, passed over Maximilian to leave Austria and the Empire to *Ferdinand I*, and urged that Maximilian not succeed Ferdinand. To assuage Catholic concerns, before ascending the throne Maximilian swore to remain Catholic (1562) and agreed that his heirs undergo Catholic education in Spain. He raised an Imperial army to fight the Ottomans but did not press ahead with war. Instead, in 1568 he agreed to pay tribute to *Selim II* for suzerainty over part of Hungary. From 1568–1571 he signed "Toleration Edicts" that legalized the Protestant parishes of Lower Austria and even approved their reformed prayer book and liturgy. He was more tolerant of Protestantism than his successors, but was so weak personally that he proved unable to stand against fanatic imposition of the *Counter-Reformation* in Bohemia and Austria later in his reign. He was elected King of Poland in 1575 but died while still readying to invade and claim the crown, which went instead to *Stefan Báthory*. Maximilian was succeeded by *Rudolf II*.

Mayenne, duc de (1554–1611). Né Charles of Lorraine. Younger brother of *Henri, duc de Guise*. He became head of the Guise family and commander of the army of the *Catholic League* upon the murder of his brothers, the duc and cardinal, by *Henri III* on December 23, 1588. Mayenne led the League as it struggled unsuccessfully to prevent the ascension of Henri de Navarre to the throne as *Henri IV*. As Marshal Ney would later promise Louis XVIII about Napoleon, Mayenne promised to kill Navarre or bring him back to Paris "in an iron cage." He was instead beaten by Navarre at *Arques* (1589), after which Mayenne was more dependent on aid from Spain and less admired within France. He was beaten by Henri again at *Ivry-la-Bataille* (1590). He entered Paris on November 28, 1591, and deposed the radical *Sixteen*, a rival to the League among Catholics. After that, he was the undisputed leader of the League and Catholic cause. He tried to rally support to continue the civil wars after

> *Mayenne promised to kill Navarre or bring him back to Paris "in an iron cage."*

1593. However, his reputation never recovered from the defeats of 1589–1590 and this denied him many followers. Also, Henri's abjuration of Calvinism gained him acceptance as the legitimate king among most French Catholics, while Mayenne's alliance with Spain during the *Franco-Spanish War* (1594–1598) won him no admiration in most of France. After losing Dijon and all Burgundy to Henri, Mayenne looked to recover his governorship (which he had held for 22 years before 1595), but Henri refused to return it. Instead, in 1596, Mayenne was made governor of Ile-de-France and three fortified towns while Henri also paid off his war debts. Several weeks later, Mayenne ritually submitted before his shrewd and victorious king.

Mazarin, Jules (1602–1661). French statesman. Educated by *Jesuits*, he began his diplomatic career as papal nuncio for *Urban VIII* at the French court, 1634–1636. He became a naturalized French subject and joined the French diplomatic corps. Mazarin was elevated to cardinal through the influence of *Cardinal Richelieu*, whose anointed successor as advisor to *Louis XIII* he became in the final years of the *Thirty Years' War*. When Richelieu and Louis XIII died, Mazarin effectively ruled during the regency of Louis XIV. He likely was, but may not have been, the queen-regent's lover. He oversaw the triumph of French arms from 1643 to 1648 and the success of French diplomacy in permanently weakening and dividing Spanish from Austrian Habsburg power, an achievement enshrined in the *Peace of Westphalia*. He also began the prolonged French policy of supporting the rising state of Brandenburg as a counterweight to Sweden in northern Germany. Mazarin was the central target of the divers "frondes" that followed the end of the German war in 1648 and played a key role shaping French policy toward the Anglo-Dutch wars during the 1650s.

Mecklenburg, Duchy of. Mecklenburg, a duchy from 1348, was forced into the *Thirty Years' War* in 1625 because the Danes occupied parts of it. In 1628, with *Christian IV* driven from the war, *Ferdinand II* declared the lands and title of the Mecklenburg dukes forfeit by cause of treason, and handed both to *Albrecht von Wallenstein*. This was an act of revolution by constitutional standards: as with the *Edict of Restitution* by which he bungled religious affairs, Ferdinand hugely overreached his authority on matters political and dynastic. Henceforth, no prince of the Empire felt save from Imperial fiat and their anger focused on getting rid of Wallenstein to reduce the great captain's independence and, indirectly but more importantly, also to constrict and constrain the excessive ambition of Ferdinand.

media culebrina. See *culverin*; *demi-culverin*.

media falconeta. See *falcon*; *falconete*.

media sacre. See *minion* (2); *saker*.

Medici. The wealthiest and most powerful family in Florence during the *Italian Renaissance*. Medici money came from banking and political power from intrigue, assassination, and intimate intelligence about Florentine politics. Outside Florence, the family produced two French queens and four popes, and dominated much of the political and cultural life of Italy and France. See also *Henri IV, of France*; *Luther, Martin*; *Machiavelli, Niccolò di Bernardo*; *Medici, Catherine de*; *Medici, Marie de*.

Medici, Catherine de (1519–1589). Queen of France, 1547–1559; Queen Mother, 1559–1589. After the accidental death of her husband, *Henri II*, she exerted great influence behind the scenes during the reigns of three sons, *Francis II, Charles IX*, and *Henri III*. Her daughter Elizabeth was Queen of Spain by virtue of marriage to *Philip II*. When Francis II died in 1560, leaving *Mary Stuart* a 19-year-old widow, power in France was seized by the *Guise* over Catherine's opposition. She fought for influence over Francis, who was more attuned to his Guise uncles than to his mother, then again with Charles. Although a believing Catholic, she was a pragmatist in politics who opposed radicalism and intolerance, whether among the *Huguenots* or as practiced by the Guise and *Catholic League*, as detrimental to national unity and domestic peace. Following the premature death of Francis she declared herself regent for 11-year-old Charles and released *Condé*, whom the Guise had marked for death in wake of the *"conspiracy of Amboise."* Pursuing a policy of moderation, Catherine sought to prevent the outbreak of the *French Civil Wars* (1562–1629) by appointing the King of Navarre lieutenant-general of France, releasing all religious prisoners, and ending heresy trials and executions. Her efforts to reconcile all French within the Gallican Church failed, and in 1562 the first of the French Civil Wars broke out. It is likely her tolerance was eroded and her policy changed after the failed Huguenot attempt to kidnap Charles IX in 1567.

Catherine's role in the events leading to the *St. Bartholomew's Day Massacres* have been much misunderstood. Generations of historians portrayed her as madly jealous of *Coligny's* influence over her son. She was accused of organizing the murder of Coligny and slaughter of the Huguenots to forestall a plan by Coligny to persuade the king to invade the Netherlands and make war on Spain in support of Dutch Protestant rebels. More recent research has shown that, in fact, she was a would-be peacemaker whose plans for national and royal reconciliation fell foul of popular religious hatred and violence, at least until the night of August 23 when she joined in the decision of a royal council to strike at the Protestant leadership gathered in Paris. This was a gross political miscalculation and despite her efforts at peacemaking her consent to the council's decision that night lays the lion's share of blame for the bloodshed that followed at her feet, along with her weak-willed son and other Catholic grandees.

Catherine lost most of her power upon the ascension to the throne of a third son, *Henri III*. Older and less easily influenced than his brothers, Henri shared his aging mother's preference for toleration and a return to social tranquility. Catherine was therefore shocked at Henri's impolitic murder of Guise and arrest of leaders of the Catholic League on December 23, 1588. She scolded him for foolhardiness just before she died on January 5, 1589. She was quickly proved right: things fell apart, the Catholic League turned against the king, and Henri was himself assassinated in August 1589. His death ended the Valois line.

Suggested Reading: R. Knecht, *Catherine de Medici* (1998); N. M. Sutherland, *Catherine de Medici and the Ancien Régime* (1968).

Medici, Marie de (1573–1642). Second wife of *Henri IV* (from 1600); mother of *Louis XIII*. In 1614 she betrothed Louis to Anne of Austria, daughter of *Philip III* of Spain. That Catholic alliance provoked a court rebellion nominally led by *Condé* (Henri II, de Bourbon). Each side sought alliance with the Huguenots, which had the effect of tumbling the Protestants back into rebellion. When Louis seized power from Marie de Medici in 1617 he had her favorite adviser murdered, recalled his father's advisers to Court, and exiled his mother to Blois. Although Marie's influence thus was sharply curtailed during the reign of her strong-willed son, she yet played a key role in elevating *Cardinal Richelieu* to power.

Medina Sidonia, duque de (1550–1615). Né Alonso Perez du Guzman. See also *Invincible Armada*.

Mediterranean system (of war at sea). See *galley*; *war at sea*.

Mehemet I. See *Muhammad I*.

Mehemet II. See *Muhammad II*.

Melegnano, Battle of (1515). See *Marignano, Battle of*.

Melilla. A Spanish *enclave* inside Morocco captured by Castile in 1497. See also *Ceuta*; *Morocco*.

Melo, Francisco di (1608–1666). Portuguese general. He fought for Spain in Flanders in 1639, and against the French. In 1643 he led a Habsburg army into France but was defeated at *Rocroi* by the *Great Condé*, and was captured.

Meloria, Battle of (1284). In this naval battle the Genoese fleet bested the Pisans, dropping Pisa from the front rank of Italian and Western Mediterranean naval powers, with Genoa and Venice taking its place. Vast numbers of Pisans were taken to Genoa as prisoners of war.

men-at-arms. "homme d'armes," "homines armati," "Lanze." A third category of armored men, usually but not always lesser in wealth, status, armor, and arms to *bannerets* and *knights*. In England they included *sergeants*, *esquires*, and *valets*. In France they were more usually called sergeants early in the 13th century but esquires after its close. Generally, they could not afford to themselves keep esquires or large clutches of retainers. It is important to note, however, that there was no single, standardized type of "men-at-arms." The status was sometimes determined by social pedigree, but more often by the quality of armor a man could afford to wear into battle and the number and quality of *warhorses* he owned or was allowed to take on expeditions. The main battle mount of most men-at-arms was seldom a true *destrier*, which was so expensive only great nobles and the wealthiest men-at-arms could afford one.

A humbler man-at-arms might take possession of a destrier from a dead or captured enemy, along with all his armor, so that some were better mounted and armored than higher knights. But the usual mount was a simple *rouncey* or *courser*. This did not mean that men-at-arms were light cavalry like *Turcopoles*. They are more accurately described as medium-to-heavy cavalry, clearly distinguished by their mode of mounted combat from mounted archers such as *hobelars* and from all infantry. Starting in the 13th century it became more difficult to distinguish men-at-arms from full knights (*milites*). This was because many minor nobles began to refuse the dubbing ceremony so as not to incur the obligation of 40 days free military service that accompanied full knighthood. This shift in attitude marked an important stage on the road from a feudal-service military to paid systems of military recruitment. Beginning in the 14th century—in the armies of *Edward III* from the 1330s and French armies from the 1350s—men-at-arms dismounted to fight, primarily as a defense against skilled archers. They would remount to charge if an opportunity for shock action was presented, or to pursue a broken and fleeing enemy. France had a surfeit of men-at-arms, many thousands more than any other country. They therefore made up the majority of French soldiers (and casualties) in such battles as *Crecy* (1346), *Poitiers* (1356), and *Agincourt* (1415). Other kingdoms more often used men-at-arms as the mandrel of an army, around which they wrapped less expensive town militia and peasant or yeoman levies. The individual man-at-arms provided the core of the mid-14th century *lance* on which a new-style army was built. See also *condottieri*; *White Company*.

mendum. See *warhorses*.

menzil-hane supply system. See *logistics*; *magazines*; *Ottoman warfare*; *Tatars*.

mercenaries. Professional soldiers (or sailors) who fought for pay or plunder, not for any national or religious cause or because they were conscripts. Mercenaries have been found garrisoning forts or on the battlefield almost as long as men have made war: they marched alongside Roman Legions as auxiliaries, and fought against them; Song emperors deployed mercenaries in China in distant garrisons and used them in field armies from the 12th century; they guarded the great trans-Saharan trade routes for the African slave empires of *Mali* and *Songhay*; they fought for the Crusader states of the Holy Land, as well as against them in several Muslim armies. The *Aztec Empire* was built in blood by a ruthless people who began as tributary soldiers in the paid service of a more advanced and wealthy city-state, Tepaneca, in the Central Valley of Mexico. In parts of Medieval Europe primogeniture ensured that many young men were forced to turn to arms to earn a living. This produced the necessary forces to eventually defeat the great waves of invasions over some 600 years by Vikings, Mongols, Arabs, and other warlike raiders. A growing surfeit of warriors produced by a whole society structured for war but with a newly rising population was then sent off to fight the

Crusades, while others went mercenary and fought ever closer bound to the king's war chest at home.

The collapse of the monetary economy in Western Europe following the fall of Rome left just two areas where gold coin was still used in the 10th century: southern Italy and southern Spain (*al-Andalus*). Ready gold drew mercenaries to wars in those regions as carrion creatures draw near dead flesh. Also able to pay in coin for military specialists and hardened veterans was the Byzantine Empire, along with the Muslim states it opposed and fought for several centuries. The rise of mercenaries in Western Europe in the 11th century as a money economy resumed disturbed the social order and was received with wrath and dismay by the clergy and service nobility. Early forms of monetary service did not necessarily involve straight wages. They included fief money and *scutage*. But by the end of the 13th century paid military service was the norm in Europe. This meant that local bonds were forming in many places and a concomitant sense of "foreignness" attached to long-service soldiers. Mercenaries were valued for their military expertise but now feared and increasingly despised for their perceived moral indifference to the causes for which they fought. Ex-mercenary bands (*routiers, Free Companies*) were commonplace in France in the 12th century and a social and economic scourge wherever they moved during the *Hundred Years' War* (1337–1453). Their main weapon was the crossbow, on land and at sea. In the galley wars of the Mediterranean many Genoese, Pisan, and Venetian crossbowmen hired out as specialist marine archers. Much of the *Reconquista* in Spain was fueled by the mercenary impulse and concomitant necessity for armies to live off the land. The hard methods and cruel attitudes learned by Iberians while fighting Moors were then applied in the Americas by quasi-mercenary *conquistadores*. Mercenaries— "*condottieri*," or foreign "contractors"—also played a major part in the wars of the city-states of the *Italian Renaissance*.

French "gen d'armes" and Swiss pikemen and halberdiers fought for Lorraine at *Nancy* (1477). By the start of the 15th century Swiss companies hired out with official Cantonal approval or as free bands who elected their officers and went to Italy to fight as condottieri. With the end of the wars of the *Swiss Confederation* against France and Burgundy, Swiss soldiers of fortune formed a company known as "das torechte Leben" (roughly, "the mad life") and fought for pay under a *Banner* displaying a town idiot and a pig. Within four years of Nancy some 6,000 Swiss were hired by *Louis XI*. In 1497, Charles VIII ("The Affable") of France engaged 100 Swiss halberdiers as his personal bodyguard ("Garde de Cent Suisses"). In either form, the Swiss became the major mercenary people of Europe into the 16th century. "Pas d'argent, pas de Suisses" ("no money, no Swiss") was a baleful maxim echoed by many sovereigns and generals. Mercenaries of all regional origins filled out the armies of *Charles V*, and those of his son, *Philip II*, as well as their enemies during the wars of religion of the 16th and 17th centuries. By that time Swiss mercenaries who still used pikes (and many did) were largely employed to guard the artillery or trenches or supplies. Similarly, by the late 16th century German *Landsknechte* were still hired for battle as shock troops but they were considered undisciplined and perfectly useless in a siege.

In Poland in the 15th century most mercenaries were Bohemians who fought under the flag of St. George, which had a red cross on a white background. When Bohemian units found themselves on opposite sides of a battlefield they usually agreed that one side would adopt a white cross on a red background while their countrymen on the other side used the standard red-on-white flag of St. George. In the Polish-Prussian and *Teutonic Knights* campaigns of the mid-15th century the Brethren—by this point too few to do all their own fighting—hired German, English, Scots, and Irish mercenaries to fill out their armies. During the *"War of the Cities"* (1454–1466) German mercenaries were critical to the victory of the Teutonic Knights at *Chojnice* (September 18, 1454). When the Order ran out of money, however, Bohemian soldiers-for-hire who held the key fortress and Teutonic capital of *Marienburg* for the Knights sold it to a besieging Polish army and departed, well paid and unscathed by even a token fight.

The social and economic dislocations caused by confessional ferocity during the *Thirty Years' War* (1618–1648) forced many men into the profession of arms, especially if they came from the fringe peoples of Europe or borderlands such as Scotland, Ireland, or the Balkans, where wars of raid and counter-raid were endemic. Thus, when a "Swedish" army assaulted Frankfurt-on-the-Oder a Scots Brigade made the attack against a defending "Imperial" Army made up wholly of Irishmen under Colonel Walter Butler. In fact, the great bulk of European armies during the first half of the 17th century were comprised of mercenaries who owed little ethnic, class, or religious loyalty to the causes for which they fought. This was because kings and great captains owed such men little more than pay, out of which soldiers were expected to buy their own food, weapons, clothing, and provide shelter. In some armies musketeers were even expected to buy their own black powder, so of course they were loathe to spend it on combat. Even this primitive

Not all were Catholics—Wallenstein himself was an agnostic mystic.

system was subject to great abuse and corruption as quartermasters and colonels skimmed payrolls, troops exposed themselves to minimal danger, and captains used their tactical skills to escape rather than win battles. One result was a tendency for armies to maneuver constantly, eating out enemy territory rather than seeking out combat. The mercenary presence on the battlefield thus led to fewer pitched battles but much longer wars, conditions which best satisfied the interest of military professionals in prolonged but also cautious and relatively nonsanguinary service. During the Thirty Years' War many top officers were mercenaries, notably on the Habsburg side under *Wallenstein*. Not all were Catholics—Wallenstein himself was an agnostic mystic. They came from Scotland, England, Ireland, the Swiss cantons, and the many overrun and warring German states. In 1500 most European armies contained about one-third mercenary troops. Shortly after *Gustavus Adolphus* intervened in the Thirty Years' War 130 years later his "Swedish Army" had become, through casualties and new recruitment, 80 percent foreign mercenaries wrapped around a core of Swedish veterans.

Among the most important effects of large numbers of greatly skilled, highly mobile, and utterly disloyal mercenaries, combined with the lethality of the cannons and firearms they employed, was to so threaten any self-respecting sovereign that it became essential to establish *standing armies* to protect the dynasty and realm. The answer to the anarchy, terror, and destruction caused by "Free Companies" of heavily armed and homeless men all over Europe thus became the law of kings. This was then enforced by soldiers in royal service who dressed in the king's colors, were paid regularly and sheltered year-round in barracks, who had stables for their mounts, magazines full of shot and powder, and national foundries and small arms industries to supply military needs. In short, the answer to mercenary anarchy was the modern state. See also *appatis*; *Armagnacs*; *baggage train*; *Bashi-Bazouks*; *Bernhard von Sachsen-Weimar*; *Bestallungbrief*; *Black Company*; *Catalan Great Company*; *galloglass*; *Hawkwood, John*; *Holk, Heinrich*; *itqa*; *kerne*; *Leslie, Walter*; *Mansfeld, Count Ernst Graf von*; *redshanks*; *Saracen*; *siege warfare*; *stradiots*; *Trabanten*.

Suggested Reading: S. Brown, "The Mercenary and his Master," *History*, 74 (1989); K. A. Fowler, *Medieval Mercenaries*, Vol. 1 (2001); M. E. Mallett, *Mercenaries and Their Masters* (1974); J. F. Verbruggen, *The Art of Warfare in Western Europe During the Middle Ages* (1977); David Worthington, *Scots in Habsburg Service, 1618–1648* (2004).

Mercy, Franz von (1590–1645). Imperial general. He joined the Austrian army at age 16 and rose through the ranks. He saw action at *First Breitenfeld* (1631) where he was wounded. Afterward, he fought *Bernhard* in the Rhineland. In 1638 he joined the army of the *Catholic League*. He defended Bavaria against the French in 1643 and won at *Tüttlingen*. He was pushed back from *Freiburg* (1644) by the *Great Condé* and *Turenne*. Mercy bested Turenne at *Mergentheim* (1645). He was defeated and killed three months later at *Second Nördlingen*.

Mergentheim, Battle of (May 2, 1645). One of the last major battles of the *Thirty Years' War*. It was sparked by *Turenne*'s marauding into Bavaria, as far south as the Tauber River. There, his men demanded a halt, made camp, and many went in search of fresh provisions. A Bavarian army under *Franz Mercy* caught the camp unprepared and poorly defended, at dawn. A short fight gave all of the baggage train and the French artillery to the Bavarians. Turenne fled with the survivors, to rejoin the *Great Condé* on the Rhine, preparatory to another drive south.

merlon. The solid block between two *crenels* on a castle or town wall providing protection to defenders firing on besiegers below or in an opposing *bastille* or *belfry*.

Mesopotamia. See *Iraq*.

Mestre. "Master." In the Iberian *Military Orders* the Mestre was the senior commander, with powers to call out the Brethren for combat or assign them to other duty.

mestres de camp. A German rank comparable to *colonel.* Not the same as the French *maître de camp.*

Methven, Battle of (1306). See *Scottish Wars.*

Metz, Fortress of. See *Cateau-Cambrésis, Peace of; Guise, François; Thirty Years' War; Westphalia, Peace of.*

Mewe, Battle of (1626). See *Gustavus II Adolphus.*

Mexico. See *Aztec Empire; conquistadores; Cortés, Hernán; disease; Moctezuma II; real patronato; requerimiento; Tenochtitlán, First Siege of; Tenochtitlán, Second Siege of.*

Mezókeresztes, Battle of (1596). See *Thirteen Years' War.*

midshipman. One of several classes of petty officers on an English warship in the 17th century.

Mikata ga Hara, Battle of (1572). See *Tokugawa Ieyasu; Unification Wars.*

Milan. See *armor; artillery train (2); condottieri; expulsion of the Jews; Francis I; Giornico, battle of; Italian Renaissance; Italian Wars; Italy; Leonardo da Vinci; Lodi, Peace of; Marignano, battle of; palace guards; Sforza, Ludovico; Sforza, Maximilian; standing army; Swabian War; Venice.*

miles. A medieval warrior of the noble class or his armed retainers; a mounted and armored warrior, the ultimate soldier of the Middle Ages, not a peasant or town militiaman. While they formed a military and social elite, they were not a wholly closed class or order. Men of lower status could rise on their merits as soldiers to become miles, if they displayed rare courage in battle. This was solely an individual matter: the class as a whole excluded lower social orders in order to maintain a monopoly on military profits and prestige. Miles were fundamentally distinguished by wearing expensive *armor.* They wore mail to begin, but later plate or a combination of both. From the 11th century many wore conical helmets and used the *couched lance,* in addition to a double-edged sword and a mace or other clubbing weapon, and carried a shield. Their armor, weapons, and skills thereafter evolved with more general changes in war in Europe. See also *cavalry; knight; men-at-arms.*

Militargrenze (vojna krajina). "Military frontier." In 1527, *Ferdinand I* of Austria established a frontier zone of land-based military obligations for Serbs and Bosnian Vlachs migrating northward, away from the territorial advance of the Ottoman Empire. These were not so much feudal ties as a form of frontier garrisoning using local troops that did not draw down the treasury while redirecting bandit energies back against the Ottomans. To this end, the newcomers were left undisturbed to practice their Orthodox faith. Troops of the Militargrenze elected officers ("vojvode") who led them on plundering expeditions. On the other side of the frontier the Ottomans also employed local Christian troops, so that each empire fought the other (or kept a long, hostile peace) via Vlach and Serb proxies. The Militargrenze grew in time into a band of territory that ranged from 20 to 60 sixty miles in width and over 1,000 miles in length. See also *Thirteen Years' War*; *voivodes*; *Voynuqs*.

military colonies. See *amsār*; *arma*; *Bedouin*; *commandery*; *conquistadores*; *Crusades*; *Great Wall*; *Hongwu emperor*; *Ireland*; *Livonian Order*; *Military Orders*; *Ming Army*; *Morocco*; *Normans*; *Ordensstaat*; *Saracen*; *Spain*; *Teutonic Knights, Order of.*

military discipline. There was almost no punishment in any medieval army in Europe for mistreatment of *civilians*, even if a soldier's crime included rape or murder. On many occasions, such as *Edward III*'s great *chevauchée* of 1339, even a king's order to spare a town from plunder and sack might be ignored by men whose interest in the campaign was just such profits and illicit pleasures. Outright disobedience even of the king in such matters did not usually incur punishment. As for infractions against company rules, most armies of the period could ill-afford to house or guard men who transgressed against their brother soldiers. As a result, whenever military punishment was applied it was swift, harsh, brutal, and physical. The *Janissary Corps* had to instill obedience in slave boys from the age of 6, raising them in all-male barracks far from their families with men as old as 40. A common penalty was beating the soles of their feet. After suffering a beating the offender was expected to kiss the hand of his beater to signal contrition and gain reacceptance into his unit. Janissary officers could be demoted, beaten, or executed, according to their particular crime. Execution methods were beheading or strangulation.

Maurits of Nassau tightened discipline in the Dutch "new model army," publishing a modern code of military conduct in 1590 and setting up special tribunals inside garrisons to enforce it. The new code was read out to all recruits upon enlistment and annually to every unit in the army. For serious breaches capital punishment was the norm, notably hanging for rape or murder. So effective were these efforts, so sure the application of Dutch military justice, and so well and regularly paid were the troops, that well-behaved garrisons proved highly profitable for local traders in everything from foodstuffs to beer, clothes, nursing, and sexual services. By the early 17th century Dutch towns competed to host garrisons—an extraordinary request in an era where most everywhere else in Europe soldiers were feared, for excellent reasons, and loathed as the dregs of humanity with no place in civil society.

Gustavus Adolphus was a severe disciplinarian who punished for religious offenses as well as military ones. The punishments he employed, which spread from the Swedish Army to other armies in Germany from 1630, included *running the gauntlet*, putting men in stocks, public whipping, dunking offenders in icy ponds, and execution by firing squad. Unusually, like Maurits of Nassau, the great Swede punished for transgressions against civilians—the main sources of labor, provisions, and intelligence on enemy movements and operations—by assigning additional sentry or other tedious duty, or for more serious offenses, public humiliation, and flogging. Across the valley in the Imperial Army, *Albrecht von Wallenstein* had men decapitated for cowardice in battle while officers were executed for desertion of their posts or undue haste in surrendering strongpoints. The *New Model Army* in England encouraged internal and personal spiritual discipline, pointing to the example of the Lutheran piety of the Swedes. But Puritans took spiritual idealism to a new level

> *The punishments he employed . . . included* running the gauntlet, *putting men in stocks, public whipping . . .*

of expected decorum that was close to the virginal rules imposed by the näif girl, *Jeanne d'Arc*, on French soldiers 200 years earlier, and beyond what might be reasonably expected of any company of men, let alone soldiers. Copies of the Puritan "Laws of War" were read out to each Roundhead regiment upon enlistment. Duly warned, men were thereafter punished for blasphemy, swearing, drunkenness, homosexual acts, adultery, unauthorized plunder, and avoiding religious services, along with the more usual military crimes of cowardice, rape, murder, theft from fellow soldiers, *mutiny*, and *desertion*. Punishment ranged from shaming, flogging, and the stocks to hanging. This level of zeal was only possible—leaving aside whether it was desirable—because the New Model Army was an unusually homogenous and mostly volunteer force united by confessional allegiance and political ideology. See also *Art of War*; *drill*; *Invincible Armada*; *Ivan IV*; *keel-haul*; *Laws of Olèron*; *Nachrichter*; *samurai*; *"skulking way of war."*

military flail. A *staff weapon* of the late medieval period combining the best offensive features of a *mace* with the greater reach of a *lance*.

military fork. A *staff weapon* of the late medieval period. Two or three iron prongs were mounted on a stout staff along with iron hooks for snagging and unhorsing riders. It was used to stab through armor while the enemy was mounted or after he was pulled off his perch to flounder on the ground.

military labor. See *askeri*; *Baghdad, Siege of*; *beldar*; *camp followers*; *casting*; *culverin*; *gabions*; *Gustavus II Adolphus*; *Janissary Corps*; *lağimci*; *Maurits of Nassau*; *Ottoman warfare*; *war finance*.

military medicine. See *disease*; *wounds*.

Military Orders. In the latter half of the 11th century charitable Orders of lay Brethren were organized to run hospitals and alms houses to assist Christian pilgrims arriving in the "Holy Land" in the wake of the early success of the *Crusades*. Major hospitals were founded (in Jerusalem, and later on Cyprus, Malta, and Rhodes) in which the Brethren succored the ill and wounded, even as they learned and employed the advanced medical knowledge of the Muslim world. Through their hospices scattered across Western Europe they helped conduct this knowledge to the Latin world. Naïve and vulnerable pilgrims also needed protection from robbery, rape, murder, or kidnaping for ransom or sale into the slave markets of the Middle East. This prompted some nursing Brethren to arm. Once armed, the chronic need for military aid by the undermanned and thinly populated Crusader states encouraged formation of full-scale Military Orders. These each took their "rule" from an established monastic order (Cistercian and Augustinian were the most popular), and some received charters from the pope. This made them members of the clergy—"warrior monks"—within the tripartite feudal system of warriors, clergy, and laity. Members of Military Orders took vows of poverty, chastity, and obedience, venerated the cults of the "Virgin Mary" and the "Immaculate Conception," and rode forth to convoy Christian faithful to and from the Holy Land. As a result the Military Orders were swept up into a greater Latin armed migration eastward, and quickly became the steel tip of the spear of the Latin *holy war* which aimed at conquest and occupation of Palestine and Syria. In the words of historian Desmond Seward, the Military Orders were also "the first properly disciplined and officered troops in the West since Roman times."

The three most important Military Orders to emerge out of the wars of the Middle East were the *Hospitallers*, *Templars*, and *Teutonic Knights*. Other truly international Military Orders were *Montjoie* and *St. Thomas*. More Brethren organized knightly Orders on regional lines, especially in Iberia. Most of these also crossed borders (which meant little in the time of the *res publica Christiana*) and had overseas *commanderies* but to a lesser extent than the major Orders. While such local Orders sent a few knights on crusades to the Middle East or the Baltic they usually fought against Muslims, pagans, or "heretics" closer to home. Several large Iberian Military Orders headed the *Reconquista*: the Knights of *Alcántara, Calatrava*, and *Santiago*. These knights manned fortified strongpoints in defense at first, but later conquered, occupied, and protected and cultivated lands that unarmed Christian peasants could not till for fear of Muslim *razzia* and *rabitos*. The Iberian Orders protected the valley approaches to Toledo and other urban centers of Christian rule and power. The *Order of Avis* rose to ultimate authority in Portugal, setting its head on the throne in 1385 as Juan I, and ruling Portugal until 1580 as the Aviz dynasty. Smaller independent Orders included *Monte-Frago, Santa Maria*, and *Turgel*; *Montesa* and *Christ*, made up of fragments of the broken Templars; *Knights in the Service of God in Prussia* ("Brothers of Dobrzyn"); and the Knighthood of Christ in Livonia (*Livonian Order*). Military Orders spread throughout the Latin world until members of the ruling elites of all Western countries that counted themselves Christian were well represented in one or another. Society at large supported the Orders into the 15th century by sending them postulant knights, sergeants, clerics, and huge sums of money raised from dedicated lands, pious bequests, and wills. See also *Art of War*; *Johannitterorden*; *Knights of Santo Stefano*; *Ordensstaat*; *professed*; *Schlegelerbund*.

Suggested Reading: A. Forey, *Military Orders* (1992); Desmond Seward, *Monks of War* (1995).

military revolutions. See *artillery*; *broadside*; *Edward III*; *fortification*; *gunpowder weapons*; *infantry*; *revolution in military affairs*; *trace italienne*.

military slavery. See *Berbers*; *Devşirme system*; *galley slaves*; *ghulams*; *Janissary Corps*; *Maghreb*; *mamlūks*; *slavery and war*.

milites. *Knights* or mounted *men-at-arms*, not ordinary foot soldiers ("pedites"). See also *belatores*; *miles*.

militia. Town (or "commune") militia were especially important in this period in wars fought in Italy and Flanders, regions that hosted large towns and cities throughout the Middle Ages and early modern era. French monarchs drew heavily on militia to supplement *heavy cavalry* from the 13th century forward. Most raising of militia resulted from the need of towns to defend themselves from marauding bands of *Free Companies*. Large towns might raise several thousand during the 13th century, rising to tens of thousands by the 15th century. See also *arrière-ban*; *Brustem, Battle of*; *Cassel, Battle of*; *cavalry*; *Charles the Rash*; *condottieri*; *Courtrai, Battle of*; *Dithmarscher*; *Dutch Army*; *exact militia*; *feudalism*; *Flanders*; *French Civil Wars*; *German Peasant War*; *goedendag*; *gunpowder weapons*; *Hermandad*; *Indian Wars (North America)*; *infantry*; *Italian Renaissance*; *Italy*; *Landwere*; *lanze spezzate*; *Laupen, Battle of*; *Leiden, Siege of*; *Lipsius, Justus*; *Machiavelli, Niccolò di Bernardo*; *partisan (2)*; *Pequot War*; *Piyadeğan militia*; *Prussia*; *Roosebeke, Battle of*; *routiers*; *Rumania*; *Saint-Denis, Battle of*; *schutterijen*; *standing army*; *St. Bartholomew's Day Massacres*; *Swiss Confederation*; *Tenth Penny*; *"Time of Troubles"*; *trained bands*; *Treuga Dei*; *uniforms*; *waardgelders*; *war finance*.

militia Sancti Petri. "Army of St. Peter." See *Papal States*.

milling. See *corning/corned gunpowder*.

Ming Army. The Ming dynasty (1368–1644) early on employed hereditary troops who lived in self-supporting military colonies on large grants of land straddling the Inner Asian frontier. They were organized into brigades of roughly 5,600 men, subdivided into 5 battalions of 10 companies each. Forty men in every company were designated as spearmen, 30 as archers, 20 as swordsmen, and 10 were armed with early handguns. The Ming also maintained several training divisions. Three were located near Beijing with others outside Nanjing. One of the Beijing divisions conducted special training in firearms, a second taught tactics, and a third was for reconnaissance. Ming officers were often court eunuchs or trusted bureaucrats, a measure designed to prevent some general repeating the warlord's path to power taken by the Ming founder, *Hongwu*. An exception to this was the northern frontier, where the constant threat of *Mongol* raiding forced the Ming to commission generals attached to frontier garrisons. Eunuchs also controlled much military production—including of cannons and personal firearms—along with the central Ming armory, although a separate Weapons Bureau made mail, armor, swords, and spears. Strong in infantry, to counter the Mongol light horse the Ming hired Mongol auxiliaries to serve as light cavalry. By 1400 the Ming Army numbered over 1 million troops, making it by far the largest *standing army* in the world in sheer numbers, though not by proportion to available population. However, a century later many Ming soldiers had deserted while military families had died out or moved away from the frontier military colonies. By 1500 the Ming Army probably numbered fewer than 250,000 men, with many of dubious quality. See also *mutiny*.

Ming dynasty (1368–1644). See *China*; *Ming Army*.

Mingolsheim, Battle of (April 22, 1622). *Graf von Mansfeld* tried to prevent a Bavarian army under *Johann Tilly* from joining forces with a Spanish army. At Mingolsheim, Mansfeld successfully blocked and defeated Tilly, but this action merely delayed the junction of the Catholic armies the next month and did not prevent their ultimate conquest of the Palatinate. See also *Thirty Years' War*.

mining. Tunneling under the walls of a castle or town to undermine the foundation and allow gravity to open a breach. *Mottes* were especially susceptible to mining since they were usually surrounded by a dry ditch rather than a moat. When undermining a stone wall fires were lighted in a cavity dug below the base, with dead swine or other animal carcasses added to bring fat to the fire and increase the heat to levels that cracked stone. Once gunpowder arrived at siege sites the hollow under the wall could be packed with black powder and exploded. This was quicker than fire but much more expensive, and not as common in Europe as it was in medieval Indian warfare, where powerful fortified cities presented much greater obstacles to the attackers. If a breach was opened the defenses might be taken by *storm*. The best defense against mining was to counter-mine, or tunnel under the attacker's tunnel to make it collapse before it reached the wall. To this end defenders placed bowls of water atop drums on the ground or on stretched skins on pegs, to observe ripples caused by disturbance of the earth by enemy miners. If counter-mining failed one could always drop boiling oils and water or heavy stones on the heads of attackers, or build a secondary wall behind the breach to shoot them as they climbed through. See also *Constantinople, Siege of*; *fortification*; *Maastricht, Siege of*; *siege warfare*.

minion (1). A small early cannon or even "handgun." These were ultra-light pieces that fired small stone balls or darts or arrows. They were a design dead end that gave way to the *arquebus* and *musket*.

minion (2). "demi-saker," or "media sacre." A 16th-century medium class of cannon that fired 6-pound shot to 450 yards effective smashing range and 3,500 yards maximum lobbing range.

miquelet. The most popular lock mechanism for *muskets* in Spain for over two centuries, beginning in the 17th century. It was preferred even to the advanced *flintlock* used elsewhere in Europe. Although it employed a flint, because of a distinct design and firing action it is not generally classified by historians with other flintlock weapons.

misericord. A short, double-edged dagger carried by *knights* during the latter Middle Ages. It was used mainly to deliver the coup de grâce to a fallen enemy by piercing his armor or plunging into unarmored zones such as the armpit or groin, or through the visor and eye into the brain.

missile weapons. See *arquebus*; *artillery*; *catapult*; *crossbow*; *longbow*; *muskets*; *pistols*; *trebuchet*.

Missio Hollandica. The Catholic political and confessional revival in Holland. It made substantial gains during the *Twelve Years' Truce* (1609–1621), peaking again in the late 17th century. See also *Jansenism*.

missionaries. See *Toyotomi Hideyoshi*; *Jesuits*; *jihad*; *Kongo, Kingdom of*; *Nagasaki*; *requerimiento*; *Sofala*; *Tokugawa shoguns*.

mitaille. See *grapeshot*.

mitrailleuses. Primitive, multi-barreled cannon or handguns. They were more commonly known as *ribaudequins*.

mizzen. See *masts*; *top*.

moat. A water-filled barrier surrounding a *castle* or a fortified town, principally to impede attackers from reaching and scaling the walls. They were less common than dry ditches. See also *fortification*; *motte-and-bailey*.

mobility. See *armor*; *artillery*; *Bedouin*; *cavalry*; *Cortés, Hernán*; *fortification*; *galleon*; *galley*; *gun carriages*; *Gustavus II Adolphus*; *infantry*; *logistics*; *Maurits of Nassau*; *Mongols*; *revolution in military affairs*; *Wallenstein, Albrecht von*; *warhorses*.

Moctezuma II (c.1470–1520). "Montezuma" or "Motecuhzoma." Emperor of the *Aztec Empire* (r.1502–1520). From the beginning of his reign he continued the Aztec (Mexica) expansion of an already vast theocratic empire via conquest of neighboring Mezoamerican cities and tribes, and added new levels of authoritarianism to Aztec governance. This continued right up to his fateful encounter and dealings with *Hernán Cortés* and the *conquistadores*, including four unsuccessful wars with Tlaxcalan which ripened the hate of the Tlaxcalans for Tenochtitlán just before the Spanish arrived. The nature of Moctezuma's rule helps explain why the Spanish were able to muster so many anti-Aztec allies. Mesoamericans hated the Aztecs for their theocratic tyranny, arrogance, and enormous demands for human sacrifice and other tribute, and were happy to see Moctezuma and his empire fall. They used Cortés to that end as much or more than he used them. Moctezuma initially greeted Cortés with cautious diplomacy. Contrary to popular stories, he probably did not believe that Cortés was an incarnation of the Aztec god Topiltzin Quetazalcoatl, whose return out of the East (the traditional direction of authority among Mesoamericans) was prophesied for that year ("1 reed" of the Aztec calendar, which codified a

> *Moctezuma was probably murdered on the order of Cortés. Or he may have been killed by accident . . .*

powerful religious belief in a recurring cycle of historical events). Moctezuma's military option was instead bound to the harvest season which was underway and which kept most of his army in the fields. And he needed to gather intelligence about the strange little army around which too many of his vassal tribes and enemy cities were already rallying in rebellion and opposition.

Moctezuma next tried the stratagem of luring the Spanish into the center of Cholallan, a nearby Aztec vassal city, where he planned a lethal ambush by troops hidden on the rooftops. The idea was a good one, but it was betrayed to Cortés by rebellious Indians and the Aztec ambush was instead itself ambushed by the Spanish. Moctezuma then made the fateful decision to allow Cortés to enter Tenochtitlán. He likely did this out of a pragmatic military motivation as well: he probably hoped to trap his enemies in an even larger and more hostile city. However, within two weeks Cortés sprang his own trap, seizing Moctezuma and holding him prisoner for six months. Moctezuma's failure to call for an immediate assault on Cortés was his major and ultimately fatal error. In early 1520 he formally declared his vassalage to *Charles V*. The Aztecs were enraged by Moctezuma's call for peace after so much bloodshed and the desecration of their most important shrines by the Spanish, and deposed him in favor of his brother Cuitláhuac. Moctezuma was probably murdered on the order of Cortés (the Aztec version). Or he may have been killed by accident during the *First Siege of Tenochtitlán* by missiles thrown by his own people out of contempt for his failure and appeasement of Spanish and Tlaxcalan occupiers (the Spanish version). One of his descendants later served as Spain's viceroy, 1697–1701.

Mogul Empire. See *Mughal Empire*.

Mohács, Battle of (August 29, 1526). The Hungarians were led by King Lajos (Louis) II against a huge Ottoman army under *Suleiman I*. To disrupt the alliance between Lajos and *Charles V*, and to expand his European provinces, Suleiman attacked up the Danube Valley starting in June 1526. The Hungarians, with about 25,000 men, chose to stand at Mohács. The Ottomans reached the field with about 60,000 men, having left tens of thousands behind as garrisons or strung out as stragglers. The sharp and bloody fight that ensued lasted only a few hours. Ottoman units arrived piecemeal, so that they were initially devastated by the concentrated Hungarians. Once the *Janissaries* and *timariots* arrived along with the main body, however, the Hungarians were badly overmatched not just in manpower but in martial skill and weaponry. The Hungarian right advanced enthusiastically but without proper support and was soon isolated. The Hungarian line was then broken by skilled Ottoman musketry and artillery, in which they had a great advantage since the Hungarians had only about 20 cannon to reply to Suleiman's nearly 300 heavy guns. The main event came when the Hungarian *heavy cavalry* was stopped cold by Janissary firepower, their devastating musketry well-supported by accurate artillery. Thousands of Hungarians were killed in just two hours of combat. When the fighting stopped thousands more were taken prisoner, then summarily beheaded. Ottoman losses were high but were more readily absorbed by a richer and more populous state. Mohács finished, in death and despair, the medieval army of Hungary. It also eliminated the last opposition to Ottoman control of the Balkans. Suleiman proceeded to conquer much of the region with the best trained, equipped, and financed army of the early modern world. The fight also made immediate military operations by Charles V in Germany against Lutheran princes impossible, thereby helping survival of *Martin Luther* and the *Protestant Reformation*.

Mohi, Battle of (1242). See *Hungary*; *Mongols*.

Moldova. This territory was progressively absorbed by the Ottoman Empire from the 15th century, and thus became an active frontier between the Ottomans, Austria, Poland, and the rising power of Muscovy. See also *March*.

monarchia universalis. "Universal Monarchy." A key motif of anti-*Habsburg* propaganda, especially during the *Eighty Years' War* (1568–1648) and the *Thirty Years' War* (1618–1648). It argued that the Habsburgs were intent on restoring, or imposing, "beastly Spanish servitude" and Catholic orthodoxy over all of Europe. While this view was often sincerely held by contemporaries, research on Spanish foreign policy does not sustain the argument for a conscious drive for Spanish hegemony, certainly not past the reign of *Philip II*. See also *Lerma, Duke of*; *Olivares, conde-duque de*; *Philip III, of Spain*; *Philip IV, of Spain*.

Moncontour, Battle of (October 3, 1569). Following the Huguenot defeat at *Jarnac*, Moncontour was the second Protestant battlefield calamity in as many engagements during the third of the *French Civil Wars*. Movement of the Royalist army enticed *Coligny* to lift his siege of Poitiers and offer battle. He met the Royalist force of some 26,000 men at Moncontour, in Poitou. The Huguenots were reinforced by German and Swiss mercenaries, but they were still heavily outmatched by the Catholics. A Royalist cavalry charge dispersed the Protestants with heavy losses. In hard fighting, some 5,000 Huguenots and German *Landsknechte* were killed (many of the later by the Swiss after they had surrendered). About as many more were wounded or captured. Most of Coligny's baggage train was lost in a panicky retreat. The Royalists lost but a few hundred men. The future *Henri III* was nominally in command on the Royalist side, thus gaining an early military reputation that he later failed to secure. On the Huguenot side, the young *Condé* earned his spurs while taking a slight wound to his face.

Mongols. The most expansive land empire in world history (Chinggisid Empire) was carved out by Mongol khans during the 12th–14th centuries. Their unparalleled martial success derived from superb mounted archers, superior battlefield communications and tactical coordination, and utter ruthlessness in dealing with all who resisted their cavalry "Blitzkrieg." It did not derive from the higher arts of civilization, which the Mongols, a people without permanent cities or great works of writing or science, did not possess. Mongols led hard, unforgiving nomadic lives. Males were fitted to the saddle with ropes by age 3, and most were skilled with a small bow at age 5. This turned every boy who survived (not all did) into a tough and resourceful horseman and every horseman into a warrior, while leaving equally tough and skilled women and children to handle the tents and herds. The Mongols thus mobilized a huge percentage of their otherwise thin population (about two million in 1200) for war. Horsemanship and superb mounted archery—the Mongols used short stirrups that allowed them to stand and shoot accurately while at a gallop—were key to Mongol success, both as hunters and as predatory raiders and conquerors.

Mongol warriors could survive on dried milk and meat, horse blood when necessary, and whatever they secured by the hunt while on the move. This made them remarkably mobile and often gained complete tactical surprise over more plodding armies of foot or armored *heavy cavalry*. Mongol warriors were armed with composite bows and several quivers of arrows, and they carried hooked lances to dehorse enemy riders. Some used scimitars (curved swords) for close-in work. As mounted archers they could not carry shields, so they made speed and accuracy of arrows their best defense. They had a superb command and control system that rested on wide scouting and advance intelligence, brought to commanders via a steppe "Pony Express" of couriers and fresh horse stations. And they enjoyed the great advantage of the steppe as a safe haven: on their grass-fed ponies they could raid and strike, or retreat, when and where they chose, living off the fat of the rich lands of China, India, the Middle East, and Russia. Their settled enemies employing grain-fed horses could neither adequately supply their own cavalry armies nor survive long if they ventured too deep into the Mongols' natural domain.

Expansion and Empire

For centuries the tribes of Mongolia were disunited and involved in petty civil wars. They only realized their latent military power when united in 1206 by Temüjin (1162–1227), better known by his warlord title of Chinggis (or Ghengis) Khan, which meant "Mighty Ruler." By 1218, Chinggis subdued all Mongol rivals and some Turkic and Siberian nomads. One of his generals overran Kara-Khitay that same year. The next spring Chinggis led an army across the Jaxartes, invading Muslim lands for the first time. In 1220 he split his force into four armies. He circled around Bukhara with 40,000 horsemen, then took it by surprise from the west. He had the population butchered as an example to all who would resist him, then razed the city before returning to his tents. This was normal practice: the Mongols often sacked and plundered cities, but they had no taste for them otherwise and no intention to reside in them. Meanwhile, lieutenants took Samarkand and other great Muslim centers of learning and civilization, and more slaughter followed. The Mongol invasion thus permanently depopulated much of Central Asia by murder and pillage, two trademarks of Mongol warfare against settled civilizations. The next year commenced the Mongol conquest of eastern Iran.

Chinggis overran most of northern China 1217–1223; successors completed the Mongol conquest of the Jin Empire in 1234. The election of Kublai Khan (1214–1294) was contested, a fact that pulled many hordes back into Mongolia to fight out a succession war. This may well have saved Muscovy and even Central and Western Europe from invasion, defeat, and occupation. After Kublai Khan was secure in power he completed the conquest of China. The Southern Song held out for five years during the siege of their fortress city, Hsiang-Yang (1268–1273). The end of the Song dynasty came swiftly, however, after a final naval battle off Guangzhou (Canton) in April 1279, during which the last Southern Song child-emperor drowned. Thereafter, the Mongols ruled all China from Beijing as the Yuan dynasty, until they were ousted by *Hongwu* and the Ming in 1368. In the span of three generations after Chinggis the Mongols had conquered much of Eurasia, overrunning most of Russia, Central Asia, and large parts of the Middle East. They deeply frightened Western Europe and interrupted the long wars between Muslims and the Crusader kingdoms.

In 1234 the Mongols did what no sultan had been able to: they drove the *Assassins* from their mountain fastness at Alamut. In 1240, Mongol armies defeated the Iranians at Jand and added western Iran to the empire of the Great Khans. In April 1241, a Mongol army defeated the Poles at Cracow, then the *Teutonic Knights* at Liegnitz. A year later a horde wiped out the Hungarians at Mohi. In 1243 the Mongols crushed the *Seljuk Turks* in Anatolia. At mid-century they attacked into Georgia and Armenia and scouted northern Iraq. Now began a concerted effort to conquer all the Islamic lands of the Middle East. In 1258 an Asian horde reinforced by the Golden Horde of Russia and led by Hulagu, a Buddhist convert married to a Christian, moved against the Abbasid caliphs in Baghdad. In the greatest humiliation suffered by Islam they breached Baghdad's walls and sacked the city for a week, putting most of the population to the sword. They captured caliph al-Musta'şim and his family and entourage, and put them all to death. That closed the classical age of Islam and ended the preeminence of Baghdad and Iraq in the Muslim world as the remnants of the Abbasids fled to Egypt.

Even so, the destructive impact of the Mongols on Islam can be exaggerated. Recent scholarship suggests that while occupied Muslim lands suffered greatly, in Syria, Egypt, and North Africa Islamic regimes and societies held their own. Indeed, at *Ayn Jālut* ("The Spring of Goliath") in Galilee a *mamlūk* army out of Egypt defeated the Mongols in 1260, forestalling a planned invasion of Egypt and North Africa. The mamlūks subsequently blocked multiple Mongol attempts to invade Syria, annexing it themselves as a protected province of their slave soldier empire. Also, the Golden Horde Mongols eventually converted to *sunni* Islam. That divided them from other hordes and encouraged a semi-alliance with the Mamlūk overlords of Syria and Egypt. The Golden Horde then clashed with an Asian horde at the Terek River in 1262. This horde suffered a second defeat in Syria at mamlūk hands at Homs (1281). Meanwhile, the governing Mongols (Il-Khans) in Iran converted to *shi'ia* Islam in 1295 and governed fairly well thereafter through the literate Iranian elite.

Although the Mongols were the dominant land power of the 12th–14th centuries, they were not so adept at sea. Kublai Khan sent vast armies to invade Japan, carted there by Chinese and Korean junks and pilots. These attempts were repulsed at *Hakata Bay* in 1274 and again in 1281 by a combination of bad weather and determined defenders. The Mongols also tried amphibious invasions of Burma, Java, Siam, and Vietnam during the 13th century, and failed in every case.

A wave of Turkic invaders conquered north India ahead of the Mongols: the Khaljis took control of Delhi in 1290. The Muslim state they established there beat back a Mongol invasion out of Afghanistan during the first decade of the 14th century, though not without seeing Delhi partially sacked and plundered. These Turkic invaders may thus have preserved India from worse depredations by the Mongols, deflecting the hordes instead into Ukraine and southern Muscovy. Various Mongol regimes ruled parts of Central Asia until defeated by *Timur*. The Mongol "Khanate of the Golden Horde," a sunni Muslim and largely Kipchack state, ruled the Caucasus, Ukraine, and southwestern Russia

> *In the mid-15th century Mongolia revived after a century of depression of its population due to the* Black Death.

from the 13th to 15th centuries. It was pushed onto the defensive after a defeat by Muscovy in 1380. In the mid-15th century Mongolia revived after a century of depression of its population due to the *Black Death*. Extensive raiding of Ming China followed and provoked a Ming invasion of Mongolia itself. That led an entire Ming army to be outmaneuvered and wiped out at *Tumu* in 1449. After 1474 the Ming concentrated on adding hundreds of miles of *Great Wall*, behind which they huddled in fear of the Mongols (and Manchus). A Ming army sallied against the Mongols and won in 1517 and in 1522 Mongol trade privileges were revoked, but that only led to annual border warfare through the 1540s as Mongol warlords tried to force a restoration of trade. In 1550, Altan Khan skirted the Great Wall to the north then raced south to savage the suburbs of Beijing for three days, unchallenged by the city's frightened garrison.

Legacy

What was the Mongol legacy? Modern scholarship has revised the older view that in all places barbarism, cruelty, and the fundamentally parasitical nature of Mongol warrior culture worsened local despotic traditions and held back ideas and social forces which might have advanced civilization and hastened modernity. This more extreme view was succinctly put by the Russian poet Alexandr Pushkin, who contrasted medieval Muscovy's misfortune under the Mongols with the more fruitful encounter between Islam and Western Europe. The Mongols, he said, were "Arabs without Aristotle or algebra." In Iraq, this older view of devastation and decline of classical Islam under the Mongols holds true. Elsewhere, while Mongol warfare was terrifying and destructive, their regimes did not significantly alter classical Islamic or Chinese civilization. There were even some positive results from the Mongol conquest, albeit effects not intended by the Great Khans. For instance, Iran enjoyed relative peace and stability after it was overrun, though a cultural renaissance only occurred in the post-Mongol era (13th–14th centuries). The Mongols actually restored long-term order in several lands previously disrupted and opened to repeated invasion by local tribal feuds and endemic nomad and clan warfare. Finally, the unity of the Mongol empire facilitated a revived trade along the old Silk Road and led to diffusion of civilian culture and military technology alike from Asia to the Middle East and Europe, and thence back to Asia. This had far-reaching effects on those parts of the Islamic world the Mongols occupied. And it afforded Christians in Europe more contact with Asia by eliminating Muslim middleman regimes that had previously blocked direct travel overland to China. See also *Bedouin*; *Inner Asia*; *Ming Army*.

Suggested Reading: S. Adshead, *Central Asia in World History* (1994); R. Amitai-Preiss and David Morgan, eds., *The Mongol Empire and its Legacy* (1999); Nicola Cosomo, *Warfare in Inner Asian History, 500–1800* (2002); Leo de Hartog, *Ghengis Khan, Conqueror of the World* (1989); Luc Kwanten, *Imperial Nomads* (1979); J. Langlois, ed., *China Under Mongol Rule* (1981); David Morgan, *The Mongols* (1986); Paul Ratchnevsky, *Ghengis Khan* (1992); Morris Rossabi, *Khubilai Khan* (1988).

Monk, George (1608–1670). English general. He was an experienced soldier, fighting in Flanders and Germany from 1629 to 1638 well before the outbreak of the *English Civil Wars*. A pragmatist isolated among confessional and class fanatics, he began on the Royalist side but switched to fight for Parliament after being taken prisoner. He fought in Ireland from 1646 to 1649, and at

Dunbar (1650). His most important exploits occurred during the later Anglo-Dutch Wars and in English domestic politics during the 1650s–1660s. He also played a key role in the Restoration. See also *Art of War*.

Mons-en-Pévèle, Battle of (August 18, 1304). Just two years after the spectacular Flemish militia victory over a French army of *heavy cavalry* at *Courtrai* (1302), Philip IV ("The Fair") sent another chivalric army into Flanders to reassert his overlordship. This time the Flemings did not have the advantage of marshy ground, though to their rear they lashed together disabled wagons with chains. For several hours the two sides did nothing. Hoping to provoke the French, the Flemings finally advanced. Although when the clash came the Flemings held as steady as they had at Courtrai, the French horse this time broke their formation, allowing men-at-arms to come among them with lance and sword. As the Flemings ran the terrible armored men on *destriers* rode them down, killing as many as 6,000 in a blood revenge taken without mercy.

Monsieur, Peace of (1576). See *Edict of Beaulieu*; *French Civil Wars*.

Montecuccoli, Raimundo (1609–1680). Habsburg general. He first saw action in 1625 at age 16. He fought in the Imperial defeats at *First Breitenfeld* (1631) and *Lützen* (1632), and the Imperial victory at *First Nördlingen* (1634). He was taken prisoner by the Swedes at *Wittstock* (1636) and held to 1642. He defeated a Swedish army at Troppau (1642). From 1644 to 1646 he fought in Hungary. In 1647 he beat the Swedes again, at Triebel; however, he was defeated at *Zusmarshausen* (1648). His more famous military exploits were performed after 1648, when he also composed his even more influential writings.

Montezuma II. See *Moctezuma II*.

Montfort, John. See *War of the Breton Succession*.

Montfort, Simon de (d.1218). See *Albigensian Crusade*.

Montiel, Battle of (1369). See *Pedro the Cruel*.

Montihéry, Battle of (1465). See *League of Public Weal*; *Louis XI*.

Montijo, Battle of (1644). Four years after regaining independence from Spain, Portugal invaded western Spain in retaliation for continuing Spanish plots against the Portuguese monarchy. With Spain still bogged down in the *Eighty Years' War* with the Netherlands and another long war with France, the Portuguese won an easy victory that secured them from further interference for a dozen years, though it did not bring formal peace.

Montjoie, Knights of. See *Knights of Our Lady of Montjoie*.

Montmorency, Anne, duc de (1493–1567). Marshal of France; Constable of France. He fought in the *Italian Wars* for *Francis I*, who raised him to the rank of maréchal in 1522. Along with his king he was captured at *Pavia* (1525). In 1538 he was made Constable of France, de facto head of the French Army. At *Saint Quentin* (1557) Montmorency was again bested by the Spanish and taken prisoner. He was a close friend of *Henri II*, a fact that initially led the radical Catholic *Guise* to shut him out of power after Henri's accidental death in 1558. Setting aside old differences, Montmorency joined the Guise in 1561 in a grand Catholic alliance that sought to drive armed Protestantism from France. He was a leading figure on the Catholic side in the first *French Civil War*, despite the fact that three of his nephews from Châtillon fought against him as fresh converts to the Huguenot faith, most notably *Gaspard de Coligny*, Admiral of France. Montmorency was captured for a third time at *Dreux* (1562). Five years later, at age 74, he was fatally wounded in the midst of his victory at *Saint-Denis* (1567). Shot in the spine during a mêlée, he was carried from the field by his sons and died two days later.

Montpellier, Peace of (1622). See *French Civil Wars*.

Montrose, Marquis of (1612–1650). Né James Graham; Scottish soldier. A *Covenanter* in 1638, he served under *Alexander Leslie* in the *Bishops' Wars*. He was hounded out of the Covenanter army by his lifelong enemy, the *Marquis of Argyll*. Montrose turned coat and led the Royalists in Scotland. He was always able to strike fast and boldly (he took Aberdeen four times), but never had the resources or men to hold what he took and was repeatedly compelled to retreat to the Highlands. A desperate *Charles I* named him Captain-General in Scotland in 1644. Montrose bested a Covenanter army at *Tippermuir* (September 1, 1644). At Inverlochy (February 2, 1645) he crushed a force of Campbells, and three times in the summer of 1645 he beat superior Covenanter forces: at *Auldearn* (May 9), *Alford* (July 2), and *Kilsyth* (August 15), where he bested Argyll. Glasgow and Edinburgh both submitted. That was as much success as should have been expected, but Charles wanted far more. He called Montrose south to invade England, a move far beyond his meager resources. Montrose obeyed only to meet disaster at *Philiphaugh* (1645), after which Charles characteristically repudiated him in a vain effort to make peace with the Scottish Covenanters. Montrose left for five years in exile. He returned to Scotland in 1650 with 1,500 men to fight for Charles II. Some Highlanders rallied to his flag; most of his countrymen did not. Montrose was taken by surprise and routed at *Carbiesdale* (April 27). He was betrayed out of hiding and hanged by Argyll at Edinburgh (May 21), his corpse dismembered and scattered. A master of *la guerre guerroyante*, Montrose was a faithful servant of faithless masters who paid with his life for serial political misjudgments.

Monzón, Treaty of (May 1626). As *Huguenot* rebellion broke out again in January 1625, *Cardinal Richelieu* turned away from potential alliance with

Protestant England and the Netherlands to seek a temporary rapprochement with Catholic Spain. He negotiated this treaty surrendering the strategic alpine valley of the *Valtelline*, permitting Spanish troops and supplies to again move between the Tyrol and Milan along the *Spanish Road*. As he regained strength in the early 1630s, he again moved to block Spanish movements and oppose Madrid's ambitions and policies.

Mookerheyde, Battle of (April 14, 1574). Fought near the River Meuse early in the *Eighty Years' War* (1568–1648). *Louis of Nassau* led a mixed Dutch, Huguenot, and German mercenary force 7,500 strong. The Spanish opposed with 6,000 men, about 90 percent tough *tercio* infantry fighting under *Luis Requesens y Zúñiga*. At the start of the battle the Germans deserted Louis of Nassau and the Dutch troops were routed with heavy casualties. Louis and Henry of Nassau were both killed.

Moors. Berber and Arab peoples of the Maghreb and Muslim Iberia. See also *Castile*; *expulsion of the Moors*; *Granada*; *Inquisition*; *mudéjar*; *Philip II, of Spain*; *Philip III, of Spain*; *Philip IV, of Spain*; *Spain*.

Morat, Battle of (June 9–22, 1476). "Murten." Swiss lack of cavalry contributed to a failure to pursue and finish off the Burgundians at *Grandson* (March 2, 1476). That allowed *Charles the Rash* to withdraw and to reform an army of 22,000 ducal, Milanese, and mercenary troops (including English longbowmen and *Landsknechte* infantry). He also cobbled together a new artillery train to replace the 400 guns lost at Grandson. Within three months he was ready. On June 9, 1476, he besieged the garrison town of Morat. There he faced his old Grandson guns which the Bernese had emplaced atop the walls. Several rash Burgundian assaults were repelled by the guns, but Charles was able to get his largest siege pieces into position by June 17 and these blew great gaps in the city's defenses. Into these breaches he sent infantry to take the city by storm. After a full day of hand-to-hand fighting the Swiss still held, guarding the smoking gaps. Meanwhile, a relief column of 25,000 tough troops from the *Swiss Confederation* and another 1,800 Lorrainer cavalry made for Morat. Learning this, Charles personally chose the ground for the coming battle and fortified it with a "Grünhag" (earthwork palisade) paralleling a forward-lying ditch. His rear rested securely at the foot of a wooded hill. For a week the Burgundians manned the Grünhag and waited as Charles grew ever more impatient with each false alarum. He sent out scouts to locate the Swiss encampment then rashly repositioned the bulk of his army in fields in front of the Grünhag, leaving just 3,000 men to hold the earthworks.

Seeing this, the Swiss seized the initiative. They sent a 5,000 man *Vorhut* forward to pin the Burgundians down with harassing fire from crossbows and arquebuses. The Vorhut was supported by a 12,000-man *Gewalthut* moving in echelon, which was highly unusual for the Swiss, on the left. Free to maneuver to either flank or to assault the rear of the Burgundian position was a third square, a 7,000-man *Nachhut*. The Vorhut, along with allied cavalry from Lorraine, attacked the Grünhag directly. The advance was slowed by sharp casualties inflicted by longbowmen and Charles' artillery, which was in fixed position behind the Grünhag. The main square recovered and with "push of pike" swept over the earthworks, killing most of the defenders. This released the Vorhut to continue its advance toward the main Burgundian force. When the Vorhut collided with Charles' men neither side was in tactically disciplined formation: the fighting was disorderly, hand-to-hand, and extremely bloody. Also charging into the Burgundians was the oversized Gewalthut, supported by hundreds of allied horse from Lorraine. In the interim, the smaller Nachhut completed a planned encirclement of the main Burgundian position aided by a distracting sortie by the Swiss garrison out of Morat. A mêlée ensued during which most of the Burgundian foot were slaughtered with the usual Swiss efficiency and ignorance of quarter. Many men-at-arms were driven into the water of nearby Lake Morat, where they drowned under deadweight of their own armor. Or they were cut down along the shoreline after discarding armor and weapons to better run from the pursuing Swiss foot and ruthless Lorrainer cavalry. Confederate casualties ranged between 400 to 500 men, whereas Burgundian dead reached close to 12,000. And Charles had again lost his artillery train, further weakening him even as its capture strengthened the Swiss. After Morat came the climactic battle of the Burgundian Wars, at *Nancy* (1477).

Moray's Rebellion (1565). See *Mary Stuart, Queen of Scots*.

Mordax. A small Swiss battle axe, cousin to the *halberd*. It was mainly used by the close guard of the *Banner* in the midst of a *Swiss square*. It was swung or thrown as need and opportunity dictated. It also proved useful in felling trees and rough construction of defensive earthworks and palisades (*Letzinen*).

More, Thomas (1478–1535). See *Cromwell, Thomas*; *Henry VIII, of England*.

Morgarten, Battle of (November 15, 1315). The battle was provoked by a raid made by men of the Canton of Schwyz against a neighboring abbey at Einsiedeln, which was under Habsburg protection. Duke Leopold I led an Austrian force of 2,000 knights and 7,000 foot to punish Schwyz. The Swiss numbered only 900 "oath brothers" ("eidgenossen") from Schwyz, plus 300 auxiliaries from Uri and 100 more from Unterwalden, the other "Forest Cantons." They took position behind earthen fortifications built across a narrow alpine valley blocking the pass at Morgarten. The Austrians made a fatal mistake; they advanced up the narrow valley in column, with knights in the van. Obstacles on the trail forced the Austrians onto a narrow path between the mountain and Lake Aegeri, one not easily navigated by *destriers* and armored men. The steep terrain made it impossible to form for a charge, the standard tactic of medieval *heavy cavalry*. When the van reached a preselected clearing a detachment of Swiss blocked its advance, harassing the knights with crossbows fired from behind earth-and-log barriers. With the column fixed, follow-on knights clogged the clearing. More Swiss felled trees to block the way back and took up firing positions behind the van, cutting it off from the Austrian infantry strung out along the mountain path and well out of the fight.

The main body of Swiss attacked the confounded knights, running downslope into an ill-formed and confusedly milling body of armored horsemen. Some Swiss rolled logs and boulders into the clearing, breaking the legs of warhorses and unseating riders. Others hurled stones at the knights or fired crossbows at close-range from behind the cover of trees. Finally, the Swiss closed for the kill swinging *halberds* and battle-axes, wreaking bloody mayhem among the Austrians. Panic set in as knights turned to flee the clearing but found themselves trapped. Many floundered in reeds of a broad marsh that abutted nearby Lake Aegeri. As the knights and their mounts struggled to

> *Finally, the Swiss closed for the kill swinging* halberds *and battle-axes, wreaking bloody mayhem . . .*

escape the mud Swiss peasants and townsmen from the Forest Cantons cooly dispatched hundreds, showing no mercy as they pulled nobles from aloof saddle perches and butchered them on the ground. Hundreds were hacked and stabbed to death; some had their hearts cut out as trophies by the ferocious Swiss. About 1,500 to 2,000 Austrian knights were killed while the Swiss suffered only modest losses. As all this was happening the Austrian infantry fled the pass and retreated from the valley.

It remained to be seen whether the Swiss could handle heavy horse on open plains, but in their mountain homes henceforth they were unassailable. And when they next met knights in battle halberdiers and axemen would be protected by more pikes and crossbows and the emerging tactics of the *Swiss square*. Politically, the Swiss victory at the pass of Morgarten strengthened ties among the cantons and advanced consolidation of the Swiss Confederation. Some scholars think that Swiss tactics owed something to the lessons of the famous Flemish victory at *Courtrai* (1302), but the difference in terrain (mountains versus marshland) and the offensive posture of the Swiss ambush militate against that conclusion.

Suggested Reading: Douglas Miller and Gerry Embleton, *The Swiss at War, 1300–1500* (1979).

Morgenstern. "Morning Star." A staff weapon of the late medieval period in Germany. It combined hitting characteristics of the *mace* with the greater reach of a *lance*.

morion. A 16th-century, open-faced steel helmet with a broad outer rim and cheek pieces. It was roughly descended from the *chapel-de-fer*. It was lined, with a chin strap and plume holder. Because they offered an unobstructed view they were the favored helmets of musketeers and archers. A fancy variant was the "comb morion," which had a drooped brim and upturned peak, like a rooster's comb. See also *cabasset*.

Moriscos. Iberian Muslims who converted to Christianity either sincerely or more often to avoid expulsion, fines, or the fires of an *auto de fe*. See also *conversos*; *expulsion of the Moors*; *Inquisition*; *mudéjar*; *Philip II, of Spain*; *Philip III, of Spain*; *Philip IV, of Spain*.

"Morning Star." See *Morgenstern*.

Morocco. From the 11th to mid-13th centuries, North Africa and southern Spain were ruled by a *Berber* dynasty (Almohads) based in Morocco. The Marinds succeeded the Almohads in 1248 and moved the Imperial capital to Fez. By the 15th century Morocco entered a long decline related to, and paralleling, the rise of rival Portuguese naval power which circumvented its erstwhile monopoly on the trans-Saharan trade in gold, salt, and slaves. In 1415 the Portuguese took *Ceuta* and in 1471 they captured *Tangier*. In 1472, Wattazid viziers seized the sultanate from the Marinds. At the start of the 16th century Portugal took control of several Moroccan ports. Morocco might have become a mere coastal colony of Portugal had not radicalized Muslims from the desert, led by *marabout* sharifs of the Atlas Mountains, expelled the Portuguese and Wattazid "usurpers" by 1550. The sharifs later divided, as holy men in power are wont to do. Some allied with Christian Portugal while others sought aid from the Ottoman Empire. This provoked a long civil war that ended only when a Portuguese invasion led to the "Battle of the Three Kings," or *Alcazarquivir*, in 1578. The winner of the struggle died shortly after the battle; his brother, Mawlai Ahmad al-Mansur (r.1578–1603), then seized power. He proved a spectacular success: he introduced firearms and mercenaries to the army, moved the capital to Marakesh, and expanded into the desert, seizing control of the caravan trade. He sent a large military expedition through the deep Sahara, 1590–1591, to conquer distant *Songhay*, taking Gao, Jenne, and Timbuktu. Songhay's medieval army succumbed to the Moroccans' superior military technology despite outnumbering them by 20:1. Morocco thus gained a vast desert and tributary empire stretching as far as Timbuktu and Jenne. The tie was broken in 1618, however, when the continuing fruits of conquest and occupation failed to meet expectations and most Moroccans lost interest in their distant military colony. The "Moors of Timbuktu" held onto power deep inside the desert, de facto independent while still governing de jure in the name of Morocco. Even that ended when the *arma* broke the imperial tie. Meanwhile, Morocco fell into yet another succession crisis and did not regain internal stability until the 1660s when the Alawids, a new dynasty of marabout sharifs, seized power.

    Suggested Reading: Weston Cook, *The Hundred Years' War for Morocco* (1994).

Morozov riots (1648). See *Muscovy, Grand Duchy of*.

mortar. A stubby, short-range artillery piece with thin barrel walls designed to lob heavy solid shot or shells at high angles (45° or more) on a parabolic trajectory, so as to bring indirect fire down beyond the walls of fortified enemy positions. Another use was shore-to-ship fire, though this can hardly have been successful other than by occasional luck or accident. Early mortars were little more than small pots fixed to boards or dug into the earth. Later, in Germany, multiple mortars mounted on a turntable were cast, allowing for rapid firing at the same target. Next came the pedrero class, which fired a stone ball as far as a cannon might fire an iron one. An "average" pedrero weighed 3,000 pounds and could lob a 30-pound stone ball to 500 yards effective range and 2,500 yards maximum range. "Heavy mortars" (the term referred to the weight of shot, not the gun, which weighed five tons or more) were used exclusively in siege warfare. They took whole bales of black powder to throw 200-pound stone shot to 1,000 yards effective range and 2,000 yards maximum range. At the siege of *Constantinople* in 1453 the Ottomans deployed a heavy mortar to lob ordnance over the triple walls of the city, landing incendiaries and crushing living quarters. See also *bombard*.

Mortimer's Cross, Battle of (1461). See *Wars of the Roses*.

Mossi states. Ouagadougou, Tengkodogo, and Yatenga. From the 11th century, like other desert and Sahel polities, they relied primarily on armored cavalry to conduct slave raids into neighboring lands. The Mossi states held off the more powerful *Mali* and *Songhay* empires into the 16th century. Then the whole region was buffeted by larger imperial clashes stemming from the slave trade, the gunpowder revolution finally reaching West Africa, and a fundamentalist revival of *Islam* in the deep desert.

motte. See *castles, on land*; *motte-and-bailey*; *Normans*.

motte-and-bailey. A motte was an artificial earthen mound (though often sited on a natural rise) built up as a basic *castle* (or *fortification*). Its sloped face aided defense against cavalry and gave a height advantage to missile troops. Mottes have been measured at 50 or 60 feet high and 90 to 100 feet in diameter, but most were smaller than that. They were normally surrounded by a *bailey*, a ringwork timber fort on the other side of a moat or dry ditch dug around the motte while building up its height. The motte and the bailey were then connected by a small bridge or a drawbridge that could be broken or burned in the event the bailey was stormed and a last stand was called for from the motte. The bailey permitted livestock and villagers to take refuge inside a basic fort and allowed stockpiling of supplies. Additional baileys were added as need arose or population grew. The motte-and-bailey fort probably originated in Anjou, where Duke William of Normandy ("The Conqueror") first learned of them. When he launched the Norman conquest of England in 1066 he built a motte-and-bailey fort as soon as he landed, at Pevensey, and another at Hastings two days later, before the arrival of the Wessex army under King Harold. As the Normans moved inland they dotted the countryside with at least 500 motte-and-bailey "castles." These acted in an

613

offensive as well as defensive role, securing ever more territory with small garrisons. The great weakness of motte-and-bailey forts was their high susceptibility to breach of the bailey by *mining* or *fire*. Still, they were so cost-effective that it was only much later that a stone *keep* was built atop the motte and the simple wooden bailey replaced by a stone enclosure. Motte-and-bailey forts were built from Scandinavia to Italy and Iberia, as well as in Anjou, Normandy, and England. They were still being built in militarily backward Ireland and Scotland and other fringe areas in the 13th century, well after stone castles replaced them most everywhere else. See also *Bergfried*; *donjon*; *keep-and-bailey*.

mounted shock combat. See *shock*.

Mountjoy, Baron of (1562–1606). Né Charles Blount. English general. He fought for *Elizabeth I* in Flanders and was in the squadron which *Richard Grenville* saved by his sacrifice in the Azores. In 1598, Mountjoy was appointed to lead the Queen's armies in Ireland fighting the *Nine Years' War* (1594–1603) against the rebellious Earl of Tyrone and his Spanish allies. Mountjoy trounced the Irish-Spanish armies at *Kinsale*, on Christmas Eve, 1601. Later, he urged clemency for his defeated enemies.

mourning war. A practice of the Indian nations of eastern North America wherein the emphasis in war was placed on taking prisoners who were then adopted into the tribe. This was one way of maintaining population levels critical to military success in face of extraordinary rates of death from new epidemic diseases that arrived with European settlers and African slaves.

moyen/moyenne. A cannon of intermediate size. It was one of six standard French guns from the mid-16th century.

Mozambique. See *Sofala*.

mudéjar. Muslims subjected to Christian rule as the *Reconquista* advanced over Iberia. Many were used as agricultural slaves on the estates of the Christian *Military Orders*. See also *Ferdinand II, of Aragon and Isabella I, of Castile*; *Inquisition*; *Knights of Calatrava*; *Moors*; *Philip II, of Spain*; *Portugal*; *Spain*.

mufflers. Sleeves of *mail* that covered the outer hands; usually worn in combination with a *hauberk*.

Mughal Army. The great Muslim empire in India maintained the second largest *standing army* in the world in this era, in terms of sheer numbers of men and beasts (horses, bullocks, and camels). Tens of thousands of permanent troops were maintained, along with an *elephant* corps. From the 15th century the Mughals attached an artillery train. The bulk of the army was poorly trained infantry, so that its real striking power remained *heavy cavalry* well into the 17th century. See also *fitna*; *mansabdari*; *mulkgiri*; *Panipat, Battle of (November 5, 1556)*; *warhorses*.

Suggested Reading: W. Irvine, *The Army of the Indian Mughals* (1903).

Mughal Empire (1526–1857). "Mughal" is a corruption of "Mongol," which accurately referred to the *Timurid* origins of its founder, *Babur*, King of Kabul. Mughal rule was established on the ruins of the *Delhi Sultanate* a decade after Babur was forced to retreat from Samarkand to Kabul by the *Uzbeks*, in 1512. Restless in barren Afghanistan, he looked to fragmented, ill-defended northern India to seize a rich new patrimony. Babur defeated and killed the last Delhi sultan at *Panipat* (1526), and erected the Mughal Empire in place of the older Muslim state, which he secured by victory over the *Rajputs* at *Khanwa* (1527). Consolidation of this new *"gunpowder empire"* took from 1526 to 1555, with extensive fighting against *Sher Khan*'s rival empire based in Bengal, until Sher Khan chased Babur's son Humayun into Iran and mounted the Mughal throne from 1540 to 1545. The Empire reached its southern limits at the Deccan where Mughal artillery was harder to move and deploy and resistance to conquest by the *Marathas* more effective.

The *sunni* Mughals ruled most of northern India for 200 years. In 1572 they conquered and annexed *Gujarat*. With the conquest of Bengal the Mughal Empire straddled northern India and controlled its rich seaborne commerce. Humayun's son, *Akbar*, seized power from his regent in 1562. He encouraged broad tolerance of *Hindus* and other non-Muslims, and thereby ruled effectively a huge state of perhaps 100 million souls which was stable as well as fabulously wealthy and powerful. While broadly tolerant of various religious groups, the Mughal state was harsh, inequitable, and often cruel in its treatment of individuals. And it was extravagant: Emperor Shah Jahan (1592–1666) commissioned assembly of the Peacock Throne and built the Taj Mahal as a tomb for his wife, Mumtaz Mahal (d.1631). This took 20 years and 20,000 laborers, all to indulge a latter-day Pharonic display of unchecked power, exploited labor, and expropriated wealth. The main threat to Mughal power at first was *Safavid* Iran. Intermittent warfare continued along the northwest frontier for many decades. The Hindu Deccan was also a *March* of war. Its independent warrior societies revolted repeatedly against the Mughals. Opposition might be provoked by famine but drew as well on a resilient Hindu resistance to Muslim overlordship. In 1646, Shah Jahan dispatched a two-year expedition to capture the dynasty's ancestral capital, Samarkand. It failed. See also *fitna*; *mansabdari*; *mulkgiri*; *Panipat, Battle of (November 5, 1556)*.

Suggested Reading: M. Alam and S. Subrahmanyan, *The Mughal State, 1526–1750* (1998); John Richards, *The Mughal Empire* (1993); Douglas Stresusand, *The Formation of the Mughal Empire* (1999).

Muhammad I (r.1413–1421). Ottoman sultan. His father, *Bayezid I*, committed suicide after his capture by the Tatar-Mongol army that sacked Damascus and Baghdad and then was led to victory by *Timur* at *Ankara* (1402). There followed an 11-year war of succession among Bayezid's several sons, with Muhammad finally winning over his brothers in 1413. His reign was always troubled by internal rebellions, however. It was left to his successor, *Murad II*, to restore stability and resume the Ottoman march of conquest.

Muhammad II (1430–1481). "Fatih" ("The Conqueror"); "Mehemet" (in Turkish); Sultan, 1451–1481. *Janissary Corps* disgruntlement over pay led to a mutiny at Buçuk Tepe in 1446 that delayed the planned ascent of Muhammad to the throne until his father's death in 1551. Muhammad was a military reformer of great note. He expanded the Janissary Corps, adding whole divisions, improving weaponry, and making these professional troops central to his military system. He then deployed the reformed Ottoman army to achieve a long-desired goal of the Ottoman Empire and of all prior Islamic empires in Anatolia: he besieged and took *Constantinople* in 1453 and extinguished the last embers of the Byzantine Empire. To accomplish this he transferred a fleet of warships overland to avoid Byzantine naval defenses on the Bosphorus. He ordered construction of a greased plank road over a mile long, along which his ships and guns were towed until they deployed into the Golden Horn, behind its chain boom. The fleet bombarded the city from one side while his land-based artillery pounded it from the other with 70 big guns. Several were huge *bombards* such as "Elipolos" ("City-Taker"), a monster with a 26-foot barrel, weighing 20 tons that hurled 600-pound stone shot at the city walls. The bombardment lasted 55 days. When the city fell there ensued merciless taking of life, including hundreds butchered inside the 1,000-year-old Orthodox cathedral of Hagia Sophia ("Church of the Holy Wisdom"). Muhammad stopped the killing only after it had nearly run its full bloody course.

> *When the city fell there ensued merciless taking of life, including hundreds butchered inside the . . . Hagia Sophia.*

His use of bombards earned him wide recognition as the first great artillery captain in the history of the gunpowder age. It should be noted, however, that he was greatly aided by a Hungarian master gunner known as "Urban" and that the city was actually taken by stealth, through a small open gate, not by artillery breach of its triple walls.

Having given the Ottoman Empire a commanding position on the Bosphorus that would last half a millennium, Muhammad invaded the Balkans, where he laid siege to Belgrade in 1456. He was beaten back by the Hungarian general *János Hunyadi*. Muhammad reinvaded the Balkans in 1458, overrunning Serbia by the end of the year. He then turned his highly aggressive attentions to Greece and the Aegean Islands, which he conquered from 1458 to 1460. He took over Bosnia, 1463–1464, while starting what proved to be a long naval and island war with Venice. He penetrated Croatia and Dalmatia in 1468, the same year he conquered Albania. In 1470 his fleet and marines took Negroponte from Venice, but in 1473 he was counterattacked on both strategic flanks by armies and fleets of an Iranian–Venetian alliance. After dealing with Iran he rolled up several Venetian colonies along the Dalmatian coast and threatened to invade northern Italy. That brought much fear to the divided city-states of Italy, and panicky rather than convincing talk from the pope about proclaiming another anti-Muslim crusade. Muhammad was intent to secure the entire eastern Mediterranean as a Muslim sea and watery highway between his Arab and Balkan provinces, where he was still stymied in his attempt to capture *Rhodes* (1479) by stout resistance from the *Hospitallers*. However, he took Otranto in 1480. Muhammad died while campaigning in Iran, leaving that problem as well as final conquest of the Balkans to *Suleiman I*. In addition to Muhammad's martial success and territorial conquests he oversaw an important codification of Ottoman law.

Suggested Reading: Franz Babinger, *Mehmed the Conqueror and His Time* (1978).

Mühlburg, Battle of (1547). The *Duke of Alba* won a major victory for *Charles V* when he crushed the Protestant rebel army in this climactic battle of his war with the *Schmalkaldic League* (1546–1547). After fording the Elbe, Alba marched on Leipzig with 13,000 Imperial troops. At Mühlburg he was met by and bested a smaller princely army made up mainly of Saxon troops.

mujahadeen. Muslim fighters who were, or thought they were, or who just said they were, engaged in jihad. See also *Assassins*; *ghazi*; *"holy war."*

mukai-jiro. "facing fort." In Japanese warfare, an earth-and-wood palisade built opposite a besieged fort.

Muley Hacen (d.1484). "Abdul Hassan." See *Granada*.

mulkgiri. A military expedition in India. They usually began in October after the monsoon passed and the fall harvest was collected, and ended in March or April before the onset of high heat. *Mughal* mulkgiri were enormous affairs in which the entire Court—tens of thousands of people and animals—migrated along with the army.

mullah. In Muslim nations, a title of respect for persons learned in sharia (Islamic) law.

Münster, Siege of (1534–1535). See *Anabaptism*.

Münster, Treaty of (January 30, 1648). The peace treaty between Spain and the Netherlands ending the "Revolt of the Netherlands," or *Eighty Years' War* (1568–1648). It followed a 1647 truce. In part, its terms reflected growing unease among the Dutch about French plans for expansion in Flanders and domination of Germany. But mostly it codified the fact that Spain could not defeat the Netherlands after eight decades of trying. With signature of the treaty Dutch independence was formally accepted by Madrid. Limited freedom of religion was granted to Spaniards conducting business in the

Netherlands, and vice versa, reestablishing trade relations between the former belligerents. See also *Westphalia, Peace of.*

Münster, Treaty of (October 24, 1648). One of two major peace treaties (the other was *Osnabrück*) signed simultaneously on October 24, 1648, ending the *Thirty Years' War* in Germany. Münster was signed by the Holy Roman Empire and France, as well as other Catholic princes and German *Estates*. See also *Westphalia, Peace of.*

Müntzer, Thomas (c.1490–1525). See *German Peasant War.*

Murad I (c.1326–1389). He was the first Ottoman ruler to claim the title "sultan." During his reign (1362–1389) he continued expansion into southern Europe. He overran Macedonia, planted it with his vassals, and moved his capital to Adrianople (1360). In 1373 he compelled the much weakened Byzantine Empire to pay tribute to the Ottomans. His reign witnessed the beginnings of the *Janissary Corps* as newly conquered Christian populations were drawn into Ottoman military service by selective enslavement and conversion of male children. He defeated the Serbs twice, decisively at the *Maritza River* (1371) and definitively at *Kosovo* (1389). Murad was assassinated by a disguised Serb soldier following his victory at Kosovo. He was succeeded by his son, *Bayezid I.*

Murad II (r.1421–1444; 1446–1451). Ottoman sultan. He resumed the Ottoman march of conquest that had been severely set back by the capture and suicide of *Bayezid I* at *Ankara* in 1402. Murad II's main theater of operations was southeastern Europe. There, he took territory from the remnants of the *Crusader* knightly orders, and from Greeks, Hungarians, and Serbs. He defeated the Hungarians at *Kosovo Polje* (1448), but his army took heavy casualties that day from the superior and more numerous gunpowder weapons of the enemy. Murad II's thirst for conquest was eventually slaked and he settled into patronage of advanced Islamic arts and sciences and the daily life of his Court. His successor, *Muhammad II*, resumed Ottoman conquests starting with the great siege of *Constantinople* in 1453.

Murbräcker. "Wall-breaker." Large caliber siege guns. They were in use in Germany much longer than elsewhere. Barrels were often inscribed with boasts of special prowess in knocking down fortifications, praise for their royal owners, or religious pieties. See also *artillery*; *basilisk*; *Gustavus II Adolphus.*

murder holes. Small holes cut in the roof above the passageway running from a castle gate to the interior of the castle proper. Through them defenders dropped large rocks on attackers who breached the outer *portcullis*, or poured down on their heads heated sand, quicklime, burning oils, or boiling water.

Muret, Battle of (1213). See *Albigensian Crusade.*

murtat. Serbian infantry archers of mixed Christian-Muslim stock in the Ottoman army. Some were hereditary soldiers descended from fathers or grandfathers once held as prisoners of war.

Muscovite Army. See *Muscovy, Grand Duchy of*; *pishchal'niki*; *Pomest'e cavalry*; *servitor classes*; *strelt'si.*

Muscovy, Grand Duchy of. The *Mongols* ruled what later became Russia for two centuries, under the Golden Horde and several independent khanates in the southern steppes. Mongol *light cavalry* remained unchallenged as the dominant military force even into the era of firearms. They took everything from the subject Slavic populations, but gave almost nothing in return during the time of social chaos known as "Appanage Russia" (after the splintered landholding, or "udel," or appanage system which kept each local prince weak but also independent of the others). A strong state slowly emerged in the north around the fortified city of Moscow, under Alexander Nevsky (1220–1263). Moscow's Prince Dimitri first beat the Mongols at Kulikovo, on the Don (September 8, 1380). During the 15th century Muscovy absorbed all other north Russian principalities, reaching 2.8 million square kilometers by 1533. When Muscovy broke the "Mongol yoke" 100 years after Kulikovo, in 1480, its people and leaders looked to the past glory of Orthodox Byzantium as a model of cultural and religious guidance. Yet, Muscovy was a harsher state and society for its many decades of subjugation by the Mongol khans. As it shifted from Dukedom to Empire, it would be ruled by tsars instead of dukes for over 400 years, from the renunciation of vassalage to the Mongols in 1480 to the end of the Romanov dynasty in 1917.

Muscovites took to gunpowder artillery late, not casting their own cannons until the end of the 15th century when *pishchal'niki* first appeared. That was likely because the main threat to Muscovy was fleet horsemen of the divers steppe peoples on the southern frontier, who could not be stopped by immobile early cannon. To counter the cavalry threat from *Tatar* and *Cossack* hosts who entered the Russias at will on extended raids, Muscovy built a complex defensive system of earthworks, log forts, and trenches. The defensive line these formed was garrisoned and patrolled by *servitor cavalry* established by *Ivan III* (1440–1505). It was their job to move rapidly to reinforce threatened positions upon receiving warnings by sentries in hundreds of guard posts built at six- to eight-mile intervals. Later, bribed or cowed *Cossacks* were brought into the system and helped buffer Muscovy from the *Tatars*. During the first quarter of the 16th century the Muscovite army was organized into five regiments comprised largely of cavalry and named according to their predetermined position in battle: the Advanced (the van), Left Wing, Right Wing, Main, and Guard (rearguard). A smaller Reconnaissance regiment was available by 1524, joined subsequently by Transport and Artillery regiments. Specialized troops who drilled and fought under instruction and command of Western military advisers were called "New Formation Units."

Muscovy expanded westward during the reign of Ivan III and under his successor, Vasily III (1479–1533, r.1505–1533). It lost an army of 40,000 to a force of just 12,000 Brethren of the *Livonian Order* and auxiliaries at the Seritsa River (January 1501). Three months later, 100,000 Muscovites and 30,000 allied Tatars annihilated the Livonian Knights at Dorpat. However, the Muscovites suffered another major defeat at Smolino River (September 1502) and in 1503 a truce was agreed upon. By 1510, Muscovy had advanced deep to the south, while acquisition of Novgorod and Pskov made it a Baltic Power. Under *Ivan IV* (1530–1584), Muscovy's *appanage* princes were brought to heel through terror and murder. Muscovy next expanded northward and then in all other directions: south against the Tatars, where successor khanates to the Golden Horde of Kazan (1552) and Astrakhan (1556) were overrun; east into the vast expanses of Siberia; and west during the *First Northern War* (1558–1583) against Livonians, Poles, and Lithuanians. The western thrust was the least successful because it was the most heavily resisted by equal or superior military forces. Indeed, it was still possible in 1600 that Poland rather than Muscovy might emerge from a century of war and palace intrigue as the dominant power in "The Russias." Even to the far south, wrongly thought tamed by 1510, Muscovy faced powerful enemies: Crimean Tatars sacked Moscow in 1571 and again in 1591.

> *From 1604 to 1613 came the* "Time of Troubles," *characterized by social unrest* ...

Worse awaited. From 1604 to 1613 came the *"Time of Troubles"* (Smutnoe Vremia), characterized by social unrest, famine, peasant uprisings, and harsh repression. All that was aggravated by dynastic struggles among several claimants to the throne, starting with the "False Dmitri" during the reign of *Boris Godunov*. Poland also invaded twice, in 1610 and 1612. This baleful period for Muscovy ended with establishment of a new dynasty under *Michael Romanov* in 1613. More war with Sweden and Poland over Livonia and the eastern Baltic ports followed, 1617–1618, as Wladyslaw tried to claim the Muscovite throne his father, Sigismund III, first claimed for him. There was also fighting with Poland from 1632 to 1634. Otherwise, Michael I's reign restored the old religion, politics, and social order. Under Michael, Muscovy could field over 92,000 men in its armies. Of these, 28,000 were strel'sty, 27,000 were servitor cavalry, 11,000 were Cossacks, 10,000 were Tatars, 4,300 were artillerymen, and the rest were foreign mercenaries. In 1648, just as religious peace broke out in Germany, the Morozov riots broke out in Moscow as outbursts of rabid and violent piety directed against the boyar retainers of Tsar Alexis frightened him into undertaking a bloody purge. Muscovy did not resume its drive to the west until the second half of the 17th century. See also *Oprichnina*.

Suggested Reading: Gustave Alef, *Ruklers and Nobles in 15th Century Muscovy* (1983); R. Crummey, *The Formation of Muscovy, 1304–1613* (1987); R. Hellie,

Enserfment and Military Change in Muscovy (1971); Lindsay Hughes, ed., *New Perspectives on Muscovite History* (1993); J. L. Keep, *Soldiers of the Tsar* (1985); C. B. Stevens, *Soldiers on the Steppe* (1995).

musketeers. See *Haiduks*; *infantry*; *Janissary Corps*; *musket*; *revolution in military affairs*; *strel'sty*; *tercio*.

muskets. The musket was a later and much heavier weapon than the *arquebus*, which led the first generations of musketeers to be recruited among big men (who also received more pay). It was first used effectively by a Spanish army at the siege of Parma in 1521. The early "Spanish musket" was six feet long, weighed at least 15 pounds (more often 18–20 pounds), took two men to carry and load, and could only be aimed and fired using a fork rest stuck in the ground or hooked to a wall or *pervase*. Still, it could shoot a heavy ball (1½ ounces) with sufficient force to pierce plate armor out to 240 yards, making it the anti-tank weapon of its day. While this punching power greatly exceeded that of any other missile weapon, muskets were extremely poor weapons in several regards. They were too heavy and inaccurate, with an effective sniping or aimed range barely passing 50 yards. They were difficult and very slow to load and reload, with a poor rate of fire; one 1607 English military manual depicted 28 discrete steps needed to reload a musket. Powder and match did not work well in damp weather and not at all in rain. And muskets could not be reloaded while on horseback or easily held or fired by a cavalryman even if preloaded. By comparison, archers had few weather restrictions beyond high wind, a very high rate of fire and much greater maximum killing range (especially the *longbow*). Normal bows, though not *crossbows*, might be shot from horseback (though mounted archery as practiced by the Mongols or other horse peoples was virtually unknown in Europe). Nor did muskets equal composite bows in accuracy until the 18th century, or match a bow's rate of fire until the 19th century. And yet, tactical systems using musketeers evolved from a support role for pikes and archers to equality with those arms, to displacement of both from the battlefield with invention of the plug bayonet in the second half of the 17th century.

Why would any army adopt the arquebus or musket over bows, given such facts? The answer is that they did not, at least not immediately. Instead, they mixed arquebusiers and musketeers into existing pike-and-bow or pike-and-halberd infantry formations, initially at the outer edges as in the Spanish *tercio*. Other experiments put musketeers inside the pike square for protection, or in front, where they lay or knelt under the bristling hedge of pike points during an enemy attack. A desire for more firearms among the infantry grew with incremental improvements in musket design, *locks*, and firing characteristics. A strong preference for firearms also grew from the fact that it was easier and far quicker to train an inexperienced peasant or town boy to use a musket than a bow. This suited non-noble armies such as the Swiss or the town militia of Flanders. It also pleased kings and magnates who fielded larger armies of lower class troops that were cheaper and more easily expendable politically and socially than feudal levies. Specific national or cultural circumstances also dictated the pace of change: English armies adopted the musket later than most because of a romance about the longbow that lasted in places to 1595. After the *Hundred Years' War* (1337–1453) England ceased to be a major military power on land, saw little action in continental wars, and thus was not pressured to reform by being defeated by better-armed foreigners. All this inhibited weapons or tactical innovation as the old missile weapons repeatedly proved "good enough" in fights with Scots or Irish or fellow English.

Another effect of introducing muskets was to put an end to most battlefield armor because not even the heaviest plate could stop the penetrating power of a musket ball cut at 12 to a pound of lead. By 1570 such a heavy "Spanish musket" firing a 1½-ounce ball with refined *corned* powder could penetrate 4mm of plate at 100 meters range. As muskets multiplied on the battlefield armor was discarded, which in turn obviated the need for heavy muskets so that these were replaced by smaller, shoulder-fired weapons that shot a 1-ounce ball (cut 16 to a pound of lead). These guns were closer in size to the original arquebus though with improved firing mechanisms and faster reloads. As differences in size and weight among personal firearms eroded, the term "musket" came to be used for all shoulder-fired *smoothbore* infantry weapons. The standardized patterns and bores of "Dutch muskets" set by *Maurits of Nassau* in the 1590s were widely copied by other armies. As this was still a heavy gun, later versions reduced weight by shortening the barrel. In addition to the weight of his gun, a musketeer was burdened with several yards of *slow match*; a flask of fine priming powder; a horn filled with coarser gunpowder for the main charge, fitted with a nozzle to measure each charge; a small sack of lead bullets; a pouch of lead bars and cutting tools for making new bullets; and various stabbing weapons and personal comforts. During the early 17th century the powder flask or horn was replaced by a bandolier that contained premeasured charges in wooden plugs. Later, the invention of fixed *cartridges* made from paper and kept in a side pouch eliminated both the bandolier and the bars of lead.

The Chinese obtained European-style muskets—which they called "bird-guns"—before the mid-16th century, and replaced their own models soon thereafter. The Japanese acquired mid-16th-century guns from Portuguese merchants blown ashore in 1543. Within a few years thousands of Japanese-made muskets were in use and over the next 50 years changed the face of warfare in Japan. See also *bastard musket*; *breech*; *caliver*; *child-mother gun*; *gunpowder weapons*; *heavy cavalry*; *infantry*; *Janissary Corps*; *mamlūks*; *matchlock*; *revolution in military affairs*; *rifled-bore*; *strel'sty*; *wheel lock*.

muster. At sea: assembling the men needed to man a war fleet; alternately, calling the roll of sailors and fighting men that made up a ship's company. On land: calling fighting men to order; alternately, raising and counting troops prior to a military expedition.

mutilation. See *atrocities*; *Aztec Empire*; *samurai*; *scalping*; *Toyotomi Hideyoshi*; *Tenochtitlán, First Siege of*; *Tenochtitlán, Second Siege of*; *wounds*.

mutiny. Mutiny was more common in the early modern than the medieval period. This was due to the shift to money economies and a new and heavy reliance of sovereigns on *mercenaries* instead of *servitor* classes or broad feudal levies. Primitive war finance and the poor quality bureaucracies of early modern states could not meet the *logistics* challenges they faced or pay the arrears of wages promised to restless companies of hardened, well-armed men. This tendency to mutiny over pay in arrears had a direct effect on battle and on whole wars. For example, the *Teutonic Knights* won at *Chojnice* in 1454 with German mercenaries, but their inability to meet the huge payroll that military professionals demanded led to disaster: two years later unpaid Bohemian mercenaries mutinied and betrayed the Teutonic capital Marienburg to the Poles without a shot or arrow fired. In 1515, Ottoman troops mutinied after defeating the Safavids and refused to invade Syria for *Selim II*, though mainly because it was just too hot and too late in the campaign season rather than over issues of pay.

The *Army of Flanders* mutinied 46 times between 1572 and 1607, mainly over arrears of pay caused by Spain's repeated bankruptcies. This led to the *Spanish Fury* in Antwerp in 1576 that made it impossible for the rebel Dutch to see Spanish rule as any longer legitimate. Mutinies were common in all armies during the *Thirty Years' War*. Even military reformers such as *Gustavus Adolphus* and *Cromwell* faced occasional mutinies, while *Oxenstierna* was held captive by mercenaries in his own army after *First Nördlingen* (1634), until he agreed to pay all arrears. In 1641 no fewer than 20 mercenary colonels of regiments in the Swedish Army refused to fight until arrears were paid.

A drought in northern China in 1628 triggered *Ming Army* mutinies that spread to central China and deeply undermined Ming prestige and control. A related mutiny in Shandong in 1631 led to internecine fighting the next year that wiped out an entire *war wagon* brigade the Ming had just organized with the aid of several dozen Portuguese advisers, which they hoped to use to stop the *Manchus*. In 1642 a Ming mutiny in the south rolled into a more general peasant uprising, and several powerful warlords and rival armies emerged that collapsed Ming power at the center. In 1644 one of these mutinous warlords took Beijing, where the last Ming emperor hanged himself in despair. See also *contributions*; *Kazan*; *Laws of Olèron*; *Levellers*; *Provost*; *round robin*.

muzzle-loader. Any gunpowder weapon that was loaded via the muzzle (mouth) of the gun, rather than through the end or *breech*. See also *artillery*; *casting*; *chamber*; *corning/corned gunpowder*.

Myongnyang, Battle of (1597). See *Korea*; *Toyotomi Hideyoshi*.

Myton, Battle of (1319). See *Scottish Wars*.

Nachhut. The smallest and rearmost of three formations in the traditional deployment of a *Swiss square*.

Nachrichter. The official executioner in a *Landsknechte* company or regiment. Some dressed in red and carried a two-handed executioner's sword and a noose, the latter serving as symbol of their office.

Näfels, Battle of (1388). As they had done in several earlier battles, at Näfels the Swiss waited behind earthwork palisades (*Letzinen*) and let the enemy come on. But this time the Austrians broke through with relative ease. The Swiss were rescued by a tactically cunning withdrawal to nearby high ground by a contingent from the Canton of Glarus, from where they used stones and other missiles to harass the Austrians. They followed with a downhill charge that broke the Austrian attack and carried the field.

Nagakute, Battle of (1584). See *Tokugawa Ieyasu*; *Toyotomi Hideyoshi*.

Nagasaki. From the 16th century this ancient port served as Japan's "window on the West." Iberian traders were followed by *Jesuits*, Dominicans, Augustinians, and other missionaries. In 1597 *Toyotomi Hideyoshi* turned on the missions and had 26 Franciscans crucified at Nagasaki. In 1635, Chinese traders were confined to Nagasaki, which thereafter remained the hub of an important China trade for two centuries. After 1641, all Westerners were strictly confined to the artificial island of *Deshima*.

Nagashino, Battle of (1575). *Oda Nobunaga* brought 3,000 *arquebusiers* to this battle and fought to aid his ally *Tokugawa Ieyasu*, who was under assault by Takeda Katsuyori. Nobunaga placed his musketeers front and center, behind wooden palisades. They were trained in *volley fire* and armed with

European-style *muskets*. The Takeda mustered 15,000 men for the battle and their confident *samurai* cavalry attacked straight at the musketeers. Like the French *knights* at *Agincourt*, brave Takeda samurai charged again and again only to be cut down by missile troops. The slaughter of the Takeda was immense.

naginata. A Japanese *polearm* consisting of a stout staff with a large curved blade attached. It was an infantry weapon used by "grooms" of the *samurai*.

Nájera, Battle of (April 3, 1367). "Navarrete." *Pedro the Cruel*, King of Castile and León, and the *Black Prince* used infantry tactics developed by *Edward III* to win this fight against a Franco-Castilian army that outnumbered their own 3:2. Most of the *routiers* who took part were killed. The English-Gascon intervention was provoked by a challenge for the throne by Pedro's half brother (later, Henry II of Castile), who was supported by France. That drew in the Black Prince as ruler of neighboring Aquitaine. Although Pedro and the Black Prince won the battle, their opponents won the civil war in Castile within a few years. In addition to routiers, *knights* of the Iberian *Military Orders* fought on both sides. See also *Hundred Years' War*.

Nancy, Battle of (January 5, 1477). Following the catastrophic defeat of the Burgundians at *Morat* (June 22, 1476), the fortunes of *Charles the Rash* declined as his enemies moved to take advantage of weakness. He had lost his army and *artillery train*, the latter for the second time. And now his finances, always strained, also failed. Unpaid *mercenaries* mutinied, deserted en masse, and one by one handed over his garrison towns to a regional rival, Duke Renatus of Lorraine. The garrison at Nancy surrendered to the Lorrainers on October 6, 1476. That was a loss Charles could ill afford. He managed to assemble a small army of 12,000–13,000 men, and moved with his usual recklessness against Nancy, despite the winter cold and snows. The *Swiss Confederation* declined to fight directly for its sometime ally Duke Renatus, but allowed him to recruit mercenaries within the cantons. He was able to raise an army of over 26,000—including 5,000 horse—comprised of ducal troops from Alsace and Lorraine and 10,000 Swiss.

Charles made the first move, away from his siege of Nancy toward the approaching Swiss and Lorrainers. He set up a blocking force in pike squares across a narrow valley, supported by the few-dozen artillery pieces he had left from the once magnificent and unrivaled Burgundian train. He placed his cavalry in standard position on either flank of his concentrated infantry and guns. The Swiss sent a large *Forlorn Hope* forward as a decoy, to disguise a pincer move into flanking positions by the main bodies of their *Vorhut* (van) and *Gewalthut* (center). An unusually small *Nachhut* (reserve) of just 800 men, armed mainly with arquebuses, followed behind the Forlorn Hope at the center, ready to move as reinforcement toward either of the main squares, working their way stealthily through snow and forest-covered hills. By mid-afternoon, the Gewalthut was in position above the Burgundian right flank.

Supported by Lorrainer cavalry, the Swiss formed a pike-and-gun wedge and moved smartly downslope into the right flank. Charles' immobile canon could not traverse to break up the attack, which crashed into the Burgundian squares in a great shock of gunfire, impalement, splinters, and spraying blood. The Vorhut overran Charles' artillery and scattered his cavalry on the left flank. The Burgundian foot was now exposed and outnumbered. Men broke formation and fled, uncovering their comrades to a merciless assault and slaughter. To the rear, fleeing men were held by a minor noble allied in the morning to Charles, who turned coat in the afternoon and handed erstwhile comrades-in-arms to the savage Swiss in a treacherous parlay of their lives for his. Charles also tried to flee, but was hooked down from his horse by a halberdier and hacked to death on the ground. Thus ended the *Burgundian-Swiss War* (1474–1477).

Nantes, Edict of (1598). See *Edict of Nantes*.

Nantwich, Battle of (1644). See *Fairfax, Thomas*.

nao. A Spanish merchant ship of the *carrack* class. Columbus' flagship, the *Santa Maria*, was a nao.

naphtha. Arabic: "naft." A Middle Eastern oil-and-sulphur-based incendiary comparable to *Greek fire*. It was not much used after 1200 except by the *Mamlūks*. See also *Alexandria, Siege of*.

Naples revolt (1647). A revolt of peasants and lower bourgeoisie whose origins were local grievances directed at the nobility and Church. A Neapolitan republic was declared with an ordinary fisherman, Tommaso Aniello (Masaniello) pushed forward as quasi-messianic leader ("Captain-General of the People"). He lasted just nine days in "power." Within six weeks he was murdered by a conspiracy of grain merchants anxious to return to religious and mercantile normality. The defeated rebels were treated with brutal severity that included public beheadings.

nariada. A late-14th-century Muscovite cannon that was essentially a metal tube affixed to a wooden block or sledge.

Narrow Seas, Battle of (1588). See *Invincible Armada*.

Naseby, Battle of (June 14, 1645). *Charles I* started north with 9,000 men on June 12, 1645, but could not elude the pursuing *New Model Army* under *Thomas Fairfax*. Some 15,000 Roundheads caught up to the King at Naseby and deployed in the dead of night along an east-west ridge. *Oliver Cromwell* commanded 3,500 *Ironsides* on the right, cavalry and dragoons, and *Henry Ireton* 3,000 more on the left. Fairfax commanded the main body of Roundheads in the center. The Royalists also deployed blocks of infantry in line at the center and cavalry supporting either wing. *Prince Rupert* attacked prematurely, opening himself to a counterattack by Ireton. However, Ireton botched the assault and Rupert skillfully recovered and smashed the Roundheads. Typically, Rupert overpursued a fleeing enemy; he soon got bogged down fighting with defenders of the Parliamentary supply train. Meanwhile, at the center the Royalists beat off an attack by Fairfax and counterattacked to good effect. While Fairfax reinforced the center, Cromwell rode around to the left—thinking the situation desperate there—and found dragoons in good order, holding steady and engaging enemy infantry. Cromwell joined the attack, scything toward the center of the battlefield to meet Fairfax coming from the right and to collect surrendering Royalist infantry. Rupert returned from the baggage just in time to join a general withdrawal forced on Charles by the weight of Parliamentary numbers and the collapse of his center. The Royalists lost 4,000 foot that day, and 300 more horse killed over 13 miles of pursuit; the Roundheads lost fewer than 300 dead. The King lost his baggage train and a fair number of cannon, along with any realistic hope of continuing the war. After the fight, Fairfax's men murdered several hundred women they called "Irish whores," out of several thousand traveling with the baggage. Most of the rest were later deported overseas as indentured servants.

Nassau, William of. See *William the Silent*.

National Contingent. See *Polish Army*.

National Covenant (England). Passed by Parliament under the guidance of John Pym in 1643, in the wake of a failed Royalist coup, it bound all Parliamentarians by oath to stand against *Charles I* as long as any "papists" (Catholics) remained under arms within the "Three Kingdoms."

National Covenant (Scotland). See *Covenanters*; *Knox, John*.

naval warfare and tactics. See *war at sea*.

Navarre. A small, independent kingdom straddling the Pyrenees between France and Spain. It backed the Cathars during the *Albigensian Crusade* and participated in the *Reconquista*. After 1500 Navarre was squeezed between the expanding and feuding powers of France and Spain. It was a center of *Huguenot* and Bourbon military power, and gave French Protestants their great champion in Henri de Navarre. The Parlement of Paris would not permit Henri to rule Navarre as a discrete kingdom after his coronation as *Henri IV* of France, so it was instead annexed. See also *French Civil Wars*.

Navarrete, Battle of (1367). See *Nájera, Battle of*.

nave. See *nef*.

Navigation Acts. Laws compelling national trade to make use of the home country's merchant marine. Most seafaring nations passed such laws, but the most important historically were a series of acts by the English Parliament that were crucial in developing the early law of the sea as a support for English naval and commercial predominance. The first was passed in 1382 and the second in 1463. Each of these early acts sought to restrict trade between English ports on either side of the Channel to English ships alone, but neither

> *...the truly historical Navigation Act was not passed by* Oliver Cromwell *until 1651.*

was enforceable in the absence of a permanent navy or a coherent sense of national maritime policy. The Tudors added to the legislation but the truly historic Navigation Act was not passed by *Oliver Cromwell* until 1651. It gave voice to a self-conscious idea of Great Britain as a world sea power, which justified and required construction of a powerful and permanent navy.

navy royale. See *Royal Navy*.

Nayakas. Local Hindu military elites that dominated the deep south of India well beyond *Mughal* control. Elsewhere such groups were called *Marathas* or *Rajputs*.

nef. "Nave." A two-masted medieval roundship rigged with *lateen sails*, native to the Mediterranean.

nefer-i am. The Ottoman conscription system. See also *Devşirme system*; *Janissary Corps*; *sekban*.

Negora Temple. A key site of the martial arts in medieval and early modern Japan and a center of the *sōhei* (warrior monks). It trained mercenaries and in 1543 manufactured copies of Portuguese muskets, powder, and shot, the first modern weapons to be produced in Japan.

Negroponte, Battle of (1470). *Muhammad II* sent his fleet and marines to storm this Venetian outpost in 1470. The Ottomans won a quick and decisive victory.

Nemçe (Nemse). "Germans" (or "Austrians"). The generic term used by the Ottomans in reference to their *Habsburg* enemies, whether Austrian, German, or the Christian Balkan peoples of the *Militargrenze*.

Nêmecký Brod, Battle of (January 10, 1422). "German Ford." An early battle of the long *Hussite Wars*. It was fought just four days after *Kutná Hora* (January 6, 1422), where *Jan Žižka* led the Hussites to a spectacular victory over Catholic troops under Emperor *Sigismund*. Žižka had pursued the Imperials, who regrouped fifteen miles from Kutná Hora at Nêmecký Brod, about sixty miles south of Prague. Žižka had 12,000 men against 23,000 Imperials. Once again the Hussite *tabor* and gunpowder weapons told the tale: the Imperials were confused, stunned, and bloodied by the firepower coming from the tabors. By the end of the fight nearly 10,000 Imperial troops had fallen. Sigismund fled, barely escaping personal capture and a likely cruel revenge for his betrayal of *Jan Hus*.

Nemours, Treaty of (July 1585). Increasingly weak as a result of royal bankruptcy and *Guise* influence among French Catholics, *Henri III* capitulated to the *Catholic League* by revoking all prior concessions to the *Huguenots*. Nemours forbade all Protestant preaching and denied even freedom of conscience, as it ordered abjuration from heretical belief within six months on pain of death or exile. Huguenot fortified towns were to be surrendered, their army disbanded, and none could hold public office. The effort of the League to impose the treaty by force brought on the eighth of the *French Civil Wars*. Nemours' terms were reaffirmed and extended in the *Edict of Union* (July 1588).

Netherlands. Two-thirds of the Netherlands was land reclaimed from the sea after 1200, using dikes, dams, and polders; hence, the folk saying, "God made the world but the Dutch made Holland." Holland then expanded, overtaking Zeeland in the 13th century, then conquering parts of Friesland in the early 15th century. The *Black Death* only lightly touched the area as it emerged as a center of shipbuilding and trade. In 1428, the Low Countries were linked to *Burgundy*. Holland fought the rival *Hanse* from 1438 to 1441, displaying a latent capacity to raise funds and field armies and navies it would demonstrate again in protracted war with Spain. After *Charles the Rash* was killed at *Nancy* (1477) the Netherlands fell under Habsburg rule through a dynastic marriage that linked Burgundy to Austria. Holland rebelled against Habsburg control and the "Grand Privilège" secured by the southern provinces of Flanders and Brabant. A major anti-Habsburg revolt lasted from 1487 to 1492, led at first by Ghent and Bruges in alliance with France, but not supported by the Netherlands nobility. Rotterdam was starved into surrender in June 1489; Ghent held out until July 1492. Gelderland was invaded in 1504–1505 but still would not submit. Intermittent fighting also took place within Holland and Friesland until *Charles V* mounted the Spanish throne in 1517 and the Netherlands was placed into regency under Margaret of Austria (1517–1530). Charles did not return to the north until 1531 when he made his ineffectual sister, Mary of Habsburg, regent (1531–1540). Charles set in motion administrative reforms in the 1530s that aimed at suppression of confessional divisions even as he cooperated in further Netherlands expansion. From 1516 to 1549, lesser and outer provinces were attached to the larger states of the Netherlands (Brabant, Flanders, and Holland), unifying it "north of the rivers." In turn, Gelderland, Utrecht, Overijssel, Friesland, Groningen, and Drenthe were overrun. In this military-political effort, Holland's interest in regional hegemony aligned with Charles V's interest in unifying his northern domains with Habsburg holdings in the south.

The Netherlands was highly urbanized. During the *Protestant Reformation* many townsfolk north of the rivers converted to reformed religion. The countryside and most of the south remained Catholic. In 1521, Charles V and the *Diet of Worms* banned all Lutheran writings. That led to book burnings in the Netherlands and in July 1523, the first burning of "heretics." There followed many more burnings, particularly of *Anabaptists*. In 1550, the *Inquisition* defined new punishments for heresy: men were to be beheaded, women drowned, and the unrepentant or relapsed burned. From 1523 to 1565, some 1,300 were executed, provoking deep opposition to the Habsburgs. From the 1540s, the Netherlands were drawn into the Habsburg war with France, hitherto confined to Italy. Many new *trace italienne* fortresses were constructed along the frontiers. Netherlanders thus suffered from new war taxes (a sevenfold increase), along with billeting of foreign troops. The key political change came in the 1550s when much of the noble and intellectual elite switched to Calvinism. This process began in the Dutch refugee communities in Germany and London, and was not at first connected to Calvinist communities in Geneva or France. The crisis built from 1559 to 1566, just as the *Italian Wars* ended, aggravated after 1562 by the start of the *French Civil Wars*. That freed *Philip II* to concentrate on suppressing Protestantism in the Netherlands, and moved him to do so by the baleful example of the *Huguenot* revolt in France. *William the Silent* assumed the leadership role in the early phase of the "Netherlands Revolt" that followed, and which evolved into the *Eighty Years' War* (1568–1648), a bitter and protracted conflict few foresaw. From 1582, the United Provinces became a republic, though they were still governed by a hereditary aristocracy and embraced a courtly political and military culture.

War and confessionalism divided the Netherlands: the Catholic *Union of Arras* formed in the south in early 1579. In reaction, the anti-Spanish and Protestant *Union of Utrecht* took shape in the north. The ten provinces of the Union of Arras remained tied to Spain within a truncated "Spanish Netherlands." The seven provinces of the Union of Utrecht became the "United Provinces" when their tie to Spain was formally repudiated in 1581. The region had long been a sanctuary of free thinking (and free trade), and welcomed religious and political refugees from across Europe: Jews from Spain after 1492, Protestants from Bohemia and Germany after 1520, Huguenots from France after 1562, Calvinists from the Spanish Netherlands in the 1580s, and divers German and other Protestant nobles from deposed dukes to pauper princes in the 17th century. For this reason and out of considerations of the balance of power, the United Provinces emerged as a major opponent of the hegemonic ambitions and religious policies of Spain under the three Philips. In the process it became a close ally of Protestant England under *Elizabeth I* and a more wary ally of Catholic France. The key internal struggle from 1600 to 1618 was between *Maurits of Nassau* and a dogged Calvinist war party on the one hand, and *Johan van Oldenbaarneveldt*, *Hugo Grotius*, and a moderate *Arminian* peace party on the other. With Holland—which had assembled and effectively governed the United Provinces—thus bitterly divided, princely power emerged as a viable alternative to the *Generality*. In 1618, Maurits launched a coup d'état, diminishing the role of Holland and the Generality until a revival of Holland's power during the final years of the Stadholderate of his half-brother, *Frederik Hendrik*. With Maurits in charge the war with Spain resumed in 1621 when the *Twelve Years' Truce* (April 1609–April 1621) expired. Fighting quickly overlapped with the *Thirty Years' War* (1618–1648) because of Maurits' support of *Friedrich V* against *Ferdinand II*. When the fighting finally stopped in 1648, the United Provinces were recognized by Spain as fully sovereign. By that time the Netherlands had acquired a world empire and was the dominant commercial, shipping, and naval power in the world. See also *Alba, Don Fernando Álvarez de Toledo, duque de*; *d'Anjou, duc*; *Army of Flanders*; *Don Juan of Austria*; *Dutch Army*; *English Fury*; *iconoclasm*; *Leicester, Earl of*; *Louis of Nassau*; *Margaret of Parma*; *Nonsuch, Treaty of*; *Parma, duque di*; *Raad van State*; *schutterijen*; *Sea Beggars*; *"Spanish Fury"*; *Spanish Road*; *Tenth Penny*; *Vereenigde Oostindische Compaagnie*; *waardgelders*.

Suggested Reading: W. Brake, *Regents and Rebels* (1989); Jonathon Israel, *Conflicts of Empires: Spain, the Low Countries, and the Struggle for World Supremacy, 1585–1713* (1997) and *The Dutch Republic: Its Rise, Greatness and Fall, 1477–1806* (1995); Jan De Vries and Ad Van Der Woude, *The First Modern Economy* (1997); Charles Wilson, *The Dutch Republic* (1969).

Neville's Cross, Battle of (October 17, 1346). See *Scottish Wars*.

Nevsky, Alexander (1220–1263). See *Livonian Order*; *Muscovy, Grand Duchy of*.

Newburn, Battle of (1639). See *Bishops' War, Second*.

Newbury, First Battle of (September 20, 1643). *Essex* lifted the siege of Gloucester by *Charles I*, but his path back to London was blocked at Newbury, northwest of Reading. The Royalists failed to secure the key high ground on the battlefield, Round Hill, so Essex planted his artillery and some infantry there. While fighting took place on the flanks, the main action was at Round Hill, where the Royalists suffered heavy casualties as they struggled upward and were met by withering Roundhead fire. *Prince Rupert*, as he often did, attacked prematurely and impetuously. This time the *trained bands* stood their ground, bristling with pikes and pouring deadly musketry into the Cavaliers. Essex then advanced the main Parliamentary infantry against the Cavalier flank, where they poured volleys into densely packed troops. Casualties were heavy on both sides and Essex expected to renew the fight in the morning. But Charles, nearly out of gunpowder, left during the night.

Newbury, Second Battle of (October 27, 1644). See *English Civil Wars*.

New England. See *Indian Wars (North America)*.

New English. An ascendancy of Protestant military men sent to Ireland to help suppress the *Kildare Rebellion*, some of whom remained to officer the new English garrison army established in *The Pale* after 1535. They became part of the landowning elite with estates granted them by the Tudors and Stuarts from confiscated Irish lands. While that joined their economic interests to the Catholic *Old English* and *Old Irish* they remained separated from those older landowning groups by confessional differences. See also *English Civil Wars*; *Ireland*.

New France. See *Indian Wars (North America)*.

New Model Army. The term was applied to several early modern armies patterned on the army of the United Provinces imagined by *Justus Lipsius* and Willem Lodewijk, equipped with standardized weapons by the *Generality*, and drilled and commanded by *Maurits of Nassau*. The Swedish Army reshaped by *Gustavus Adolphus* on the Dutch model was also widely regarded as a "new" and "model army." In English historiography, the term is applied to the army founded on February 17, 1645 by Parliamentary ordinance, trained in the Dutch and Swedish fashions, and infused with Puritan zeal. It was principally the creation of *Thomas Fairfax*, its first commander, who pushed for it over objections from *Manchester*, the *3rd Earl of Essex*, and the House of Lords. *Oliver Cromwell* was responsible for the *Ironsides* cavalry. In place of regional association armies it formed a single command of 12 regiments of foot (1,200 men per regiment) and 10 troops of 600 cavalry each. Another cavalry troop was added later, so that the New Model Army boasted nearly 15,000 foot and 7,000 cavalry and dragoons. Its first battlefield test was *Naseby*. Two other Parliamentary armies, the Northern and Western, were subordinated to Fairfax's overall command. See also *countermarch*; *drill*; *Eastern Association Army*; *Eighty Years' War*; *English Civil Wars*; *Fifth Monarchists*; *Ireton, Henry*; *military discipline*; *regiments*; *Thirty Years' War*; *volley fire*.

New Monarchies. A term employed about the centralizing national monarchies of Europe, which first took shape in England and France during the *Hundred Years' War* (1337–1453); and in Spain by 1500. The "New Monarchies" are said by historians who favor the term to have shared a novel sense of royal authority, and a more effective and centralized bureaucracy and systems of taxation and law, while also institutionalizing the medieval principle of royal governance by consent. That may well have been true of Europe, but globally there was nothing particularly new or modern about centralization: the conservative empires of China, the Mughals, and the Ottomans long had fairly centralized military administrations and highly capable bureaucracies. See also *Augsburg, Peace of*; *gunpowder empires*; *Holy Roman Empire*; *res publica Christiana*.

New Ross, Battle of (1643). See *Ormonde, 1st Duke of*.

New Spain, Viceroyalty of. A composite colony of the Mexican and Central American conquests of Spain formed in 1535. It hosted one of just two viceroys in the New World in Mexico City (the other was in Peru). It stopped short of modern Panama (then part of Gran Colombia) and excluded all holdings in South America. However, the Philippines fell into its jurisdiction. See also *Aztec Empire*; *Black Legend*; *conquistadores*; *Council of the Indies*; *real patronato*; *requerimiento*.

Ngola. Portugal's partnership with *Kongo* and patronage of Christianity lasted only to the death of Afonso I in 1543, by which time Portugal had shifted its slaving interests south to Ngola (Angola). In 1556, a Kongo army was defeated by Ngola troops using Portuguese firearms. Kongo thereafter went into decline, itself raided by Ngola armies and *Yaka*. The first Portuguese settlers landed on Luanda Island in 1575. There followed a century of armed penetration of the interior in pursuit of slaves for the markets of Brazil, usually in partnership with Imbangala slavers. The Dutch took and held Luanda from 1641 to 1648, during the final years of the *Eighty Years' War*.

Nichiren Shonin (1222–1282). Né Zennichimaro. A Tendai monk who launched the national strand of Buddhism known as "Nichiren Shu," or "Nichiren Shoshu," which helped inspire part of the population of Japan to resist two attempted *Mongol* invasions (1274 and 1281). He insisted on a reformed and unified national faith (Buddhism with Japanese characteristics) based on "Lotus Sutra." This reform version of Buddhism made some of the higher meditative practices of classical Buddhism available to the common people, greatly increasing its popularity among the lower social orders. His major reform was to suggest that salvation via the Buddha lay more in individual ethical action than purity of faith.

Nicopolis, Battle of (September 25, 1396). Seven years after the *Battle of Kosovo* (June 20, 1389), Pope Boniface IX proclaimed a crusade against the Ottomans. *Sigismund* of Hungary gathered a Christian coalition at Buda, which may have totaled 50,000 knights and men-at-arms from across Europe. This horde ate out the Christian lands as it moved toward Nicopolis, which it besieged for two weeks. Meanwhile, Sultan *Bayezid I* broke off his siege of Constantinople and marched to lift the Christian siege. A body of 2,000 French knights did not wait for Sigismund's order; they charged the Muslims headlong and were overwhelmed. Bayezid ordered a massive counterattack that overran the whole Christian position. Many thousands died on the field; more drowned in the Danube. Afterward, Bayezid had 10,000 prisoners slaughtered. Nicopolis ended the Latin Christian adventure in the eastern Mediterranean dating to the *Crusades*.

> *Many thousands died on the field; more drowned in the Danube.*

Nieuwpoort, Battle of (July 2, 1600). *Maurits of Nassau* led 11,000 foot and a small force of cavalry to forestall the *Siege of Ostend* (1601–1604). He was met along the shoreline by *Albert, Archduke of Austria* at the head of a veteran Spanish army. Maurits' well-drilled troops, new flexible formations and tactics, and "Dutch muskets" gave the Netherlanders a rate-of-fire advantage over the Spanish. Albert's heavy *tercios* also found it difficult to maneuver over a broken terrain of dunes and drifts. The smaller Dutch formations adjusted and moved with relative ease, not least because they deployed wooden mats developed by Maurits for conducting siege warfare in a water-soaked theater of war. The mats supported the Dutch artillery on the shifting sands so that their guns could be repositioned quickly after firing, whereas recoil of the Spanish guns drove them crookedly into the soft dunes. After exchanges of infantry volleys, the Dutch cavalry brushed aside the Spanish horse, which had the sun in its face. Supported by advancing infantry, Maurits' cavalry smashed right through the Spanish infantry lines and the full rout was on. The victory brought no strategic gains, however, as Maurits dawdled and failed to prosecute sieges of the *privateer* bases at Nieuwpoort or Dunkirk, and then withdrew.

Nijmegen, Siege of (1591). See *Maurits of Nassau*.

Nine Years' War (1594–1603). In the mid-1590s, the great lords of Ulster, Red Hugh O'Donnell, Hugh O'Neill, and Hugh Maguire formed a rare alliance of their private armies and quickly drove the English from Ulster. By 1598, the war spread across Ireland to become a genuinely national rebellion. At its outbreak, the English garrison in Ireland numbered just 1,500. This swelled to 10,000 men by 1598 and peaked at over 20,000 in 1601. The key figure on the Irish side was Hugh O'Neill (1540–1616), Earl of Tyrone, head of the O'Neill clan. In 1594, Tyrone and the other Ulster lords moved into effective rebellion against *Elizabeth I*. The fighting was sporadic before 1598, broken by parlays and local truces and paced to the cautious strategy pursued by the undersized English garrison. At the "Battle of the Biscuits" (1594), an English supply column was attacked and routed by the rebels. A more significant rebel win came against a relief column at Clontibret (1595). Tyrone's major victory took place outside Armagh at "Béal Atha Buí" (or Yellow Ford or the Blackwater River) on August 14, 1598. The English garrison was forewarned of an ambush but marched out anyway in a heavily armed column. Tyrone's musketeers and artillery fired point-blank into the English from behind well-prepared and partly concealed positions. English casualties surpassed 2,000 killed and wounded, plus 300 more who deserted to the rebels. This stunning victory prompted fresh rebellions all over Ireland.

The Tudor state massively reinforced its Irish garrison, sending the *2nd Earl of Essex* over the Irish Sea with 17,000 reinforcements. But Essex would not fight. Instead, he signed a humiliating truce while allowing thousands of men to die in barracks from typhus and other camp diseases. The *Baron of Mountjoy* replaced the disgraced Essex (who returned to England to plot treason against

Elizabeth's life). Mountjoy penetrated rebel holdings in Ulster with surprise amphibious landings, and he scorched the countryside. The major fight came once Spain intervened in support of the rebellion, landing troops in Ireland in 1601 at Kinsale, in Cork. Mountjoy besieged the Spanish in Kinsale, forcing Tyrone to march south to relieve his allies. On December 24, 1601, Tyrone led 8,000 Irish and *redshanks* Scots, supported by 4,000 Spanish veterans attacking from the other side, against an English army of just 6,500, many of whom were deathly ill, but who were most ably led by Mountjoy. Tyrone attacked and suffered a bloody repulse from the tactically skilled Mountjoy. The Irish lost nearly 3,000 casualties. The Spanish surrendered and were shipped home. The loss at Kinsale ended Spanish interest in the Irish rebellion while dispiriting Irish lords and troops alike. The Irish army broke up as men disbanded to defend their homes with the traditional Irish *guerre couverte*, or went into hiding or exile. Famine then struck as a delayed result of English scorched earth tactics in Ulster. O'Donnell went into exile while O'Neill fought on until March 30, 1603, a week after Elizabeth I died. He surrendered to Mountjoy and was given generous terms by *James I*.

Suggested Reading: Nicholas Canny, *Elizabethan Conquest of Ireland* (1976); John McCavitt, *Flight of the Earls* (2004); Hiram Morgan, *The Battle of Kinsale* (2004).

ninja. Little that is historically reliable is known about the ninja of *Sengoku* Japan. Most likely, they were spies and assassins rather than the super warriors of popular culture. Almost certainly, they did not dress in all black but blended in with the local people of the garrison or town on which they were spying.

Noblesse d'epée. "Nobility of the Sword." In France, the hereditary nobility that traced its rank and privileges to military prowess and service.

Noblesse de robe. "Nobility of the Robe." Nobility acquired through holding an office from the French king. This was usually a privilege of the clergy in the medieval period, but the literate bourgeoisie later moved into its ranks as they joined the civil service of the early modern state.

nobori. Long, narrow, colored flags carried vertically on poles and used in early modern Japanese warfare to signify unit positions and rally points. See also *flags*; *hata jirushi*; *sashimono*.

"Noche Triste" (1520). See *Otumba, Battle of*; *Tenochtitlán, First Siege of*.

Nonsuch, Treaty of (August 20, 1585). It was agreed between *Elizabeth I* and the *Raad van State* of the United Provinces, the first treaty entered into by the new Dutch Republic. Elizabeth provided money and troops to aid the Dutch rebellion, then on the point of defeat at the hands of the *duque di Parma*, in exchange for input into rebel strategy. It was agreed that she would nominate the top commander and be represented in the Raad. In return, she sent 6,350 foot and 1,000 horse to the Netherlands and paid half their expenses, on condition that her favorite, the *Earl of Leicester*, both command and receive high public office. See also *Oldenbaarneveldt, Johan van*.

Nordic Seven Years' War (1563–1570). Fought between Sweden and a Danish-Lübeck alliance. Each side initially fielded just under 30,000 men, but much reduced numbers later. Denmark also deployed a large fleet from the outset; Sweden built one during the war. The Danish army was comprised of German and other mercenaries and some poorly trained Danes. Poorer Sweden fielded a more "national" force of native levies, led by the mad Erik XIV, supplemented by mercenary officers. Some historians describe Erik as a military genius, citing his early experimentation with pike-and-musket tactics, deployment of smaller units, and fewer ranks. However, he had few chances to try these ideas in the field: there was a skirmish among a few thousand men at Mared (1564), and just one sizeable battle, at Axtorna in 1565, where the Danes prevailed. Along with the usual sieges, much of the war consisted of small *chevauchées* that destroyed the Swedish countryside. Denmark captured Älvsborg in 1563 after four days of bombardment by land and sea. The cost of foreign mercenaries and their mutinous mutterings forced the Danes to pare back, allowing Erik's levies to take Trondheim in 1564 and Varberg the next year. Sweden then returned to defensive warfare. Sweden did better in the war at sea from 1565, winning two naval battles and drawing a third that summer. Still, it regained Älvsborg only by payment of a large indemnity under terms of the Peace of Stettin (1570). Little was changed by this war on the fringe of Europe's burgeoning struggles over religion and empire, beyond ruining villages, towns, and lives. Meanwhile, the *First Northern War* (1558–1583) continued.

Nördlingen, First Battle of (September 5–6, 1634). An Imperial army of 20,000 infantry and 13,000 cavalry besieged a large Swedish garrison in Nördlingen. A Swedish relief army of 16,000 infantry and 9,000 cavalry attacked the Imperial left, which was anchored on high ground, at dawn on September 5. The fight on the left lasted nearly eight hours before the attacking Swedes withdrew, crossing the rear of the Protestant center. Seeing this, the Imperials attacked directly into the Swedish center. They broke the line, pushing survivors back on top of the withdrawing left wing. Carnage followed: the Swedes lost 17,000 dead and wounded and another 4,000 captured out of 25,000 engaged, along with 80 guns. They lost mainly due to poor execution of tactics that had served them exceptionally well under *Gustavus Adolphus* two years earlier at *Lützen* (November 6, 1632). This was partly a result of the heavy casualties they suffered before and at Lützen, which meant that the *Swedish Army* at Nördlingen was no longer the premier force that landed in Pomerania and marched through Germany singing Lutheran hymns with Gustavus. Death, wounds, disease, and desertion had long since eroded veteran formations. And replacements were fewer and not of the same quality as those who fought so brilliantly for the dead king, and no longer met the stringent training and skill requirements demanded by Gustavus. Disastrously, at Nördlingen they still went into battle thinking they were superior to their opponents. Overconfidence thus was the second reason they lost the battle. The remnant of the army was marched away by *Bernhard von Sachsen-Weimar*, to shelter with the French until they entered the war in 1635. See also *Olivares, conde-duque de*; *Richelieu, Cardinal Armand Jean du Plessis de*.

Nördlingen, Second Battle of (August 3, 1645). *Turenne* and the *Great Condé* (Louis II) jointly invaded Bavaria with 12,000 men. An Imperial-Bavarian army of comparable strength under *Franz von Mercy* and *Johann von Werth* moved to met them at Nördlingen. Mercy entrenched there, barring access to the Danube. When Condé arrived he attacked directly into the Catholic lines, driving them back until they reached the river. With casualties approaching 50 percent on each side, mutual exhaustion caused the armies to separate and forbade any pursuit.

Normaljahr. "Normative year." In conferences and treaties such as the *Peace of Prague* (1635) and the several treaties of the *Peace of Westphalia* (1648), which abolished the *reservatum ecclesiaticum*, this was the temporal marker for resolving disputes over prior secularization of ecclesiastical lands and benefices. In the *Treaty of Hamburg* (1638) France and Sweden demanded 1618 as the Normaljahr. At Westphalia, radical Protestants insisted on 1618, rolling the settlement back before the recatholicization of Bohemia and the Palatinate; fanatic Catholics demanded 1630, the apex of *Habsburg* martial success and subsequent to the *Edict of Restitution* (1629). It was finally agreed to use January 1, 1624.

Normans. "Northmen." The Normans were descendants of pagan Scandinavian invaders (Vikings) who conquered, settled among, and were subsequently Christianized by the Gothic and Frankish peoples of northwestern France. During the 11th century, the Normans emerged as the most aggressive, dominant warrior-people of Europe, a position they kept for 200 years. Duc William (1027–1087), "William the Conqueror," led an extraordinary amphibious operation across the Channel to England in 1066, winning the bloody Battle of Hastings against King Harold of Wessex and seizing the crown. William completed the conquest by 1070 with ruthless massacres and suppression of rebellion, but mainly with creeping encastellation of town and countryside. England thereafter was the main base of Norman power, from which they conquered parts of Ireland and Scotland. Yet, the Norman monarchy they established may have led to a prolonged partition of Great Britain rather than its early unification.

Other Normans took Malta, raided the Adriatic provinces and commerce of the *Byzantine Empire*, and ripped portions of southern Italy away from Byzantine control, including Sicily. Their reputation for rapine and brutality was so great even among fellow Christians, and their aggression so successful, Pope Leo IX (r.1049–1054) organized an expedition by Byzantine, Lombard, and Swabian troops to drive the Normans from Italy. The effort failed at

Civitate (June 17, 1053), where papal, allied Italian, and German soldiery were destroyed by the *heavy cavalry* of the Normans. Gains in Italy (Apulia and Calabria), as well as the conquest of Muslim Sicily made by the magnates Robert and Roger Guiscard, owed much to the military pressure that *Seljuk Turks* exerted against the eastern borders of the Byzantine Empire. Palermo fell in 1072 and the rest of Sicily by 1099. It is notable that in these conquests it was not the Normans' heavy horse that won but their expertise in naval blockade and amphibious invasion. At the end of the 11th century, Norman knights were in the van of the *Crusades*. It was their military architecture, with regional modifications, that built the great Crusader castles of the Middle East such as Krak des Chevaliers (in modern Jordan).

Norman strategy and tactics combined in a typical pattern of aggression. Wherever the Normans invaded they first built *motte-and-bailey* castles of mounds of earth and timber, only later adding stone *keeps* and towers and walls. From 1066 to the death of William I in 1087, it is thought the Normans built as many as 500 castles with which to hold England, starting at the Channel ports and concentrating on river fords and other strategic sites, notably London and Coventry. From these bases Norman cavalry sallied to drive the region into submission through raids of calculated terror and burning of surrounding towns and villages. This was also a way of paying for military service, as lands taken from the Anglo-Saxon aristocracy who were slaughtered or fled were redistributed to Norman barons who built more motte-and-bailey garrison forts to hold their domain and subjugated population. By 1100, *subinfeudation* settled a new aristocracy, ruthless and armed to the teeth, over most of England. In time, crusading and other military misadventures overstretched the Norman social and recruitment system. They

> *...in these conquests it was not the Normans' heavy horse that won but their expertise in naval blockade...*

adapted somewhat by bringing larger numbers of the lower social classes to the battlefield to supplement the armored cavalry of their landed nobility and knights. These troops were armed with new weapons, most notably the Welsh-English *longbow*, but also with *pikes* and *crossbows* and an English variation on the *halberd*, the *brown bill*. Such Norman innovations did not prevent Normandy itself being overrun by Geoffrey of Anjou and his successors from 1136 to 1144. See also *feudalism*; *Franks*; *fryd*; *Holy Roman Empire*.

Suggested Reading: Marjorie Chibnall, *Normans* (2001); David C. Douglas, *The Norman Achievement, 1050–1100* (1969); C. W. Hollister, *Military Organization of Norman England* (1965); John Le Patourel, *The Norman Empire* (1976); Jack Lindsay, *Normans and Their World* (1974).

Northampton, Battle of (1460). See *Wars of the Roses*.

Northern Army. After founding the unified *New Model Army*, Parliament retained two other armies, a Western and a Northern. These, too, were under the overall command of *Thomas Fairfax*.

Northern War, First (1558–1583). Also known as the "Livonian War." In 1558, *Ivan IV* invaded Estonia. His army massacred 10,000 at the *sack of Dorpat* (1558), went on to sack 20 more towns, and captured Narva. The *Livonian Order* brought in *Landsknechte* with guns, but were unable to staunch the assault. The Order fought its last battle at *Ermes* (August 2, 1560), then disbanded. This collapse of the Brethren in face of Ivan's *strel'sty* and *servitor* cavalry opened Livonia to partition as Poland-Lithuania, Muscovy, Sweden, and Denmark all looked to gain territory. The Muscovite invasion marked the end of the wars of crusade in the Baltic region, but not the end of wars of imperial ambition. These would continue, almost uninterrupted, to 1667.

Despite initial success, Ivan was unable to take other key towns: Reval and Riga held out with Swedish and Polish aid. In 1563, the war spread: Denmark and Sweden fought each other at sea and Ivan attacked into Lithuania. In 1564, the Lithuanians won huge victories over Muscovy at Czasniki and the Ula River, driving Ivan farther into a madness that triggered gross excesses and terror against his own *boyars*. This *Oprichnina* lasted to 1571, temporarily taking Muscovy out of the war. The end of the *Nordic Seven Years' War* in 1570 threatened Ivan with fresh enemies in the west. He responded by ending the terror at home and invading Livonia in 1572–1573, leaving much fire and destruction in his wake. Then he turned to defend against the Ottomans and *Tatars* in the deep south of his huge empire. In 1575, a Muscovite army besieged Reval unsuccessfully then ravaged the surrounding lands. The next summer's campaign was the largest and most destructive of the entire war. In 1577, Ivan personally returned to attack Reval with 30,000 men, then Dünaburg and Kokenhausen. He was nearly killed by a cannonball at Wenden. Enraged, he threatened terrible punishment against the whole town. Whether by accident or with the suicidal intention of escaping the tsar's wrath, 300 men, women, and children blew themselves up. But Ivan was defeated at Wenden by September 1578 and offered to make peace. He was rebuffed by *Stefan Báthory* at the head of an army of the new union of Poland-Lithuania (*Union of Lublin*). Báthory led three expeditions into Russia in 1579, 1580, and 1581–1582, forcing Ivan to surrender his earlier Livonian conquests. This only ensured that fighting over the carcass of Livonia continued in future northern wars in the 17th century.

Suggested Reading: Robert Frost, *The Northern Wars, 1558–1721* (2000).

Novara, Battle of (1500). See *Sforza, Ludovico*.

Novara, Battle of (June 6, 1513). In the second decade of the *Italian Wars* (1494–1559), Swiss mercenaries fighting in service of the *Holy League* defeated a French army under Louis de la Trémoille, forcing France to abandon its effort to hold onto the Duchy of Milan. The Swiss nominally restored Duke *Maximilian Sforza*, but remained in effective occupation of the Duchy themselves, then milked it with oppressive taxation and the burden of upkeep of their 20,000-man army. French fortunes were reversed two years later when *Francis I* won a crushing victory over the Swiss at *Marignano*

(1515), where the future reformer *Huldrych Zwingli* served as a chaplain in the Swiss ranks.

Noyon, Peace of (1516). A temporary halt in the *Italian Wars* (1494–1559), partitioning north Italy between France and the Habsburgs. It did not long survive the further ambitions of either party.

Nuremberg, Congress of (June 26, 1650). This follow-on conference to the *Peace of Westphalia* (1648) set the demobilization plan and schedules carried out after the *Thirty Years' War* (1618–1648).

Nurgaci (1559–1626). "Nurhaci." A dynamic *Manchu* leader who united the Jürchen clans of *Manchuria* into a single martial culture and state. In 1601 he instituted major military reforms, shaping the *banner system.* Formally a Ming vassal, in 1610 Nurgaci shook off this status. Six years later he proclaimed himself "khan" and his Manchurian domain an empire in its own right, the "Later Jin," a title that deliberately echoed the "Jin" ("Golden") empire that ruled northern China out of a Manchurian power base from 1122 to 1234. In 1619 Nurgaci launched a protracted war against the Ming with an initial force of 60,000. China mobilized 100,000 men and moved into Manchuria to oppose him. At *Sarhu* (1619), Nurgaci devastated the ill-led and divided Ming infantry, defeating each of four columns in turn. By 1621 he had conquered all Liaodong and Shenyang. In 1625 Nurgaci set his capital at Shenyang (Mukden). Nurgaci now made up for Manchuria's small population by absorbing into his army many Chinese and Mongolian prisoners, who were made to shave their foreheads and adopt the Manchu "queue" as an act of formal submission. They added crucial firearms and siegecraft expertise to what until then was a cavalry army. This enhanced Manchu military prowess once Nurgaci trained his cavalry to collaborate with artillery in an effective, early-modern combined-arms system. Still, the Ming were not defeated. In fact, Nurgaci was beaten in 1626 by a Ming counterattack. It was left to his eighth son, Hong Taiji, and his heirs to conquer Inner Mongolia (1632), make Korea a tributary state (1638), overthrow the Ming and establish Qing rule over northern China (1644).

nüzül. The internal supply system of the Ottoman Empire. See also *logistics*; *magazines.*

O

Oberster Feldhauptmann. A commanding officer of Swiss cantonal troops. See also *Banner (Swiss)*; *Swiss square*.

Oberster Feldweibel. The officer responsible for setting the order of battle in a *Landsknechte* company.

Obrist. "Colonel." In predominantly German-speaking mercenary companies, the officer appointed to command. Directly comparable to "colonel" in other companies. Modern German usage is "Oberst."

Obrona Potoczna. "General Defense." See *Polish Army*.

ocak. An Ottoman regiment.

Oda Nobunaga (1534–1582). Japanese warlord. Born in Owari during a period of chronic warfare (*Sengoku*) and perfidy among *samurai*, in the 1540s and 1550s Nobunaga trained in the martial arts and prepared for a life of war. He won a major victory in 1560 at *Okehazama*, securing his eastern flank with *Tokugawa Ieyasu*. These two warlords formed an enduring alliance, with Nobunaga occupying the senior position. Together they waged the key early battles of the *Unification Wars*. In addition to innovative use of firearms, Nobunaga introduced a 20-foot pike to Japanese warfare to protect his arquebusiers and infantry archers. He also seized key centers and towns that manufactured guns, gaining an early lead on opponents by fielding a trained corps of arquebusiers. Utterly ruthless (one specialist historian called him "a cruel and callous brute"), he used bribes, threats, killing of hostages, maniacal massacres, burnings of towns and forts with hundreds still inside, and other terror methods to advance his unification by conquest. It was his policy to kill defeated *daimyo*, then to kill their entire extended family. He had his brother-in-law's head pickled and displayed at banquets.

Nobunaga occupied Kyoto in 1568, but did not claim the shogunate; he intended to hollow it out instead. In 1570 a league of northern daimyo formed to oppose him, but in alliance with Tokugawa he defeated these enemies at *Anegawa* (July 22, 1570). Nobunaga treated all enemies with great brutality, but he was specially ruthless in persecuting *Buddhists*. In 1571 he burned down the Tendai monastery on Mt. Hiei, massacring thousands of monks and blotting out a major center of Japan's medieval life and economy. Two years later he encircled and burned Kyoto to punish and depose the last Ashikaga shogun, who had not understood the limits of his allowed power. His most ferocious opponent was the *True Pure Land* sect of Buddhists. He exterminated many with great savagery in Nagashima and besieged the survivors for 10 years in their exquisitely sited fortress (at the narrow end of a lake) of *Honganji* at Osaka. At *Nagashino* (1575), Nobunaga used a corps of some 3,000 arquebusiers to rout the army of an enemy daimyo. With fire and firearms, he conquered one-third of Japan by 1580. Death came in 1582: trapped in a Buddhist temple in Kyoto by the troops of a treacherous vassal, he either died in the fiery climax of the attack or committed seppuku. His destruction of Buddhist and monkish military bastions and his reduction of daimyo fortifications and power greatly advanced the unification of Japan that was later completed by *Toyotomi Hideyoshi* and Tokugawa Ieyasu. See also *castles, on land*.

Suggested Reading: Jeroen Lamers, *Japonius Tyrannus: The Japanese Warlord Oda Nobunaga Reconsidered* (2000).

odoshi ge. See *armor*.

officer. Any person holding a commission or warrant to command in a regularly constituted military force. The term derives its modern meaning from the great military reform in France of 1444, in which the problem of untrustworthy mercenary leaders was partly solved by appointing men who served at the pleasure of the king. These new commanders were "office-holders," or officers, in the royal service. The idea that officers should also be nationals of the state which employed them arose much later, and was still not general practice before the French Revolution. With some exceptions, during the medieval and early modern periods most officers were nobles, still considered the outstanding warrior class.

On naval ranks and related matters, see *admiral*; *boatswain*; *boatswain's mate*; *captain*; *constable*; *coxswain*; *general*; *Kapudan-i Derya*; *lieutenant*; *master*; *master carpenter*; *master gunner*; *master's mate*; *midshipman*; *patron*; *petty officer*; *purser*; *quartermaster*; *quartermaster's mate*; *rear admiral*; *standing officer*; *tarpaulin*; *vice admiral*; *warrant officer*.

On army ranks and related matters, see *alferes*; *banneret*; *captain*; *Cebici başi*; *cihuacoatl*; *colonel*; *constable*; *Constable of France*; *Çorbasi*; *cornet* (1); *corporal*; *Cossacks*; *dead-pays*; *dirlik yememiş*; *dziesietniks*; *ensign*; *Feldobrist*; *Feldweibel*; *Field

Marshal; *general*; *Generalfeldobrist*; *Generallissimus*; *Generalobrist*; *general officer*; *Grand Vezier*; *Hauptmann*; *Hochmeister*; *Hurenweibel*; *kaim mekam*; *knight*; *knight marshal*; *Kreisoberst*; *lieutenant*; *Lieutenant-général du royaume*; *Lieutenant-General (Germany)*; *locumentems*; *maître de camp*; *maréchal de camp*; *maréchal de logis*; *Marshal*; *Mestre*; *mestres de camp*; *Ming Army*; *Oberster Feldhauptmann*; *Oberster Feldweibel*; *Obrist*; *Ordensmarschall*; *otaman*; *Pfenningmeister*; *podestà*; *porucznik*; *Prévôt des maréchaux*; *Prior Mor*; *Provost*; *provost marshal*; *quartermaster*; *ransom*; *rota*; *rotmistrz*; *Rottmeister*; *sanack bey*; *Schultheiss*; *serdar*; *sergeant*; *Shogun*; *shugo*; *"skulking way of war"*; *starosty*; *starshnya*; *subashi*; *Swiss Army*; *uniforms*; *vintenar*; *Wachmeister*; *Yeniçeri Ağasi*; *Zeugherr*.

Oikoumene. "The inhabited lands." A world historical term for the densely populated, interconnected landmasses of northern Africa, Europe, the Middle East, and continental Asia. Its dominant civilizations were Arabic, Roman (Latin), Hellenistic, Sanskrit, and Chinese. The major religions produced by these civilizations, overlapping one another in frontier zones, were *Christianity, Islam, Hinduism, Buddhism,* and *Confucianism.* What justification for the term there is derives from the fact that most of the world's population lived in the Oikoumene and that technology as well as political, military, economic, and religious ideas spread rapidly there among diverse cultures, more so than in isolated areas such as sub-Saharan Africa, the Americas, Southeast Asia, or Australasia.

Okehazama, Battle of (1560). In 1560, a massive army of 45,000 was sent by a powerful *daimyo*, Yoshimoto Imagawa, to invade the domain of the warlord *Oda Nobunaga.* The latter kept his battle plan secret from his captains, fearing treachery and even betrayal on the battlefield. (In later campaigns, Nobunaga used offers of protection and vassalage to win over enemy daimyo and gain victories.) With only 5,000 men Nobunaga daringly attacked Yoshimoto's camp and won overwhelmingly over his more tactically staid, and utterly surprised, enemy. This remarkable victory inspired generations of Japanese officers, including those who launched the Pacific War in 1941, to believe in the superiority of will and daring over material reality and enemy numerical advantage. More immediately, the victory secured Nobunaga's eastern flank with *Tokugawa Ieyasu.*

okka. The standard Ottoman measure of *artillery* caliber: 14 okka guns fired the equivalent of 40-pound shot; 11–22 okka guns fired 30–60-pound shot; a 24-okka gun fired the equivalent of 68-pound shot.

Oldenbaarneveldt, Johan van (1547–1619). "The Advocate." Dutch statesmen and reformer. Although a diplomat by profession, he was strangely lacking in diplomatic skills. He came from a family with long anti-*Habsburg* credentials and for 30 years was the leading official in the *States General*, rising to hold the office of "landsadvocaat." He was an early supporter of *William the Silent.* With long experience in dike supervision and engineering, he oversaw the flooding of fields around Leiden to permit *Sea Beggar* boats to relieve the siege of that city in 1574. He helped negotiate the *Treaty of Nonsuch* with *Elizabeth I*. He was instrumental in securing hegemony for Holland in the Union of Utrecht and over the United Provinces. He played a lead role in launching the *Vereenigde Oostindische Compaagnie* (VOC). He supported the *Twelve Years' Truce* (1609–1621), but over its course he lost power and influence to hardline Calvinist preachers (he leaned to the *Arminian* side in the religious disputes of the period), and *Maurits of Nassau*, with whom he was increasingly at odds from 1600. What ultimately doomed Oldenbaarneveldt was opposition of the regents and Dutch merchants to overseas commercial concessions he made to Spain to secure the Truce in 1609. This issue came to a head in 1617, as he led the "peace party" that hoped to extend the Truce or perhaps even arrive at a permanent peace. He was also opposed by fervent Calvinist refugees from France, Flanders, and Brabant, who tended to be more rigid in their religiosity than most Dutch. In August 1618, Maurits had the Advocate arrested. His trial for treason dragged on into 1619. He was convicted on May 12 and executed the next day, much to his surprise.

Old English. The Catholic ruling and landowning class descended from the *Norman* conquest of Ireland and later medieval migrations. They were dominant in *The Pale* where they acted for the crown, but did not rule outside it where the *Old Irish* lords held sway. After the *Kildare Rebellion* (1534–1535), the *New English* Protestant military class challenged both older groups for leadership. In 1641, the Old English joined the Old Irish in rebellion against the possibility that *Covenanter* success in England and Scotland might lead to further Protestant "plantations" in Ireland. Old English control of ports in Wexford and Waterford was crucial to the logistics of sustaining the Irish rebellion, and for *Confederacy* naval attacks against English shipping. See also *English Civil Wars*.

Old Irish. Gaelic lords, survivors of the *Norman* conquest of the 12th century. Hardline Catholics, they included most clerics and viewed any peace with Protestants after 1641 as obtainable only at the price of their religious liberty, and so voted consistently for war. They were prominent in the *Confederation of Kilkenny* (May 10, 1641), expelling any Catholics from the Confederacy who wanted the peace offered by *Ormonde*.

Olivares, conde-duque de (1587–1645). Né Gaspar de Guzmán y Pimentel. Also duke of Lerma and "Valido" (chief minister) to *Philip IV* from 1622 to 1643. He headed the "Junta Grande de Reformación" that sought to reform all Spanish government from banking to royal finance to military affairs. Like so many centralizers of the era, notably his great sparring partner, *Cardinal Richelieu*, Olivares sought to give his king one country under a single faith. To that end he supported purging activities of the *Inquisition* and proposed a "Union of Arms" wherein all parts of the Spanish kingdom and empire were allotted a military tax and recruitment contribution. This was not welcomed outside heavily burdened *Castile*, but its intent and structure revealed a long-term plan for centralization under a powerful monarch. Olivares core military strategy from 1625 was to shift the long war against the Dutch rebels to sea, because on land little progress was possible and Spain's costs were unsustainable. Hence, he reduced the *Army of Flanders* until it could no longer fight a major offensive campaign unaided, even though it was still asked to blockade Dutch overland trade in support of the war at sea that aimed to smash *Sea Beggar* fleets and strangle the Dutch economy. Olivares could not get the Austrians to agree to this strategy, which entailed their assault on several Baltic ports that handled the Dutch northern trades. *Albrecht von Wallenstein* tepidly invested *Straslund* and began to build a Baltic fleet, but he never fully supported Olivares' project either.

Olivares was personally devout and served a devout Catholic king in domestic affairs, but he did not pursue an exclusionary Catholic foreign policy: he was not a confessional fanatic or even idealist when it came to raisons d'état. He thus supported the *Huguenots* against the Catholic kings of France because he thought war with France was unavoidable as long as Cardinal Richelieu was in power. That led Olivares to make a major mistake in 1629: he involved both branches of the *Habsburgs* in a losing war with France in northern Italy, the *War of the Mantuan Succession* (1627–1631). That left *Johann Tilly* undermanned and alone in Germany to face *Gustavus Adolphus* and the German Protestant powers. Olivares seems to have envisioned a short war against France in which such heavy blows would be landed by Spain's putatively superior *tercios* that Richelieu would be toppled. He was wrong, and Spain was thereafter drawn more deeply into the German war, on top of its Dutch war, in addition to protracted war with France, as well as ongoing

In 1639 Olivares sent 20,000 reinforcements north in a convoy of 100 ships . . .

naval wars with the Ottomans and the Barbary emirates. Olivares was extremely worried by Richelieu's steady advance of French garrisons across the Rhine from 1632 to 1634. Once the Habsburgs won at *First Nördlingen* (1634), he took aggressive measures designed to lure France into the German war (after the *Treaty of Regensburg* in 1630, he no longer trusted *Ferdinand II* as an ally). This was part and parcel of his long-term policy of mobilizing Austrian Habsburg resources to advance the interest of Spain, in this case by tying down and fighting the French in Germany.

In 1639 Olivares sent 20,000 reinforcements north in a convoy of 100 ships, only to have nearly the entire fleet destroyed at *The Downs* (October 21, 1639). The defeat was strategically worse than the disaster of the *Invincible Armada* of 1588. The defeat gutted Olivares' naval strategy. Then the *Revolt of Catalonia* began in May 1640, provoked by his high war taxes. That was followed in December by a coup and rebellion in Portugal. Uprisings against Spanish rule also broke out in *Naples* and Andalusia, Philip was sorry to see Olivares go; but the country was not and Queen Isabella saw that he did. Olivares was never as abstract as Richelieu and had to contend with a vast overseas empire that did not burden the Cardinal. He did not seek to reshape the European order so much as to preserve Spain's position in it. Given the long-term decline of Spain vis-à-vis France, this he could not do.

Suggested Reading: J. H. Elliott, *The Count-Duke of Olivares: The Statesman in an Age of Decline* (1986).

olive line. See *Castile*; *Reconquista*.

Oliwa (Oliva), Battle of (November 28, 1627). A small naval battle in which 10 Polish ships, some crewed by experienced Dutch sailors and Scottish mercenaries, defeated six Swedish ships near Danzig. The Swedes were trying to impose a blockade against Danzig that affected Polish and Dutch mercantile interests in the eastern Baltic. The Poles lost fewer than 50 men, but that figure included their admiral who was killed by a cannonball. The Swedes lost 350 killed and 70 captured.

Oñate, Treaty of (March 1617). A secret treaty between Spain and Austria negotiated by the Spanish ambassador, Count Oñate. It was intended to clear the way for resumption of war with the Netherlands upon expiration of the *Twelve Years' Truce* in 1621. Oñate committed *Philip III* to waive his formal pretensions to the crowns of Bohemia and Hungary in exchange for *Ferdinand II* ceding an Austrian claim to Alsace. This cleared the way for Ferdinand to receive Spanish military aid in his war with Venice, but also pulled Spain into the *Thirty Years' War* after 1621. It thus reversed *Lerma's* policy of staying clear of war north of the Alps.

O'Neill, Hugh. See *Nine Years' War*.

O'Neill, Owen Roe (c.1583–1649). Irish Confederate commander. He served in the Spanish *Army of Flanders* for 40 years before returning to Ireland aboard a "Dunkirk frigate" with a regiment of tough veterans to join the great rebellion in 1642. He fought mainly in Ulster, winning one of the most signal Irish victories ever over a British force at Benburb on June 5, 1646. This gave the Catholic Irish armies superiority for the first time and thereby greatly extended the rebellion. See also *Confederation of Kilkenny*.

Ōnin War (1467–1477). It began the period in Japanese history generally known as *Sengoku jidai* or "Warring States." It was rooted in the failed balance of power between the Ashikaga *shoguns* and their *shugo* and *daimyo* even in the central provinces, or Kantō region. The trigger was resignation of a weary emperor, which set off an intense succession struggle between the Yamana and Hosokawa daimyo and their *samurai* retainers, each with great compounds within the Imperial capital. Most of the fighting took place in Kyoto between an "eastern army" and a "western army," coalitions named for the location of their base camps within Kyoto. The city was destroyed by a decade of combat and arson carried out by hordes of *ashigaru* who joined with samurai in the protracted fight. With the succession decided by 1473, and the city reduced to ashen ruins, samurai drifted away. All fighting stopped inside Kyoto in 1477. In the interim the fighting had spread, merging with local conflicts across Japan. For that reason, some historians view the Ōnin War as merely the first decade of the *gekokujō* and a "Japanese Hundred Years' War."

Suggested Reading: H. Varley, *The Ōnin War* (1994).

Opbud. See *Denmark*.

open order. In the cavalry, a spacing of one horse length (about six feet) between ranks in a troop. In the infantry, a loose formation used on the march. Units moved into *close order* for battle. See also *drill*.

Oprichnina. "Government apart." Originally this referred to the quixotic decision by *Ivan IV* ("The Terrible") to divide the administration of *Muscovy* into the "Oprichnina," a territory free of troublesome nobles which he governed directly, and the rest of Muscovy, or "Zemshchina" ("The Land"). However, the term is more commonly used about his reign of terror, torture, and arbitrary arrest and executions. The anarchy lasted seven years (1565–1572), taking Muscovy temporarily out of the *First Northern War* (1558–1583) while encouraging Poland and Lithuania to form the *Union of Lublin* in 1569. Ivan's "oprichniki"—quasi-warrior monks who dressed in all black and carried dog's heads and broomsticks to sniff out and sweep away evil—purged and slaughtered with abandon. In 1570, four thousand were killed in Novgorod alone and the city was gutted. The chaos was so extreme that the ranks of the *Cossacks* swelled with new recruits and the Crimean *Tatars* reached and sacked Moscow in May 1571, destroying large parts of the city. They also sacked Tula, Riazan, and several other cities. The combination of depredations by the oprichniki and the Tatar raid left large parts of the Oprichnina desolate and fallow. In 1572, Ivan liquidated the liquidators. That was a model of political terror and control that appealed to an admiring Joseph Stalin nearly 400 years later.

Orange, Principality and House of. See *Eighty Years' War*; *Hendrik, Frederik*; *Maurits of Nassau*; *William the Silent*.

Ordensmarschall. The commanding officer and spiritual leader in a German *Military Order*.

Ordensstaat. The lands of the *Teutonic Knights*, stretching at their greatest extent from the Baltic coast of Prussia into western Poland and Russia, nearly to the area occupied by modern St. Petersburg. It was the main product of the most successful West European colonization project of the Middle Ages. It had no archbishop, instead combining internal administration and foreign policy under the Hochmeister. Towns were guarded by huge citadels and *commanderies* speckled and controlled the countryside.

Order of Aviz. See *Aviz, Order of*.

Order of the Garter. A decadent order of *chivalry* founded in 1348 by *Edward III*. It had more to do with tame tournaments than the battlefield, with the later pretend ideals of Thomas Mallory's *Le Morte d'Arthur* than with Edward III's real life slaughter of Scots and Frenchmen. Its emasculating purposes and effects were later closely paralleled by the Burgundian *Order of the Golden Fleece*.

Order of the Golden Fleece. Founded by Philip of Burgundy in 1430, it was a decadent mimicry of the older ideal of *chivalry*. Its "knights," all leading nobles, might once have set out as Crusaders or at least as warriors of the realm. Instead, they became feckless courtesans and courtiers fawning for favors from the dukes. Its purpose was twofold: to celebrate the sovereign and emasculate the old landed aristocracy. It met 23 times from 1430 to 1559.

Order of Trufac. See *Knights of Our Lady of Montjoie*.

Order States. States founded or sustained by one or other of the *Military Orders*. See also *Lithuania, Grand Duchy of*; *Livonia*; *Livonian Order*; *Malta*; *Ordensstaat*; *Prussia*; *Rhodes, Siege of (1444)*; *Rhodes, Siege of (1479–1480)*; *Rhodes, Siege of (1522–1523)*; *Teutonic Knights, Order of*.

Ordinary. In the English navy in the 16th–17th centuries this was a fixed sum supposed to cover the cost of the routine (peacetime) activities of the king's/queen's ships.

ordu bazar. An Ottoman army market where food was bought from local villages at fair prices and craftsmen repaired boots, fixed weapons, or cut hair, all inside large tents.

Orgelgeschütz. "Organ gun." German term for small bore, multi-barreled pieces that elsewhere were known as *ribaudequins*.

Orléans, Siege of (1428–1429). See *Fastolf, John*; *Hundred Years' War*; *Jeanne d'Arc*; *Rouvray, Battle of*.

Ormonde, 1st Duke of (1610–1688). Né James Butler. Anglo-Irish soldier and statesman. Made commander-in-chief of English forces in Ireland in 1640, within a year he faced a major rebellion. He led Royalists in relieving sieges of Dublin and Drogheda in 1641, and to victory at New Ross (March 18, 1643). In 1644 he was made Lord Lieutenant of Ireland. In that role he contended with the miasma of Irish civil war, papal intrigue, and the sordid political machinations of *Charles I*. Bowing to reality, and never a fanatic, he accepted that most of Ireland was controlled by the *Confederation of Kilkenny*. He tried to restore peace in 1646 ("First Ormonde Peace") by offering the

Confederates religious toleration. The *Old Irish* rejected the offer in June 1647. Ormonde surrendered Dublin to the *Confederate Army* and left for France. Many in Parliament thought him too closely associated with the king, whom he attended in his Hampton Court captivity. Returning to Ireland, Ormonde arranged the "Second Ormonde Peace" (January 17, 1649) that secured Catholic rights and linked the Confederate Army with his Royalists. When Charles I was executed two weeks later (January 30, 1649), Ormonde declared against Parliament and for Charles II. When *Oliver Cromwell* arrived in Ireland with 12,000 men of the *New Model Army* in August, Ormonde—who had failed to secure Dublin—again went into French exile.

Orta. A large unit within the *Janissary Corps*, roughly akin to a battalion. See also *wounds*.

Orthodox Churches. National churches of the Balkans, Eastern Europe, and Muscovy followed the Byzantine rite and Nicene creed, a statement of fundamental principles set out at the *Ecumenical Council* held in Nicene in 325 C.E. After centuries of contention that began in the 8th century, a full schism with the Latin *Catholic Church* came about in 1054. The divide was confirmed by the sack of Constantinople, the capital of the Orthodox faith, by Latin knights during the Fourth Crusade (1204). Kiev became a holy site for Slavic Orthodox when it hosted Prince Vladimir's conversion in 988. The Muscovite Orthodox Church grew more independent of the Greek Church once *Constantinople* was captured by the Ottomans in 1453, a pattern followed in Bulgaria, Cyprus, Georgia, Rumania, and Serbia. The Muscovite Church was made thoroughly subservient to the tsars and the state, markedly so even as it was elevated to a full patriarchate independent of Constantinople. It remained a close servant of tsarist autocracy, inculcating among the peasantry the claim of tsars to a unique legitimacy based in divine grace and holiness. In short, in a land of mass illiteracy tamed priests served as powerful propagandists for the regime, as they did also among Catholics in Spain. A similar role was played by sunni mystics in the Ottoman Empire and the *Qizilbash* in Iran. See also *Militargrenze*; *Union of Brest*.

Suggested Reading: J. M. Hussey, *The Orthodox Church in the Byzantine Empire* (1986).

Osaka Castle, Siege of (1615). Toyotomi Hideyori, son of *Toyotomi Hideyoshi*, gathered the last opponents of *Tokugawa Ieyasu* at Osaka Castle in 1614: Toyotomi clan loyalists and retainers, defiant *samurai* left over from earlier defeats in the *Unification Wars* (1550–1615), soldiers of fortune, and civilians brought there by misfortune. Ieyasu surrounded Osaka with a huge army of 200,000 men and began the first ever bombardment of a Japanese stone fortress with modern cannon (*culverins* and *sakers*). The defenders could reply only with old-style Chinese cannon (early model breech-loaders) and torsion catapults. Hideyori led his troops outside the castle defenses to fight on the field at Tennoji (June 3, 1615). The fighting was intense and the slaughter immense. The battle lost, Hideyori retreated into the burning castle and committed seppuku (ritual suicide). His eight-year-old son was murdered to prevent a later political claim against Ieyasu's heirs.

Osman I (1259–1326). Founder of the Osmanli dynasty for which the *Ottoman Empire* was named. The *Seljuk Turks* awarded him for military service with lands they wanted him to hold for them along the frontier with the *Byzantine Empire*. From there he raided constantly into rich Byzantine provinces. As the Seljuk state collapsed Osman moved into the political and military vacuum. He was a successful border warlord so he attracted freelance fighters to his banners, including many former Seljuk warriors. He failed to take Nicaea or Nicomedia in a two-year campaign, 1302–1304. In 1317 he began a nine-year siege of *Bursa*. He died before the city fell. Orkhan, his son and successor, moved the Ottoman capital there once it did.

Osnabrück, Treaty of (October 24, 1648). The second of the major treaties of the *Peace of Westphalia* which, together with the *Treaty of Münster* signed on the same day, brought peace to Germany and most of Europe and ended the *Thirty Years' War* (1618–1648). Osnabrück was a heavily detailed agreement which resolved hundreds of long-standing religious and territorial disputes within Germany. For instance, it clarified the legal standing of the Protestant branch—*Johannitterorden*—of the Knights of St. John, as distinct from the still-Catholic Order of Malta, and returned five *commanderies* to the Maltese. More generally, it clarified the titles and claims of various German princes and bishops, reformed the election provisions of the constitution of the *Holy Roman Empire*, and confirmed as sovereign some 300 political entities in greater Germany. In that it carried forward recognition of the German *Estates* agreed in the *Imperial Diet* at Regensburg in 1641. It also granted Sweden an indemnity of five million Taler that was crucial to Sweden agreeing to withdraw its unpaid army from Germany.

Ostend, Siege of (1601–1604). After losing at *Nieuwport* (July 2, 1600), *Archduke Albert of Austria* laid siege to Ostend. An initial effort to storm the defenses failed and the Spanish settled in for a siege that became known throughout Europe as the "new siege of Troy." In 1602 *Ambrogio di Spínola* took charge of the Spanish trenches but fared no better than his predecessor. *Maurits of Nassau* brought in troops to relieve the siege, supplying them and the city via the sea. This enabled the Dutch to continue to resist long after traditional limitations of supply would have forced a surrender. However, Spínola likewise made use of the sea for resupply. The result was that both sides were able to last for three years—a record for sieges of that time—until the city fell to Spínola on September 22, 1604. Most of its Protestants departed along with surviving defenders and settled in other garrison towns along the Scheldt. Ostend was important in spreading new military technologies and siegecraft to other lands, as hundreds of young nobles and more military engineers made their way to Ostend to observe the new methods firsthand.

otaman. Leader of a *Cossack* host. See also *hetman*.

Otterburn, Battle of (August 15, 1388). After decades of minor border raids and skirmishing, and with England tied down in the *Hundred Years' War* with France, the *Scottish Wars* flared up again in 1388. A combined French-Scottish army crossed into northern England to conduct a raid-in-force. The English, hoping to literally catch the allies sleeping, attacked their camp at night. But an alarm was raised and the fighting was sharp. About 2,000 English were killed by Scots pikemen and their French allies, and many English nobles were captured and held for ransom. Untamed by English military power, Scottish raiding continued unabated across the border into the 15th century.

Ottoman Army. The sultans had a *standing army* of real size before most European states: the *Kapikulu Askerleri*. At its core was a professional firearms-bearing corp of military slaves, the *Janissary Corps*, who added expertise in gunpowder weapons in the early 15th century to their original skill as archers. They were supported by quasi-feudal levies of *timariot* light cavalry, and six regiments of elite household *sipahis*. In 1527 the Ottoman army boasted some 11,000 musketeer infantry, 5,000 auxiliary light cavalry, 2,000 artillerymen, and 90,000 timariot horse (seasonal troops). By 1609 the force swelled to 47,000 Janissaries plus irregular peasant infantry, 21,000 cavalry, 8,000 artillerymen, and 140,000 timariots. During the 16th century the Ottomans boasted a large early modern army that was more than a match for any army in Europe, a fact proven by continued conquests of new provinces carved out of western Iran and southeastern Europe. In any discussion

During the 16th century the Ottomans boasted a large early modern army . . .

of the period it should be noted, as does Geoffrey Parker, that it was Ottoman armies that besieged European cities such as Buda, Belgrade, and Vienna and not Europeans who besieged Constantinople (Istanbul). See also *Acemi Oğlan*; *akincis/akinjis*; *Azaps*; *Beyliks*; *Bostancilar*; *camp followers*; *cavalry*; *Cebicis*; *Cecora, Battle of*; *Celâli Revolts*; *Dar al-Harb*; *dead-pays*; *desertion*; *Hungary*; *Kazan*; *Khotyn, Battle of*; *Kosovo Polje, Battle of*; *Kur'aci*; *magazines*; *Marj Dabiq, Battle of*; *Militargrenze*; *Mohács, Battle of*; *murtat*; *ocak*; *ordu bazar*; *Ottoman Empire*; *Ottoman warfare*; *Piyadeğan militia*; *revolution in military affairs*; *Rhodes, Siege of* (1444); *Rhodes, Siege of* (1479–1480); *Rhodes, Siege of* (1522–1523); *Sekban*; *Sis, Battle of*; *Tatars*; *Thirteen Years' War*; *Top Arabacs*; *Topçu*; *trace italienne*; *Tüfeçis*; *Voynuqs*; *Yaya infantry*.

Ottoman Empire. The Ottoman Empire arose from, and was centered on, successor Turkic military power in Anatolia. The first Turkic empire, in the 6th–7th centuries, was based in Turkestan, from where Turkic-speaking nomads dominated Inner Asia for centuries. They mounted raids into China and north India, and overran Central Asia and most of the Middle East. The

Seljuk Turks helped pave the way in Anatolia for the later Ottomans by a decisive victory over the *Byzantine empire* at Manzikert (1071). That catastrophe started the Greek empire on the path to degradation and extinction. The Ottomans expanded out of their base in western Anatolia along the Byzantine border region of Bithynia, with the founding conventionally dated to 1300. The Ottomans moved into a vacuum of power and *overlordship* left by the defeat of the Seljuks by the *Mongols*, aided by *Crusader* occupation of Constantinople from 1204 to 1261. The Empire was ruled by the Osmanli dynasty, named for its founder *Osman I* (or Othman, 1259–1326). Its expansion proceeded from the 13th century through the 16th century, with its outer limits in Europe only made clear late in the 17th century. Some historians depict the rise of the Ottomans as a leading example of a *gunpowder empire* made possible by the willingness of martial classes to harness black powder technology to territorial expansion. Others see that as an overly technologically deterministic thesis.

Expansion

The Ottomans captured *Bursa* in Anatolia in 1326 after a nine-year siege of that Byzantine city. They made it their temporary capital as they moved on to assault and take Nicaea (1331) and Nicomedia (1337). They acquired their first territory in Europe at Gallipoli in 1354, which they followed with the conquest of Adrianople in 1360 under *Murad I*. That ancient Roman town became their new capital and major military base in Europe from 1362. Constantinople was encircled by conquering the lower Balkans, an advance marked by key victories over the Orthodox Serbs at *Maritza River* (1371) and *Kosovo* (1389). These martial successes were followed by political and territorial absorption of much of Greece. Byzantium's second largest city, Thessalonika, fell in 1387. Next came conquests in Bulgaria, Macedonia, and Serbia proper. *Bayezid I* (r.1389–1402) completed the conquest of Anatolia, incorporating all smaller Turkic states there into the Ottoman Empire. The Ottomans final surge against the defenses of Byzantium was interrupted by an advance into their strategic rear in Anatolia by the last of the great Mongol-Turkic hordes, led by *Timur*. Bayezid was defeated and taken prisoner by Timur at *Ankara* (1402). There followed a decade of civil war among Bayezid's sons, until *Muhammad I* emerged as sultan in 1413. He was followed by *Murad II*, who retread the Ottoman path of conquest by capturing parts of Anatolia lost to the *Timurids* and taking new territory in Greece, Hungary, and Serbia.

Around 1390 the Ottomans initiated a new recruiting system for their *Janissary Corps*. The *Devşirme system* drew boy slaves from newly conquered Christian subjects in a "levy of tribute children." The system was not wholly unpopular among Christian peasant families. In addition, the relative tolerance of the Ottoman state for religious minorities, along with tax incentives to convert to Islam, meant the old Greek and Slav military elites found a niche in the Ottoman military. After Murad came the spectacular reign of *Muhammad II*, "The Conqueror," usually ranked among the greatest of sultans. He took *Constantinople* in 1453 and moved the capital there from Adrianople, where it remained as the center of power in the Islamic world into the 20th century. Muhammad conducted sweeping campaigns into southern Europe, overrunning the last holdout territories in Greece and finally subduing all of Serbia and Bosnia: northern Serbia was overrun in 1459, Bosnia fell between 1463 and 1466. What is now Albania was invaded in 1468 and the Negroponte was wrested from Venice in 1470. Muhammad put down a Turkoman revolt in eastern Anatolia and Iraq in 1473 and landed troops in Italy, at Otranto, in 1480. From this point the Empire moved away from its older, overt religiosity and Muslim ideology as justification for expansionist wars. It assumed a more mature internationalism in foreign policy and cosmopolitan toleration at home, such that *Bayezid II* welcomed tens of thousands of Jewish refugees from Christian persecution in Iberia and Italy after 1492.

After the Timurid dynasty in Iran collapsed, the Ottomans conquered most of the older Islamic lands directly west of the new *Safavid Empire* in Iran, and penetrated deep into the southern Arab lands of Syria and Palestine. The first half of the 16th century saw enemies consolidate in the east (Safavid Iran) and the west (singular union of Spain and Austria under *Charles V*). In 1514 *Selim I* reversed his father's toleration and ordered a mass slaughter of dissident Muslims (*shi'ia*) within the Empire. He followed up with an aggressive campaign against Iran. Following victory over the *Mamlūks* of Egypt at *Marj Dabiq* (1516), Selim set up Damascus and Aleppo as administrative capitals of two new provinces carved from Syria. In the first months of 1517 Janissary musketeers twice more defeated the conservative, firearms-abjuring mamlūks: at al-Raydaniyya in January and Giza in April. This led to the conquest of Cairo itself. Control of Egypt also made the Ottomans masters of the *Hejaz* (and hence, of Mecca and Medina) and provided a crucial stream of revenue used to support garrisons in Hungary.

The Ottomans next embarked on a prolonged curl of expansion around the south shore of the Mediterranean basin. If the long contest between Spain and the Ottoman Empire in the Western Mediterranean ultimately left the *Barbary corsairs* of North Africa—based in *Algiers*, *Tunis*, and *Tripoli*—only nominally under Constantinople's control, still these *Berber* states were mostly loyal and useful allies, especially in naval warfare. Another opportunity lay due west, against the *Nemçe* (*Habsburgs*) in Europe. As the *Protestant Reformation* split the Latin West it opened confessional fissures that might be exploited with Ottoman arms and diplomacy. The first moves came with the conquest of Belgrade (1521) and *Rhodes* (1522). Some Protestants looked to Constantinople to counterbalance Catholic Vienna, even as the former challenged the latter for physical control of the Balkans and Hungary. The Ottomans found an eager anti-Habsburg ally in Catholic France, under *Francis I*. Overall, after the fall of Buda in 1541 the Ottomans were mostly preoccupied with consolidation and defense of their Trans-Danubian territories and naval wars with Venice and Spain.

Consolidation

The cultural peak of Ottoman civilization came under *Suleiman I* (r.1520–1566), who ruled a population of nearly 20 million and an empire over 800,000 square miles in size. However, Suleiman was succeeded by thirteen weak and ineffectual sultans. His son, *Selim II*, lost the Ottoman galley fleet to a Western alliance at *Lepanto* in 1571. He also lost an Ottoman army in Astrakhan to *Muscovy*, a dangerous new enemy and rival empire encroaching on the northern frontier. Under a progression of bumbling sultans the Ottomans began to lag Europe in military technology and cultural and scientific innovation, though the gap was not large before c.1680. Some historians suggest that Ottoman social cohesion began to fray and economic productivity lagged from the end of the 16th century. If so, such long-term decline was well disguised by Ottoman military strength, which abided well after Lepanto and Astrakhan. The size of the empire brought strength and security, not just more hostile borders and vulnerability. And even with relative economic decline, Ottoman wealth was still immense and the military more self-sustaining from local resources than the new militaries of Europe or Muscovy.

The *Thirteen Years' War* (1593–1606) broke out with the Habsburgs over local quarrels in the *Militargrenze*. It ended in stalemate partly because neither side was really committed to the fighting, but also because in 1603 the Ottomans were distracted by renewal of war with a reformed and revived Safavid Iran led by *Abbas I*. The Ottomans were stunned by the new Safavid army at *Sis* (1606), and during the next quarter century lost considerable ground in the east, including Iraq after the Ottoman garrison in *Baghdad* switched to the Safavids. The Ottomans concentrated on retaking Baghdad, which they besieged three times (1625–1626, 1630, and 1638). Iraq was restored and accommodation reached with Safavid Iran in the *Treaty of Zuhab* (1639), which more or less kept peace to the end of the Safavid regime in 1722. Despite protracted Ottoman-Safavid wars, it should be noted that there were also long periods of peace, compromise, and a spirit of mutual recognition by the orthodox and heterodox Muslim empires. Similarly, while Paris and Constantinople found a common enemy in the Habsburgs during the first half of the 16th century, a military-political equilibrium in the west was established with Austria by the end of the Thirteen Years' War that both sides respected until 1660.

In the first half of the 17th century the Ottomans were mostly relieved of war in the west by the agonizing and destructive descent of Austria and the Holy Roman Empire into the *Thirty Years' War* (1618–1648). In addition, by 1650 the Ottoman Empire reached the outer logistical and administrative limits of expansion and became increasingly devoted to defense of immense territory already gained. It is a grand irony that this was precisely the moment Europe began to view the Ottoman Empire as a lasting security threat. Note: Although contemporary Europeans and later historians called the Ottomans "*Turks*," the term is inaccurate. For instance, reflecting the great cosmopolitan basis of the Ottoman Empire, no sultan after 1362 was ethnically Turkish; most were Slavs, Georgians, or Circassians. See also *Amasya, Peace of*;

artillery; askeri; Azaps; Chaldiran, Battle of; Derbençi; dirlik yememiş; Ethiopia; Eyâlet Askerleri; ganimet; Kapikulu Askerleri; Kur'aci; levend/levendat; magazines; Martolos; Raya; Sekban; sipahis; terakki; timariots; Voynuqs; Yaya infantry; Yeniçeri Ağasi; ziamet; Zsitva Torok, Treaty of.

Suggested Reading: Jason Goodwin, *Lords of the Horizons: A History of the Ottoman Empire* (1999); Marshall Hodgson, *Gunpowder Empires and Modern Times* (1974); Colin Imber, *Ottoman Empire, 1300–1650* (2002); H. Inalcik, *The Ottoman Empire: Conquest, Organization and Economy* (1978); C. M. Kortepeter, *Ottoman Imperialism during the Reformation* (1992); Justin McCarthy. *The Ottoman Turks* (1997); V. J. Parry, *History of the Ottoman Empire to 1730* (1976); A. Stiles, *The Ottoman Empire, 1450–1700* (1989).

Ottoman-Safavid Wars. See *Abbas I; Amasya, Peace of; Chaldiran, Battle of; Iran; Muhammad II; Ottoman Empire; Ottoman warfare; Safavid Army; Safavid Empire; Selim I; Sis, Battle of; Suleiman I.*

Ottoman warfare. The medieval and early modern Western image of the Ottoman soldier as motivated principally by fanatic Muslim (*ghazi*) belief, and the *Ottoman Empire* as driven by a core mission of *"holy war"* (jihad), is a gross caricature that has nonetheless been purveyed by generations of historians. For one thing, jihad applied principally to defense of the *Dar al-Islam* ("Abode of Islam"), and the central Ottoman lands were almost never under threat. More recent work has shown that Ottoman imperialism operated out of a complex web of secular as well as religious motivations and interests, with the former more prominent than the latter after 1600. Also, it must be remembered that Ottoman armies were highly heterodox in terms of religious affiliation and that the Ottomans were far more tolerant in religious matters than contemporary states in Europe which engaged in decades of confessional war. Ottoman armies operating in the Balkans were comprised of local Christian soldiers; Crimean scouts and foragers of dubious, if nominal, Islamic belief; professional *Janissaries* taken as boys from Christian families and raised to *Islam*; traditional sunni *heavy cavalry* from Anatolia; and other Muslim troops drawn from tolerated sufi or regional sects. It is difficult to see how such religiously cosmopolitan armies were driven by a supposed fanatic devotion to Islam. It seems far more likely that they were moved by more normal interests in martial glory, imperial expansion, and especially greed for land and plunder.

> *...Ottoman armies were highly heterodox in terms of religious affiliation...*

By the end of the 16th century the distance of the western frontier from Constantinople meant that local raiding and private wars in the *Militargrenze* prevailed, sometimes even against the wishes of the sultan. Large armies and prolonged campaigns were still fought into the mid-16th century, though during the first half of the 17th century there was mostly peace along the frontier with Christian Europe as the Ottomans dealt with a revived and reformed *Safavid* Iran. The pattern of Ottoman warfare was also different in the east where greater distances from supplies and harsher climate and rougher terrain conditions, along with widespread public disapproval of making war on fellow Muslims, placed sharp limits not just on Ottoman generals but on the capacity of their armies to sustain military operations. A second hoary myth—that the Ottomans progressively fell behind the West in military technology and capabilities after c.1500—also has been exposed. Most historians of Ottoman warfare now agree that significant technological divergence did not begin until c.1680. Moreover, before the 18th century the Ottomans were more advanced than Europe in military organization and specialization. In addition to the universal specialization of all early modern militaries into infantry, cavalry, and artillery, the Ottomans had a sophisticated commissariat and supply system ("menzil-hane"), a transportation service, and even special assault commandos (*Serdengeçti*). And far more Ottoman troops were well-trained professionals rather than last-minute seasonal conscripts, as was so often the case in Europe.

Rhoads Murphey has identified important material and fiscal constraints on Ottoman warfare. Materially, military technology was the least-constraining factor as the Ottomans imported *renegade* military engineers and generally kept pace with developments in the West prior to the late 17th century. *War finance* was more restrictive, as it was in all early modern warfare. Yet, the Ottomans had major advantages over their enemies in the Christian West and in Safavid Iran in this arena, too: they were less involved in expensive naval warfare; they had a vast empire and productive economy that allowed them to avoid special war taxes, debasement of currency, or periodic bankruptcy; they had self-sustaining allies (*Tatars*), freelance auxiliary cavalry (*akinci*), and unpaid frontier troops (*Voynuqs*), all financed mainly through a share in plunder. They also used regular troops as military laborers, thereby reducing fortification costs, where European troops disdained spade work before the 1590s. A greater constraint on Ottoman operations was climate, especially the heat of the eastern deserts of Iraq and Iran. Limited fodder for huge *timariot* cavalry armies along with difficult terrain restricted operations in the Balkans. Seasonal rains and the cycle of the growing season placed sharp logistical limits on military operations, as they did on all early modern armies, confining activity to the six months between May and November. All in all, the early modern Ottoman military was more Habsburg than Prussian in its military and ethnic diversity and internal divisions, its size and ineluctable clumsiness, and the costs and distractions of multiple fronts and wars. But then the Habsburgs, too, governed a successful cosmopolitan empire that was often underestimated in its military and organizational capabilities by outside observers and later historians. See also *armories*; *artillery*; *askeri*; *Azaps*; *Baghdad, Siege of*; *Chaldiran, Battle of*; *Derbençi*; *dirlik yememiş*; *Eyâlet Askerleri*; *fortification*; *ganimet*; *Hormuz*; *Kapikulu Askerleri*; *Kur'-aci*; *Lepanto, Battle of (October 7, 1571)*; *levend/levendat*; *magazines*; *Martolos*; *Militargrenze*; *rations*; *Raya*; *sekban*; *siege warfare*; *sipahis*; *Sis, Battle of*; *standing army*; *terakki*; *Yaya infantry*; *Yeniçeri Ağasi*; *zarbzens*; *ziamet*.

Suggested Reading: Rhoads Murphey, *Ottoman Warfare, 1500–1700* (1999).

Otumba, Battle of (July 2, 1520). *Hernán Cortés* and the bloody and wounded survivors of the *"Noche Triste"* (June 30, 1520) who escaped from the *first siege of Tenochtitlán* were caught on the open plain on July 2, partway through their flight to the Tlaxcalan capital. Possibly as many as 40,000 enraged Aztec warriors, led by the newly proclaimed Emperor Cuitláhuac, caught up to and surrounded the staggering Spanish and their remaining Tlaxcalan allies. Outnumbered as few armies have been in the history of warfare, the small *conquistadore* and Tlaxcalan force fended off repeated attacks for more than six hours. The decisive action came, according to Spanish accounts, when Cortés led a charge of the last lancers right at the *cihuacoatl* (commander) of the main Aztec formation. The brittle military-theocratic hierarchy of the Aztecs worked to their disadvantage as once the cihuacoatl and his lieutenants fell and regional musters of Aztecs scattered, leaderless and demoralized. This allowed the surviving Spanish and Tlaxcalans to escape to Tlaxcala, where Cortés regrouped prior to embarking on the *second siege of Tenochtitlán* (1521).

Outremer. Also "Oultremer" ("over the sea"). The Crusader states in Palestine and Syria. These took different shape at different times, but for nearly two centuries some territory survived as a Latin Christian military burr in the side of Arab-Muslim civilization. In 1187, as *Salāh-al-Dīn* approached Jerusalem, the full complement of Outremer's *knights* (600) and *sergeants* (20,000), along with its *Turcopoles* and infantry, moved to meet him. Most of them by that time were native to the area, not Europeans. It was the last time Outremer fielded such a force. See also *Crusades*.

outworks. Defensive structures built outside the main *enceinte*. See also *crownwork*; *hornwork*; *redan*; *redoubt*.

overlordship. In many pre-modern societies from Europe to the Ottoman Empire, overlordship was the key relationship holding together not just armies but society itself. Men were bound to their lords in complex ways, including obligations of military service. Their lords were bound in turn to overlords—kings or emperors—through the retinue system of the major magnates. Even kings and whole states might be bound to others by subservient relations of *tribute* that arrayed in complex patterns crafted by conquest or dynastic marriages and inheritance. See also *bushidō*; *Crusades*; *feudalism*; *Holy Roman Empire*; *Hundred Years' War*; *samurai*; *Scottish Wars*; *servitium debitum*; *servitor classes*; *Teutonic Knights, Order of*; *tribute*.

Oxenstierna (1583–1654). Swedish Chancellor from 1611 to 1654. He assumed a dominant position on the death of *Karl IX* in 1611, with the boy-king *Gustavus Adolphus* still just seventeen. He assisted Gustavus during the *Kalmar War* (1611–1613) with Denmark and a series of wars with *Sigismund III* of Poland. By 1627–1628, Oxenstierna determined that Sweden would have to enter the *Thirty Years' War* to clear the Baltic coast of the *Imperial Army* ensconced there under *Albrecht von Wallenstein,* and to block plans by *Olivares* of Spain to pursue a maritime war against the Netherlands in the Baltic. Crucially, Oxenstierna sought to preempt a *Habsburg*-Polish alliance. Finally, he and Gustavus were devoted Lutherans. Their confessional interest in the war was real and influential on their decision-making, and was reinforced by the connection between the Vasa dynasty and the success of Lutheranism in Sweden (as against the rival Catholic claims of Sigismund III). Oxenstierna thus encouraged Gustavus to sign the *Truce of Altmark* in 1629, freeing him to make his key intervention in Germany from 1630 to 1632.

Following the death of Gustavus at *Lützen* in 1632, stewardship of Swedish armies and interests in Germany fell to Oxenstierna as head of the regency council that governed Sweden. The death of the aggressive, ambitious Gustavus changed Sweden's war aims from imperial expansion and *overlordship* to peace, but not at any price or on any terms. Oxenstierna retrenched, withdrawing all Swedish units from central Germany to the Baltic coast in 1633, but he hoped to fight on through proxies in the manner of *Cardinal Richelieu.* That came down to substituting France for the *Heilbronn League* as the fulcrum of Sweden's diplomatic and military efforts. But Oxenstierna and Sweden lost badly at *First Nördlingen* on September 5–6, 1634, severely undercutting his negotiating position. A few months later, Oxenstierna was taken prisoner at Magdeburg by non-Swedish mercenaries who by then made up the bulk of the "Swedish Army," and who demanded arrears of pay Sweden did not have the ability to meet. The gap in prestige evident between Oxenstierna and the dead king, and Sweden's weakened finances, was such that further mutiny was forestalled only with major concessions of lands and plunder so that the Swedish Army, too, became a plague even to the lands and Protestant peoples it had liberated. Moreover, only France's intervention in the war in 1635 permitted Sweden to make a slow recovery after Nördlingen. To speed this process, Oxenstierna made peace with Poland at Stuhmsdorf (September 20, 1635). To forestall Denmark's re-entry to the German war in 1643, Oxenstierna launched a preemptive attack (*Torstensson's War*). He then presided over Sweden's interests in the negotiations leading to the *Peace of Westphalia* in 1648. See also *Hamburg, Treaty of.*

o-yoroi. See *armor; samurai.*

P

Pacification of Ghent. Following the "*Spanish Fury*" of November 4–5, 1576, delegates from Catholic Brabant and Protestant Holland and Zeeland agreed, at Ghent, to join Utrecht and *William the Silent* in driving out all Spanish troops and forming a new government for the Netherlands. *Don Juan of Austria*, the new Spanish governor, was forced to concede initially, but within months returned to active hostilities.

pacifism. See *Albigensian Crusade*; *Anabaptism*; *Arianism*; *Lollards*; *Pax Dei*; *Tartaglia, Niccolò*; *Treuga Dei*.

Pacta Conventa. Charters limiting royal constitutional and military powers sworn by the monarchs of Poland-Lithuania. They codified the weakness of the monarchy vis-à-vis the *Sejm* and noble classes.

page. In the later Middle Ages, the son of a noble became a *knight* in stages. As a page he learned how to tend to the great *destrier*, to clean and keep weapons, and began to imbibe the mores of *chivalry*. The next step in a knight's apprenticeship and military education was *esquire*.

palace guards. Early medieval monarchs in Europe used extended family members and trusted retainers as personal guards. In England this was the function of the *housecarls*. Monarchs and magnates hired elite palace guards of professional troops starting around 1350. Their main function was still to act as bodyguards, but an important secondary role was to display the grandeur of the prince or king. Such units should be seen as part of the long process of developing *standing armies*, since they were well-armed personal troops of the sovereign. In time, purely ceremonial functions were served by various courtiers, sergeants-at-arms, and the like while palace guards took on an important military role. In battle, *Edward III* employed Cheshire mounted archers dressed in green and white as his bodyguard. The Avignon popes had a personal guard (not yet Swiss) of over 100 armed men; the Visconti of Milan kept a palace guard of 700 cavalry during the 1420s, which later grew to more than 2,000 "familiares ad arma." In England, the "Yeoman of the Guard" was established in 1486 with an initial complement of 200, rising to 600 by the coronation of *Henry VIII*. In Spain the royal bodyguard, the "guardas reales," numbered 1,100 *men-at-arms* and another 130 *jinetes* (light cavalry) in the 1490s. In France the household or palace guard was made up of nearly a thousand men in 1500, including 200 *knights*, 100 Scots Archers, 100 *franc-archers*, 200 ordinary archers, and the famous "Les Cent-Suisses." *Charles the Rash* outdid French kings in this, as in all things pompous, retaining 2,000 armed men as a personal guard, including eight companies of English archers and another eight companies of infantry. When *Henri III* hired Swiss guards for his Paris residence he so alarmed the citizenry that they rebelled on the *Day of the Barricades* (May 12, 1588), driving the king from Paris. See also *eunuchs*; *Haiduks*; *Kapikulu Askerleri*; *strel'sty*.

palanka. See *çit palankasi*.

The Pale. The key administrative area of Ireland under Norman/English rule from the 12th to the 16th centuries. It centered on Dublin but included parts of the modern counties of Louth, Meath, and Kildare.

palfrey. A cheaper breed of horse that carried knights or men-at-arms to battle; not a charger. See also *warhorses*.

***Pancerna* cavalry.** In Polish, "jazda pancerna." Before 1648 they were known as "Cossack cavalry" ("jazda kozacka"), and in their earlier days had been raised in fact from *Cossack* hosts. Later, the term Cossack meant any horseman, registered or not, armed with saber, bow, and spear. From 1648, "Pancerna" was used for Polish medium cavalry to distinguish them from the Zaporozhian and Cossack light cavalry. They used sabers in preference to lances but also bows and short spears; many wore little or no armor. They were thus much cheaper to raise and maintain than *hussars*, whom they progressively replaced over the course of the 17th century until the Pancerna constituted 80 percent of Polish cavalry. By 1650 they were no longer predominantly Cossack by origin but were mainly Poles who rode and fought in the Cossack style. They sometimes employed the *caracole* in battle and generally rode on the flanks or in front of infantry columns on the move. The same style of cavalry in Lithuania was known as "Petyhorcy."

Panipat, Battle of (December 17, 1398). *Timur* invaded north India in September 1398. On the strategic plain of Panipat, 90 miles north of Delhi, his Timurid army crushed the host of the *Delhi Sultanate*. That left Delhi open to sack and burning. For ten days the Timurids ran amok, killing, raping and looting, in accord with Timur's normal cruelty and habits.

Panipat, Battle of (April 21, 1526). A major battle fought between an invading army under *Timur*'s grandson, *Babur* (1483–1530), and the *Delhi Sultanate*, whose forces were led personally by Sultan Ibrahim Lodi. Delhi's army included nearly 1,000 elephants. Its 40,000 infantry and horse cavalry far outnumbered Babur's 10,000–15,000 Afghans, Mongols, and Turks. The Indian army was armed in the manner traditional to the subcontinent, with swords, javelins, and bows. Babur's troops carried those weapons but also had cannons and muskets. Babur formed a defensive line with his right wing abutting the town of Panipat and protected by cavalry. On his left his troops felled trees to form field obstacles parallel to his flank, where he placed some cavalry. He concentrated musketeers and artillery at the center behind field works made from hundreds of overturned wagons lashed together to form a *Wagenburg*. Babur placed his cavalry reserve to the rear, ready to exploit breaks in the Indian lines. The battle would turn on action at the center where Babur's firepower was concentrated. Knowing this, Babur ordered harassing fire and cavalry forays to provoke an Indian attack on his strong defensive position. But for a week the lumbering Indian army refused the bait, and in fact did little, if anything, as its commanders argued over strategy and who should exercise command authority.

On April 19 Babur ordered a night attack in force. Although it became disoriented and was largely ineffective, it finally provoked the Sultan to attack. At sunrise on April 21 Ibrahim ordered his host to advance toward the Afghans. His elephant corps did little, either because Ibrahim held them back as a reserve or due to the elephants' fear and indiscipline in face of the unfamiliar noise of cannon and musketry. This left the Indian infantry to advance alone in three columns, line abreast. Ibrahim aimed at Babur's right in an effort to flank the Afghans with his main force. Babur's right held, musketeers and artillery doing severe damage to the Delhi infantry. As the Indians were strung out across the center-right, Babur attacked into their semi-exposed flank. Meanwhile, he ordered cavalry on the left to encircle the Indian rear areas while his cavalry reserve charged through gaps left in the wagon line into the floundering Indian infantry. Musketeers, cannon, and now cavalry made a great slaughter of the Indian ranks. When it was over perhaps 20,000 Delhi troops were dead, carpeting the path to a new empire in north India. After the battle most of the Sultan's elephant drivers switched sides and swore allegiance to Babur. Within the week he took Delhi and established the *Mughal Empire*.

Panipat, Battle of (November 5, 1556). Troops loyal to the teenage emperor *Akbar*, grandson of *Babur*, defeated an Indian army at Panipat north of Delhi, preserving Mughal rule in India. Once more, a vastly numerically superior (100,000) Indian army was bested by a smaller (20,000) Mughal force that had superior discipline and more and better gunpowder weapons. Akbar's army used modern artillery obtained from the Portuguese to support mobile Mughal cavalry and smash the elephant and infantry corps of the forces trained and once led by *Sher Khan*. After the battle Akbar shrewdly incorporated many prisoners into the Mughal army, thus consolidating Mughal rule in north India.

papacy. See *Albigensian Crusade*; *Cambrai, League of*; *Catholic Church*; *Charles V, Holy Roman Emperor*; *corpus mysticum*; *Counter-Reformation*; *Crusades*; *Ecumenical Councils*; *Elizabeth I*; *Great Schism*; *Guelphs and Ghibellines*; *Henri IV, of France*; *heresy*; *Holy Roman Empire*; *Hus, Jan*; *Hussite Wars*; *Index Librorum Prohibitorium*; *Inquisition*; *Italian Wars*; *Italy*; *just war tradition*; *Line of Demarcation*; *Lollards*; *Pax Dei*; *prohibited weapons*; *Protestant Reformation*; *real patronato*; *res publica Christiana*; *Thirty Years' War*; *Treuga Dei*; *two swords, doctrine of*; *Urban VIII*; *War of the Eight Saints*; *Westphalia, Peace of*.

Papal States. The Catholic popes controlled significant territories in central Italy under land grants dating to a succession of Carolingian kings of the Franks in the 8th century. Their more expansive territorial claims were based on a title rooted in a clear forgery: the infamous "Donation of Constantine." This parchment purported to document a 4th-century grant of vast central and south Italian lands to the popes by the Emperor Constantine I, the first Christian ruler of the Roman Empire. Papal power over temporal affairs inside Italy thereafter waxed with the talents and fortunes of several powerful popes during the early decades of struggle with the German emperors of the *Holy Roman Empire* over "Investiture" of clergy and related issues, a contest that occupied much of the 11th–12th centuries. Gregory VII (1073–1085) set the marker for superior papal claims and was the first pontiff to envision a papal army (militia Sancti Petri) to enforce them. Warrior popes were heavily engaged during the wars of *condottieri* in Italy. Along with the influence exercised by popes over devout and powerful Catholic princes, the papacy was a significant secular as well as spiritual authority. The nadir of medieval papal authority and influence was reached in 1303 when a protracted dispute with France led Philip the Fair to send an army to Rome to kidnap Boniface VIII, who had threatened to excommunicate the French king. This began the "Avignon Captivity" of the popes, a period which saw a dramatic weakening of ecclesiastical—not just papal—authority throughout Europe and left the Papal States rudderless within Italy.

This baleful episode was followed by the *Great Schism*, by the end of which no fewer than three popes claimed Peter's crown and struggled to control the See of Rome and the Papal States. During the *Italian Renaissance* the Papal States were expanded by successive warrior popes who made war and intrigue with the same fury and disdain for personal morality and restraint as secular princes. Like other Italian city-states, the Papal States were swept into conflict between outside Great Powers known as the *Italian Wars* (1494–1559), during which Rome was sacked and occupied (1527) by troops sent to punish the pope by *Charles V*. Five hundred years of Guelph instinct and policy strained to oppose this powerful emperor, but to do so could only weaken the Catholic cause in Germany at the outset of the *Protestant Reformation*. Also, popes were forced to maneuver between Catholic France on one side and Catholic *Habsburg* power in Austria and Spain on the other. It was a balancing act they performed with ever greater difficulty in the 16th century and at which they failed entirely during the great religious wars of the first half of the

17th century. See also *Cambrai, League of*; *Carafa War*; *Catholic Church*; *Henri IV, of France*; *Italy*; *Philip II, of Spain*; *Urban VIII*; *War of the Eight Saints*.

Suggested Reading: Owen Chadwick, *Popes and European Revolution* (1981); J. A. Thompson, *Popes and Princes, 1417–1517* (1980).

Pappenheim, Graf zu (1594–1632). Imperial and mercenary cavalry general. Raised a Lutheran, Pappenheim converted to Catholicism and served the Catholic side in the *Thirty Years' War*. Like *Gustavus Adolphus* Pappenheim was a student of Polish cavalry tactics, preferring their aggressive shock techniques to the overly dainty *caracole*. He taught Polish skills to his regiment of cuirassiers. He fought in Bohemia and the Rhineland from 1618 to 1622, and in Italy. At the head of a Bavarian army he savagely repressed a peasant uprising in Upper Austria (May–November 1626). This accorded with a general reputation throughout his career for brutality, pillaging, and rough enforcement of *contributions*. It was Pappenheim who stormed and sacked *Magdeburg* (May 20, 1631), butchering its population in the worst atrocity of an atrocious war. At *First Breitenfeld* (1631) a precipitous charge by his cuirassiers unsettled the Imperial lines, but then his troopers broke and ran before Gustavus' musketeers and a counterattack by Finnish horse. He nearly won the day with a late charge into disarranged Swedish horse at *Lützen* (1632), but was instead killed by a cannonball. His men galloped off and the battle was lost. See also *Maastricht, Siege of (June–August 1632)*.

> *Pappenheim . . . sacked* Magdeburg, *butchering its population in the worst atrocity of an atrocious war.*

parapet. Earth or stone defense works raised to screen defenders from enemy observation and provide extra cover against hostile fire. In permanent fortifications it protected against missiles, whether arrows or shot, and so was raised on top of the main wall or earthen rampart. In field works it was no more than a bank of earth quickly made by piling dirt removed from the trench along the side of the trench facing the enemy. It hid defenders while absorbing shot, especially from artillery. At its foot was a raised firing step called a "banquette."

parcq en champ. A siege camp.

"Pardon of Maynooth." See *Kildare Rebellion*.

parias. Tribute paid by the *taifa states* of *al-Andalus* to Iberian Christian states. "Parias" was paid in place of annual *razzia* that Christians otherwise inflicted on Muslim cities of the south. Among the Muslim cities that paid this protection money were Badajoz, Granada, Seville, Toledo, and Zaragoza.

Parlement (of Paris). The highest court under the French king; not a representative assembly. A prime function was to register royal edicts, which it frequently refused to do during the *French Civil Wars* (1562–1629) when it was dominated by radical Catholics. There were also seven provincial "parlements."

Parliament. See *Charles I, of England*; *Cromwell, Oliver*; *English Civil Wars*; *Estates*; *New Model Army*.

Parma, duque di (1545–1592). Né Allesandro Farnesse. Son of *Margaret of Parma*. The fourth in a line of Spanish commanders sent north by *Philip II* to crush the Dutch revolt. Under his cousin, *Don Juan of Austria*, Parma led the Spanish cavalry in routing a Dutch army at Gembloux (1578). When Don Juan died, Parma replaced him as governor and set out to moderate Spanish policy in Catholic Flanders while reducing Protestant outposts by force. This policy backfired. In 1579 his troops sacked *Maastricht*, murdering over 10,000 civilians. He took Tournai in 1581 and Bruges, Ghent, and Ypres in 1584. With the outposts taken he conducted a *Siege of Antwerp*, which fell in 1585 after holding out for 14 months. *Zutphen* surrendered to his siege in 1586. He failed to join his army with the escorts of the *Invincible Armada* in 1588, a plan he opposed from the start. The next year Parma reluctantly intervened in the *French Civil Wars* on Philip's orders, again a plan he opposed in preference for using his military resources against the Dutch rebels. See also *Eighty Years' War*; *Netherlands*.

Parthian shot. "Parting shot." Firing a bow to the rear while fleeing on horseback. The light cavalry of the ancient Parthian Empire, which also deployed heavy armored cavalry, was noted for this skill. Few later cavalries, other than those of steppe nomads such as the *Mongols*, could make the shot.

partisan (1). A *halberd* type marked by a long central spike flanked by double side blades of various forms. Closely related to the *gisarme*, it was used mainly by foot soldiers in the 16th and 17th centuries. Also used in reference to militia or other soldiers armed with this weapon.

partisan (2). A lightly armed irregular soldier used to forage, scour and scorch the countryside, lay in ambush, and to attack and harrass isolated outposts. The term originated in the German "Parteigänger" or "Partisanen," irregular troops employed by Austrian dukes and emperors. They were mostly Croats, Serbs, and Greeks who fought the Ottomans in the 16th–17th centuries along the *Militargrenze* frontier where cross-border raids were common and warfare was endemic, even a way of life. The modern meaning of volunteer fighters resisting a foreign occupation, or guerilla warriors, did not apply in this period.

pasavolante. A 16th–17th century standardized gun of the *culverin* type. It weighed about 3,000 pounds and fired 6-pound *shot* to an effective range of 1,000 yards and a maximum range of 4,500 yards.

Passau, Convention of (1552). A treaty between *Ferdinand I* in behalf of his brother, *Charles V*, and the Protestant princes of the so-called "Fürstenverschwörung" or "Conspiracy of Princes." Charles conceded partial religious toleration for Lutherans in northern Germany. Passau left unresolved key questions such as the secularization of church lands, control of disputed bishoprics, and rights to consecrate Protestant bishops. See also *Augsburg, Peace of*; *Edict of Restitution*; *Schmalkaldic League*.

pata. A long Indian sword with attached gauntlet that grasped an iron bar as a handle. It was wielded like a lance or spear as well as serving as a cutting weapon. It was used primarily by *Maratha* cavalry.

patache. A small Spanish reconnaissance ship. They were an integral part of most treasure fleets. The type was closely related to the *zabra*.

Patay, Battle of (1429). See *Hundred Years' War*; *Jeanne d'Arc*; *Talbot, John*.

patis. See *appatis*.

patron. In Mediterranean *galley* warfare, the commander of a single galley. See also *captain*.

pauldrons. French: "epaulière." Also called "spaudlers." Plate armor for the shoulders. As they grew in size *gardebraces* were sometimes added to their back side.

Paul IV (1476–1559). Né Giovanni Pietro Carafa. *Counter-Reformation* pope. See *Carafa War*; *Elizabeth I*; *expulsion of the Jews*; *Index Librorum Prohibitorium*; *Inquisition*; *Philip II, of Spain*.

Pavia, Battle of (February 23–24, 1525). The climactic battle of the opening half of the *Italian Wars* (1494–1559), and one confusing and obscured to historians by the dense fog in which it was fought. In January 1525 *Francis I* led a combined force of 24,000 French and 4,000 Swiss into northern Italy and laid siege to Pavia. The local militia of 6,000 held out until an Imperial army of 23,000 arrived to relieve it, led personally by *Charles V*. The Imperials failed in an initial effort to break through the French trenches. They dug *lines of circumvallation* around the French lines and each side deployed artillery. Francis had about 50 cannon of various types and calibers; Charles had fewer than twenty. Neither bombardment had much effect on dug-in positions. In a daring night attack, partly concealed by wild weather and a fresh bombardment, Imperial troops crossed a small river and caught the left of the French position by complete surprise. Three thousand Spanish under the *Marchese di Pescara*, victor of *La Bicocca*, used their "Spanish muskets" to great effect. Maneuvering independently of pike protection but sheltering behind trees and hedges, they poured fire into the French flank, joined by 1,500 Basque crossbowmen. The garrison in Pavia saw its chance and attacked the few French left in the siege trenches, showing no mercy. In an action that took less than two hours, musketeers and archers killed 8,000 French.

French cannon proved of little use since their rate of fire was too slow to turn the tide of the assault. Francis I was captured, and held in Spain until he agreed to end his claims in Italy and Burgundy (a promise he renounced immediately upon his release). It is often written that Pavia ended the era of armored lancers on heavy horses. That is not so. Noble cavalry units remained active all through the *French Civil Wars* (1562–1629), for instance. Pavia shook their reputation for effectiveness, but it did not eliminate them from battle. What Pavia decided was the fate of Italy for several generations, ensuring that it remained an Imperial protectorate to be exploited for decades as a source of revenue and a recruiting ground for Habsburg *tercios* thrown against the enemies of Spain and the Empire. Although the long and mutually impoverishing Italian Wars continued for another three decades, there was almost no change in territorial holdings or in the regional balance of power after the French defeat at Pavia, nor was there another major set-piece battle for nearly a generation. This was because opponents of Charles V, an excellent cavalry soldier who showed his mettle at Pavia, were unwilling to meet the deadly tercios on the field of battle. Instead, they cleaved to cautious campaigns of maneuver or hunkered down inside stout fortifications defended by artillery towers and skilled musketeers. See also *Alba, Don Fernando Álvarez de Toledo, duque de*; *German Peasant War*; *Henry VIII, of England*.

Suggested Reading: Angus Koustam, *Pavia 1525: Climax of the Italian Wars* (1996); Catherine Whistler, *The Battle of Pavia* (2003).

pavisade. A large but movable wooden shield wall employed on warships from the 13th to the 15th centuries. While they blocked arrows and other early missile weapons, the advent of effective *arquebuses*, *swivel guns*, and other gunpowder *cannon* overwhelmed them and made all wooden shielding obsolete.

pavisare. Shield-bearers who were tasked to protect crossbowmen with their "pavois" (great bucklers) or "*pavise*" while the archers reloaded.

pavise. A large, oblong, convex shield made of wood and hide and used at sea as well as in land warfare. Possibly originating in Pavia, the land versions were about five feet high and just over two feet wide, and had wood braces and spikes along the lower edge that enabled them to stand unaided in soft ground so that archers could fire from behind cover. Some *pervase* had ring-and-stave assemblies that allowed them to be propped at an angle like a modern picture frame. Late models had a firing slot cut out of the top edge enabling crossbowmen or arquebusiers to fire at shoulder height. See also *hackbut*; *pavisade*.

Pax Dei. "Peace of God." Efforts by the Medieval Church, supported by a broad lay movement to protect lands, property, and persons (clergy and nuns, but also widows and the poor) in time of war by placing such persons and property under protection of the Church. It began in the 9th century and grew thereafter into a powerful social movement. It included an effort to end feuds as these led to local private wars that were destructive of public peace. In extreme cases of unrepentant marauding by magnates or kings, the Church might impose penalties of excommunication and interdict. In the same year that Pope Urban II preached the First Crusade at Clermont in 1095 against the Muslims of the Holy Land, he endorsed the Pax Dei in Europe. See also *Crusades*; *Treuga Dei*.

Suggested Reading: T. Head, and R. Landes, eds., *The Peace of God* (1992).

Pax Hispanica. "The Spanish Peace." The condition of demilitarization and relative absence of warfare in Italy after 1560 which resulted from the policies of *Philip II* and his successors. A second meaning was the period of retrenchment of Spanish power after his death which resulted from peace treaties or truces signed by *Philip III* with France (1598), England (1604), and the Netherlands (1609–1621). Finally, the term is used with respect to the absence of war in most of the territory of Spain's American colonies for several centuries after colonization. While those areas saw violent Indian rebellions and political repression, there were no interstate wars (because there were no states) such as were common in European affairs. The "Spanish Peace" would break down in the early 19th century with, and following, the wars of Latin American independence. The antonym of Pax Hispanica in meaning and in historiography of the colonial era was the *Black Legend*.

Peace of God. See *Pax Dei*.

peasants. See *Alcántara, Battle of*; *appatis*; *ashigaru*; *Aztec Empire*; *Black Death*; *Bondetal*; *Bonnets Rouges*; *Catalonia, Revolt of*; *Český-Brod, Battle of*; *Chojnice, Battle of*; *chevauchée*; *chivalry*; *Confederation of Kilkenny*; *Counter-Reformation*; *contributions*; *Cossacks*; *Devşirme system*; *Dithmarscher*; *drill*; *Edict of Nantes*; *encomienda*; *feudalism*; *Free Companies*; *French Civil Wars*; *Gardetal*; *gekokujō*; *German Peasant War*; *Gustavus II Adolphus*; *Hongwu emperor*; *Hundred Years' War*; *Hussite Wars*; *infantry*; *Jacquerie*; *Karsthans*; *kerne*; *Landsknechte*; *logistics*; *maryol taifesi*; *muskets*; *Naples revolt*; *petering*; *pioneers*; *Polish Army*; *"Poor Conrad" revolt*; *price revolution*; *Protestant Reformation*; *pulk*; *quarterstaff*; *Razats*; *Sengoku jidai*; *Sufism*; *Tard-Avisés*; *taille*; *taillon*; *Teutonic Knights, Order of*; *timariots*; *"Time of Troubles"*; *Toyotomi Hideyoshi*; *Treuga Dei*; *True Pure Land*; *war finance*; *War of the Cities*.

pedites. Foot soldiers, not *milites*.

pedrero. A short-barreled, breech-loading *swivel gun* in common use on Spanish warships. It fired stone *shot*. Also used in reference to a *mortar* that lobbed stone shot. The English term was *perrier*.

Pedro the Cruel (1334–1369). King of Castile and León. He came into his inheritance as a boy of sixteen. He murdered his female regent the next year, which provoked her sons to rebellion. Pedro had few troops and little money for the fight so he turned to the *Military Orders*, deposing their *Mestres* until he found suitable sycophants. His reign was marked by more murder (of his brother, in 1358), treachery, cruel tortures, and endless wars with Aragon and Granada. He allied with the *Black Prince* and used the infantry tactics of *Edward III* to win at *Nájera* (1367). However, he lost the trust of his foreign allies and was routed at Montiel (1369). When he tried to kill another brother he was tipped over by a page, his belly armor was raised as he turtled on the ground, and he was stabbed to death through the stomach.

> *...his belly armor was raised ...and he was stabbed to death through the stomach.*

penal settlements. Colonies initially peopled by convicts or exiled religious or political dissidents. While usually maintained by naval empires, some land powers—Russia and China—settled convicts in penal colonies in distant and unpleasant corners of their empires. São Tomé and Principe were settled by *transportation* of Portuguese convicts in the 1490s; Cape Verde also received criminal deportees from Portugal. In the 17th century England shipped criminals and political prisoners to Virginia where they were sold as indentured laborers or servants. The latter category included Irish and Scots rebels and hundreds of women captured at *Naseby* (1645). Alternately, some Scottish felons served as penal conscripts in regiments in Germany during the *Thirty Years' War*, including women prisoners.

Penenden Heath, Battle of (1648). See *English Civil Wars*.

pennant. "Pennon." At sea: A triangular or split-tailed *flag* flown by warships as a unit or royal or national designation. On land: A fork-tailed personal ensign flown by a *knight* on his lance to designate his status as a chevalier or bachelor. Larger versions were later flown by whole units of *heavy cavalry*. See also *banneret*; *Jeanne d'Arc*; *tournaments*.

pennon. A crossbar below the lethal tip of a lance to limit its penetration of an enemy's body by making contact with his ribs. This permitted it to be more easily extracted and used again.

peones. Spanish foot soldiers, as distinguished from *men-at-arms* and *jinetes*.

Pequot War (1636–1637). Imperial, racial, and religious tension led to individual atrocities by Pequot Indians and English colonists against one another in 1636. This turned into open, communal war in 1637. Settler *militia* and Mohican Indian allies, and some Narragansetts, launched a punitive expedition in May. On June 5 they took a stockaded Pequot settlement near

Stonington (Mystic), Connecticut, by surprise and overcame the defenders. The Connecticut militia proceeded to slaughter nearly 600 Indians, including women and children. Most Mohican braves departed, refusing to murder the women and children. The few survivors who escaped were hunted down and killed on July 13. The settlers lost just two killed and 20 wounded. Further expeditions, along with Indian slavery, subsequently destroyed the Pequot nation.

permanent navies. The third Ming emperor, *Yongle*, commissioned transoceanic voyages by Admiral *Zheng He* from 1405 to 1433 in ships that outclassed all others in the world. However, in 1433 the Xuande emperor dry-docked the fleet, forbade overseas trade, and banned new construction of ocean-capable ships. Some Italian city-states had small but permanent navies from the 13th century. Venice maintained a navy that peaked at about 300 ships in 1450 (with some hulls and guns kept in storage in peacetime in the Venice Arsenal). This galley fleet protected and carried out Venice's vital trade with the dangerous eastern Mediterranean. The Ottomans began to acquire a permanent navy under *Bayezid I* from 1390. Under *Bayezid II* a century later they expelled the Venetians from the eastern Mediterranean. While the Atlantic states had large fleets of ocean-going vessels (the United Provinces had 1,800 by the 1560s), they only deployed true permanent navies in the 16th–17th centuries. See also *Armada Real*; *Barbarossa*; *charter company*; *Cinque Ports*; *convoy*; *cruising*; *flota*; *galleon*; *Great Ships*; *Invincible Armada*; *Lepanto, Battle of (October 7, 1571)*; *piracy*; *privateer*; *Royal Navy*; *Sea Beggars*.

"Perpetual Peace." Following a crushing defeat of the Swiss confederate army at *Marignano* (1515), the Cantons agreed to the Peace of Noyon with France establishing a "perpetual peace" between the two nations. It lasted 300 years, until the wars of Napoleon Bonaparte.

perrier. A 16th-century, large-caliber *artillery* piece that fired only stone *shot*. Its thin barrel meant it was often undercharged by gunners to reduce risk to themselves. This meant it hurled stone at low velocity. The Spanish term was *pedrero*.

Persia. The European name for *Iran*. More exactly, Persia (Persis) was the name of the province of Fars (Pars), lying along the southwest "Persian Gulf" coast.

Peru, Viceroyalty of (1544). The Spanish administrative area from 1544 to 1739. It encompassed all Spanish possessions in South America, including Brazil from 1580 to 1640 (when Portugal and its empire were annexed to Spain), and what is today Panama but was then part of Colombia (or rather, "Peru"). The other Viceroyalty was *New Spain*. See also *Black Legend*; *conquistadores*; *Council of the Indies*; *encomienda*; *Inca Empire*; *Jesuits*; *Pax Hispanica*; *real patronato*; *requerimiento*.

pervase. See *pavise*.

Pescara, marchese di (1490–1525). Né Fernando de Avalos. Imperial general. Trained as a *condottieri*, he fought in the *Italian Wars* for *Charles V*. He won at *La Bicocca* in 1522, and was the great victor of *Pavia* in 1525. He was a competent general who knew how best to use his high-quality Spanish veterans to good effect by taking advantage of position and terrain, as at La Bicocca, or novel tactics, as at Pavia.

petering. Making crude saltpeter from animal or human manure. It became a major peasant industry in Europe, which lacked large saltpeter deposits and so had to import expensive supplies from China.

petite mottes. See *corning/corned gunpowder*.

petrariae. See *petrary*.

petrary. A generic term for any medieval stone-throwing siege engine, though sometimes excluding the well known *catapult* and *trebuchet*.

petronels. Mounted *arquebusiers*, originally firing stone ammunition.

petty officer. A senior rating on a warship.

peytral. Equine *plate armor* that protected the chest of a *warhorse*. See also *armor*; *chanfron*.

Pfenningmeister. "Penny master." The officer in charge of a *Landsknechte* company's common funds.

phalanx. See *drill*; *infantry*.

Philip II, of Spain (1527–1598). Son of *Charles V*; king of England, 1554–1558; king of Naples, 1554–1598; king of Spain, 1556–1598; king of Portugal (as Philip I), 1580–1598; son-in-law to *Catherine de Medici*. Philip first exercised power as regent in Spain at age sixteen. As his father declined, despaired, and was defeated in Germany, Philip was made king of Naples in 1554 and the next year sovereign in the Netherlands. In 1556 he succeeded his father as king of Spain and thus also of most of South and Central America. His conquest of the Philippines in 1565 would make him ruler of the first true globe-spanning empire, albeit one superficially united at best and lacking geographical, legal, or cultural cohesion. He invaded and seized the vacant crown of Portugal in 1580, adding its vast overseas empire—coastal Brazil and key African and Indian coastal enclaves—to Spain's. He resided in Portugal only from 1580 to 1583. The aggressive spirit of his imperialism was captured in his motto "Non suffict orbis" ("The World Is Not Enough"). He anchored one end of his grand strategy in the reserves of wealth and strength of Castile; he failed completely to anchor the other end in the rising modern economy and human capital of the Netherlands. His main hope was to consolidate that rich *Habsburg* province as a bulwark of Catholic and Spanish power, via thorough re-Catholicization, military occupation, and suppression of Calvinist and other "heresy" through the *Inquisition*. Instead of adding to Spain's strength his policies provoked the *Eighty Years' War* (1568–1648) that slowly bled Spain white, drained its coffers, and fatally eroded its power and prestige.

Limits of Absolutism

The Spanish Empire was a vast undertaking and its complex finances Philip's main concern. Somehow, he had to find the money to maintain a hugely expensive standing army of 90,000 fighting in Flanders fields. Reinforcing these troops from Italy and Castile was done via the *Spanish Road*, which meant keeping thousands more troops in garrisons. Another 70,000 troops manned the overseas empire. He also needed to build and maintain an immense navy required to hold together a seaborne empire that at his death girdled the globe. He was usually at war on several oceans and continents at once. That meant not merely building warships, but harbors, warehouses, overseas bases, and all the paraphernalia of world naval power and empire. And since he lost several fleets in battle in whole or part, he had to rebuild more than once. The best recent scholarship argues that Philip indeed pursued a "grand strategy" of empire, and that he well might have succeeded but for the independent and chance course of events. Also intervening were the restraints of his personality. Fortune and character allowed lesser powers—in particular, the Netherlands and England—to frustrate his grand design and defeat his ambitious plans. Among his negative personal traits was an inability to let go the minutest detail of administration: Philip spent the greatest part of his adult life diligently reading and signing in person literally hundreds of petitions and itemized bureaucratic orders each day. In the end this tendency to micro-management overwhelmed him psychologically and badly hampered Spain's responses to mounting crises on multiple fronts.

Like most monarchs of his day, Philip did not really understand state finance. As a result, and despite the flow of treasure ships carrying New World gold and silver to his coffers, he faced constant money worries and serial bankruptcies which undermined his strategic plans and led to repeated mutinies. Spanish troops mutinied in 1576, then sacked Antwerp with such wanton murder and mayhem their depredations are remembered still as the "Spanish Fury." The *Army of Flanders* mutinied no fewer than 46 times between 1572 and 1607. The main grievance was the inability of Philip II or his son and successor, *Philip III*, to pay soldiers' wages many months in arrears. This situation was not helped by Philip II's naval policy, where he imposed embargos on all trade with the United Provinces from 1585 to 1590 and on English trade from 1585 to 1604 (the latter period including continuation of the embargo by Philip III from 1598 to 1604). At times money concerns so overwhelmed Philip that he took recourse in feigned illness and prolonged convalescence: consumed with fiscal and strategic worries and fretting over details of his plans for dispatching an armada to invade England, he stayed in bed from February to July, 1587.

A devout Catholic, with all that meant on the part of a 16th-century monarch, Philip believed he had a divinely anointed mission to crush Protestantism in Europe and that God would aid him directly in this effort. He spent state funds lavishly on devotional edifices such as El Escorial, his great monastery-like palace and retreat which cost as much as the 1588 Armada. He spent more endowing or building churches, pilgrimages, mausoleums, reliquaries, and shrines. Such pious projects importantly underlay his chronic penury, but were inseparable from why he made policy as he did. As much from piety as politics, he launched Spain on a perpetual crusade to crush the Calvinist rebellion in Flanders, later reaching out to cower heretic England as well. His messianic faith led him to rely on miracles where he knew his resources were actually insufficient to meet his military goals. This led to baffled interpretation of his military defeats as an expression of divine judgment on his statecraft. He once chided an official whose zealotry was less than his own: "You are engaged in God's service and in mine—which is the same thing." To pious ends, he encouraged the terrible persecutions of the Spanish Inquisition at home, sent rude Inquisitors north to scour Flanders, supported *Jesuit* missions throughout his overseas empire, and established courts of Inquisition in Lima and Mexico City by 1570. This devotion to the *Counter-Reformation* did not mean that Philip always got on well with popes. Far from it: in 1557, Pope *Paul IV* excommunicated Philip and declared war on Spain. The pontiff was tamed within a few months when Philip cut off Rome from its Sicilian grain supplies as a demonstration of whose sovereign writ really ran in Italy. Thenceforth, Philip was deeply involved in wider church politics and in the affairs of the *Papal States*, intervening with money and threats to prevent the election of popes who opposed him.

> *"You are engaged in God's service and in mine—which is the same thing."*

Grand Strategy

Philip's "grand design" was encouraged by a paralysis of French diplomacy resulting from forty years of confessional civil war between *Huguenots* and Catholics. That left Philip free to intervene in France when he chose, rather than face the stratagems of a powerful once and future foe of his and other Habsburg designs. France's misfortune was also Spain's external opportunity: Philip was thus free to prosecute a long war against the Dutch rebels in Flanders. Even as that crisis deepened and a naval war expanded to all the world's oceans, in Granada a major rebellion by the "Moriscos" broke out and in 1570 the *Ottoman Empire* resumed a naval war in the eastern Mediterranean when it attacked Cyprus. Yet, Philip failed to take full advantage of the *French Civil Wars* to hamstring France permanently. He was instead repeatedly drawn into futile conflict with the Ottoman Empire, as his father had been, and with the *Barbary States*. At *Lepanto* (1571), Philip's galley fleet destroyed the Ottoman galleys and killed 40,000 men. That was the great victory in the eastern Mediterranean which for decades had eluded his father. Did Philip follow up with occupation and fortification of the eastern islands, and a Mediterranean alliance? His attention was instead drawn to wars in other parts of his empire. The triumph of Spanish naval forces was thus ephemeral as the Ottomans remade their ship losses remarkably quickly and forced a truce on Philip in 1578. Philip had appeared a colossus, but rapid Ottoman rebuilding of their Mediterranean fleet and catastrophic loss of his own armada in the Atlantic in 1588 eliminated any geostrategic advantage to be gained from Lepanto. All that was worsened by his serial bankruptcies and the continued success on land and growing success at sea of the Dutch "beggars."

In 1554 Charles V arranged a dynastic marriage of Philip and *Mary Tudor*. Philip spent fourteen dreary months in England but never learned to love his wife or win over suspicious Protestant subjects. He abandoned Mary to a hysterical-pregnancy depression and a lonely death in 1558. When the outwardly Catholic but inwardly Protestant *Elizabeth I* ascended the throne Philip offered to marry her to continue the alliance of England and Castile. She demurred. At first Philip supported her, but as she moved to establish Protestantism a diplomatic revolution occurred that aligned Protestants in Scotland and England with Dutch rebels against Philip. During decades of cold war between England and Spain Philip indulged a mounting messianism that it was God's plan that he annex England. To that end he plotted against Elizabeth's life and throne with *Mary Stuart*, whom Elizabeth had under close arrest. (Similarly, he paid for the assassination of *William the Silent*). These plots were discovered by *William Cecil* and, as an eminent historian put it: they "turned England from a neutral observer into a covert enemy." Several times Philip thought of invading England, but pulled back. However, when Elizabeth finally executed Mary Stuart in 1587, he made the decision for war. In his mind the conquest of England—like his invasion of Portugal seven years earlier—was essential to the security of Spain, a form of defensive imperialism. In the spring of 1588 the *Invincible Armada* sailed on a mission to carry out what in weak private code Philip called "my Enterprise of England," which he saw as the solution to all his military problems. Instead, the Armada was scattered and broken by English fireships and the "Protestant Wind" that blew from the Channel to the North Sea. The next year, an Anglo-Dutch fleet burned surviving ships and put ashore landing parties to wreak stores and terrify Philip's subjects. He rebuilt the fleet at great cost and planned to try again, even as he was drawn into the climactic battles of the French Civil Wars.

Tragedy

Now God, too, failed Philip: his fleets were wrecked, his armies dashed and defeated, his treasury as empty as his hopes, and a lifetime of pious service rewarded only with personal tragedy (he buried several wives and children) and political and military failure. These were crushing blows, for Philip genuinely believed in direct divine intervention in the affairs of nations and sovereigns. He had no truck with Machiavellian "fortuna," instead believing that "God will find a way" where material resources were lacking and men proved wayward. Yet, battles had been lost to heretic armies and fleets sunk as storms blew unpredictably on God's high seas. What did God want from him? How was it that he had failed his Lord? His last years were consumed with these thoughts. In 1597 his armies in France and the Netherlands mutinied yet again, as did his navy; both refused to fight and he had not the will or the money to make them. In the famous imagery of one of Philip's soldiers, Miguel de Cervantes (1547–1616), a lifetime spent tilting at Protestant windmills had emptied Philip and ruined Spain. Nor was it over: Philip set Spain on a course that led to another fifty years of losing war in Flanders, and more decades of war with the Ottomans and unbowed Barbary emirates, and with France. Philip's wars were so costly in blood, treasure, goodwill, and trust that Spain never recovered: throughout the caldron of confessional and Great Power warfare to the mid-17th century, his son and grandson cast new failures from the molds Philip set for them. See also *Alcántara, Battle of*; *Augsburg, Peace of*; *Catholic League (France)*; *Gravelines, Battle of*; *Guise family*; *Joinville, Treaty of*; *Netherlands*; *Pax Hispanica*; *real patronato*.

Suggested Reading: Henry Kamen, *Philip of Spain* (1997); Geoffrey Parker, *The Grand Strategy of Philip II* (1998).

Philip III, of Spain (1578–1621). King of Spain and Portugal, 1598–1621. From his father, *Philip II*, the 20-year-old Philip III inherited a nation and empire already past its fiscal and military prime and badly overcommitted to too many wars on too many fronts. The *Duke of Lerma* was Philip's "Valido" (first minister) from 1598 to 1618. They started badly by confirming the embargo against England (to 1604) and reimposing an ill-advised embargo on the United Provinces (1598–1609). The embargos damaged the Spanish economy far more than they did England or the Dutch Republic, which were spurred to build more ships and overseas entrepôts. Yet Philip also made peace: with France in 1598, England in 1604, and the Dutch in the *Twelve Years' Truce* (1609–1621). Recent scholarship contends that the embargos reflected real policy and that peace was a ruse forced on Spain by debt and exhaustion with war and intended to allow it to recover only to fight again. Yet, Philip simultaneously weakened the economy by forcible *expulsion of the Moors* from 1609 to 1614. Like his father, Philip III believed in Spain's Catholic and imperial mission and that to serve both the Dutch must be forced back into the Spanish Catholic fold. Yet, most European and even several Muslim states saw this would never happen and recognized the United Provinces as independent from 1609. Philip agreed to the *Treaty of Oñate* (1617) with the Austrian Habsburgs to set the stage for Spain to resume its war with the Netherlands and enter the *Thirty Years' War* (1618–1648) in Germany, repeating his father's key error of military overextension. In addition to the Dutch and German wars, Philip took Spain into war with Savoy and Venice (1615–1617). None of these problems were resolved by the marriage of his daughter, Anne of Austria, to *Louis XIII*. See also *Nine Years' War*.

Suggested Reading: Paul C. Allen, *Philip III and the Pax Hispanica 1598–1621: The Failure of Grand Strategy* (2000).

Philip IV, of France (1285–1314). "La bel." See *Courtrai, Battle of*; *Knights Templar*; *Philip VI, of France*.

Philip IV, of Spain (1605–1665). King of Spain, Naples, and Sicily, 1621–1665; king of Portugal, 1621–1640. Son of *Philip III* and grandson of *Philip II*. He was styled "rey planeta" ("Planet King"), claiming with an Aristotelian metaphor the central place in the political universe, presaging Louis XIV's later use of a Copernican metaphor to claim the same position, from which France had by then displaced Spain. Philip appointed *Olivares* as "Valido" (first minister), leaning on him heavily from 1621 to 1643. That was a mistake, as Olivares had overly ambitious plans that greatly exceeded Spain's ever diminishing military, economic, and diplomatic resources. Philip was a devout Catholic, raised from his first thoughts and words to sustain Spain's divinely appointed Imperial mission and the Catholic faith. He was seldom seen in public outside appearances at Mass, though in theatrical imitation of Jesus of Nazareth he washed the feet of thirty poor men each year. He oversaw war with France over the *Valtelline* in 1622 and the *War of the Mantuan Succession* (1627–1631). He presided over the last three decades of the *Eighty Years' War* (1568–1648) with the Dutch and recklessly took Spain into the *Thirty Years' War* (1618–1648) against France and Sweden; the Spanish-French war continued to 1659. In 1640 began the *Revolt of Catalonia* and the "guerra dels segadors" that lasted to 1652. Portugal also broke away in 1640 after 60 years of Spanish occupation. In 1647 Naples revolted unsuccessfully against his rule. Philip finally agreed to end the Dutch war and recognize the United Provinces in the *Peace of Westphalia* (1648). While a disastrous foreign policy leader, he is well-remembered in portraiture by some of the greatest artists of the Spanish school, including Velázquez.

Suggested Reading: J. H. Elliot, *Count-Duke of Olivares* (1986).

Philip VI, of France (1293–1350, r.1328–1350). "The Fortunate." Immediately upon his ascent to the throne, which he gained with aid from a narrow interpretation of *Salic Law*, he moved to crush the Revolt of Flanders that had gained ground with the Flemish militia victory at *Courtrai* (1302) over the knightly army of Philip IV. Philip VI's army defeated the Flemish militia at *Cassel* (1328), and he restored his vassal as Count of Flanders. His dispute over feudal vassalage with *Edward III* was a casus belli of the *Hundred Years' War* (1337–1453).

Philiphaugh, Battle of (September 13, 1645). The *Marquis of Montrose* had taken Glasgow and Edinburgh with a Highland army. At the behest of

Charles I he moved south to try to rescue the lost Royalist cause in *England*. He was met by 4,000 *cavalry* under *David Leslie* at Philiphaugh. Betrayed and surrounded, the Scots were to a man put to the sword immediately or secured as prisoners to be executed later as traitors. Montrose, at the head of his cavalry, barely escaped with his life. Less fortunate were Irish prisoners and 300 Irish women captured with the baggage: all were murdered by *Covenanters* and locals.

Philippines. Starting in the 14th century, *Islam* arrived with the trade winds from India and perhaps also directly from the Arabian Gulf, making inroads in Mindanao and other southern islands. Possession of the Philippines was disputed by Portugal and Spain during negotiations over Pacific extension of the *Line of Demarcation*. The archipelago was granted to Madrid despite lying inside Lisbon's sphere. That was because it had been discovered in 1521 by Ferdinand Magellan (1480–1521) while in service to *Charles V*, King of Spain. The islands were occupied in 1565 by *Philip II*, for whom they were renamed. In 1577 Philip quashed wildly fanciful proposals by local factors, Jesuits, and a governor to use the Philippines as a base for invasions of China and Japan. And he rejected requests by settlers to expel all Muslims from the archipelago. An "audiencia" (royal court) was established at Manila in 1583. The town was fortified in 1585 and became the Spanish legal, administrative, and military forward base in Asia.

Piatka River, Battle of (1591). See *Ukraine*.

picchieri. Italian infantry of the late 15th century. They were armed with *pikes*.

Piccolomini, Ottavio (1599–1656). Italian general. He was a loyal servant of *Habsburg* masters. He fought for *Ferdinand II* in Bohemia in 1618 and as a cavalry commander in Hungary in 1619. *Albrecht von Wallenstein* made Piccolomini his aide and captain of his bodyguard in 1627. He was loyal to the Czech mercenary even after the Emperor turned against him. At *Lützen* (1632) he fought well and bravely, receiving multiple wounds. As Wallenstein flirted with treason, Piccolomini moved to the opposite camp, conspiring to do in the Czech and perhaps replace him in command. He fought in several small actions against France in the latter 1630s. He also fought at *Second Breitenfeld* (1642), losing many men and the battle. After 1648 he retired to enjoy his great wealth and many titles.

picorreurs. French light infantry used as scouts and skirmishers.

pike. An infantry spear with a deadly (to armored man or horse) three-foot iron point mounted on an eighteen-foot wooden shaft. The pike probably originated in Italy (Turin), but was most famously deployed in the *Swiss square* and Spanish *tercio*. The Swiss made the pike the principal weapon of their infantry after a near defeat of halberdiers and axemen in square at *Arbedo* (1422). But they came to the choice only slowly, after more than a century of fighting mainly with *halberds* and axes. After Arbedo the Swiss Confederation ruled that other weapons should take second place to the pike, which came to dominate their tactics and occupy the front ranks of all their squares. During the late 15th century, Swiss pike infantry upset the military balance in Europe when they formed tightly disciplined and ferociously aggressive squares ("Haufen") to block, and then to defeat and destroy, the *heavy cavalry* of *Charles the Rash*. They did this twice in 1476, at *Grandson* and *Morat*, and again at *Nancy* in 1477. Imitative pike formations developed as offensive infantry in 15th- to 17th-century warfare in Europe, based on these Swiss successes. Most notably, the German *Landsknechte* became direct competitors. Later-period pikes grew to monstrous lengths. In 1486 German troops were recorded as carrying ash-wood pikes 24 feet long; pikes up to 30 feet long were carried by some Swiss against the Burgundians. Such ponderous weapons were unwieldy if carried on the shoulder when marching: they vibrated badly with each rhythmic footfall. Instead, they were dragged on the ground behind each pikeman, or they were bundled and hauled to battle in carts.

In combat, pikes were held with both hands, a fact that left pikemen unshielded and vulnerable to archers and other missile infantry. Normally, the first four ranks extended their pikes at varying angles calculated to hit man or horse in the waist, chest, neck, or face. All horses and most men were bright enough not to charge headlong toward impalement on a hedgehog of deadly iron-tipped spears. That many died this way, nonetheless, resulted from being pushed from behind by the forward rush and momentum of the back ranks of their own side. To avoid this, some cavalry thinned their lines. More often, it became standard tactics to move archers or *arquebusiers* forward to break up the defending pike formation so that the heavy cavalry could charge into gaps created in the ranks and files and break it up further with lance and saber. In the typical new-measure-prompts-countermeasure pattern of all tactics and war, that device was countered by placing archers and musketeers inside the pike squares, or at its corners as in the Spanish tercio, or on its wings, from where they ran to the back of the square after firing off their weapon at the enemy's missile troops. Such changes were incremental during the 16th century as missile weapons improved and more specialists were added according to battlefield experience.

Offensively, individual pikemen were next to useless because of the sheer unwieldiness of their weapon and their immobility and vulnerability if caught in the open. Pikemen therefore drilled in moving together, leveled pikes to the forefront with back ranks holding their spears vertical. Squares formed tightly packed hedges that bristled with ranks of lethal spears. Densely packed formations then moved on command into a forward trot, and kept pace to a chant or beaten drum. This presented the enemy with an unstoppable frontage of iron-tipped spears that combined *shock* with deadly momentum and penetration ("push of pike"). Facing a massed square of several thousand men, rear ranks pressing and pushing with shoulders down against the backs of men in front, the whole body moving as one, no cavalry could stand and few tried. Only another pike square might hope to hold its place in defense, pushing back after the stunning initial collision. Modern recreations have demonstrated that pike formations of 10,000 men could compress into an essentially impenetrable square 60 feet by 60 feet. Such formations pushed aside whatever resistance they met from archers or slow-firing fixed artillery, which they usually overran. Axe men and halberdiers in the back ranks then hacked apart any wounded enemy, as the square literally rose over and trod on the bodies of their enemies. Pikes were used in European warfare until the invention of the socket bayonet (1687) made every musketeer his own piker.

Pikes were also used in war in Asia. They were incorporated in Japanese armies to protect infantry archers and defend against cavalry from about 1300. However, in Japan and on the steppe, mounted archers remained the dominant arm into the 16th century. Once firearms were introduced to Japan in 1543, the pike was readily adapted to protect musketeers as well, notably by *Oda Nobunaga*. See also *Bannockburn*; *Breitenfeld, First*; *brown bill*; *Courtrai, Battle of*; *drill*; *Falkirk, Battle of*; *Frastenz, Battle of*; *Gevierthaufen*; *goedendag*; *Haiduks*; *half-pike*; *Halidon Hill, Battle of*; *La Bicocca, Battle of*; *Laupen, Battle of*; *Marignano, Battle of*; *mercenaries*; *Morgarten, Battle of*; *Näfels, Battle of*; *picchieri*; *Sempach, Battle of*; *Stirling Bridge, Battle of*; *St. Jacob-en-Birs, Battle of*.

pike court. See *run the gauntlet*.

pikemen. See *Landsknechte*; *pike*; *Swiss square*; *tercio*.

pillage. See *attrition*; *bellum se ipse alet*; *chevauchée*; *contributions*; *guerre guerroyante*; *logistics*; *raiding*; *razzia*; *requisition*.

Pilsen, Battle of (1618). See *Thirty Years' War*.

Pinkie Cleugh, Battle of (September 10, 1547). An English army of 12,000 foot and 4,000 horse crossed the Tweed into Scotland on September 1, 1547. Most were armed in the old English style, with *longbows* and *brown bills*. They were accompanied by a contingent of mercenary mounted *arquebusiers*, or "hackbutters" as the English called them, and a large *artillery train*. Offshore, a naval force added its guns to the English arsenal. A large force of Scots, perhaps 25,000, awaited them. Among them were some light cavalry, but most were infantry armed with pikes, halberds and axes, bows and *crossbows*, and handguns and claymores. On September 9 the Scottish horse was overmatched by English demi-lancers in a running fight and played no great role the following day. The English fleet, everything from *galleys* to great *galleons*, bombarded the Scots position without effective reply. The Scots infantry formed like the Swiss, into three *battles* bristling with pikes level and forward, supported by other arms. They also pushed a number of *arquebus à croc* mounted on heavy wagons toward the English position.

> ...*most were infantry armed with pikes, halberds and axes, bows and* crossbows, *and handguns and claymores.*

English offshore batteries broke the first infantry charge, then the English heavy horse were committed—regiments of "Gentlemen Pensioners" and other *men-at-arms*. As the main armies locked, the artillery did bloody work with solid and hail shot. The Scots broke, scattering as they could. English dead numbered around 500, but more than 5,000 Scots died and another 2,000 were captured. The political effects of the battle were minor: the English advanced deeper into Scotland, but met there stiff Scottish resistance reinforced by French military advisers. Troubles at home led to a desultory English departure in 1550 from Edinburgh. This was the last major battle in centuries of feudal conflict fought between national armies from England and Scotland; thereafter, war in the north had more the character of rebellion and occupation than a clash of nations. Long ignored as politically inconsequential, more recent research suggests that Pinkie Cleugh was the first "modern battle" fought in Britain, with both sides deploying new weapons and combined arms tactics imported from the wars of the continent. That was certainly true in part, but the overall reliance on traditional weapons and the relative paucity of guns, other than artillery, speaks against the further conclusion that Pinkie Cleugh was the spearpoint of the continental *revolution in military affairs* penetrating the British Isles.

pinnace. A small warship—the largest were 60 tons—but capable of *cruising*, especially maneuvering in jagged coastal waters from which larger ships steered clear. The smallest of these auxiliary warships were not much more than a large ship's boat. Some were towed to the Caribbean by *galleons* or *frigates*, where they were used in close shoreline actions and to pursue fast merchant *prizes* that might otherwise escape the slower mother ship. Some employed oars as well as sails. See also *bark*.

pioneers. Poorly paid, unskilled peasant laborers who accompanied the *artillery train*. On the march they mended roads over which the big guns passed. In a siege they dug trenches (*saps*) and mines. They were viewed as the bottom of the barrel in any early modern army and not usually counted among its regular company or considered soldiers. See also *uniforms*.

piracy. Due to the difficulties of long-distance *cruising*, in this period even more than later pirates congregated around narrow channels which other ships were forced to use: the Taiwan strait, where *wakō* lurked and preyed; the Straits of Dover, where English pirates swooped down on the trade of the *Hanse* and the "Flanders fleets" that went to and from the Mediterranean, and French pirates raided the rich Gascon wine trade with England; the Strait of Otranto off Italy's rich eastern coast; around Gibralter, where *Barbary corsairs* waited to pounce on poorly defended or unescorted ships; the Skaggerak between Denmark and Norway, through which moved heavy *cogs* and other roundships carrying the rich herring trade; and the Sicilian Channel, the only seaway that bypassed "Scylla and Charybdis" in the Strait of Messina. Medieval jurists recognized piracy as a crime in theory, but in practice there was little distinction among piracy, *war at sea*, and even "peaceful trade" prior to the mid-17th century. Until the work of *Alberico Gentili* and *Hugo Grotius* was adopted in secular international law, the law of the sea was crude and virtually nonexistent. The oceans thus remained "Hobbesian" in their legal and daily character, a realm of "war of all against all" in which the ruthless barbarity of pirates was matched in kind by royal warships, privateers, and armed merchants.

Merchants, pirate ships, and royal warships looked and fought more or less the same prior to 16th century specialization in warship design. Pirates and navies both attacked without warning, often tortured captured officers to extract information, and drowned ordinary crew or passengers who did not warrant a ransom. Peacetime piracy was tolerated in part because it produced wartime seamen useful to kings, but mostly because medieval and early modern states lacked the strong navies to counter piracy. *Henry V* was unusual in using his battle fleet to suppress English and other piracy, but the practice revived after his death as the fleet was sold off during the regency of Henry VI and as West Country pirates adopted the new *caravels*. English pirates were feared all over Europe. They were financed by merchant interests, protected by bought judges and juries, and accepted by seaside towns, where generations of pirate families lived and spent their booty. At least one "Admiral of England" owned a pirate barge. This corruption reflected the fact that Admiralty Courts provided income in the form of shares of *prizes*. Royal officers thus had a direct financial interest in tolerating piracy and the disorder at sea it created, even if that ran counter to the "national interest" by creating hostility among neutral nations and potential allies. At one time or another precisely that happened concerning Aragon, Brittany, Castile, Denmark, the Hanse, and the Netherlands. Neutrals were frequently taken on the thin excuse that they failed to acknowledge England's "*sovereignty of the sea*" by some gesture of submission. In 1449, piratical seizure of the Hanse's annual salt convoy though the Channel led to counter-seizure of all English property in the Baltic and a naval war costly to both sides. Four years later, hostile navies from *La Rochelle*, Brittany, and Castile cut off England from reinforcing its garrisons in Gascony, which the French then overran. That conclusively ended the *Hundred Years' War*. The oscillations in later English sea power and national prosperity corresponded closely with the rise and fall of the fortunes of English pirates. For instance, in the three years that followed the Armada campaign of 1588 English ships captured 299 Spanish and Portuguese prizes, an equivalent value of a full year's national income.

Sovereigns sometimes paid compensation when subjects they could not control attacked neutral shipping. But just as often monarchs profited from piracy more than from its suppression. Famously, *Elizabeth I* invested in the piratical and *privateer* adventures of the *sea dogs*, while the *corsairs* of North Africa engaged in state-supported piracy and slave trading for centuries. States did not build modern, permanent navies to be rid of pirates but to fight other states. Nevertheless, a beneficial side effect of the new navies was slow constriction of private warfare at sea beginning in the late 15th century. Even so, piracy was still endemic in the 16th and 17th centuries in select areas. In the Carribean, most pirates were Dutch, English, or French by origin, or *cimarónes* (free blacks, mainly escaped former slaves). They preyed on Spanish colonies and ships of the annual *flota*. In Jamaica, Henry Morgan (c.1635–1688) was so successful as a pirate he was knighted and made governor, which was more cost-effective than hunting him down. The Mosquito Coast of Central America was infested with English pirates from the 1630s, along with colonies of cimaroons. In times of war between Spain, England, and the Netherlands, the usual state of affairs from c.1570 to 1648, English and Dutch pirates sailed as privateers with official support from their home governments. See also *junk*; *Malta*; *Sea Victuallers*; *Zheng He*.

Suggested Reading: Angus Konstam and Angus McBride, *Elizabethan Sea Dogs, 1560–1605* (2000); James G. Lydon, *Pirates, Privateers, and Profits* (1970); So Kwan-wai, *Japanese Piracy in Ming China during the 16th Century* (1975).

pishchal. An early-16th-century Muscovite small *cannon* or heavy harquebus. It was the signature weapon of the original *pishchal'niki*.

pishchal'niki. The first Muscovite firearms troops. They were garrison artillery troops named for the small cannon they operated, the "pishchal," a heavy harquebus fired as a wall hook gun or from a stand. They evolved into mobile infantry using these guns as shoulder-borne "hand cannons" or harquebuses. Some pishchal'niki were mounted and served as *dragoons*. Others later graduated into the *strel'sty*.

pistolade. A tactic invented by *Henri IV* for the *Huguenot* cavalry. It involved riding toward enemy infantry en masse to discharge pistols at close range, then charging home with sword and *arme blanche*.

pistols. Ottoman: "tabanca." Czech: "pistala" or "firing tube." Primitive *matchlock* pistols came into use as early as matchlock *arquebuses* and *muskets*, as all developed from the same early "hand cannons." The first true pistols were made utilizing the *wheel lock*. This made them available to *cavalry* since the problem of keeping the match alight while riding was solved by discarding the match altogether. However, the effective range of these short-barreled hand guns remained just six to ten feet, so the only cavalry tactic available to pistol troops was the elegant but rather feckless *caracole*. It was widely noted by contemporary observers that pistol-bearing cavalry tended to fire while out of effective range because of the longer range of the infantry weapons they faced. Ottoman cavalry began carrying pistols in the 1600s but only as a supplement to their sabers. Design experimentation continued throughout the period, including several multi-barreled designs. A famous effort was the so-called "duck-foot pistol" which had five or more barrels fixed to a single stock in a splayed pattern. Some ship's captains were drawn to such designs, thinking they might be handy in a mutiny. Otherwise, they proved to be mere novelties. See also *hussars*; *pistolade*.

Piyadeğan militia. Turkish urban militia, often run by associations of dervishes. On occasion, they reinforced the *Seljuk* armies as well as those of minor Muslim states (*Beyliks*). Their more usual roles were to keep order in larger cities and to patrol and protect the roads and caravan routes.

Pizarro, Francisco (c.1478–1541). He was part of expeditions to coastal Colombia in 1509 and to Panama in 1519. He first encountered *Inca* outposts in northern Peru in 1528. He returned to Spain to gain a royal contract for the conquest. In 1531 he led an expedition to Peru, departing from Panama with 183 *conquistadores*, including several brothers, 37 horses, and some small cannon. He moved with caution, not advancing down the Andes until September 1532. Unbeknownst to him, but of fundamental importance in explaining his subsequent success, the Inca were in the midst of a major civil war and succession struggle. On November 16 Pizarro surprised and seized the Sapa Inca, Atahualpa, who had invited him to a parlay. The Spanish slaughtered 2,000 Inca guards with their cannon, muskets, swords, and pikes, protected from lethal wounds by their Toledo steel armor, which Inca weapons could not penetrate. Pizarro extorted a massive ransom for Atahualpa's release (a large room literally filled with gold), then murdered him anyway (July 1533). Pizarro then marched on the Inca capital at Cuzco. Reinforced with new arrivals, the Spanish fanned out from Cuzco to conquer the rest of Peru and most of northern Chile. One Pizarro brother, Juan, was killed in an Inca insurrection in 1537. Another conquistador, Diego de Almagro, who led an expedition into Bolivia and Chile, lifted an Inca siege of a small Spanish garrison in Cuzco and re-occupied the city. Pizarro sent his other brothers to defeat this rival, whom he had garrotted and beheaded (1538). Pizarro was himself killed in his home in Lima in 1541 by rebellious conquistadores allied to Almagro and enraged at his murder.

placard. Or "plackart." A thin sheet of supplementary *armor* worn over the lower *cuirass*.

place d'armes. A parade ground or concentration area for troops preparing an assault, especially if enclosed by the works and trenches of a besieging army.

place de sûreté. "Surety towns." Legally recognized fortified towns which the *Huguenots* were permitted to garrison starting with four towns named in the *Edict of Saint-Germain-en-Laye* (August 8, 1570): *La Rochelle*, La Charité, Cognac, and Montauban. The number rose to eight in the *Edict of Beaulieu* (May 6, 1576), and to nearly 200 in the *Edict of Nantes* (April 13, 1598). Thereafter, they were reduced by *Louis XIII* and *Cardinal Richelieu*, culminating in the siege of La Rochelle and revocation of the military brevets of the Edict of Nantes.

plantations. See *Cromwell, Oliver*; *Ireland*; *James I*; *New English*; *Old English*; *Ulster*.

plate armor. Shaped slabs of iron or steel worn to protect against penetrating missile weapons, and to deflect glancing blows of *swords* and spears. Plate armor only slowly supplemented *mail*. The earliest plate was the roughest iron or just hardened leather (*cuir-bouilli*), shaped to protect the critical joints at elbow and knee. Articulated plate fingers replaced "mail mittens" much later. Plates covering the lower legs were called *greaves*. Over time, plate covered the feet, calves, then all extremities. The transition started in the mid-13th century and was not completed until the late-15th-century development of the fully articulated "suit of armor." The shift away from mail was initially a response to the penetrating power of the *couched lance*. Later plate responded to missile weapons, as improved bows and crossbows and then handguns appeared on the field of battle. Its adoption was also affected by technological and economic factors. Early medieval forges were limited to making small iron blocks which were then hammered into plates that were attached to a cloth or leather garment to form a "coat of plates." Slow advances in forging technology,

> *...small iron blocks...were then hammered into plates that were attached to a cloth or leather garment...*

notably mastery of temperature-controlled forging, made larger pieces of plate possible by the 14th century. And once large pieces of plate were "mass-produced," at least by the standard of the day, in addition to offering greater protection they proved far less expensive than the labor-intensive methods required to make mail. The early *surcoat* of multiple small plates was thus replaced with a solid breastplate by the 14th century. The entire complex armor system was held together by "leathers," a generic reference to any number of leather belts and rivets which attached the various plates to each other. See also *arquebus*; *besegaws*; *bodkin*; *bracers*; *couters*; *crossbow*; *cuisses*; *elephants*; *fauld*; *gauntlets*; *gorget*; *lance* (1); *longbow*; *muskets*; *poleyns*; *sabatons*; *sarmatian armor*; *schynbalds*; *shields/shielding*; *tassets*; *vambraces*.

Pluderhosen. Outlandishly torn or heavily pleated trousers and stockings worn from the mid-16th century by *Landsknechte* infantry. They were part of an overall trend among the Landsknechte to appear tattered and wildly unconventional and became a signature feature of these German *mercenaries*.

plunder. See *Bedouin*; *chevauchée*; *conquistadores*; *contributions*; *Cortés, Hernán*; *"holy war"*; *lines of supply*; *logistics*; *magazines*; *mercenaries*; *Mongols*; *pillage*; *piracy*; *raiding*; *razzia*; *Sempach, Covenant of*; *Teutonic Knights, Order of*; *Thirty Years' War*; *Wallenstein, Albrecht von*.

poczet. "Post." The smallest unit in the *Polish Army*, equivalent to a *lance*, the medieval unit from which it evolved. It was centered on a *knight* or "comrade" ("towarzysz"), supported by retainers ("pacholeks") numbering anywhere from one to as many as twenty soldiers.

podestà. The chief executive, and therefore also the commander, of one of the communal armies of the central and northern city-states of Italy in the 12th–14th centuries.

point-blank range. Extremely close range, preferred by early gunners so that there was minimal fall of shot (due to gravity and ballistic trajectory) before it smashed into the target. This lent much greater accuracy to the most elemental aim and to correspondingly high velocity and impact force when the shot made contact. Later, the term applied to the firing range determined technically by the point at which the line of flight of a cannonball cut across the "line of metal," the gunner's line of sight looking straight down the muzzle from the base.

poison. See *Akbar*; *Assassins*; *Invincible Armada*; *logistics*; *prohibited weapons*; *rations*; *siege warfare*; *Ukraine*.

Poissy, Colloquy of (1561). See *French Civil Wars*.

Poitiers, Battle of (September 19, 1356). A key battle of the first phase of the *Hundred Years' War* (1337–1453). The English again used the tactic of the *chevauchée* to force the French to battle, this time cutting a wide swath of destruction through to the Ile-de-France. On the field at Poitiers, the *Black Prince* repeated the tactics of his father, *Edward III*, at *Crécy*: he set a defensive trap to lure the French *heavy cavalry* into range of carefully positioned and well-protected longbowmen set in flanking "V" formations. The English *men-at-arms* again fought dismounted, protected by natural obstacles on ground parallel to an old Roman road. A small cavalry detachment was held back in a nearby wood, a hidden reserve to exploit and pursue should the French files and ranks break and run. Outnumbered over two to one (13,000 French to some 6,000 English), the Black Prince remained on the tactical defensive, as his father taught him. He feigned flight of his right wing, a ruse that lured several hundred foolhardy French knights forward, accompanied by numerous German mercenaries. Most met death hissing down in flights of goose-grey arrows shot by archers aligned along the flanks. The longbowmen concentrated on the horses, using *broadhead arrows* to carve great wounds in flank or leg or chest, bringing them down and unseating their riders. The French made desperate charges, each broken by arrow storms that killed and maimed men of rank indiscriminately with common soldiers and writhing, gravely wounded *destriers*.

The French at last took account of the extreme vulnerability of their horses, dismounted and advanced on foot. That only made them slower and easier targets for the archers, who leveled their bows and fired plate-piercing shots at *point-blank range*. Once the longbowmen exhausted their arrows they drew stabbing weapons and joined the English men-at-arms in hacking and slashing at the dismounted French. The third French *battle* had not yet engaged. Observing the carnage it fled, abandoning comrades to death or capture. The infantry and dismounted men-at-arms of the first two battles who stayed, or who could not flee because of the press of their own dead and dying fellows, fought bravely but without hope. Their courage began to tell as the number of English dead mounted, too. Finally, some French broke through their swarming enemies and ran. The Black Prince now committed his cavalry reserve. His small force emerged from a nearby wood and tore into the rear of the fleeing French. As they rode down stragglers, what began as a battle turned into a bloody rout, then a gory slaughter. King Jean II ("The Good," 1319–1364) was taken prisoner. Around him the common wounded were dispatched with dirk or sword while knights were made prisoner, to be stripped of arms and armor and held for ransom. Some 1,900 French men-at-arms were taken that day. Another 2,500 knights, *sergeants* and *esquires* lay dead or dying on the field. The king was later paroled, literally for a king's ransom: France paid the equivalent of two years' national income to recover Jean II. In 1360 he was forced into a peace entirely favorable to England, the *Treaty of Brétigny*, which gave the Aquitaine as a personal fief to the Black Prince. English occupation did not sit well with the French, however, and the great war resumed in 1370. See also *Jacquerie*; *routiers*.

Suggested Reading: David Green, *The Battle of Poitiers, 1356* (2002).

Poitou, Battle of (April 15, 1622). A rare battle during the last of the *French Civil Wars* (1562–1629), the *Huguenot* loss of 2,000 men, and even more the loss of the revenues and defensible towns of Poitou, was the beginning of the end of the Huguenot state-within-a-state in southern France. Within a few years *La Rochelle* was besieged on all sides. It held out a few more years, but without hope.

Poland. Most of the population in Poland, primarily of Slavic origin, was converted to Catholicism in the 9th century. Poland formed a widely recognized if loosely organized and ephemeral kingdom from the 11th century. Poland numbered among the larger powers of the Middle Ages, expanding across the great plain between the *Holy Roman Empire* to its west and the fractured chaos of "Appanage Russia" in the east. It reached new heights under Casimir III, the Great (1310–1370, r.1333–1370), who made peace with Bohemia and the *Teutonic Knights*, consolidated the monarchy, codified Polish laws, and improved the lot of Jews and peasants in a reign that was unusually just and benign by the standards of the Age. He also invaded Ukraine, shifting Poland's strategic frontier from west to east. Following the Union of Krevo (1385), the *Jagiello dynasty* took power on condition of acceptance of Catholicism. The dynasty cemented control with a historic victory over the Teutonic Knights at *Tannenberg* (1410). During the *War of the Cities* (1454–1466), *Casimir IV* hired Bohemian mercenaries to counter the numerous Bohemian and German mercenaries in the pay of the Teutonic Knights. This greatly strained his treasury. Worse, Casimir's call-up of peasant levies could be filled only by making major concessions to noble demands for a devolution of power from the center, fatally weakening the monarchy for the long term. For the moment, however, Poland added "Royal Prussia" to its huge land holdings after securing victory in 1466.

From the middle of the 15th century a new threat appeared in the south: the advance of the *Ottoman Empire* into southeastern Europe and the Balkans. The threat drew closer with the Ottoman occupation of Hungary in 1526, severing that land's long connection to Poland-Lithuania. The *Eternal Peace* was signed with the Ottomans in 1533, formally surrendering Hungary. Four years later, Poland lost Smolensk to the *Grand Duchy of Muscovy*. In 1548 the last Jagiello king ascended the throne, *Sigismund August II* (r.1548–1572). During his reign religious tolerance was permitted and the tie to *Lithuania* was elevated to a full constitutional union (*Union of Lublin*) in 1569. Polonization of Ukraine was also advanced. Poland fought Muscovy for control of *Livonia* during the *First Northern War* (1558–1583). It came under pressure from the expanding Ottomans in the latter 16th century, and though scoring some defensive victories entered a long, tortuous military and political decline. Sigismund II's death ended the Jagiellonian line. From 1573, Polish kings were no longer hereditary but elected: the first elected king was Henri Valois, who left Poland after 118 days to become *Henri III*, of France. He was succeeded by *Stefan Báthory* of Transylvania.

Since the Polish nobility comprised 10 percent of the population compared to 2–3 percent in most of Europe, and since most nobles were fiercely egalitarian within their own ranks while highly oppressive of their peasants and disdainful of the bourgeoisie, their predominance guaranteed national weakness in a new era of increasingly powerful monarchs. Noble resistance to political centralization under the crown fatally disabled Poland when it came time to face powerful and aggressive centralized monarchies in Sweden in the 16th–17th centuries, then Russia and Prussia in the 17th–18th centuries. In 1595 the *Union of Brest* joined with the Catholic Church all Orthodox in Ukraine who objected to the claims of religious authority by the new patriarchate in Moscow. From 1606 to 1609 Protestant nobles rebelled out of fear of Catholic *confessionalism* as promoted by the Jesuits. This opposed a minority of Calvinist nobles, and some who adopted *Arian* views, against the majority of Catholic Poles. Religiously more diverse and fragmented than any other country in early modern Europe, Poland was also physically vulnerable to invasion. Essentially a broad plain dissected by several major but fordable rivers (Dnieper, Nieman, Vistula) and tributaries, it was cut off from Lithuania by marshland that formed each year after the spring rains.

The main story of 17th-century Poland is usually depicted as decline, but there were moments of expansion and renewed hope as well. *Sigismund III* occupied Moscow from 1608 to 1613 and elevated his son as would-be tsar. The Muscovite expedition failed, however, when he refused to accept *boyar* demands that Crown Prince Wladyslaw convert to Orthodoxy in order to keep the throne. Instead, it went to *Michael Romanov*: Moscow, unlike Paris, apparently was not worth the Mass. Fighting in the east continued to 1619. From 1621 to 1629 Poland fought with Sweden, losing Riga but not every battle to *Gustavus Adolphus*. The 1630s to 1640s were quieter. By 1648

Poland, a sprawling empire of eleven million souls, was twice the size of France and bigger than the European holdings of Muscovy. As Robert Frost noted: "A confederal, consensual, decentralized, multi-ethnic state had waged almost constant warfare.... It had coped with the constant threat of *Tatar* raids, and had significantly extended its borders." It also fended off invasions by Muscovy, Sweden, and the Ottoman Empire. In fact, along with Sweden, Poland was a victor in the *First Northern War* (1558–1583) with Muscovy the major loser. Given that record it is hard to accept the usual portrait of 16th- to 17th-century Poland as failing to adapt to the challenge of the *revolution in military affairs* and the centralized fiscal-military state as it developed in Western Europe, even if the 18th century would tell a different tale. See also *Sigismund I*; *Sigismund August II*.

Suggested Reading: J. K. Fedorowicz, ed. *A Republic of Nobles: Studies in Polish History to 1864* (1982); K. Friedrich, *The Other Prussia: Poland, Prussia and Liberty, 1559–1772* (2000); Robert Frost, *The Northern Wars, 1558–1721* (2000); Norman Davies, *God's Playground: A History of Poland*, vol. I (1981).

polearm. Polearms went by many names including *brown bill* and *poleax*. They were widely employed by infantry facing cavalry in Europe, the Ottoman Empire, the Mughal Empire, Central Asia, China, and Japan. Dismounted cavalry started to use them in Western Europe in the late 14th century. A polearm was any cutting or thrusting staff weapon whose lethal top spike and blade were mounted on a wooden shaft of varied length. Polearms were cousin to *halberds*, though usually mounting a smaller blade and sporting a war hammer rather than a rear-facing iron spike. They gave the wielder the option of using the top spike to punch through armor or crushing an opponents skull or breaking bones with the hammer. The blade was used to slash at infantry or the exposed legs and flanks of horses. Period fighting manuals describe polearms as good for jabbing, leveraged moves, and hacking axe blows. See also *kumade*; *naginata*.

poleax. A medieval weapon combining the features of axe and hammer, with a spike or cue on the end for repeated jabbing into the flesh of the enemy. The killing devices were mounted on a stout staff or handle. From the 14th century poleaxes were used by infantry in preference to the traditional battleaxe. They were equally effective against cavalry or infantry. See also *axes*; *halberd*; *polearm*.

poleyns. *Plate armor* shaped to fit the knees above the *schynbalds*. They were attached to *cuisses*.

Polish Army. The Polish infantry in the 14th and 15th centuries was composed of conscripts (townsfolk and peasants). These were organized by clan or region and commanded by "szlachta," noblemen bound by hereditary service obligation to the king. Large numbers of *mercenaries* were also hired, mostly Czechs and a few Silesians. Polish infantry were placed on a firm footing by *Stefan Báthory* in 1578 to supplement the predominant notable cavalry with peasant levies. Báthory set up "drafted" or "chosen infantry" ("Piechota wybraniecka"). These soldiers were freed from labor-service demands, which allowed them to develop professional military skills. Each was armed with axe, saber, and musket, and sustained by the serf and peasant population of Poland's royal estates at a tax ratio of one soldier to every twenty households. The wybraniecka had to be supplemented by traditional peasant infantry levies, as only about 2,000 were raised in any year and many of these deserted at the first sign of real fighting. Still, this system served Poland's infantry needs until the mid-17th century. Báthory also reduced the number of pikemen, halberdiers, and axemen, in favor of massed musketeer firepower. While early firearms were deployed (siege cannon, bombards, pistols, and arquebus), the main weapon remained the crossbow. Pikes, axes, and other thrusting, hacking, and slashing weapons were also in wide use among Polish infantry.

The core of the Polish Army, as befitted the feudal structure of the kingdom, was *heavy cavalry*. *Hussar* units were added as early as 1500. Starting in 1511, the Poles set up a force of 3,000 cavalry and a few hundred infantry for "General Defense" ("Obrona Potoczna"), to deal with *Tatar* raids along the southern frontier. While permanent and professional, the Obrona Potoczna was not a true *standing army* as its soldiers were part-timers who owed local lords or the king labor service. From 1566, it was known as the *Quarter Army* ("wojsko kwarciane"), from the fraction of crown income devoted to its maintenance until 1652.

> ..."*Cossack cavalry*" ...*dressed in wildly irregular ways, and used many types of weapons.*

The revenues came from Poland's royal lands, though in practice the ratio was hardly reached. The predominance of cavalry spoke to much greater requirements for mobility in the east as compared to France or Germany due to vast distances, fewer fortified towns, and flatter topography. Polish cavalry was variegated: until 1648, medium cavalry, regardless of ethnicity, were known as "Cossack cavalry" ("jazda kozacka"). These units painted their horses with red dye, dressed in wildly irregular ways, and used many types of weapons. They liked sabers in preference to lances but also used bows and short spears. After 1648, they were known as "jazda pancerna" or *Pancerna* cavalry.

The tension in the Polish Army between cavalry and infantry reflected a strategic dilemma faced by Poland: the *light cavalry* it needed to deal with the Tatars in the south were mostly useless against Swedish infantry, artillery, and field fortifications in the north, while Polish infantry and artillery needed to fight Swedes were highly vulnerable when facing Tatars. Starting in the 1630s, the army was divided into two parts: the "National Contingent" ("autorament narodowy") was sustained by the "towarzysz" system; the second part of the army, the "Foreign Contingent" ("autorament cudzoziemski"), was originally made up mostly of Tatars and Ukrainians, including *Cossacks*, but later came to include many Germans. Later, while the Foreign Contingent always employed some non-Polish mercenaries, most of its troops were in fact recruited within the vast lands of Poland-Lithuania. From 1613 to 1635 the *Sejm* steadily increased direct taxes to pay for the new army as Baltic customs duties declined. This force was tested after mid-century by a huge Cossack rebellion and war: the Khmelnitsky Uprising (1648–1654). See also *Cecora, Battle of*; *choragiew*; *Dziesietniks*; *Haiduks*; *hetman*; *karacena*; *Lisowczyks*; *poczet*; *porucznik*; *pulk*; *sejmiki*.

Suggested Reading: R. Brzezinski, *Polish Armies, 1559–1696*, 2 vols. (1987).

Polish-Lithuanian Commonwealth (*Rzeczpospolita*). See *Jagiello dynasty*; *Lithuania, Grand Duchy of*; *Poland*; *Polish Army*; *Union of Lublin*.

Polish-Muscovite War (1609–1619). See *Sigismund III*; *"Time of Troubles."*

Polish-Swedish War (1600–1611). See *Karl IX*; *Sigismund III*.

Polish-Swedish War (1621–1629). See *Gustavus II Adolphus*; *Sigismund III*.

politiques (France). In most older and some recent French historiography, "politiques" were presented as secular men of power who first appeared in the wake of the *Edict of Beaulieu* (1576), and who later looked to *Henri IV* and the *Edict of Nantes* to impose a "modern"—that is, national and non-religious—solution to the *French Civil Wars* (1562–1629). For contemporaries the term was actually a pejorative used by the *Catholic League* for any other Catholic who disagreed with their radical intolerance. The politiques are thus better understood to have been moderate Catholics who sought compromise with Protestantism for the sake of short-run peace and social order, not some early version of secular humanists. Most recent scholarship argues that the politiques sought a respite from confessional wars but not religious toleration in the modern sense. Instead, they hoped to reconvert *Huguenots* to Catholicism and thereby restore confessional and social unity to France in accord with the ancient maxim of the Gallican Church: "un roi, une foi, une loi" ("one king, one faith, one law"). Nevertheless, many were violently purged by the radicals of the League during the siege of Paris by Henri IV in 1590. When their later efforts to convert the Huguenots failed, under *Cardinal Richelieu* and *Louis XIII* most politiques abandoned their limited toleration of Protestantism in favor of a policy of national unity through suppression and enforced exile of remaining confessional dissenters.

politiques (Netherlands). Leading Dutch nobles, notably *William the Silent* and his sons *Maurits of Nassau* and *Frederik Hendrik*, who opposed repression of individual conscience on religious matters. This stance drove the politiques into political rebellion once the *Habsburgs*, starting with *Alba*, executed hundreds of nobles for "heresy" and crushed the traditional liberties of the Netherlands Estates.

Pomerania. See *Gustavus II Adolphus*; *Thirty Years' War*; *Wallenstein, Albrecht von*; *War of the Mantuan Succession*; *Westphalia, Peace of*; *Wolgast, Battle of*.

Pomest'e cavalry. In the Muscovite system, *servitors* ("pomeshchiki" or "pomest'ia") held land from the tsar in exchange for a lifetime of military obligation. Such men usually supplied their own mounts and served as the tsarist cavalry. Their numbers grew greatly with acquisition of Novgorod and redistribution of its lands. Still more served and were rewarded during campaigns in Lithuania. Unlike the Polish *hussars* who were mainly medium cavalry, the Muscovite pomest'ia remained a light force. See also *soyughal.*

"Poor Conrad" revolt (1514). "Armer Konrad." A peasant revolt centered on the Rems Valley near Stuttgart. It was sparked by imposition of new and heavy taxes by Duke Ulrich of Württemberg, with an additional grievance of government cheating of the peasants using falsified weights and measures in assessing taxes-in-kind. The revolt was brutally and swiftly repressed by the Duke's *men-at-arms* and followed by over 1,000 retaliatory beheadings of peasants. The underlying grievances were not resolved by this repression and fed into the still more violent and widespread *German Peasant War* of 1525.

Poor Knights. See *Knights Templar.*

port. See *gun port*; *port piece.*

portcullis. An iron or wood grill or grate hanging from the interior roof of the passage behind the gate of a castle or fortified town. It would be dropped to block inward passage of attackers who breached the outer gate, whereupon defenders speared the enemy or shot crossbows or handguns into them as more enemy pushed from the rear, pinning comrades against the portcullis. See also *castles, on land*; *murder holes.*

port fire. An alternate term for *quick match.*

Portland Bill, Battle of (1588). See *Invincible Armada.*

portolan chart. Sailing directions based on the collective experience of a community of maritime navigators, compiled in graphic form. Portolan charts for various coastlines were available from the late 13th century, with the first known use aboard ship in 1270. See also *maps.*

port piece. A breech-loading *swivel gun* frequently mounted on 16th-century warships and merchants. The Spanish term for this gun was *bombardetta.*

Portugal. Portugal emerged as a distinct country during the *Reconquista* (1071) and became a separate kingdom in 1143. In the early 13th century it completed conquest of the Algarve. From 1383 to 1411 it fought off neighboring Castile. It was united under the *Aviz* dynasty, beginning with Juan I, (r.1385–1433). In the 15th and 16th centuries it was the leader among all maritime powers, capitalizing on its location near Africa with easy access to the Mediterranean. The initiative was taken by *Enrique the Navigator* (1394–1460). He captured Ceuta in 1415 and founded a school of navigation from which later explorers graduated to map the coasts of Africa, India, and South America, all in search of gold, spices, and slaves. These expeditions of exploration were followed by traders, missionaries, soldiers, and settlers, as the barely one million people of Portugal—which had been ravaged by the *Black Death*—built an overseas empire on the coasts of three continents. Madeira was colonized in 1419; the Azores from 1439. Portugal again fought Castile from 1474 to 1479, with the war ending in agreement to leave the Azores and Madeira with Portugal and give the Canaries to Castile. Portugal's king might have formed a union of the crowns with Castile had not *Ferdinand* of Aragon won Isabella's hand instead. That union survived a Portuguese attempt to overthrow it, and catapulted Aragon-Castile ("Spain") to the forefront of the Reconquista and beyond Portugal in power and prestige. This trend continued with Spain's acceptance of the surrender of *Granada* in 1492. Still, the Portuguese controlled the early Atlantic slave trade and broke into the spice trade running from Cape Verde to Mozambique, India, China, and Japan.

In 1493 the pope granted Portugal a monopoly on trade in the eastern half of the globe marked by the *Line of Demarcation*, amended the next year in the Treaty of Tordesillas. In 1500 Portugal discovered and claimed Brazil, but over the next 150 years Portuguese settlers barely penetrated beyond a long strip of coastline on which they thinly settled. Portugal was never a major European or imperial power. Even against minor North African states it quickly found its military limits. A Portuguese invasion of Morocco was defeated at *Alcazarquivir* (1578), where Portugal lost its king. Two years later, it was itself invaded by *Philip II*, following betrayal by its noble class and defeat of a commoner army at *Alcántara*. During its overseas expansion Portugal became a major market for imported cannon, as ship-building, commercial expansion, and colonial fortification increased its need for artillery even as Imperial profits provided the means to buy guns in the booming cannon markets of Europe (principally Flanders and Germany). The problem was that not enough cannon could be cast in Lisbon due to a shortage of skilled labor. Portugal thus became dependent during the 16th century not just on foreign guns but on foreign gunners; to the end of the 17th century it was chronically short of artillery, a situation exacerbated by its absorption by Spain, which cut Portugal off from the Flanders cannon market during the *Eighty Years' War*. That led to establishment of local foundries in India and Macao, where indigenous materials and labor were used to cast guns for the Asian fleets and forts of the Portuguese Empire. After it regained independence in 1640, Portugal was free to again buy guns from the Dutch, who extracted a high price from their old foe and new ally against Spain.

Hampered by a small population, Portugal did not deeply penetrate or settle the interior of its African or Asian claims prior to the 19th century. Instead, it concentrated on control of sea lanes and sought a monopoly on ocean-borne trade. The interiors of Africa and Brazil were viewed as locales from which to take slaves and draw tropical products for sale in European markets. The Empire was a thinly settled, coastal archipelago of heavily fortified entrepôts scattered over three continents, not an empire of permanent settlement and colonization. From these forward bases armed merchants and warships conducted a lucrative trade in gold, spices, and slaves. In southern Africa the Portuguese destroyed virtually every native state into which they came in contact, including *Kongo*, not by conquest but through participation in local wars and especially by sponsorship of expanded slaving. From the moment Portuguese *caravels* first appeared in the Indian Ocean at the turn of the 16th century they enjoyed a huge military advantage over the Arab and Indian *galley* fleets they encountered. In 1501 a fleet of five Portuguese caravels and three smaller ships destroyed an Indian galley fleet off Calicut. In 1507 the Portuguese took *Hormuz*. Two years later a small Portuguese fleet decimated a far larger *Mamlūk* and *Gujarat* galley fleet at *Diu* (1509). After that,

> *. . . English, Dutch, and French privateers . . . burned overseas settlements and entrepôts.*

Portugal enjoyed a monopoly on the spice trade of the Indian Ocean and cut sharply into Venice's share of the overland trade—through Iran and the Ottoman Middle East—by going directly to the Asian sources of valuable spices. They maintained control of the Indian Ocean for most of the 16th century, defending Hormuz from several Ottoman attacks from 1551 to 1554. In 1589 Portuguese ships destroyed an Ottoman galley fleet that slowly sallied down the coast of East Africa, taking from 1585 to 1588 to make the voyage. It was long-distance Portuguese traders who first brought advanced European firearms to China and Japan and established trade relations with the Far East in the mid-16th century. But already by the early 17th century the Portuguese were displaced from most of Southeast Asia and from Japan by the Dutch.

From 1580 to 1640 Spain pulled Portugal into all its wars: with England, France, the Netherlands, over northern Italy, and with the Ottomans and Barbary emirates. The cost to Portugal was high: English, Dutch, and French privateers took Portuguese *prizes* and burned overseas settlements and entrepôts. From 1620 to 1640 the Portuguese Empire shrank even more quickly than it had expanded. Military pressure came from the English and Dutch, who supported Muslim and Hindu enemies of the Portuguese and carried out direct attacks. Portugal lost a series of key overseas bases and entrepôts: Hormuz fell to the *Safavids* (aided by the English *East India Company*) in 1622; from 1631 to 1640, it lost Pernambuco, Elmina (Gold Coast), Luanda (Mozambique), Ceylon, Malacca, and *Deshima* to the Dutch. It also had to fight off a Dutch occupation and several English amphibious raids along coastal Brazil, a war waged mainly by local settlers. By 1640, Spain faced internal unrest and rebellion in several provinces over high war taxes and too many defeats. In early 1640 the *revolt of Catalonia* broke out. Portugal, too, struck for independence in 1640. As with the Catalans, Portuguese were resentful of high taxes that were of so little benefit to themselves: the Dutch had stripped them of many overseas bases and occupied parts of coastal Brazil, yet Spain paid little attention to the defense of Portuguese overseas territories. During the 1630s there had been a series of minor tax revolts within Portugal, each put down by Spanish troops. Now a coup in Lisbon was backed by the nobility and merchant classes and received secret French aid. The rebellion, or "Restauracão" ("Restoration"), was nearly bloodless. Lisbon was seized and the Duke of Bragrança elevated as King João IV on December 15, 1640. Spain refused to accept dissolution of the 1580 forced union and attacked. The Portuguese fought off the Spanish at *Montijo* in 1644, after which they were de facto independent even if it took fighting until 1668 for Spain to recognize this status. See also *d'Albuquerque, Alfonso de*; *Aviz, Order of*; *expulsion of the Jews*; *Portuguese India*.

Suggested Reading: B. Diffy and G. Winius, *Foundations of the Portuguese Empire* (1977).

Portuguese India. "Estado da India." The first Portuguese foothold in *India* was Goa, seized in 1510 by the architect of Portugal's Indian empire, the religious fanatic and skilled admiral Viceroy Dom *Alfonso de d'Albuquerque* (1453–1515). He took the port from Bijapur with just 1,500 men, losing under 100 to Indian losses in the thousands. In 1509 the Portuguese bested an Arab navy at *Diu*, but they did not take Diu for another 22 years. In 1531 they directly assaulted Diu and took it from Gujarat, despite the latter receiving some artillery and musketry aid from the Ottomans. In 1541 Gujarat tried but failed to retake Diu. The next year the first *Jesuits* arrived in Goa, where they introduced the *Inquisition* in 1560. In 1580 *Philip II* of Spain took control of all overseas Portuguese territories. In 1638 Goa was nearly lost to the *Marathas* but was held with aid from the Mughal emperor. Portugal recovered these bases from Spain after 1650.

porucznik. In the Polish Army, a junior officer (lieutenant) serving in a *choragiew* under the *rotmistrz*.

pots de fer. "Fire pots." Bell-shaped, primitive gunpowder artillery. They were cast by bell makers. Because they were fired from a ground board rather than a stabilizing *gun carriage*, they were wildly inaccurate. Contemporary etchings and descriptions suggest that they shot thick arrows wrapped in leather to fit the mouth of the vase and seal in propellant gasses. The powder was placed in the rounded end and touched off by a heated wire or match. These weapons were unreliable and probably served as little more than noisemakers. There is a record from 1338 suggesting that the French used pots de fer from ships, an extraordinarily risky tactic, during a raid on the English coast. Once it became possible to manufacture large cannon with the *hoop-and-stave* method the term pots de fer shifted in meaning to refer to pre-loaded breeches or pots that contained the charge, wadding, and cannonball inserted as one into breech-loading *bombards*. Neither sense should be confused with a still later incendiary sometimes also called a "firepot." See also *alcancia*.

powder scoop. A common gunner's tool. Powder scoops on land were long handled. Aboard ships they were short handled because of limited room. Some were made from copper alloy, but more normally they were wooden to eliminate the chance of striking stray sparks that might set off the black powder. They were used to load loose, unpacked gunpowder into the guns.

Powhatan War (1609). See *Indian Wars (North America)*.

Powick Bridge, Battle of (1642). See *English Civil Wars*; *Rupert, Prince*.

Prague, Battle of (1420). See *Hussite Wars*.

Prague, Peace of (May 30, 1635). Mutual exhaustion brought a number of German territorial princes to terms with Emperor *Ferdinand II* in an effort to end the *Thirty Years' War*. An armistice ("Preliminaries of Pirna") was agreed on November 25, 1634, wherein a reluctant Ferdinand accepted to weaken the *Edict of Restitution*. His dynastic interest trumped his fanaticism: he needed the German princes to elect his son, the future *Ferdinand III*, as "King of Rome," the traditional stepping-stone to the Imperial throne. On the other side, *Johan Georg* of Saxony led a cluster of Protestant princes who were either unhappy with Swedish domination of the war or eager to end its expense and destruction. Georg broke with the Swedes in 1634 after they lost at *First Nördlingen*. Peace talks opened in Prague on April 2, 1635, with an accord reached on May 30 declared binding on Ferdinand, the *Estates*, and any prince willing to accept its terms. These included a 40-year suspension of the Edict of Restitution and an end to the *reservatum ecclesiaticum*. Instead, there would be restoration of lands Ferdinand seized from Protestants based on a *Normaljahr* set at November 12, 1627. That protected northern princes while leaving the south solidly Catholic. The bishoprics of Halberstadt, Bremen, and Verden taken from *Christian IV* in 1629 would remain under Imperial control. An amnesty was offered to rebel princes who agreed to abide by the Peace of Prague in return for which they accepted Imperial military obligations. This reflected a growing proto-nationalism in Germany in reaction against prolonged tramping and trampling of foreign armies on German soil. A key exception to the amnesty was any prince at war with Ferdinand prior to the landing of *Gustavus Adolphus* in Germany in 1630. That was intended to ban in perpetuity the heirs of *Friedrich V*, whose lands, rights, titles, and Electorship were granted to *Maximilian I of Bavaria*.

Excluded from the peace were most Calvinist princes, including the Landgrave of Hesse-Kassel, who was also dispossessed. The Calvinist Elector of Brandenburg was too important to bar, and was explicitly admitted. Only one Lutheran, the Duke of Württemberg, was excluded. Rights of Lutheran worship were confirmed in specified states and Saxony gained significant territory. In the Habsburg hereditary lands Catholicism was confirmed as the established and sole legal religion, while elsewhere in southern Germany traditional rights of *Reichsritter* (knights) and *Reichsstädte* (free cities) were severely truncated in favor of Catholic princes. Finally, the *Catholic League* was dissolved and all other internal or external princely alliances declared null and void. Most princes acceded within six months. The Peace of Prague did not resolve all confessional issues in Germany, but the religious question was sufficiently abated after 1635 that internal calm returned to large parts of the Empire. Some Lutheran princes even supported Ferdinand III in the general war that continued with France and Sweden. Prague failed in the short run—the great German war continued—because it never took account of the conflict's international dimension, which was predominant by 1635. No peace made solely by Germans for Germans could stand given the facts of powerful foreign armies and interests engaged in the war. The Peace of Prague may even have prolonged the war by moving the fulcrum of anti-Habsburg opposition outside Germany into the hands of powerful foreign sovereigns. Fighting thus continued until the general European settlement of the *Peace of Westphalia* in 1648, which in its German treaties and clauses confirmed many of the details agreed at Prague. See also *Arnim, Hans Georg von*; *contributions*; *Imperial Diet*.

Prague, Siege of (1645). See *Thirty Years' War*.

Prague, Siege of (1648). See *Thirty Years' War*.

prangi. An Ottoman breech-loading *swivel gun*. It was widely used in Mediterranean *galleys*.

predestination. See *Arminianism*; *Calvinism*; *Luther, Martin*; *Protestant Reformation*; *Zwingli, Huldrych*.

Preliminaries of Pirna (1634). See *Prague, Peace of*.

Presbyterianism. See *Bishops' War, First*; *Bishops' War, Second*; *Covenanters*; *English Civil Wars*; *Knox, John*.

press gang. See *impressment*.

Prester John, Legend of. See *Crusades*; *Exploration, Age of*.

Preston, Campaign of (August 17–20, 1648). An army of 10,000 Scots and English Royalists invaded England on July 8, 1648. *Oliver Cromwell* advanced north from Wales gathering *trained bands* as he moved. He surprised 3,500 Royalists (the enemy had badly divided his forces) on August 17, quickly routing their horse but facing tough resistance from the infantry. Cromwell advanced his infantry to Preston, mauling the Scots' rearguard and seizing control of a key bridge, cutting off the main body of Scots from a return to Scotland and separating them from their ammunition wagons and stores. The Scots-Royalists were forced to retreat south, away from home and safety, closely pursued by Cromwell. The armies fought again at Winwick on August 19, where Cromwell killed or captured 3,000 enemy. The next day he caught up with the survivors at Warrington, where 4,000 Scots surrendered. As Scottish stragglers wended their way back north local countryfolk attacked and murdered many more.

Preussische Bund. "Prussian Confederation." A corporation founded in 1444 at Marienwerder by Prussian burghers and Junkers. It grew to include 21 towns and to rival the *Teutonic Knights* within Prussia. In 1454 the Bund was ordered to submit by the Holy Roman Emperor, but refused. In 1455 the *Holy Roman Empire* banned the Bund and the pope threatened to excommunicate its officers, members, and allies. It defiantly renounced allegiance to the Hochmeister of the Sword Brothers, and all Prussia rose with it against the Knights. The Bund captured over 50 castles inside two months and offered the crown to Poland. These events set off the thirteen-year *War of the Cities* (1454–1466).

Preveza, Battle of (1538). A naval fight opposing yet another "Holy League," this time comprised of Venice, the Papal States, and *Charles V* against the Ottoman Empire. *Andrea Doria* led the Christian fleet to Greece where it engaged the Ottomans under *Barbarossa*, only to lose seven *galleys* without sinking a single Muslim ship.

Prévôt des maréchaux. A military magistrate whose task was to police deserters and stragglers.

price revolution (of the 17th century). A spectacular, prolonged inflation which beset all economies in Europe from the discovery of the New World through the climactic confessional wars of the period, peaking in the 17th century. While many of its causes and effects remain subject to intense academic debate there is agreement on two main causes. First, the influx of gold and silver from Spain's American colonies vastly increased Europe's supply of monetary metals. Second, decades of deficit financing of protracted wars encouraged debasement of most currencies. The 17th century thus witnessed a steady climb in commodity prices aggravated by a rising population logistic and a corresponding decrease in real wages. The price revolution undermined the political and social position of landed aristocracies and impoverished peasants, whose lot was declining with population growth and agricultural changes anyway. Inflation benefitted urban merchant classes but especially debt-ridden monarchs, allowing them to pay off old loans with debased currency. On the other hand, it destabilized industries and entire economies, aggravated social, religious, and international conflicts, turned the expanding city populations into deep pools of immiseration and therefore potential revolution, and in significant measure underlay the larger political, social, military, and religious crisis of the 17th century that wracked European civilization. See also *mutiny*.

prickers. Yorkist term for *light cavalry* used during the *Wars of the Roses* in England.

printing. Moveable type (letterpress printing) was invented in Germany by Johannes Gutenberg (1400–1468), probably in 1454. The new method meant that Bibles were printed and circulated en masse where previously a single copy had required 300 sheepskins. By 1500, Paris boasted 75 presses and most other large towns in Europe experienced a similar printing boom. This had a huge impact on religious affairs, as it did on all realms of human activity. Permanent records and the transmission of new ideas in printed form led to wider diffusion of practical knowledge and a concomitant change in metaphysical outlook. Printed bibles and tracts greatly aided the spread of Protestant ideas, adding to confessional divisions across Europe. From 1517 to 1520 *Martin Luther* wrote 30 tracts that were printed in over 300,000 copies. His translation of the Bible into German was circulated in printed editions. The English translation of the Bible by William Tyndale (who was strangled, then burned, for heresy in 1536) was widely circulated by *Thomas Cromwell*, who believed that "enlightened religion" among the people was conducive to patriotism. In fact, it conduced to sectarian conflict and indirectly to religious civil war.

Printing also had direct military effects. Among the first and most important military outcomes was translation and reproduction of artillery tables and manuals which hitherto were written out in limited, and often also secret, editions. These manuals reproduced what otherwise existed only in the heads and private notes of master gunsmiths: alloy ratios and methods for bronze casting; recipes for gunpowder, including advanced techniques of *corning*; and tables of inclination and weight-of-powder-to-shot. Standardized knowledge of the latter greatly increased accuracy and professionalized the role of *bombardiers*. Printing also improved government record keeping. This greatly enhanced central administration, which led to more efficient systems of taxation that were essential to meeting the growing burden of *war finance*. And printing contributed to standardization of major languages, strengthening development of "national" identities and hostilities in the early modern world. See also *Art of War*.

Prior Mor. In the Iberian *Military Orders*, the officer below *Mestre*. His duties were largely ceremonial and internal to the workings of the Order.

prise. In 13th-century England, this was a system of compulsory purchase of food for military purposes at prices set by the state. It was deeply unpopular. The later term for this practice was "purveyance."

prisoners of war. During the knightly era, as endemic warfare threatened men of property and title with death or capture that would lead to catastrophic losses, a convention arose within the code of *chivalry* whereby wealthy prisoners taken in battle were held for ransom rather than killed. While this helped preserve the hereditary class structure it provided a new incentive for raiding and war: profit through ransom. Protection did not extend to ordinary soldiers who were hacked, stabbed, and bludgeoned to death with happy abandon by their armored and lawfully protected social superiors. This attitude was reciprocal: neither Flemish militia nor Swiss country lads took nobles captive. The Flemings massacred French *knights* at *Courtrai* (1302) while the Swiss butchered and mutilated young nobles at *Morgarten* (1315), *Laupen* (1339), *Sempach* (1386), and *Näfels* (1388). In 1444 Zurich tried to restrain its more passionate soldiers from ripping out the hearts of dead enemies as trophies and dismembering corpses. In the other direction, Lucerne passed an ordinance in 1499 stipulating that no prisoners were to be taken at all. Irish peasant *kernes*, too, had a reputation for ferocity and routine murder of prisoners.

The medieval ideal of the *jus in bello* could lead to strange results. During the *Scottish Wars* England regarded Scots soldiers as rebels and often butchered prisoners, whereas the Scots felt they were fighting nation-to-nation and felt bound by the laws of war to protect English prisoners. Similarly, the English regarded France as a legitimate sovereign enemy and therefore respected high-class French prisoners and held them for ransom (though they killed commoners and Genoese mercenaries in French service). A notable exception occurred at *Agincourt* in 1415 where *Henry V* ordered a massacre of French knights, possibly because he feared they would attack his rear. His own knights refused to do the deed, but his lower-class archers were happy to cut some 1,000 noble throats. Large numbers of casualties in battle were almost always suffered by the losing side, usually after the outcome was made clear by a formation being broken and the men in it running or riding for their lives. This exposed their backs to pursuers who more easily cut them down.

> *...Zurich tried to restrain...soldiers from ripping out the hearts of dead enemies...*

In the Middle East the *Catalan Great Company* slaughtered all Ottoman males over the age of ten. The Ottomans also killed prisoners of mature ages, but kept able boys to be converted to *Islam* and raised as military slaves. Overseas, small and isolated European armies engaged in colonial conquest, such as the *conquistadores* in the Americas, usually took few prisoners and slaughtered those they did in order to even the military odds. On the other warrior side, the *Aztec Empire* avoided direct killing in order to take large numbers of prisoners to be slaughtered in ritual sacrifice.

In general, prisoners were killed or roughly treated in situations where one side felt secure from retaliation by the other. Thus, *Alba* routinely hanged all captured Dutch rebels, but only until 1573 when one of his favorites was captured by the Dutch. This led to a reciprocal agreement on regular prisoner exchanges. During the *Thirty Years' War* the large number of *mercenaries* in all armies meant that ordinary soldiers taken prisoner were usually afforded the opportunity to change sides, and did so. Officers would be released upon payment of a ransom to the commander of the enemy regiment. But this could be financially ruinous to the captured officer. In France, the king paid ransom for any captured "maréchal de France." To reduce his personal risk, *Bernhard von Sachsen-Weimar* negotiated similar treatment in the event of his capture. By the end of the war it was common for monarchs to pay ransoms for all their captured troops, national or mercenary. The sum to be paid was set by rank and governed by formal agreement between opposing armies. For example, a *Field Marshal* was worth 20,000 florins. This system reduced personal financial risks for officers while redirecting the spoils of war out of their purses into the *war chest* of rising territorial princes. An exception to this was the "War of the Three Kingdoms," or *English Civil Wars*, fought within and among England, Ireland, and Scotland. These wars were intensely religious in character. As a result, Irish soldiers serving in England were subject to summary execution while Royalist, Confederate, Scots, and Parliamentarians in Ireland all killed prisoners unless a ransom or exchange proved possible. See also *Albigensian Crusade*; *Charles I, of England*; *Constantinople, Siege of*; *cuartel general*; *Dunbar, Battle of*; *German Peasant War*; *guerre mortelle*; *infantry*; *Knights Templar*; *Mohács, Battle of*; *mourning war*; *murtat*; *Nicopolis, Battle of*; *Philiphaugh, Battle of*; *piracy*; *Salāh al-Dīn*; *"skulking way of war"*; *stradiots*; *Tannenberg, Battle of*; *Vienna, Siege of*; *Wallace, William*; *Worcester, Battle of*.

privateer. A privately owned warship and/or its captain issued *letters of marque* or *letters of reprisal* by a monarch authorizing capture or destruction of enemy shipping. Taking ships captive as *prizes* was the preferred action. Privateers usually carried large crews, useful for boarding actions and from which skeleton crews could be split off to sail captured ships into ports with *prize courts*. The Prussians hired privateers to fend off more powerful ships of the *Teutonic Knights* during the *War of the Cities* (1454–1466). French (*Huguenot*) and Dutch (*Sea Beggar*) privateers preyed on Spanish commerce through the 16th and 17th centuries, while Flemish privateers in Spanish service and based in Dunkirk and Ostend from the 1620s preyed on the rich Dutch trade that bottlenecked in the Channel. By far the most wide-ranging privateers were English *sea dogs*, sailing under such reckless and daring captains as *Francis Drake*, *John Hawkyns*, *Walter Raleigh*, and *Martin Frobisher*. During *Elizabeth I's* protracted war with *Philip II*—undeclared before 1588 but open after that—100 English privateers were given letters of marque to prey on Spanish ships from the Channel to the Caribbean, off the coast of Spain and Portugal, and along the treasure and supply lanes of the several Atlantic passages. Dutch and English privateers carried the war even to Asia, where they preyed on Iberian ships in the Indies but also on Chinese junks and other local traffic. Historian Kenneth Andrews argues that privateering was "the characteristic form of Elizabethan maritime warfare." That was because no permanent navy was available beyond a few "royal ships" and there was no consistent naval policy or doctrine that appreciated the advantages to England of pursuing sea power in a more modern sense ("command of the sea"). In general, sailors much preferred to serve on a privateer where they shared in the *prize money* than on a royal ship owned by the monarch which paid poor or even no wages. See also *Confederation of Kilkenny*; *Glyndŵr's Rebellion*.

Suggested Reading: Kenneth Andrews, *Elizabethan Privateering* (1964).

Privilegium minus. See *Holy Roman Empire*.

prize. Any enemy merchant ship or warship taken on the sea and returned for sale of the ship and its cargo in a *prize court*. See also *booty*; *privateer*.

prize court. An ad hoc naval court established to decide conflicting claims over what was, or was not, contraband. Prize courts were originally established to assess the competing claims of *privateers* and merchants and to give the monarch a stake in any *prize* or goods seized during privateering or naval warfare.

prize money. Enemy goods or vessels seized or captured at sea in wartime were sold in a *prize court*, from which monarchs always took "a piece of the action." In 14th-century England, prizes were divided thus: one-quarter to the king, one-quarter to the warship's owners, half to the captain and crew (with the lion's share going to the captain) that captured the prize. There was, of course, much concealment and cheating in order to reduce the monarch's share. See also *booty*.

Procopius the Great (d.1434). Czech: Prokop Holý. Radical priest and *Hussite* general. He served under *Jan Žižka* and fought at *Kutná Hora* (1422) and *Německý Brod* (1422). He replaced Žižka as overall Taborite commander when Žižka was killed in the first Hussite civil war (1424). He won a major victory over the Imperial Army at *Ustí nad Labem* (1426). He then led the Hussites on a prolonged offensive into Austria, Hungary, and Germany, 1429–1430. When the *Council of Basel* offered an olive branch to moderate Hussites, Procopius and the radical Taborite rebels again faced civil war with Utraquists, who were allied this time with Bohemia's Catholics. Procopius commanded at *Český-Brod* (1434) where he was killed in a losing fight in which the Taborites took heavy casualties.

Procopius the Little (d.1434). Czech: Prokupek. *Hussite* general. He served under *Jan Žižka*, seeing action with the Taborite army at *Kutná Hora* (1422) and *Německý Brod* (1422). He then served with *Procopius the Great*, fighting at *Ustí nad Labem* (1426). He led a somewhat more moderate group of Taborites (Orebites) in an unsuccessful siege of Pilsen (1432–1434). Like his greater namesake he was killed while fighting at *Český-Brod* (1434).

professed. A warrior monk of one of the *Military Orders* who took full vows of chastity, poverty, and obedience.

prohibited weapons. The effort to prohibit certain weapons from use in warfare is ancient. The Greeks banned poisoning of a besieged city's water supply and poison-tipped arrows, though Romans, Byzantines, and Ottomans saw nothing wrong with either method of killing. During the *Crusades* Christians first encountered the *crossbow* and recoiled from the devastation it wrought among *knights*. In 1139 Pope Innocent II declared a ban on crossbows in fighting among Christians (though he granted a dispensation for use against Muslims or pagans). But the crossbow was simply too effective a weapon to suppress and was soon in wide use in Christian armies and wars. Similarly, when the *longbow* appeared on the continent during the *Hundred Years' War* it cut down the flower of French chivalry. This led to another useless papal ban: the longbow was also far too efficient a killing system to suppress for merely metaphysical reasons, even in an age of faith, and was deployed in bloody-minded defiance of the papal ban. When gunpowder first became known in Europe in the late 13th century, the *Catholic Church* tried to ban all weapons that employed it, proclaiming them to be the product of daemonic arts and purposes. So valuable did "black powder" weapons prove in battle no one other than a few theologians paid any attention to protests from Rome. See also *serpentine*; *wheel lock*.

propaganda. See *Affair of the Placards*; *Antichrist*; *Black Legend*; *Calvinism*; *Congregatio de Propaganda Fidei*; *Counter-Reformation*; *"Defenestration of Prague" (May 23, 1618)*; *Ferdinand II, Holy Roman Emperor*; *Fifth Monarchists*; *French Civil Wars*; *iconoclasm*; *Inquisition*; *Jesuits*; *kerne*; *Luther, Martin*; *Mali Empire*; *monarchia universalis*; *Philip II, of Spain*; *printing*; *Protestant Reformation*; *Songhay*; *"Spanish Fury"*; *Suleiman I*; *Third Rome*; *Thirty Years' War*; *Vienna, Siege of*; *witchcraft*.

Propositions. A Parliamentary *contributions* system especially important for the supply of cavalry mounts during the *English Civil Wars* (1639–1651). In 1643 "donations" were made compulsory.

Protestant Reformation. A great 16th-century shattering of the unity of Latin Christian civilization (the larger Christian world had split into Catholic and Orthodox branches centuries earlier). It was both an extension of trends flowing from the *Italian Renaissance* and a reaction against them; it was a call for basic reform of clerical abuses and corruption and a partial rejection of the claimed authority of the clergy. Christian humanists such as Erasmus and Lefèvre d'Etaples were active within the *Catholic Church* before the great theological divide of the 16th century. They rejected scholasticism, arguing for direct textual study of the Bible and new approaches to devotion, piety, and theology. Yet, they insisted on the essential unity of the Church and hence were not "proto-Protestants." The term Protestant was first attached to the followers of *Martin Luther*, more specifically to all who registered protests against resolutions of the *Imperial Diet* of 1529 called by *Charles V* to deal with the confessional split and religious rebellion in Germany.

Genesis

Clerical in origin and mostly confined to the towns at first, the Reformation took varying shape in certain core areas before spreading unevenly across the "Christian Commonwealth" (*res publica Christiana*). It took early and deep root in Germany where Luther led lower clergy and regular orders in opposition to widespread corruption in the Church and to medieval penitential practice, but even more in protest against scholasticism and Aristotelian ethics. The goal of scholastic theology was rational exposition of a "faith seeking understanding" ("fides quaerens intellectum"), within the context of divine love ("caritas") rather than faith as the cardinal religious idea. Lutherans and other Protestants instead championed a highly individualistic piety that spoke to popular longing for religious emotion left unsatisfied by mere habitual public observance and hollow rituals. They proposed a new theology developed using the textual and critical tools of humanism and an ethics rooted in "justification by faith" alone ("sola fides"). In thus committing theology, under another name the reformers continued the scholastic search for "true doctrine," or revelation affirmed by reason. This set the stage for later all-out war over which doctrines were true and whose were false.

Alternate reform communities gripped parts of Switzerland. *Huldrych Zwingli* led the revolt in Zurich which moved into the open in 1522 with defiant eating of sausages during the Lenten fast. Jean Calvin fled France and took up residence in Geneva, where he pushed too hard too soon for political control. After five years away from Geneva he returned and became master of the city. From Geneva, *Calvinism* spread to the Netherlands, Scotland, France and the Rhineland. Other charismatic preachers proclaimed and wrote tracts promulgating new doctrines and distributed bibles for direct study by the laity. In this way subsidiary reform doctrines and movements inevitably arose that were evermore distinct from the original Lutheran protest. In France, too, early conversions occurred mainly among the clergy, notably of Cordelier, Jacobin, many Augustinian monks, and several bishops who declared their conscience and surrendered their sees to go preaching or into hiding. Missionaries sent by Calvin from Geneva after 1555 made inroads among the French nobility of the Midi and their clients, setting the stage for the protracted tragedy of forty years of the "Wars of Religion" in France. The Reformation took a much different path in England, driven at first by the carnal lusts and dynastic and financial interests of *Henry VIII* rather than any doctrinal disputes. Only slowly did the English Church move away from Catholicism in matters of faith, doctrine, prayer book, and ritual, consolidating England as a Protestant country under *Elizabeth I* and making it an enemy of Catholic power.

Everywhere the Reformation was fundamentally occasioned by demographic, economic, social, and political changes which presented an opportunity to offer an alternative lay piety to the spiritual and intellectual dominance of the Catholic clergy. The impulse to reform was rooted in widespread disgust over the rank secularism and corruption of higher clergy, and open concubinage and raw spiritual and doctrinal ignorance of most lower clergy and parish priests. There was widespread resentment over large and small fees charged by clerics for everything from blessings at weddings to candles at funerals, to absolution for rape, infanticide, and murder. More deeply, there was widespread emotional dissatisfaction with a mere "religion of habits" among the multitudes, who were instructed in external and often spiritually hollow ritual observance while being stripped of money by unscrupulous hucksters playing on superstitions at shrines, festivals, and on pilgrimages. Still, many challenges to Catholic orthodoxy and Church practices had been made before 1500, including some where doctrinal revolt took intense political and social form. In order for demands for reform to become actual revolution and religious warfare it was necessary for spiritual disquiet to marry political unrest, and together conceive military conflict.

Martin Luther

The most intense phase of religious ferment and demand for institutional and moral reform, which led directly to permanent division of Latin Christianity, began in 1517 when Martin Luther nailed a scroll of 95 theses to a church door in Wittenberg. These protested corrupt clerical practices, especially sale of "indulgences" (promissory notes on reduced punishment in "Purgatory," Catholic antechamber of the afterlife). By 1521 significant elements in the German church were in de facto schism from Rome. They broke openly with promulgation of the *"Augsburg Confession"* of Lutheran principles nine years later. While watchful and concerned, Charles V was unable to venture into his Empire before 1530, so preoccupied was he with wars with France and the Ottoman Empire. When he did turn to the religious revolt in Germany the reformed faith was already deeply rooted. Given translation of the Bible into vernacular languages (the German translation was made

Radicals . . . painted the Catholic Church . . . as the "whore of Babylon" . . .

by Luther himself), its mass production on the new Gutenberg press, and chronic scandal among the clergy, reference by the laity to the direct authority of scripture had wide appeal. Punching through the barrier of the priesthood clung to by Catholics, reformers offered direct access to scripture. In reform congregations laity needed no priest to instruct them in correct dogma, paid no petty clerical fees, and were freed in their daily practices and piety from the conjoined asceticism and puritanism of clerical spiritual and sexual ideals. Radicals went much further, reviving and reveling in ancient apocalyptic traditions that painted the Catholic Church—with its many attachments to secular power—as the "whore of Babylon" and every reigning pope as the *Antichrist*.

For all the vitriol and rhetoric, the reformed faith spread almost solely in the towns during its first seven decades, mainly among clergy and literate laity in the professional classes. Some historians thus regard the Reformation as essentially a bourgeois movement. While that seems extreme, it is true that reform barely touched the vast peasant masses during the 16th century other than by wars and forced migrations it suffered or provoked, or in villages tied economically to a nearby Reform town. In part, indifference to *confessionalism* on the part of the majority reflected the arcane complexity of the doctrinal disputes at issue, championed by theologians on either side who felt little need to make their points more plainly for plain folk. Most peasants thus continued to visit reliquaries, go on pilgrimages, join in sometimes wild religious processions and festivals, wait sullenly in coerced attendance at services, accept spiritual tutelage from the mouths of priests as illiterate and ignorant as themselves, and uphold folk practices and beliefs alien and repugnant to Protestant and Catholic elites alike.

Jean Calvin

That is why Calvin was so important. He made Protestant theology comprehensible and teachable to the many, if not quite the multitude, by producing a reform catechism for "Everyman." His *Institutes of the Christian Religion* was first published in 1536 and thereafter printed and reprinted in several revised versions and on a truly vast scale. Calvin's lucidity as a writer, along with his early legal training, permitted him to make complex theological arguments with a direct simplicity and clarity rare for disputants of the day. This made his work accessible to lay folk who could read it themselves or, more often, who listened to readings from his pamphlets and texts. The immediacy of his writings made them far more powerful than Zwingli's or Luther's distant, arcane, and angrily polemical treatises. (The Catholic Church recognized the challenge this posed. It finally matched Calvin's catechism with one of its own, the simplified *Roman Catechism* produced by the *Council of Trent*.) Despite the fact that on most issues of doctrine Calvin agreed with Luther, militant "Calvinists" came to reject Lutheranism and Catholicism in near-equal measure, not least because their contempt was returned in full measure by Catholics and Lutherans who joined in rare union to deny formal legal protection to Calvinists in Germany that they afforded to each other in the *Peace of Augsburg* (1555). As Catholicism concentrated and consolidated after Trent, Protestantism divided to became a multi-colored cloak, adding new swatches with the rise of some charismatic preacher in the Netherlands or Scotland or Bohemia who fixed on this or that narrow scriptural passage and worried it into an extreme claim held above all others, and around which gathered a fanatic following utterly convinced that only he, and they, possessed God's truth.

So what united Protestants? Devotion to individualistic piety framed in the core tenet that no third person was needed as intermediary between oneself and God: no corruptible priesthood with a monopoly on interpretation of scripture, no hierarchy of doctrinal or administrative authority, and no pope. Protestants also rejected the notion of the intercession of saints and despised cults of veneration of saints organized around reliquaries or shrines and represented in images and statuary in churches, many of which were smashed by furious Protestant mobs. Where Catholics looked to the pantheon of Christian saints as models of godliness worthy of respect and emulation by the masses, overly fervent Protestants expected the masses to be saints. Not all Protestants were so radical in the changes they sought or the doctrines they preached. But there was a shared and fierce rejection of the Catholic view that there were two distinct paths to holiness and salvation. The first, chastity, self-abnegation, and "mortification of the flesh" guided by prayerful devotion, was a life of holiness designed for the clergy but imposed during the Middle Ages as the ideal held out for the laity as well. The alternative was personal, familial, and social conformity with Church teachings, along with participation in certain sacraments and observance of holy and feast days and other public rituals. This path was of lower spiritual value but was provided to laity, including all nobles and kings, as a poor but acceptable second to the truly godly life of clerics. What united Protestants was rejection of this notion of alternate lay and clerical paths to salvation. They instead upheld the idea of a unified piety, or a "priesthood of all believers."

Political Effects

This had an unforeseen yet powerful political effect. Protestants persecuted by Catholic kings, as in the Netherlands and France, moved toward denial of the old idea of the *corpus mysticum*, eventually rejecting the notion of a unique physical holiness for kings as they already did the unique spiritual holiness of despised Catholic clergy. In place of veneration of the king's "divine body," an even older medieval idea took hold in new form: kings ruled by consent or they ruled by mere force of arms. The latter case gave rise to the modern idea, first opposed by all Protestant theologians but later endorsed by some, that a king who ruled unjustly via the sword could be justly pulled from his throne by the people. In different ways in different countries at varying times this intellectual revolution of the first order found expression in pamphlets and arguments, then in riots, civil wars, and revolutions. *Huguenots* in southern France, Calvinists in the Netherlands, English Puritans and Parliamentarians, all came to the same conclusion by different historical paths: "godly men and true" had no more need of kings than they did of priests or popes. Elsewhere, in Lutheran Denmark and Sweden and much of northern Germany, monarchs converted to Protestantism and so were not challenged. Instead, they became the main protectors of the reformed religion, which thereby took on a territorial and national aspect. The enemy, in caricature and in reality, became the Habsburg ambition to hegemony that was tied to the *Counter-Reformation*.

From the middle of the 16th century to the middle of the 17th century bloody wars of religion ensued as every side dug in doctrinally. Protectors among the monarchs and great princes of Europe were secured, towns fortified, armies raised, and a ferocious military struggle began. Even more sharply, the fight was over confessionalizing the still largely uninvolved and uncaring masses. Radical ideas, men, and policies found ready hearings in the highest courts as Protestants and Catholics together burned the last bridges connecting them to one another as Christians; then they burned each other. Fanatics took the lead most everywhere, condemning the enemy not just in this life but more deliciously also in the next, as a "heretic" on some ferociously debated arcana of angelic, apostolic, catechistic, or doctrinal interest. As the

Counter-Reformation won back whole countries for Catholicism (Bohemia, Inner Austria, Flanders), Protestantism rushed to marry regional and secular autonomy, in some places also sheltering constitutionalism as a mistress. Wherever Protestantism survived it did so because it was defended by territorial princes when confessional conflict led to religious wars and bloodletting widened confessional divides. Not all wars of the period were caused by disputes occasioned by the Reformation: the *Italian Wars* (1494–1559), for instance, were waged by Catholics against Catholics and the *Nordic Seven Years' War* (1563–1570) was fought exclusively among Lutherans. Yet, the names of the greatest wars of the era point to the intractability of their causes, rooted in religious passions and hatreds: the *Eighty Years' War* (1568–1648) and the *Thirty Years' War* (1618–1648). Other great nations were torn apart from within by religious fissures: France during the *French Civil Wars* (1562–1629); and England, Scotland and Ireland during the "War of the Three Kingdoms" or *English Civil Wars* (1639–1651). European civilization as a whole was violently tossed and tumbled for more than a century. Old alliances were discarded and new ones took shape; old balances of power were broken and new ones arranged. When it was all over, Europe was unrecognizable diplomatically, politically, militarily, or spiritually.

The wars of the Reformation and Counter-Reformation also drove parties outward, to engage the wider world in a search for profits and martial advantage to be used in mortal combat at home in Europe. The Americas saw scenes of battle between Iberian Catholics and English and Dutch Protestants and their navies, and religious massacres of native and colonial populations from Florida to New England. The coasts of Africa and India were scouted by rival traders and the interiors penetrated by missionaries. Storm-tossed conquerors eager to deny any advantage to enemies thousands of miles away made deals with local Muslim potentates in the Gulf and Indian Ocean. Coastal China was brushed by Reformation winds when European *privateers* attacked trade junks, while company diplomats strove to persuade Ming emperors to deny China's trade to their confessional and commercial rivals. The *Jesuits* fanned over the Americas and across Asia in a fierce competition for converts, protecting Indians in the Amazon from slavers or turning master gunner for a Chinese or Manchu emperor. The *Inquisition* reached into Mexico, Peru, and the Philippines, looking for signs of Protestant infection and heresy. In Japan, Catholic missionaries and Protestant traders vied for favor from the profoundly suspicious warlords *Oda Nobunaga* and *Toyotomi Hideyoshi*, and the more calculating *Tokugawa Ieyasu*. Hundreds of thousands converted only to be left behind when the missionaries were ordered out, and then slaughtered in the 1630s by the Tokugawa shogunate. *Kirishitan* survivors were hunted and driven underground into secret devotions until the 19th century, a communal island of memory of Europe's long-forgotten wars of religion.

Yet, when European states and empires finally emerged from the religious wars they were flush with extraordinary commercial, military, and political energy. Where did it come from? From the concentration of mind and power caused by 150 years of the prospect of being hanged in the morning by some other European state or empire. Masters of parts of five continents, armed with navigational, technological, and commercial innovations born of decades of cutthroat warfare and ferocious economic competition, flush with wealth from the springtime of capitalism, a newly secular Europe's appetite for still more overseas profit and land would grow with the eating.

Conclusions

Wilhelm Dilthey and Jacob Burkhardt saw the great changes of the Reformation as reinforcing the intellectual openness first seen in the *Italian Renaissance*. Georg Hegel was also an admirer, especially of Luther, depicting the Reformation as part of an unfolding of greater historical self-consciousness. Max Weber famously proposed a thesis linking Protestantism in its Calvinist and Puritan forms with the rise of capitalism. In his *The Protestant Ethic and the Spirit of Capitalism* (1904), Weber argued that piety and asceticism ("the Protestant ethic") made Calvinists more "thrifty" than others, leading to a higher savings rate. Then, worldly success was read into the doctrine of predetermined salvation to produce a virtuous economic circle of savings, investment, and prosperity, leading to more saving. But the thesis does not stand up. Many early capitalists were not Calvinists, and many Calvinists were never capitalists. It is more likely that the special connection between Calvinism and capitalism, insofar as there was one, had more to do with the urban concentration of Calvinists. Thus, they were disproportionately involved in the expansion of commerce which matured first in the larger cities of northeastern Europe, rather than in the economically declining states of the Mediterranean where most people remained rural and Catholic. Even then, Weber's thesis failed to account for the fact that recognizable capitalism was first evident in the city-states of the (Catholic) *Hanse* in the 14th century and in (Catholic) Italy before and during the Renaissance. Secular critics of Dilthey's and Burckhardt's positive view of the Reformation, most notably Ernst Troeltsch, saw it as more medieval than modern, replacing outward observance with inward piety to be sure, but stuck still in a false claim to revelation over reason while invoking new dogma and superstitions to replace the old. That said, secularists praised the Reformation for its modernizing rejection of monastic spiritual and sexual idealism, its promotion of natural law and the modern state (discounting too readily, perhaps, a notable impulse in practice to theocracy and support for authoritarianism), and Protestantism's embrace of humanistic reforms and lay education. Catholic critics disputed positive interpretations as well, though on much different grounds.

Judged in terms of its departure from medievalism rather than from the secular vantage point of the 21st century, the Reformation achieved a great deal. First, it was a genuine religious revolution in an age and civilization where religion informed all aspects of human endeavor, from birth to death, in private and in public affairs. In some regions it conduced to social and political revolution as well as religious upheaval, but this was not its intent or main effect. In most locales, whether defiantly Protestant or stubbornly

Catholic, the dominant elites were notably changed in their spiritual outlook but not in their persons. In spite of all the wars and dislocations associated with the Reformation, despite utopian religious projects and dystopian reality and mass suffering, there was no social or political equivalent in Europe of the 16th century *gekokujō* in Japan. The tripartite medieval social order remained in place; where it was challenged in cities and towns that had more to do with commerce than confessionalism. On the other hand, the Reformation left a rich legacy of nonconformism with religious tyranny and took tentative steps toward nonconformity with political tyranny as well. There was still an enormous distance to travel from the "priesthood of all believers" to the sovereignty of the common man, but history had been nudged closer to that destination—against the will and intention of reformers—by the Reformation. Yet, for all that, judged in terms of its own declared aspirations to uplift people to new levels of spiritual engagement and capacity, the Reformation singularly failed. As do all utopian schemes.

Globally, the Reformation was a key act in the play of world history, not just a localized religious struggle in Europe in the 16th–17th centuries. The wars of the Reformation and Counter-Reformation reframed Europe as a state system instead of a "res publica Christiana" and gave its states a uniquely sharp separation of church and state. This idea was enshrined as the core principle of interstate affairs and international law in the *Peace of Westphalia* (1648). That great settlement brought confessional peace to Germany and Europe not though the triumph of one sect over the others but by elevating secular powers to a near absolute authority over subject populations (thus, balefully perhaps, burying the feudal ideal of consensual monarchy), while rejecting claims to supranational religious authority. That shift away from "The Christian Commonwealth" toward a new world order of competing Leviathans had much to do with the ideas and events of the Protestant Reformation. See also *Anabaptism*; *Cromwell, Thomas*; *Erastianism*; *Habsburgs*; *Henry VIII, of England*; *Holy Roman Empire*; *Hus, Jan*; *Hussite Wars*; *iconoclasm*; *Knox, John*; *Lollards*; *Mohács, Battle of*; *Philip II, of Spain*; *Prague, Peace of*; *Savonarola, Girolamo*.

> *...the Reformation...took tentative steps toward nonconformity with political tyranny...*

Suggested Reading: Thomas Brady, *The Protestant Reformation in German History* (1998); Owen Chadwick, *The Reformation* (1972); A. Duke, *Reformation and Revolt in the Low Countries* (1990); G. Elton, *Reformation Europe* (1963); H. Gelder, *The Two Reformations of the 16th Century* (1961); Mark Greengrass, *The French Reformation* (1987); C. Haigh, ed., *The English Reformation Revised* (1987); R. P. Hsia, ed., *The German People and the Reformation* (1988); Richard Marius, *Martin Luther* (1999); Steven Ozment, *The Age of Reform, 1250–1550* (1981); James Tracy, *Europe's Reformations, 1450–1650: Doctrine, Politics, and Community*, 2nd ed. (2002).

Protestant Union. A mutual-defense alliance of German Protestant princes agreed for ten years on May 12, 1608. It was a reaction against Imperial occupation of Donauwörth in violation of the traditional rights of the *Reichskreis*. Its membership included nine princes and 17 Imperial free cities. It was held together to wage war by the "godly against the Antichrist," but beyond that useless slogan it had no political program. Thus, the effort of *Christian of Anhalt-Bernburg* to take it to war as part of his policy of brinkmanship with the Empire failed. In addition to promoting *confessionalism*, the Union increased princely autonomy from the Empire. Not all Protestant princes joined (most notably, Saxony remained outside the Union). Its formation provoked founding of the *Catholic League* in 1609. The Protestant Union signed alliance treaties with England (1612) and the Netherlands (1613) during its failed intervention in the *Jülich-Kleve* crisis. The Catholic League signed a treaty of neutrality with the Protestant Union at Ulm in 1620, in a joint effort to limit the fight that ultimately became the *Thirty Years' War* to just Bohemia and Austria where it had begun in 1618. Protestant disunity and the early defeat of the armies of *Friedrich V* led to formal dissolution of the Union in May 1621.

Providence Island. A zealous and overly ambitious English colony was established on this island, off the shore of the Mosquito Coast (modern Nicaragua), from 1630 to 1643. It was intended as a base from which Spanish-Catholic holdings in the Americas might be raided and challenged, but it failed in that purpose. Some investment was recovered and applied by *Oliver Cromwell* to Protestant plantations in Ireland.

Provost. The officer responsible for maintaining *military discipline* in a company or regiment. In a *Landsknechte* regiment or army he was often the most outlandishly dressed man in a company of men famous for strange and flamboyant attire. He was responsible for what today would be called "military policing" of the camp. This included not merely prevention of *desertion* or *mutiny* but keeping the men happy by overseeing markets set up by *sutlers*, in return for which he got a piece of the sutler action. The Provost also profited from a percentage of the business done by the *baggage train*, including laundry, gambling, whoring (a duty shared with the *Hurenweibel*, or "whore sergeant"), and sometimes nursing. See also *Prévôt des maréchaux*; *provost marshal*.

provost marshal. The executive officer, reporting to the *knight marshal*, of the English garrison army in Ireland. The office was first appointed in 1570 and confirmed in 1583.

Prussia. The early history of Prussia was linked with that of Livonia and conquest by the *Livonian Order* in association with the *Teutonic Knights*, from 1237. The "Sword Brethren" built stone castles to mark and hold territorial conquests in Prussia, most notably at Königsberg (1254). The native tribes of the *Ordensstaat* rebelled in 1240 and again in 1269, but by 1340 the Brethren completed the conquest of Prussia. The Ordensstaat was then heavily colonized by immigrant German *knights*, nobles, and free peasants. There followed a sustained war with Lithuania. By the 15th century the Ordensstaat's affluent cities and local nobility chafed at the economic restrictions imposed by the Brethren and the rights and monopolies they kept for themselves. They looked to Poland as a model of constitutionally protected civic and noble freedoms. But the Brethren would not go easily or peaceably from power, until they were beaten by a huge Polish-Lithuanian army at *Tannenberg* (1410), during the "Great War" of 1409–1411. After that defeat many Prussian estates pledged allegiance to the *Jagiello dynasty*. However, the Poles failed to consolidate their victory by capturing the Teutonic stronghold and capital of *Marienburg* (Malbork), and the Knights thereafter forced Prussia back into submission. Formation of the *Preussische Bund* meant that by 1440 Prussian cities, the Junkers, and other Estates were moving toward rebellion. In 1453 legal relief was sought from the Holy Roman Empire for grievances against the Teutonic Knights, but the Prussians were flatly denied help. That pushed them into the arms of the Polish king, *Casimir IV*, whom they asked to incorporate Prussia into Poland. He agreed, and Poland and the Bund declared war on the Teutonic Knights in 1454, commencing the *War of the Cities* which lasted to 1466.

At the time, Prussia mounted a small army comprised mainly of conscripts with core units raised as militia from the larger towns and cities. The largest militia was about 750 men. All told, Prussia's towns yielded an army of 16,000 partially trained and reasonably well-armed militia, supported by several thousand ill-trained and poorly armed but inexpensive peasant infantry. The great strength of the Prussians was a sizeable artillery train, outstripping even that of Poland, along with well-defended castles, fortresses, and fortified towns. Once the war began the Prussians also quickly proved able to raise a decent-sized and effective navy by arming their merchant ships and hiring *privateers* from the fleets of neutral Baltic cities. "Royal" (or Polish) Prussia was lost to Poland as a result of the War of the Cities. The Teutonic Knights formally converted their remaining lands into the secular duchy of Prussia in 1525, which became an effective fief of the Polish monarchy. The small north German state that remained was called "Brandenburg-Prussia" upon the acquisition of Brandenburg and *East Prussia* by Albert of *Hohenzollern* in 1618. A rising power after 1650, it was only a minor and impoverished Baltic state at the end of the *Thirty Years' War*.

Suggested Reading: F. L. Carsten, *The Origins of Prussia* (1954); H. W. Koch, *History of Prussia* (1978).

Prussian Confederation. See *Preussische Bund*; *Prussia*; *War of the Cities*.

psychological warfare. See *battle cries*; *Granada*; *siege warfare*.

Pubei rebellion. See *Wanli Emperor*.

pulk. A large tactical unit of the *Polish Army* equivalent to a medieval *battle*. It was formed out of anywhere from 2 to 20 or more *choragiew* (or "banners").

It was an ad hoc unit without permanent structure of command or staff. It differed from the medieval battle by combining several arms, from peasant levies to professional infantry to noble cavalry. It was capable of independent maneuver and fighting, if necessary.

punishment. See *military discipline*.

Puritans. Austere English Protestants opposed to all traces of Catholicism in the Reformed Church. Persecuted under *Charles I*, Puritan emigrants founded religious colonies in New England. Those who remained to fight the *English Civil Wars* rose to prominence in the officer corps of the *New Model Army* and later, in the Commonwealth government of *Oliver Cromwell*. Their bans of Christmas, Maypole dancing, and other folk traditions went a long way to revive royalist sentiment in the 1650s and newly linked the king to popular customs. See also *Arminianism*; *Calvinism*; *"Root and Branch" petition*.

purser. On a wooden warship, one of four *warrant officers* and later *standing officers*. His main job was to secure victuals (edibles, beer, and wine) for the crew and to distribute ship's pay. Both responsibilities were matters of crucial importance in that if they were not carried out promptly and well they could and did cripple ship and fleet actions and cause naval missions to fail.

purveyance. In 14th-century England this was a system of compulsory sale of food to the army at prices set by the state. This term replaced the earlier *"prise."*

push of pike. See *pike*; *Swiss square*.

Pym, John (1583–1643). See *English Civil Wars*; *National Covenant*.

Pyongyang, Battle of (1592). See *Korea*; *Toyotomi Hideyoshi*.

Qing dynasty. See *banner system (China/Manchuria)*; *China*; *Manchus*; *Nurgaci*.

Qizilbash. "Redheads." So named because they wore red turbans. This was a radical *shi'ia* movement that embraced the theology of the Sufi mystic Sheik Safi al-Din (1252–1334). The Qizilbash raised the *Safavid* regime to power in Iran when it supported the candidacy of Shah Ismail I (1486–1524) in 1502. The Qizilbash order controlled provincial governorships and the military, resisting modernization and reforms that might disturb the Safavid social order during much of the 16th century. This ended with the reforms introduced by *Abbas I*. Thereafter, the Qizilbash sustained the Safavid regime by giving religious legitimation to its rule, but also giving its policies a zealous character and keeping the fires of religious war (the *ghazi* spirit) burning on two fronts with the rival *sunni* regimes of the Ottomans and Uzbeks.

quarrel. A thick-shafted short arrow fitted with a square head and fired from a *crossbow*. A synonym was *bolt*. Large quarrels were sometimes fired from *pots de fer* or other primitive cannon, but the practice was a design dead end. Most quarrels were made from yew or ash and had a quadrangular head. Three stiff fletchings, about half the quarrel length, were made from wood or hardened leather or metal. More rarely, fletchings were stiff feathers from an older bird.

quarter. Mercy, or abstaining from killing an enemy who was clearly trying to surrender or had already done so. This was an expectation of the *just war tradition*. However, there were permitted exceptions: where no quarter was offered none was required to be given; and no one was obliged to offer quarter twice. If a foe indulged in a *"ruse de guerre"* such as faking surrender to gain advantage in combat, killing could be legitimately resumed and continued until the enemy was utterly repressed. See also *battle cries*; *guerre mortelle*.

Quarter Army. "Wojsko kwarciane," from the Polish "Kwarta" ("Quarter"), which referred to the share of rent from royal lands taken as tax to sustain these troops. This system allowed Poland to maintain a small, but permanent, cavalry force from 1566 to 1652. In practice, the sums raised were closer to one-fifth of revenues. The troopers were lightly armed and hardly armored at all, with an increasing reliance on firearms in the 17th century. They peaked at about 3,000–5,000 light-to-medium cavalry. See also *light cavalry*; *Polish Army*.

quarter deck. A small deck erected above the main deck in the aft of a ship.

quartermaster. A petty officer (usually a *warrant officer*) tasked to help the *master* oversee the general handling of a warship. On land this was the officer (or contractor) in charge of riding ahead of an army to arrange food and quarters (lodging). In the French Army his title was *maréchal de logis*.

quartermaster's mate. A subordinate of the *quartermaster*.

quarterstaff. A six-to-eight-foot-long stout pole. One end was usually wrapped in hammered iron to give it a killing weight. It served as a cheap and easily manufactured peasant weapon. See also *staff-weapons*.

quarto-cannon. A 16th-century medium-sized gun that weighed about 2,000 pounds and could launch 12-pound *shot* to an effective range of 400 yards and a maximum range of 2,000 yards.

Québec. See *Indian Wars (North America)*.

quick match. Also called "port-fire." A metal tube holding rapidly flammable materials. They were usually made from threads of cotton wick soaked in a solution of gunpowder and gum arabic, dried and rolled in *corned* powder. A quick match was lighted by touching it to the *slow match* held in place in a *linstock*. The quick match was then applied directly to fine powder in the vent (touch hole) of the cannon. When a given firing action ended or guns needed to be repositioned, the burning end of the quick match was snipped off, while the slow match remained lighted and secure in the linstock. Using quick match to set off the main charge significantly improved safety for gun crews.

R

Raad van State. "Council of State." The body that took control of government in the United Provinces following the death of *William the Silent*. It oversaw military operations and finance and administration of the navy and army. Under terms of the *Treaty of Nonsuch* (1585), *Elizabeth I* gained representation in the Raad, to which she named the *Earl of Leicester*. In the 1590s the Raad lent important support to the military reforms of *Maurits of Nassau*. Later, it lost effective political power to the Holland regents.

rabito. A border patrol by troops from an Iberian Muslim *ribat*. They were cousins to the *razzia*. Christians mimicked their success with formation of more formal *Hermandades*.

race-built. See *galleon*; *Invincible Armada*.

rachat. The purchase of domestic slaves for use in military formations. It was an ancient practice among slave empires such as the *Mamlūks* in Egypt.

raiding. Wherever an economy of plunder and tribute existed or strong government was absent, as throughout most of Europe during the Middle Ages, for a thousand years around the Mediterranean following the collapse of Roman power, and for two millennia along the Inner Asian frontier with China, raiding thrived as the principal form of warfare. Raids were conducted by land and sea, by small parties or large forces, according to time, place, and expected opposition. Raiding became systemic as sedentary populations paid protection money to fend off raiders. For example, the "Danegeld" was paid to reduce Viking raiding into Saxon England. Unintentionally, raiding circulated and redistributed wealth in the form of precious metals and captured slaves and livestock. Where tribute was late or refused raiders might burn rather than carry goods away, "pour encourager les autres." Most raiders traveled light, the better to carry off plundered goods or herds of cattle or slaves. Raiders relied on surprise and speed and hence tended to be horse soldiers (except the Vikings, whose longships could stealthily navigate hundreds of miles of inland waterways). Such cavalry raids were so preeminent and memorable special terms for them were embedded in different languages: *cavalgada, chevauchée, razzia*. Foot soldiers also raided, of course, but only cavalry had the mobility to conduct the true chevauchée or razzia. Raiders generally tended to run rather than fight when met by stout defense or a solid *fortification* that was not taken by a raid unnoticed and unannounced by careless watchers. If an alarm was raised, armed men in the fields would escort civilians and livestock to a prepared place of defense, a *motte-and-bailey* fort in the 12th century or a more substantial stone or brick castle after that. This resulted in running fights between the escort and the raiding party, with the latter unimpeded and able to move to attack with superior speed while the former herded old people, women, and children while running and fighting themselves. Combat was sharp and deadly, as one group of armed men tried to steal a living in harsh times while the other fought desperately to protect families, flocks, and fields. See also *civilians*; *Crusades*; *Inner Asia*; *March*; *Militargrenze*; *prisoners of war*; *slavery and war*.

Rain, Battle of (April 15, 1632). Following his victory at *First Breitenfeld* (September 17, 1631), *Gustavus Adolphus* took his army of 25,000 out of winter quarters and invaded Bavaria. He crossed the Danube on April 7 and next looked to ford the River Lech, where *Johann Tilly* was positioned to stop him with 20,000 Imperial and Bavarian troops. Gustavus employed a novel tactic: at a carefully chosen bend of the Lech his main army forded while hidden by a smokescreen made from burning straw and covered as they crossed the river by Swedish artillery fire. This secured a beachhead into which he next crossed over the artillery and from where it hammered the Imperial lines. The Catholic position, which once seemed unbreachable, broke down in confusion as men fell back through their camp that was now part of a battlefield. During this action 4,000 Imperial troops were killed and Tilly was mortally wounded (he died five days later). The victory at Rain allowed Gustavus to take Augsburg and Munich and his troops to eat out unprotected Bavaria.

Rajputs. From "rajaputra," or "son of a chief." A martial caste of *Hindu* warriors who established themselves under local potentates in various locales, with a concentration in northwestern India. Their precise origin is disputed. Some assert they arose from original clan/communal formations (traditionally, there were 36 Rajput clans) which climbed to local prominence through warfare and offering protection to the peasantry, to then found discrete states and kingdoms. These histories ascribe to the Rajputs what they claimed for themselves: a vedic pedigree as the "first kshatiyas" in the caste system. Others argue they descended from early Central Asian invaders of India (Hunas). If so, these peoples and the states they founded in western India were subsequently Indianized and Hinduized, possibly with the aid of hired Brahman scribes, and thereby transmuted into "Rajputs" who laid claim to the vedic tradition. "Untouchables" were drawn to the Rajputs as military service enabled them to rise above their assigned station in the caste system.

Whether homegrown or imported, Rajput states and chiefs strenuously resisted later invasions of India from the 8th to the 13th centuries by Turkic, Mongol, and mixed Muslim warrior peoples. They held out against invasions by the Ghaznavids, Ghurids, *Mamlūks*, and Khaljis, with the latter overrunning Delhi in 1290. Sultan Ala-ud-din (r.1296–1316) of the *Delhi Sultanate* for a time overran the northern Rajput states, and therefore was able to invade even more ancient Tamil states they had buffered to the south. The Rajputs acquired cannon sometime in the mid-14th century, and gunpowder weapons were in wide use in Rajput wars by the 1360s. Conflict with the later *Mughals* could be horrific: in 1568, when *Akbar* threatened to conquer the Rajput states, some Rajput warriors responded with massacres of their own women and children rather than allow them to fall into Muslim hands. Other Rajput chiefs allied with Akbar since he showed that any who resisted would be exterminated. This lesson had been taught when Akbar razed the Rajput city of Chitor and ordered the slaughter of 30,000 of its inhabitants. Others allied with the Mughals because there were huge rewards available in the *mansabdari* system. See also *Khanwa, Battle of*; *Rana Sangha*.

Suggested Reading: Dirk Kolff, *Naukar, Rajput, and Sepoy* (1990); R. Saxena, *Army of the Rajputs* (1989).

rake. Firing along the length of a flanked position of enemy troops or line of ships. This avoided exposing oneself to a volley of ship's guns, or *broadside*, while bringing maximum fire to bear on the enemy. This became a key tactical objective when in *line ahead* or *line astern* formations.

Rakoczy, George (1593–1648). Prince of Transylvania; king of Hungary, 1630–1648. His lands were a region of *guerre guerroyante* between the *Habsburgs* and the *Ottomans* to the end of the *Thirty Years' War* in 1648. He allied with Sweden from 1630 against the common Habsburg foe, continuing the practice of his predecessors of aligning with Protestant enemies of the Habsburgs. In 1644 he declared war on *Ferdinand III* and forced a peace on the Empire at Linz (1645) that was favorable to Hungarian political and religious liberties.

Raleigh, Walter (1552–1618). Raleigh was born into the Devonshire nobility, which had longstanding investments in the rough trades of *piracy* and *privateering*. At age 15 he fought for the Huguenot cause in France. In 1580 he served in Ireland and participated in a massacre at Smerwick. His decision to become a "gentleman adventurer at sea" was thus an almost natural transition from family life. In 1585, after the fall of Antwerp to the Spanish, Raleigh sailed to harry the Iberian fishing fleet off Newfoundland. His subsequent expedition to what later became North Carolina was a failure, with

719

the colony he founded at Roanoke eventually abandoned and lost. He did not take an active part in defense against the *Invincible Armada*, and in 1589 left court and settled in Ireland. He organized a privateering expedition in 1592 but fell out of favor with *Elizabeth I* over his secret marriage in late 1591 to one of her maids of honor, Bess Throckmorton, and was sent to the *Tower of London* along with his bride as the ships sailed. He was released when they returned with a rich prize of a fully loaded Portuguese *carrack*. In 1595 he sailed to find "El Dorado" in the Amazon. In 1596 Raleigh led one squadron of an assault by 30 Anglo-Dutch warships and 8,000 men against Cadiz, led by *2nd Earl of Essex* and *Charles Howard* of Effingham. The English burned or took as prizes 40 Spanish ships and held Cadiz for six weeks. Raleigh fell out with *James I* after a whispering campaign at court poisoned the king against him. He spent years in the Tower upon being convicted of high treason. He was released in 1616 and sailed for South America to again search for El Dorado. He was ordered not to disturb James' peace with Spain on pain of death, but one of his captains attacked and captured a Spanish port, during which Raleigh's son was killed. The Spanish ambassador demanded restitution. Raleigh tried to flee to France but was arrested and beheaded on James' order in 1618.

Suggested Reading: Paul Seaver, *Sir Walter Releigh* (2004).

ramming (of guns). Wooden rams were used to force the powder charge, wadding, and *shot* down the muzzle of *cannon* so that it reached the *breech* and the charge lay under the vent (touch hole). Whether in big guns or *muskets*, early charges were served as loose powder; by 1560 powder and wadding were bagged in a *cartridge* or sack. In either case, the powder and shot had to be rammed. Shot for muskets was generally a lead ball about one-half ounce in an *arquebus* (cut 32 to a pound of lead) and 1 ounce for a musket (cut 16 to a pound of lead). Ottoman firearms and the "Spanish musket" fired balls weighing $1\frac{1}{2}$ ounces (cut 12 to a pound of lead). For cannon, shot could be any of a stone or iron cannonball or a variety of specialized naval bar shot, or it might be *canistershot*, *case shot*, or *grapeshot*. Wooden ramrods slowed the rate of fire of big and small guns, as if not used carefully they jammed weapons or broke inside the barrel. Nevertheless, the simple solution of switching to iron ramrods did not catch on until the second half of the 17th century. Ramming was faster and cleaner in a *smoothbore* than a *rifled-bore* barrel, which conduced to infantry preference for less-accurate smoothbore muskets that had a higher rate of fire. See also *sponge*.

ramming (of ships). See *galley*.

rampart. A raised earthen structure forming the main defense line shielding defenders from enemy artillery fire. It was usually topped by a stone *parapet* and was often wide enough for troops and guns to move along to reinforce other areas of the defense perimeter. In the absence of *artillery towers*, ramparts supported the main defensive artillery. See also *casemate*; *casement*; *chemin de ronde*; *curtain wall*; *terre-plein*.

ramrods. See *ramming (of guns)*.

Rana Sangha (r.1509–1527). Né Maharana Sangram Singh. *Rajput* king of Mewar. His expansionist wars against neighboring states gained him recognition by most Rajputs, but his consolidation of power was interrupted by the invasion of north India by *Babur*. After Babur overthrew the *Delhi Sultanate* in 1526 the Rajputs united under Rana Sanga and fielded a confederate army. At *Khanwa* in 1527 superior Moghul artillery and musketry firepower defeated the much larger but politically divided Rajput army.

ransom. Ransom was an essential part of war in the Middle Ages in both Christian and Muslim societies. The practice also extended well into, and indeed past, the early modern period. Captured monarchs such as Richard I ("Coeur de Lion") of England, or the French kings Jean II and *Francis I*, were held literally for a "king's ransom." Holding nobles and officers for ransom, while killing commoners, was so commonplace that to avoid bankruptcy of wealthy prisoners regular schedules of payment were agreed; mercenary captains even took out insurance contracts in which their employers were obliged to pay their ransom as part of the service agreement. During the *Thirty Years' War* (1618–1648) mutually agreed tariffs for captive officers were published that ranked the worth of a general at 25,000 thalers and a captain at just 100, with rankings in between for colonels, princes, and other ranks. See also *Agincourt, Battle of*; *Brétigny, Treaty of*; *chevauchée*; *chivalry*; *condottieri*; *Crécy, Battle of*; *Crusades*; *cuartel general*; *herald*; *hostage-taking*; *Hundred Years' War*; *infantry*; *Italian Wars*; *Jacquerie*; *Jankov, Battle of*; *knight*; *Knights of Our Lady of Montjoie*; *Knights Templar*; *Military Orders*; *Otterburn, Battle of*; *piracy*; *Pizarro, Francisco*; *Poitiers, Battle of*; *prisoners of war*; *Salāh al-Dīn*; *Scottish Wars*; *shock*; *Torstensson, Lennart*; *Yellow Waters, Battle of*.

> *...to avoid bankruptcy of wealthy prisoners regular schedules of payment were agreed...*

Rathmines, Battle of (August 2, 1649). *Ormonde* led an Irish army against the *Roundhead* garrison in Dublin, but while he was still preparing to assault the Parliamentarians attacked his camp at Rathmines. Several thousand of Ormonde's men were killed or taken, and most of his artillery was captured.

rations. During the medieval and early modern periods staple foodstuffs in Europe and Asia were few in number and difficult to preserve. This was especially a problem for war at sea. Various grains were used to bake bread or hard biscuit. Some historians think biscuit formed 70 percent of a sailor's diet, supplemented by cheese and beer, cider, or wine, according to local custom. Horses also traveled by sea, often great distances. They were generally fed oats. Meat (cattle, pigs, chickens, sheep) sometimes traveled live, but more often animals were butchered and their salted meat was stored in the ship's hold. Fish was always available, but usually salted in casks rather than caught fresh. Fruits and vegetables were virtually unheard of, other than onions, especially in northern latitudes. Scurvy was not a great problem prior to the 16th century, however, because few ships made long-distance voyages. It was some time after the discovery of the New World that a connection was noticed and understood between eating fruits and avoiding scurvy. By the 17th century ships sailing to or in the Caribbean had access to fresh fruits, sugar, and barrels of rum.

Food and drink supplied to soldiers varied greatly by national custom, diet, and locale. Ottoman *Janissaries* were guaranteed one meal per day—boiled cracked wheat and butter—cooked in the *Orta's* large copper kettle (which also served as the unit icon), the *Kazan*, and plentiful hardtack when bread was not available. But they usually ate much better than that owing to a sophisticated commissary system that was the envy of Europe, through which victualing was carefully organized and funds dispersed. In addition to basic rations, each Janissary company received extra cash to buy bread and meat. While on campaign additional allowances were dispersed and tens of thousands of animals from the Imperial herds were slaughtered. Ottoman troops were (mostly) sober, unlike those of European or Asian armies. English soldiers expected salt meat, butter, hard biscuit, cheese, and small beer, even if they had to steal it themselves. The beer was important for more than recreation: water supplies in foreign lands were unmapped and possibly unsafe or poisoned. French armies took large ovens and supplies of grain with them on the march, pausing every several days to bake thousands of loaves of fresh bread. Wine, rather than small beer, was the French or Burgundian or German soldier's preference, and he drank it in huge quantities. Danes, Dutch, and Portuguese expected large quantities of fish in their rations.

Globally, soldiers' diets varied widely. North American forest Indians could march 30–50 miles in a day, for days on end, subsisting on acorns and small nuts, animal entrails, squirrels, skunks, or hares, marrow sucked from old bones, small snakes, and river or lake trout. If fortunate and not being pursued, they might bring down and feast on a deer. Mongols were expert huntsmen who picked up game along the way to supplement a basic diet of beef and bovine cheese washed down with cow's blood mixed with milk. Chinese, Viet, and other Asian troops subsisted on rice, which traveled further than most Western foods. *Aztec* warriors fed on supplies sent to Tenochtitlán as tribute before the campaign season: maize cakes and meal, beans, chile, pumpkin seeds, local fruits, and salt. Following a victory, they consumed roasted human flesh. During the *Thirty Years' War* (1618–1648), the standard ration in most European armies was 1 kg of bread, $\frac{1}{2}$ kg of meat, and 2 liters of wine or beer. Of course, that measure was not always met. All soldiers in all wars—whether African, Ottoman, English, German, Spanish, or Chinese—supplemented daily rations with opportunistically plundered food and drink. In the 16th–17th centuries, that fact of military life was systematized by *Albrecht von Wallenstein* in the *contributions* system that epitomized the early modern principle that "war should pay for itself" (*bellum se ipse alet*).

ravelin. A small defense structure, triangular or arrow-headed in shape, set between two *bastions* in front of the *curtain wall*.

Ravenna, Battle of (April 11, 1512). Fought during the early phase of the *Italian Wars* (1494–1559), Ravenna was a clash of two armies in transition from the *feudal* to the modern. Perhaps 20,000 French under *Gaston de Foix*, along with 8,500 Swiss and German mercenaries, met 18,000 Spanish led by *Pescara*. Each side brought cannon to the field, with the French artillery outnumbering the Spanish by 50 guns to 30. The French artillery pounded the Spanish heavy horse but the Spanish infantry remained protected in well dug-in positions along the Ronco River. The French manhandled several guns across the river and began to fire into the rear of the Spanish position. The Spanish fled their suddenly exposed trenches in panic but could only flee from the guns to their rear by advancing into the teeth of the main French position. As French horse and infantry closed on breaking Spanish ranks a terrible slaughter commenced. The Spanish lost nearly half their men. French casualties were also heavy, totaling over 4,000 dead. Among them was the impetuous Foix.

Ravenspur, Battle of (1471). See *Wars of the Roses*.

rawcon. A late-medieval *halberd* type with a long central spike flanked by double side blades.

Raya. Or "Reaya." The tax-paying, strictly civilian population of the *Ottoman Empire*. Sultans and the *Janissaries* tried to keep Raya disarmed by law (as did the *samurai* concerning townsfolk and peasants in Japan). As the Empire's military needs grew and infantry displaced traditional *heavy cavalry*, segments of the Raya were allowed to own bows or guns and some were recruited into Ottoman auxiliary corps.

al-Raydaniyya, Battle of (1517). See *Mamlūks*; *Ottoman Empire*.

Razats. French peasants in Provence who rebelled against royalist forces from 1578 to 1580. Comparable peasant rebellions broke out in Dauphiné and Vivarais. The Razats formed armed bands with complete indifference to the confession of their members, despite the raging of confessional conflict all around them. They were driven by the deprivations of chronic warfare—especially the practice of billeting troops in peasant homes and at their expense. In addition to the usual violence and atrocities of a peasant rising against the local seigneury and royal tax collectors, the Razats specially targeted local military garrisons as the main authors of want and misery. In Dauphiné the end came when over 1,000 peasants were slaughtered by royalist troops at Morains on March 26, 1580. Throughout the southeast of France, after the main revolts died down peasant guerillas remained active in the forests and mountains. See also *French Civil Wars*; *Jacquerie*; *Tard-Avisés*.

razzia. "Raid." A traditional style of *Bedouin* warfare in which small units of *light cavalry* swept into a town in search of plunder or as a form of ritualized warfare intended to humiliate and demonstrate the weakness of the enemy. It was widely mimicked by the Christian states of Iberia in their own dealings with the Muslim *taifa states* of the south. See also *parias*; *rabito*; *raiding*; *tribute*.

real patronato. "Royal patronage." This was a grant of extraordinary governing powers by Spanish monarchs to the *Catholic Church* in Latin America, but nowhere else in the Spanish Empire. It intertwined the politics of Catholic monastic and priestly orders—notably, Augustinians, Dominicans, Franciscans, and *Jesuits*—with the interests of the crown. Also at stake were raw politics of settlement, Indian conversion and the matter of Indian slavery, and other troublesome issues raised by extension and adaptation of the crusading system of *encomienda* to conquest and control of the Americas. The Church's "Christianizing mission" among the Indians was deepened, broadened, and subjected to more clear hierarchical authority under instructions issued by *Philip II* in 1574. In return, the crown reserved the right to name bishops and other high clergy and thereby control the social, class, and racial make-up of the colonial Church.

reaming. An early modern (c.1550) method of making barrels for iron or bronze *cannon*. The barrel was cast as a solid piece then laboriously slow-bored by a mechanical device called a "reamer" that was powered by animal treadmills or water wheels. A touch hole was later drilled at right angles to the reamed bore. This method made much stronger barrels, and made casting of barrels with *trunnions* and other innovations much easier.

rear admiral. In the 16th–17th centuries among the Atlantic nations, an admiral who was the third ranking commander in a fleet, behind the *admiral* and *vice admiral*.

Reconquista. "The Reconquest." In 711 C.E. an army of Islamicized Moors crossed from North Africa and began the Muslim conquest of Visigoth Iberia. Within twenty years they reached the Frankish frontier, across which they raided in force on several occasions. Behind this army tens of thousands of civilian Moors migrated into Iberia while many Visigoth serfs converted and lent support to the Muslim displacement of the old Visigoth aristocracy. This migration-cum-conquest threatened the Frankish lands (formerly Roman Gaul) as well. The Moors' northward advance was not stopped until they suffered defeat, c.732–737, and were forced to stay south of the Pyrenees by an army of Franks led by Charles Martel, "The Hammer" (c.688–741). The Muslims united under a powerful *caliphate* (the Umayyads) based in Córdoba until 1008, while petty Christian kingdoms (Aragon, Castile, Galicia, Léon, Navarre, and Barcelona) in the north fought each other as well as the Moors. For centuries the quality of Muslim civilization in *al-Andalus* far surpassed that of the Christian states to the north. Muslim societies were more urban, more prosperous, and considerably more literate and learned, especially in Córdoba and *Granada*. Muslim universities ("madrassa") here and in Sicily were major conduits for the transmission of Graeco-Roman classical knowledge to Europe, via Arabic translation.

A long Christian "reconquest" began under Alphonso II (866–911). As each new territorial gain was secured by construction of town-fortresses, the Reconquista took on its essential character of a slow migratory advance, with progressive extension of Christian principalities and kingdoms at the expense of Muslim power and control. The pattern included frequent interruptions by successful Muslim counterattacks. Still, on the whole the Christians advanced at Muslim expense. Asturias migrated southward to be reorganized around a new capital at Léon; Navarre emerged as a discrete kingdom early in the 10th century; and Castile arose as a Christian territory by 950, a half century before the caliphate in Córdoba broke up into several weak and warring emirates. Portugal was a distinct principality by 1071 and a kingdom by 1143. Into this long and multi-faceted war were drawn "foreign" fighters at different times: *Berber* and *Tuareg* tribesmen, *jihadis* from Muslim Africa, and Frankish and other Christian *knights* from all over Europe. The military exploits and volunteerism of the latter prefigured and foretold the coming *Crusades* to the Middle East.

While it might seem that for over 700 years Christians and Muslims waged war for control of Iberia, in fact for much of the period the situation was more politically confused. Muslim and Christian sometimes allied with each other to fight coreligionists over such material interests as land, trade, and *parias* (forced annual tribute). The emirs of Córdoba imported Berber warriors from North Africa and *mamlūk* slave soldiers from the east, but they also employed Christian mercenaries. The most famous Christian warrior of the Reconquista, "El Cid" (né Ruy Díaz de Vivar), once served the emir of Zaragoza. Christian kings allied with Muslim rulers against fellow Christians or to raid and plunder some third Muslim power. This changed as *Norman* invaders captured Sicily from its Muslim masters and Latin Christendom launched the First Crusade to the "Holy Land." Christian warriors-cum-bandits, stirred by religious zeal, committed to an Iberian crusade depicted as a reconquest of the peninsula from Islam, but also richly rewarding in land and serfs. Christians benefitted from Muslim division into dozens of petty and rival *taifa states*, even taking Toledo in 1085.

Almoravids and Almohads

The Almoravid caliphs of North Africa intervened at the behest of taifa Muslims, riding in on a wave of Berber and Tuareg jihadis from Africa. Castile was defeated at Badajoz and at Sagrajas (1086), and Christian borders were pushed back by a newly united and militant Muslim power. A short-term turning point came in 1094 when El Cid captured Valencia for Castile following a sustained and terrible siege. But the city was retaken by the Almoravids in 1102; Zaragoza fell in 1106, then Majorca and Ibiza in their turn. By 1117 the Almoravids had themselves overrun and annexed all the taifa states, which had angered Emir Yusuf ibn Tashufin by their failure to unite with him against the Christians. Some taifa states had even sought Christian protection from the radical Almoravids. As the sole Muslim power left in Iberia, the Almoravids settled in to govern their extended empire from Córdoba. Neither side could establish military dominance; a temporary balance of power in Iberia was attained.

The Almoravid homeland in Africa was still peopled by tough, desert jihadis. They remained fanatically puritanical, compelled by the moral aesthetic of the desert, while their Almoravid cousins in Córdoba settled into a comfortable urban and semi-assimilated existence that looked decadent when viewed from the dunes of North Africa. And so the Empire began to pull apart, as an African revivalist challenge raised up a radical challenger, the Almohads, to oppose Córdoban doctrinal softness and toleration. A second set of fourteen taifa states thus emerged between 1144 and 1146, as Muslim fragmentation returned to Iberia with the Almohad assault on the Almoravids in Africa. This fatally undermined the Almoravids across the Gibraltar Strait. A Christian coalition led by Castile took advantage to capture Almeria while the Portuguese took Lisbon, assisted by English

> *. . . the Portuguese took Lisbon, assisted by . . . Crusader knights.*

and Flemish Crusader knights. In reaction, Almohad jihadis rode out of the desert and crossed over the water to Iberia in 1148, tossing aside the last Almoravid resistance. They came prepared for a long campaign, with pack camels and swift Arabian ponies in tow, intent on cleansing Iberia of the Christian infection. They began by overrunning the taifa states, then retook Almeria from Castile in 1157. By 1172 Almohad fighters were in full control of all the Muslim lands of Iberia. In 1195 the full strength of the African-Andalusian martial empire of the Almohads was directed against Castile. In a major battle at Alarcos (July 18, 1196) Castile's main army was crushed by the Almohads. In 1203 Majorca fell.

Turn of the Tide

Despite these defeats, Iberia's Christians retained three significant military advantages. First, their social-military culture and organization of knights and retainers provided a semi-professional edge, and a deeper recruiting pool, compared with the less-efficient Muslim system of tribal levies. Second, new *Military Orders* were founded to take up the fight—the *Knights of Calatrava* in 1164 and the *Knights of Santiago* in 1170—in response to proclamation of an Iberian crusade by Pope Innocent III (1161–1216). Their strategic role was to hold exposed cities and key valleys. The knights and retainers of the Military Orders, holy warriors in their own right, provided an effective and efficient counter to the Muslim jihadis. They gave Christian rulers a large force of well-trained, highly disciplined, religiously inspired troops. This was first made clear when a large number of knights from all over Europe gathered at Toledo in the spring of 1212. The clash with the Almohads occurred at Las Navas de Tolosa (July 16, 1212). The Christian victory there opened up the crucial

Guadalquiver Valley. Muslim losses were so great, especially among the Moorish aristocracy, that the defeat marked the beginning of a terminal decline of the Almohads. Las Navas de Tolosa was thus the most important battle in the 700 year history of religious warfare in Iberia. After it, Ferdinand III (1217–1252) united Castile with León in 1230 and, in alliance with James I ("The Conqueror") of Aragon (1208–1276), sent Christian armies to capture a sequence of important territories from the Muslims: the Balearic Islands (1229–1235), Majorca (1229), Córdoba (1236), Valencia (1238), Murcia (1243), Jaen (1246), and Seville (1248). Portugal took advantage of these multiple blows to Muslim power to conquer territory along the Algarve coast.

All this enhanced the third Christian advantage: interior lines. Once the central plain of Iberia fell to Castile-León, Christians controlled the headwaters of the major rivers of a parched land and the main roads critical for trade and war, all of which traveled through the river valleys. Moorish *razzia* slowly petered out over fifty years while Christian raiding correspondingly increased. This strategic shift drained Muslim wealth and manpower and eroded Muslim territory. By the end of the 13th century Castile crossed the "olive line" to control Toledo and its hinterland, while Muslim Seville was forced into tributary status. Castile tended to strip conquered Muslims of all land and forcibly remove them from cities, pushing tens of thousands of refugees toward Granada. Aragon was more tolerant, leaving a large Muslim population in Valencia, for example. Alfonso XI (1312–1350), whose people feared his autocratic ways more than they feared the Moors, decisively defeated a combined Iberian and African Muslim army at Río Salado (October 30, 1340). The follow-on *Siege of Algeciras* destroyed much of the city before it fell to *conquistadores* from Castile and Léon in 1344. Self-governing Muslims were thereafter confined to mountainous, and therefore defensible, Granada. Despite chronic border warfare the main "Reconquista" now stalled. The *Black Death*, Christian civil and inter-kingdom wars, and Castile's involvement in the *Hundred Years' War* (1337–1453) all slowed its march. A long peace of mutual toleration therefore followed, with much social, intellectual, cultural, and economic interaction between the major faiths, with Jews also broadly tolerated by Muslims (though less so by some Christians).

Intense religious hostility increased again in the 15th century as the final conquest of Muslim Spain was launched following the union of Aragon and Castile under *Ferdinand and Isabella*. The campaign began on February 28, 1482, with a surprise assault on the garrison fortress of Alhama de Granada, two dozen miles southwest of Granada. There was a new spirit of barbarism infecting Spanish arms in the final push on Granada and even a new savagery in Iberian Christianity. This was noted at the time by Italians who saw it firsthand in the Aragonese conquest of Sicily and Naples and by Europe as a whole as Spain besieged, conquered, and enslaved the entire population of Málaga in 1487. After the fall of Granada it was evident in rapacious behavior by conquistadores in the New World, and later in *Alba*'s brutal mistreatment of the Netherlands and the *"Spanish Fury"* in Antwerp. In Iberia this mood took the form of a new ferocity in treatment of Jews and Muslims before and after the fall of Granada, which finally negotiated its surrender after a 10-year siege. There followed a military procession led by Ferdinand and Isabella into the city on January 2, 1492, an event read as a divine blessing by the monarchs and by many of their subjects. Queen Isabella, a rather dim Catholic ideologue, celebrated by expelling Jews from Castile, forcibly converting Muslims, and financing the first voyage of Christopher Columbus.

The Reconquista poses an interesting counterfactual: had its course gone otherwise, South and Central America could well have been conquered by a Muslim power based in Iberia rather than the two Christian states which colonized them in fact. The effect on the native populations of the Americas likely would have been broadly similar: mass death from African and European diseases, enslavement and displacement of survivors by a self-regarding superior civilization that thought itself specially favored by God and was comfortable with slavery. The effects on world history, however, would have been enormous, though wholly unpredictable. See also *Catalan Great Company*; *jinetes*; *Santiago Matamoros*.

Suggested Reading: P. Cachia, *A History of Islamic Spain* (1965); Hugh Kennedy, *Muslim Spain and Portugal* (1996); L. Lomax, *The Reconquest of Spain* (1978).

recruitment. How a society recruits soldiery is of fundamental importance to its politics, social order, class structure, and military-political success. The recruitment systems of the societies covered in this work paralleled in diversity the great range in the forms of medieval and early modern societies themselves, from tiny city-states and fortified medieval towns to fragmented feudal orders in Europe and Japan where the "state" per se hardly existed, to monarchies with advanced bureaucratic systems, to the huge empires of the Ottomans and Chinese. For most of Western Europe during the Middle Ages the *servitium debitum* dictated who owed military obligations and under what conditions. This was paralleled by the *itqa* system of smaller Islamic emirates. In other Muslim societies slave soldiers (*mamlūks*) occupied a prominent place. In general, during the 13th century the medieval idea in Europe slowly gave way to paid military service, including for the knightly orders, and a greatly expanded recruitment base. Recruitment was determined by much more than the shape or strength of the state, however. Culture and technology played key roles, especially once the "infantry revolution" took hold and warring societies and military elites adapted to the arrival of new social classes on the field of battle. See also *beat the drum*; *"coat-and-conduct" money*; *Cossacks*; *dead-pays*; *Denmark*; *Devşirme system*; *dirlik yememiş*; *Dithmarscher*; *Doppelgänger*; *English armies*; *French armies*; *ghazi*; *ghulams*; *Grand Vezier*; *Imperial Army*; *Janissary Corps*; *Kur'aci*; *maryol taifesi*; *men-at-arms*; *Military Orders*; *militia*; *Ottoman Army*; *Ottoman warfare*; *Polish Army*; *Raya*; *rusttjänst*; *schutterijen*; *sekban*; *sipahis*; *Spanish Army*; *Swedish Army*; *Swiss Confederation*; *Swiss square*; *timariots*; *war finance*; *Yaya infantry*; *ziamet*.

redan. An elementary fieldwork of right-angled faces so emplaced as to present a series of "teeth" to the enemy. In permanent fortifications they were used to cover weak points in the main structure or where it was feasible to use them in place of more expensive *bastions*.

"red barbarian cannon." A Chinese term for European-style *cannon* recovered by the Portuguese from a sunken English (or Dutch) ship in 1621, delivered to Ming gunsmiths who made copies for use in the ongoing Ming war with the *Manchus*.

redoubt. An isolated outwork defending an important position forward of the *enceinte*. Alternately, a small self-contained fort built within a larger structure as part of its layers of defense.

redshanks. Scots *mercenaries* who hired out seasonally for wars in Ireland from the early 15th century. The term may have derived from their tendency to sunburn. Their terms of service were more flexible than the expensive, hereditary *galloglass* and they were far more numerous. During the Tudor conquest of Ireland thousands crossed the water. Some also fought in Ireland during the *English Civil Wars*.

Red Turbans. Actually, the "turban" in question was a topknot of hair tied with a red cloth. This gave a distinctive appearance to soldiers of a military offshoot of the millenarian White Lotus, a *Buddhist* sect which challenged the Mongol (Yuan) dynasty in the wake of the ravages of the *Black Death* in parts of China from c.1331, and the catastrophic southward shift of the course of the Yellow River in 1344. Their rebellion broke apart the Mongol Empire in China, reducing the country to warring provinces. They were not able to secure either power at the center or broad enough popular support to take control themselves. However, one of their generals, the squat, famously ugly Zhu Yuanzhang, captured Nanjing in 1356. He split from the Red Turbans and upon ousting the Yuan from central China proclaimed a new dynasty with himself at its head: the *Ming* (1368). He took the reign name *Hongwu*. See also *Lake Boyang, Battle of*.

reflex bow. A composite bow whose tips were curved back against the direction of the draw, which imparted additional velocity and penetrating power to the arrow.

reformadoes. Originally, unemployed officers who organized in 1641–1642 to intimidate Parliament into giving them military commissions; some accompanied *Charles I* to bully the Commons and arrest five leaders of the Parliamentary opposition. In 1647 reformadoes and deserters were brought into regiments in London loyal to Parliament in its losing argument with the *New Model Army*.

Reformation. See *Protestant Reformation*.

regard. A military bonus paid to *knights* in service on campaign with their king.

regementsstycke. "Regiment guns." See *Gustavus II Adolphus.*

Regensburg, Treaty of (1630). A peace treaty between *Ferdinand II* of the Holy Roman Empire and *Louis XIII* of France in the midst of the *War of the Mantuan Succession.* It isolated the Spanish *Habsburgs* while also convincing *Olivares* that Ferdinand was an untrustworthy partner in war or peace.

Regensburg Diet (1640–1641). See *Imperial Diet.*

regiments. European armies shifted to a regimental from a *company*-based administrative and tactical system following the successful Dutch military reforms of *Maurits of Nassau.* The English lagged behind, maintaining no standing regiments through the 1630s. That sharply hampered the effectiveness of English intervention in the early part of the *Thirty Years' War.* During the *English Civil Wars* of the mid-17th century, regiments were formed in one of two ways: the *New Model Army* organized regiments in seven small companies of 100 men each plus larger companies of 140, 160, and 200, under a sergeant-major, lieutenant-colonel, and colonel respectively. The Royalists deployed smaller regiments of 1,000 men divided evenly among ten companies. See also *uniforms; wounds.*

Reichsgrafen. Counts of the *Holy Roman Empire.*

Reichskreis. "Imperial Circles" of the *Holy Roman Empire.* Regional defense associations set up in 1500 by *Maximilian I* and given responsibility for policing a specific territorial jurisdiction. They elected their own military commanders (almost always a prominent local prince), issued coin, and were responsible for raising troops and regional defense. The original Imperial Circles were: Bavaria, Swabia, Upper Rhine, Lower Rhine-Westphalia, Franconia, and Lower Saxony. In 1512 four new circles were added: Burgundy, Austria, Upper Saxony, and the Rhine Electorate. Excluded from the system were Bohemia, Switzerland, and Reich territory in Italy. Attempts at cooperation among the circles were few, and by 1600 they were incapable of defending their members. This system was directly violated in 1607 with the Imperial-Bavarian occupation of Donauwörth. German territorial princes then broke the system apart by forming confessional alliances: the *Protestant Union* and the *Catholic League.* Further violation by *Ferdinand II* of the tradition of regional courts and policing was part of the constitutional struggle within the Empire that led to war in 1618. See also *Christian IV; Leipziger Bund; Lübeck, Peace of.*

Reichsritter. German *knights.* See *Prague, Peace of; Westphalia, Peace of.*

Reichsstädte. "Free cities." See *Holy Roman Empire; Prague, Peace of; Schmalkaldic League; Westphalia, Peace of.*

Reichstag. The *Imperial Diet* of the *Holy Roman Empire* which met at Ratisbon and was comprised of representatives of the seven *Kurfürsten*, along with those of some 300 dukedoms, bishoprics, baronies, fiefdoms, and free cities which made up the *Estates* of the Empire.

Reisläufer. A Confederate (Swiss) mercenary. By the late 15th century they were often decked out in multi-colored hose, puffed sleeve shirts, and ostrich-plume hats. The *Landsknechte* made fun of them, but imitated and carried their sartorial extravagance to still further extremes of flamboyant disdain and display. See also *German Peasant War*.

Reiters. "Riders." French: "reîtres." Italian: "raitri." German *light cavalry* in the wars of the 16th–17th centuries, armored with at least a *cuirass* and helmet and from the mid-16th century deploying *wheel lock* pistols while fighting in the *caracole* style. A Reiters' great advantage was that he could shoot on the move, and did not have to stop and dismount like a *dragoon* or stop and stand in his stirrups to fire. Like their *Landsknechte* countrymen, however, Reiters were widely thought to be undisciplined and unreliable. See also *Black Riders*; *Dreux, Battle of*; *French Civil Wars*; *Thirty Years' War*.

reîtres. See *Reiters*.

Religionsfriede. "Religious peace." See *Augsburg, Peace of*; *Passau, Convention of*; *Westphalia, Peace of*.

Renaissance. See *Italian Renaissance*.

renegades. Arms dealers, master gunsmiths, and other military advisers who sold strategic goods and skilled services to lords other than their own, especially if they crossed confessional lines. Many Christians did so despite royal or church bans on arms sales and papal threats of excommunication. Muslim and Christian renegades sold their services in India, and Dutch, German, Italian, and other Europeans sold military expertise to the Ming and to the warlords of Japan. See also *armories*; *artillery*; *Barbarossa*; *bombard*; *Farangi*; *folangji*; *India*; *Invincible Armada*; *Iran*; *Janissary Corps*; *Landsknechte*; *Ottoman warfare*; *Rhodes, Siege of (1479–1480)*; *Rumis*; *Shirley, Anthony*; *Shirley, Robert*; *technology and war*; *Urban*.

Rennfahne. Noble *light cavalry* of the *Swabian League*. See also *German Peasant War*.

requerimiento. Following morally baleful encounters between *conquistadores* and Mesoamericans in the Caribbean, *Ferdinand II* of Aragon summoned a panel of Spanish theologians to advise on the status of natives facing conquest in the New World. The panel drew up the "requerimiento" based on the Book of Deuteronomy (20:10–16), demanding that all natives accept the spiritual authority of the *Catholic Church* and the political authority of the United Crowns of Castile and Aragon (Spain). Further, the document demanded that they permit Catholic missionaries to move and preach freely anywhere in their lands. The requerimiento was to be read aloud by all would-be conquistadores prior to making war on Indian nations in the Americas. If its "reasonable demands" were refused or ignored the conquistadores might, with full religious and legal sanction, commence slaughter and conquest unimpeded by qualms of conscience. The requerimiento was first read out in 1514 to a group of utterly baffled Indians who did not understand its exotic foreign language, let alone its alien religious doctrines, and who did not foresee its profound import for the looming destruction of their freedoms and societies. See also *just war tradition*.

requisition. A basic *logistics* wherein an invading army demanded billets and food from the civilian population. In this period what distinguished requisition from simple *plunder* was that it was usually done under the pretense of payment in the form of promissory notes. These usually proved worthless.

rerebrace. Upper arm armor. See *bracers*.

reservatum ecclesiaticum. An amendment to the *Peace of Augsburg*, added without the approval of the Protestant *Estates*, which mandated that any ecclesiastical prince who converted to Lutheranism must resign all Church offices and benefices (that is, was not afforded the right of *"cuius regio eius religio"*). This reservation guaranteed survival of Catholic communities while leaving open the possibility of reconversions to Catholicism whittling away Protestant positions. Thus, when the Archbishop of Cologne converted to Lutheranism in the 1580s and refused to give up his offices and income he was forcibly chased away from his bishopric by Spanish and Burgundian troops. Protestants largely ignored the reservatum, which thereby importantly contributed to confessional animosities leading to the *Thirty Years' War*. During the war, the issue of the reservatum came up with tragic consequences at *Magdeburg*. The reservatum ecclesiaticum was abolished in the 1635 *Peace of Prague*, clearing the way for a final religious and political settlement in the *Peace of Westphalia* (1648). See also *Declaratio Ferdinandei*.

> *During the war, the issue of the reservatum came up with tragic consequences at* Magdeburg.

resfuerzo. A Spanish supply ship. They were used between colonies as well as between Spain and its overseas holdings. They also accompanied the great armadas and treasure fleets.

res publica Christiana. "Christian Commonwealth." A medieval European concept expressing an admixture of pride in the putative Roman heritage of

Latin Christian law and civilization, and genuine faith in the existence of a single godly community ("Corpus Christianum") of all Latin Christians. The Christian Commonwealth overarched feudal and dynastic ties, in theory. It began to break down with the "Avignon Captivity" of the papacy (1314–1362) and the *Great Schism* (1378–1417). Still, it provided deep cultural resistance to the emergence of the *new monarchies* and later, secular nation-states. It did not survive, other than as a romantic memory and papal pipe dream, the political and intellectual storms of the *Italian Renaissance*, the breakup of Latin Christianity during the *Protestant Reformation*, and the attendant rise of self-seeking states and absolutist monarchs. The great legacy of the res publica Christiania was a common body of law, both natural and canon, much of which was incorporated by secular legal theorists into modern international law. See also *Grotius, Hugo*; *Machiavelli, Niccolò di Bernardo*.

Suggested Reading: Garrett Mattingly, *Renaissance Diplomacy* (1955).

restaur. See *warhorses*.

retirata. A freestanding rampart made from dug earth and used as a field obstacle to break the momentum of an attacking infantry square or a cavalry charge. It was developed early in the *Italian Wars* (1494–1559).

retrenchment. An interior fortification within a larger fortress to which a defending force retreated if the outer walls were breached; an inner line of defense. Alternately, an emergency trench dug by defenders behind a pending or existing enemy breach.

"Revenge," Fight of. See *Flores, Battle of.*

Revolt of the Netherlands (1487–1492). See *Netherlands.*

Revolt of the Netherlands (1568–1648). See *Eighty Years' War*; *Netherlands.*

revolution in military affairs. The academic theory of a "revolution in military affairs" in early modern Europe was first broached by Michael Roberts in 1954 and has since become generally, though not universally, accepted. What remains in dispute is when the "military revolution" occurred and what drove it. Roberts pointed to the period from 1550 to 1650, and especially to reforms undertaken in the Netherlands and Sweden. Subsequent studies, notably by Geoffrey Parker, stretched the term to cover the period 1450–1800. Other historians demurred, contending that any historical process which took a century or more to gestate could not in any meaningful way be termed a "revolution." That was not an inconsiderable point: was "military evolution" a more appropriate descriptor than "military revolution"? In its original form, the thesis identified an expanded utility and deployment of mass *infantry*, a new emphasis on *drill* and professional discipline, adoption of firearms and *artillery* through the full flowering of *gunpowder weapons*, and a corresponding counter-adoption of new techniques of *fortification*. Battle again was mobile and decisive, in contrast to the static and indecisive form that preceded the military revolution. Above all, a vast expansion in the size and cost of armies and navies put enormous new fiscal, technical, bureaucratic, and cultural demands on early modern states and societies. Standing armies and permanent navies were seen as the key change. Also, commanders were forced to make tactical adjustments to new technologies employed on the battlefield and states had to devise new methods of garnering revenues needed to sustain expanding forces. In the end, most military historians came to accept Roberts' thesis in modified form, recognizing that even if the processes of change in military doctrine, technology, and institutions were mostly evolutionary in the 16th–17th centuries, they still resulted in truly revolutionary effects.

To encompass the new armies, emerging nation-states of early modern Europe were compelled to undertake a wholesale reorganization of their societies and economies. They often did so in ways that concentrated and centralized power without regard to the surface constitutional form of the state, or longstanding traditions of civic liberty or noble privilege. This was necessary to raise the vast sums the new armed forces consumed on a year-round basis and to sustain the bureaucratic organization that so distinguished modern states and militaries from their Medieval predecessors. The great exemplars of the change were the Netherlands during the regime of *Maurits of Nassau* and the *Eighty Years' War* (1568–1648); Sweden under *Gustavus Adolphus* in the *Thirty Years' War* (1618–1648); and the *New Model Army* in England under *Thomas Fairfax* and *Oliver Cromwell* during the mid-17th century *English Civil Wars* (1639–1651). Other noteworthy features of the revolution in military affairs pointed to by historians were an inexorable trend toward establishment of national *standing armies* under centralized state control; heavy financing of artillery by monarchs, in places leading to royal monopolies on the manufacture, export, and possession of cannon; and commissioning hugely expensive royal warships to supplement *privateers*, leading ultimately to permanent professional navies.

The trend toward more massive, firearms-bearing armies culminated in the first half of the Thirty Years' War. Whereas in 1567 the *Duke of Alba* marched to repress the Revolt of the Netherlands with just 10,000 men—three infantry *tercios* of 3,000 men each, and supporting cavalry—by the end of the 16th century the *Army of Flanders* was 60,000 strong, yet it was but one of several armies maintained by Imperial Spain. Just three decades later armies as large as 100,000 fought in and over Germany. In the latter years of the German war, however, army size decreased considerably due to the logistic inability of lands already eaten out several times over to sustain such large forces. In addition, there had been a dramatic general decline in population in Germany and a specific decline in men and boys of military age, caused mostly by death from exposure to plague and other highly contagious camp diseases, and by starvation, rather than massacres or death in battle. This mid-17th-century drop was only a temporary downturn, however, in a long-range secular trend: 18th-century armies in Europe surpassed 150,000; nearly all major 19th-century armies exceeded several hundreds of thousands of men (for instance, Napoleon took 620,000 men into Russia in 1812); in the 20th century millions would fight for the belligerents of World War I and tens of millions wore uniforms of the major armies of World War II. The trend line did not break until after World War II when the mass killing technologies made such enormous concentrations of soldiers and material militarily fool-hardy, as well as unnecessary.

It is noteworthy that early debate over the military revolution was confined to developments in Western Europe where military technology was said to evolve dramatically over two centuries via progressive adaptation of winning weapons systems and tactics. At first scholars did not note or notice the same changes elsewhere. Even concerning so closely related a military arena as eastern Europe, the old ways were said to have remained largely intact. This was mainly, it was argued, because the dominant military power for most of the period—Poland—enjoyed such success with its traditional cavalry against still more "backward" armies such as that of Muscovy, that battlefield in-centive to change was minimal. This condition supposedly lasted until the Poles were bested by the reformed Swedish Army under Gustavus Adolphus in the 1620s. Yet, topographical factors and the nature of the enemy faced, *Tatar* and *Cossack* light cavalry armies, almost certainly played a greater role in Polish deployment of large cavalry forces than any putative military primi-tivism in eastern Europe.

Nor, it was said, did the *Ottoman Empire* adopt new ways. There, too, scholars saw short-term victory as the handmaiden of long term military stagnation and "backwardness." Throughout the period it was the armies of Constantinople that were on the march, and usually winning, against Euro-pean armies in the Balkans and southeastern Europe. That is why there was no obvious need or effort by the sultans to undertake socially disruptive military reforms. Or so said the academic theory. Yet, that view grossly un-derestimated the adaptability of Ottoman armies. Recent research suggests that significant divergence in adoption of new military technologies from those employed in Europe did not occur until the 1680s. Up to that point it is almost certainly more accurate to say that the Ottomans had the most ad-vanced commissary and logistics system and a sounder basis of *war finance* than any state in Europe. And the Ottomans (and Safavid Iran, too) imported *renegade* master gunners and cast cannon and made muskets broadly compa-rable to anything in the West to the end of the 17th century.

As for great empires further afield, Mughal India absorbed some firearms technology but did not shift to European-style military recruitment, organi-zation, or tactics. Imperial China, whose wealth and advanced civilization should have enabled it to follow suit with ease, forewent the advanced naval artillery encountered aboard visiting European ships in favor of retention of the old methods of ramming the enemy, followed by grappling and boarding by marines. On land, on the other hand, both *Ming* and *Manchu* readily adopted Portuguese and *Jesuit*-made cannon and muskets. In Japan the military revolution triggered such profound changes in warfare it contributed to vast political upheaval. The introduction of firearms to Japan in 1543 upset centuries-old military traditions and the internal balance of power among the *daimyo*. During the bloody *Unification Wars* this led to an end to fractious political divisions which had for centuries torn that island realm. In place of the ravages of *ashigaru* and the chaos of the *Sengoku jidai*, a political and social revolution took place under the *Tokugawa Shoguns* which rendered Japan at internal peace for over 250 years.

In Africa the introduction of firearms by Portuguese, Dutch, Danish, and English coastal traders tipped the balance of military power away from the armored cavalry of the Sahel and desert peoples, who had dominated the tribes of the coastal forest zone for over 1,000 years, in favor of their longtime victims. Why? Because it was the forest tribes who hugged the West African and Angolan coasts of Africa who first encountered European ships and traders, from whom they acquired firearms. With guns they drove back the horse-borne knights of the sword and spear of the old desert empires and began to build large states and empires of their own. Thus, *Songhay* and *Mali* fell to the *arma* of Morocco. In the southeast *Ngola* bought Portuguese muskets

> *...firearms ...upset centuries-old military traditions and the internal balance of power ...*

and decimated *Kongo*. This did not happen in North or South America, however, where other factors—disease, population loss, and rapid external conquest of the major Indian states—utterly destroyed pre-Columbian military regimes and military culture. There, *conquistador* and later firearms armies overthrew old Indian political orders and displaced the pre-gunpowder elites socially and economically as well. See also *armor*; *contributions*; *Edward III*; *English armies*; *rifled-bore*; *smoothbore*.

Suggested Reading: Brian Downing, *The Military Revolution and Political Change* (1992); MacGregor Knox and Williamson Murray, eds., *The Dynamics of Military Revolution, 1300–2050* (2001); Geoffrey Parker, *The Military Revolution*, 2nd ed. (1996); Clifford Rogers, ed., *The Military Revolution Debate* (1995).

Rex christianissimus. "Most Christian King." The ancient title of French kings denoting ordination by God, reinforced in the *sacre*, and surpassing in age and prestige newer appellations given by popes to England's *Henry VIII* ("Defender of the Faith") or to *Ferdinand and Isabella* ("Catholic Crowns"). See also *corpus mysticum*.

Rheinfelden, Battle of (March 2–3, 1638). *Bernhard von Sachsen-Weimar* led a Protestant investment of Rheinfelden, near Basil. As he was maneuvering for the siege he was met by a surprise attack by the Bavarian army under *Johann von Werth*. This caught Bernhard's men strung out while crossing the river. During the night Bernhard moved upstream those men already across the river, crossed back over, marched downstream to Rheinfelden, and took the

Bavarian army by surprise from the rear. The victory was total, with even Werth taken prisoner.

Rhodes, Siege of (1444). The *Hospitallers* had operated as "Sea Brothers," or pirates, out of Rhodes for decades. In 1440 Cyprus submitted to Egypt, leaving Rhodes the last outpost of the *Crusades* still facing ascendant Muslim power in the eastern Mediterranean. The *mamlūk* navy first attacked in 1440. Hospitaller *galleys* met the Muslims ships in the outer harbor with hymns and cannon fire, and again along the coast, and the Muslims fled. In 1444 the mamlūks returned with 18,000 men and laid siege. They pounded Hospitaller defenses with 3,500 cannonballs over six weeks. With the walls of the citadel breached late in the evening, the Brethren gathered overnight and in the morning they charged into the astonished besiegers. The mamlūks bolted for their galleys and rowed away, leaving their entire *artillery train* behind.

Rhodes, Siege of (1479–1480). The *Hospitallers* mustered 600 Brethren and hired 1,500 mercenaries to face an invasion force of 70,000 Muslims led by *Muhammad II*. The Muslims landed on May 23, and blockaded the main port with 50 *galleys*. When the Muslim assault troops landed they were massacred by gunfire from the walls. The Christians also sent *fireships* into the harbor to chase away the Muslim galleys; other galleys were sunk by fortress artillery firing incendiaries. Muhammad had several large *bombards* cast on the island and set up as a battery to pound the defenses of the main citadel with heavy stone balls. The casting and firing of this artillery was directed by a *renegade* German gunner, Meister Georg. When he feigned desertion to the Knights, possibly to spy out weakness in the walls for his guns to smash, they hanged him for his troubles. On July 28 thousands of Muslim troops stormed through a partial breach. Street fighting ensued. The Knights pushed the attackers back, pursued to their camp, and chased the survivors back to their galleys. The Muslims hurriedly burned their supplies and left.

Rhodes, Siege of (1522–1523). The siege began on July 28, 1522 as *Suleiman I* landed some 80,000 men on Rhodes to face walls rebuilt after the siege of 1479. These first arrivals were later supplemented by many tens of thousands more Muslim troops. It took a month for engineers to sap trenches and set up the Ottoman siege artillery, which was numerous and powerful. Thousands of cannonballs, incendiaries, and other projectiles were fired at the garrison's walls and bastions. Receiving this fire were about 700 *Hospitaller Knights* and sergeants and 6,000 mercenaries. Casualties were extremely heavy on both sides from mutual bombardment and repeated assaults. But it was mining with gunpowder, not bombardment, that breached the walls of the outer bastions and allowed the siege to creep inward. Repeated attempts to storm the citadel were beaten back. As the Knights ran low on saltpeter to make more powder, fear and hunger also began to tell; desertions, military and civilian, rose. On December 16 a *galley* filled with Cretan archers ran the blockade, but it was not enough: on December 21, 180 surviving Knights and 1,500 infantry surrendered and were given safe passage off the island with all their goods. They paraded out of the ruble and left for Crete on January 1, 1523, some carried there on the Sultan's ships. Suleiman had won the fight and made a magnanimous peace even though he had lost half his army to combat or disease. *Charles V* said of this last act of the *Crusades*: "Nothing in the world was so well lost as Rhodes."

ribat. A fortified outpost of Muslim warriors. They were almost miniature monasteries whose garrisons lived ascetic lives, patrolled the borders of the *taifa states*, and carried out much-feared "*rabitos*" or raids.

ribaudequin. Latin: "ribaldi." Also "ribauld" or "ribaude" or "ribaudiaux." Originally, any mean gun of cheap quality. Later, small multi-barreled *cannon*. They first appeared in Flanders in the 1330s and were always best known and most widely used there. Some had up to twelve barrels, others six or seven. Most ribaudequins could be fired singly or in volley; some were fired in multiple volleys of three or more barrels at a time. When the Veronese fought the Paduans under *John Hawkwood* at Castagnaro (March 11, 1387), the former deployed ribaudequins in carts that held 144 guns in three banks of 48 barrels each, of which 12 could be fired in volley. The Veronese still lost the fight. By the 1380s some were mounted on wheeled carts, a feat which was a significant innovation for early *artillery*. By 1500 ribaudequins were usually mounted on a *gun carriage* and thus formed an early light field artillery, but they were not very effective and never decisive. The real solution to massing firepower in battle was the musketeer.

Richard III (1452–1485). See *Wars of the Roses*.

Richelieu, Cardinal Armand Jean du Plessis de (1585–1642). "Éminence Rouge." Cardinal of Luçon, statesman, molder of the French state and much modern diplomatic practice. Richelieu trained for military service but also at the Sorbonne, where he became interested in reform of the *Gallican Church*. He entered the clergy to secure his family's hereditary claim to a French bishopric, and was made bishop in 1607 at age 22. From the court influence of *Marie de Medici*, in 1616 he was made secretary of state for foreign affairs. He wore a cardinal's hat from 1622 and was made *Louis XIII*'s first minister two years later, serving in that capacity to his death in 1642. Richelieu's first goal was to centralize authority and administration under the monarch. He did this through a system of direct rule by royal officials (intendants) who were sent into the country but reported directly to the crown. Provincial courts and medieval towns previously governed by free charters came under the authority of his intendants. Like most royalists and Catholics, he identified "heresy" with sedition, treason, and social disorder. He and Louis thus revoked the special political and military privileges enjoyed by the *Huguenots* under the *Edict of Nantes*, launched southern campaigns against the Huguenots from 1622 to 1625, and finally starved the last Protestant stronghold,

La Rochelle, into submission in 1628. That victory was tempered by a return to religious toleration with the *Edict of Alès* (1629), a settlement that contrasted starkly with the *Edict of Restitution* in Germany that same year.

When Richelieu was done consolidating the home front the monarchy was nearly unchallenged and able to pursue a new concept in governance and statecraft: raison d'etat. This 17th-century equivalent of the "national interest" became the mark of Richelieu's policy. Hence, he objected to the involvement in national politics of so many women among the *dévots*, viewing them as responsible for the devotional and confessional excesses he so despised. For Richelieu, piety and religious conformity was good for domestic tranquility and conduced to a more peaceful world, but only if religion was not indulged to excess by the governing classes. His tastes were most inclined to a monarchy of grandeur and classical harmonies, and he much preferred the "natural hierarchy" of aristocratic rule to the disruptive confessional politics of dévots, Huguenots, or troublesome *Estates*.

Keeping the Peace

The conventional view is that Richelieu built up a powerful national army and navy to break the *Habsburg* "encirclement" of France, destroy Louis XIII's enemies, and make France preeminent in Europe. Further, he is said to have done this without regard for the ideological content of the great struggle between Catholics and Protestants then driving the politics and wars of all surrounding powers. It has been said that Richelieu was a "Father of the Church" but no Catholic ideologue: Paris, not Rome, hosted his cathedral and commanded his deepest loyalties. Besides, he viewed the ostentatious Catholicism of the Habsburgs as a fig leaf concealing raw secular ambition. He thus beat them at their own best game with court intrigue, ruthless diplomacy, and clever dynastic marriages. Richelieu could also use force with rapier-like skill, waging war-by-proxy as an adjunct and instrument of his diplomacy. That is why he subsidized *Christian IV* and *Gustavus Adolphus* in their successive interventions against Habsburg power in the *Thirty Years' War*. While there is much truth in this view, other interpretations abound. Many French, and not just foreigners, hated and thought the worst of Richelieu in his own day, attributing to him base personal, material, and family motives in place of high policy. Some historians, especially Germans, call him overly aggressive and warlike and portray his reign as a disaster for France and Europe. Most French historians see him as dedicated to "la grandeur" of France, even as sacrificing selflessly to that goal. He is also depicted as the great practitioner of the balance of power, a coldly calculating realist of the thoroughly modern sort. Still others view him as informed by a sense of high religious duty, as a sincere Catholic and not just a French statesman, who tried to bring a universal and just peace to all Europe. A few English historians paint him as instead driven by coarse material gain for himself and his family rather than high principle, whether religious or secular.

Out of all this disagreement this much is clear: From 1625 Richelieu began to ready France for a definitive war with the Habsburgs which he thought inevitable, a view shared by his Spanish counterpart, *Count Olivares*. From then until his death, Richelieu accrued enormous power and powerful enemies as a result of this policy, especially the dévots. Many hated his war taxes and resented his nepotism, influence with the king, and his court favorites. Richelieu's initial moves were to arrange the marriage of Louis XIII's sister to *Charles I* of England and to ease relations with the Dutch. However, when the Huguenots rebelled in January 1625, Richelieu was compelled to forge a temporary alliance with Spain instead, in the *Treaty of Monzón* (1626). The next year he intervened against Spain in Italy. From the *War of the Mantuan Succession* (1627–1631) until he died, he and France were at war continually with Spain, undeclared before 1635 and openly after that. In 1630 he led a French army into Italy to occupy and annex Savoy when France was also indirectly at war with the Austrian Habsburgs.

A consensus view is that after the Mantuan war ended in 1631 Richelieu sought to avoid an all-out confrontation with Spain. He had learned that the *tercios* were superior to French troops in battle (as they remained until the sharp French victory at *Rocroi* in 1643), while at home any war with the Habsburg powers threatened conflict with radical Catholic dévots. As was then happening also in England, where Charles I faced opposition from "The Godly" (soi-dissant), in the 1630s Richelieu and Louis XIII faced confrontation with dévots whose hysterical piety turned them into political zealots. In short, Richelieu's humanist authoritarianism clashed with a pietistic mass movement convulsing French Catholicism that made overt opposition to the Habsburgs difficult and open alliance with Protestant powers near impossible. Fortunately, a third option appeared in the north where the Swedish king stood to be played as the greatest of Richelieu's anti-Habsburg champions, saddled with French gold and sent to fight in Germany; but the great Swede also turned out to be the proxy the Cardinal least controlled. Richelieu shrewdly mediated the *Truce of Altmark* to free Sweden of its war with Poland then subsidized its entry into the German war by paying Gustavus Adolphus 400,000 Taler (rix-dollars) under the *Treaty of Bärwalde* (1631). If domestic constraints meant he could not fight the Habsburgs with French troops then he would fight to the last Swede or mercenary that French gold could buy.

> ...*he and France were at war continually with Spain, undeclared before 1635 and openly after that.*

Making War

Following the death of Gustavus Adolphus at *Lützen* (1632), Richelieu sought to stay out of the German war by finding another anti-Habsburg champion to finance. None was up to grade. While the Swedes fought on under *Oxenstierna*, Richelieu garrisoned the Rhine frontier. Brilliantly combining foreign and domestic interests, he forced Lorraine to accept French troops in 1632: that threatened to cut the *Spanish Road* militarily while politically undercutting both the *Guise* and Gaston d'Orléans, brother of

Louis XIII, the French heir presumptive (to 1638) and husband to Marguerite of Lorraine. Richelieu also sent troops to occupy the bishopric of Trier. Alsatian free cities and small principalities were occupied in 1634–1635. Most importantly, Richelieu took the fortresses of Ehrenbreitstein and Philippsburg. In December 1634 he marched into Heidelberg in the Palatinate. Defeat of the Swedish Army at *First Nördlingen* (September 5–6, 1634) and a mutiny in the Swedish Army that took Oxenstierna captive convinced Richelieu that France had to enter the war directly, that his policy of confrontation of Habsburg power through subsidized allies was no longer sufficient to achieve France's vital interests. In 1635 he committed France wholesale to the war in Germany and against both branches of the Habsburgs in Italy and Flanders, and also at sea. Thus began the "French Phase" of the Thirty Years' War.

It did not start well: a series of peasant rebellions broke out protesting the spectacular rise in taxes resulting from Richelieu's multiple wars, and through 1636 little of note was accomplished in Germany by French arms, despite massive expenditure. And there were assassination attempts against the Cardinal supported and financed by the Guise. All opposition was put down with ruthless military and juridical violence, with even nobles going to the block. When a Spanish army threatened Paris, Richelieu actually strapped on a sword and personally led a force of 30,000 infantry and 12,000 cavalry to do battle. His advance pushed the Spanish back and out of Picardy. In 1638 the French finally won a field victory at *Rheinfelden* (March 2–3, 1638). By 1640 France's advantages in population and wealth were brought to bear and its armies had learned how to fight by fighting. Fissures now appeared in the enemy camp. Spain's economy groaned to supply overstretched armies and fleets, and its disparate peoples grew war weary and rebellious: first Catalonia then Portugal rebelled. The French began to win in Germany, too, by 1642.

If Richelieu had by then set France on a path to hegemony, or at least to preeminence and "greatness," he did not live to see it: he died in December 1642. Nevertheless, his influence survived the grave: before he departed this Earthly coil he drafted the principal instructions later used by French envoys in negotiating the *Peace of Westphalia* in 1648. His legacy was complex but at the least included a newly centralized crown and powerful French state, army and navy, and predominance within the European state system. He also began a critically important codification of the new, secular international law. He reformed and advanced the forms and practices of modern diplomacy and set state espionage on a permanent footing. It is probably wrong to say, however, that he sought a just and universal peace for all Europe. His core motives appear to have been a mix of accrual of personal and family power along with attaining a preeminent position for France in the new, postwar order. He was, in sum, a man and a statesman. See also *Castelnaudary, Battle of*; *Jansenism*.

Suggested Reading: Joseph Bergin and Laurence Brockliss, eds., *Richelieu and His Age* (1992); Henry Bertram, ed. and trans. *Political Testament of Cardinal Richelieu* (1961); M. Carmona, *Richelieu, L'Ambition et le pouvoir* (1983); W. Church, *Richelieu* *and Reason of State* (1972); J. H. Elliott, *Richelieu and Olivares* (1984); David Parrott, *Richelieu's Army: War, Government, and Society in France, 1624–1642* (2001).

Riddarhus. "House of the Knights." Established as a reform measure by *Gustavus Adolphus* in 1626. The Riddarhus reform marked the formal creation of the Swedish national nobility, thereby cementing the loyalty of the noble classes to the *House of Vasa* and to an expansionist foreign policy.

rifled-bore. A gun or cannon with a grooved and spiral bore. This spun the bullet as it traversed the barrel, giving it greater accuracy and range by a factor of five over comparable *smoothbore* weapons. The first rifles were made about 1500 for hunting or sport, not war. *Louis XIII* and the Landgrave of Hesse introduced rifled *muskets* to their armies, but insufficient advantage was gained while rates of fire dropped, so that the experiments were ended. As late as the end of the 17th century rifles were rare in battle. The main reasons for the lack of interest in rifles were first, the tight fit of the bullet in a muzzle-loading rifle made it much harder to ram, which in turn reduced its rate of fire. It was necessary to service the gun through the muzzle since muskets were welded shut at the breech to prevent the highly pressurized gasses produced by *corned gunpowder* escaping into the face of the musketeer. Second, musketry tactics had already evolved a strong preference for reloading speed over accuracy or range. The opposite was true in Japan at the start of the 17th century, but once that nation dropped out of international conflict under the *Tokugawa* shoguns in the 1640s innovations to gun design ceased and developments in Japan did not affect the wider world. Most weapons of the era covered in this work remained smoothbore and highly inaccurate at anything beyond *point-blank ranges*. Rifled guns remained the weapon of choice of hunters, who needed an accurate single-shot musket rather than a fast reloader. See also *artillery*; *gunpowder weapons*.

Riga, Siege of (1621). See *Gustavus II Adolphus*; *Sigismund III*.

rigging. The complex system of ropes and pulleys that supported and controlled a sailing ship's *masts*, *spars*, and *yards*. Footropes—or ratlines, ropes looped through holed wooden blocks called "deadeyes" or "deadmen's eyes"—were introduced during the 15th century. This reduced the size of the crew needed to raise, lower, and handle the huge sails of new ship designs, thereby making *carracks*, *caravels*, and other ships of sail more valuable as long-distance armed transports or warships. Also, footropes allowed for divided sails to be rigged to divided masts, reducing the cost of rigging. See also *cruising*; *sails*.

"right to the bells." See *strategic metals*.

Rigksdag. The assembly of the four Swedish *Estates*: Lutheran clergy, nobles, burghers, and peasants.

Rigsdag. The assembly of Danish *Estates*, sometimes including representation for the peasantry.

Río Salado, Battle of (I340). See *Algeciras, Siege of*; *Reconquista*.

Ritter des Deutschordens. See *Teutonic Knights, Order of*.

Ritterstand. The lower nobility of the *Holy Roman Empire*; the knightly order, that class of nobles and armed retainers owing feudal military service to the Holy Roman Empire in the Middle Ages. After the *Battle of the White Mountain* (1620) the Ritterstand in Bohemia was marginalized by redistribution of their lands to those most loyal to *Ferdinand II*. There and in Moravia and Austria they were displaced by a Catholic class of noble magnates, many of foreign (German, Italian, Irish, and Spanish) origin, united by religious and political ties to the Imperial court. See also *Imperial Army*.

robinet. A class of relatively standardized early-16th-century small *cannon*. While size and caliber could vary within this class, most had a 37mm caliber and could fire *solid shot* up to one-half kilogram in weight.

rockets. War rockets were employed in China almost from the discovery of gunpowder. They were also used in Indian warfare from the 13th century, if not earlier, where they constituted the first *gunpowder weapons*. They were seldom if ever used in Europe in this period. The British learned of war rockets from the Indians in the 1700s and thereafter used them in various theaters (most famously, in an attack on Fort McHenry during the War of 1812 that is remembered in the American national anthem).

Rocroi, Battle of (May 19, 1643). Led by *Francisco di Melo*, an Imperial army of 19,000 foot and 8,000 horse comprised of Italians, Germans, Walloons, and Spanish, besieged the French fortress town of Rocroi. They were met by the *Great Condé* (Louis II), then just 22 years old and yet to earn his famous nom de guerre. He marched to lift the siege with 16,000 infantry and 7,000 horse. Each side deployed traditionally: infantry to the center, cavalry on either wing. Condé opened the fight with a charge on the right, moving Spanish cavalry on that flank off the field. The Spanish cavalry on the left flank did the same to the French, driving their horse backward. Condé turned and rode daringly across the entire battlefield, right through the Imperial infantry at the center. This split solid Spanish veterans from less-reliable *Habsburg* infantry, many of whom turned and ran. Emerging on the other side, Condé's troopers fell on the rear and flank of exposed Spanish cavalry. Seeing this, the surviving French on that flank turned, so that the Spanish were trapped between two bodies of French horse, slashing and stabbing at them and firing pistols into their faces. As the last Spanish horsemen fled from this trap the Spanish *tercios* were left standing alone at the center and were quickly assaulted from all sides by French horse and foot. The Spaniards fought bravely, in many cases to the death of whole companies. Their casualties reached 7,000 dead and 8,000 captured from the tercio infantry alone, compared with 4,000 French casualties. Rocroi was so complete a victory it is often cited as marking a transition point: the moment France displaced Spain as the dominant land power in the European system. Even if true, that had as much or more to do with the earlier closing of the *Spanish Road*, which meant that Spain could not make good its losses at Rocroi.

Rohan, Henri, duc de (1579–1638). The main *Huguenot* military leader during the last of the *French Civil Wars* (1562–1629). He submitted to *Louis XIII* upon the fall of *La Rochelle*.

Romanov, Michael (1586–1645). Tsar, 1613–1645. His election as tsar closed the *"Time of Troubles"* ("Smutnoe Vremia"), which had seen defeat of several pretenders and an invasion by *Sigismund III* of Poland. Two new wars with Poland followed, 1617–1618 and 1632–1634. Otherwise, Michael I's reign saw restoration of the traditional religion, politics, and social order of *Muscovy*. It was most marked by the powerful Orthodox patriarchy of his father, Philaret (d.1633), and deeper enserfment of the peasantry.

Rome, Sack of (1527). See *Charles V, Holy Roman Emperor*; *Cognac, League of*; *Italian Wars*; *Landsknechte*.

rondel. See *daggers*.

ronin. Wild *samurai* unbound to any lord, usually because of the death or disgrace of their *daimyo*. They were comparable in low social status and high brigandage to *routiers*, *Free Companies*, and *Ecorcheurs* in Europe.

Roosebeke, Battle of (November 27, 1382). "Rozebeke." The revolt of Flanders against French overlordship revived in the 1380s as France bogged down in the *Hundred Years' War* (1337–1453) with England, key commercial ally and military supporter of Flemish independence. Unfortunately for the Flemings, their militia were not the same tactically disciplined force that faced the French at *Courtrai* in 1302. At Roosebeke, an army of ill-trained Flemish militia was supplemented by peasant levies and led by Philip van Artevelde. This patchwork force was met by French *heavy cavalry* and *men-at-arms* under Olivier de Clisson. Pinned by repeated charges and cut off by the superior mobility of the French horse, the Flemings were cut down without mercy and slaughtered almost to a man. Louis II (de Malle) was restored as Duke of Flanders. Within three years the Flemish revolt was crushed and Flanders passed to Burgundy by agreement with France. The point of long memory, class hatred, and revenge was driven home when the 500 sets of spurs taken from dead French *knights* at Courtrai were recovered to France after Roosebeke.

"Root and Branch" petition (December 1640). A petition against episcopacy circulated by Puritan clergy, signed by over 15,000 people and presented to Parliament. It blamed discontent in England on toleration of prelates (Presbyterianism), identifying the path to peace as a godly government—or rather, government by the self-proclaimed godly—which would strictly enforce public morals and inculcate sound commercial values. See also *English Civil Wars*.

Rostjeneste. The feudal military obligation of the Danish nobility to serve in the cavalry, or provide substitutes, as part of their service obligation to the monarchy.

rota. The roster of a company of infantry or troop of cavalry, notably in the *Polish Army*, where units of 100 men were subdivided into files of 10 led by *dziesietniks*. A "rotamaster" was the officer in charge of the rota (roughly, a captain). The term went out of favor in the late 17th century. See also *rotmistrz*; *Rottmeister*.

rotmistrz. "Rotamaster." The rotmistrz was the military contractor who agreed to raise a quota of men and lead them to the muster under his flag. In battle he commanded a *choragiew* or *banner* (company) of men. In the *Polish Army* the *poczet* ("post" or "lance") of a rotmistrz was larger than most others because it included a number of *dead-pays* used to pad the income of the whole unit, to the extent that as many as 10 percent of names on the paper muster might be fictitious.

Rotte. A squad of ten *Landsknechte* mercenaries. It was the basic tactical unit of a *Fähnlein* or company.

Rottmeister. "Rotamaster." A minor officer in a *Landsknechte* company. When in pike square or *Gevierthaufen* formation each Rottmeister was in charge of a file of about 20 men.

rotularii. Italian infantry of the late 15th century armed with small, round shields and a variety of hand weapons.

Rouen, Siege of (1418–1419). See *Hundred Years' War*.

Rouen, Siege of (1449). See *Hundred Years' War*.

Rouen, Siege of (November 1591–April 1592). *Henri IV* undertook a siege of Rouen supported by 5,000 English troops sent to him by *Elizabeth I*. Although *Parma* was suffering from gout and his men were mutinous from want of pay, he invaded Picardy with a large Spanish army out of the Netherlands. Henri left his trenches to interdict the Spanish en route. Leading a raiding party of just 1,000 horse, he was cut off and slightly wounded. Parma approached Rouen in late February but failed to lift the siege, instead moving on Neufchâtel and into Picardy. Henri's Dutch allies cut off Rouen from the sea, provoking its population to riot for food. Parma finally marched to relieve the siege. He and *Mayenne* entered Rouen on April 21, 1592.

rouncey. An average *warhorse* that bore the bulk of the armored *cavalry* of the European knightly class. It was neither as large nor as expensive as a *destrier* nor as fleet as the small *courser* that was preferred by most riders on a *chevauchée*. It was an average animal of average price, as little as one-twentieth the cost of a prime destrier, and thus affordable to poorer *knights*, *men-at-arms*, and other armed retainers.

roundel (1). A small, round shield.

roundel (2). A round turret in a fixed fortification.

Roundheads. The sobriquet of the Parliamentary forces in the *English Civil Wars* (1639–1651). See also *Cromwell, Oliver*; *drake*; *English armies*; *Ironsides*; *Lobsters*; *New Model Army*.

round robin. A petition of grievances drawn up by a naval crew in the form of a complete circle. This was done to prevent the ship's officers from determining which man had signed first and was the likely ringleader, who could then be singled out for rough punishment. Round robin petitions were often, but not always, precursors to outright mutiny.

roundship. Round-hulled sailing ships, as opposed to flat-bottomed ships used in shallow coastal waters or the sleek hull of a *galley*. See also *balinger*; *barge*; *clinker-built*; *cocha*; *cog*.

Roundway Down, Battle of (1643). See *English Civil Wars*; *Hopton, Ralph*; *Waller, William*.

routiers. Rootless, roving, impoverished, unemployed mercenary "routes" (bands) that lived off the land by intimidating the peasantry of medieval France. They came mostly from the towns of Flanders and Brabant or from Provence and Navarre, regions where poor soil and overpopulation drove men to desperation and banditry. They were notorious for harassing and robbing religious houses and terrorizing civilians. They organized in bands of several thousand heavily armed men, which made some bands of routiers as large as major armies commanded by the greatest kings of the period. Their depredations provoked formation of a vigilante group known as the "White Hoods" ("Capuciati"), a band of pious warriors drawn mostly from the towns and peasantry to fight off the routiers. It later became a radical religious sect. In 1185 the social radicalism of the White Hoods frightened the nobility more than the threat from routiers and they were crushed by a combined force of nobles and hired routiers. So many routiers were killed at Bouvines (1214) and in the *Albigensian Crusade* (1208–1229) that France enjoyed a long domestic peace, reinforced by eight decades of cross-Channel peace with England. Both factors encouraged a shift from traditional claims by the great magnates to a right of private warfare to limiting that right to the king. A leading medieval military historian, Philippe Contamine, therefore called this "the great peace of the 13th century."

Routiers reappeared during the 14th century as France was devastated by the terrible English *chevauchées* of the *Hundred Years' War* (1337–1453). Their ravages were supplemented by still worse atrocities committed by *Free Companies*, violent gangs who adopted names like "Smashing Bars" and "Arm of Iron." In the 1350s–1360s routiers and Free Companies spread chaos through most of France, including the Île-de-France less than 15 miles from Paris. These "Anglo-Navarrese" companies took and held towns, monasteries, and other strongpoints. Between 1356 and 1364 more than 450 strongholds were held by various bands of routiers or Free Companies. Occupation could last a considerable time, as long as 15 years in the case of the Abbey of Louroux. These routiers were different from earlier bands in that they did work of destruction and conducted a war of economic attrition in the name of the kings of England, though not necessarily in their pay. They used terror to extort *appatis* and

> *With the nobility dead or in despair, routiers roamed the country . . .*

had almost unobstructed freedom to ravage the French countryside, especially after the disaster for French chivalry at *Crécy* (1346) and *Poitiers* (1356). With the nobility dead or in despair, routiers roamed the country, seizing whole towns and holding them as bases for exploitation of surrounding lands. That this was part of English policy was confirmed by the fact that many routiers gave up their strongholds upon signature of the *Treaty of Brétigny* (1360). The legal cover afforded by *Edward III* gave routiers status as soldiers under the *just war tradition* instead of that of the criminals and bandits most of them were. Clifford Rogers has therefore aptly called routiers the *privateers* of 14th-century land warfare, reserving the even greater opprobrium of "pirates" to unlicenced Free Companies. See also *akutō*; *ashigaru*; *aventuriers*; *Ecorcheurs*; *guerre couverte*; *Nájera, Battle of*; *ronin*; *wakō*.

Suggested Reading: Philippe Contamine, *War in the Middle Ages*, Michael Jones, trans. (1984; 1990); L. Siméon, *Histoire de Bertrand du Guesclin et de son époque* (1867).

Rouvray, Battle of (February 12, 1429). "Battle of the Herrings." *John Fastolf* commanded 1,000 longbowmen and 1,200 Burgundians escorting a supply convoy heading to the English army besieging Orléans when it was attacked by the French. He formed a *Wagenburg* from the carts, behind which his archers delivered arrow storms against the French, who charged repeatedly but could not overcome this novel obstacle. Fastolf went on to deliver his cargo of salt fish and flour to Orléans. His tactic was innovative but not strategically important as *Jeanne d'Arc* lifted the siege later in the year.

rowbarge. A small, 16th-century oared warship peculiar to England; not a flat-bottomed barge of the modern type. They were square-rigged for sail, with 16 oars per side. They fought in the 1545 Anglo-French war, opposing French *galleys*.

Royalists. See *Cavaliers*; *Charles I, of England*; *English Civil Wars*.

Royal Navy. Naval forces played an important role in successive English invasions of Scotland, Ireland, and Wales, and in the defense of those lands by their Celtic populations. Ships were also essential to English fortunes in the *Hundred Years' War* (1337–1453), which had a crucial naval component that is too often overlooked. English monarchs back to the 11th century purpose-built fleets of warships, but each time the effort to sustain a navy lapsed and the ships were sold off to private interests. Even the *"Great Ships"* commissioned by *Henry V* were left to rot by his successors, sold off after his death, or burned by accident. In the 14th century a rudimentary naval administration was set up under the "Clerk of the King's Ships." Naval financing was managed within the royal household through accounts in "The Chamber" and "The Wardrobe" (later, "Great Wardrobe"), which eventually took responsibility for naval gunnery and small arms, delivery of ships and crew, repair and resupply. The state of "royal ships," or warships owned directly by the crown, from the 14th to the 17th century reflected the state of the monarchy: the "navy royal" waxed under the vigorous later Tudors but waned under the maladroit early Stuarts. Upon the death of *Henry VIII* in 1547 the Royal Navy had 53 warships of all types and sizes. The fleet declined briefly under Edward VI and *Mary Tudor* but building and repair resumed under *Elizabeth I*, with special attention paid to *galleon* construction and *cruising* warfare. In J. R. Hill's words, the Royal Navy finally arose "through a blend of fear, ambition, curiosity, and trial and error." A consensus among naval historians assigns the pedigree of the modern Royal Navy to the fleet of warships assembled by Elizabeth. At its height the Elizabethan navy consisted of 34 royal ships, 13 of which exceeded 500 tons displacement, with many more *privateers* sailing under *letters of marque*, along with impressed and armed merchant ships.

The Royal Navy deteriorated spectacularly under the early Stuarts. *James I* and a tepid House of Commons laid up the royal ships or sold them off or allowed them to rot in port. Great corruption returned to naval administration and privateering was abolished by James (who actually beheaded *Walter Raleigh* for it), even though the English merchant marine was exposed to predations by Dunkirk and Barbary pirates operating from the Newfoundland and Iceland fisheries to the Narrow Seas. This shift surely came about in large part because, except for pirates, there was no continental threat to England during this period: Europe was exhausted by war, embraced the

Twelve Years' Truce (1609–1621), then plunged into the first years of the *Thirty Years' War* (1618–1648) with indifference to England. *Charles I* and *Buckingham* did no better in terms of management and much worse in combat, bringing humiliation to English seamanship and England's naval tradition.

Despite the Royal Navy's Elizabethan heritage, most naval historians date England's true permanent navy, and especially its conscious national policy of pursuit of sea power, to the *English Civil Wars* (1639–1651) and Commonwealth era. The victory by Parliament, which most navy men supported, put naval finance on a sound footing for the first time. From 1649 to 1660 Parliament built or purchased 207 new warships, adding these to an original fleet of just 39 ships. The Puritan revolution also raised to power men opposed to the monopoly charter companies favored by the monarchy. These new men wanted naval protection from Channel pirates and foreign privateers which the Stuart kings failed to provide. They were devoted to radical Protestantism, colonialism, and the self-conscious idea of England as a major sea and world power. They supported financing for a permanent navy to be used to block Catholic nations from overseas expansion while protecting their, and England's, commercial and colonial interests. The Commonwealth navy subsequently demonstrated professionalism, seamanship, and martial superiority against a comparably fine Dutch navy during the Anglo-Dutch Wars. Reconstituted as the Royal Navy upon the Restoration, sea power took a special place in English national consciousness and policy ever after. See also *Cinque Ports*; *convoy*; *Drake, Francis*; *Edward III*; *Flores, Battle of*; *Frobisher, Martin*; *fryd*; *Hawkyns, John*; *Howard, Charles*; *ship money*; *Sluys, Battle of*; "*sovereignty of the sea*"; *tarpaulin*; *Tower of London*; *war at sea*.

Suggested Reading: J. R. Hill, ed. *Oxford Illustrated History of the Royal Navy* (1995); David Loades, *The Tudor Navy* (1992); N.A.M. Rodger, *The Safeguard of the Sea: A Naval History of Britain*, vol. 1 (1997).

Royal Prussia. See *Gustavus II Adolphus*; *Poland*; *Teutonic Knights, Order of*; *Torun, Second Peace of*; *War of the Cities*.

royal ships. See *privateer*; *Royal Navy*.

Royal Touch. See *corpus mysticum*.

Rudolf II (1552–1612). Holy Roman Emperor, 1576–1612. He was not as tolerant of Protestantism as his father, *Maximilian II*: he had greater interest in alchemy than transubstantiation. His direct support to the *Counter-Reformation* in Germany helped harden confessional positions. He suffered bouts of deep depression and even insanity, and progressively lost power to his brother, Matthias. He faced a rebellion in Transylvania in 1604 backed by the Ottomans, just as his powers declined. In 1606 Matthias signed the *Treaty of Zsitva Torok* ending the *Thirteen Years' War* (1593–1606). He responded to the Bocskay Rebellion in Transylvania (1604–1606) and civil war in Hungary by conceding toleration to Protestants, including Calvinists. In 1608 Rudolf ceded governance of Austria, Hungary, and Moravia to Matthias. In 1609 Rudolf decreed toleration in Bohemia, but was forced to cede that province to Matthias in 1611 after a threatened civil war was averted. The tempest and ineptitude of his reign in Bohemia, Hungary, and the Empire greatly contributed to the grave crisis that led to the *Thirty Years' War* after his death.

Rumania. Rumania was a province of the Roman Empire (known as Dacia) until the 3rd century C.E. Like most outlying provinces of Rome, over the next seven centuries it was alternately overrun and settled by barbarian tribes. In the 13th century, the *Mongols* reached and raided Rumania. The Ottoman Empire conquered Rumania only with difficulty, as local warlords raised effective infantry from urban militia, stiffened the ranks of townsmen with Italian, Bulgarian, or Polish mercenaries, and fortified against conquest. In time, Muslim armies overran the "Danubian Principalities" of Moldavia (Moldova) and Wallachia, which remained Ottoman provinces into the late 19th century. See also *Militargrenze*; *Thirteen Years' War*.

Rumelia. The largely Christian and exclusively European territories of the Ottoman Empire, as distinct from the core Muslim lands of Anatolia and Arab lands to the south. Rumelia included most of modern Albania, Bulgaria, Croatia, Bosnia, Greece, Macedonia, Thrace, and Serbia.

Rumis. A Mughal term for Turkish or other Ottoman artillery specialists in the service of their emperors. See also *Farangi*; *renegades*.

run the gauntlet. From the Swedish "gantlope," a military punishment introduced to Europe during the *Thirty Years' War* (1618–1648) by *Gustavus Adolphus*. An offending soldier was made to run between files of men who beat him as he passed. It was always brutal and sometimes fatal. The *Landsknechte* had an earlier version of this punishment, the "pike court," which may explain why the Swedish variant spread so quickly through Germany. The Landsknechte pike court made an offender run between two files of pikemen who stabbed him as he passed. Almost no one survived, as any man refusing to stab the offender would be sent to take his place.

Rupert, Prince (1619–1682). Cavalry general and admiral. Nephew of *Charles I*, son of *Friedrich V*, Elector Palatine. He went to war as a teenager for the Dutch against the Spanish in the Netherlands. Captured by the Spanish in 1638 he was released to Charles I in 1641 upon the intervention of *Walter Leslie*. Rupert took command of the *Cavalier* cavalry immediately upon the start of the *English Civil Wars*. He had trouble making professional soldiers of the continental style out of the stubborn English noblemen he commanded, but in the early years they were still the superior of any horsemen Parliament could raise. He thus beat a small enemy force at Powick Bridge (October 23, 1642), his first action. He could not restrain his own high spirits or those of his men, however, which often led him and them to disastrous overpursuit, as at *Edgehill*. In 1643 he took Bristol, a major supply point for the whole Royalist cause, but he behaved badly at *First Newbury*. The next spring he advanced north in a protracted *chevauchée* and also lifted the siege of York. On May 24, 1644, he sacked Bolton, massacring 1,600 soldiers and civilians. At *Marston Moor* (1644) once more his Cavaliers overpursued, this time costing the Royalists the battle. In the aftermath, Charles nevertheless named Rupert overall commander (at age 25). He led the Royalists into the fight against the *New Model Army* at *Naseby* (1645), where yet again his Cavaliers dispersed beyond hope of recall while the Parliamentarians stood firm and destroyed the rest of the Royalist army. Rupert retreated to Bristol, which he later surrendered to *Thomas Fairfax*. His enemies at court used this to turn Charles against him: he was stripped of command, humiliated and exiled, with no thanks given for his many acts of military service to the king. He subsequently revived Royalist naval fortunes, displaying genuine skill in making war at sea.

ruse. See *Forlorn Hope*; *karr-wa-farr*; *Mongols*; *Morgarten, Battle of*; *ruses de guerre*; *Swiss square*; *Uzbeks*; *Wittstock, Battle of*; *Yongle Emperor*.

ruses de guerre. Within the *just war tradition*, "ruses de guerre" had a special meaning of deceptions or tricks in the course of combat viewed as illegitimate because they abused the norms of war that were designed to protect noncombatants. They included false surrender or firing from protected places. See also *quarter*.

Russia. See *Muscovy, Grand Duchy of*.

rusttjänst. "*Knight* service." The *feudal* military obligation of the Swedish nobility to serve in the cavalry, or provide substitutes, as part of their *servitor* obligation to the monarchy.

Ruthven, Patrick (c.1573–1651). English general. He served under *Gustavus Adolphus* in Germany during the *Thirty Years' War* (1618–1648). Back in England, he joined the *Cavaliers* in support of *Charles I*. In 1643–1644 he served his king as overall commander of the Royalist armies. He was overshadowed for Charles by the early exploits of *Prince Rupert*.

sabatons. Broad-toed foot armor made from articulated pieces of *plate*. It first appeared in Europe around 1320. Sabatons left only the heel exposed and most versions accommodated spurs.

Sablat, Battle of (June 10, 1619). In the second year of the *Thirty Years' War*, a contract "Protestant" army of 20,000 mercenaries under *Graf von Mansfeld* moved against the Catholic fortress of Budweis (České Budějovice) in Bohemia. It was intercepted en route by *Bucquoy* at Sablat. In a day-long fight, Mansfeld lost over 1,500 men along with his baggage train. See also *White Mountain, Battle of*.

Sachsen-Weimar, Bernhard von. See *Bernhard von Sachsen-Weimar*.

sack (of a city). See *Alexandria, Siege of; Ankara, Battle of; Byzantine Empire; Charles V, Holy Roman Emperor; chivalry; civilians; Cognac, League of; Constantinople, Siege of; Delhi Sultanate; Dorpat, Sack of; Drake, Francis; Drogheda, Sack of; Eighty Years' War; English Civil Wars; English Fury; French Civil Wars; Haarlem, Siege of; Holy Roman Empire; Hospitallers; Ivan IV; Jerusalem; Knights of St. Thomas Acon; Knights Templar; Maastricht, Siege of (1579); Magdeburg, Sack of; military discipline; Mongols; Northern War, First; Papal States; Pappenheim, Graf zu; Parma, duque di; Rupert, Prince; Selim I; siege warfare; "Spanish Fury"; Tatars; Timur; Tunis; War of the Mantuan Succession; Wexford, Sack of*.

sacre (1). See *saker*.

sacre (2). The coronation ceremony of French kings, dating to Charlemagne, which emphasized the sacerdotal and consecrated nature of the monarchy (as against secular constitutional understandings). The ceremony was usually held at Reims and bound the "Most Christian King" of France to defense of the Catholic faith as well as the realm. The coronation oath to "expel from my land...all heretics," greatly aggravated the confessional struggle and search for peace during the *French Civil Wars* (1562–1629).

Safavid Army. Iran had an available force that seldom exceeded 20,000 before 1600. Defeat is the true teacher in all war, however, and Iranian armies were regularly defeated in the 16th century by more modern and regular Ottoman troops. *Abbas I* therefore fundamentally reformed Iran's military, importing Ottoman technology and Western advisers (the *Shirley* brothers, and others) to set up a *standing army* comprised of firearms troops supported by artillery with ancillary cavalry. With this force Abbas retook most of Iraq from the Ottomans in the first quarter of the 17th century. See also *Baghdad, Siege of*; *Chaldiran, Battle of*; *ghazi*; *ghulams*; *Qizilbash*; *Sis, Battle of*.

Safavid Empire. The Safavid Empire was a successor state to Timurid Iran, the prior dynasty descended from *Timur* (Tamerlane). It was founded in Tabrīz in 1502 by Shah Ismail I (1486–1524, r.1502–1524). It was militantly *shī'a* in orientation and religious ideology, a *ghazi* stance kept fresh by the *Qizilbash*. It warred constantly with the Uzbeks and Ottomans, both orthodox sunni states. The more advanced *Ottoman Army* crushed the Safavids at *Chaldiran* (1514). The Iranians remained overly reliant on traditional cavalry archers for most of the 16th century, despite this defeat by Ottoman firearms infantry. An accommodation with the Ottomans was reached in the *Peace of Amasya* (1555). That same year, the Safavids removed their capital to Qazwin from Tabrīz. Peace lasted until an Ottoman offensive in 1578, timed to take advantage of a period of weak Safavid rule under Muhammad Khudabanda (r.1578–1587). Safavid military and political fortunes changed with the brilliant, expansionist, modernizing reign of *Abbas I* (r.1587–1629). Abbas moved the capital again, to Isfahan (1597), reformed the Safavid Army, won at *Sis* (1606), and took Iraq temporarily from the Ottomans. After his death the dynasty went into long-term decline, losing Iraq in 1638. It reigned in name only after 1722. That it lasted and excelled militarily before that was remarkable given that it was smaller and weaker than its great Ottoman enemy and had to fight on the Uzbek front as well.

safeguard the sea. "Keeping the sea." An early attempt to build a battle fleet and use warships not just for escort but for patrolling sea lanes, notably the English Channel (the "Narrow Sea") and the key trade route from England to Gascony. It could also entail bringing an enemy fleet to decisive battle. Either by patrolling or battle, the essential idea was to preserve England and its seaborne trade from hostile attack. This was a largely unachievable goal until the creation of a permanent *Royal Navy* in the 16th and 17th centuries. See also *Henry V, of England*; *Hundred Years' War*.

sail. A count of ships, as in "eighty enemy sail were sighted."

sails. By the late 16th century, standard English terminology for sails was well-established, dividing them into two classes: square sails, set outside the *rigging* and hung across the ship; and "fore-and-aft" sails, set inside the rigging and lying along the centerline, moving side to side with the wind. The "foresail" was the lowest rigged square sail, held aloft by the foremast; the "headsail" was set on a *spar* forward of the foremast; the "mainsail" was the lowest and largest square sail, rigged to the main mast; the "studding" was a lightweight sail rigged outside the mainsail, or the topsail, to take extra wind on light days; the "topsail" was a square canvas rigged to the topmast; the "topgallant" was a smaller square sail, rigged to the topgallant mast, above the topsail. "Stay sails" were rigged between masts. Most "square rig" sails were actually rectangular, with their broad sides fitted along *yards* running horizontal to the mast. Yards rotated on the masts at right angles to the centerline of the ship, which allowed tacking into the wind. "Fore-and-aft" sails were subdivided into lateen sails, gaffsails, spritsails, and lugs.

Lateen sails, which greatly improved handling, were large triangular canvases hoisted to mastheads by long yards (or gaffs or sprits) secured to the deck with rope and tackle. Originating in the Mediterranean, they were adopted by Atlantic and Baltic shipbuilders during the 15th century and made already "weatherly" ships handle even better. Thereafter, lateen sails were integral in development of the great hybrid ships of sail: *galleons*, then *frigates* and the *man-of-war*. The "spritsail" was set below the bowsprit of a large ship, secured with ropes called bowlines. The spritsail-topsail was a signature rig of major warships by the first half of the 17th century. Spritsails were deployed solo in river barges. Staysails were lateen or lug in shape but fitted without yards beneath the stays. Lugs were square sails hung obliquely on their yard. In Europe, they were commonly used in ship's boats. In China, lugs were the main sail type on all *junks*. See also *make sail*; *masts*; *shorten sail*; *tackle*.

Suggested Reading: R. C. Anderson and Romola Anderson, *A Short History of the Sailing Ship* (1926; 2003).

Saint-Denis, Battle of (November 10, 1567). The only major battle of the second of the *French Civil Wars*. Under *Montmorency*, a Royal army of 3,000 horse and 16,000 foot (10,000 Parisian *militia* and volunteers, and 6,000 Swiss) moved out to fight a smaller *Huguenot* force that was blockading Paris. Led jointly by *Condé* and *Coligny*, the Protestants had just 2,000 horse and 4,000 foot, including some Scots mercenaries. The Huguenots formed a single line between two small villages, with Condé heading the cavalry on the right and Coligny commanding the van. Montmorency lined up his Parisians on the left, Swiss infantry and gendarme cavalry of the *compagnies de l'ordonnance* in the center under his direct command and more French infantry on his right. He began the fight with a bombardment. He then ordered an attack without assessing the damage, if any, done by his guns. The enthusiastic but inexperienced Parisians were easily repelled by Coligny's line of *arquebusiers*. Then Condé charged the Royalist center, passing right through it. During the mêlée, Montmorency was fatally wounded. This loss greatly diluted the Catholic victory even though the Protestants were compelled to retreat south to link up with German mercenary reinforcements.

Saint-Quentin, Battle of (August 10, 1557). *Graaf van Egmont* invaded northern France out of the Habsburg Netherlands at the head of a Spanish army. *Montmorency* hurriedly raised a force of 26,000 and rushed to stop Egmont. He and *Coligny* tried to sneak around Egmont's flank but were caught fording the Somme. In a sharp action, the French lost 14,000 men and Montmorency and Coligny were taken prisoner. *Henri II* was forced to terms and Spanish military prestige soared across Europe. *Philip II* was now free to resume his twin crusades against Islam and Protestantism.

Saka. "Water carriers." A specialized support unit within the *Janissary Corps* responsible for bringing water to fighting men on the battlefield and doubling as a hospital corps tending to wounded Janissaries.

saker. "Sacre." An early, light *artillery* piece. Size and range varied considerably, but by the late 15th century, saker generally referred to a gun capable of throwing stone or iron five-pound *shot* to a maximum range of 350 meters. Accuracy was low, but sakers had the advantage of mobility and could be employed on carts for field combat. By the end of the 16th century, saker referred to a bigger gun class that was reasonably standardized at 1,600 pounds weight and capable of firing nine-pound shot to an effective range of 500 yards and a maximum range of 4,000. A *demi-saker* (or *minion*) was a smaller version of this type, which fired six-pound shot to an effective range of 450 yards.

salade. A light, globular infantry helmet. See also *sallet*.

Salāh al-Dīn (1137–1193). Né Yusuf ibn Ayyub. "Saladin." Sultan of Egypt and Syria. His father was a Kurd and provincial governor at Tekrit under the *Seljuk Turks*. In the service of Nur al-Din, emir of Syria, Salāh al-Dīn served in Egypt from 1167 to 1168. He became *Grand Vizier* in 1169, under the tottering Fatamid *caliphs*. He deposed the *shī'a* dynasty of the Fatamids in 1171 and proclaimed himself sovereign in Egypt, at the head of the *mamlūk* slave soldiery imported from the north. He signaled the return of Egypt to *sunni* orthodoxy by nominally recognizing the Abbasid caliphs in Baghdad, a gesture which cost him nothing in terms of power but helped pacify the sunni majority in Egypt and consolidate his family's claim to the sultanate. From his base in Cairo he expanded westward across North Africa and eastward into the Arabian peninsula. After Nur al-Din's death he incorporated most of Syria and Palestine (but not the mountain fastnesses held by the *Druse* and *Assassins*) into his empire, along with Mesopotamia (Iraq). The Seljuks in Syria paid him homage and tribute as the leading prince of the Muslim world.

Salāh al-Dīn next turned to face the Christian threat, in the form of the *Crusader* states. The direct provocation was Christian castle rustling (*raiding*) and attacks on trade caravans. In 1187 Salāh al-Dīn inflicted a massive defeat on a Crusader army at Hattin, near Tiberias in Galilee. After the battle he ordered all *Hospitaller* and *Templar* prisoners killed. On October 3 his troops overwhelmed the remaining defenders of Jerusalem and recaptured the city for Islam. Subsequently, he battered down Crusader castles along the Syrian coast, earning respect among the Latins for his military skill and *chivalry*. A Christian counterattack, led in person by King Richard I (Coeur de Lion, 1157–1199) of England and King Philip of France, retook Acre in 1191, but was unable to retake Jerusalem in two advances against it. Richard defeated Salāh al-Dīn at Caesarea and Jaffa, exacted from him a three-year treaty and departed the Holy Land (to be later captured and held for ransom in Germany at Christian hands). Salāh al-Dīn is remembered not merely for his conquests but for wise and benevolent government, and for promoting economic prosperity through rebuilding of roads and canals. His Ayyubid dynasty ruled Egypt until 1250, when his successors were overthrown by the Mamlūk general Baybārs.

> *...Salāh al-Dīn inflicted a massive defeat on a Crusader army at Hattin, near Tiberius in Galilee.*

Suggested Reading: M. C. Lyons and D. Jackson, *Saladin: Politics of the Holy War* (1982).

Salic Law. From "Salian Franks." The Salic Law governed the succession in France from the 7th century, restricting it to male inheritance of "Salic land," or the royal inheritance. This was thought critical to avoid infighting in a *feudal* society divided among military *fiefs*. Yet, only after the original Salic lands ceased to exist was the old law opportunistically cited by rival dynasts to deny the inheritance of the crown to one royal family as against another. The most important episode concerned rival French and English claims that contributed to the outbreak of the *Hundred Years' War* (1337–1453). The issue was again important during the *French Civil Wars* (1562–1629). To deny the throne to the *Huguenot* prince, Henri de Navarre, the *Catholic League* asserted a radical doctrine that Catholicity trumped the Salic Law. However, in June 1593, the paramountcy of the Salic Law was reaffirmed by a majority of Catholic deputies in the Estates General. That, and Henri's abjuration of his Calvinist faith a month later, cleared the way for acceptance of Henri de Navarre to mount the throne as *Henri IV*, the legitimate king of France.

sallet. An open-faced helmet in wide use toward the end of the European Middle Ages. It was a German redesign of the Italian 'celāta' or *barbuta* style. It could be worn with or without a visor.

salute. The origin of the military salute appears to be the raising of a *knight*'s visor to permit identification of opposing knights in *tournaments*. Once the armored helm disappeared only the ghost of the gesture remained as a tribute to a fellow warrior.

salva guardia. "Safe conduct" passes sold to merchants or nobles wishing or needing to pass through a region controlled by an occupying army. A lucrative variant was a guarantee of protection offered by the commanding officer to specified buildings placed off limits to plundering upon receipt of a set fee. Entire fortified towns might buy protection for themselves and for outlying villages this way.

samurai. "Those who serve." The warrior class of *feudal* Japan. At their height, hundreds of thousands served as retainers and vassals of the *daimyo.* They were elite warriors who fought as *light cavalry,* firing bows with deadly accuracy while riding small ponies. They were accompanied by "grooms," the rough equivalent of *pages* or *esquires,* running on foot and armed with a *kumade* or *naginata.* Samurai were richly armored and decorated. Their battles were fought at arrow range until the supply was exhausted. Then they closed to fight with *swords,* trying to unhorse an opponent then dismounting to kill him and take his head. After battle an "inspection of heads" ("kubi jikken") of enemies was carried out to determine individual rewards, usually a parceling of lands of the dead. Samurai were dedicated to a romantic ideal of self-sacrifice ("*kenshin*") and code of honor ("*bushidō*"), that in the extreme denied surrender and called for ritual suicide by disembowelment ("seppuku") to honor one's fallen daimyo or avoid the disgrace of capture, or when ordered to do so as a military punishment. This honor code and samurai loyalty broke down badly during the *Sengoku jidai* period. During the *Unification Wars,* especially under *Toyotomi Hideyoshi,* some samurai served as a de facto rural constabulary barracked in *jōkamachi* (castle towns) that were built along the inland roads. At this time many samurai shifted to spears from bows and the mounted charge against *ashigaru* arquebusiers was introduced. Reflecting the shift to guns and cannon in Japanese warfare, *Tokugawa Ieyasu* elevated skilled gunners to the rank of samurai. The last stand of the old samurai took place at *Osaka Castle* in 1615. Later, separation from the land and the long peace under the Tokugawa shoguns slowly reduced the samurai into a parasitic social class. Samurai had broad rights and legal exemptions and were kept at state expense, but many sank into decadence and poverty over time as they became militarily obsolete and socially useless. See also *Anegawa, Battle of*; *armor*; *gekokujō*; *Hakata Bay, Battle of (1274)*; *Hakata Bay, Battle of (1281)*; *Honganji fortress, Siege of*; *Nagashino, Battle of*; *Okehazama, Battle of*; *ronin*; *Sekigahara, Battle of.*

Suggested Reading: William Farris, *Heavenly Warriors: The Evolution of Japan's Military, 500–1300* (1992); K. Friday, *Hired Swords: The Rise of Private Warfare in Early Japan* (1992); Stephen Turnbull, *The Samurai: A Military History* (1977).

sanack bey. An Ottoman commander of local troops; not a major general.

Santa Cruz, marques de (1526–1588). Né Alvara de Bazán. Spanish admiral. In command of the reserve line at *Lepanto* (1571), his quick action saved the Christian center from a flank attack by Muslim *galleys* and helped turn the battle. He led an Atlantic fleet in support of *Philip II*'s conquest of Portugal (1580). Two years later he decisively defeated a French fleet off the Azores at *Terceira*, and fended off a second French fleet the next year. He was the leading proponent of a Spanish invasion of England from an early date. As the leading Spanish sailor of the day, he was given command of the king's great "Enterprise of England" but died before the *Invincible Armada* sailed. He was replaced by Medina Sidonia.

Santiago, Knights of. See *Knights of Santiago*.

Santiago Matamoros. "St. James the Moor Killer." The patron saint of the *Reconquista*, believed by Iberian Christians to have descended from heaven to lead the crusade against the Moors. His shrine at Compostella was among the most visited by pilgrims in Medieval Europe.

sap. In *siege warfare*, a tunnel and pit dug toward or underneath a *curtain wall* or other defensive work to undermine its integrity. "Sapping" was the process of digging covered trenches, usually zig-zagging in direction, leading ever closer to the enemy works to position offensive artillery or close with the wall to carry out *mining*. Saps were usually covered to provide protection from missiles.

Sapa Inca. "Sole Inca." See *Inca Empire*.

sapper. A military engineer or laborer employed in undermining trenches or fortifications. See also *mining*; *sap*; *siege warfare*.

Saracens. Originally, Syrian nomadic tribes encountered and conquered by the Roman Empire. Later, a generic *Crusader* term for any Muslim warrior, especially the grand coalition assembled at the end of the 12th century by *Salāh al-Dīn* which retook *Jerusalem* and held off the Christian counterattack led by the *Norman* Crusader King, Richard I ("Coeur de Lion"). Saracens also fought as mercenaries for Christian rulers. *Friedrich II*, Holy Roman Emperor, planted a colony of some 35,000 Saracens near Lucera, Italy. For many decades this colony provided German emperors with 5,000 archers per year. This unit was wiped out in fighting with the Angevin monarchy at Benevento in 1266. See also *surcoat*.

Sardinia. In the 12th century, the Dorias of *Genoa* took control of Sardinia. In 1353 *Aragon* landed a force on the north of the island. In the campaign that followed the Aragonese forced the Genoese onto their *galleys* and off Sardinia. The island remained securely controlled by Aragon for 400 years.

Sarhu, Campaign of (1619). After suffering a deep *Manchu* (Qing) raid in 1618, the *Ming* organized a punitive expedition into *Manchuria*. The Ming made a basic mistake of advancing in four columns, whereas the Qing Army, led by *Nurgaci*, concentrated to achieve local superiority and defeat its enemy in detail. The first Han (Ming) column lost its war-wagon brigade at an unfordable river crossing; it was destroyed near Sarhu. As the Manchu van made contact with a second Ming column the next day, the Han troops panicked and ran, offering no resistance. The third Ming column withdrew on hearing news of the loss of the first two, but the fourth ran into an ambush and was wiped out. Manchu cavalry closed quickly in face of slow-loading Han gunmen and slaughtered the Chinese infantry. The loss finished the Ming in Manchuria. That had the odd and unintended effect of shortening Ming defensive lines, but it was not enough to save the dynasty from falling to the Qing in 1644.

sarmatian armor. Scale *armor* made with small iron plates sewn onto a deerskin leather jerkin in an overlapping manner, like scales on a fish. It was named for the region north of the Black Sea known in Roman times as Sarmatia. In Poland this style of armor was known as *karacena*. It was labor-intensive to produce and hence very expensive. For all that, it offered less protection than *plate*. It was usually worn as double armor, over *mail*. Polish nobles still wore such armor in battle as late as the 1760s.

sashimono. A small *samurai* banner, often displaying family or *daimyo* heraldic devices. It was attached to a bamboo pole inserted into brackets in back of a mounted warrior's upper armor.

saubannerzug. Bands of Swiss hooligans and young quasi-soldiers, frequently apprentices from the guilds, who gathered under an infamous *Banner* of a pig to raid local towns, threaten peasants, and extort money from merchants. They were militarily significant in that they provided weapons training to youths, principally with the *pike*, and in emergencies could be mustered to defend the cantons.

sauve-garde. See *salva guardia*.

Savonarola, Girolamo (1452–1498). Italian religious reformer. He was trained as a Dominican monk. He moved among several church postings in northern Italy without exhibiting a particular talent for religious oratory. In 1489 he was posted to Florence, where he was received by the devout as an inspired moralist. In 1493 he led a reformation of the Dominicans in Tuscany. His preaching became overtly political—essentially, apocalyptic and theocratic—that year. At first he greeted the French invasion at the start of the *Italian Wars* (1494–1559) as an opportunity for civic redemption. In the chaos that followed the French withdrawal, Savonarola and his followers ("Weepers") set up a radical, puritanical theocracy in the guise of a "Christian commonwealth." Clothing and ornaments deemed temptations to sexual vice were destroyed in a "bonfire of the vanities," public burnings of forbidden things that presaged subsequent burning of people who read censored books or upheld forbidden doctrines. Public hysteria was fed by the general reformist discontent of the times, the dislocations caused by the French invasion, and fresh outbreaks of plague. In 1495 Savonarola was called to Rome to answer charges of heresy but refused to go. He was excommunicated in 1497. The next year he oversaw a second great "bonfire of the vanities." But when the *Medici* family returned to power, his days were numbered. The full powers of the church were brought to bear and charges of heresy and false prophesy made. Savonarola was tortured, confessed, recanted, and convicted. He was both hanged and burned on May 23, 1498.

Saxony. See *Georg, Johan*; *Prague, Peace of*; *Protestant Union*; *Reichskreis*; *Schmalkaldic League*; *Thirty Years' War*; *Westphalia, Peace of*.

scalping. Some revisionist historians ascribed the practice of scalping—slicing off the thin flesh and attached hair from the head of a dead or dying enemy—to European settlers. More recent research confirms the original view that this was a common, though not universal, practice of North American Indians that some Europeans later adopted. Scalps were war trophies, tokens of a brave's courage and success in battle. They were comparable to the *samurai* taking of enemy heads ("kubi jikken") and the head-hunting of Balkan *stradiots* in the pay of Venice. Women's scalps were especially prized as a sign the warrior had raided deep into an enemy's lands and hurt him in his most vital interests: his home and family. Not all those who were scalped died, though most scalps were taken from the dead. The practice changed in the 17th century when colonial governments offered bounties for Indian scalps. This had the baleful effect of inducing unscrupulous whites to kill and scalp friendly or even allied Indians, which was always much easier than facing a hostile brave in combat. See also *Indian Wars*; *"skulking way of war."*

scarp. See *escarp*.

schiltron. "Wall of spears." A Scottish infantry formation of the 12th–14th centuries in which spearmen or pikemen formed circles in hedgehoglike defense against *heavy cavalry*. These formations could also move in offense and on occasion push even cavalry backward. See also *Bannockburn*; *caracole*; *Falkirk, Battle of*.

schiopettari. Italian infantry of the 15th century armed with a variety of handguns. Until the 1430s they were mostly confined to garrison duty but by mid-century they were used in field campaigns. Their weapons produced so much smoke that the field of battle was often obscured.

Schladming, Battle of (1525). See *German Peasant War*.

Schlegelerbund. "Mauling band." An alliance of largely reactionary nobles formed in the mid-14th century, an exclusive order of *knights* to oppose the independence of the cities of the *Swabian League*. They were ultimately defeated. See also *Swabian War*.

Schmalkaldic League. A defensive alliance of German Protestant princes and 20 *Reichsstädte* (free cities) formed in February 1531, to oppose the policies of *Charles V* after he ordered all Protestant territories to resume traditional religious practices as of April 1531. War in Germany was averted only because Charles was again distracted by war with the Ottomans. This led to a compromise at Nuremberg postponing action on the religious issue in Germany while Charles fought two more foreign wars with *Francis I* and *Suleiman I*. The German problem came to a head in the "War of the Schmalkaldic League" (1546–1547). On April 24, 1547, the *Duke of Alba* won a major victory for the Imperials by crushing the Leaguers at *Mühlburg* (1547) and capturing several leading princes. Magdeburg was one of the few Reichsstädte to stand successfully against the emperor, and so became a potent symbol of resistance to Catholic tyranny in following decades. Meanwhile, the Protestant dukes of Saxony cleaved to Charles, establishing a special relationship with the emperor that proved more rewarding for the Saxons than Protestant solidarity for nearly a century prior to the *Thirty Years' War*.

Schnepper. A 16th-century German *crossbow* that fired a round bullet instead of a *quarrel*. It came with a steel stock. Some versions could be modified to also shoot quarrels.

Schultheiss. The officer responsible for overseeing all legal matters in a *Landsknechte* company or regiment, including reading out and enforcing the *Articles of War* and rulings by the *Provost*.

schutterijen. Dutch civic *militia*. They were far better troops than most militia and have been described by one historian as a military "elite of the second rank." Recruited from among the bourgeoisie at a rate of 100–150 men per 5,000 population, they regularly drilled, paraded, patrolled, and fought. See also *Alkmaar, Siege of*; *Eighty Years' War*; *Maurits of Nassau*; *uniforms*.

Schweizerdegen. A medium-length *sword* with a simple pommel and cross-guard that was favored and made famous by Swiss mercenaries.

Schweizerdolch. A long *dagger* carried by Swiss mercenaries. It became the main symbol of their status as professional warriors.

schynbalds. *Plate armor* positioned to protect the lower leg. It was introduced during the 14th century.

scorched earth. See *Abbas I*; *ashigaru*; *Black Prince*; *castles, on land*; *chevauchée*; *Ecorcheurs*; *Edward III*; *French Civil Wars*; *Hundred Years' War*; *Ōnin War*; *Mongols*; *raiding*; *routiers*; *Sengoku jidai*; *siege warfare*; *Timur*; *Unification Wars*; *wasters*.

Scotland. Like their English counterparts, Scottish kings had recourse to feudal service obligations of an enfeoffed nobility. In addition, there was a tradition of communal military service among the free male population known as "communis exercitus" or the "servitium scottianum." During and after the *Scottish Wars* of the 13th–14th centuries, Scotland cleaved to the 'Auld alliance with France, which presented a natural alliance out of mutual propinquity to a common enemy. That proved of little worth at *Flodden Field* (1513) where an English army sent north by the young *Henry VIII* defeated the Scots, who lost their young king, James IV (1488–1513), and many lairds and clansmen that day. Another day of defeat and despair came in 1547, at *Pinkie Cleugh*. The association with France was temporarily strengthened by

> *Elizabeth kept the fires of dissent alive with money and subversion of Scottish political stability.*

England's turn toward the reformed religion under Henry and then *Elizabeth I*, which alienated Catholics in Scotland and France who shared ties of kinship and faith through *Mary Stuart* and the *Guise*. It broke down, however, as more Scots converted to a severe version of the new religion during the full-throated *Protestant Reformation*. The dour preachings of *John Knox* and the new national faith of the *Covenanters* reshaped the Church in Scotland into the Presbyterian Kirk. The historical prop of the 'Auld alliance and French support of Scottish political independence was kicked away.

Matters came to a head during the reign of Elizabeth I and the interrupted reign of Mary Stuart, who was supported by Catholic powers in her claim to the Scottish and English thrones but was opposed by many of her Scottish subjects for her Catholic faith and ties to foreign powers. Elizabeth kept the fires of dissent alive with money and subversion of Scottish political stability. In the end, Mary Stuart lost the Scottish throne and her personal freedom (1567), then her life to an English executioner (1587). Her son was elevated as James VI of Scotland (1566–1625) and later as *James I* of England (1567–1625), mounting the southern throne after the childless Elizabeth died in 1603. This *union of crowns* between England and Scotland brought peace along the border. However, trouble lay ahead: the Lowlands accepted union with the ancient enemy, to which the Lords had grown closer and more alike over the centuries from shared holdings on either side of the Tweed; but the Highlands remained wild, hardly governed at all, and fiercely independent and resentful of England.

For a time this social and cultural division among Scots was obscured by the dominance of the religious question in Scottish and international politics. During the *Thirty Years' War* large numbers of Scots served as *mercenaries* in various armies. Arcane doctrinal and ecclesiastical disputes pulled Scotland deep into the *English Civil Wars* (1639–1651) as Scottish nobles and Covenanters backed the English king, *Charles I*, then betrayed him to Parliament, then fought Parliament and the military dictator, *Oliver Cromwell*. Following losses at *Dunbar* (1650) and Worcester (1651), thousands of Scots prisoners were transported to the West Indies as indentured laborers and Scotland became permanently subservient to England. See also *Argyll, Marquis of*; *Bannockburn*; *Burnt Candlemas*; *chevauchée*; *Edward III*; *Falkirk, Battle of*; *galloglass*; *Halidon Hill, Battle of*; *Montrose, Marquis of*; *Otterburn, Battle of*; *penal settlements*; *redshanks*; *Stirling Bridge, Battle of*; *Wallace, William*; *Whiggamore Rising*.

Suggested Reading: I. Cowen, *The Scottish Reformation* (1978); David Stevenson, *The Scottish Revolution, 1637–1644* (1973).

Scots Archers. A famously fierce, and fiercely anti-English, unit of Sottish troops closely allied to the French crown. It was in regular French military service from 1419 when 150 Scots *men-at-arms* and 300 archers landed at *La Rochelle*. Another 17,000 followed during the final decades of the *Hundred Years' War*. The Scots provided what little backbone the dauphin (the future *Charles VII*) exhibited in military affairs prior to the advent of *Jeanne d'Arc*. See also *uniforms*; *Verneuil, Battle of*.

Scottish Wars (13th–14th centuries). *Edward I* sought English *overlordship* in Scotland, in part to force the Scots to accept ruthless taxes he needed to impose in order to pay for his wars in Gascony and Flanders. He repeatedly send lumbering armies north without sufficient attention to problems of supply by sea. On the Scottish side, these early wars saw one of the first efforts by a medieval government to address problems of military organization in a comprehensive manner. The Scots generally avoided battle, wisely letting repeated English failures of *logistics* wither most offensives. Still, battle was sometimes unavoidable. In 1296 Edward I reduced Berwick Castle, crushed a Scots army at Dunbar (April 27), captured Edinburgh, forced John de Baliol to abdicate, sent the Coronation Stone of Scone to England, and proclaimed himself overlord and king of Scotland. However, at *Stirling Bridge* (1297) the Scots won a surprising victory over Edward's heavy horse, partly as a result of the inspired leadership of *William Wallace* and in part because of blunt English cavalry tactics, overconfidence, and error. The next year, at *Falkirk*, the weight of English numbers and *longbows* overwhelmed the Scots. But once again, bad logistics forced Edward to withdraw before full victory was achieved. Another English campaign in 1301 produced no battles and no result. Fortunately for Edward, the French were stunned by the Flemings at *Courtrai* (1302), which freed English troops in Gascony and others intended for Flanders to campaign in Scotland. His 1304 campaign was successful: all the Scottish lairds capitulated and Stirling Castle fell.

The Scottish Wars waxed and waned over the following years and decades, lasting more than a century. After Wallace's execution in 1305 the Scots were led by Robert Earl of Carrick, crowned Robert I (Bruce), at Scone in 1306. That challenge to English overlordship provoked Edward I to send another army north, to Perth. It was met at Methven by Robert and a small Scots army that was easily crushed. That sent Robert into exile in the northern isles (where the legend says he was inspired to renewed resistance by watching the determined web-building efforts of a country spider). More likely, he did not enjoy residence in the isolated and uncomfortable northern isles. Robert returned to Scotland to raise an army and fought the English at Loudon Hill (1307). There, his *schiltrons* met the rash and headlong charge of English heavy horse and won handily, inflicting serious casualties to English knighthood. For seven years following the death of Edward I, just after Loudon Hill, England was governed by the weak Edward II. At first he left Scotland alone. That permitted Robert to consolidate his claim by marrying the daughter of King Philip ("The Fair") of France, confirming the '*Auld alliance*. Next, Robert rousted most English garrisons along the frontier and the Tweed. The Scots boldly laid siege to the last two English strongholds, the great castles at Berwick and Stirling, in 1314. That provoked Edward II to send north the largest English army ever to invade Scotland. The Scots used tactics learned from the Flemings to best the English cavalry with numerically inferior infantry at *Bannockburn*, five miles from Stirling.

Edward II spent the rest of his reign a detested and severely weakened king. He gained marginally from a civil war over the succession in Scotland between King David II and Edward de Baliol and "The Disinherited" (Scots nobles). After the Scots defeated another English army at Myton (September 20, 1319), a brief peace was agreed that lasted into 1322. With a baronial revolt underway in England, "The Bruce" crossed the border to raid northern England in force. Edward II learned something from his defeats and altered his tactics sufficiently to win over his barons at *Boroughbridge* (1322). Then he advanced into Scotland to retaliate against the Scottish invasion. But "The Bruce" chased Edward out, routing him at Byland (October 14, 1322). Edward formally accepted Scotland's independence and a long truce was agreed.

In 1327 Edward II was deposed and murdered by an invasion force organized by his Queen, Isabella. In what became popularly known as the "Cowardice Peace" or "Shameful Peace" of 1328 (officially, the Treaty of Northampton), *Edward III* was forced to renounce his claim to the Scottish throne. The young king overthrew the regency in 1330, rejected the settlement, revived England's claim to overlordship in Scotland and resumed the Scottish Wars. At Dupplin Moor (1332), a Scots host ten times the size of the English army it faced was routed, leaving 3,000 dead on the field to go along with the deaths of the Regent of Scotland and four out of five Scottish earls (the fifth was captured). Why this extraordinary victory by a far smaller force? Because Edward III had implemented an advanced military doctrine that led to a true infantry revolution in English arms. He tried out his new ideas in Scotland, before carrying them across the English Channel to France during the first decades of the *Hundred Years' War* (1337–1453). In both regions he used the old trick of a *chevauchée* to provoke his enemy to a battle in which he held to the defensive and slaughtered his foes with massed archery and dismounted *men-at-arms*. That is how he beat the Scots again, at *Halidon Hill* (1333), despite a 2:1 disadvantage in raw numbers. An Edwardian army drove another chevauchée into Scotland in 1346, which again provoked the Scots to fight. This time they lost not just the battle but also their king, David II, at Neville's Cross (October 17, 1346). That battle was nearly lost for England when the archer wings broke, but when the men-at-arms held the center the archers rallied and returned to the fight. King David was held for a literal "king's ransom" to be paid by Scotland over ten years.

The loss of their king did not dismay the Scots. Also, they were more successful in war at sea where Highland *galleys* raided down the English coasts and the Channel Islands. And a Scots army beat back the 1356 *Burnt Candlemas* chevauchée led by Edward III in person. The Scots took the offensive as Edward III settled into a long and decadent decline, but they could only hope to punish, not conquer their English foe. For several decades more the Scottish wars were marked mainly by cross-border raids and skirmishes and occasional deeper chevauchées, along with harassment and capture of *prizes* at sea. Major fighting erupted again in 1388 when a Franco-Scottish army invaded northern England and fought a rare night battle at *Otterburn* (August 15). The Scots continued to raid unchallenged along the border for another fifteen years after that. They were badly beaten, however, at Homildon Hill (September 1402) by an English army utilizing large numbers of longbowmen who stood back and decimated the Scottish ranks with long-range missile fire, softening them up for a heavy cavalry charge. The Scots were rescued from further defeats by the outbreak of civil war in England, from the deposition of Richard II in 1399 to the fight at Shrewsbury in 1403.

Suggested Reading: E. Miller, *War in the North* (1960); Ranald Nicholson, *Edward III and the Scots: Formative Years of a Military Career, 1327–1335* (1965).

Scottish Wars (15th–17th centuries). See *Charles I, of England*; *Covenanters*; *Cromwell, Oliver*; *Elizabeth I*; *English Civil Wars*; *Henry VIII, of England*; *Mary Stuart, Queen of Scots*; *Pinkie Cleugh, Battle of*; *prisoners of war*; *Scotland*; *Wars of the Roses*.

scourers. Lancastrian term for *light cavalry* used during the *Wars of the Roses* in England.

scurvy. See *cruising*; *disease*; *Exploration, Age of*; *rations*.

scutage (*scutagium*). Cash payments to a liege lord or king in lieu of military "service in the host." Rather than award of a *fief* and jurisdiction in return for vassal military service, nobles recruited *men-at-arms*, or archers and other military professionals, and paid them to serve in the liege lord's host. This system was progressively adopted in England from the 12th century but later in France and Germany. It was not used in the Crusader states in the "Holy Land," however. There, a knightly vassal wishing to escape or limit military service was required to surrender his fief for a year and a day, rather than pay a cash settlement. This harsher system and deterrent penalty was made necessary by the acute shortage of military manpower in the Latin kingdoms established by the first *Crusades*. See also *feudalism*; *servitium debitum*.

scuttle. To sink a ship by drilling, cutting, or knocking a hole in its hull below the waterline. This might be done to deny the ship to an enemy or more often, to sink it as a *blockship* in a river mouth or harbor.

Sea Beggars ("*Gueux*"). They took their sobriquet from a famous insult delivered to 200 nobles by *Margaret of Parma* on April 5, 1566, as she rejected their "Petition of Compromise." The Beggars established a naval force in 1568, as a rebellion against Spain broke out that ultimately became the *Eighty Years' War* (1568–1648). Most Sea Beggar officers were Hollanders and Frisians; a few hailed from the south. The ferocious anti-Catholicism of the Sea Beggars was well-represented by their chosen symbol, a crescent Moon with the bold inscription "Better Turkish Than Roman." They often killed prisoners and clergy with special cruelty. They were not highly regarded by all Protestants, either. Dutch Calvinists admired Sea Beggar martial feats but dreaded their presence in port and bad moral example: many Sea Beggar crews were little short of pirates in their manners and sexual habits. From 1568 to 1572, the Sea Beggars operated out of England against Spanish shipping in the Channel, under *letters of marque* issued by *William the Silent* in his sovereign capacity as Prince of Orange. The *Duke of Alba* countered by garrisoning the mouths of the Scheldt and Maas. In early 1572, *Elizabeth I*, under great pressure from Spain, closed English harbors to the Sea Beggars. In need of a new haven, on April 1, 1572, the Sea Beggars took *Brill*, then

> *…many Sea Beggar crews were little short of pirates in their manners and sexual habits.*

Flushing, and with the aid of local *schutterijen* held out against Alba's counterattack. In 1573 the Sea Beggars defeated an inland Spanish fleet and lifted the *Siege of Alkmaar*, then bested Alba's ships and a fleet from royalist Amsterdam at the Zuider Zee (October 11, 1573). In 1574 they finally overran the last Spanish garrison on Walcheren, at Middelburg, then dramatically lifted the *Siege of Leiden*. They failed to lift the *Siege of Antwerp* in 1585, despite a determined amphibious effort. From the 1590s they dominated the Spanish in the Channel and open sea, blockaded the Scheldt estuary and Flemish ports, privateered against Iberian shipping on several oceans, supported the Dutch invasion of Brazil and capture of Portuguese entrepôts in the Far East, and aided the rise of the United Provinces to globally dominant commercial and naval power in the 17th century. See also *Boisot, Louis*; *fireships*; *French Civil Wars*; *Tromp, Maarten van*.

Sea Brothers. See *Hospitallers*; *Rhodes, Siege of (1444)*; *Rhodes, Siege of (1479–1480)*; *Rhodes, Siege of (1522–1523)*.

Seacroft Moor, Battle of (1643). See *Fairfax, Thomas.*

sea dogs. *Privateers* and sometime *pirates* who earned a deserved reputation for ruthlessness and often indiscriminate violence at sea. Most were seamen of the ports of the West Country of England where skilled sailors joined common cause with aggressive local gentry, enjoyed protection by the local courts and magistrates, and often were backed financially and legally by the monarch. The most famous English sea dog captains were *Francis Drake, John Hawkyns, Walter Raleigh,* and *Martin Frobisher,* all of whom preyed on Iberian shipping with (though at other times, without) the blessing of *Elizabeth I* in her protracted war with *Philip II.* The Spanish viewed the sea dogs as common pirates, which they surely were in spirit and in practice; they also feared them greatly, especially Drake ("El Draque"). Piracy shaded into privateering when it was formally sanctioned and heavily invested in by the Queen. The crossing of class lines, the importance of privateering to the English economy, and the alliance of merchants with the monarch reflected and encouraged an emergent English patriotism and defiant Protestantism. Even so, profit was first and nearly always the prime motivator of these men, as was best shown during the Armada fight in 1588 when Drake slipped away from the battle to escort a Spanish *prize* into port.

    Suggested Reading: Angus Konstam and Angus McBride, *Elizabethan Sea Dogs, 1560–1605* (2000); Neville Williams, *The Sea Dogs: Privateers, Plunder and Piracy in the Elizabethan Age* (1975).

sea power. See *ships; war at sea.*

Sea Victuallers. Swedish *pirates* in the Baltic, based on Gotland, who preyed on ships of the *Hanse.* They were driven off Gotland in 1398 by the *Teutonic Knights,* after which *Denmark* undertook to suppress them and protect the Baltic trade.

seclusion decrees. See *Japan; Kakure Kirishitan.*

secret. A mid-17th-century iron skull cap, sewn (secreted) inside a cloth hat. With full helmets out of fashion and no longer useful against *muskets,* this hidden head *armor* still provided some protection against sword cuts in a cavalry-to-cavalry fight.

Sefarad. The Hebrew name for Spain before the *expulsion of the Jews* in 1492.

sefer bahşişi. A campaign bonus customarily paid to active troops of the *Kapikulu Askerleri.*

Sejm. The assembly (Diet) of the Commonwealth of Poland-Lithuania. It had an upper Senate and a lower Chamber of Envoys. In 1505, the statute "Nihil Novi" ("Nothing New") was passed, forbidding any legislation without consent of the Sejm. Through this law and institution the nobility (*szlachta*) exercised great influence over monarchs, even deciding the size, command, and financing of armies. See also *Lithuania, Grand Duchy of*; *Poland*.

sejmiki. Professional troops, whether native Polish or foreign *mercenaries*, paid for by Sejmiki: provincial assemblies modeled on the *Sejm* and replicating its baronial autonomy on the local level.

sekban. Ottoman infantry, with some mounted as dragoons to keep up with *timariot* cavalry. Sekban units were formed from frontier auxiliaries in the Balkans at first; later they were recruited via universal conscription ("nefer-i am") in Anatolia, to a wartime strength of about 10,000. They were deployed only temporarily, to supplement the permanent forces of the *Kapikulu Askerleri*. They shared their name with the "sekban" of the *Janissaries*, but otherwise were unrelated to that elite professional corps. At the end of campaigns it was sometimes hard to disband sekban infantry who wished to remain employed by the sultan. By the mid-17th century, some outside observers considered them to be better troops than the later Janissaries, as the Corps succumbed to a certain decadence. Others disagreed. See also *Celâli Revolts*.

Sekigahara, Battle of (September 15, 1600). After months of careful planning by *Tokugawa Ieyasu* nearly 170,000 troops met in this climactic battle of a century of *daimyo* warfare of the *Sengoku jidai*. Ieyasu led a coalition eastern army of 75,000 men in a final battle that established his control over Japan, confirming his succession to *Toyotomi Hideyoshi* (d.1598) and blocking the path to power of his minor son, Toyotomi Hideyori. The enemy was a western coalition of 82,000 led by Ishida Mitsunari, nominally backing Hideyori. Ieyasu maneuvered to bypass the western army in Ōgaki castle during the night, but it moved to meet him in a narrow valley at Sekigahara. The fight began at 8:00 a.m. after a thick fog lifted that had obscured the valley. The outcome was foreordained by secret agreements between Ieyasu and key western army daimyo who sat and watched the battle from on high, without joining it. That left just 30,000 Toyotomi loyalists to fight the Tokugawa. At noon one of the traitor Toyotomi daimyo revealed his shift in allegiance by charging down the mountainside into the Toyotomi right flank. This treachery was repeated by other commanders, serially collapsing the Toyotomi line. After six hours of heavy fighting Ieyasu won a crushing victory. Sekigahara was the culminating fight of the *Unification Wars*, but not the end. That finally came when Ieyasu destroyed the last *samurai* holdouts at *Osaka Castle* in 1615.

Selim I (1467–1520). "The Grim." Ottoman Sultan. In 1512 he deposed his father, *Bayezid II*, with the help of the *Janissary Corps*. He put to death several brothers and nephews, eliminating all potential claimants to the throne. The bloody path to his ascension left Selim in debt to the Corps his whole reign.

Intent on imposing hardline religious conformity within his realm, something alien to most Ottoman sultans, in 1514 Selim ordered a mass slaughter of *shī'ia* and other heterodox Muslims preparatory to campaigning against the *Safavids* in Iran. He defeated the Iranians at *Chaldiran* in 1514 and went on to crush the Kurds of Iraq. However, in 1515 his *kuls* (including Janissaries) refused his orders to invade Syria, complaining of the desert heat and the lateness of the campaign season. He returned the next year to destroy a *mamlūk* army out of Egypt at *Marj Dabiq*. That enabled him to secure Syria, Palestine, and the Hejaz to the Empire. In early 1517 the Janissaries twice more defeated firearms-abjuring mamlūk armies, at *al-Raydaniyya* in January and *Giza* in April. Selim bombarded Cairo, destroyed much of it, then let his men sack the city. He killed all potential leaders among the Mamlūks, overthrew the last Abbasid *caliph*, and brought Egypt into the empire as a tributary province. He was succeeded and surpassed by his son, *Suleiman I*, who repudiated his father's religious intolerance and eastern aggressions but kept the new provinces that he inherited and further consolidated them within the Empire.

Selim II (1524–1574). Ottoman sultan. Decadent and incompetent successor to his father, *Suleiman I*. During his reign but not because of it, the *Ottoman Empire* took control of the remainder of the Arabian peninsula (it already held the Hejaz) in 1570. He occupied Cyprus in 1571 which provoked a Christian alliance to counterattack: Selim lost his whole fleet at *Lepanto* as a result. He also lost three-quarters of a large army to a new enemy, *Muscovy*, which he sent on an ill-fated expedition to Astrakhan.

Seljuk Turks. A nomadic warrior people from Central Asia who constructed a large empire on top of prior Arabized peoples and *caliphates* in the 11th–12th centuries. They were named for Seljuk ("Selchuk") who led them in conquest of the failing empire of the Turkic and Islamicized Ghaznavids in Afghanistan and the Punjab (1040). The Seljuks were drawn into Anatolia by the usual forces of Central Asian martial expansion: overpopulation, land hunger, and access to steppe horses and military technology that made *raiding* settled civilizations an attractive way of life. They quickly overran northern Iraq, taking Baghdad in 1055. Contact with the Abbasid caliphs led to a military alliance against the *shī'ia* of Iran, cemented in a dynastic marriage following conversion of the leading Seljuks to *sunni* Islam. The Seljuks next overran Armenia. Their greatest and most portentous victory was won over the Byzantines by Sultan Alp Arslan (r.1065–1072) at Manzikert (1071). This stunning victory was followed by further expansion under Sultan Malik Shah (r.1072–1092). The Seljuks governed their ethnically and religiously diverse empire within a tradition of broad tolerance of Christians and Jews, even during the *Crusades*. They were far more intolerant of heterodox Muslims, the shī'ia, whom the freshly converted and hence fervently orthodox Seljuks regarded as heretics and with whom they fought all along their Iranian frontier. The Seljuk empire was never fully consolidated and was sharply weakened by the depredations of Asia Minor by the *Mongols*. The Seljuks were superceded by the *Ottoman Empire*, the creation of one of their Anatolian clients, Osman (1280–1326). See also *Normans*; *Piyadeğan militia*; *Turks*.

Suggested Reading: Mehmet Koprulu, *The Seljuks of Anatolia*, Gary Leiser, trans. (1992).

Seminara, Battle of (June 28, 1495). An early battle of the *Italian Wars*. A Franco-Swiss army defeated a Spanish force under *Gonzalo di Córdoba*. Following the battle *Charles VIII* still held Naples, which he had seized in February. See also *Cerignola, Battle of*.

Sempach, Battle of (July 9, 1386). The Austrians were led at Sempach by the young Duke Leopold III, who sought to reassert Austrian control over the Swiss and avenge the humiliation suffered at the hands of the *Forest Cantons* at *Morgarten* (1315). Leopold moved against the Swiss with about 4,000 *knights*, including a number of *mercenaries*, split into two columns. The Swiss Confederation, much expanded since Morgarten, fielded an opposing force (mainly from Lucerne) of 1,600 men. They advanced in the soon-to-be famous *Swiss square*. At the head of the lead Austrian column, Leopold ordered his knights to dismount, form ranks, and face the approaching Swiss van with lances level. The Swiss were mainly *halberdiers* with a few hand gunners, and were only partly protected by *pikemen* (the Swiss did not routinely deploy large numbers of pikers until after *Arbedo* in 1422). At first, the Austrians held their own and killed many lightly armed and armored Swiss. But the exceptional maneuverability of Swiss formations and tactics came into play as a separate detachment was formed from the rear ranks and sent to attack into the Austrian flank. This side assault was reinforced by fresh troops arriving at the run from Uri. The Austrian line was breached: Swiss halberdiers pushed into the gap swinging weapons at head height, beheading and mutilating hundreds of knights. The Austrians fought constricted by their armor and with an awkward main weapon—the *lance*—never meant for use on foot. Their rear ranks and the second column panicked as the Swiss broke through the front ranks. The Austrian infantry turned and ran, taking most of the wagons and nearly all the horses with them. Abandoned and on foot, knights were slaughtered en masse by the utterly unmerciful Swiss. It is thought that 1,800 Austrians—mostly knights, and including Leopold III—were killed, to just 200 Swiss.

Sempach, Covenant of (1393). An agreement among the Swiss cantons to coordinate their military efforts brought about by the external threat from Austria and Burgundy but also in the wake of Swiss successes at *Morgarten* (1315), *Laupen* (1339), and *Sempach* (1386). It is sometimes said to mark the beginning of the *Swiss Army* as a national force. In addition to the usual provisions and pledges required to facilitate joint military action, it was agreed that training of Swiss troops would continue on a canton-by-canton basis. The covenant also elaborated a fairly advanced code of conduct, including protection of designated holy places (churches, shrines, monasteries) and of civilians ("defenseless persons"). It did so not to limit collateral damage or to encourage moral behavior, but to reduce conflict between men from different cantons by regulating in advance each man's share of goods acquired through *plunder*.

Sengoku daimyo. Japanese provincial warlords (*daimyo*) in the *Sengoku jidai* period.

Sengoku jidai (1467–1568). "Country at War" or "Warring States." The anarchic period in Japanese history starting with the *Ōnin War*. The Ashikaga shogunate was reduced to impotence while regional *daimyo* waged protracted war to satisfy predatory *samurai* greedy for conquered lands and willing to prostitute their vassalage to get it. So unusual was this phenomenon of once honorable and loyal samurai switching sides on the eve of a battle and behaving little better than *ronin*, and so revolutionary were its political, economic, and social upheavals, the period is also called *gekokujō* ("the lower overthrowing the higher"). That term denotes the new role of peasants and townsfolk in Japanese warfare, in which they participated in numbers hitherto unknown and using brutal tactics of scorched earth and razing hundreds of castles and towns. Most fighting was seasonal and local rather than national with chronic small battles rather than large decisive ones. There were few expensive or protracted sieges. Some 40,000 forts (*honjō* and *shijō*), were built by all sides. While these were easily reduced by fire, remote *jōkaku* and *yamajiro* in the mountains, fortified monasteries, and strong *jōkamachi* (castle towns) astride inland roads were harder to overcome. The period came to an end with *Oda Nobunaga*'s triumphal entry into Kyoto during the *Unification Wars*. See also *akutō*; *ashigaru*.

> *. . . Japanese warfare . . . using brutal tactics of scorched earth and razing hundreds of castles and towns.*

Seoul, Battle of (1592). See *Korea*; *Toyotomi Hideyoshi*.

serasker. See *serdar*.

Serbia. See *Austria*; *Kosovo, Battle of*; *Maritza River, Battle of*; *Murad I*; *Ottoman Empire*.

Serb Sindin ("Serbian Defeat"), Battle of (1371). See *Maritza River, Battle of*.

serdar. Or "serasker." The personal command representative of an Ottoman sultan, placed in full charge of the army according to terms laid out in a diploma of office. Even when a sultan went on campaign the serdar retained control of most deployment and tactical decisions and had full powers to punish troops. Because the post was so powerful it was an object of intense competition among senior *kuls*.

Serdengeçti (serden-geçtiler). "Head riskers." Elite, all-volunteer Ottoman commando and assault units. They were recruited among the *Janissaries* and *sipahis.* They undertook the most dangerous assignments in return for promises of unusual material rewards, defined in advance in written contracts. Some led the wild and frantic Janissary charges that so often overcame enemy infantry; others were the first through a breach in the enemy's wall or over it on scaling ladders. Their casualty rates frequently exceeded 70–90 percent. See also *Kapikulu Askerleri; uniforms.*

serfdom. See *Cossacks; feudalism; German Peasant War; Muscovy, Grand Duchy of; Poland; Ukraine.*

sergeant. A rank common among *men-at-arms.* In France it was replaced by *esquire* by the end of the 13th century. In England, sergeants were distinct from squires (esquires) and *valets.* Elsewhere, as with the *Military Orders,* they formed the real backbone of medieval armies.

Seritsa River, Battle of (January 1501). See *Muscovy, Grand Duchy of.*

serpentine. This term had three distinct meanings in the medieval and early modern periods. First, it was used about early mealed (as opposed to *corned*) gunpowder in apparent reference to the presumed Satanic origins of a technology whose employment of fire in war the *Catholic Church* regarded as the inspiration of the devil and tried to ban. Next, the *matchlock* firing device on a mid-15th-century *arquebus* had a serpentine shape and the term attached to it. Finally, serpentine described a class of small cannon that fired half-pound shot to an effective range of 250 yards and a maximum range of 1,000 yards. Serpentine also qualified other gun types such as *cannon-serpentine.*

serving the vent. See *wounds.*

servitium debitum. The feudal military obligations of a medieval European lord and his *knights* and retainers (*men-at-arms*). It invoked three main obligations. The first was *chevauchée,* or riding service, the basic means of assembling early medieval cavalry. This faded out of existence over time. The second duty under the servitium debitum was "watch" or garrison service. Over time, this too was replaced by a substitution of money (tax) in lieu of service. Finally, there was "service in the host" or the responsibility to give 40 days free military service when called to arms by one's liege lord. Once more, over time this was eroded by the practice of instead paying *scutage,* in England in particular. Elsewhere, it was undermined by the success of vassals in placing sharp geographical and time limits on their service, which forced monarchs to seek out professional troops instead. By 1300, recourse to the servitium debitum was seldom made in England or France. See also *English armies; feudalism; French armies; Imperial Army; war finance.*

servitium scottianum. See *Scotland.*

servitor classes. The *Tatar* servitor system was called *soyughal*. Ottoman servitor classes included *askeri*, *sipahis*, and *timariots*. Servitors in the Muscovite military and social system could be patrimonial (votchina), principally the *boyars*, or non-hereditary (pomest'e). A servitor cavalry (*pomest'e cavalry*) was established by *Ivan III* in the late 15th century. These horsemen were recruited from a new landholding class seeded by Ivan over the countryside to control newly conquered lands, in exchange for several months per year of military service. Often, this involved patrolling the semi-fortified southern frontier against raids by Tatars or *Cossacks*. Pomeshchiki horsemen were required to provide their own mounts, weapons, and supplies. *Ivan IV* set up a servitor palace guard of infantry musketeers, the *strel'sty*, in 1550. Their special privilege was exemption from taxation. Other servitor units included artillery. Servitors on the southern frontier of the Muscovite empire had to serve south of the "chertva lines" in one of eight regular patrols made by 70–100 horsemen each. They departed on precise schedules from April through November, serving about three months active duty. See also *feudalism*; *fief*; *knight*.

sesto. "Sixth." A division of the northern Italian communes, each tasked to produce units of infantry and cavalry for the common defense.

Sforza, Ludovico (1451–1508). Although he was formally Duke of Milan only from 1494 to 1499, he governed in fact from 1480. His alliance with Charles VIII of France helped trigger the French invasion of Italy that began the *Italian Wars* (1494–1559). In 1495 he tried to switch sides, leading the French to depose him. He mediated an end to the *Swabian War* (1499) in order to release Swiss troops for his own effort to recover Milan. In 1500 he was defeated at Novara and captured. He died in a French prison.

Sforza, Maximilian (1493–1530). "Massimiliano." *Ludovico Sforza* lost Milan to France in 1499. In 1512, the Swiss (nominally as members of the *Holy League*) captured Milan in the name of his son, Maximilian. The Swiss in fact kept control of Milan, milking it for themselves until a stunning defeat at *Marignano* (1515). After that Milan reverted to French control. See also *Francis I*; *Italian Wars*.

shaffron. See *chanfron.*

shallop. Originally, a small sloop-like warship, predominantly a cruiser in shallow coastal water. In the 16th–17th centuries this term was used more often about a small class of ship's boat.

shell-keep. A round stone *keep* built on top of, or around, an older *motte.*

shells. During the early 16th century, experiments were made with hollow explosive projectiles fired from cannon; these were called "shells" for the obvious reason. Early shells were fitted with primitive wicks or fuses. These were highly risky as they had to be lighted at the same time the gun (usually, a *mortar*) was loaded. They were also inaccurate since nonstandardized fuses burned at irregular rates or according to the skill and experience of the master gunner. A fast-burning or short (cut) fuse might explode the shell before it reached its target while a really short fuse could detonate the shell inside the gun barrel. A slow or long-burning fuse was likely to go out when the shell hit the ground or be put out by a courageous enemy after the shell landed. Experimentation partly solved this problem by loading in a manner that permitted igniting the fuse on the shell simultaneously with the main powder charge that propelled the shell down the barrel. However, final resolution of the problem was not achieved until just before the French Revolution. Even so, after 1450 improvements to artillery shells were impressive: bronze explosive shells were available from 1463; incendiary shells appeared in 1487; an early "shrapnel" was invented in 1573; hot shot was in use from 1575; reliable explosive shells appeared in 1588; percussion fuses were invented in 1596. See also *artillery*.

Sher Khan (1486–1545). "Sher Shah." Mughal emperor, 1540–1545. He was a leading general in *Babur*'s Afghan army that invaded north India and established the *Mughal Empire* after defeating the *Delhi Sultanate* and the *Rajputs*. He split with Babur's son and successor, Humayun, setting up a rival state in Bengal. He defeated Humayun in 1539 and again in 1540, after which he gained control of the Mughal Empire, adding to it his holdings in Bengal. He was succeeded by Humayun's son, *Akbar*.

shī'a Islam. "Shī' atu Ali" ("The Party of Ali"). The most significant minority sect within *Islam*. The shī'a early on broke with the *sunni* majority to develop their own forms of piety and follow their own historical and theological path. Shi'ites accept as legitimate four *caliphs* whom they agreed with sunnis correctly succeeded Prophet Muhammad, up to Muhammad's son-in-law Ali (d.661 C.E.), the fourth caliph. However, they rejected the sunni (Umayyad) caliphs who then followed Ali. Thus, they denied legitimacy to the fifth caliph, Mu'awiya, founder of the sunni dynasty known as the Umayyad Caliphate (661–750), and all his sunni successors. Shī'a proclaimed only the descendants of Ali and Fatima, or the family of Muhammad, as the rightful— that is, anointed by Allah—successors to the Prophet and ruler of all Muslims. These shī'a shadow candidates became known as "Alids." There were variants on this position of differing subtlety or obscurity. A deeply eschatological, quasi-messianic variant called "Twelfth-imam shi'ism," or colloquially just "Twelvers," recognized eleven specially anointed *imams* who lived in historical time while awaiting the arrival (future return) of the 12th, or "Hidden Imam," who was said to be the true caliph. In contrast, *Ismailis* (Fatamid) were sometimes called "Seveners" because they believed the rightful succession stopped in 765 C.E. with the death of the sixth caliph, the last visible to earthly eyes after Muhammad. Some Ismailis (Nizari) divided further, following only until the fourth caliph. All of this represented theological adjustment to historical reality, in which the devout were encouraged to believe that Muhammad's true successors exercised hidden influence in the interest of the community of believers. Shī'a thus became the main repository of Islam's original highly apocalyptic vision that was similar to, and rooted in, that of Christianity and Judaism, after the first several generations waited in vain for the great and promised transformation. This tradition became embodied in the idea of the "mahdi," a quasi-cult notion which looked to the arrival of a divinely guided, heroic figure—the true or hidden imam—who will transform and end all history.

Over the centuries this latent messianism had great political significance: it was possible to create much turmoil and conflict in devout Islamic societies if some claimant to political power could, sincerely and legitimately or not, assert a claim to an Alid nature and candidacy. Shī'a communities also displayed a tendency toward exclusivity, indeed a real elitism contrary to the great spiritual leveling which made original Islam so attractive to so many, and still does. This flowed from a temperamental tendency in shi'ia theology which, rather like the clergy of the Medieval Latin Church, held the larger mass of faithful sunni (let alone non-Muslims) in some disdain as non-privileged by—and probably incapable of—the highest truths of the faith. A fundamentalist variant of shī'a thus utterly rejected the right of Muslims to select their own rulers. It was not enough for a community of believers to establish laws based upon the Koran, said these fundamentalists. Muslims must also have among them the physical presence of a true imam, one in genuine (Alid) descent from the family of the Prophet. This imam was to be be received as the spokesman of the divine will on Earth. Only such a ruler was seen as fit to govern Muslims because only such a man (women were wholly excluded) was anointed by Allah. Any leader not within the tradition, however devout, was scorned as a usurper. Such radical believers would, from time to time as circumstance permitted, challenge sunni Muslim leaders they regarded as not Alid, or whom they declared to have supplanted the legitimate rule of a true imam. Among Muslims the shī'a were closest to having an interpretive priesthood ("mujtahids") and had the most highly developed and distinctive mystical traditions, notably *Sufism*. Yet, despite their more vehement political tradition, the great corpus of shī'a doctrine was akin to sunni doctrine and practice. Nevertheless, deep communal tensions often led to war between the main branches of Islam. See also *ayatollah*; *flagellants*; *Iran*; *Iraq*; *Islam*.

Suggested Reading: John Esposito, ed., *Oxford History of Islam* (1999); Marshall Hodgson, *The Classical Age of Islam* (1974).

shields/shielding. Early European and most Arab and Berber shields were simple and round. In Europe these "bucklers" were a mark of warrior status as well as armaments. While Muslims retained round shields, European *knights* shifted to hefty kite-shaped shields. Smaller triangular shields were in use by the 13th century. At the end of the 14th century a notch was cut in the right top corner to afford greater protection to the rider by his not having to lower the shield along with the *lance* which he rested upon it. As *armor* evolved from *mail* to *plate*, shields became redundant and were eventually abandoned by most cavalry. In Scotland, clansmen still used a "targe," many of which had a 12-inch spike at the center for offensive use as a lethal stabbing weapon. Similarly, warriors in India used a *madu*, a one-armed shield with horns or spikes attached for stabbing at the enemy in hand-to-hand combat. Japanese infantry carried a large wooden shield, the "tate," for defense against *samurai* archers. Similar infantry shields were used in Europe by *pavisare*, special defensive troops who carried heavy wooden and iron shields into battle to protect crossbowmen who clustered behind them when reloading. *Henry VIII* ordered special gun shields from Italian armorers for his musketeers. These were small and circular, made from wood and attached plates of iron with a shooting hole at the center, above which there was a small grill for the musketeer to peer through. These were expensive and wholly impractical, and were not widely adopted. See also *adarga*; *artillery*; *bretasche*; *cat*; *chimalli*; *dhal*; *enarmes*; *escutcheon*; *gambeson*; *Mamlūks*; *manteletes*; *pavisade*; *pavise*; *sipar*; *sow*; *targe*; *targhieri*; *testudo*.

> *In Scotland, clansmen still used a "targe"...as a lethal stabbing weapon.*

shi'ite. An adherent of *shī'a Islam*.

shijō. Japanese branch forts, usually simple wooden affairs supporting the main *honjō*. They were prevalent in the *Sengoku jidai* era.

Shimabara Rebellion (1637–1638). See *Japan*; *Kakure Kirishitan*.

shino-gote. See *armor*.

ship money. A tax imposed on coastal counties of England in 1634 by *Charles I* to support a royal navy to defend the Channel. It supported construction of 19 royal warships and 26 armed merchants. In 1637 Charles extended it to the inland counties. As this was all done without the consent of Parliament, "ship money" became a synonym for royal dictatorship and taxation without representation and thereby significantly moved the country toward the violent conflict of the *English Civil Wars* (1639–1651).

ship-of-the-line. Any warship in the "Age of Sail" powerful enough to join a *line ahead* or *line astern* formation to wage *broadside* battle alongside the most powerful warships, without constituting a weak point in the line. See also *frigate*; *galleon*.

ships. Ships of the period often doubled for war and trade. War at sea in the Mediterranean saw specialized warships in ancient times that were all variations on the galley, the most successful warship design in history. Among ships of sail there was a much slower trend toward building specialized warships. However, this accelerated in the 14th–17th centuries as more iron *cannon* became available to be mounted on warships and new designs and methods of hull manufacture were laid out to accept heavy guns. Ship design varied by region with even closely connected seas such as the Mediterranean and Atlantic seeing different ship-building designs and techniques. Indian Ocean, Japanese, and Chinese junk designs were radically different from European craft.

On ship types, see *balinger*; *barge*; *bark*; *birlin*; *brigantine*; *caravel*; *carrack*; *coaster*; *cocha*; *cog*; *cromster*; *dhow*; *drekkar/drekki*; *dromon*; *frigate*; *Fujian ships*; *fusta*; *galleass*; *galleon*; *galley*; *galliot*; *Great Galley*; *Great Ships*; *Guangdong*; *hulk*; *junk*; *longship*; *lymphad*; *man-of-war*; *nao*; *nef*; *patache*; *pinnace*; *resfuerzo*; *rowbarge*; *shallop*; *sloop-of-war*; *tarides*; *xebec*; *zabra*.

On related matters see *admiral*; *admiralty*; *aftercastle*; *Almiranta*; *astrolabe*; *battery*; *battle*; *blockade*; *blockship*; *boarding*; *bow(ing)*; *breeching*; *brig*; *broadside*; *burden*; *Capitana*; *captain*; *castles, on ships*; *chase gun(s)*; *clinker-built*; *compass*; *convoy*; *cross-staff*; *cruising*; *dead reckoning*; *demurrage*; *fathom*; *fireships*; *flags*; *Greek fire*; *gun-deck*; *gun port*; *gun tackle*; *haul close*; *haul wind*; *heave to*; *Invincible Armada*; *keel-haul*; *knot*; *last*; *Laws of Olèron*; *league*; *line abreast*; *line ahead*; *line ahead and astern*; *line astern*; *line of battle*; *longboat*; *make sail*; *maps*; *master*; *master gunner*; *master's mate*; *masts*; *muster*; *officer*; *patron*; *piracy*; *portolan chart*; *privateer*; *quarter deck*; *quartermaster*; *quartermaster's mate*; *rations*; *rigging*; *round robin*; *Royal Navy*; *safeguard the sea*; *sail*; *sails*; *ship money*; *ship-of-the-line*; *ship's boys*; *shipyards*; *shorten sail*; *skeleton-built*; *"sovereignty of the sea"*; *spar*; *sternpost rudder*; *sweeps*; *swivel gun*; *tackle*; *tier*; *tonnage*; *top*; *"tunnage and poundage"*; *van*; *victualer*; *waft*; *wafter*; *warp*; *wear*; *weather*; *weather gauge*; *weatherly*; *windlass*; *windward*; *yard*; *yardarm*; *Zheng He*.

ship's boys. Upper-class boys might be apprenticed to the captain and study navigation and command; lower-class boys were assigned to assist carpenters, gunners, and other specialized crew functions. Boys were added to English naval crews in the 14th century. They worked aloft in the new multi-masted sailing ships, nimbly moving among footropes and rigging of the upper *spars* that might not support the weight of a grown man, or replacing a heavier crewman sitting on a *yardarm* as it was hoisted aloft. Sometimes, as in the *St. Augustine massacre* (1565), their lives were spared in battle; other times, not.

ship-smashers. "ship-killers." Large-caliber ship's guns cast from alloyed gun metals such as brass or bronze, though sometimes from strengthened cast iron. They were capable of severely damaging or even holing and sinking an enemy ship. Their introduction reduced the need for boarding, thereby reducing the size of crews over time as well as eliminating the fighting *castle* from new ship designs. In order to accommodate their great weight they tended to be placed amidships and fired through holes cut in the upper deck. In later designs they were dropped to the lower decks and fired through gunports with moveable outer doors. See also *galleon*.

shipyards. Specialized yards to build warships could be found in Venice from 1104 where the famous "Arsenal" grew into a marvel of concentrated state and merchant commitment, capital investment, and skilled craftsmen (carpenters, caulkers, coopers, oar carvers, rope makers, sailmakers, and others). Aragon kept a shipyard in Barcelona that specialized in building *galleys* from the end of the 13th century. Before and during the *Hundred Years' War* (1337–1453), the French crown built warships in a royal yard at Rouen. Burgundian ships were built at Bruges, largely overseen by Portuguese master shipwrights. England arrived late to the game of royal shipyards, relying for many decades on scattered armed merchants and *privateer* ships, with small production from yards on its east and south coasts. Korea had a large shipbuilding industry from the 12th century. Most of China's capacious shipyards were located along the southern coast. These were captured by the *Mongols*, who lacked any navy but used captured and coerced Chinese and Korean *junks* and pilots to attempt two invasions of Japan, in 1274 and 1281. The Ming dynasty built vast fleets of the world's largest ships into the rein of the *Yongle Emperor*, but then abandoned oceanic voyaging and banned bluewater ships. The Ottoman Empire maintained the largest shipyards in the world in the 16th century, employing over 160,000 in the yards at Constantinople alone. The Ottomans were thus able to replace their staggering losses of over 200 galleys and galliots at *Lepanto* (1571) within just nine months. However, they were never able to replace the skilled pilots and crews.

Shirley, Anthony (1565–1635). English adventurer and mercenary. Shirley's first military experience came with the English contingent fighting in alliance with the Dutch against Spain in the 1590s. He also took part in a military expedition to Normandy in 1591 during which he was knighted by Henry of Navarre (later, *Henri IV*). This displeased *Elizabeth I* and led to his brief imprisonment in England. In 1596, Shirley undertook a *privateering* mission to West Africa and the Caribbean (Jamaica and the Gulf Coast of North America). But some crews mutinied, and he was forced back to England with just one ship (1597). The next year he led English mercenaries to Italy to fight for Ferrara. From there he and his brother, *Robert Shirley*, left for Iran. He impressed Shah *Abbas I*, who made him a prince and gave him rich trade privileges. Abbas commissioned him as ambassador and sent him to Prague, Moscow, Rome, and Venice (where he was again imprisoned, this time for several years). His own government would not readmit him to England. In 1605 Emperor *Rudolf II* made him a count of the *Holy Roman Empire* and dispatched him as ambassador to Morocco, Lisbon, and Madrid. Once in Spain, he was appointed admiral and given a fleet to make conquests in the

Levant. In this he failed, being repulsed at Mitylene and losing his command in 1609. He retired to Madrid, spending his final years in quiet poverty.

  Suggested Reading: D. W. Davies, *Elizabethans Errant* (1967).

Shirley, Robert (c.1581–1628). English mercenary. He traveled with his older brother, *Anthony Shirley*, to Iran in 1598. There, he married a Circassian woman and remained long after his brother left on a diplomatic mission for Shah *Abbas I* in 1599. Over the next nine years he was instrumental in helping modernize the new *standing army* Shah Abbas deployed, playing a key role as technical adviser in establishing Iran's first effective *artillery train* and musket corps. In 1608 Sir Robert was sent by Abbas as an envoy to *James I* of England (the king would not receive Shirley's brother). En route he visited Poland, Bohemia, Florence, Rome, and Spain, finally arriving in England in 1611 to be received at the court of James I. In 1613 he went back to Isfahan. In 1615 he went to live with his brother in Madrid. He made a final trip to Iran in 1627, where he died the next year.

shock. Delivering a stunning, smashing attack directly and bluntly into an enemy line or square with the weight and force of a whole military unit. This was the principal role of *heavy cavalry* in medieval Europe from the early 12th century, a tactic made possible by the *couched lance*. In a charge by 1,500–2,000 heavy cavalry, a line four ranks deep was about one mile wide. It did not move all at once, but in sections. Most often it swung down from the right, each section moving on a clear signal. The horsemen kept formation as they increased speed by stages, each time upon another signal. The central aim was to break through enemy *infantry*, to disarrange their ranks and files. This was often accomplished without a blow being struck as infantry unprotected by *pikes* or archers frequently ran at the terrifying spectacle of serried ranks of mounted *knights* pounding toward them, *lances* lowered for the kill at about 50 paces. If the enemy unit was also *cavalry*, however, the aim became dehorsing riders so that *esquires* and other retainers could finish them off on the ground, or more likely hold them for ransom. If the charge failed for any reason (terrain alone might break up momentum), heavy cavalry would withdraw and form up for a second charge. If the charge was met by a hedge of infantry spears and courage, as it was increasingly from the late 13th century, a heap of dead men and horses formed in front of the pike-and-halberd or *schiltron* hedge. The lead rank of horses could not turn aside due to the push of over-eager knights and hard-pounding mounts to its rear and would be impaled or dehorsed. If that happened, heavy cavalry lost the battle. Infantry were also capable of employing offensive shock tactics. In the early 15th century, the *Swiss square* represented a remarkable tactical innovation for infantry shock based on tightly packed pike-and-halberd formations moving across the field of battle. See also *Aztec Empire*; *battle (2)*; *chivalry*; *destrier*; *Landsknechte*; *men-at-arms*; *tournaments*; *warhorses*.

Shogun (*"Sei-i-tai-shogun"*). "Great-barbarian-subduing general," or "genera-lissimo." From the 8th century until the triumph of the Minamoto clan in the

12th century, this was the title of generals commanding pacification campaigns against indigenous Ainu in the north. Under the Minamoto, Shogun became a hereditary title for the head of the great warrior households. The Kamakura shogunate (1185–1333) passed, after a three-year interlude, to the Ashikaga clan (1336–1603). The *Tokugawa shogunate* took form in 1603 and lasted to the Meiji Restoration in 1868. With the Tokugawa, warrior rule was ascendant: the 15 Tokugawa shoguns of Edo ruled in fact while a succession of emperors reigned in Kyoto as figureheads, though some were more beholden to the *bakufu* than were others. The shogunate ended with the Meiji Restoration. See also *daimyo*; *Japan*; *shugo*.

shorten sail. When a sailing ship dropped or reduced canvas in order to leave the wind and slow or stop.

shot. A generic term for firearms troops, as in "he had with him 300 archers and 100 shot." Alternately, any projectile fired from a gunpowder weapon. See also *artillery*; *ballot*; *canister shot*; *case shot*; *chain shot*; *dice shot*; *grapeshot*; *hail shot*; *hot shot*; *okka*; *small shot*; *solid shot*.

Shrewsbury, Battle of (1403). See *England*; *Scottish Wars*.

shugo. "Constable." Semi-autonomous warlords, one for each of Japan's 66 provinces, nominally answerable to the *Shogun*. See also *daimyo*.

shynbalds. See *schynbalds*.

sich. A fortified *Cossack* camp and permanent headquarters.

Sicily. See *Aragon*; *Byzantine Empire*; *Catalan Great Company*; *Ifriqiya*; *itqa*; *Normans*; *War of the Sicilian Vespers*.

Sickingen, Franz von (1481–1523). German *knight*. Something of a Germanic Don Quixote, he protected *Martin Luther* and other reformers during the so-called "Knights' War" of 1522–1523, in which he led the last German knights in arms against forces of the episcopacy in Germany. He besieged Trier, put under an Imperial ban, and himself was besieged by the bishops in 1523. He was later memorialized by Johann Goethe as a romantic German hero.

siege engines. See *artillery towers*; *bastille*; *belfry*; *cat*; *catapult*; *mangonel*; *pertrary*; *sow*; *testudo*; *trebuchet*.

siege train. See *artillery train (1)*.

siege warfare. Surrounding, isolating, and attacking a *castle* or walled town was a characteristic form of warfare from the 11th century onward, as thickened stone walls or towers and a spate of castle-building made defenses nearly unbreachable. The nature of slow siege warfare did not change much until the advent of effective gunpowder *artillery* speeded the whole process, until adoption of defensive *cannon* and reinforcement and lowering of military architecture restored the balance. Siege tactics followed a basic pattern. They began with savage threats of massacre and pillage, presented along with an offer of fair treatment should quick surrender ensue. Most commanders were justly hesitant to frontally assault a fortified position. Prudently, besiegers instead tried indirect methods of attack, such as *blockade*, seizure and destruction of outlying livestock and grain and blocking or poisoning any water source that flowed into the castle or town. They might even attempt biological warfare: diseases were spread that weakened or killed defenders by catapulting infected animal carcasses or bodies of plague victims over the walls. In one siege in France hundreds of cartloads of manure were flung over the walls, filling the besieged town with disease and a choking stench. If all that failed direct assault followed. Moats and dry ditches were filled with faggots of wood or rubble or stones to gain access to the walls. Trenches were dug and palisades erected to protect *sappers* and engineers in their work, while batteries of artillery provided covering fire. The besieging army might also resort to knocking down walls with *catapults* or *trebuchets*, if they had these weapons; or use these and other siege engines to launch great stones over the walls to smash houses and public buildings and inspire fear, or hurl incendiaries to the same end. They were also likely to try raw intimidation by hurtling heads and body parts of dead defenders over the walls.

Assaults

Once the moats and ditches were filled in besiegers would roll towers close against the walls to serve as archery platforms in exchanges of fire with the defenders, while miners and sappers worked to undermine the base of the wall, perhaps protected as they dug trenches and cavities by a *sow* or *testudo*. More daring or reckless, or just desperate, besiegers might try a direct assault over the wall, firing and crossing over from a huge siege tower such as a *belfry* while comrades kept up fire from a nearby *bastille*. But siege towers, even when protected with lead or copper, could be smashed by huge rocks dropped or rolled out by defenders, or they might be burned down with flaming oils or resins, or destroyed by trebuchet or catapult fire by the defenders. Scaling ladders were even more exposed. Besides, many defending walls were built too high for any storming attack to succeed. Most attempts to directly *storm* fortress walls were physically impossible, or promised to be too costly in the lives of expensive soldiers. That left the gates, at the same time the most vulnerable and the best-defended point of any fortified wall. A battering ram would be mounted to smash the gates. Close against the wall and gate there were special dangers facing attackers: defenders used their height advantage to drop crushing stones and inflammables or scalding water through *murder holes*, and fired point-blank into the chests or faces of attackers through firing slits or the *portcullis*.

Commanders were thus most often compelled to resort to *mining*— weakening the foundations of a defending wall by digging beneath it to remove all earthen support, or building an intense fire in a cavity to crack the stones so they fell into the pit. Mining was of course met with countermining. A long siege added hunger and thirst, with the latter more quick and deadly, to the attackers' arsenal and the defenders' list of miseries. Yet, those were weapons that cut both ways: the duration of any siege was limited by the capability of surrounding lands to support the attacking force. If the area had been "eaten out" in a prior campaign it was next to impossible for the attackers to sustain their siege due to the severe limitations of supply that marked the *logistics* of warfare in this period. The best method to win a siege was the simplest: bribe or threaten and cajole defenders into surrender. This did not mean that bombardment did not take place: talk and killing were simultaneous, as in most wars. Just as was the case with so forbidding a structure as the *Great Wall* of China, the easiest way past fortified defenses in Europe or the Middle East or India was not over or under or through the walls but walking un-

Victories . . . gave the winner a reputation for invincibility and made conquest look inevitable.

molested through the gate: offering good terms to induce surrender spared everyone involved. In most countries a convention persisted wherein defenders could expect greatest mercy if they gave in to attackers early in a siege. The more difficult the defenders made things for attackers the more likely that they would be put to the sword when their resistance collapsed. However the surrender occurred, it if was of a renowned fortress many lesser forts could change hands suddenly, swinging a whole region from one overlord to another. This happened several times during the *Hundred Years' War* (1337–1453), where the fall of some great city or complex led the subordinate garrisons of entire provinces to quit. Victories over field armies might have the same effect: they gave the winner a reputation for invincibility and made conquest look inevitable. But victory in a siege also gave the victor land and booty and a fortress into which to move.

Indirect Approach

The heavy advantage enjoyed by the defense from c.1000 to 1450 in Europe encouraged indirect offense in the form of economic warfare against the lands and villages surrounding a besieged castle or town. This ranged from local raiding and aggressive foraging by the besieger to the grand strategy of the *chevauchée*, which could encompass enormous destruction of whole regions and cut a swath through several countries. In the case of cities, any suburbs outside the walls became prime targets. Thus, "El Cid" ravaged the suburbs of Valencia in a successful effort to force its capitulation in 1094. On the other hand, *chivalry* and the *just war tradition* played some role in mitigating excesses and atrocities and establishing conventions governing sieges in practice. To apply these rules it was important for both sides to know when a siege officially began. Initially, the signal was a thrown javelin bearing announcement of siege. With the advent of gunpowder cannon a single report sufficed to alert all within earshot that a siege had commenced. If a truce was agreed upon both sides hearing of the likely arrival of a relief force, hostages were given as a guarantee that besiegers would not bring troops or siege engines forward or complete their saps, defenders would not repair damaged walls or towers. Cheating by either side broke the truce: hostages would be killed in sight of the other side and left on display as a warning and a threat. If the truce held, the agreement extended to the army marching in relief. It was instructed to meet the besiegers at a given time and place to offer and accept *battle*. If the relief failed to arrive by the appointed time, the defenders were obliged to surrender. If a siege was ended by negotiation, a process usually mediated by clerics in Europe, waving a white flag or handing over the keys to the town gates were the usual signals of submission. In most cases, the lives of defenders and civilians were spared, or perhaps just the men were killed. If the siege was short or the attackers suffered few casualties, defenders might be allowed to carry out necessities of life. In a famous example of observation of the strict letter of agreement, women in one French town were told they could leave with whatever they could carry but that the lives of their husbands were forfeit; so they carried out their husbands. At the other extreme, if *guerre mortelle* was declared or the siege ended in storming, defenders and civilians could expect to be put to the sword.

By the mid-14th century the rate of fire, accuracy, and reliability of siege guns was such that the average length of sieges was shortened from several months to several weeks. For instance, Dinant fell to *Charles the Rash* after just seven days of bombardment even though it successfully resisted 17 prior sieges. This resulted from greater reliance on battering power as opposed to medieval practices such as encirclement, *raiding*, burning, blockade, and starvation. *Gunpowder weapons* thereby probably reduced the overall destructiveness of sieges. The pattern was the same in *Ottoman warfare*. From the 15th century, the Ottomans estimated the length of sieges not by months or weeks but by the number of cannonballs they were likely to expend before enemy walls were breached. Surviving Ottoman plans and dispatches refer to a "seven-hundred shot siege" or a "two-thousand shot siege" and other durations. The first guns fired at the walls from close range. Later, long-range *culverins* were brought to sieges to provide protective fire to engineers digging approach trenches. At the start of the 16th century siege defenses caught up with offensive firepower. New methods of fortification proliferated while older forts were reinforced with earthen escarpments and thickened walls or squat artillery towers to support heavy defensive cannon firing through low-level gun ports cut into stone walls. All that, and especially the new *trace italienne* style of bastioned artillery fortress, revived sieges at the expense of battles by the mid-17th century. See also *abatis*; *Albigensian Crusade*; *Alexandria, Siege of*; *Algeciras, Siege of*; *Alkmaar, Siege of*; *Antwerp, Siege of*; *attrition*; *Baghdad, Siege of*; *bellum hostile*; *bombard*; *Boulogne, Siege of*; *bretasche*; *Bursa, Siege of*; *Calais*; *Castillon, Battle of*; *casting*; *Chaul, Siege of*; *chevaux de fries*; *Constantinople, Siege of*; *Courtrai, Battle of*; *crossbow*; *Cyprus*; *Eighty Years' War*; *engineers*; *fire*; *fortification*; *Franco–Spanish War*; *Freiburg, Battle of*; *galley*; *garrisons*; *Gustavus II Adolphus*; *Granada*; *grenades*; *Haarlem, Siege of*; *herald*; *Héricourt*,

Battle of; Honganji fortress, Siege of; hot shot; infantry; Italian Wars; Jeanne d'Arc; Laupen, Battle of; Leiden, Siege of; Le Tellier, Michel; lines of circumvallation; lines of contravallation; lodgement; Maastricht, Siege of (1579); Maastricht, Siege of (1632); Magdeburg, Sack of; Malta; Marienburg, Fortress of; Maurits of Nassau; Morat, Battle of; mortar; Muhammad II; mukai-jiro; Oda Nobunaga; Ostend, Siege of; Pavia, Battle of; place d'armes; Rhodes, Siege of (1444); Rhodes, Siege of (1479–1480); Rhodes, Siege of (1522–1523); Rouen, Siege of; Straslund, Siege of; Sturmgeld; Tenochtitlán, First Siege of (1520); Tenochtitlán, Second Siege of (1521); Thérouanne, Siege of; Thirty Years' War; Uzbeks; Vienna, Siege of; wakō; War of the Cities; Wars of the Roses.

Suggested Reading: Jim Bradbury, *The Medieval Siege* (1992); C. Duffy, *Siege Warfare: The Fortress in the Early Modern World, 1494–1660* (1979); Christopher Gravett, *Medieval Siege Warfare* (1990).

Sigismund (1368–1437). Elector of Brandenburg, 1376–1415; king of Hungary, 1387–1437; Holy Roman Emperor, 1411–1437; king of Bohemia (disputed), 1419–1437; In 1396 he was badly defeated by the Ottomans at *Nicopolis*. His response to rebellion and religious dissent in Bohemia was to call the *Council of Constance* (1414–1418) in an effort to end the schism. However, he failed to uphold the safe-conduct he had granted to *Jan Hus*, who was burned at the stake instead. That sparked the long *Hussite Wars* (1419–1478) as rebellion broke out when Sigismund tried to mount the Bohemian throne.

Sigismund I (1466–1548). King of Poland, 1506–1548. The *Protestant Reformation* unfolded during his reign, unsettling Poland as it did all Europe. More immediately, Sigismund lost Smolensk to the expanding state of *Muscovy*. He was partly compensated with Moldova. In 1537 the Polish nobles rose against his authority; the concessions the rebellion forced from him permanently weakened the Polish monarchy.

Sigismund III Vasa (1566–1632). King of Poland-Lithuania, 1587–1632; king of Sweden, nominally, 1592–1604. He was the offspring of a dynastic marriage intended to unite the ruling families of Sweden and Poland-Lithuania. Sweden was a rising power in the western Baltic while Poland-Lithuania was on a protracted descent from weak medieval monarchy and empire to tremulous victim of three rising and territorially rapacious empires of the north: Russia, Sweden, and Prussia. Sigismund ruled Sweden and Poland-Lithuania as an unbending, convinced Catholic monarch. That led to chronic arguments with the Polish nobles. Ultimately, his persecution of Protestants led to war with Sweden, defeat at Linköping (1598), and deposition from Sweden's throne in favor of a Calvinist-leaning cousin, *Karl IX*, whose faith was also suspect but closer to the reformed Lutheranism of most of the Swedish population. Sigismund never accepted the loss of his northern kingdom and actively sought to regain it during the Polish-Swedish war of 1600–1611, again during the *Kalmar War*, and yet again against *Gustavus Adolphus* to 1629.

Sigismund supported the "False Dmitri" against *Boris Godunov* during the *"Time of Troubles"* ("Smutnoe Vremia"). He invaded Muscovy and put his son on the throne as would-be tsar, but was compelled to abandon that position in 1613 to *Michael Romanov*. From 1621 to 1622 and again from 1626 to 1629 Sigismund led Poland in a losing campaign against Sweden over control of Riga and Estonia. He closed his life in bitter defeat, shut out of Sweden by Gustavus and finally lost in self-pitying devotions and extravagant acts of piety.

Sigismund August II (1520–1572). King of Poland-Lithuania, 1548–1572. He extended religious tolerance to Polish Protestants, who multiplied greatly during his reign, especially among the nobility. He elevated the old tie to ducal Lithuania to full constitutional union, and advanced Polish colonization of Ukraine. From 1557 to 1558, he waged a war against Muscovy over control of Livonia. Unable to garner full military support from the powerful Polish nobility he allied with remnants of the *Teutonic Knights*. See also *Northern War, First*; *Union of Lublin*.

signals. See *battle cries*; *flags*; *Harsthörner*.

Sikhism. A blend of *Hinduism* and *Islam* which developed in Punjab. Over time it became a distinct religious tradition. It was founded by Nānak (1469–1538), its first Guru, as a syncretic fusion of Muslim rejection of the Hindu caste system but retention of other Hindu beliefs. It was broadly tolerant and rejected all religious extremes in India: the radical asceticism and self-abnegation found in Hinduism and Islam alike on one hand, and the highly ritualized and rigid caste system which engulfed Hindus on the other. *Akbar* donated land in Amritsar to the Sikhs who built the Golden Temple upon it. The faith only acquired a martial character later, under Guru Gobind Rai (1666–1708), when Sikhs responded militarily to persecution by the Mughal emperor and Muslim zealot Aurangzeb (r.1658–1707). Gobind Rai formed an "Army of the Pure" to defend Sikhs. He took the surname "Singh" ("lion") which all Sikhs used thereafter, and instituted distinguishing features of Sikh males including beards, turbans, and carrying of a comb and ceremonial dagger.

silahdars. "Swordsmen." Ottoman household infantry, part of the *Kapikulu Askerleri*. Like the *sipahis* they were among the most expensive troops to maintain. During the 17th century the state whittled away their numbers and used the savings to hire more modern infantry and cavalry.

Silesia. A mineral rich German province, long a *Habsburg* possession and integral part of the *Holy Roman Empire*. It was for centuries a theater of struggle between medieval Austria and Poland. Wracked by the *Protestant Reformation*, it was a frequent battleground during the wars of religion of the 16th and 17th centuries. As its nobility and most of its towns were Lutheran, it allied with *Gustavus Adolphus* when he intervened in the *Thirty Years' War*, though more from fear of Swedish depredations than any firm confessional convictions. Subsequent occupation by the Austrian Empire saw reconversion of many Silesians to Catholicism under the influence of the *Counter-Reformation*. See also *War of the Cities*; *witchcraft*.

Simon de Montfort (d.1218). See *Albigensian Crusade*.

sipahis. "Horsemen." Ottoman *heavy cavalry* drawn mainly from Anatolia and Rumelia. They were granted nonhereditary fiefs by the sultans in return for which they raised, armed, and supplied a given number of horse soldier retainers (*Cebelu*). Sipahis were known for wearing heavy *mail* and, along with *timariot* light cavalry, were the mainstay of Ottoman armies into the 15th century. Despite their origins as cavalry, some sipahis served as marines on the sultan's *galleys*. Given the dominant role of cavalry in *Ottoman warfare*, campaigns were confined to summers by the need for fodder. Sipahis decisively defeated mixed Balkan-Serb armies at the *Maritza River* (1371) and again at *Kosovo* (1389). They remained the keystone of Ottoman military power well past the advent of the *Janissary Corps* and other elite infantry and *gunpowder weapons* corps. However, slowing Ottoman expansion in the 16–17th centuries limited lands available to support an enfeoffed cavalry army. The growing importance of guns further encouraged a shift to infantry, includ-

> *Despite their origins as cavalry, some sipahis served as marines on the sultan's* galleys.

ing Imperial garrisons and various auxiliaries. By the end of the 16th century, six regiments (about 2,400 horsemen) of highly privileged, richly rewarded sipahis ("alti bölük sipahileri") were assigned to the *Kapikulu Askerleri* at court. These older troops served in noncombat administrative roles ("divanî hizmet"). Because they were the most expensive of all Ottoman troops to maintain they were more exposed to demotion or even expulsion from the ranks. Sipahis were listed on a register, delisting from which was the ultimate punishment since it entailed loss of revenue and prestige. Over the course of the 17th century, sipahis rolls were steadily and deliberately reduced by the sultans to contains costs and shift military resources to recruitment of cheaper regular infantry. The sums saved were so substantial that the Ottoman Empire, unlike most European states, was able to meet the great cost of raising more modern infantry and artillery formations with relative ease. Purges of the sipahis rolls, sometimes involving thousands of names, were also tied to the ebb and flow of court intrigue and politics. See also *Serdengeçti*; *Thirteen Years' War*.

sipar. A Persian-Mughal style of small round shield. It was made of beaten and polished steel with a small boss in the center of four or five smaller bosses. Carried in the left hand, it was principally used by swordsmen or javelin troops.

Sis, Battle of (1606). The newly modernized Iranian Army, under *Abbas I*, deployed their *gunpowder weapons* and *artillery* corps when they met, and then destroyed, an Ottoman army at Sis. Perhaps 20,000 Ottoman dead were left on the field. The victory for Iran did not end the long Ottoman-Safavid and *shi'a* versus *sunni* Muslim war that had darkened the common frontier since *Chaldiran* in 1514. However, it marked the end of Ottoman predominance in battle, the emergence of a more powerful because reformed and modernized Iranian military, and a revival of the Iranian Empire in Central Asia.

Sixteen, The. See *Catholic League (France)*; *Day of the Barricades*; *French Civil Wars*.

skeggøx. See *axes*.

skeleton-built. The predominant shipbuilding technique of the Mediterranean world which constructed ships by first erecting a skeleton of the hull, then adding planking. Its northern counterpart was the *clinker-built* ship, which constructed the hull from the keel up and out, with layers of planks. Skeleton-built ships were lighter but less sturdy. From the 15th century there was some blending of the methods to create successful hybrids such as the *carrack*. See also *caravel*; *galleass*; *galley*; *galliot*.

"skulking way of war." The stealthy native style of warfare of the Indians of eastern North America. It was essentially the mode of the natural guerilla and lightening raider. It avoided direct assault on heavy fortifications that cost too many lives; it employed guile and ruses; and it used ground and forest cover in making the approach, to spring ambushes, and for refuge in retreat or defeat. "Skulking" bewildered settlers, *militia*, and European regulars during the *Indian Wars* in North America, at least until some learned it themselves and began to succeed on the battlefield. It also enraged Europeans as supposedly opposed to the "rules of war." It should not have: Europeans had for centuries themselves "skulked" along wild frontiers in Ireland, or on the Scottish and Hungarian borders, and in the Balkan *Militargrenze*.

Well-adapted to its environment, the "skulking way of war" also reflected native cultural and ritualized religious values, some admirable but others less so. At its core was the Indian brave, who was a warrior rather than a soldier. A brave was usually young—training began no later than age 12—exceptionally fit, and capable of greater speed and physical endurance on the march than his European allies, enemies, or prisoners. He was an expert marksman, taking the white man's firearms and powder and shot in exchange for furs, and excelling in use of the rifle in hunting and war. He possessed, as Armstrong Starkey has shrewdly noted, "the skills and discipline of modern commandos and special forces." He could move and survive in winter by using snowshoes and eating scraps from the forest floor, while white troops stayed huddled in wooden huts awaiting the spring or died starving and frozen in the deep snow. In summer he moved over river and lake in stealthy birchbark canoes that gave his war party unparalleled mobility and tactical surprise. His officers were "elected" based on demonstrated bravery, audacity, and cunning, not mounted stiffly in a saddle by accident of birth or from a purchased commission.

Indian *military discipline* was based on personal honor rather than hard punishment. Indian tactics aimed at victory achieved with minimal loss of the lives of attackers. Tactical retreat or refusing to fight in the face of superior numbers or fortified works was thus commonplace. This infuriated European commanders who misunderstood Indian battlefield prudence as cowardice or fecklessness toward the "cause," further misreading the fact that Indians fought in white men's wars for reasons of their own. A brave's ethics were also akin to a modern commando's, notably when it came to prisoners. They would take prisoners if chance permitted or slaughter all their enemies because they could not move quickly with old men and women and children in tow. While contemptuous of enemy males who surrendered, a warrior could still treat a prisoner gently and adopt him (or her) into his nation. Or he might slow torture or burn him (or her) to death. Unlike European or Asian soldiers for whom rape was a ubiquitous part of war, out of mystical taboo Indian warriors rarely molested captive women. In sum, braves could be as kind and humane, or as callous and cruel, as any other soldier in any era.

Most eastern Indians quickly adapted to firearms (exclusively *matchlock* weapons prior to 1660), abandoning bows and arrows. Starkey argues that they did this because the ability of most braves to dodge arrows became an impossible feat when facing bullets. In short, Indians appreciated the greater hitting power of firearms, which they often loaded with several bullets to maximize a gun's wounding or killing effect. Moreover, Indians much preferred rifles to muskets for hunting and in war, domains they did not always distinguish. Most became expert riflemen well beyond the skills exhibited by settlers, who were mainly farmers who occasionally supplemented their winter larder with wild game. European regulars sported *smoothbore* muskets and fired in *volley*, were not trained in marksmanship, and did not aim at individual targets. Braves aimed, fired, moved to new cover, fired again, and moved again. This emphasis on aimed fire did not mean that they fought merely as individuals. War parties conducted skilled advances and retreats "blackbird fashion," where braves with loaded guns covered those reloading or moving, rather as a modern commando unit moves in urban warfare from cover to cover under suppressing fire. The "skulking way of war" also reduced casualties, a great concern of Indian societies once demographic decline set in from contact with virgin, settler-borne diseases.

Suggested Reading: Patrick Malone, *The Skulking Way of War: Technology and Tactics among the New England Indians* (1991); A. Starkey, *European and Native American Warfare* (1998).

slavery and war. Slavery and war are ancient cousins, closely and causally related. Slave raiding was a common practice from ancient times, with women especially targeted by raiders from underpopulated areas. Interestingly, this was not true of Europe during the Middle Ages. As the European population expanded from the 12th century, chronic labor shortages ended and slavery became economically unnecessary in most of its regions. As one result, traditional German slave raids into Celtic and Slavic territories came to an end. Raiding continued, but it targeted livestock and portable wealth rather than human chattel. Other peoples who lived in thinly populated areas, including Celts and Slavs, still practiced slavery and therefore also slave-raiding, but on the whole Medieval Europe did not see wars originating from a slave economy. In the 16th century, however, Europe's overseas expansion created a new demand for slaves leading to a huge expansion in slave wars in Africa. After 1500, West and then Central Africa suffered ever-increasing demographic losses to this overseas slave trade, with a much older but smaller Arab slave trade draining people from East Africa and the sudan. These losses were uneven: many African societies found it rewarding to commit fully to the trade and became devoted to slave-raids against weaker neighbors. Few Africans were actually captured by European or Swahili Arab traders; most were brought to the coast by other Africans and sold to merchants servicing the overseas slave markets. Other African states exchanged captives of war for firearms. The guns were then used to acquire more slaves, to be sold for more guns.

Even at the peak of the African slave trade the awful truth is that more Africans were likely toiling as slaves of other Africans than were hauled away by sea or across the desert by camel caravan. The *Hausa* forced nearby pagans onto slave villages which surrounded and sustained their city states; *Benin* and the great *Yoruba* cities enslaved weaker tribes, raiding westward and throughout the Niger delta; *Songhay* expanded its use of slaves in the 16th century, raiding far afield and south of the Niger bend. The later jihads of the *Fulbe* were justified by enslavement of pagans. For such empires cavalry was the key to slave raiding: cavalry operating on the sudan and savannah easily ran down helpless villagers during slave raids hundreds of miles from Africa's coasts, caravan routes, and imperial capitals. The introduction of firearms in the 16th century dramatically changed the balance of power: guns made slaving easier but also war more costly, requiring still more slaving to pay for the new military technology which now sustained or overturned local balances of power. Firearms thus strengthened formerly weak coastal and forest tribes—who obtained them first from European traders—against the traditionally dominant slave-raiding states of the savannah and desert, which continued to rely on the armored cavalry that had served them so well since the 13th century but now became obsolete.

Beyond Africa other empires rested upon a foundation of military slaves. The Umayyad Caliphs of *al-Andalus* and Córdoba used northern and western European slaves captured as boys, castrated, and trained as local *mamlūks*. Other Europeans were taken from south Russia and the Caucasus, converted to Islam, and turned into mamlūk slave soldiers by emirs and caliphs in Damascus or Cairo. The Mamlūks eventually took over Egypt in all but name, forming a slave dynasty that eventually also ruled Palestine and Syria. The

Ottomans, too, kept a converted slave force: the *Janissary Corps*. Military slaves were commonplace in medieval India where different Mamlūks also, but only briefly, achieved supreme power in the Muslim-dominated north. And around the shores of the Mediterranean over the millennia tens of thousands of slaves pulled oars to which they were chained on the war *galleys* of Phoenicians, Romans, Byzantines, Persians, Ottomans, Spanish, Venetians, Genoese, corsairs, sultans, and popes.

Suggested Reading: David Ayalon, *Islam and the Abode of War: Military Slaves and Islamic Adversaries* (1994); Patricia Crone, *Slaves on Horses: The Evolution of Islamic Polity* (1980); D. Davis, *The Problem of Slavery in Western Culture* (1966); Daniel Pipes, *Slave Soldiers and Islam: Genesis of a Military System* (1981).

slave soldiers. See *military slavery*; *slavery and war*.

sling. A small *artillery* piece fitted on a swivel mount and deployed on castle or town walls as an anti-personnel weapon. These weapons came into use in Europe in the 15th century; some were still in use in European forts in Asia as late as the 17th century.

sloop-of-war. A mid-size warship in the Age of Sail with *cannon* on just one deck.

slow match. A slow burning wick or fuse, several feet long and lighted at both ends. It was made by soaking a thin hempen cord in a solution of limewater and saltpeter. This imparted a burn rate of about five or six inches an hour. *Arquebusiers* used slow match to ignite the powder in the pans of their weapon using a *matchlock* device. Slow matches were the source of many bad accidents, as a gust of wind carried embers into contact with exposed powder sacks or casks. Alternately, damp fog or rain would extinguish the slow match and render guns useless. For the *artillery*, the slow match was held aloft on the curved arms of a *linstock* planted firmly in the ground between each pair of guns. In the early days a gunner would lift the linstock to touch the slow match directly to the vent hole, setting off fine powder in the vent that ignited the main charge of coarser grains wadded and rammed down the muzzle. Later, gunners touched a *quick match* to the slow match then applied the quick match to the touch hole.

Sluys, Battle of (June 23, 1340). The largest naval battle of the 14th century, fought during the opening phase of the *Hundred Years' War*. The English sent out from 120 to 160 ships to face over 200 French ships, including 6 *galleys* and 22 *barges*. The English fleet worked up the coast and gained the *weather gauge*, which it used to stand off from the numerically superior French fleet and defeat it in detail. English and Welsh longbowmen used positional advantage to fire "arrow storms" at the French ships, decimating rowers and marines. The French probably lost more men and ships than necessary when their commander declined the advise of a Genoese technician and thereby lost the benefit of wind and tide which might have been used to cut the range to the English fleet, or to escape. The other key to the battle was that the English ships carried thousands of archers, where the entire French fleet had only 150 *men-at-arms* and 500 crossbowmen, and thus no effective reply to the long-distance archery tactics of their enemy. The French lost 190 ships at Sluys and 16,000–18,000 men, more Frenchmen than died at *Agincourt* (1415) or even Waterloo (1815). Despite this devastating defeat, Sluys did not establish the English claim to *"sovereignty of the sea,"* which was beyond enforcement by navies of the day.

small shot. Any *shot* fired from a handheld firearm whether a musket ball or some form of *hail shot*.

small war. See *Glyndŵr's Rebellion*; *guerre couverte*; *Indian Wars (North America)*; *Ireland*; *Korea*; *Martolos*; *Militargrenze*; *raiding*; *Razats*; *Scottish Wars*; *"skulking way of war"*; *Toyotomi Hideyoshi*; *Wallace, William*; *William Louis, of Nassau*.

Smolino River, Battle of (1502). See *Muscovy, Grand Duchy of*.

smoothbore. A *musket* or *cannon* with a bore that was not rifled (grooved) but smooth, giving it far less accuracy and range than a rifled weapon. Estimates based on famous 1886 tests are that early smoothbore muskets, most of which fired one-ounce lead balls about 300 yards, inflicted just one casualty for every 200–500 aimed shots. The reason for smoothbore inaccuracy—shots missed by five or more feet from the target at 200 yards range—was that the spin imparted to the ball by the barrel was random and the ball itself was not aerodynamic. The effect was comparable to a slicing golf shot or an American baseball pitcher's curve ball. Modern testing of smoothbore muzzle velocities recorded speeds about half that of a late-20th-century assault rifle, but a little faster than a Colt '45. The main point was that spherical shot lost speed to drag and deflection three times as fast as a shaped modern bullet, greatly lowering impact. This had a direct effect on tactics, limiting smoothbore muskets to firing at densely packed infantry or cavalry from close ranges of 50 to 75 yards. Hence, in early *volley fire* the initial command was not "aim" before giving the order to fire, it was "level guns."

> *...early smoothbore muskets...inflicted just one casualty for every 200–500 aimed shots.*

Smutnoe Vremia (Smuta). See *"Time of Troubles."*

snacca. See *longship*.

Society of Jesus. See *Jesuits*.

Sofala. The port of Sofala in Mozambique was an outpost of "Swahili Arab" trade for centuries before Vasco da Gama's ships landed there in 1497. In

1505 a military-trade expedition tried to oust the Arab slavers from Sofala; this was finally done in 1515. Portuguese factories took over the slave trade, and traded with Great Zimbabwe. Further north, Portuguese ships acted essentially as *pirates* with regard to Arab shipping. In 1575 Portugal signed a treaty with the Mwene Mutapa that permitted mining and trade and allowed for resident missionaries. The interior remained in the hands of Shona states (Kiteve, Mandanda, Manyika, Mutapa; in the 17th century, Barwe and Butwa). The Portuguese interfered only on matters of coastal trade and competition with Muslim slave powers active in the region.

sōhei. Japanese warrior monks. See also *Japan*; *Oda Nobunaga*; *Toyotomi Hideyoshi*; *True Pure Land*.

Sold. The unit of pay earned each month by a *Landsknechte* mercenary: 4 guilders. Over the course of the 16th century this rate did not change, which showed the declining value placed on pikemen of the Landsknechte sort as musketeers came to dominate the battlefield. See also *Doppelsöldner*; *mercenaries*.

solid shot. Stone or iron cannonballs, or what the French at first called "pierres de fer" or "iron rocks." For most of the period, solid shot had a theoretical long range but in practice all effective gunnery took place at short ranges so that the shot did not bury itself harmlessly by traveling along too high an arc. The idea was to shoot below head height to do maximum damage. Gunners sought, but rarely achieved, enfilade positions that permitted solid shot to bore raw tunnels through many more ranks of men. Solid shot's effect, if not reduced by *balloting*, was to bore straight through enemy ranks killing several men instantly as they stood in what became in a split second a "tunnel of destruction." If the ground was not dampened and the shot absorbed by rain-sodden turf, or if the cannonball landed inside a stone castle or town, it might ricochet among the enemy, decapitating some and smashing limbs and bones of others (though deliberate ricochet fire was invented, by Vauban, only in 1688). For technical reasons—sheer weight, problems of cartage, and limited mobility—field artillery lagged far behind siege guns. In *siege warfare*, solid shot was used to weaken walls as an assist to *mining* or *fire*, or if very heavy guns were available (possibly cast on site) they could independently batter down stone fortifications or force a breach. In war at sea, if fired at ships from a *raking* position (where solid shot penetrated thin planking at the fore or aft end of the enemy vessel), an iron cannonball might travel through the guts of a ship killing or maiming a dozen gunners and smashing into cannon and gun carriages. When solid iron shot was fired broadside at point-blank ranges it could penetrate decks or side beams and hole a ship below the waterline, if it was caught on the up-roll. Even a broadside hit that did not penetrate the wooden hull could kill: huge splinters exploded inward at high velocity from the inside of the impact point, impaling and terribly wounding men so that they died quickly from loss or blood or slowly from sepsis.

sollerets. Molded *armor* protections for the feet.

Songhay. "Songhai." This Mande-speaking, West African empire straddled the great bend of the Niger, profiting as middle broker in the trans-Saharan salt, gold, and slave trades since the days of early medieval Ghana. Like *Kanem*, its original ruling house claimed to have Yemeni roots, though in the case of Songhay the claim was more likely a propaganda effort to gain legitimacy among its population following numerous conversions to Islam. Songhay was briefly a tributary of *Mali*, which cut it off from the desert trade in the 13th century. It broke free of Mali in the 14th century. Resurgent under a military innovator and conqueror, Sunni Ali (r.1464–1492), from 1464 to 1484 it utilized mounted knights to expand into several former Mali provinces and displace Mali as the major power in the region. Songhay captured Timbuktu from the *Tuareg* in 1469 and took Jenne with a riverine fleet in 1473. It greatly expanded the role of slavery in the economy, raiding south of the Niger to replenish its slave population. Under Muhammad Ture (r.1493–1528), it expanded westward and northward and raided in force as far south as the *Hausa* states. Ture was deposed by his sons in 1528, leaving Songhay divided between Animists and Muslims.

In 1591 Songhay was invaded and extinguished by a Moroccan army equipped with firearms. The Moroccans made an extraordinary trek across the desert to capture Timbuktu. Songhay's spear-cavalry and bowmen simply were no match for the Moroccan musketeers. The original conquerors were reinforced, but the tie to Morocco was slowly then definitively broken by 1618 when the fruits of the conquest failed to meet expectations in Marrakesh. The soldiers abandoned in Songhay clung to power and over time formed an ethnically distinct ruling class called, prosaically enough, the "*arma*" (gunmen). In the 1660s a succession crisis in distant Morocco provoked the arma to formally repudiate the Moroccan tie. Steeped in desert mysticism they were intolerant of the older and gentler Muslim tradition of Timbuktu and grew contemptuous of the cosmopolitan city they left behind on the coast.

Suggested Reading: David Conrad, *The Songhay Empire* (1998).

Sound Tolls. The entrance to the Baltic Sea narrows to just a small lane of water known as The Sound, lying between Denmark and the southern tip of the Scandinavian peninsula. It was a principal interest of Danish foreign policy and a major financial support of the monarchy, navy, and state to compel all ships traversing the Sound to pay tolls for the privilege. This occasioned frequent disputes and naval wars whenever Denmark was weakened, notably in conflicts with Sweden and the United Provinces. Nevertheless, the Danes levied tolls from the 1420s until 1857. See also *Christian IV*; *Dominum Maris Baltici*; *Kalmar War*; *Knäred, Peace of*; *Torstensson's War*; *Wallenstein, Albrecht von*.

Southern Route Army. See *Hakata Bay, Battle of* (1281).

Sovereign Military Order of Malta (SMOM). See *Hospitallers*.

"sovereignty of the sea." An English naval and political doctrine proclaimed in 1293 by *Edward I*, who had been summoned before a Paris court to explain why he had permitted his Gascon subjects to attack their liege lord, the king of France (the Gascons had burned part of *La Rochelle*). The doctrine held that English kings had "time out of mind...been in peaceable possession of the sovereign lordship of the English sea and the islands therein" (that is, the Channel). This was an effort to redefine a dangerous dispute with France as an internal English problem, and to elevate the English king to equal status with the king of France. On the water it was an idle boast: no one respected the English claim to jurisdiction, and England had no navy to enforce what, in Mahanian terms, today would be called "command of the sea." The assertion's most lasting effect was to sometimes embarrass the crown to pay compensation to foreign victims of English pirates. It was most often cited by foreign monarchs keen to embarrass their English counterpart, or by wily Flemish or Dutch merchants eager to recover goods lost to English *piracy*, or cynically by English pirates as an excuse to raid neutral shipping that "failed to honor" the claim. For two centuries English monarchs trotted out the claim to "sovereignty of the sea" but intermittently, only when it was enforceable or politic. Not even the staggering naval victory at *Sluys* (1340) permitted England to enforce this premature claim, which would have demanded a permanent navy to effect.

sow (*truies*). A type of moveable hut protected on the roof with copper sheeting or hides. It was used to protect *sappers* and engineers as they approached the walls of a fortification. They were used extensively in medieval warfare on the continent. They were still in wide use in Ireland during the *English Civil Wars* after 1641, even though they were no longer effective when facing *muskets* or *cannon*.

soyughal. The Kazan Tatar *servitor class* system of provisional tenure of landed estates in return for military service. It is not known whether the Tatar system directly influenced the Muscovite system of *Pomest'e cavalry*, which it closely resembled.

spahis. See *sipahis*.

Spain. In 711 C.E. Moors from North Africa swept into Iberia, a poor and arid peninsula with few natural resources, claiming most of it for *Islam*. Over the next eight centuries Iberia witnessed a see-saw battle between Christian and Muslim rulers and states in the long and culturally formative *Reconquista*, with the fortunes of war eventually favoring the Christians. In 1469 the union of Aragon and Castile, through the dynastic marriage of *Ferdinand and Isabella*, set the stage for the final battle. In 1492 the last surviving Moorish state (*Granada*) fell to their crusading armies. In celebration, they sent Columbus west to search for an alternate route to the China trades but also hoping to find a strategic backdoor to the Middle East. The relative tardiness of other Europeans in following the Spanish example of conquest and settlement of overseas colonies in the Americas has often been seen as a historical "problem" to be explained. Yet, it seems clearly the case that Spain was unique in its initial fortune: it encountered wealthy Indian empires that, once conquered, were easily exploited economically. Its colonial policy was also unique: Spain pursued armed settlement as an overseas continuation of its centuries-old pattern of military colonization during the Reconquista. Not even Portugal emulated Spain in this regard, barely penetrating coastal Brazil and Africa with entrepôts while France and England did not grip their first colonial toeholds for nearly a century after Spain had established a vast New World empire.

Catholic and *Habsburg* power looked to Spain as its champion with the ascent to the throne of *Charles V* in 1519. Spain's powerful infantry—the *tercios*—dominated land warfare in Europe for 150 years, along with the service of mercenary armies bought with the plundered silver of the *Aztec* and *Inca Empires*. In the 16th century Spain enjoyed a "golden age" of prosperity, internal (though not external) peace, and artistic achievement. It built a vast overseas empire, the first "world empire" in history, and was "primus inter pares" (first among equals) among the Great Powers of Europe. Imperial Spain faced no threat to the south, but was badly overstretched north to the Spanish Netherlands, east into Italy and parts of Germany, and west across the Atlantic to the Americas and into the Pacific. Its great advantages were that it enjoyed what one historian has aptly called the "precocious modernity" of a semi-modern state. It enforced religious uniformity in an age of doctrinal upheaval through persecution of Jews and Moors by the monarchy and *Inquisition*, culminating in the *expulsion of the Jews* and later *expulsion of the Moors*. Spain also benefitted from a "power vacuum" in Europe caused by prolonged internal disorder in its greatest enemy, France, during the *French Civil Wars*. Finally, it drew upon vast reserves of American silver to support protracted Catholic and Imperial crusades, though this bounty was a mixed blessing that brought with it a terrible *price revolution*, chaotic financial crises, and repeated royal bankruptcy.

> *...religious uniformity...through persecution of Jews and Moors by the monarchy and* Inquisition *...*

Dissolution of the marriage of *Philip II* to *Mary Tudor* (1558) marked the high tide of Habsburg "encirclement" of France. Philip made Madrid the permanent capital of his empire in 1561. With the French tearing out their own vitals during 40 years of civil war from 1562, Philip was free to seek to impose religious conformity on the Netherlands and even in England. A revolt of the Moors in 1566 was quashed, but pointed to latent internal instabilities and weakness. Undeterred, Philip expanded: he seized Portugal and its vast overseas empire in 1580, gaining in Lisbon the best fortified anchorage in southern Europe. That also added to his naval strength the Portuguese fleet of superb *galleons* and tens of thousands of able and experienced seamen, and gave him access to a store of several generations of secret maritime maps and navigational knowledge (*portolan charts*). On the other hand, taking Portugal also added additional overseas bases to defend against English, Dutch, and French *privateers* and *pirates*. Philip II sent Spanish armies into Flanders via the *Spanish Road* and sent the *Invincible Armada* (the first of three failed invasion fleets) north against England in 1588. The armies made little headway in decades of fighting and the Armadas were all lost.

Philip III completed Spain's economically and intellectually disastrous expulsion of its most educated and commercially advanced classes, which had begun a century earlier: from 1609 to 1614 he expelled remaining Jewish "conversos" and also forced into exile all "moriscos," suspect converts from Islam. He negotiated peace with France in 1598, with England in 1604, and with the Dutch in the *Twelve Years' Truce* (1609–1621). All that may have been done in order to refinance and rearm. In any event, the *Eighty Years' War* (1568–1648) resumed in the year of his death (1621) and was prosecuted until 1648 by *Olivares* and *Philip IV*. Spain's dramatic martial and geopolitical decline was underlain by economic backwardness and inflation brought on by military expenditure and fiscal mismanagement. But the main problem was its pursuit of an unsustainable "Weltpolitik" (world policy) rooted in a medieval European vision of universal empire, the *monarchia universalis*, that did not match the emerging early modern world. Spain pursed protracted, debilitating, losing wars when peace might have been arranged on several occasions. But how could any part of a great empire which God had given Spain be handed over to heretics? While there is little question that Spain pursued a grand strategy of overseas empire and Catholic hegemony in Europe, the thesis should not be overstated, as Spain's international strength was always more a product of the weakness or internal division of its enemies than any fundamental national advantage. By the start of the 17th century Spain was still primus inter pares among the European powers, but the end of its preeminence had begun with de facto breakaway of the Netherlands and humiliation at the hands of England's *sea dogs* and navy.

By 1610 many within Spain's governing elite accepted that Catholicism could not be reimposed on certain parts of the empire or in Europe as a whole, and hence that Dutch and English heretics should simply be left to go to Hell after their own fashion. But that was not the view of Olivares or Philip IV. What changed fundamentally in the first half of the 17th century was not Spain but France: the re-emergence of a populous rival power after decades of internal chaos forced a basic shift in the balance of power in Europe. This was made evident by repeated defeats of Spanish forces in the 1640s, on land and at sea, by the Dutch and French. In the interim, Spain contended with serial revolts against rising war taxes in a losing cause in Catalonia, Portugal, Naples, and Castile itself. The Catalan and Neapolitan revolts were suppressed by force of arms, but Portugal broke free and took its empire with it, giving Spain multiple more fronts on which it thought it had to fight. The new balance of power in Europe was codified in the *Peace of Westphalia* (1648).

Yet, so complex was the relationship with France that even after the great war in Germany ended Spain and France still fought over Catalonia, where the lingering "guerra dels segadors" lasted until 1652. Final agreement on peace was only reached in 1659 in the Treaty of the Pyrenees. See also *Armada Real*; *Black Legend*; *Catalonia, Revolt of*; *Ceuta*; *conquistadores*; *Council of the Indies*; *cruzada*; *encomienda*; *Gibraltar*; *Lerma, Duke of*; *Line of Demarcation*; *Melilla*; *Naples, Revolt of*; *New Spain, Viceroyalty of*; *real patronato*; *requerimiento*.

Suggested Reading: Raymond Carr, ed., *Spain* (2000); J. H. Elliott, *Imperial Spain, 1469–1716* (1964; 1970); D. Goodman, *Spanish Naval Power, 1589–1665; Reconstruction and Defeat* (1996); L. Harvey, *Islamic Spain, 1250–1500* (1990); Henry Kamen, *Imperial Spain* (1983); A. Mackay, *Spain in the Middle Ages* (1977).

Spanish America. All New World possessions of the Spanish Empire, c.1500–1898, governed by the "Spanish Monarchy" as the empire was then known. At their greatest extent these stretched from Mexico through Central America to New Granada, and select Caribbean islands: Cuba, Puerto Rico, and most of Hispaniola. It included all South America except Brazil, which was Portuguese other than the period of Spanish control from 1580 to 1640.

Spanish Armada (1588). See *Invincible Armada*.

Spanish Army. The Christian armies of the *Reconquista* relied on Iberian *Military Orders* and the *Hermandades*. During the 14th–15th centuries, only 3,000 *men-at-arms* were kept in permanent service in Castile, with another 4,000 in a reserve on half-wages. (The Spanish Army that so impressed Europe, the army of the *tercios*, only took shape after the Reconquista.) The Brethren organized *militias* to supplement Castilian and Aragonese men-at-arms and the thinning ranks of the Iberian Military Orders. But once Spain moved to make war against other European powers the Brothers and militia were insufficient to meet Spain's manpower needs. Major reforms were introduced in 1493 that built the forces under royal command. The army was then critically shaped by the "Ordinance of Valladolid" of 1496, issued by *Ferdinand and Isabella*. This introduced conscription whereby 1 man in 12, age 20 to 45, was bound to royal military service. Volunteers were also recruited directly by the crown, and many served gladly as *conquistadores* in the 15th–16th centuries. As Spain's military fortunes declined in the 17th century rural landlords had to compel their tenants to enlist. In addition, Spain enforced penal conscription whereby felons were forced to serve out their sentence in arms, or sentences were commuted in return for military service.

A "colonel" was put in command of the basic unit of the Spanish Army, a regiment or "coronelia" of 3,000 soldiers, made up in turn of companies of 500 men. Two of these companies were armed exclusively with *pikes*; the others comprised combinations of *arquebusiers* and swordsmen. Each coronelia had attached to it a unit of 500 to 600 mixed *light cavalry* and *heavy cavalry*. Although the Spanish failed to standardize *artillery*—well into the *Thirty Years' War* (1618–1648) they used over 50 types of guns across some twenty calibers—their use of cannon and arquebus in support of the pike-and-sword *tercios* made Spanish infantry the best troops in Europe for over a century. Under *Philip II*, in 1584 Spain could raise 200,000 troops all told. It kept nearly 150,000 employed on a regular basis, mostly in garrisons, including 20,000 infantry and 15,000 cavalry in Spain; 60,000 infantry and 2,000 cavalry in the *Army of Flanders*; 24,000 infantry and 2,000 cavalry in Naples and northern Italy; 15,000 infantry and 9,000 cavalry in Portugal; and scattered smaller garrisons in many overseas colonies. The financial burden of these huge numbers, added to the extraordinary costs of warships, dockyards, and convoy escort, was staggering, and ultimately fatal. See also *Alba, Don Fernando Álvarez de Toledo, duque de*; *Córdoba, Gonzalo di*; *Cortés, Hernán*; *Parma, duque di*; *Pizarro, Francisco*; *Santa Cruz, Marques de*; *Spínola, Ambrogio di*; *Zúñiga, Louis Requesens y*.

"Spanish Captivity" of Portugal (1580–1640). See *Brazil*; *Eighty Years' War*; *Invincible Armada*; *Philip II, of Spain*; *Portugal*.

"Spanish Fury" (November 4–5, 1576). The Spanish *Army of Flanders* mutinied after receiving no pay and no supplies as a result of a bankruptcy declared by *Philip II* in late 1575. Its starving veterans sacked several small towns from July through October, then ravaged the countryside to the point that opposing councils in Flanders and Holland united to drive the marauding Spanish and mercenaries away. But the militia of Brabant could not protect Antwerp where the Spanish ran amok, sacking the city. Over 1,000 buildings were razed, thousands of women were raped, and hundreds of civilians were robbed and murdered (Dutch propagandists claimed 18,000 dead). See also *Black Legend*; *Eighty Years' War*; *English Fury*; *Pacification of Ghent*.

Spanish Inquisition. See *Inquisition*.

Spanish Main. Originally, the north coast of South America. By the 16th century it referred also to the Caribbean coast of Mexico and the United States or even the entire Caribbean coastline. Along these shores Spanish ships formed into annual *convoys* to ply their way to Spain filled with slave-mined silver and gold from the Americas. Treasure ships were preyed upon by English *pirates*, French *buccaneers*, and in times of war—which was virtually constant at sea in the 16th and 17th centuries—by French, Dutch, and English *privateers* sailing under *letters of marque*.

Spanish Monarchy. See *Spanish America*.

"Spanish musket." See *La Bicocca*; *muskets*.

Spanish Netherlands. The southern half of medieval Burgundy (*Flanders*). It remained largely Catholic during the *Protestant Reformation* and thus split away from the rebellious Calvinist provinces during the *Eighty Years' War* (1568–1648). See also *Burgundy*; *Netherlands*.

Spanish riders. Sharp stakes driven into the ground at a forward angle by infantry anticipating a cavalry attack, but also useful as a defense to blunt advancing enemy infantry. In Sweden these were known as "Swinesfeathers."

Spanish Road. "Le chemin des espagnols." The main *Habsburg* supply route from Italy to Flanders. It was of vital strategic and economic importance during the *Italian Wars* (1494–1559), the *Eighty Years' War* (1568–1648), and the *Thirty Years' War* (1618–1648), especially in those periods when French or Dutch or English naval power denied Spain the sea route to its northern possessions. It ran through Lombardy, several Swiss cantons, and into the Rhineland. Passage through parts of the Rhineland was often hotly contested. The Spanish Road hosted a remarkable postal service, a "pony express" of early modern Europe dating to 1504, when the Taxis family first created a chain of 106 relay stations supplied with fresh mounts to connect territories bound together by the new union of the crowns of Burgundy and Castile. In 1516 the young *Charles V* signed a contract with the Taxis family guaranteeing delivery times, and in 1518 Charles and *Francis I* of France agreed to extend diplomatic immunity to official couriers using a mutually advantageous service. *Philip II* deployed similar services connecting his new capital at Madrid with Rome and Vienna. In 1567 the *Duke of Alba* set up a new chain of postal relay stations. From 1572 riders from these stations carried copies of all letters to and from Philip II. Large bullion shipments also took this road to pay and support Spanish and Italian troops in Flanders, though other bullion shipments traveled by galley to Savoy and thence overland to the Netherlands. The route also had semi-permanent stations (*étapes*) where food, fodder, and other provision were brought by villagers and townsfolk for sale to the troops marching north. Later, *sutlers* were hired to supply the stations. This was quite advanced *logistics* given the state of the art in that era. In 1592 the first serious Franco-Dutch efforts were made to cut this vital Spanish artery in Lorraine. That led to a treaty securing Spanish access across *The Grisons*, by then a Protestant alpine valley, as long as the troops moved in small units and carried only *swords* (all other military equipment had to be carted separately).

Another critical choke point was the still-Catholic *Valtelline*. In 1595 *Henri IV* declared war on Spain and threatened the passage through Franche Comté, forcing the Spanish to march further to the east. Two years later Henri attacked the route in Savoy. Most issues appeared settled in the *Peace of Vervins* (May 2, 1598), but in 1600 Henri invaded Savoy, adding the pont de Grésin to France in the Treaty of Lyon (1601). That squeezed the Spanish Road down to a single route through a narrow valley and permitted France to cut it virtually at will. *Spínola* led 8,000 men through the pass in 1601 and more companies traversed it in 1602. Nevertheless, after 1601 Spanish troops could only move along this route upon French sufferance, a fact that greatly hampered Spain's military efforts in Flanders. As relations with France deteriorated, ultimately to end in protracted war, Spain was hard-pressed to resupply its troops in the north. There was intermittent fighting over control of the mountain valley passes—the Protestant Grisons and the Catholic Valtelline—from 1607 to 1617, involving Spain, Savoy, Venice, and France. In 1620, Spain occupied the Valtelline and Grisons with 4,300 men. Within a year another 3,600 Habsburg troops were garrisoned in Alsace and 5,000 in the Palatinate, protecting the road north. But the next year the spread north of the German war cut off most roads from Italy to Flanders. In 1633 the French occupation of Lorraine cut all overland routes between Spain and Flanders. From 1635 the Spanish Road was more often than not blocked by French troops, who were garrisoned throughout the Rhineland. That forced the Spanish to reinforce their northern armies via the sea, with every convoy harassed by French and Dutch warships. Spectacular defeat of a heavily armed and escorted relief convoy at *The Downs* (1639) resulted in progressive strangulation of the Army of Flanders and reduction by the Dutch of the outer, fortified perimeter of the Spanish Netherlands. See also *besonios*; *Monzón, Treaty of*; *Rocroi, Battle of*.

Suggested Reading: Geoffrey Parker, *The Army of Flanders and the Spanish Road, 1567–1659* (1972).

spar. Any stout pole on a ship forming a *mast* when vertical, or a boom, *yard*, or gaff when horizontal.

spaudlers. *Plate armor* protecting the shoulders; also called "pauldrons." See also *bracers*.

spears. See *lance (1)*; *pike*.

Speicher (Vögelisegg), Battle of (1403). See *Appenzell Wars*.

Spice Islands. The Portuguese first landed in 1512, after which these Moluccan islands became a great prize in the 16th century contest among European sea empires for control of the spice trades. In 1529 Spain renounced its claim in return for a heavy payment from Portugal. The islands were seized by the Dutch during the latter part of the *Eighty Years' War* (1568–1648).

spice trades. For centuries, spices from Asia (cloves, various peppers, curry powders, cinnamon, and others) formed one of the world's richest international trades. The direction of trade was from China and southeast Asia, Ceylon (Sri Lanka), and India, through Central Asia to the Middle East, and on to Europe. Arab middlemen, and in a real economic sense also Arab civilization, thrived from and depended upon this trade. In the Mediterranean, Venice dominated spice exchange, which made it and Italy rich, and underwrote and sustained the wars as well as cultural accomplishments of the *Italian Renaissance*. The Venetian monopoly was threatened by the Ottoman conquest of *Constantinople* in 1453, as the Ottomans at first denied market access to Venetian traders before later agreeing to a Venetian monopoly on the westward carry trade. That calamity (from Europe's point of view) married a longstanding search (dating at least to the 13th century) for a new way to the fabled spice lands of the east with revolutionary new means of travel and transport: ocean-capable ships of sail that at last made it possible for Europeans to outflank Muslim control of the overland trade routes to Asia.

Once the Portuguese circumnavigated Africa they also bypassed Venetian control of the Mediterranean terminus of the spice trades, contributing significantly to the economic and military decline of Venice. Armed Portuguese merchantmen reached the Indian Ocean following the voyage of Vasco da Gama to the Calicut coast in 1497–1498. By 1510, Portuguese *carracks* had decisively defeated local Arab and Indian fleets of *dhows* and gained direct access to rich sources of cloves, cinnamon, and black pepper. Meanwhile, the Genoese explorer Christopher Columbus sailed west in 1492 in search of spices and other riches of Asia. In the *Line of Demarcation* decision made upon his return in 1493, Portugal was awarded a paper monopoly by the pope over the spice trade of the eastern hemisphere. Lisbon was never able to secure effective control of the sources of all the major spices, however. After a few decades of unchallenged profits, it lost the old monopoly on knowledge of the trans-African oceanic routes. In the mid-16th century Portugal surrendered the *Spice Islands* to the highly aggressive Dutch. Regardless of who controlled the spice trades at a given historical moment, for the better part of two centuries they were a major mover in European expansion and in naval and amphibious warfare in southeast Asia. See also *d'Albuquerque, Alfonso de*; *Diu, Battle of*; *East India Company*; *Fugger, House of*; *Portuguese India*.

> *Portuguese* carracks...*gained direct access to rich sources of cloves, cinnamon, and black pepper.*

Suggested Reading: Kristof Glamann, *The Dutch-Asiatic Trade* (1958).

spiking (guns). The poor rate of fire and the limited range of early gunpowder *artillery* were inherent weaknesses that led opposing armies to adopt a simple and effective counter: wait until the enemy's guns fired, then rush the position and overwhelm the gun crews. From the early 15th century the additional precaution was taken of "spiking the guns." Once the guns were taken, iron spikes were hammered into the touch hole, which was the quickest and surest way to put *cannon* out of action. This rendered them inoperable even if the position was retaken by the guns' original owners. This threat to the artillery led to ever larger protective contingents of *infantry*, which meant more men on the other side were dedicated to charging the guns, which led to still more defenders, and so on. Over time, the proportion of an army's strength devoted to protecting or attacking artillery grew to a considerable size, much of it on the defensive side devoted to digging blocking trenches in front of the guns or constructing earthworks and palisades, and manning them. See also *Breitenfeld, First*; *Lützen, Battle of*.

Spínola, Ambrogio di (1569–1630). Italian mercenary general in the service of *Philip III*. In 1602 he raised an army of 9,000 *mercenaries* and hired it out to Spain. He was commander of the *Army of Flanders* from 1603 to 1628. Upon first arrival in Flanders, he relieved *Albert, Archduke of Austria* at the *Siege of Ostend*, finally forcing the city to surrender in September 1604. A highly aggressive commander, he reduced or stormed numerous Dutch strongholds and towns, often using his field army to screen siege operations from interference by his nemesis, *Maurits of Nassau*. This partially revived Spanish military fortunes from 1605 to 1606, just before the *Twelve Years' Truce* (1609–1621). As a member of a prominent Genoese banking family, Spínola was instrumental in obtaining loans to support Philip's war effort. He was also singularly responsible for modernization of the *Spanish Army*, in particular its system of *logistics*. One incentive was the chronically poor state of Spanish finances which several times forced Spínola to pay troops out of his own resources. He was a proponent of the Twelve Years' Truce and hoped to see it extended. When it ended in 1621, he resumed the fight with the Dutch and intervened in the Lower Palatinate, as the *Thirty Years' War* (1618–1648) merged with resumption of the *Eighty Years' War* (1568–1648). In 1625 he besieged Breda. In 1628, with the war in the Netherlands temporarily stalemated militarily, he left to become governor of Milan. He died during a siege of Casale. See also *contributions*.

sponge. The process of swabbing out a *cannon* or *bombard* after firing as well as the dampened felt or brush sponge (on the end of a long wooden handle) used to do this. It was critical to extinguish any smoldering wadding or burning powder that might remain inside the barrel. Failure to properly sponge out a gun could lead to catastrophic ignition of a new charge as it was loaded and *rammed* down the muzzle, which would kill the crew. For this reason buckets of water were kept near the guns to soak the sponge (and to cool the barrel by wrapping it from time to time with wet cloth). Sometimes acid was added to the water to wash out the barrel. See also *worm*.

springald. A ballista (arbaleste), dating in its main idea to at least Roman times, used to shoot large iron bolts stabilized by wooden "feathers." If fired into a mass of men, the bolt might pass through several enemy. The wounds it caused were almost always lethal, ripping great holes in bodies and leaving large splinters to later cause sepsis. Given its compact structure and size and the nature of its projectile, the springald was more often used in defense against a siege than by attackers. Springalds were not normally used as engines of bombardment, but they could throw stone ammunition in bombardment if necessary.

Spurs, Battle of (1302). See *Courtrai, Battle of*.

Spurs, Battle of (1513). See *Henry VIII, of England*.

squadron. Under the Dutch system introduced by *Maurits of Nassau*, each *company* was subdivided into three squadrons, each under a *corporal*. This system was copied, with variations, by many armies.

square rig. See *sails*.

squares. See *Arbedo, Battle of*; *arquebus*; *artillery*; *Banner (Swiss)*; *battle* (1); *Breitenfeld, First*; *Brustem, Battle of*; *Calven, Battle of*; *cavalry*; *crossbow*; *Dornach, Battle of*; *drill*; *Fähnlein*; *flags*; *Forlorn Hope*; *Frastenz, Battle of*; *Gevierthaufen*; *Giornico, Battle of*; *Grandson, Battle of*; *Gustavus II Adolphus*; *Haiduks*; *Harsthörner*; *heavy cavalry*; *Héricourt, Battle of*; *infantry*; *La Bicocca, Battle of*; *Landsknechte*; *Laupen, Battle of*; *Marignano, Battle of*; *Maurits of Nassau*; *Maximilian I*; *Morat, Battle of*; *mordax*; *Morgarten, Battle of*; *muskets*; *Nancy, Battle of*; *pike*; *Sempach, Battle of*; *shock*; *St. Jacob-en-Birs, Battle of*; *stradiots*; *Swiss square*; *tercios*; *Tilly, Count Johann Tserclaes*; *uniforms*; *Vienna, Siege of*; *wounds*.

squire. See *esquire*; *knight*; *men-at-arms*.

Sri Lanka. "Ceylon." Its indigenous people were conquered by *Buddhists* from India around 545 B.C.E. The Buddhist conquerors intermarried with the native Sinhalese to form the majority population. Also migrating to the island were ethnic Tamils and other *Hindus*, on and around the Jaffna peninsula. In 1505 Portuguese traders first made landfall. In 1515 Vasco da Gama secured the *spice trade* of Ceylon for Portugal. The Portuguese later lost out to the Dutch *Vereenigde Oostindische Compaagnie* (VOC), who controlled the island trade until displaced by the *East India Company* ("John Company") in 1796.

Stadholder. A representative of the *Habsburgs* in the Netherlands, with the exceptions of Brabant and Mechelen. They were always leading nobles from Flanders. The Habsburgs traditionally appointed three in the north, though under *William the Silent* these offices were combined into one Stadholderate. The title survived in the United Provinces after the outbreak of the *Eighty Years' War* (1568–1648). While often linked to the captaincy-general of the Dutch Army, it remained a political rather than military title. See also *Hendrik, Frederik*; *Maurits of Nassau*.

Stadtlohn, Battle of (August 6, 1623). The army of the *Catholic League* under *Johan Tilly* met a Protestant army of 15,000 under *Christian of Brunswick*, who had recklessly marched into Saxony. Christian withdrew on first contact but Tilly pursued. In Westphalia, just a few miles shy of the Dutch frontier, Tilly caught up with Christian's less fit and ill-disciplined troops and forced the fight. Both sides deployed in the traditional manner: infantry at the center flanked by cavalry. With heavy attacks, Tilly broke both Protestant cavalry wings and trapped the fleeing enemy infantry against an impassible bog. At least 6,000 Protestant troops died and another 4,000 were captured. The fool Christian escaped, running with under 2,000 surviving horse. The defeat pushed *Friedrich V*, the "Winter King," out of the *Thirty Years' War*, sent the Dutch of nearby Gelderland into a near panic, and brought thousands of refugees into the United Provinces by river and overland.

staff-weapons. Beyond the simple *quarterstaff*, staff weapons were any stout pole to which an axe head, war hammer, bill (blade), trident, or spiked tip was attached. See also *brown bill*; *gisarmes*; *goedendag*; *halberd*; *military flail*; *military fork*; *Morgenstern*; *polearm*; *poleax*.

St. Albans, First Battle of (1455). See *Wars of the Roses*.

St. Albans, Second Battle of (1461). See *Wars of the Roses*.

standardization (of weapons). See *artillery*; *ballot*; *bullets*; *Burgundy, Duchy of*; *cannon*; *corning/corned gunpowder*; *culverin*; *falcon*; *Gustavus II Adolphus*; *Henri II, of France*; *Invincible Armada*; *Le Tellier, Michel*; *Maurits of Nassau*; *muskets*; *New Model Army*; *pasavolante*; *printing*; *quarto-cannon*; *robinet*; *saker*; *shells*; *Spanish Army*; *Torstensson, Lennart*; *volley fire*.

standing army. "Militum perpetuum." The permanent, professional army of a state; one not demobilized in times of peace. Several ancient empires had large standing armies, notably Rome and Persia. The *Byzantine Empire* at its height had a powerful standing army and a permanent navy supported by an advanced military bureaucracy and tax system. The first standing army in the Islamic world was set up by the Abbasid *caliphs* of Baghdad. This lessened their dependence on Arab tribal levies (*Bedouin*) while allowing newly converted, non-Arab populations to rise to social and political prominence within what was still an Arab empire. The *Mughal Army* had several hundred thousand permanent troops while the *Ming Army* was by far the largest of the period; it may have had 1 million men under arms in 1400, though this fell to just 250,000 a century later. The Japanese deployed large permanent armies toward the end of the *Unification Wars* (1550–1615) and in their two invasions of Korea in the 1590s. The rise of standing armies occurred later in Europe, paralleling a slow emergence of centralized monarchies and states (which came first remains a matter of intense debate). It was not until after 1650 that most powers in Europe adopted professional standing armies, in part to reduce the old reliance on untrustworthy *mercenaries* but also to concentrate military and political power under the sovereign. Creation of a standing army thus was not solely the result of evolution of military institutions or even a reaction to external military pressure. It primarily reflected changes in the social composition of states and armies and in popular attitudes toward both. This usually meant prior establishment of a stable tax system and a more advanced and literate bureaucracy, and expansion of social involvement in battle to include large infantry formations drawn from previously non-martial classes in countryside and town. Once the new militaries were in place they augmented trends toward national identities as represented by wearing *uniforms*, use of distinctive emblems and *flags*, and stable national military cultures. Note: It is normal to discount *militia* or reserves or potential conscripts when calculating the size of standing armies. See also *Austrian Army*; *barony*; *contributions*; *Dutch Army*; *English armies*; *feudalism*; *French armies*; *Holy Roman Empire*; *housecarls*; *Hungarian Army*; *Imperial Army*; *Military Orders*; *Mughal Empire*; *Muscovy, Grand Duchy of*; *palace guards*; *Polish Army*; *Safavid Army*; *Spanish Army*; *Swedish Army*; *Swiss Army*.

standing navies. See *permanent navies*.

standing officer. In the *Royal Navy*, from the 17th century this was any of four *warrant officer* positions appointed to a ship on a permanent footing.

Stangebro, Battle of (1598). See *Karl IX*; *Sigismund III*.

starotsy. Polish officials in Ukraine responsible for protecting the frontier against *Tatar* raids.

starshnya. The *Cossack* officer elite.

States General. A governing body formed by the seven provinces that comprised the United Provinces in revolt against Spain. A special committee oversaw military operations. See also *Eighty Years' War*; *Generality*; *Maurits of Nassau*; *Nonsuch, Treaty of*; *Oldenbaarneveldt, Johan van*; *Raad van State*.

St. Augustine Massacre (1565). Following the defeat and massacre at *Fort Caroline*, a hurricane damaged a *Huguenot* fleet so that its survivors crawled ashore at St. Augustine, Florida. A Spanish military expedition ran down, caught, and killed all the men there, sparing only five *ships' boys*. Three years later, on April 6, 1568, a small Huguenot fleet surprised the Spanish garrison at San Mateo (Fort Caroline) and hanged every man in retaliation for the 1565 massacre.

St. Bartholomew's Day Massacres (August 24, 1572). This key event in the history of the *French Civil Wars* (1562–1629) still sparks fierce controversy among historians over who was responsible for the bloodshed. It was once thought that *Catherine de Medici* and the *Guise* together plotted the violence, but most specialist historians reject that thesis. Instead, the Queen Mother is portrayed as looking to end the confessional warfare and heal the nation's wounds by tying Catholics and *Valois* to *Huguenots* and *Bourbons* with one stroke (though with a long-term hope of reconversion of most Huguenots): a dynastic union of Valois and Bourbon via the marriage of her daughter, Margaret de Valois, sister of King Charles IX, to Henri de Navarre (*Henri IV*). However, this proposal was made against a backdrop of several years of rising popular violence and zealotry. The prospect of a Valois marriage to a heretic prince of the blood thus deepened rather than assuaged Catholic fears about secret Protestant influence at Court, and hardened opposition to any compromise with heresy and rebellion. This ugly mood was aggravated by efforts of some Huguenots to send military aid to Dutch rebels and news that a small Protestant army had seized Mons en route to the Netherlands. Catholics also falsely assumed that Charles IX was under the strong influence of the Huguenot commander *Coligny*, and again falsely that Coligny had persuaded Charles to support the Dutch against Spain. The planned union of Valois and Bourbon through the marriage of Margaret and Henri de Navarre went ahead on August 18, 1572. But over the next few days and the following six weeks, instead of reconciliation France was shaken by an explosion of extreme religious violence in which thousands of Huguenots were hunted down and the Fourth Civil War began.

The Massacres

The first of four key phases of the events known as the "St. Bartholomew's Day Massacres" came on August 22 with a failed attempt to assassinate Coligny, who was in Paris along with several thousand Huguenot nobles to attend the wedding. Coligny was shot in the arm and hand but only wounded superficially. As a result of the failed attempt on his life and his refusal to leave until the culprits were found, he and the majority of Huguenot nobles were still in Paris two nights later when the city exploded with violence. Modern research has largely cleared Catherine de Medici of the long-standing charge of organizing the assassination attempt and the massacres. No consensus exists on who to blame instead. Some scholars point to the Guise from whose house the shots were fired at Coligny and who stood most to gain from his death and renewed war with French Protestants. Others tried to save the traditional interpretation that blamed the Queen Mother. Still other historians marshaled evidence pointing to this or that culprit or claimed conspiracy. What is clear from the newest research is that the mass violence that followed was not directly linked to the assassination attempt: it was instead both popular and spontaneous rather than planned, and grew out of levels of extreme confessional tension within Paris that had been building for years. On the night of August 23, a Royal Council was called at which Charles and the Queen Mother agreed to make a preemptive strike against the Protestant leadership, that it was best to kill the top Protestant leaders all at once rather than face them again in battle. Heightening tension was the presence of a small Huguenot army outside the city walls and the presence of thousands of armed Catholic and Protestant nobles inside the city, men who had only recently taken up arms against one another.

Coligny was shot in the arm and hand but only wounded superficially.

Whether the order was given after long planning or impetuously out of fear and opportunity, the king's Swiss Guards, accompanied by soldiers loyal to the Duc d'Anjou, were dispatched into the hotels and the homes of leading

Huguenots to act as royal assassins. They startled awake Protestant leaders and their families and cut their throats or put them to the sword. The city militia was sent out to guard the streets and keep order while these bloody deeds were done. Coligny was killed personally by *Henri Guise, duc de Lorraine*, as part of an old vendetta between two noble families, Châtillon and Guise. Several dozen Huguenot nobles quickly followed Coligny into death. His blood lust and feud satisfied, Henri Guise protected other Huguenots from murderous Catholic mobs over the next several days. However, the Royal Council's plan for selective killings quickly got out of hand as ordinary Parisians, awakened by the death cries and screams of murdered Protestants, partook of an extraordinary and indiscriminate frenzy of ritualized murder, dismemberment, and drowning. Three awful days and nights of butchery in the streets, houses, and hotels of Paris ensued, joined in by some militia but carried out in the main by civilians rather than the Guise's or the king's men. Barbara Diefendorf has convincingly demonstrated that while Catherine and Charles did not plan these massacres, and despite the fact that they made some effort to stop the killing, their decision to murder the top Huguenot leaders betrayed such reckless disregard for confessional tensions in Paris and across the kingdom that they must be held responsible for them nonetheless.

At least 2,000 Huguenots were slaughtered in Paris by Catholics aroused to an exterminationist fury by the sounds and screams of official murders. The victims were not just killed: they were butchered with ritualized cruelty in sickening accord with Catholic rites of violent purification of the body social. Hence, special cruelties were enacted against pregnant women and their unborn babies, and hundreds of Huguenots were drowned in the Seine, perhaps symbolizing purification of Catholic France by lethal baptism. Others were vivisected and dismembered and their corpses (including Coligny's) and houses and religious places burned: "purification by fire" was an accepted method of expurgating *heresy* from the community of the godly. Historians also explain that the mobs thought they were carrying out the will of the king by holy purging of his, and their, confessional enemies. Even more important, pamphlet and other contemporary evidence points to a widespread belief that the killings were not just condoned by the king but were seen as the will of God, as signaled in dark portents and omens and affirmed on the spot by blessing of the murders by blood-spattered priests.

The massacres spread to the provinces during the next six weeks as a near-genocidal slaughter of the Huguenots gripped Catholic France. Another 3,000 were killed outside Paris in twelve provincial cities, all towns with Catholic majorities that moved to carry out a final solution to the Protestant problem by cleansing the Huguenot pollution from their godly communities. As in Paris, in the provincial cities civilians took the lead in the killings, repeating the pattern of ritualized humiliation and butchery of erstwhile neighbors. In several cities killings were carried out to the accompaniment of minstrels and musicians. In some towns civic leaders organized the butchery. In others they placed Protestants into protective custody, only to see the city's prisons stormed by frenzied Catholic mobs who hauled out the prisoners and dispatched them in the streets.

Legacy

Most of the top Huguenot leaders were dead by October. That left only Henri de Navarre, who escaped murder by virtue of his new relationship with Charles IX and the fact that he abjured *Calvinism*. He was not the only one: many thousands of terrified Huguenots accepted reconversion to Catholicism. In some provincial cities fifty times as many Huguenots abjured their reformed faith as were killed in the massacres; thousands more emigrated to England or the Netherlands. The impact of these conversions and departures into exile on French Protestantism was catastrophic: Huguenot communities shrank to a fraction of their former size as despair set in, or they disappeared entirely, reconverted and reabsorbed into suspicious Catholic majorities. This happened well beyond the 12 massacre towns and Paris: public abjurations were made all over France. At the same time, and for the same reason, Catholic morale and confidence soared. The massacres thus marked the beginning of the end of the Huguenot movement in France and were the key turning point in the civil wars. Henceforth, Huguenots mainly hunkered down behind the walls of their fortified towns, which prolonged the civil wars by leading to fewer battles and more drawn-out sieges.

Nor were the massacres a signal event in France alone: they resonated across a divided Europe, bringing fear but also resolution to Protestant communities in face of widespread bloodthirsty celebrations by Catholics. The pope ordered a "Te Deum" chanted, struck a commemorative medallion, and had fresh frescoes painted in the Vatican depicting angelic approval of the French massacres. Catholic princes across Europe sent heartfelt congratulations to the Queen Mother and to Charles. Protestants drew a much different conclusion, forgetting and forgiving that Huguenot mobs had sometimes murdered Catholics without mercy and had also tortured priests, nuns, and monks in imitation of the *Inquisition*. And just as the French Civil Wars ended, across Europe various confessional communities gathered for the climactic phase of the wider "Wars of Religion," with all sides asserting a renewed sense of righteousness and a new dedication to military resolution of old religious antagonisms. See also *Edict of Beaulieu*.

Suggested Reading: Denis Crouzet, *La nuit de la Saint-Barthélemy* (1994); Barbara Diefendorf, *Beneath the Cross: Catholics and Huguenots in 16th Century Paris* (1991); Mack Holt, *The French Wars of Religion, 1562–1629* (1995).

St. Bernard of Clairvaux (1090–1153). See *Crusades*; *Knights Templar*.

St. Denis, Battle of (1567). See *Saint-Denis, Battle of*.

Stegeborg, Battle of (September 8/18, 1598). See *Karl IX*; *Sigismund III*.

sternpost rudder. The sternpost was a straight timber rising upright from the keel to reinforce weakly built sterns and support a rudder that was fitted at the center. First used in Germany or the Netherlands at the end of the 12th century, the sternpost rudder was a key invention that displaced single and double steering oars and changed north European ship design. It greatly improved maneuverability and helped make possible the true sailing ship, which first evolved in the Baltic and Atlantic as the *cog*.

Stettin, Peace of (1570). See *Nordic Seven Years' War*.

stiletto. An Italian gunners' gauge in the form of a fine, thin dagger marked as a ruler and used for measuring both the caliber of a gun and the weight of shot and powder to be used. It also served as a personal weapon of last resort should the guns be overrun.

Stirling Bridge, Battle of (September 11, 1297). An early battle in the *Scottish Wars*. *Edward I* sent a large army north to secure his claim to *overlordship* of Scotland. At Stirling, *William Wallace* waited in ambush with a passionately inspired Scots army made up mostly of Highland infantry supported by small detachments of noble and retainer cavalry. They waited until perhaps a third of the English *heavy cavalry* crossed a narrow bridge over the Forth, then rushed to cut off the lead *knights* from the still-crowded bridge. While some Scots fought the English still on the bridge, others tore into knights milling about near the banks of the Forth. Many were pulled from their mounts and slaughtered, others were driven in panic to drown in the Forth under the weight of their armor. Stirling suggested that infantry could in fact stand against heavy horse, the arm that had dominated feudal warfare for two centuries, though its unique topography cast doubt on how general the lesson might be. The Scottish defeat at *Falkirk* the next year did not advance the argument for infantry. More clear was the stunning Flemish victory over French knights at *Courtrai* four years later.

St. Jacob-en-Birs, Battle of (August 16, 1444). An *Armagnac* army 40,000 strong invaded the Swiss Confederation in 1444. They were opposed by a force of just 1,200 regulars, plus 300 auxiliaries from Basle. After two minor skirmishes with Armagnac scouting parties the Swiss ranks and files grew eager for a fight, forcing their officers to continue an advance they wished to avoid. The Swiss forded the River Birs and were set upon along the far bank by the Armagnacs. The Swiss were badly positioned: the river at their backs limited prospects for any kind of tactical retreat. The outnumbered Swiss therefore formed their standard three squares of "Vorhut," "Gewalthut," and "Nachhut," and immediately attacked the Armagnac horse. Close-order fighting is said to have lasted for five hours, until the sheer weight of Armagnac numbers wore down the Swiss. The Swiss retreated to a nearby hospital where they gained some cover but still took heavy fire and casualties from French artillery and archers. The cannon fire particularly withered the

Swiss ranks. Then the Armagnac foot charged and overran the Swiss. In the last hand-to-hand fighting every Swiss was killed. The Armagnacs had won the day but their losses—estimated at over 4,000—were a testament to the courage and ferocity of their enemies. Conversely, Swiss losses were confirmation of the new power of artillery on the battlefield, something the Swiss sorely lacked prior to their war with *Charles the Rash* of Burgundy.

St. Lazarus, Knights of. See *Hospitallers*.

Stolbova, Peace of (1617). "Stolbovo." A treaty of peace that ended the war between Russia and Sweden fought off and on since 1609, during Muscovy's *"Time of Troubles"* ("Smutnoe Vremia"). Sweden kept Ingria and Kexholm, but returned Novgorod to Muscovy.

stop-rib. A inverted v-bar on a breastplate designed to stop an enemy's *lance* from riding up the chest and penetrating the throat.

storm. To rush a *breach* in a wall or other fortification en masse. Usually carried out by infantry, this was a costly and risky tactic. At sea, the same tactic was called *boarding*. Whereas most infantry in most armies shied away from this dangerous task, the Ottomans had special units of volunteer commandos (*Serdengeçti*) who were the first through any breach. See also *artillery*; *belfry*; *castles, on land*; *fortification*; *siege warfare*; *solid shot*; *Sturmgeld*.

Stormakstid. "Great Power Period." A term employed by Swedish historians about the period after 1621 when *Gustavus Adolphus* began to win a series of important victories and established *Sweden* as the new Great Power in the north. Usually said to have ended with the decisive defeat of Karl XII during the Great Northern War (1700–1721) against Russia.

Stoss, Battle of (1405). See *Appenzell Wars*.

Stow-on-the-Wold, Battle of (1646). See *English Civil Wars*.

St. Quentin, Battle of (1557). See *Saint-Quentin, Battle of*.

stradiots. "Stradioti." Mercenary *light cavalry* mainly from Dalmatia and Greece. They were semi-barbaric, with a reputation for great ferocity and routine cruelty to prisoners. They wore distinctive "top hats" and light or little *armor*. While they carried *shields* and close-order weapons, notably a curved Turkish *sword*, most were *lancers*. Some also carried *crossbows* which they dismounted to use in the manner of *dragoons*. The Venetians recruited stradiots from 1479 to support their heavier cavalry and to contend with Turkish and Moorish raiders by fighting them in their own style of warfare. Using stradiots was also a calculated response to the intervention of the *Swiss square* and *pike* tactics in the wars of northern Italy. Venice paid stradiots by a count of the enemy heads they delivered to the paymaster at the end of a raid. See also *heavy cavalry*; *mercenaries*.

Straslund, Siege of (May–July, 1628). *Albrecht von Wallenstein* dispatched an Imperial force to besiege the city of Straslund, an important port on the Baltic, an old opponent of Imperial power, and a target of *Olivares'* new policy of squeezing Dutch trade by attacking the *Hanse* ports. Although not yet ready to enter the *Thirty Years' War* directly, Sweden's Protestant champion *Gustavus Adolphus* sent aid by ship to Straslund to aid *Heinrich Holk* and the *Earl of Leven* (Alexander Leslie) resist the Imperials. Denmark also send aid. Wallenstein arrived and took command in early July. He made two failed assaults on the city then lifted the siege and moved off to fight at *Wolgast* (September 2, 1628).

strategic metals. The main metal used in warfare nearly everywhere outside the Americas during the medieval and early modern periods was iron, which was used to make weapons of war ranging from spear tips and bodkins to *armor*, to *hoop-and-stave* and cast *cannon*. Bronze—an alloy of copper and tin—was also known and in wide use, especially later in this period. Indeed, it was the preferred metal for casting larger *artillery* pieces due to its malleability during casting, general sturdiness, and much greater resistance to cracking and premature explosion. Its great disadvantage was expense. Copper, the basic metal used to make bronze, was found in quantity in Europe in Bohemia, Hungary, and Saxony. From the 16th century, large supplies of copper were imported by Spain from mines in Cuba, Mexico, and Peru. During the 16th and 17th centuries the Portuguese, and then the Dutch, exported copper from Japan to gun foundries scattered over Asia. In Europe, tin mining was largely confined to England, Germany, and Spain. A lively trade in these metals characterized the period, accelerating from the early 16th century but also concentrating in several key markets: Nuremberg, Bolanzo (Italy), and Antwerp. Bronze gun casting was done anywhere that skilled artisans and sufficient capital were brought together, sometimes even when an army was on the march (hence, into the 19th century some armies maintained a "right to the bells" by which their chief *gunner* could claim the best bronze bell in any captured town, later to be melted down and recast as cannon). See also *casting*; *Fugger, House of*.

> *...some armies maintained a "right to the bells"...later to be melted down and recast as cannon.*

strategy. See *Art of War*; *attrition*; *bellum se ipse alet*; *castles, on land*; *chevauchée*; *fortification*; *guerre guerroyante*; *Gustavus II Adolphus*; *logistics*; *Machiavelli, Niccolò di Bernardo*; *Maurits of Nassau*; *Normans*; *Philip II, of Spain*; *Philip III, of Spain*; *siege warfare*; *trace italienne*; *Wallenstein, Albrecht von*.

Stratton, Battle of (1643). See *English Civil Wars*; *Hopton, Ralph*.

strel'sty. "Musketeers" or "harquebusiers." A permanent corps of 3,000 nonhereditary Muscovite infantry armed with *arquebuses* (later, muskets), some of whom were selected from the *pishchal'niki*. The corps was established by *Ivan III* sometime between 1545 and 1550, probably in the wake of the disastrous Russian campaign in Kazan, 1549–1550. They were employed from 1550 by the tsars as an elite household guard then as an elite infantry corps that first saw combat in 1552. Some served as *dragoons* ("gunners at the stirrup") and special guards of the tsar. Others served as auxiliaries performing household or constabulary functions. They were incorporated into a modified *servitor* system they owed the crown military service rather than taxes and they were not allowed to own serfs. Over time they evolved into a hereditary military caste, which lessened their military effectiveness. In wartime they formed the core of a tsarist army that otherwise was comprised of masses of ill-trained peasant conscripts supported by *pomest'e cavalry*. They fired from platforms while protected by cavalry or from *Wagenburgs*. By 1600, there were 25,000 strel'sty, with 2,800 serving in 28 elite companies in Moscow. Many later strel'sty remained Old Believers, alienated from the tsarist court after the schism within Russian Orthodoxy sparked by the reformed ritual introduced by Patriarch Nikon (1605–1681). They were savagely repressed by Peter I.

Stuart, Mary. See *Mary Stuart, Queen of Scots*.

Stuhm, Battle of (June 17–27, 1629). "Honigfelde." After the Imperial victory over the Danes at *Wolgast* (September 2, 1628), *Albrecht von Wallenstein* sent 12,000 troops to aid *Sigismund III* against *Gustavus Adolphus* in Livonia. The Swedes advanced toward Warsaw but were blocked by a Polish-Imperial army at Stuhm, where *dragoons* seized the crossing over the Leibe. The Swedes were badly beaten by *Reiters* and *Cossacks*, with much of the fighting hand to hand. Gustavus, as always in the thick of it, was nearly killed or captured twice. *Cardinal Richelieu* then negotiated a peace with Poland that freed Sweden to intervene in the *Thirty Years' War* (1618–1648).

Stuhmsdorf, Truce of (September 12, 1635). An extension of an earlier peace between Poland and Sweden. It allowed Swedish troops to move to Germany, where they met and bested an attack by an Imperial-Saxon army at *Wittstock* (October 4, 1636).

Sturmgeld. "Storm money." Extra pay given to soldiers who volunteered to take part in *storming* a *breach*, one of the riskiest of all military operations.

subashi. An Ottoman provincial prefect.

subinfeudation. Dividing *fief* lands held under *feudal* law and granting them to an inferior on the same conditions by which they were held by the higher lord. It was abolished in England in 1290, but survived for centuries longer in Scotland.

sub utraque specie. "In both kinds." In the Catholic Mass, serving the sacrament in the form of wine (blood of "The Christ") and bread (body of "The Christ"). In the 15th–16th centuries it was a significant reform issue whether only clerics should take the sacrament in both kinds (the Catholic position) or whether it should be so distributed to lay believers as well. See also *Calixtines*; *Hus, Jan*; *Hussite Wars*; *Utraquists*; *Zwingli, Huldrych*.

Sudan. When the majority of Egyptians converted to *Islam* in wake of the Arab conquest, Arabic Sudanese closely tied to Egypt by culture and economics followed suit. The ethnically African southern Sudan remained mixed animist and Christian. Between 1300 and 1500, much of Sudan was overrun by nomadic Muslim tribes, fragmenting and pushing inland the older Christian kingdom of *Alwa*. Central Sudan was controlled by the "Funj Sultanate," a cavalry-based military power, from the 16th to the 19th centuries.

Sud-Beveland, Battle of (1574). See *Boisot, Louis*; *Sea Beggars*.

Sudler. A cook who traveled with the *baggage train* but cooked for the troops.

Sufism. The great mystic tradition of the Muslim world. It helped craft a grand compromise under the *Seljuk Turks* between purer forms of desert and ascetic mysticism on one hand, and *sunni* orthodoxy and set legal and religious doctrine on the other. Sufism supplemented the grand sunni revival of the 11th century, which had been largely an urban and elite movement, by appealing to peasants and the nomads of the Arabian desert and Central Asian steppe and grafting these groups to a unifying mystical pietism. The Turkic tribes which converted to Islam were particularly attracted to Sufism. As a result, from the 13th century the majority of Muslims were bound to each other in a body of religious sentiment and identity that had as much or more to do with Sufism than with the earlier formed, but by then rigidified doctrines of legal theorists and theologians. See also *Qizilbash*; *shī'a Islam*.

Suleiman I (1494–1566). Süleyman "The Magnificent." Ottoman sultan, 1520–1566. He succeeded and repudiated his brutal father, *Selim I*, expanding into Europe instead of warring with the *Safavids*. In a series of thirteen major campaigns Suleiman sought to complete the northward-moving conquest of the Christian peoples of the Balkans pursued by his predecessors, but blocked since the 1456 victory at Belgrade over *Muhammad II* won by *János Hunyadi*. Suleiman conquered outlying Serb provinces then undermined and assaulted fortified Belgrade in 1521, having first defeated the feudal cavalry levies of King Lajos of Hungary with his highly disciplined *Janissary Corps*. Although he lost many tens of thousands of men over six months of bloody fighting, he achieved what Muhammad failed to do. Building up the navy, he also succeeded in the south: he defeated the *Hospitallers* in a great *Siege of Rhodes*, 1522–1523, ending their protracted threat to the Muslim southern flank. In 1524 Suleiman made peace with Poland so that he could concentrate on attacking the Hungarians. Accompanied by an *artillery train* of 300 guns hauled by barge up the Danube, he advanced into Hungary with 100,000 men in the summer of 1526. He was met by a Hungarian force of 25,000 on the field at *Mohács* (1526), where he utterly destroyed the overmatched Hungarian army. Having decimated its feudal nobility, Hungary lay prostrate and compliant before him. Buda fell in September.

When fortune shifted, the Hungarians later recanted their surrender. Although Suleiman expended vast amounts of Ottoman and Balkan blood and treasure trying to complete the conquest of Hungary, he was never able to do so. His aggression brought him also into direct conflict with *Habsburg* Austria. He personally conducted an unsuccessful *Siege of Vienna* (1529), possibly in tacit alliance with *Francis I* who sought an Ottoman alliance against *Charles V*. Suleiman was repulsed at Vienna and his army harassed and badgered bloody during its long withdrawal to Buda. As he pulled back, having overstayed the usual campaign season, his troops and cavalry suffered much want of grain and fodder.

Suleiman next attacked eastward into Asia Minor and Iran. It is important to note that his use of religious propaganda was aimed more at the *shī'a* "schismatics" and "heretics" of Iran than at Christian Europe: he was no *ghazi* in spirit, but was instead a sophisticated ruler of an increasingly cosmopolitan and tolerant empire. In 1532 he attacked Austria again, but neither side could win outright and Hungary settled down as a region of *guerre guerroyante* between the Ottoman and Austrian empires, with both sides content to leave it as a buffer between them. In 1538 Suleiman sent his navy to make war on Venice, threaten coastal Italy, and raid the coast of Spain. He tried but failed to capture Malta in 1565. He spent his last 25 years expanding and defending the difficult territory taken north of the Sava, as did his successors for another 100 years after that. Suleiman constantly intrigued with European powers, taking advantage of divisions within Christendom occasioned by the *Protestant Reformation*, the *Italian Wars*, and the first civil and religious wars in France. Suleiman was a life-long patron of arts, culture, and building, though even in such areas his instincts and tastes were imperial and martial. He died at age 72, still campaigning in Hungary, during the siege of Szigetvár.

Suggested Reading: André Clot, *Suleiman the Magnificent: The Man, His Life, His Epoch* (1992); Metin Kunt and Christine Woodhead, eds., *Süleyman the Magnificent and His Age* (1995).

Sully, duc de (1560–1641). See *Henri IV, of France*.

sultan. Arabic: "sovereign." The sovereign ruler of an Islamic nation. The title became more common once agreement on the proper succession to the *caliphate* ended. A sultan ranked above emir but did not claim to rule all Muslims everywhere by right, as did the first caliphs. The Ottomans used the title from the early 16th century (Venetians called the Ottoman sultan "Gran

Signor"). The Mughal rulers also used the title. Lesser sultans ruled lesser Muslim states in the Maghreb, Iberia, and in parts of southeast Asia.

sultanate. A territory ruled by a *sultan* as a secular prince, a Muslim religious authority, or both. See also *caliphate*.

sumpter. A baggage horse; not a *warhorse*. While never used as a battle mount for a *knight*, sumpters were indispensable in transporting his *armor*, weapons, and other effects to and from battle.

sunni **Islam.** The main body of believers in *Islam*. Sunnis accepted the historical succession of *caliphs* and honored the Sunna, or tradition (life example) of the Prophet Muhammad. Four streams of accepted interpretation developed within sunni Islam, each reasonably tolerant of the others: (1) Hanafi, officially sanctioned by the Ottoman Empire and dominant in Central Asia, India, Iraq, Syria, and Turkey; (2) Maliki, predominant in North and West Africa and Sudan; (3) Shafii, spread through Arabia, East Africa, Egypt, and Southeast Asia; and (4) Hanbali, largely confined to inner Arabia. See also *Ismaili*; *shī'a Islam*; *Sufism*.

supply lines. See *lines of supply*; *logistics*.

surcoat. A long coat, usually white, worn by *knights* over their *hauberk* or other *mail*. It was called "coat armor" because it consisted of a hardened leather coat reinforced with plates of iron. It preserved *armor* from exposure to rain and, perhaps more important, deflected the baking heat of the sun. The surcoat may have been copied from the *Saracens*. See also *jupon*.

surety towns. See *place de sûreté*.

Susa, Peace of (1629). See *Charles I, of England*; *La Rochelle*.

sutlers. Large scale merchants (sutlers, in the full sense) carted goods in great wagons in the *baggage train* of armies. Sometimes, they heaped bulk goods on pole-driven barges that plied navigable rivers that paralleled the route taken by their customers. Sutlers also sold goods to garrisons and armies encamped for a siege. Armies were, in effect, large mobile marketplaces, often exceeding in size all but the largest cities. It made commercial sense to follow them on campaigns. Sutlers played a critical role in medieval and early modern warfare, not least since soldiers were responsible for obtaining their own food, clothing, arms, and equipment. Sutlers thus became a regular feature of the logistical systems of early modern armies as well, which could not have maneuvered as they did without such contracted supplies from civilian sources. At the start of a campaign sutlers might be dispatched along the anticipated line of march with orders to establish markets before the troops (and their families) arrived. Along the *Spanish Road* such sutler markets became more or less permanent over time.

Swabia. "Schwaben." A large region of southwestern Germany originally including parts of Alsace, Baden, Bavaria, the Swiss cantons, and Württemberg. See also *Swabian League*; *Swabian War*.

Swabian League. A series of confederations of south German towns mainly located within Swabia. The first Swabian League was formed in 1331 by 22 towns led by Augsburg and Ulm. Initially, the Leaguers enjoyed support and protection from the *Holy Roman Empire*, which promised to uphold their constitutional rights and foreswore mortgage of their interests. The level of Imperial support for the League waxed and waned. In the 1360s feudal nobles who opposed emerging civic freedoms formed a counter-alliance called the *"Schlegelerbund"* ("mauling band"). With support from the emperor, the Bund moved to suppress the League, leading to fighting across Swabia from 1367 to 1372. League resistance was crushed by the Schlegelerbund under the Count of Württemberg. In 1376, 14 Swabian towns led by Ulm formed a new Swabian League and once again war broke out with the Bund. The emperor declined to support the nobles this time, possibly because he was bribed into effective neutrality by the Leaguers. The League *militia* army quickly prevailed over the *knights* of the Bund. This encouraged additional towns and cities in Bavaria, Franconia, and the Rhineland to join. In 1382 the Swabian League allied with Austria and was reaccepted into the Empire. The threat from the Schlegelerbund ended in 1395 when the headquarters fortress of its knights at Heimsheim was captured by a League army from Württemberg.

After nearly a century of religious and military quietude in Swabia, in 1488 the "Great Swabian League" was formed as a composite of knights and nobles of the "Company of the Shield of St. George" and a number of towns, all nominally accepting the authority of the emperor. The new League's military headquarters was in Ulm. Its army was comprised of noble *light cavalry* ("Rennfahne"), supplemented by "poor knights" hired by the member cities, and *Landsknechte* infantry. In 1499 the Leaguers supported the Holy Roman Empire during the *Swabian War* with the Swiss Confederation. In 1525 the Great Swabian League raised an army of 1,500 horse and 7,000 infantry to help put down the peasant rebellion in Germany and Austria known as the *German Peasant War*. The Swabian League was dissolved in 1534 because of growing and incompatible confessional differences, and hence dividing allegiance to the emperor, arising from the ferment of the *Protestant Reformation* in Germany.

Swabian War (1499). The Great Swabian League supported Holy Roman Emperor *Maximilian I* in his frontier claims against the *Swiss Confederation*. In January 1499, Imperial troops invaded and occupied a rich monastery in Graubünden ("The Grisons"). Fighting was actually sparked by taunts from Imperial troops shouted across the Rhine to passing Swiss from Uri ("moo, moo" was a favorite), along with more provocative suggestions that all Swiss were "cow herds" or bumpkins, and that they partook of intimate relations with their herd animals: "milchstinker" ("milk stinker"), "chueschnäggler" ("cow cuddler") and "chuefigger" ("cow fucker") were among the coarse insults hurled across the river. The Swiss responded good-naturedly, by burning down a nearby village. Within weeks they returned in force and retook the Graubünden monastery and a series of sharp fights ensued. The first clash came at *Frastenz* on April 20, where the Swabians were flanked and routed. The next came a month later at *Calven* (May 22), where the Swabians were again put to flight. The key battle was *Dornach* (July 22), where the Swiss for the first time met *Landsknechte* in battle (Germans trained in the Swiss style to beat them at their own game of infantry shock and "push of pike"). The Landsknechte were fairly quickly crushed. The Treaty of Basel that ended the war was signed two months later, on September 22. An unrelated event affected this outcome: the *Italian Wars* had left Duke *Ludovico Sforza* bereft of his duchy of Milan. Anxious to recover it, Sforza mediated the Peace of Basel to free Swiss troops who tied down fighting Imperial armies in Swabia, so that he could hire them for the fight he wanted to wage to regain Milan. The three quick yet decisive Swiss victories secured formal Imperial recognition of the Swiss Confederation. Within 15 years several more cantons joined the Confederacy, raising their number to 13. While Swiss soldiers sallied forth repeatedly to fight in other people's wars, their homeland was not again invaded before the late 18th century.

> *...along with...suggestions that all Swiss...partook of intimate relations with their herd animals...*

Swahili Arabs. Arabic: "Sahel" or "coastal." Sometimes called "Congo Arabs," this mixed Swahili and Arab population (Bantu speaking but using many Arabic words) dominated the east African *slave* and *spice trade* between Oman and Zanzibar. Predominantly Muslim, from the 16th century they fought against competition from Portuguese slavers. Their own plantation economy on *Zanzibar* demanded slaves be taken from the interior. Surplus captives were sold into the Arabian and Indian Ocean markets. They were overwhelmed by the Portuguese in the 16th century.

Sweden. Sweden was founded as a Viking kingdom with extensive interests throughout the Baltic and deep inside Russia, where ancient Swedes ("Varangians") were the likely founders of the first Russian state: Kievan Rus. Sweden was united with Denmark and Norway in 1397 in the *Union of Kalmar*. It broke this *union of crowns* in 1523 with the ascension of *Gustavus I*. He established *Lutheranism* but met deep resistance to most other reform measures he attempted. As Sweden rose to become an important regional power by the mid-16th century it faced constant hostility from Denmark, whose navy controlled the Baltic Sound and demanded payment of *Sound Tolls*. Sweden fought the *Nordic Seven Years' War* (1563–1570) with Denmark, and although it built a navy and even won a naval victory it was defeated on land and forced to pay a large indemnity to regain Älvsborg. In the eastern Baltic, given the decline of both the *Hanse* and the *Teutonic Knights*, the Swedish navy was unchallenged and Sweden established several coastal enclaves. Expansion was furthered, but also complicated, by a dynastic marriage with the Catholic rulers of Poland-Lithuania. King *Sigismund III* was the offspring of that union but was deposed in Sweden in 1589 by *Karl IX*. Sigismund raised a Polish force that was met by a Swedish army that was still semi-feudal, consisting mainly of peasant levies and *mercenaries*. The reformed religion gave Sweden a rallying cry against Catholic Poles and Orthodox Russians, in addition to the ancient Scandinavian urge to war provided by prospects of plunder. During the long war that followed Sigismund's deposition, the economy and army was strained to the limit and Sweden's empire proved more a burden than boon. Out of this baleful experience Karl IX determined to prepare his son, *Gustavus Adolphus*, not just to conquer but also to govern shrewdly a kingdom mobilized for aggressive war. This emphasis on sound administration was crucial, as Sweden had only 1.5 million people, or less than a third the population of England and but one-tenth that of the Crown Lands of the *Habsburgs*.

Sweden was beaten in the *Kalmar War* with Denmark, 1611–1613, which was ended upon the death of Karl IX and by his son bribing the Danes to peace with an indemnity of 1 million riksdalers. Gustavus used the time bought to reform the army and fight off *Muscovy*. In 1621 he went on the offensive and took Riga (September 25), a city three times the size of Stockholm and thereafter a source of rich revenue sustaining his and Sweden's wars. During the 1620s, Gustavus pushed the Poles further out of Livonia and fought Sigismund for possession of Royal Prussia, 1626–1629. *Cardinal Richelieu* then arranged a peace to free Gustavus to intervene in the *Thirty Years' War* (1618–1648). Sweden's intervention in Germany had a huge impact, rolling back earlier Imperial and Catholic advances and securing north Germany against the Habsburgs. Overnight, Sweden became champion of the Protestant cause. However, it lost its great king in battle at *Lützen* in 1632, and thereafter struggled to hold early gains with an army increasingly mercenary rather than national, and a population and economy that strained under the burden of decades of war despite dramatic growth in demands for Sweden's iron ore and fine cannons. The fiscal strain was offset by French subsidies, Livonian revenues, profitable foundries that cast for export Sweden's famed regimental cannon (and cannonballs), and other tools of early modern war for the export markets of northern Europe. From 1635 Sweden remained mired in the German war but no longer directed the grand strategy of the anti-Habsburg alliance—that role was assumed by France. For 16 years Sweden fought on, trying to hold on to at least some of the territorial and political gains Gustavus had earlier made for it in Germany. In the *Peace of Westphalia* (1648) Sweden retained enough German territory to confirm it as a major power, while in the Baltic it remained the unchallenged hegemon for another fifty years. See also *Oxenstierna*; *Swedish Army*.

Suggested Reading: Robert Frost, *The Northern Wars, 1558–1721* (2000); Michael Roberts, *The Swedish Imperial Experience, 1560–1718* (1979).

Swedish Army. The traditional Swedish recruitment system was known as "Gardetal," wherein levies were raised from homesteads rather than a strict head count of male peasants. This was later reversed and replaced by the "Bondetal" (from "Bonde," or peasant), in which levies were made by head count and not homestead. The overall system was known as "Utskrivning" ("Registration"). As with the army of its rival and ofttime enemy Denmark, Swedish soldiers were assigned to farms according to "allotments" ("Indelningswerk"), where they lived and worked as tenant farmers in peacetime. This kept a ready reserve in place while shrewdly displacing costs of military upkeep from the cash-poor crown to the productive countryside. Again paralleling the draft system in Denmark, if Sweden was attacked its kings could call up emergency levies by exercising the "Uppbåd," their constitutional right to raise emergency levies of one man out of every five. This right was strictly defensive, however, and could not be used to raise troops to wage aggressive wars beyond the agreed borders of Sweden.

Beyond peasant infantry the Swedish nobility provided cavalry under the *rusttjänst*, a feudal military obligation to knightly service. If a noble wished to avoid personal riding service to the crown he was required to provide and pay for the upkeep and arming of a substitute. Much of this changed under *Gustavus Adolphus*, who introduced the first true national conscription in Europe (though still exempting the nobility). According to records kept by *Oxenstierna*, in its first year the system raised 15,000 men "but afterwards, when every man had time to think of some evasion, not more than six or seven thousand." Once the Swedish Army entered the *Thirty Years' War* (1618–1648) in Germany and took heavy casualties, Gustavus and later captains resorted to hiring *mercenaries*, which they wrapped as best they could around a core of several thousand Swedish conscripts and noble and retainer cavalry. After 1632 most troops in "Swedish" armies were mercenaries. See also *Alte Feste, Siege of*; *Bärwalde, Treaty of*; *Breitenfeld, First*; *brigade*; *Chemnitz, Battle of*; *Dirshau, Battle of*; *engineers*; *Hamburg, Treaty of*; *Kalmar War*; *Karl IX*; *Kirkholm, Battle of*; *"leather guns"*; *mutiny*; *New Model Army*; *Nördlingen, First Battle of*; *Northern War, First*; *revolution in military affairs*; *"Time of Troubles"*; *Torstensson, Lennart*; *Torstensson's War*; *Zusmarshausen, Battle of*.

Swedish-Muscovite War (1554–1557). See *Ivan IV*; *Muscovy, Grand Duchy of*; *Sweden*.

Swedish-Muscovite War (1590–1595). See *Muscovy, Grand Duchy of*; *Sweden*.

sweeps. Racks of elongated oars. They were usually built into hybrid ship designs that had a high freeboard but were not yet true ships of sail, such as *Great Galleys* or *Guangdongs*.

Sweinfedder. See *swine feathers*.

Swiecino, Battle of (August 17, 1462). This battle is regarded by most military historians of the region and period as the historic turning point in the *War of the Cities* (1454–1466). A Polish army of 2,000 men under Piotr

Dunin sortied from *Danzig* to meet and defeat a force of 2,700 *mercenaries* and *Teutonic Knights*. After this loss the Knights could not hope to prevail or prevent further Polish gains on land and at sea.

swine feathers. Swedish: "Sweinfedder." Sharp stakes or half-pikes driven into the ground at a forward angle by infantry anticipating a cavalry attack, but useful as well in blunting advances by enemy infantry. Elsewhere in Europe these simple but effective battlefield devices were known as "Spanish riders." They could also be used to construct *chevaux de frise*.

Swiss Army. The Swiss operated a remarkably efficient and graded system of conscription from the middle of the 15th century. Rather than using a general head count, local councils of elders in each canton and within every town and village decided who and how many would serve. Recruitment was not usually a problem due to the immediacy of cantonal or village interests at stake in early Swiss wars, and the remarkable ferocity and general bellicosity of the Swiss. The term "conscripts" applied ever more loosely, however, as the mature Swiss Army moved into profitable *mercenary* service for foreign princes, fighting far away from the home cantons.

The recruits were divided into three groups. The "Auszug" were elite units comprised of fit unmarried men under the age of 30 who fought in every war their canton waged. The "Landwehr" were mainly married or older men who served outside their canton in wars authorized by the *Swiss Confederation*. The "Landstrum" was a general levy called up only in time of "national" emergency, and demanded the presence of all Swiss males capable of military service. The Landstrum was essentially a defensive levy, bringing in older and poorer troops to fight alongside elite and well-trained younger men, but it was effective enough to present any potential invader of the home cantons with a bristling wall of many thousands of tough, experienced, and usually merciless veterans. It has been estimated that the cantons could quickly raise a formidable force of over 50,000 skilled fighters in this fashion—a huge army by 13th to 16th-century standards.

The recruits responded to a roll call ("Mannschaftsrodel") which decided who would officer the units, the number of men to be raised in each local area, and what equipment and supplies the guilds or towns needed to provide the troops. Soldiers provided their own weapons, usually, a *halberd*, *pike*, or *crossbow*, and were expected also to provision themselves with a minimum of 5 to 6 days' food supply. This gave Auszug units an unusual mobility and logistical independence which more than once caught a clumsy enemy by surprise and led him to death and desolation. Swiss troops were all well-drilled. They kept an unusually tight formation on the march and also in battle, with a degree of rigor and close-order discipline not seen in European warfare since the fall of the Western Roman Empire and the last legionnaires. For that reason *Machiavelli* called the Swiss the "new Romans of Europe" (he might better have called them the new Spartans). Unlike other medieval or early modern armies the Swiss elected their officers during a muster held in

821

each canton before embarking on a campaign. This ensured that officers knew most of the men under their command. If the army represented the Confederation an overall commander might be chosen, though rivalries among the cantons meant they sometimes fought instead under a council of war that provided collective rather than a central command.

Larger *Swiss squares* assembled under the *Banner* of a canton. Smaller than the Banner was the *"Fähnlein,"* or "small flag" tactical group organized by guild or town and numbering anywhere from 50 to 150 men. Some Fähnlein specialized in missile weapons (crossbow and later *arquebus*) to support the front ranks of pikes. The greatest tactical weakness of the Swiss was their complete lack of *cavalry*. Even when pikemen and halberdiers won a victory with "push of pike" they did not always finish off a beaten enemy because they could not effectively pursue his fleeing troopers. This happened at *Grandson* (1476), where failure to finish off the Burgundians made necessary two more battles: *Morat* (1476) and *Nancy* (1477). The great strategic weakness of the Swiss, which Hans Delbrück noted, was that "it was known that they always wished to return home again soon.... Therefore, if one succeeded in avoiding their attack and outlasting them in unassailable positions, one could hope to win the campaign without risks and without battle." See also *Appenzell Wars*; *Arbedo, Battle of*; *Burgundian-Swiss War*; *Calven, Battle of*; *Dornach, Battle of*; *Frastenz, Battle of*; *Giornico, Battle of*; *Héricourt, Battle of*; *Kappel, Battle of*; *Laupen, Battle of*; *Marignano, Battle of*; *Morgarten, Battle of*; *Näfels, Battle of*; *Novara, Battle of*; *Reisläufer*; *Sempach, Battle of*; *Sempach, Covenant of*; *St. Jacob-en-Birs, Battle of*; *Swabian War*.

> *Some Fähnlein specialized in missile weapons to support the front ranks of pikes.*

Swiss Confederation. "Schweizerische Eidgenossenschaft." This strategically located mountainous state was populated in Roman times by the Helvetii, a Celtic people conquered and assimilated by the Roman Empire. For a thousand years after the fall of Rome the Swiss maintained effective independence in their rural valleys and high mountain towns, fending off would-be conquerors from rude Christian kingdoms of the West and successive waves of pagan invaders. Swiss villages and herds were protected by stone retreats defended by local *militia*. During the 13th century, however, *Habsburg* expansion into neighboring areas threatened the fragmented Swiss cantons and provoked them to a more organized military response. In 1291 the first-known instance occurred of Swiss serving outside their cantonal borders, in Italy. The three "Forest Cantons" of Schwyz, Unterwalden, and Uri, known jointly as the "Waldstätte," formed a military-political alliance called the "Everlasting League" or "Eternal Bond of Brothers." Over the next 25 years the covenant—drafted in Latin and sworn to by oath—formed the core of a confederation of "sworn comrades" ("Eidgenossen") of the Swiss Confederation ("Schweizerische Eidgenossenschaft"), around which other cantons rallied as the threat from Austria grew. From 1332 to 1353, five more cantons joined the

Confederation: Lucerne (1332), Zürich (1351), Zug (1352), Glarus (1352), and Berne (1353).

Like nearly everyone else in Europe in the mid-14th century, the Swiss suffered despair and dislocations from the *Black Death*. This led to wild charges of witchcraft and to violence against Jews. Externally, the Swiss fought to preserve their de facto independence from powerful barons of the *Swabian League* as well as from Habsburg emperors, though they did not yet claim de jure independence from the Empire. The main instrument of their military success was the *Swiss square*. In a series of 14th-century battles, the well-drilled and ferocious "cowherds" of the Alps devastated Austrian and German *knights* at *Morgarten* (1315), *Laupen* (1339), *Sempach* (1386), and *Näfels* (1388). In several of those encounters they used terrain and cunning to even greater effect than their *halberds* and *pikes*.

In 1393 the cantons agreed on the *Covenant of Sempach*, melding their separate armies into a proto-national *Swiss Army*. The next year the Confederacy signed a twenty-year truce with Austria, which left the Swiss effectively independent while nominally still part of the Holy Roman Empire. As a result of the *Appenzell Wars* (1403–1411) the Confederacy solidified alliances with additional cantons. With the introduction of the pike in larger numbers, ordered after the near disaster at *Arbedo* (1422), the Swiss began a century of infantry domination of European warfare. They also placed restrictions on individual foreign military service from 1422. For instance, Zurich forbade its citizens from running away to serve for pay in a foreign army. Collective requests for mercenary service were another matter. The first recorded contract was agreed with Florence in 1424.

From 1436 to 1450, the cantons were wracked by a civil war provoked by territorial ambitions on the part of Zurich that clashed with Confederate interests. In 1444 the Swiss fought off an *Armagnac* invasion at *St. Jacob-en-Birs*. The Peace of Constance (June 12, 1446) set the stage for a final arrangement, and in 1450 general peace was achieved under a strengthened Confederacy. From 1474 to 1477 the cantons waged the *Burgundian-Swiss War* against *Charles the Rash*, during which the Swiss made allies of a number of south German cities and princes also threatened by Burgundian expansion. At first this move was supported by the Emperor and by *Louis XI* of France, but after just a year those monarchs withdrew and left the Swiss to face Burgundy alone. Swiss squares proceeded to destroy the vaunted Burgundian Army at *Héricourt* (1474), *Grandson* (1476), *Morat* (1476), and *Nancy* (1477). The next year, the Swiss defeated the Milanese at *Giornico* (1478). These victories elevated Swiss infantry to the premier league, while fatally damaging Burgundy. The final stage in the Swiss struggle for national independence was the *Swabian War*, which the Swiss won handily in three swift battles all fought in 1499: *Frastenz*, *Calven*, and *Dornach*. After that, Swiss infantry commanded the highest wages from Europe's warring kings and princes.

By the first quarter of the 16th century the Swiss Confederation had expanded to thirteen cantons organized in a loose but effective political, military, and constitutional association. Early in the *Italian Wars* thousands of

Swiss were hired by Duke *Ludovico Sforza* to recover the Duchy of Milan from the French. The first effort was turned back at Novara (1500), but the Swiss took Milan in 1512. They held it nominally for the old duke's teenage son, *Maximilian Sforza*, repelling the French at *Novara* (1513). Swiss rule in Milan was grim: they imposed heavy taxes on the peasantry of Lombardy and billeted 20,000 men on the city. In 1515 *Francis I* invaded the duchy with a reformed French Army, then stunned the military world by smashing Swiss squares and blunting Swiss tactics in a two-day fight at *Marignano* (September 12–13, 1515). Swiss military power was not just curtailed in northern Italy after this defeat outside Milan: the Confederation signed the *"Perpetual Peace"* with France and did not fight the French for another 300 years; nor did it again send a full national army to fight outside the cantonal borders.

In the mid-16th century Switzerland was wracked by religious civil war, with the predominantly Catholic Forest Cantons splitting from Zürich in 1528 in opposition to Protestant radicals in that city who followed the fire-brand teachings of *Zwingli*. The Zürich militias were annihilated at *Kappel* (1531), where a wounded Zwingli was dispatched as he lay on the ground after the battle. During the rest of the century Swiss hired out mainly to the kings of France and the popes, and fought repeatedly and unmercifully against German *Landsknechte* fighting for the Empire. During the *French Civil Wars* (1562–1629) Swiss mercenaries fought on both sides and so impressed the Royalists that they foreswore ever again hiring cheaper, but less reliable, Landsknechte. During the *Eighty Years' War* (1568–1648) and the *Thirty Years' War* (1618–1648), when *The Grisons* were of great strategic importance to Spain and all of Europe was in flames, Swiss mercenaries served in many foreign armies. When the fighting finally stopped in 1648 the *Peace of Westphalia* confirmed the full legal independence of the Swiss Confederation, separating it formally from the Holy Roman Empire. See also *Calvinism*; *Papal States*; *saubannerzug*; *Savonarola, Girolamo*.

Suggested Reading: Frederick William Dame, *History of Switzerland* (2001); Douglas Miller and Gerry Embleton, *The Swiss at War, 1300–1500* (1979); J. L. Murray, *History of Switzerland* (1985).

Swiss square. Swiss *"Reisläufer"* ("Confederates") were propelled to international attention—and well-paid military service—by a series of stunning victories won by tough and merciless *infantry* over the mounted *cavalry* of the Austrians, French, and Burgundians: for nearly 200 years the Swiss were the premier infantry in European warfare, almost never defeated at odds less than 4:1. The Swiss square, or "Haufen" ("heap" or company), did not deploy cavalry on the flanks. This was because Swiss tactics were rooted in alpine valley and forest warfare where cavalry could not develop or operate, and because infantry better reflected the rough egalitarian structure of Swiss society. Swiss soldiers in the 14th century were very lightly armored, usually wearing only an iron skull cap and corselet; they did not carry shields or wear *mail* or *greaves*, and never wore *plate*. This made them far lighter and swifter on the march and on the field than almost any opponent they met, especially lumbering mounted *knights* on oversized *warhorses*. By the 15th century, as lighter Italian *armor* came onto the market and Swiss soldiers took mounds of armor from the bodies of thousands of their dead enemies, armor came into greater use in Swiss warfare. Even so, generally only the front ranks wore plate: key to the Swiss way of war remained mobility and maneuver and this spoke against weighing down the Haufen with iron.

Early Swiss squares were made up mostly of halberdiers and axemen with some pikemen for protection, with crossbowmen and arquebusiers in support. The proportion of pikemen grew with time, but slowly. After a small Swiss army was nearly wiped out at *Arbedo* in 1422, the *Swiss Confederation* ordered that squares must comprise one-fifth crossbowmen and arquebusiers, one-fifth pikemen, and three-fifths halberdiers. The number of pikemen crested at about one-quarter of each square late in the 15th century. Swiss troops marched in sensible columns but as they approached the field of battle they quickly switched to parallel ranks making up three compact squares: the "Vorhut," or van; the "Gewalthut" (or "Gewalthaufen") at the center; and the "Nachhut," or rearmost square. The Vorhut had the majority of missile troops. The Gewalthut was the largest square. Its job was *shock* and push of *pike*, and it usually also protected the senior commanders. The Nachhut was the smallest but most flexible of the three squares. It moved behind the van in support of the main attack but could deploy to either side in a flank attack should the van become locked in close combat at the center.

This tripartite division allowed the Swiss to either feint or attack from either flank and to perform other complex maneuvers in the midst of battle, including complete encirclement and attacking from the rear simultaneously with a flank or frontal assault. The Vorhut might pin the enemy center, for instance, while the other two squares hit him from less well-protected angles (a tactic also used to great effect 500 years later by the Zulu). Or the Vorhut and the Gewalthut might attack in echelon with the Nachhut uncommitted and held in reserve until a decisive moment was reached. The Swiss also sometimes deployed a *Forlorn Hope* to skirmish in front of the Vorhut and act as a decoy or make minor feints. If cut off and isolated, the Swiss would form a true square with four ranks of pikes on every side with missile troops (including axemen, as some battleaxes were thrown rather than swung) in the middle. From there darts, stones, quarrels, axes, and shot were hurled toward the enemy. The front rank of pikemen would kneel with their pikes held fairly level and low; the next rank planted their pikes in the style of boar hunters, at an upward angle secured by the right foot; the third rank held their pikes level at waist height; the fourth rank held their pikes at shoulder height. This formed a defensive wall that was impenetrable by cavalry or infantry, with lethal blades set to contact the enemy at every level: gut, chest, and face. In the center, a stand of protective axemen and swordsmen defended the *Banner* and *Fähnlein*.

In attack, the Swiss deployed three front ranks presenting a hedge of iron-tipped pikes held at the level, behind which additional pikemen trotted with weapons held upright and one hand on the shoulder of the man in front, ready to fill in any gaps in the attacking lines caused by enemy success. Next came halberdiers supported by crossbowmen. The first three ranks leveled pikes at shoulder height (modern experiments confirm that employing pikes in the fourth or fifth rank threatened men of the first ranks far more than the enemy). Then the whole "square," which might be 30 or more ranks wide and 60 files deep, set off upon a shouted command or a signal from an alpine war horn. A disciplined and compact mass of 1,500–2,000 men (some later squares reached 10,000 or more) kept a tight but highly mobile and flexible formation as they moved toward the enemy. The square held shape even as the command was given for a fast trot, a pace maintained to the beat of drums or practiced chants. About 50 yards away the whole square accelerated to full battle speed and its mass slammed into the enemy, 18-foot pikes at chest or face height, punching through armor into flesh. The number of files provided the "weight" that gave this infantry charge real "shock."

The lead ranks of pikes smashed nearly irresistibly into any standing enemy, infantry or cavalry. As enemy front lines collapsed and went under foot with the momentum of the impact, follow-on "push of pike" resulted from 50 or 60 rear ranks pushing hard on the backs of the men in front. The whole square might undulate as it rose over the slick bodies of enemy (and friendly) dead, man or horse. Enemy wounded emerging from the rear of the square were hacked to death without mercy by halberdiers and axemen. If the shock of the initial charge did not break the enemy frontage but only moved him back, halberdiers left the ranks to curl around and slash at the enemy, gashing legs and horses and pulling *men-at-arms* from mounts or out of files to be finished off by a quick throat-cutting or a dirk plunged into an unprotected armpit or groin. While this was happening shot and quarrels whistled overheard, fired at point-blank range into the faces of the enemy by skilled crossbowmen at the rear and center (the national legend of William Tell, which dates to the early 14th century, had some basis in the fact of Swiss skill with missile weapons). If victory still eluded, the Vorhut and Nachhut would leave reserve positions to reinforce the Gewalthut and attack into the enemy flanks or rear.

> *The lead ranks of pikes smashed nearly irresistibly into any standing enemy, infantry or cavalry.*

On the march as on the battlefield, the Swiss appeared as moving groves that bristled with the promise of death. Their great Banners and lesser *flags* announced the arrival of men of terrible resolve and reputation. So fearsome and well-deserved was the Swiss reputation for killing prisoners and for mutilation, in 1444 a formal regulation was passed by the cantons forbidding soldiers from anymore cutting out the hearts of dead enemies as trophies (a fairly common practice of the Swiss). As the renown of the military effectiveness of Swiss soldiers grew after the great victories over Austria and Burgundy, so did fear, admiration, and ultimately emulation. For the next four decades those who could afford to do so hired Swiss mercenaries before heading into battle. Those who could not pay the price (a common lament was "pas d'argent, pas de Suisses," or "no money, no Swiss"), or whom the Swiss would not serve for other reasons, imitated their formations and tactics as best they could. The most famous mimics, with whom the Swiss shared an intense mutual and murderous hatred, were the German *Landsknechte*. See also *Appenzell Wars*; *caracole*; *Grandson, Battle of*; *La Bicocca, Battle of*; *Laupen, Battle of*; *Marignano, Battle of*; *Morat, Battle of*; *Morgarten, Battle of*; *Näfels, Battle of*; *Nancy, Battle of*; *Sempach, Battle of*; *St. Jacob-en-Birs, Battle of*; *Swabian War*; *Thirty Years' War*.

swivel gun. Small to mid-sized (up to six feet long) breech-loading cannon firing *grapeshot* or some other *canister shot* in an anti-personnel role. They were deployed as secondary artillery on *galleys* or on the high *castles* of roundships from where they could fire down onto the enemy's deck. The Chinese directly copied Portuguese swivel guns, which they called "Javanese guns" because they thought Portugal might be located near Java. Later, these models evolved in China into *folangji*. The Chinese also blended the swivel gun and *musket* to make the *child-mother gun*. See also *port piece*; *sling*; *verso*.

Sword Brethren. See *Livonian Order*; *Teutonic Knights*.

sword hunts. See *Toyotomi Hideyoshi*.

swords. Throughout this period personal blade weapons remained important on the battlefield, for self-defense in civilian life, and for sorting out matters of "honor" between gentlemen. Starting in the 9th century, the short "gladius" style inherited by Europe from Rome was displaced by swords with thinned, flattened, and tapered blades. This helped balance, reduced weight (to about 2½ pounds), and improved handling and fighting capabilities. The flat blade also took a better cutting edge, which was more useful against standard *mail*. A flat double-edged sword thus became the signature weapon of the medieval *knight*. A medieval swordmaker might take as long as 200–250 hours to finish one blade, raising the price of this weapon beyond the reach of any but the high nobility and their *men-at-arms*. Early medieval swords were made from pattern-welded steel and forged with a central groove which reduced metal content and weight without affecting strength. The blade was tapered to the hilt, improving balance and blade speed. For over 500 years, until about 1350, medieval European swords were mostly unchanged in appearance or manufacturing technique. As *plate armor* replaced mail and stabbing rather than slashing became the preferred use of blades against other armored men, knightly swords were thinned and tapered to a sharp thrusting point, usually reinforced with additional metal needed to punch through iron plate.

Swords played an enormous role in the mystique of the knight and the mores, ceremonies, and mystic symbolism of *chivalry*. Like later great *bombards*, great swords were named and passed down as prized heirlooms to successor generations. Or they were buried in a kingly grave with their royal owner. On the other hand, many were hurled into streams or lakes: the story of the watery origin of King Arthur's magical sword "Excalibur" probably had a basis in the widespread medieval practice of casting swords into rivers or lakes once their owner died (though why this was done remains a mystery). For Crusaders, the sword's importance was accentuated by coincidental resemblance to the cross, prime symbol of every Christian holy warrior. In Iberia, "Toledo steel" became synonymous with the *Reconquista*.

The medieval Japanese sword is today often popularly depicted as the signature weapon of a *samurai*, but in fact it was initially his secondary weapon: the samurai began as mounted archers first and swordsmen second. Still, in Japan as in Europe the sword achieved a mystique for warriors and in literature and legend that no other weapon came close to equaling. It was the symbol of a samurai's social status, the means by which he took heads ("kubi jikken") and won battlefield promotion, and the instrument of his ritual suicide should he decide or be ordered to perform seppuku. The medieval Japanese sword is rightly and universally admired for its supreme craftsmanship and beauty. There were many styles, including the curved "katana" that a samurai often paired with an 18 to 24 inch "wakizashi"; the single-edged "kogatana" ("small blade"); the still smaller "Tanto" (a *dagger*); and various "Daisho" pairs of large and small weapons worn together in combinations of subtle symbolism and meaning. Japanese swords are also classed by age. The oldest were "jokoto" ("ancient swords") dating to c.795. Medieval swords might be classed as "koto" ("old swords"), made between c.795 and 1596. The climax of the *Unification Wars* saw manufacture of "shinto" ("new swords") between c.1596 and 1624. Swords made in the 14th–16th centuries remain among the most highly regarded. Another typology referred not to date of forging but to the importance of warriors in Japanese society. "Bushi" ("warrior") era swords dated to the sharp rise of samurai warfare in the 10th century. Bushi swords were elegant and exceptionally keenly edged, sharper and far more refined than any contemporary European sword. The 12th century saw "Kamakura" period swords which reached so refined a peak of craftsmanship of forging and folding and refolding that the standard was set for all subsequent models. Most "national treasure" swords in Japanese museums date to the competing schools of master smiths of the Kamakura period, each of which put a unique signature on his swords by using local iron and sand in their making.

Ottoman swords and knives were mostly of Iranian, not Arab, origin. The "kiliç" was the most common blade. It was only slightly curved and did not taper to a point. The "acemi kiliç" was a curved, Iranian-origin saber. The Ottomans also used a sword with a reverse curve to the blade, the famous "yatağan," better known in the West as the "Turkish sword." It is worth noting that it was the bow, of all types, that was replaced by firearms and not the sword. In Japan, in the Middle East, in India, China, and Europe, the sword survived on the battlefield alongside the *musket* long after *longbows* and *crossbows* disappeared. As a weapon of choice of the European officer class the sword survived into the early 19th century; as a personal weapon of Japanese officers of samurai descent or pretension it survived into the mid-20th century, where officer swords were put to horrific use in World War II. The sword is still used in commissioning ceremonies of several modern armies, including the U.S. Marine Corps. See also *claymore*; *counter-guard*; *falchion*; *pata*; *silahdars*.

Suggested Reading: R. E. Oakeshott, *The Sword in the Age of Chivalry* (1964).

Syria. See *Bedouin*; *caliph*; *Crusades*; *Islam*; *Mamlūks*; *Mongols*; *Ottoman Empire*; *Timur*.

Szigetvár, Siege of (1566). See *Suleiman I.*

szlachta. The noble classes of Poland-Lithuania. In the 16th century they deepened the enserfment of Polish-Lithuanian and Ukrainian peasants. In 1505 they deprived towns of voting rights in the *Sejm*. In 1573 they gained the right to elect the monarch, severely limiting his ability to fund or wage war.

T

tabard. An outer garment worn by a knight over his armor, usually bearing the coat of arms of his liege lord. Alternately, the uniform of a *herald*, announcing his office and diplomatic immunity.

tabor. Jan Žižka, the Hussite general and military innovator, developed a horse-drawn mobile fort known for the base camp ("tabor") formed by the wagons in which Hussite families traveled with their warrior menfolk. These mobile towns of armed Hussites lent the name "Tabori" to the poorer, radical faction of the movement and to the town of Tabor where their main camp was located. See also *Bohemian Brethren*; *gunpowder weapons*; *Hussite Wars*; *Wagenburg*.

Taborites. See *Hus, Jan*; *Hussite Wars*; *tabor*; *Wagenburg*.

tackle. Cable, rope, pulleys, blocks, and other equipment necessary to raise, lower, and control *sails*.

tactics. At sea, see *broadside*; *castles, on ships*; *firing on the roll*; *galley*; *galleon*; *Invincible Armada*; *Lepanto, Battle of*; *longship*; *piracy*; *privateer*; *Sluys, Battle of*; *weather gauge*. On land, see *artillery*; *ashigaru*; *battle (2)*; *Berbers*; *caracole*; *castles, on land*; *cavalry*; *chevauchée*; *couched lance*; *drill*; *Edward III*; *fortification*; *Granada*; *Gustavus II Adolphus*; *Hussite Wars*; *heavy cavalry*; *infantry*; *Janissary Corps*; *karr-wa-farr*; *knight*; *light cavalry*; *logistics*; *Maurits of Nassau*; *mining*; *Mongols*; *muskets*; *rabito*; *raiding*; *razzia*; *ribat*; *samurai*; *siege warfare*; *"skulking way of war"*; *spiking*; *Swiss square*; *tercio*; *Tilly, Count Johann Tserclaes*; *Wagenburg*; *Wallenstein, Albrecht von*; *warhorses*.

taifa **states.** The dozens of small Muslim city-states which succeeded the Umayyad Caliphate in *al-Andalus* following the death of Caliph Abd al-Malik in 1008. They were well-established against each other by 1031 but lost all military initiative to the Christian *Reconquista* within a few years. The Umayyads employed Berber tribesmen as soldiers but increasingly used northern and western European military slaves. These troops were captured as boys, castrated, and trained as *mamlūks*. The supply of European slaves dried up, however, as the *Teutonic Knights* expanded into the slave-bearing regions of Slavic central and eastern Europe. Since the taifa were reluctant to employ politically unreliable North African Berber warriors as replacements, and since their loss of land shrank the basis of the *itqa* system of feudal recruitment, the taifa states steadily shrank and were forced into a consistently defensive posture against Christian raids and the Reconquista. The Almoravids, fundamentalist Berbers from North Africa, intervened at the invitation of some taifa emirs in the early 12th century. A Castilian army was defeated at Badajoz. By 1111 the Almoravids overran almost all taifa as well, which they then ruled from Córdoba. A second set of 14 taifa states emerged from 1144 to 1146 as Muslim fragmentation returned due to an Almohad challenge to the Almoravids in North Africa that spilled over into Iberia. See also *rabito*; *ribat*.

taille. A tax levied annually on land in France in two forms: one on all subjects (this was limited to a few small areas) and one on commoners alone—clergy and nobles were exempt from most taxation, as were some professions and whole towns. It was the only direct tax in the French system and provided exceptional revenues. This made France's kings less dependent than other monarchs on vagaries of revenues drawn from customs duties or special taxes such as the Spanish *alcabala*. The burden of the *Italian Wars* (1494–1559) forced a rise in the taille and expansion of the *taillon* to the countryside.

taillon. An older French tax that, until 1555, was confined to walled towns to cover the cost of billeting and feeding the king's men. In 1555 it was extended to the peasantry by *Henri II*, in order to pay for his increasingly expensive foreign wars (notably in Italy).

Taiwan. The island of Taiwan, or Formosa ("Ilha Formosa" or "Beautiful Isle") as the Portuguese called it, was peopled by Polynesian aborigines before 1500. They fiercely defended themselves, to the degree their primitive military capabilities permitted, as waves of different invaders arrived in the 16th century. Settlement from China was discouraged by the fact that *wakō* (pirates) settled in Taiwan after 1567, from where they preyed on shipping in the Taiwan Strait and East China Sea into the late 17th century. The Ming forced populations away from the Chinese coast to prevent interchange with wakō or emigration to Taiwan. The Dutch set up a base in Taiwan (Fort Zeelandia) from 1624 to 1662, expelling a small Spanish force in 1626. The Dutch were expelled by a Ming filibusterer, "Koxinga" (Zheng Chengong), in 1662.

Talbot, John (c.1385–1453). 1st Earl of Shrewsbury. He made his reputation in Ireland where he crushed a rebellion and twice served in the military administration. He achieved wider fame during the *Hundred Years' War* (1337–1453). He was present when *Jeanne d'Arc* lifted the siege of Orléans in 1429. "The Maid" took him prisoner when she bested the English at Patay (1429). At *Castillon* (1453), in his seventies, he led an English army into an artillery trap and to disaster. He was pulled from his horse and hacked to death by the French. Shakespeare froze him in heroic pose in *Henry VI, Part 1*, act 4, scene 6.

Tamerlane. See *Timur*.

Tangier. In 1437 the Portuguese *Order of Aviz* and the *Knights of Christ* tried unsuccessfully to conquer this Moroccan fortress city, losing with heavy casualties to the defending Moors. Tangier was attacked again in 1463 and 1464. The Marind dynasty in Fez collapsed in 1471, when a Portuguese assault with an army of 30,000 under *Alfonso V* ("The African") took the city. Further assaults were delayed by Portugal's intervention in a civil war in Castile that broke out over the succession and *union of crowns* of Castile and Aragon surrounding the marriage of *Ferdinand and Isabella*.

tanko. See *armor*.

Tannenberg, Battle of (July 15, 1410). The *Teutonic Knights* were decisively defeated by the *Jagiello* king of Poland-Lithuania, Ladislas (Wladyslaw) II, at the head of a traditional Polish-Lithuanian army of noble light horse and medium *hussars*, supplemented by Bohemian and German mercenaries. Some allied *Cossacks* and *Tatars* were led by *Jan Žižka*. The Polish army numbered 150,000 men. It faced 80,000 enemy—mercenaries, auxiliaries, and volunteers, led by several hundred Sword Brethren. The Knights were all traditional *heavy horse*. Their retainers had few firearms, though some carried steel crossbows. Before the battle each side sang Christian hymns, then the Knights charged, crying out: "Gott mit uns!" They broke the Polish left and damaged the right, but the center held while Žižka rallied the Cossacks and Tatars. The Brethren charged again and again but could not catch the lighter horse of their enemy. With the larger German mounts blown, the fleeter ponies of the Tatars and Cossacks encircled them, Polish and mercenary infantry closed in, and slaughter with axe and sword commenced. About 205 Knights, including the Hochmeister and many marshals, along with 18,000 other Germans were killed. Another 14,000 were taken captive, with many summarily beheaded after the battle. Tannenberg cost so many casualties that the Teutonic Knights' military power went into terminal decline. Their bloody Baltic crusade was finally over.

Tarasbüchsen. Czech: "tarasnice." Medium-caliber 14th-century guns mounted on stands. The *Hussites* used them in their *Wagenburgs*.

Tard-Avisés. "Latecomers." A self-descriptive term by peasants who rose in 1594 in several areas of southwest France. It referenced their earlier reluctance to arm in self-defense against the economic deprivations, looting by soldiers, and high taxation caused by the *French Civil Wars* (1562–1629). These had been fought mainly by the urban classes, among whom the clergy and nobility were exempt from most taxation. The Tard-Avisés rose for the usual reasons of peasant grievance, but notably attacked all soldiers and nobles of both confessions. The noble and bourgeois pejorative for these peasant rebels was "Croquants," or country bumpkins. Bands ranged in size from 2,000 to 10,000 armed peasants, but more importantly, swelled to as many as 40,000 in Périgord in May 1594. *Henri IV* wisely appeased them with words and by finally bringing peace to France. Historian Mack Holt has argued that their uprising convinced Henri and the nobility of the urgent social need to make peace. See also *Bonnets Rouges*; *Jacquerie*; *Razats*.

Suggested Reading: Mack Holt, *The French Wars of Religion, 1562–1629* (1995).

targe. A large flat shield.

targhieri. Italian infantry of the late 15th century bearing heavy shields (*targe*) with which they covered crossbowmen and arquebusiers while they reloaded their slow rate-of-fire weapons.

tarides. A flat-bottomed, long-distance oared transport used to carry from 25 to 40 cavalry mounts. Their great advantage over round-bottomed sailing ships, which could carry 100 or more horses, was that they were amphibian: their horse cargo could be unloaded directly onto a beach where a round-bottomed ship needed a secure harbor. See also *cog*.

tarpaulin. In the Elizabethan navy, an officer who learned his trade in the merchant marine; hence, a person of low social rank, not a "gentleman officer."

Tartaglia, Niccolò (c.1499–1557). Italian mathematician and "father of ballistic science." He was nearly killed by French troops who lacerated his cheeks and jaw with deep saber cuts when they captured his home city of Brescia in 1512, during the *Italian Wars* (1494–1559). His reputation as a mathematician came with victory in a contest to solve cubic equations algebraically. He made a great impact on military affairs when he published a paper on the application of mathematics to artillery fire in which he outlined a scientific understanding of ballistics and published the first-ever firing tables. He is best remembered for "Tartaglia's theorem," which proved that the trajectory of a projectile is always a curved line, rather than the straight line-to-target that the naked eye perceived. He thereby proved that the maximum range of a cannonball at any speed is obtained by firing at an elevation of 45°. Before that artillerists falsely believed that their cannonballs flew in a straight line after leaving the barrel, an error which often led gunners to fire short or position the guns dangerously close to the enemy. Tartaglia also invented the *gunner's quadrant* by which a master gunner calculated and set the elevation of the barrel to meet the desired range according to a preset table divided into degrees, and indicated by a plumb line. Finally, he calculated maximum effective ranges for several known artillery types. For all that, he worried about the moral effects of applying science to the art of war, once destroying his manuscript on projectiles to prevent its application in war. However, when Italy was threatened by the Ottomans he set aside his scruples and published *Nuova Scientia* (1537), which was followed by other works on military science in the 1540s.

Tartars. See *Tatars.*

tassets. Plates of metal that protected the upper thighs and hung over the upper *cuisses.* They were often attached with "leathers" to the *fauld* that protected the waist.

tatami. See *armor.*

Tatars. A Central Asian Turkic people. The term was often corrupted to "Tartar." It referred to any of several groups of steppe nomads including *Turks* (by the Russians) and *Mongols* (by the Chinese). The Tatars were in fact a blend of Mongol and Turkic horse peoples who overran the southern steppes, the Caucasus, and large sections of Anatolia and the Arab Middle East. They established Khanates in Astrakhan, Kazan, and the Crimea and waged war along the southern border of Muscovy for several centuries, marauding for booty and slaves. A Tatar army took Baghdad in 1393 and temporarily overran other parts of the eastern Ottoman Empire. Another horde

> *Tatars . . . killed the very old and very young, and dragged away thousands to be sold into Ottoman slavery . . .*

sacked Aleppo, Damascus, and Baghdad on orders of *Timur*, then captured *Bayezid I* after crushing an Ottoman army at *Ankara* (1402). After the collapse of the Timurids, the Tatars came to terms with the Ottomans and into the 18th century counted the Ottoman sultan alternately as overlord and ally in protracted Tatar wars with Poland and Russia. Some Tatars fought for the Poles against the *Teutonic Knights* during the *War of the Cities* (1454–1466).

Tatars raided deep into the "great wheat field" of Ukraine, Poland-Lithuania, and southern Muscovy almost annually in the early 16th century. Raiders reached Brest-Litovsk (1500), Minsk (1505), and Wilno (1510). They pillaged over an immense sweep of land, killed the very old and very young, and dragged away thousands to be sold into Ottoman slavery at Kaffa in the Crimea, the city Ukrainians called "vampire." Muscovy sent punitive raids south during the reign of *Ivan IV* ("The Terrible"). A Tatar army sacked Moscow in 1571 during the chaos of Ivan's *Oprichnina*. Another horde repeated the feat in 1591. From 1450 to 1650, over 160 sizeable Tatar raids were recorded in Ukraine alone. Tatar mobility meant they remained extremely dangerous to, and independent of, Russia into the 18th century. The distance to the Khanate and its strategic location on the lower Dnieper, then un-navigable below the rapids, cancelled out the Muscovite advantage in artillery. Still, the Tatars needed protection from increasing Muscovite aggression and expansion and therefore eventually accepted vassalage to the Ottomans.

Large Tatar armies thus accompanied the Ottomans in campaigns in the Balkans and Hungary during the 16th–17th centuries. Normal wartime contingents numbered from 30,000 to 40,000. A minimum of 72,000 rode whenever the han led the Tatars personally. On rare occasions, over 100,000 Tatars rode with the Ottomans. Tatar light cavalry was deployed to the front of Ottoman troops to serve as scouts and skirmishers, in a scythe-like formation that cut ahead of the main force. They fought not for pay but for a share in plunder and always under their own commanders. Yet, plunder was not the main tactical aim of this flying wedge of wild horsemen operating 10–15 kilometers ahead of the Ottoman army. Once the latter moved beyond the boundaries of the Empire and its "menzil-hane" system of supply depots, the Tatars acted primarily as foragers, gathering critical food and fodder while denying both to the enemy. Still, fighting under separate commands and employing different tactical styles meant that Tatar relations with Ottoman troops were usually marked by mutual distrust. On several occasions, Ottoman intervention in the Crimea itself deposed the reigning han and set back relations for years. See also *akincis*; *soyughal*.

tate. A large, wooden Japanese shield used to protect infantry against the mounted archers (*samurai*) who dominated medieval and early modern Japanese warfare.

taxes. See *Abbas I*; *Akbar*; *alcabala*; *annates*; *arrière-ban*; *askeri*; *avariz*; *Báthory, Stefan*; *bedel-i nüzul*; *bellum se ipse alet*; *Buenos Aires*; *Byzantine Empire*; *carbiniers*; *castles, on land*; *Catalonia, Revolt of*; *Charles I, of England*; *chevauchée*; *Chinese armies*; *club men*; *contributions*; *convoy*; *Cortés, Hernán*; *cruzada*; *Dutch Army*; *Edict of Nantes*; *Edict of Saint-Germain-en-Laye*; *Eighty Years' War*; *English Civil Wars*; *Estates*; *expulsion of the Jews*; *feudalism*; *France*; *French Civil Wars*; *fusiliers de taille*; *German Peasant War*; *Henri III, of France*; *Huguenots*; *Hundred Years' War*; *Imperial Diet*; *Islam*; *Italy*; *Jacquerie*; *jizya*; *jus pacis et belli*; *Maxmilian I*; *Netherlands*; *new monarchies*; *Novara, Battle of*; *Olivares, conde-duque de*; *Ottoman Empire*; *Ottoman warfare*; *Polish Army*; *"Poor Conrad" revolt*; *Portugal*; *printing*; *Raya*; *Razats*; *Richelieu, Cardinal Armand Jean du Plessis de*; *Scottish Wars*; *servitium debitum*; *servitor classes*; *standing army*; *ship money*; *strel'sty*; *taille*; *taillon*; *Tard-Avisés*; *Tenth Penny*; *timariots*; *Turks*; *war chest*; *war finance*; *War of the Cities*; *zakat*.

teamsters. Civilian drivers of ox, mule, or horse teams contracted by an army to haul its *artillery* and supply wagons. Teamsters were not considered or counted as part of the regular army. As a result, they seldom exposed themselves or their harness and teams to danger; instead, they ran away at its first sign. As *standing armies* were founded, permanent teamster units were formed and paid soldiers' wages.

technology and war. The pace of technological change in medieval warfare in Europe, as elsewhere, was exceptionally slow. Important changes included a shift to stone or brick over wood in castle building and city fortification, improvements in manufacturing techniques of armor, changes in material and design of crossbows, and advances in shipbuilding and navigation. Only toward the end of the period were the revolutionary effects of gunpowder artillery and firearms felt with major advances in ballistics, chemistry, and casting. Spinoffs from military activity occurred in such diverse fields as cartography, cartage, engineering, metallurgy, mechanics, shipbuilding, and transportation. There can be no doubt that military technology advanced importantly and that in some measure it contributed to shaping what has been widely called the *revolution in military affairs*. Yet, it is probably a mistake to see technology as the principal cause of enormous historical events or the essential cause of most medieval or early modern military victories and defeats. This is especially a problem with explanations of the rise of *heavy cavalry* in Europe that point to the stirrup and lance as the determinant of the entire socio-military system of *feudalism*. An even greater problem inheres in the concept of *gunpowder empires*, which purports to explain the creation of the early modern world's greatest states with a one-size-fits-all technological explanation centered on the rate of adoption and adaptation to guns.

For one thing, new military technologies were introduced only slowly, too slowly to have had decisive effects that favored one party over another in most cases. In addition, societies attacked with new weapons for the first time usually adapted their own tactics and weapons quickly, in some cases (such as the *Aztec Empire*, that lost for other reasons) within just months of the first encounter rather than years or decades. Finally, new military technology was often unreliable: ineffectiveness of new weapons, especially early guns, and not just military conservatism slowed adoption rates. Too much is also made of differential rates of absorption of military technology by warring societies. "Diffusion" of military manufacturing methods was actually quite rapid in most cases as *renegades* migrated to foreign courts and military markets, carrying with them materials, plans, and expertise. Complex social, political, and fiscal causes best explain this or that society's failure to adjust to new military technology. Military conservatism, while a genuine problem for several societies, was usually overcome by the most persistent fact of military history: defeat is the clearest instructor of the need to change and war the harshest of teachers. On related issues, see also: *artillery*; *castles, on land*; *cavalry*; *fortification*; *infantry*; *galley*; *gunpowder weapons*; *Inca Empire*; *logistics*; *Mamlūks*; *Ostend, Siege of*; *Ottoman warfare*; *siege warfare*; *Unification Wars*; *weapons*.

Suggested Reading: Martin van Creveld, *Technology and War* (1989); M. Duffy, *The Military Revolution and the State, 1500–1800* (1980); J.F.C. Fuller, *Armaments and History* (1946); A. al-Hassan and D. Hill, *Islamic Technology* (1986); D. Headrich, *Tools of Empire* (1981); Maurice Keen, *Medieval Warfare* (1999); John A. Lynn, ed., *Tools of War: Instruments, Ideas, and Institutions of Warfare, 1445–1871* (1990); Joel Moykr, *Twenty-Five Centuries of Technological Change* (1990); J. Needham et al., *Military Technology* (1986).

Templars. See *Knights Templar*.

tenaille. A defensive position for infantry built into the dry ditch before the *curtain wall*.

tenere in dominico. See *feudalism*.

tenere in servitio. See *feudalism*; *servitor classes*.

ten-eyed gun. A 16th-century Chinese invention that loaded ten cartridges and bullets into a metal tube, each with a separate touch hole. Starting from one end, the gunner fired five times, then reversed his grip and fired the next set of five. Its accuracy must be doubted, but not its ingenuity. This was part of a general trend in Chinese firearms experimentation with multi-shot or multi-barreled weapons. Some Chinese guns had as many as 36 barrels. See also *child-mother gun*; *winged-tiger gun*.

Tennoji, Battle of (1615). See *Osaka Castle, Siege of*.

Tenochtitlán, First Siege of (June 24–30, 1520). The capital of the *Aztec Empire* was far larger than most European cities at over 240,000 souls, many tens of thousands of them elite Aztec warriors. Moral arrogance or reckless stupidity or military necessity, or more likely all three reasons, led *Hernán Cortés* to depart Tenochtitlán for the coast with most of his small band of *conquistadores*, leaving just 100 Spaniards and a few hundred Tlaxcalan warriors behind under *Pedro de Alvarado*. He was ordered to hold the palace and temple complex in the center of Tenochtitlán where whole rooms already had been filled with plundered gold. Cortés thought his men and the gold were safe as he also left them holding a prize prisoner, *Moctezuma*. Meanwhile, he hurried to Vera Cruz to stave off a rival force of Spanish who had arrived from Cuba, led by Pánfilo de Narváez. After Cortés killed or wounded the leaders in a brief skirmish, the rest were persuaded to join his expedition, bringing his force to over 1,200 conquistadores. The new men also brought welcome supplies of horses, guns, powder, and shot. In the two months Cortés was away, Alvarado kept busy torturing and massacring several thousand Tenochtitlán nobles and priests in a maniacal search for yet more gold. He was clearly influenced by Cortés' example, which earlier seemed to bring good effects from killing Aztec nobles, and he may have been acting under orders. In any case, the Spanish murders, cruelty, and avarice had the opposite effect to that intended. Aztec rage was compounded by erection by Spanish priests of a large crucifix atop the Great Temple and conduct of Christian worship in full view of the city population below. This provoked the Aztecs to depose Moctezuma and purge the strangers from their city.

Indian allies along the shore of Lake Texcoco warned Cortés not to re-enter Tenochtitlán, but he went in to secure the plundered gold that Alvarado guarded. Aztec commanders let him into the city then closed the causeways and trapped the Spanish and Tlaxcalans inside, surrounding them with tens of thousands of angry Aztec warriors intent on blood revenge. From June 24 to 30, 1520, the Spanish and 3,000 allied Tlaxcalan warriors were besieged inside Tenochtitlán. Several sorties were assayed by crossbowmen and arquebusiers and the small unit of Spanish cavalry, but each was driven back. Aztec warriors at first were easily killed in large numbers, as too often they tried to trip and capture the Spaniards rather than swarming and killing them. Also, their obsidian-edged cutting weapons were not effective against Spanish plate armor and they had no reply to mounted lancers. But they soon learned to strike to kill with slings, *atlatl*, and large stones hurled from nearby temples. During the fighting Moctezuma was killed, possibly by the Spanish but perhaps by errant Aztec missiles.

Cortés ordered a set of *manteletes* built to try to break out under their cover. The manteletes provided protection for new sorties that each killed hundreds of Aztecs. Cortés also led attacks against secondary temples where his men slashed Aztec priests to death and overturned sacrificial tables, again demonstrating the physical triumph of their god over the weak gods of the Aztecs. In the closed confines of the main palace and temple, however, Spanish advantages in cavalry and cannon disappeared and casualties rose. The Spanish might kill thousands of Aztec warriors to their own dozens of dead, but they were sure to lose any fight ultimately decided by attrition. Cortés therefore decided to try to break out at night using a mobile bridge he had built to cross gaps cut by the Aztecs in the causeway. The horses were loaded with gold, their hooves bagged to muffle the sound of iron shoes clanging on paving stones, and the party set off on what became known as the "*Noche Triste*" or "Night of Sorrow" (June 30, 1520). Cortés was looking to escape, not to fight or conquer the inhabitants of a huge city where every man, woman, and child longed for his death.

> *During the fighting Moctezuma was killed ... perhaps by errant Aztec missiles.*

At first the stealthy escape went well. The leading Spanish and Tlaxcalans used the portable bridges to cross three out of four canals bisecting the causeway. Then they were spotted by chance by women on the shore: since the Aztecs did not usually fight at night they had not posted sentries, but women doing domestic work raised the alarm. Many Spaniards now learned that they were overly burdened with the weight of their greed, in the form of gold piled on top of their armor and on the horses. Hundreds of war canoes and thousands of Aztec warriors swarmed toward them. In a running fight that may have lasted six hours, disciplined Spanish formations were broken and half the conquistadores killed by stones or other missiles, drowned in their heavy armor, or bound and carried off to be ritually sacrificed. The last Spaniards and Tlaxcalans who escaped only did so because the bodies of their comrades and of Aztec dead filled in the last gap in the causeway, and they ran across. Cortés and half his men, along with a few hundred Tlaxcalans, fought their way to shore. Some 200 Spaniards and many more hundreds of

Tlaxcalans held out for a few days inside Tenochtitlán before succumbing to death or worse: capture, flaying alive, and ritual sacrifice. Most of the gold stolen earlier lay at the bottom of Lake Texcoco, along with Spanish heavy cannon. For years, courts in Spain heard cases over who was at fault for the shame, death, and worst military defeat suffered to that date by a European army in the Americas.

Tenochtitlán, Second Siege of (April 28–August 13, 1521). *Hernán Cortés* returned to Tenochtitlán with an enlarged force of *conquistadores* and much more important, large numbers of allied Mesoamerican warriors who came to complete what the Spanish had started but could not finish on their own. Cortés first systematically dismantled the supports of the *Aztec Empire*, forging alliances with vassal city-states around the interconnected lakes of the Central Valley. Tepeca and Cholula joined the Spanish alliance. Then, in a key event, Tetzcoco—on the eastern side of Lake Texcoco—long an ally of Tenochtitlán, switched sides. This gave the attackers the critical forward base they needed. Some Tetzcoco nobles sensed the end was near for Aztec hegemony; others hoped to replace their own king in the wake of the chaos to come. In short, as the brutal authoritarianism of the Aztecs collapsed, older traditions of fierce internal political rivalry among the noble classes and of independence of the city-states of the Central Valley reemerged. The Spanish were there largely to collect the pieces of the coming political, social, and demographic chaos.

The Aztecs enjoyed a major strategic advantage: they could attack at any point along the lakeshore with a vast fleet of war canoes. It was critical, therefore, that Cortés had 14 *brigantines* built in Tetzcoco using timber and struts hauled from the wrecks beached at Vera Cruz. They were pulled over the mountains by hundreds of Mesoamerican porters. The high-decked brigantines were launched on April 28, 1521, again vitally accompanied by thousands of Tlaxcalan and other allied braves in war canoes. The brigantines were unassailable by the Aztecs who could neither reach their high decks and *castles* from flat-bottomed canoes nor withstand withering fire spat at them from swivel guns and decks lined by arquebusiers and crossbowmen. They also were overwhelmed at water level by thousands of Indian enemies fighting canoe to canoe. The Aztec canoe fleet was destroyed, denying Tenochtitlán any means of resupply of food or fresh water. Meanwhile, 1,000 conquistadores and many tens of thousands of Tlaxcalan and other Mesoamericans warriors (over 95 percent of the attacking force) cut the causeways, isolating the island city.

The Spanish set up heavy cannon and some falconetes and settled in for a 93-day siege. But this was a siege with a difference: during the day, Spanish and Tlaxcalans fought down the causeways toward the city, slaughtering as many Aztec warriors as they could before withdrawing for the night. Each sortie consumed a bit more of the causeway and then the city itself, progressively opening lines of fire for the artillery and firearms troops and charging lanes for lancers. The fighting was close: Cortés was unhorsed three times and once nearly dragged off to be ritually sacrificed. Some Spanish penetrated too far in a June attack and were ambushed and taken. Fifty conquistadores were carried off along with hundreds of Tlaxcalans. All were sacrificed in view of their comrades, their hearts cut out while still beating by high priests wearing cloaks of flayed human flesh. The bodies were tossed down the blood-slicked steps of the Aztec temples, or roasted, with their skins sent at night to shoreside towns to show that the Spanish were mortal, and to promise Aztec revenge on any who aided them. The Spanish gave no quarter either: they slaughtered hundreds each day and tore down whole blocks of houses and temples, all to no greater end than a conquest that would make them rich beyond the avarice of the basest among them.

Without a hint of moral awareness, let alone remorse, Cortés wrote to Emperor *Charles V*: "The people of the city had to walk upon their dead.... So great was their suffering that it was beyond our understanding how they could endure it. Countless numbers of men, women and children came toward us, and in their eagerness to escape many were pushed into the water where they drowned amid the multitude of corpses." The Tlaxcalans took a full measure of revenge on the Aztecs, including thousands of women and children whom they slaughtered along with blood-stained priests and warriors. That caused humbug moralizing among the Spanish. On August 13, 1521, the third and last Aztec leader to face the Spanish, the boy-emperor Cuauhtémoc, surrendered Tenochtitlán. Cortés later had him murdered during an expedition to conquer Honduras in 1524.

Suggested Reading: Hugh Thomas, *Conquest: Montezuma, Cortés, and the Fall of Old Mexico* (1994); Ross Hassig, *Aztec Warfare* (1988); Richard Townsend, *The Aztecs* (1990; 2000).

Tenth Penny. A 10 percent sales tax, modeled on Castile's *alcabala*, introduced to the Netherlands by decree of the *Duke of Alba* and *Philip II* on July 31, 1571. It was enormously unpopular, contributing much to dissent and resentment of the monarchy, and riding roughshod over traditional liberties that reignited the *Eighty Years' War* in 1572 on a grand new scale. Many militia turned on their own town governments and refused to enforce the tax, thereby forcing still more towns to join the rebellion.

terakki. The Ottoman system of providing regular rises in salary for professional troops, tied to their performance in battle. This was different than cash bonuses ("*bahşiş*") or spoils ("*ganimet*").

Terceira, Battle of (1582). A fleet action off the Azores in which a Spanish fleet under *Santa Cruz* defeated a French fleet acting in support of a Portuguese pretender to the throne of Portugal, which had been seized by *Philip II* two years earlier.

tercio. "Third." The name derived from the tripartite division common to early modern infantry squares, especially the main infantry unit in the

15th–16th-century Spanish system. Tercios started at 3,000 men, but heavy tercios could have up to 6,000 men each, formed into 50 to 60 ranks with 80 men to a file. They were super-heavy units of armored and tactically disciplined pikemen, supported by arquebusiers and lesser numbers of heavy musketeers on the corners. To contemporary observers they appeared as "iron cornfields" which won through *shock* and sheer mass rather than clever maneuver. Others saw in the tercio a "walking citadel" whose corner guards of clustered arquebusiers gave it the appearance of a mobile castle with four turrets, especially after the reforms introduced by *Gonzalo di Córdoba* from 1500. He wanted the tercios to better contend with the Swiss so he added more pikes at the front but also many more gunmen to replace the older reliance on polearms. These formations might have only 1,200 men. The new tercio was still heavy and ponderous on the move, but it was a more flexible unit with much greater firepower that could dig in for defense or advance to destroy the enemy's main force as circumstances suggested. This reform first paid off at *Cerignola* (1503). At *Pavia* (1525), tercios destroyed the French under *Francis I*. For two generations after that most opponents declined battle against the tercios whenever possible, and they became the most feared infantry in Europe. They remained dominant for nearly a hundred years. Their demise came during the *Thirty Years' War* when more flexible Dutch and Swedish armies broke into more flexible, smaller regiments. These units smashed the tercios with combined arms tactics that also employed field artillery and a return to cavalry shock. See also *volley fire*.

Terek River, Battle of (1262). See *Mongols*.

terrain. On the impact of well or poorly chosen terrain on the outcome of battle, see *Agincourt, Battle of*; *Bannockburn*; *cavalry*; *chevauchée*; *Courtrai, Battle of*; *Kephissos, Battle of*; *logistics*; *Morgarten, Battle of*; *siege warfare*; *Stirling Bridge, Battle of.*

terre-plein. The flat top of the *rampart* above the talus or sloping wall, where the artillery was mounted. It also supported the *chemin de ronde*.

testudo. "Tortoise." A siege engine sporting an armored roof to fend off missiles and fire, which moved forward on rollers to cover men making a final assault on a breach in a fortified wall or gate.

Teutonic Knights, Order of. "Domus hospitalis sanctae Mariae Teutonicorum" ("Order of the Knights of the Hospital of St. Mary of the Teutons"). An order of hospitaller knights set up in 1127 in Jerusalem. In 1198 they were transformed into a *Military Order* ("Ritter des Deutschordens") after the failed Third Crusade. They had three classes of brethren: *knights*, priests, and *sergeants*. All were required to be of German birth and noble blood. Some of their hospitals admitted nursing women. On their shields and chests the Teutonic Knights bore the Crusader symbol of the order: the black and silver

"Iron Cross" that ordained, in both senses, German warriors and military equipment into the 21st century. Their fighting doctrine was, "Who fights the Order, fights Jesus Christ!" Their rallying cry was, "Gott mit Uns!" ("God is with us!"). They slept with their swords, initially their only permitted possession, practiced self-flagellation and extreme fasting and monkish devotions, and kept silent in camp and on the march. Many wore mail directly against their flesh to mortify it. They were at their worst Christian Taliban: gruesome holy warriors who welcomed martyrdom, willing killers for "The Christ."

Out of the Ashes

Unable to compete with other Military Orders in Syria, the Teutonic Knights fought in Armenia instead. In 1210 nearly the whole order was killed, leaving just 20 knights. Hermann von Salza essentially refounded the order in 1226, aided by Emperor Friedrich II ("Barbarossa"). They were given lands in Sicily and eastern Europe, a transaction approved by the pope in the Golden Bull of Rimini (1223). They now wore white tunics, an honor granted over the strong objection of the rival *Knights Templar*. They fought in behalf of the Hungarian king in Transylvania before moving into Prussia, which the *Knights in the Service of God in Prussia* had failed to conquer. The first two Knights of the order settled in Prussia in 1229; the next year 20 more arrived, along with 200 sergeants. The Brethren thereafter acted as commanders and officers in larger armies of converted Prussians who served them as auxiliaries. In battle the Knights were the panzer tip of a crusading invasion of the pagan lands of the Baltic. They ravaged and conquered Courland and Prussia and parts of Poland and western Russia, waging ruthless campaigns against "the northern Saracens." They settled in conquered lands as the new aristocracy, enserfing native populations. Their own vassalage shifted among the Empire, the king of Poland, and distant but powerless popes. The legacy of the "Drang nach Osten" ("Drive to the East") of the "Sword Brethren" was the Christianization and enfeoffment of Prussia by force of arms and merciless war with Lithuania, Poland, Sweden, and Muscovy. The northern crusades, especially the long forest-ambush campaigns of the 14th century against animist Lithuanians, were among the most ferocious of the entire Middle Ages.

The military tools of the Brethren were advanced and powerful crossbows, mailed *heavy cavalry*, stone watchtowers and fortress fastnesses, huge torsion *artillery* (*catapults* and counterpoise *trebuchets*), and *cogs* that could carry 500 troops, which gave them mobile striking power along the Baltic coast. Their early opponents had almost none of these weapons. When Knights charged native infantry ("Pruzzes") armed only with bows and axes, the panic and slaughter was terrible. The Brethren united with the *Livonian Order*, also comprised of German knights, from 1237 to 1525. To their new *Ordensstaat* (1238), the Sword Brothers brought German and Dutch colonists and peasants to secure the land, completing the most successful and brutal military colonization of the Middle Ages. Baltic cities within the Ordensstaat were permitted to join the *Hanse*, as did the Hochmeister.

The Brethren also fought constant border wars with Poland-Lithuania, a large condominium that dominated most of eastern Europe and western Russia. They were defeated by a Mongol horde at Liegnitz (April 1241), but thereafter held and expanded their territory. By 1250 the Lithuanians had adapted to new weapons and mounted tactics and under a new leader, Mindaugus, invaded the Ordensstaat. In 1254 some 60,000 Germans and Bohemians mobilized to rescue the Knights. Over the next two decades they faced war with Lithuania and a 13-year peasant revolt in Prussia, the "Great Apostasy." By the late 1270s they were triumphant in the Baltic.

In 1291 the last resistance to the Muslim assault on *Outremer* collapsed and the German Hospital in Acre was lost. In 1309 the Order's Grand Commandery was moved to Marienburg (Malbork) on the Vistula and its ties to the Holy Land faded into legend and dim memory. Marriage to natives was still forbidden because so many remained pagan and hostile: in 1343 peasants in Estonia rebelled and slaughtered 1,800 Germans in Reval. The Brethren hence had a narrow recruitment base: they boasted fewer than 500 full knights supported by 3,200 retainers, just under 6,000 sergeants, fewer than 2,000 garrison militia from six large towns, and 1,500 poor-quality conscripts who were peasant-tenants of various abbeys under control of the Brethren. The Order was reinforced by knights from across Europe when successive popes preached a new Baltic crusade against pagan Lithuania; many came for the blood sport. This was key, as Prussia's population was savaged by the *Black Death* and Crusaders from Germany grew scarce after Lithuanians converted to Christianity. Still, between 1345 and 1377, over 100 expeditions were launched by the Brethren into Lithuania. To make up the shortfall in German recruits, baptized Prussians and Slavs were recruited from 1400, and large numbers of Czech mercenaries were hired whenever the Brethren fought.

The reforms did not help: the Teutonic Knights were beaten decisively and with huge losses by a Polish-Lithuanian army at *Tannenberg* (July 15, 1410). That ended their Baltic crusade and accelerated a terminal military decline. Lands lay fallow, commanderies remained empty, castles were deserted. The Poles then raided into Prussia, but after the losses suffered at Tannenberg the Knights were loathe to offer battle. A full-scale Polish invasion occurred in 1422 and forced the Knights to cede territory. In 1440 the *Preussische Bund* was founded in opposition to the extant privileges of the Order. The end of political and military dominance by the Brethren came with the *War of the Cities* (1454–1466). The Knights fought well against the Poles at *Chojnice* (September 18, 1454), but the size of armies deployed by Poland and the Bund told against the Teutons and their mercenaries. Nor could the Brethren rely on their traditional Czech allies: *Hussite* armies, too, raided deep into the Ordensstaat. In 1455 virtually all Livonian knights were wiped out. When the purse of the remaining Brethren turned over empty, unpaid mercenaries handed over the capital and fortress of Marienburg to the Poles without even a token fight. The Teutonic Knights were reduced, humiliated, and split by the *Second Treaty of Torun* (1466). In 1498 they regained a measure of independence when they elected as Hochmeister the brother of Friedrich of Saxony, who renounced homage to Poland and demanded the return of "Royal Prussia." From 1498 to 1503 the Order fought with Muscovy, surprisingly holding its own against a more numerous foe. In 1519 the Knights attacked Poland, burning and raiding along the frontier but avoiding set-piece battles.

What finally defeated the Order was the same thing that had led to its founding: an argument about God. In 1523 *Martin Luther* wrote to Hochmeister Albrecht of Brandenburg. They met at the Imperial Diet in 1524 and Albrecht converted to Luther's views, as had the bishop of Straslund and many Brethren. The original Livonian Order broke away as a result of Albrecht's conversion. (Catholic remnants survived in Germany until 1809, but only as a landless and powerless ceremonial shell.) On April 8, 1525, Albrecht signed the Treaty of Cracow converting Prussia into a hereditary duchy under the Polish monarchy. The last significant military action of the Brethren was to support *Charles V* during his war with the Schmalkaldic League (1546–1547). The Order lost its rich Venetian commandery in 1595,

> *What finally defeated the Order was ... an argument about God.*

the same year 100 knights made a last crusade against the Ottomans in Hungary. In 1618 the Duchy of Prussia passed to the Hohenzollerns and the last knights became Prussian officers. In 1695 the Order itself was remade into a regiment, the "Hoch und Deutschmeister" of the Prussian Army. A key result of the slippage of the hold of the Teutonic Knights on the eastern Baltic was a rise in commercial and military competition for the succession to the Ordensstaat among Poland and Sweden, and later, also Russia. See also *Sea Victuallers*; *taifa states*; *Žižka, Jan.*

Suggested Reading: E. Christiansen, *The Northern Crusades: The Baltic and the Catholic Frontier, 1100–1525* (1980); Desmond Seward, *Monks of War: The Military Religious Orders* (1972; 1995).

Tewkesbury, Battle of (1471). See *Wars of the Roses.*

Thérouanne, Siege of (1543). At Thérouanne in France, *Henry VIII*'s cannon made the first confirmed use of indirect fire, against Burgundian gunners bombarding the English outworks. The Burgundians were located in a valley beyond the town and behind a hill. English observers mounted the hill and redirected the fall of shot from the garrison onto the Burgundian position. This scattered the besiegers.

Third Rome. An Orthodox doctrine with deep nationalist undertones, formulated in the 15th century to justify Muscovite westward expansion. It proposed that responsibility for the "True Church" had passed to Russia where Moscow formed the "Third Rome," the rightful capital of the Christian world. The first Christian capital, Rome, had been lost in the 5th century; in the 15th, from the Orthodox point of view, it was occupied by Catholic schismatics. The "Second Rome" was Constantinople, which fell to the

Ottomans in 1453, a conquest that stimulated Muscovite claims to spiritual succession. See also *Fifth Monarchists*.

Thirteen Years' War (1454–1466). See *War of the Cities*.

Thirteen Years' War (1593–1606). "The Long War." When dated from 1591 it is sometimes called the Fifteen Years' War (1591–1606). In either case, it was a protracted border conflict between the Ottoman Empire and the Austrian Habsburgs over Balkan territories. Conflict in the Balkans was long marked by small wars as local *beys* and Austrian nobles fought over control of some castle or valley. Sixty years of relative peace between the Ottomans and Austria was broken in 1591 not by the initiative of the sultan or emperor but by private raiding into the *Militargrenze* by the governor of Bosnia, Hasan Pasha. Two years later Vienna was late paying its annual tribute of 30,000 ducats. Grand Vezier Kica Sinan Pasha used this as an excuse to follow-up Hasan Pasha's petty raids with a full Imperial expedition led by his son. The war thus expanded, though still without real enthusiasm in either Constantinople or Vienna. Bitter frontier fighting broke out in the Militargrenze as the two empires fought over "The Principalities" of Transylvania, Moldavia, and Wallachia. Sisak fell to Hasan Pasha in September 1593, but was recovered because the Ottomans were unprepared to resume large-scale warfare on their western front. In May–June 1594, the Austrians besieged the strong fortress of Esztergom.

Caught unprepared for a real war in the Balkans, the Ottomans sent in relief only 2,000 locally recruited *Voynuqs*, who promptly defected. It took months more for a large Ottoman army to assemble. Before it departed, a vicious and complex fight broke out over the office of the Grand Vezier following the death of Sultan Murad III (January 1595). One rival candidate undermined the other's expedition to Wallachia. This split the *Kapikulu Askerleri* and brought tensions within the capital to a fighting pitch: at one point the *Janissary Corps* attacked the *sipahis*, the sultan's elite cavalry regiments, in their barracks.

The major clash of the war on the frontiers was a three-day fight at Keresztes (or Mezókeresztes), on October 24–26, 1596. An army led by Muhammad (Mehmed) III bombarded and stormed the Austrian fortress of Eger (Eğri). In 1600 the Ottomans also conquered Kanizsa and annexed the borderlands dividing Croatia from Hungary. The campaign season of 1601 was lost to another court struggle in Constantinople over who should command. The war sputtered on for another five years without major clashes or a real decision. The highwater mark for the Austrians was a failed siege of Buda and Pest (1602). Finally, Sultan Ahmad I forewent tribute from Austria in exchange for Vienna's recognition of his suzerainty over Transylvania. The terms were codified in the *Treaty of Zsitva Torok* (November 1606). See also *Celâli Revolts*.

Thirty, Battle of the (1352). See *Hundred Years' War*.

Thirty Years' War (1618–1648). The first half of the 17th century in Europe was riven with political, social, and religious crises. Also causing general turmoil and unrest were widespread economic changes, notably the *price revolution* of the 16th–17th centuries that saw real wages for most people badly outstripped by higher prices for basic staples, even as overall population and the size of cities rose dramatically. This drastic decline in living standards led to riots, urban and rural, especially within the *Holy Roman Empire* from the 1590s forward. Tensions within Germany were only aggravated once war broke out, so that German disquiet and constitutional and military trouble were exported to the rest of Europe. A widespread ferment—sometimes overstated as a "general crisis of the 17th century"—underlay this German crisis and was worsened by the horrors and destruction of the Thirty Years' War. That name for the war remains controversial, since it was not one war but several and did not really begin in 1618 or end in 1648. Spain and France, for instance, were at war intermittently from 1609 and continued fighting until the Peace of the Pyrenees in 1659. Spain and the Netherlands fought bitterly from 1566, signed a *Twelve Years' Truce* (1609–1621), then resumed their *Eighty Years' War*. The Dutch war paralleled, influenced, and then meshed with the war in Germany. Poland and Sweden also fought wars long before 1618 and fighting among northern and east European powers continued well after 1648, sometimes connecting with the German war, sometimes running parallel to it.

Yet, the conventional name for these interrelated wars was actually used at the time and captures well the conflicts fought on, across, and around the central battlefield of Germany. Within Germany, from the turn of the 17th century a longstanding constitutional struggle between territorial princes and the Emperor, and religious struggles throughout the Empire, fed a growing sense that war was coming: cities and princes alike began to arm and otherwise prepare for war. When war came in Bohemia and Austria in 1618 it was not unexpected or even unwelcome, though no one foresaw the full holocaust that followed. At the core of the German war were contested interpretations of the constitutional principles of an ancient empire newly split by tri-*confessionalism* into *Catholic*, *Lutheran*, and *Calvinist* camps. No longer united against *Islam* after the *Treaty of Zsitva Torok* (1606), and with the *Reichskreis* defense system broken after 1607, Germany's religious antagonists formed confessional alliances aimed at each other: the *Protestant Union* and the *Catholic League*. A closely related, and possibly more basic, issue was whether Germany's many principalities (duchies, free cities, and hundreds of smaller fiefs) were mere *Estates* of a larger and more powerful monarchy or were joined in a voluntary confederation which afforded them full sovereignty on matters of war, treaty-making, and taxes. Emperors had driven toward a more homogenous polity for half a century against resistance from feudal Estates, especially free cities and regional princes, asserting traditional local rights. The main actors in this underlying constitutional conflict were sometimes also confessional fanatics, including emperors and kings, territorial princes, and aroused clergy and their gullible flocks. But just as important were wholly secular-minded princes uncontrolled by any confessional group, who acted regardless of personal or public confessional affiliation. Princes seen as belonging to one or another confession thus might ally with or scheme against eschatological "heretics" or coreligionists, as their secular interests required. From the beginning powerful mercenary captains of no particular faith or loyalty were also important participants.

From 1618 to 1625 the war was mainly between *Ferdinand II* and his subjects within the Empire, with limited involvement by outside powers. But it subsequently spread to involve so many states that it became in effect a European civil war, or a war to define European civilization. Thus, while the German war might have been resolved by compromise between Ferdinand and the German Estates in 1635, in fact, fighting continued to 1648 because of the war's many and evolving external linkages. Its course and final resolution crucially affected the religious balance among the three main confessions in central Europe and the material balance of power among the Great Powers and lesser states. Outside Germany confessionalism was not generally seen as the main issue at stake in the war. Instead, the German war was viewed as a new chapter in a larger and older struggle for power that pitted Austria and Spain against France, or Habsburg against Bourbon, not Catholic against Protestant. This view had real merit, for while the Thirty Years' War was about changing the internal nature of the polities that would make up the emerging European system of states, it was also fought over the future balance of power among the greatest of those states. Most rulers thought about external security and secular alliances more than they did about doctrinal disputes, except where these had congealed into confessional communities that could undermine internal stability and constrain diplomacy. New dynasties in England and France feared a general European war that might undo tenuous consolidation of kingdoms already riven with sectarian conflict but momentarily at peace. Each feared a general war of religion would split apart their own fragile polities, as domestic factions reached out in appeal to outside powers and warring coreligionists who were already tearing apart the Netherlands and Germany. As always, issues of the rights and prestige of sovereigns, along with princely vanity, also strutted across the political stage. And such matters had little or nothing to do with confessional idealism or conflict.

Bohemian Phase, 1618–1625

War broke out over a local Protestant challenge to Habsburg control of Bohemia, which was linked to an expectation of the pending death of Emperor Matthias and succession to the Imperial throne of a known Catholic ideologue, Archduke Ferdinand of Styria (later, Ferdinand II). The succession crisis in Bohemia turned into open rebellion with the *"Defenestration of Prague"* (May 23, 1618), an event humorous to Protestants, sacrilegious to Catholics, and a casus belli to the Habsburgs. The Bohemian revolt which erupted that summer threatened the religious and political balance among the seven *Kurfürsten* who chose the Holy Roman Emperor. This struck at the heart of Habsburg-Catholic power in Germany just as Ferdinand, a fanatic advocate of the Catholic *Counter-Reformation*, was poised to ascend the Imperial throne. With Catholic ascendancy challenged doctrinally by Lutheranism and Calvinism, Imperial authority was challenged constitutionally by territorial princes and local Estates. This confluence of events and forces brought a brash Protestant prince, *Friedrich V*, the Elector Palatine, to Bohemia to secure for himself a crown which the rebels offered to any prince who would uphold Protestantism. Thus began the great conflagration of the 17th century.

The Duke of Savoy and Friedrich commissioned the contractor *Graf von Mansfeld* to raise and lead an army of 20,000 mercenaries into Bohemia in support of local forces already there under *Matthias Thurn* and *Christian of Anhalt-Bernburg*. After a day of hard fighting, Mansfeld took Pilsen on November 1, 1618. The first field battle came the next summer, at *Sablat* (June 10, 1619). Also in June, Ferdinand was hemmed into Vienna by a Bohemian army come to discuss grievances (submitted as a "Sturmpetition," or "storm petition") at pike point. He had to be rescued by the Bavarians. Ferdinand was thereafter greatly assisted by a zealous Catholic army of veteran Spaniards and another of Bavarians and *Catholic Leaguers*, as well as the usual assortment of confessionally indifferent mercenaries. Together, these Habsburg armies crushed the Bohemian rebels and their Dutch allies and mercenary hires at the *White Mountain* (November 8, 1620). Pilsen surrendered on March 26, 1621. Only a few cutoff Dutch and Scottish troops held out until October 8, 1622. By then Ferdinand had imposed a draconian religious settlement on Bohemia, bearing down with the full weight of the Counter-Reformation and doctrinal rigors of the *Inquisition* into heresy. He stripped rebel nobles of lands and titles by imperial fiat, and sometimes took their lives; and he ripped away the traditional freedoms and rights of the Bohemian Estates and *Ritterstand*.

Catholic armies then brought the war home to the Palatinate where Friedrich's feckless policies and increasing diplomatic isolation, along with weak finances and bad generalship by several of his commanders, doomed his cause to defeat. *Johann Tilly* brought the army of the Catholic League ("Liga") north to impose by force Catholic orthodoxy and Habsburg rule. In 1622 the Liga was blocked and rebuffed by Mansfeld at *Mingolsheim* (April 22). The armies fought again five days later at *Wiesloch* (April 27, 1622), before Tilly maneuvered around Mansfeld. Tilly won handily over the Margrave of Baden at *Wimpfen* (May 6), and yet again over the brash *Christian of Brunswick* at *Höchst* (June 20), when those Protestant commanders and armies failed to join. Tilly then successfully linked with an army of Spanish veterans from the Netherlands and forced Brunswick's remaining Protestants and Mansfeld's unreliable mercenaries to withdraw across the Rhine. An Imperial army crossed into the Netherlands to lend assistance to the Spanish against the Dutch rebels but was beaten at *Fleurus* (August 29) and forced to withdraw. In the Lower Palatinate Heidelberg fell to Tilly in September and Mannheim was overrun in November 1622.

Friedrich's coalition had fallen apart because war against the Habsburgs was something few Protestant princes were yet ready to contemplate. For instance, as a prince, *Johann Georg*, Elector of Saxony, wanted nothing to do with a direct constitutional confrontation with his Emperor; and as a Lutheran, he had no desire to seat Friedrich, a Calvinist, on the Bohemian throne. Another Protestant, the Landgrave of Hesse, joined Tilly in alliance with German Catholic princes and Ferdinand against the rebellion of the "Winter King." As for the Protestant north, Ferdinand appeased those German princes with what turned out to be false promises not to seek restitution of long secularized ecclesiastical properties. That kept them neutral. Even Friedrich's father-in-law, *James I* of England, sent just 2,000 troops in 1620. *Maurits of Nassau* helped the most, providing Friedrich one-eighth of his troops and heavy financial backing (but also unwisely egging him to war in the first place). It was not enough. In 1623 Christian of Brunswick was chased out of Saxony then trounced by Tilly at *Stadtlohn* (August 6). That ended Friedrich's last hope of regaining the Palatinate or otherwise returning to the status quo ante bellum. He went into exile in the Netherlands.

> *Ferdinand appeased these German princes with what turned out to be false promises . . .*

Danish Phase, 1625–1629

The Bohemian and Palatinate phase of the war had been mostly fought by powers of, and within, the German Empire. After 1624 this changed as the war became evermore internationalized and eternally confusing. The shift began when England intervened, weakly and ineptly, in 1624. In December 1625, *Christian IV* of Denmark formed the *Hague Alliance* with England and the Netherlands and entered the German war. James I promised money and men to support this new Protestant champion but sent little gold, and even fewer troops. The Dutch helped pay for a second army raised by Mansfeld. The French saw Spanish-Austrian armies positioned to their east and north in these years and were ever more uneasy about perceived Habsburg "encirclement." Momentarily, however, France made common cause with Spain against England: the two Catholic powers signed a treaty of alliance in 1627 that aimed at smashing the *Huguenot* base at *La Rochelle* and punishing England for intervening there when the religious wars had briefly flared again in southern France. England and France fought from 1627 to 1628 over *Charles I*'s support for the Huguenots, until Charles signed a peace treaty that abandoned the Protestants of La Rochelle to French Catholic besiegers.

In northern Europe, Christian IV managed to gather a weak and temporary coalition of Protestant states but Sweden refused to join. *Gustavus Adolphus* knew how little aid England was really lending the cause and would not in any event back the ambitions of Sweden's traditional enemy, Denmark. Besides, he was still at war with *Sigismund III* of Poland. As for the German princes, Johann Georg again sheltered under formal Saxon neutrality, while most north German princes were as yet far enough removed from Austria and Spain that the Habsburg threat was felt only faintly. The Dutch, always eager for allies in their long and lonely war with Spain, sent infantry to help the Danes and money to raise yet another cheap but unreliable mercenary army under Mansfeld. Meanwhile, the Habsburgs sent their greatest armies and generals north: Tilly and the army of the Catholic League, skilled Spanish *tercios* under veteran commanders, and above all the Czech captain *Albrecht von Wallenstein* at the head of a mercenary host, though one far more loyal to its commander than to the Emperor. These disparate forces contended in Germany and Flanders during the latter 1620s over the fate of Protestantism and the future of Habsburg power.

In spring 1626, Tilly and the Liga army moved north along the Elbe, pushing the Danes back into Holstein. Wallenstein destroyed three-quarters of Mansfeld's army of 20,000 at *Dessau Bridge* (April 25), hounded him from Saxony, then pursued him to Moravia where Mansfeld failed to link with *Gabriel Bethlen's* Hungarian rebels. That took Mansfield permanently out of the war. The great Czech next moved to Holstein to join Tilly. Their combined forces beat the Danes at *Lutter-am-Barenberg* (August 17/27). In early 1628 Wallenstein occupied Jutland, Pomerania, and Mecklenburg (which was given to him later by Ferdinand in reward for services rendered). Wallenstein besieged *Straslund* that summer but failed to take it. Christian IV tried one last time to invade the Empire but was crushed by Wallenstein at *Wolgast* (September 2, 1628). After four years of fighting that devastated northern Germany, Denmark was finally beaten into submission: Christian IV signed the *Peace of Lübeck* (July 7, 1629) and exited the war. He was left with his home realm intact but made to foreswear any future engagement in Imperial wars or politics.

Catholic and Imperial power was ascendant and seemed unassailable; grace, magnanimity, and toleration were called for. Instead, Ferdinand II gravely overreached, seeking to turn back 75 years of constitutional compromise with Protestantism within the Empire. Instead of pardons he issued arrest warrants; instead of toleration he proclaimed the *Edict of Restitution* (March 28, 1629). That marked the major turning point of the war. Ferdinand's Edict threatened to force princes and free cities alike to yield traditional freedoms, roll back the limited religious tolerance of the *Convention of Passau* (1552) and *Peace of Augsburg* (1555), and promised to restore to Catholics all offices and lands secularized by Protestant rulers. In short, Ferdinand sought to recover all Germany to "the one true Faith" (from the other one), and to radically increase Imperial power. Even Catholic princes saw this as a Habsburg grab for hegemony rather than a purely Counter-Reformation policy.

Protestants took heart that Straslund had fended off Wallenstein in 1628 with aid from Sweden, which they hoped presaged intervention in Germany by Gustavus Adolphus. They celebrated Dutch capture of the Spanish treasure fleet in September 1628, and Dutch occupation of northern Brazil in 1630. Always ready with a great *war chest* to support any emergent anti-Habsburg champion, regardless of confession, was the "éminence rouge" *Cardinal Richelieu*, behind whom stood all the wealth and latent military power of France. By 1628 France was already at war with Spain in their old battleground of northern Italy. That contest would continue undeclared until it overlapped with the German war from 1635. The Dutch also went on the offensive once the Spanish Chancellor *Olivares* reduced troop levels in the north to fight the French in Italy and shifted also to a more maritime strategy. In September 1629, Dutch troops took the key fortress of s'Hertogenbosch. Before Richelieu and *Louis XIII* would intervene in Germany directly, however, they waited to see what the "Lion of Midnight" could do to stop Ferdinand and offered the great Swede huge subsidies to try.

Swedish Phase, 1630–1635

Habsburg fortunes in Germany went into steep decline from 1630 to 1634. The *Imperial Diet* meeting in Regensburg defied Ferdinand's request to send 50,000 men to Italy to aid Spain wage the *War of the Mantuan Succession*. Instead, they enticed Ferdinand to sack his overly ambitious general, Wallenstein, who was also seen as too tolerant of Protestants, and reduce the Imperial Army by two-thirds, to 40,000 men. Wallenstein was thus forced into Bohemian retirement and Ferdinand's army was hamstrung. Ferdinand's policies had finally brought Lutheran Sweden, the Protestant German princes, and Catholic France together, in defense of local autonomy against Imperial authority and in opposition to a perceived Habsburg drive for European hegemony. Gustavus Adolphus at last entered the war, seeing an expansion of Swedish power as nicely linked to the Protestant cause in Germany. Not all Protestants agreed: Johann Georg wanted to stay neutral, but was compelled to join the coalition by Swedish occupation of Saxony. Likewise, Georg Wilhelm of Brandenburg at first refused to allow Swedish troops to use his territory, until Gustavus marched uninvited to take the fortress at Küstrin, then west to Berlin to capture the fortress of Spandau and force Brandenburg into a growing coalition of the unwilling and the mercenary. This move against the fortresses of north Germany secured the confluences of the major navigable rivers, which permitted Gustavus to move his artillery train down river and closer to the Habsburg heartland and to supply his armies with food and fodder gathered in the north. On April 13, he stormed Frankfurt an der Oder, smashing eight Imperial regiments and taking the city. The next month *Magdeburg* fell to Tilly, whose men put its population to the sword when Gustavus failed to relieve the city. The atrocity—the worst of the war—actually strengthened Gustavus by raising levels of fear and resolve among German Protestants.

By May 1631, Gustavus had cleared Pomerania of Imperial armies and garrisons, while in Mecklenburg only the city of Greifswald held out against him. Gustavus marched into Saxony, forcing Johann Georg to join him and swelling the ranks of his army by a further 12,000 men. With his strategic rear and supply lines secured he moved south to do battle with Tilly's army, which had taken Leipzig a few days earlier. The two armies met at *First Breitenfeld* (September 17, 1631), where Gustavus won a smashing victory despite being abandoned early in the fight when his reluctant Saxon allies fled in panic and en masse. Gustavus next took Mainz after a short siege. To the north, Spanish troops were withdrawn into fortified garrisons in the Netherlands: Gustavus had broken the link between the armies and bases of the

Austrian and Spanish branches of Habsburg military power. All armies then went into winter quarters. By spring 1632, Tilly and Ferdinand had raised a new Imperial army and Gustavus marched to meet it. The clash came at *Rain* (April 15, 1632), where Gustavus daringly forged the River Lech under enemy fire, covered by a smokescreen from his artillery. During the action Tilly was mortally wounded; he died five days later, forcing Ferdinand to recall Wallenstein to Imperial command. Meanwhile, Gustavus occupied Augsburg and Munich, ate out Bavaria, and prepared for either a feint or an actual drive to take Vienna. At that moment it seemed the ancient and Catholic Holy Roman Empire might become instead a Swedish and Protestant empire.

However, within a month a huge army of mercenaries flocked to the banner of the Czech war captain, enticed by the prospects of plunder and success that always accompanied his campaigns. Even as Wallenstein assembled this army and then marched north he secretly negotiated with Saxony and Brandenburg, arguing for a common interest in expelling the Swedes from Germany. Where his nominal superior Ferdinand thought in terms of "the Faith," Wallenstein thought of German lands and riches to be divided or despoiled. Impressed by Swedish artillery and maneuverability he chose to avoid battle. He curled behind Gustavus into Saxony, taking Leipzig and wasting the surrounding lands to pull the great Swede north. At Fürth, near Nürnberg, Wallenstein linked with *Maximilian I* of Bavaria and the army of the Catholic League. The Catholic and Protestant armies then settled into opposing trenches where each grew progressively weaker from disease, hunger, and desertion. Gustavus cracked first, precipitously attacking Wallenstein's trenches. He was rebuffed with a loss of 3,000 men, suffering a real blow to his reputation for invincibility. To draw Wallenstein out of his defenses Gustavus moved into Bavaria and threatened Vienna. Instead of following as expected Wallenstein moved back into Saxony where he again devastated an allied country and threatened Swedish lines of supply. Gustavus was forced north to fight Wallenstein at *Alte Feste* (August 24–September 18, 1632) after which the armies again went separate ways, each eating out the lands of the other's allies. The decisive clash came at *Lützen* (November 6, 1632) where, although Gustavus was shot to death during the battle, the Swedish army smashed the Imperials.

Gustavus died after just two years of campaigning in Germany, but his intervention altered the whole course of the war. He saved the Protestant cause even while revealing and confirming that the war had become mainly a struggle for raw political power and territory regardless of faith. On the other hand, his death brought the two sides back to even and thus forced each to look outside Germany for new allies: Habsburg-Catholics turned to Spain while the anti-Habsburg Protestant alliance turned to France. In the summer of 1633, some 20,000 Spanish troops moved through the *Valtelline* into southern Germany to reestablish Habsburg control while France invaded Lorraine and occupied Nancy. To the east the *War of Smolensk* (December 1632–June 1634) broke out between Russia and Poland, tying down Polish

Catholic armies. Within Germany, the two sides clawed at their own vitals rather than each others': as Swedish influence over the Protestant princes waned the alliance cracked, while Catholic princes worried the Emperor until he again dismissed Wallenstein, then had him assassinated.

French Phase, 1635–1648

Gustavus' councillor *Oxenstierna* replaced him in the field in Germany but lost badly at *First Nördlingen* (September 5–6, 1634). He was later taken hostage by his own men, who demanded all pay in arrears. Sweden did not recover from this debacle for several years. Moreover, the Habsburg victory persuaded Olivares that the moment had come to throw the French off the right bank of the Rhine, where Richelieu had been planting garrisons since 1632. Spanish troops attacked the French in Trier in March 1635 (taking the archbishop prisoner), in an effort to establish an alternative route to the *Spanish Road*, which had been cut by France. The assault on Trier was designed to trigger war between France and the Holy Roman Empire. The stratagem failed: on May 19, 1635, France declared war only on Spain. Longer term, expanded Spanish-French fighting drew Habsburg armies away from northern Germany, permitting Sweden to slowly recover. Led by a prince of the church, Cardinal Richelieu, France finally intervened in the German war only when the gains it had earlier made by stealth in the Rhineland were assaulted and eroded by Spain. It did not enter the war as a Catholic power, as Richelieu had already signed offensive treaties with Protestant Sweden and the Netherlands in expectation of fighting Catholic Austria and Spain. Why?

With Catholicism secure in France following Richelieu's crushing of the last Huguenot military resistance in 1628, France was free to act for raison d'etat (reason of state) against the Habsburg powers rather than out of delusional confessional loyalty. Besides, France and Spain had fought an undeclared but bitter frontier war for years in northern Italy and along the Spanish Road, even after the formal end of the Mantuan war in 1631. The stunning Swedish defeat at Nördlingen confirmed Imperial control of southwest Germany and seemed to re-close a strategic ring of Habsburg lands around the perimeter of France that had been broken by Gustavus. This threat persuaded Richelieu that France must enter the war directly at long last, that fighting the Habsburgs through subsidized proxies was no longer enough. France must now intervene herself in Flanders, Germany, Italy, and at sea. For four years France pursued these grand strategic goals with an inadequate military system, with poor armies badly led by inept generals. It was not until the early 1640s that France settled on sound commanders and fielded well-trained armies capable of winning the war. It was greatly aided by the cracking of Habsburg power occasioned by the *revolt of Catalonia* and another in Portugal in 1640.

French intervention—which guaranteed a great widening of the war—occurred just as Ferdinand and the German princes reached an accommodation that might have ended it: the *Peace of Prague* (May 30, 1635). However, the "German war" was no longer solely a German affair: it was a general war involving all the major powers, which meant it could not be ended by a settlement crafted by Germans alone. In addition, the anti-Habsburg coalition did not agree on what sort of peace it should force on the Habsburg powers, with Sweden concentrating on the German war and desperate for territorial and financial compensation for its ruinous military effort and France more concerned with defeating Spain. This split gave hope to Vienna and Madrid that they could still win by dividing their enemies.

And so, for 13 years more the armies battled. They marauded over Germany, Bohemia, the Netherlands, Italy, and France, sacking cities and terrorizing populations as they battened off and burned the land. Catholic fought Catholic and Protestant killed Protestant while each murdered, raped, tortured, and burned out the other, spreading famine, pestilence, refugees, cruelty, and death through the heart of Europe. Huge mercenary armies did not so much fight strategic battles as constantly maneuver, plunder, and forage, all the while collecting wages of death. Entire cities were put to the sword out of revenge or reprisal. The conflict left some areas of Germany and Bohemia denuded of half their population, while other provinces paid huge ransoms to approaching armies—of whichever side—to deflect the war elsewhere, escape with their lives, and keep town, livestock, and farms intact. As the war drew to a drawn-out and exhausted close, the armies engaged shrank in size. This was due to the inability of burned and eaten out farms or serially extorted and depopulated towns to sustain relentless demands for *contributions* to maintain forces on the huge scale seen earlier under Wallenstein and Gustavus. During these last years, given the strength of fortified defenses and the still unsolved problems of mid-17th century logistics, deep cavalry raiding was about the most either side could undertake. And most raids achieved little because of an abiding inability to supply mid-17th century armies on the move and the inherent superiority of fortified defenses.

At *Wittstock* (October 4, 1636), the Imperial Army lost heavily to the Swedes, so that once more the balance of power swung (as it had in the other direction after Nördlingen) and new hope for victory was raised among the Protestant princes of Europe. In 1638 France and Sweden signed the *Treaty of Hamburg* (March 15) providing French subsidies to Sweden and foreswearing a separate peace. At *Rheinfelden* (March 2–3, 1638) a Protestant army under *Bernhard von Sachsen-Weimar* destroyed a Bavarian army and took *Johann von Werth* captive. The Swedes followed up with a victory over the Saxons at *Chemnitz* (April 14, 1638) and occupation of Bohemia. From September 1640 to October 1641, the full Imperial Diet met for the first time since 1613, to work out the negotiating positions of the Empire for any future peace talks. Not every German prince waited: in July 1641, Friedrich Wilhelm (1640–1688), the new "Great Elector" of Brandenburg, agreed to a ceasefire with Sweden; in January 1642, the Welf dukes of Brunswick also dropped out of the war (Treaty of Goslar). These defections freed Swedish general *Lennart Torstensson* to invade Moravia and Silesia. A determinative battle was *Second Breitenfeld* (November 2, 1642) where Torstensson destroyed an Imperial army and *Ferdinand III*'s hope to avoid major concessions to Sweden in the final settlement. The other important battle of this last phase of the war was *Rocroi* (May 19, 1643), where the seasoned but sullen and shrunken Army of Flanders was defeated by a French army of 22,000 led by the "Great Condé" (Louis II). The French suffered a disaster of their own at *Tüttlingen* (November 24–25, 1643), after which *Turenne* was recalled from Italy and given command of the shattered Armeé d'Allemagne.

End Game

As the first diplomatic envoys gathered at Osnabrück and Munster in Westphalia, their deliberations were interrupted by *Torstensson's War* (1643–1645) between Sweden and Denmark. Ferdinand III sent an army to help the Danes, only to lose two-thirds of his force of 20,000. At *Freiburg* (August 3–10, 1644) the French were led by the Great Condé and Turenne. They initially failed to take the city and lost half the army's strength trying. Still, they forced the defending Bavarian garrison to withdraw to Rothenburg. Until the end of the campaign season that followed, Turenne's cavalry screened Condé's infantry while they alternately foraged and scoured the Rhineland of Catholic forces. After defeating Denmark the Swedes invaded Bohemia in coordination with an attack by a Transylvanian army into Hungary. At *Jankov* (March 6, 1645), Torstensson routed an Imperial-Bavarian army. Then he laid siege to Prague. However, the logistical deficit of a country long since denuded of people and resources meant the siege could not be sustained. At *Mergentheim* (May 2, 1645), also in Bavaria, Turenne was surprised in camp, beaten, and driven back to the Rhine to rejoin the Great Condé. A few months later two diminished armies of just 12,000 men apiece clashed at *Second Nördlingen* (August 3, 1645). They fought each other to exhaustion, separated to forage over devastated lands, and did not fight again for another two years. More important German states joined Brandenburg in signing separate peace treaties before the talks in Westphalia were even seriously under way. Saxony quit the war in 1645. Bavaria left in 1647 then reentered the fight, provoking another invasion by French and Swedish armies and total Bavarian defeat at *Zusmarshausen* (May 17, 1648). Yet, the last battle of the great German war was not fought in Germany but in northern France, at *Lens* (August 2, 1648).

Relief for all finally arrived in the form of the *Peace of Westphalia*, that great set of agreements which settled the religious question in Germany on a profoundly secular basis. In Bohemia, where it all had started and where confessional hatred and armed retribution scorched the land several times over, barely one in seven villages thriving and prosperous in 1618 were even inhabited thirty years later. The Czech population had been reduced by famine, murder, pillage, and pestilence to one-third its former size. Much of Germany and Central Europe, especially along the great riverine highways, lay in ruin. The Swedish army alone is thought to have destroyed over 1,500 towns and

> *Turenne was surprised in camp, beaten, and driven back to the Rhine to rejoin the Great Condé.*

18,000 villages. Population statistics for the 17th century are notoriously unreliable, but concerted efforts to measure the damage nevertheless have been made by historians. Their highest estimate of casualties is eight million dead, of whom 350,000 were soldiers killed in skirmishes, set-piece battles, or sieges. All the rest were soldiers or civilians lost to massacre, fire, famine, or disease. By 1648 those parts of Germany repeatedly fought over or eaten out by passing armies were below half their prewar population, but the overall loss may have been less than the oft-cited figure of one-third or one-half the entire Empire's population. Some historians estimate the loss at closer to 15–20 percent (or a reduction from 20 million prewar to 16–17 million in 1648). In either case, destitution and desperation was so great that in some areas people resorted to cannibalism of their neighbors, and in a few others even of their own children. Historians still argue over whether the economic decline of Germany in these years began before the war as part of the general economic decline of the 17th century, or was caused by it. None dispute that the damage was enormous, even catastrophic. Nor did suffering end with signature of the peace treaties: a Swedish siege of Prague continued for nine days after the peace was signed while bands of unemployed former soldiers continued petty ravages and isolated killings and extortion for years. Fighting over unresolved issues stirred up by the German war, or by the German peace, continued along the Ottoman frontier, in Lorraine, and the Baltic. Still, for most areas the war was finally over by the autumn of 1648.

Recognition of the complexity of the war's origins in competing secular and confessional interests makes it easier to understand that it ended not with triumph of one religious party over the other, but in a grand secular compromise born of physical and moral exhaustion. As the last and greatest of the "wars of religion," the Thirty Years' War detached confessional questions from interstate politics, jolted the core convictions of princes and hostile faiths even as it shook the land, and finally led to agreement that princes should conduct their affairs according to raison d'etat rather than doctrinal differences on such questions as transubstantiation, predestination, or justification by faith alone. In other words, the Thirty Years' War was the climax of a revolution in church-state affairs in Europe that had lasting, even global, significance. It was the first of the "Great Wars" of modern history, and thus shaped much that followed in ways both foreseen and hidden at the time. It spawned great commanders and national and confessional heroes and witnessed huge field armies that then dwindled in size as an extraordinary toll of death and destruction mounted; and it saw innumerable sieges, the sack of cities, and battles fought with new troop formations, weapons, and tactics. And yet no campaign, siege, or battle was decisive to the final outcome. Even the oft-cited Swedish intervention was more important for what it prevented, Catholic victory, than what it sought to promote, Swedish and Protestant predominance over Germany and Central Europe. In this as in other great wars, moral despair and physical exhaustion were more decisive than ideals or the vainglorious dreams of the usual dynastic, political, and military pretenders or idiots found on every side.

A major consequence of the war was to leave Germany weak and divided (over 300 distinct German entities were recognized at Westphalia), and so on the margins of world history and politics for another 150 years. Never again would war break out in Germany over religious division or Habsburg pretensions. The general mêlée also amounted to a fundamental crisis in European civilization, in its final phase witnessing a transition from an era of war between religious communities to a period of war among princes and states, fought not for God but for raison d'état, and ending not in confessional triumph but in stalemate and a new balance of power. More widely, it witnessed the removal of the religious question from international relations, though religious disputes remained a matter of prime political importance internally in many countries. An older age of "horizontal loyalty" to popes and emperors was over, though the full change would take decades more to become clear. A new age of "vertical loyalty" to centralized monarchies was under way. It was driven by prolonged warfare which speeded advanced state-building and military centralization, and necessary to sustain new levels and forms of taxation and wartime levels of military spending needed after the peace to keep permanent armies in barracks. First among equals of the myriad states and statelets of Europe was France, the greatest single beneficiary of the Thirty Years' War. Thus did a German conflict stemming from confessional and constitutional confrontations that seemed odd or quaint to later generations become a European-wide war, and indeed a global war with naval and amphibious battles waged as far afield as Brazil and Ceylon. See also *Bärwalde, Treaty of*; *Hague Alliance*; *Heilbronn, League of*; *Holk, Heinrich*; *Leipziger Bund*; *Lisowczyks*; *Monzón, Treaty of*; *prisoners of war*; *Uzkok War*; *witchcraft*.

Suggested Reading: Ronald Asch, *The Thirty Years' War* (1997); Geoffrey Parker, ed., *The Thirty Years' War* (1987); S. H. Steinberg, *The "Thirty Years' War" and the Conflict for European Hegemony, 1600–1660* (1966).

Three Kingdoms, Wars of (1639–1653). See *English Civil Wars*.

thughur. See *March*.

Thurn, Count Mathias von (1567–1640). Protestant general in the *Thirty Years' War* (1618–1648). He initiated the war by carrying out the "*Defenestration of Prague*" (1618). Along with *Graf von Mansfeld* and *Christian of Anhalt-Bernburg*, Thurn and his Bohemians were decisively defeated by the army of the *Catholic League*, led by *Compte Bucquoy* and *Johann Tilly*, at the *White Mountain* (November 8, 1620).

tier. The entire set of *broadside* guns on one deck of a ship.

Tilly, Count Johann Tserclaes (1559–1632). Catholic general. Commander of the *Catholic League* (Liga); Imperial field marshal. A Habsburg subject by virtue of his birth in the Spanish Netherlands, Tilly was raised by *Jesuits* to service of the Church Militant but never imbibed the full range, or scholarly inclinations, of a Jesuit education. Instead he turned to war: he spent his adult life in professional military service, earning a reputation for toughness, even callousness, an attitude that fit the Age like a mailed glove. He first saw combat at age 15 and served under *Parma* in the Netherlands to 1592. He fought for *Rudolf II* against the Ottomans in Hungary from 1600 to 1608. In 1610 he hired out to *Maximilian I* and the Catholic League. Tilly led an Austrian army into Bohemia at the start of the Thirty Years' War, crushing combined Protestant armies at the *White Mountain* (November 8, 1620). Then he marauded through the Palatinate, ripping it away from *Friedrich V*. In 1622 Tilly was beaten, but not stopped, by *Graf von Mansfeld* at *Mingolsheim* (April 22). He beat Mansfeld and *Baden* five days later at *Wiesloch* (April 27). He defeated Baden again at *Wimpfen* (May 6). He bested *Christian of Brunswick* at *Höchst* (June 20). From August to September, Tilly besieged Heidelberg; he let his troops pillage the city when it fell. The next year he won at *Stadtlohn* (August 6), destroying nearly 80 percent of Christian's army. That left only Mansfeld and his ragged mercenaries in the field on the Protestant side.

Once Denmark entered the war Tilly was effectively subordinate to *Albrecht von Wallenstein*, as Bavaria was to the Empire. Tilly scored a major victory over *Christian IV* of Denmark at *Lutter-am-Barenberg* in 1626, then worked with Wallenstein to clear Saxony, and later Jutland, of anti-Habsburg forces. After Wallenstein's dismissal from Imperial command in August 1630, Tilly was appointed to command both the Imperial and Liga armies just in time to face the spectacular intervention by *Gustavus Adolphus* and the superb Swedish Army. The 71-year-old Tilly could do nothing to prevent the Swedes occupying northern Germany. His response was to let his troops run amok: he dismissed one complaint about brutal conduct by his men against civilians with the cavalier remark, "Do you think my men are nuns?" That attitude underlay the most famous atrocity of an age of atrocities when *Pappenheim*'s cavalry, part of Tilly's Imperial Army, sacked *Magdeburg* (1631). So extensive was the rapine, murder, and destruction that Tilly could not provision his men there and had to march north. Gustavus met and beat him at *Werben* (July 22–28, 1631), forcing him into Saxony. Tilly is often criticized for being too old and too old-fashioned to keep up with the tactics of Gustavus at *First Breitenfeld* (September 17, 1631), where his army was shattered and he was personally wounded three times. But he was not as tactically backward as is sometimes said. For instance, he broke up his infantry squares into looser formations in imitation of the Swedes. While these were not copies of the brigade-sized units of the Swedish Army, they were not the old, over-massive *tercios* either. By early 1632 Tilly and Ferdinand had raised a new Imperial Army and Gustavus marched to meet it. They clashed at *Rain*, Bavaria (April 15, 1632), where Gustavus forced his way across the River Lech under heavy fire. During the action, Tilly's leg was smashed by a cannonball. It was a mortal hurt from which he died at Ingolstadt five days later, last of the great tercio captains.

timariots. Ottoman light cavalry. Like Muscovite *servitor class* cavalry, timariots were obliged to seasonal military service in exchange for a grant of land ("timar"), usually one that produced annual revenues of less than 20,000 akçes. The highest timariot ranks were sustained by generous income from a very large grant (*ziamet*), that paid revenue from 20,000 to 100,000 akçes. All were expected to tax their peasants at levels sufficient to equip themselves and support armed cavalry retainers (*Cebelu*), and to ride on military service for the sultan during the regular campaign season (May–October). Simply registering was enough to retain one's timar, but to expand it a timariot needed to display exceptional skill or combat bravery. Active participation in the sultan's wars was necessary to share in redistribution of the land revenues of dead timariots made after every battle or campaign. The distribution was made among survivors and landless volunteers who served recklessly in hope of winning a timar. Timariots provided the bulk of early modern Ottoman soldiery, numbering from a conservatively estimated reserve of 100,000 to perhaps as many as 200,000. On campaigns they mustered an average of about 75,000. In battle, timariots deployed on the wings, protecting the flanks of *Janissary Corps* infantry and artillery at the center. They were supplemented by light cavalry: allied *Tatars*, Kurds, or Christian *Voynuks*. These troops were used to scout, forage, and raid, preserving the timariots for combat. At the end of every campaign to about 1550, timariots were demobilized. Once the Empire became too expansive to use seasonal troops, timariot cavalry sometimes were held over the winter along the frontier to fight again the next year. In the main, however, sultans shifted to salaried forces during the 16th century. See also *Celâli Revolts*; *sipahis*.

> *Timariots provided the bulk of early modern Ottoman soldiery . . .*

"Time of Troubles" (1604–1613). "Smutnoe Vremia," or "Smuta" A prolonged period of social unrest, famine, peasant uprisings, dynastic and civil wars, and harsh repression in *Muscovy*. It was occasioned by complex dynastic struggles among several rival claimants to the throne, exacerbated by a frenetic climate of religious despair, schism, and millenarianism. The "False Dimitri," claiming to be the true tsar, invaded with a large but ill-disciplined peasant army during the reign of *Boris Godunov*. Rumors that the False Dimitri had a white cross on his chest and belief that he was the true tsar risen from the dead rallied peasants angry over the spread and deepening excesses of serfdom. Cynical Polish-Lithuanian nobles eager for material gain backed Dimitri and helped him take Moscow. True believers were disgusted with Dimitri, however, when he married a Polish Catholic who refused to convert to Orthodoxy. A cabal of *boyars* raised a Muscovite mob which turned on and killed Dimitri and his supporters with cries of "Death to the Poles!" A new tsar, Vasily Shuisky, was elected but represented only one faction of the boyars and could not control at all the aroused peasantry. Other boyars invited *Sigismund III*, king of Poland-Lithuania, to intervene. He did so, winning at Klushino (July 4, 1610) over a Russo-Swedish army. But then Sigismund claimed the throne for his son, Wladyslaw, in an effort to extend the already large Polish-Lithuanian empire over Muscovy. Wladyslaw refused to convert to Orthodoxy and was therefore rejected by most Russians as anathema. Orthodox boyars raised a rural militia that took Moscow back from the Poles in 1613. The zemsky sobor, or assembly of *Estates*, finally ended the chaos by uniting against the foreign, Catholic Poles. It established a new Russian dynasty by electing as tsar 16-year-old *Michael Romanov* (1596–1645).

Suggested Reading: M. Perrie, *Pretenders and Popular Monarchism in Early Modern Russia* (1995); Ruslan Skrynnikov, *The Time of Troubles*, Hugh Graham, trans. (1988).

Timur (1336–1405). "Amir Timur," or "Timur the Great." Best known in the West as "Tamerlane" (a corruption of "Timur Lang" or "Timur the Lame"). Born into a minor military family among the Jagatai Mongols, and partially lame in one leg, in 1370 Timur overthrew the Khan of Samarkand and declared himself a direct descendant of the "Great Khans." After securing his base with murder and terror, in 1380 he invaded Iran, which had split into fractious states following the collapse of the Mongol "Il-Khans." Thus began a career built wholly on warlordism and carnage. He next invaded Armenia, Azerbaijan, and Iraq. His major enemies were to the north, however, in southern Russia, which he invaded in 1390. As he attacked these Christian areas, rampaging and slaughtering throughout Ukraine and parts of Mongol-occupied Muscovy, rebellions broke out in his provinces in Central Asia and he was forced to return and reconquer those lands. Thus was set in motion a bloody and destructive, yet ultimately futile pattern of shifting personal and martial dominance, in which he ruled so harshly that in his absence rebellion frequently sprang up, only to be met with reconquest and ferocious retribution. Millions may have died at the hands of his mixed Tatar-Mongol armies. He left whole regions underpopulated and economically depressed, literally for centuries. In 1391 Timur turned from Iran into the Caucasus in pursuit of the army of the Golden Horde, which he chased into southern Russia and defeated in a massive cavalry battle involving 100,000 horsemen, at Kandurcha. He then returned to Iran to complete its conquest. In 1397 he savagely repressed a rebellion in Iran. The next year he invaded northern India on the pretext of enforcing strict Islam on the Hindu subjects of an overly tolerant *Delhi Sultanate*. Once again slaughter and pillage was the order of his days. Timur won at *Panipat* (1398), then proceeded to sack Delhi during ten days of rape and unbridled carnage by brutal, barbarian illiterates. He then abandoned India, satisfied with having destabilized it and opened its cities to longterm pillage, rape, and murder any time he chose to return.

Timur invaded Syria where he wiped out a *mamlūk* army in 1400. He rewarded his troops by letting them sack Aleppo, Damascus, and Baghdad. He did all this in spite of his nominal claim to be a Muslim: while he did spare Muslim holy places he killed Muslims in large numbers. Timur later had Baghdad razed as retribution for a brief revolt against his occupation. In 1402 he invaded Anatolia, defeating the Ottomans at *Ankara* and capturing *Bayezid I*. That victory made Timur overlord of a vast region from the Middle East to Central Asia: by 1405 he was receiving *tribute* from the Ottomans, Byzantines, Egyptians, Syrians, and several small khanates of Central Asia and southern Russia. Timur's appetite for blood and plunder was not satiated, however: he was planning a massive invasion of China when he took ill and died. Like so many of his Mongol and Turkic nomad forebears, Timur took much from more settled civilizations but gave back nothing. His death marked the end of an enormously destructive era of invasions of settled civilizations by steppe nomads, and his empire fell apart as soon as he departed it. In western Iran "Black Sheep" and "White Sheep" Turkomen clans succeeded Timur. Only in eastern Iran and Afghanistan did a branch of the Timurid dynasty survive. His great-grandson *Babur* also invaded India, but unlike his forebear stayed to found the *Mughal Empire*.

Suggested Reading: Beatrice Manz, *The Rise and Rule of Tamerlane* (1999).

Timurid dynasty. Any of several dynastic lines descending from *Timur*. See also *Babur*; *Iran*; *Mughal Empire*.

Tippermuir, Battle of (1644). A *Covenanter* army of 5,000 chased down and offered battle to a force of just 1,100 Irish and Highlanders (MacDonalds) loyal to the *Marquis of Montrose*. Highland ferocity and Montrose's tactical brilliance told the tale as the overconfident and numerically superior Covenanters suffered over 40 percent casualties. That allowed Montrose to occupy Perth and Aberdeen and keep Royalist hope alive, in Scotland at least. See also *English Civil Wars*.

Tokugawa Ieyasu (1542–1616). Né Matsudaira Motoyasu. Last of the great unifiers of Japan and founder of the Tokugawa shogunate. At age 4 he was given by his father as a hostage to a neighboring *daimyo*; he was captured en route by a third daimyo and held hostage to age 7. Once freed he continued to his original destination and resumed his family obligation as hostage to his father's loyalty and conduct until the age of 18. In 1560 he allied with *Oda Nobunaga* after paying that cruel warlord's loyalty-price of killing his wife and ordering his son to commit seppuku (ritual suicide). Ieyasu and Nobunaga fought together well and often, notably at *Anegawa* (1570). Ieyasu lost to Takeda Katsuyori at Mikata ga Hara in 1572 but crushed him at *Nagashino* three years later. The alliance with Nobunaga paid well: by 1582, Ieyasu controlled five provinces and was poised to succeed as military hegemon. However, *Toyotomi Hideyoshi* moved more quickly to defeat Nobunaga's assassin and claimed the succession. The two warlords met in an indecisive succession battle at Nagakute (1584). Afterwards, they allied and Ieyasu sealed the deal by marrying Hideyoshi's sister. In 1590 he helped Hideyoshi defeat the Hōjō at Odawara and subdue the northeast. He was then ordered to relocate to secure the conquered Hōjō domains. He settled at Edo (Tokyo), master of the richest and most strategic of all daimyo domains. Busy consolidating these new lands, Ieyasu was not involved in Hideyoshi's costly and failed invasions of Korea in the 1590s.

In 1598 Ieyasu was appointed one of five regents for Hideyoshi's minor son, Toyotomi Hideyori, but instead moved to seize power for himself as the new military hegemon. He secured this position by leading an eastern coalition to victory at *Sekigahara* in 1600. As a descendant of the Minamoto, Ieyasu did what Nobunaga and Hideyoshi were unable to do because of their humble origins: in 1603, he became *Shogun*. Two years later he raised his son to that office while still exercising power behind the scenes. Ieyasu made peace with Korea in 1605, formalized in the Treaty of Kiyu (1609). As part of his policy of concentrating all military power, in 1607 he decreed that all cannon casting must be centralized under his control at Nagahama. Gunsmiths were elevated to *samurai* status, reflecting a new respect in Japan for firearms. All cannon and musket purchases were henceforth channeled through the "Commissioner of Guns." In combination with control of Japan's coasts and radically restricted foreign trade, this order ultimately established a tightly centralized state and shogunal monopoly over firearms. As much as anything, this ensured the long peace that consolidation of the Tokugawa victory brought to Japan from 1615, when Ieyasu defeated Hideyori and reduced his last stronghold at *Osaka Castle*. The realm united and subdued, Ieyasu died in 1616.

Suggested Reading: George Sansom, *History of Japan, 1334–1615* (1961); Conrad Totman, *Tokugawa Ieyasu: Shogun* (1983).

Tokugawa Shogunate (1603–1867). See *bakufu*; *castles, on land*; *daimyo*; *Japan*; *Kakure Kirishitan*; *samurai*; *Tokugawa Ieyasu*; *tribute*; *Unification Wars*.

toleration. See *Akbar*; *Anabaptism*; *arma*; *Arminianism*; *Augsburg, Peace of*; *Augsburg Confession*; *Austria*; *Calvinism*; *Carafa War*; *Catholic Church*; *confessionalism*; *Corpus Catholicorum*; *Corpus Evangelicorum*; *Counter-Reformation*; *Edict of Amboise*; *Edict of Nantes*; *Edict of Restitution*; *Edict of Saint-Germain*; *Edict of Saint-Germain-en-Laye*; *Egmont*; *Eighty Years' War*; *Elizabeth I*; *expulsion of the Jews*; *expulsion of the Moors*; *Ferdinand II, Holy Roman Emperor*; *Francis I*; *Granada*; *Grotius, Hugo*; *Guise Family*; *Hendrik, Frederick*; *Henri III, of France*; *Henri IV, of France*; *Holy Roman Empire*; *Huguenots*; *Levellers*; *Louis XIII*; *Luther, Martin*; *Maximilian II*; *Medici, Catherine de*; *Oldenbaarneveldt, Johan van*; *Ormonde, 1st Duke of*; *Ottoman Empire*; *Passau, Convention of*; *Philip II, of Spain*; *Philip III, of Spain*; *Philip IV, of Spain*; *politiques (France)*; *politiques (Netherlands)*; *Prague, Peace of*; *Protestant Reformation*; *Reconquista*; *Richelieu, Cardinal Armand Jean du Plessis de*; *"Root and Branch" petition*; *Rudolf II*; *Thirty Years' War*; *Tudor, Mary*; *Urban VIII*; *Westphalia, Peace of*; *William the Silent*.

Tolsburg, Truce of (1618). This truce was to have brought peace between Sweden and Poland for two years but actually lasted until July 1621, when the war resumed. By September, *Gustavus Adolphus* had captured Riga. The Polish-Swedish war continued until the *Truce of Altmark* of September 16/26, 1629.

tompion. A wooden plug used to close the firing chamber in early *bombards*.

tonlet. An armored skirt that protected the stomach and hips. See also *fauld*.

tonnage. "Burthen." A measure of a ship's carrying capacity by volume (not weight), originally determined by the number of wine casks it could carry. The lost space involved in dry goods not in casks was called "deadweight stowage." A "tun" was a measure of eight barrels (36 gallons) or four hogsheads.

top. A platform located at the top of any lower mast (hence, "foretop," "maintop," "mizzentop"), serving as a foothold for men or boys spreading upper rigging and sail on the topmast. In battle, snipers might be placed in the top to fire down on enemy decks or at enemy snipers. See also *masts*; *sails*.

Top Arabacs (top arabacilar). "Gun-carriage drivers." Muleteers and other drivers of the *Janissary Corps* artillery. They were full members of the Corps, not auxiliaries. Other Janissary military specialists included *Cebicis* and *Topçu*.

top castle. See *castles, on ships*.

Topçu (Topçuar). "Gunners." One of several groups of military specialists within the *Janissary Corps*. Others included *Cebicis* and *Top Arabacs*.

topgallant. See *masts*; *sails*.

Tophane-i Amire. See *armories*.

Tordesillas, Treaty of (1494). See *Brazil*; *Canary Islands*; *Line of Demarcation*; *Zaragoza, Treaty of*.

toredar. A light *matchlock* firearm in use in India from the 15th century.

Toro, Battle of (1476). See *Ferdinand II, of Aragon and Isabella I, of Castile*.

Torquemada. See *expulsion of the Jews*; *Inquisition*.

torre alberrano. An exterior watch tower associated with a *torre del homenaje* to which it was connected solely by a plank bridge that could be cut or burned in the event of an enemy assault.

torre del homenaje. A *keep* in the Spanish style, with four corner towers and heavy machicolations to permit archery and pouring of burning oils on the heads of attackers below.

Torrington, Battle of (1646). See *English Civil Wars*; *Fairfax, Thomas*; *Hopton, Ralph*.

Torstensson, Lennart (1603–1651). Swedish artillery general, then field marshal. A companion of *Gustavus Adolphus* from youth, he served in the king's wars in Livonia and Poland in the 1620s. He spent two years of military study in the Netherlands, 1624–1625, under *Maurits of Nassau*. He was closely involved in the reform and standardization of Swedish artillery by Gustavus. Torstensson accompanied the king into Germany in 1630 in command of the field artillery. His batteries fought exceedingly well at *First Breitenfeld* (1631). He provided a smoke screen that allowed the army to cross the River Lech under enemy fire at *Rain* (1632). He was captured at *Alte Feste* (1632) during a failed attack on *Albrecht von Wallenstein*'s camp. He was held for a year then ransomed by Sweden and exchanged. He was subordinate to *Johann Banér* at *Wittstock* (October 4, 1636) but took full command of the Swedish Army at *Second Breitenfeld* (1642). He spent most of 1642 overrunning Saxony, Bohemia,

> *He marched the army across Germany . . . in a pre-emptive campaign against Denmark . . .*

and Moravia. He marched the army across Germany in 1643 in order to invade Jutland in a pre-emptive campaign against Denmark sometimes called *Torstensson's War*. In 1645 he moved against Prague, winning decisively at *Jankov* and knocking Bavaria out of the war but failing to take the well-defended city. His many years in the saddle took their toll: he resigned in ill-health in 1646 and died five years later.

Torstensson's War (1643–1645). In 1643 *Christian IV* of Denmark contemplated re-entering the German war, this time in alliance with the Habsburgs. As that would seriously jeopardize the Swedish strategic position *Oxenstierna* decided to pre-empt: he recalled *Lennart Torstensson* and the main Swedish Army from Moravia and sent them into Jutland (December 22, 1643). The Danes fell back, as was their usual military practice under Christian, and Jutland fell to the Swedes. In addition, Swedish and Dutch warships pounded and threatened Danish coastal towns and the Dutch and Swedes defied the *Sound Tolls*. Christian agreed to an armistice in November 1644, and a humiliating peace at *Brömsebro* (1645). He lost Gotland, Ösel, and the bishoprics of Verden and Bremen. The losses were confirmed in the *Peace of Westphalia* in 1648.

Torun, Second Peace of (October 19, 1466). This treaty ended the *War of the Cities* (1454–1466) between Poland-Lithuania under *Casimir IV* and the *Teutonic Knights*. The Brethren lost West Prussia (henceforth called "Polish" or "Royal Prussia") to Poland, retained possession only of East Prussia (but conceded suzerainty to Poland), and were forced to transfer their capital from Marienburg to Königsberg (modern Kaliningrad). They were also compelled to accept 50 percent Polish membership and to watch their Hochmeister pay homage to Casimir. Torun split the Teutonic Knights: the Livonian brothers elected their own commander (Landmeister), resuming their former discrete status. While neither the emperor nor the pope accepted the legality of this treaty it was a triumph for Polish statecraft. It set the stage for Poland's dominance of the eastern Baltic until the rise of Sweden to pre-eminence under *Gustavus Adolphus*.

Tournai, Siege of (1581). See *Parma, duque di*.

tournaments. Once personal armor afforded good protection (early 12th century) and the stirrup and wraparound saddle with pommel permitted European *knights* to use a *couched lance*, the warrior class developed a game of group ("conrois") sham combat called the "tournament" or "tourney." This was essentially a way to practice new cavalry techniques involving *shock* and test other weapons and combat skills. Tourneys were closely associated with *chivalry*. Knights would sometimes "wear their hearts on their sleeve" by tying a lady's scarf or other favor to their gauntlet before entering the arena. In a combat "à plaisance," light lances were used which had a coronal (blunted spearpoint) instead of the normal leaf-shaped cutting tip. Still, tourneys could be nearly as lethal as combat when a fight "à outrance" was waged. In these contests many real weapons were used—except the battleaxe, which was banned as too savage and lethal. Extra-heavy armor was developed for tourneys, with additional pieces such as the "barber" (an added layer of iron plate) worn over the *cuirasse* and *hauberk*. Saddles were adjusted to protect the legs. In later tourneys a wooden barrier called the "tilt" was introduced to jousts to keep horses and riders from colliding, which could have fatal consequences. From the 14th century the addition of lance-rests to armor increased breakage of lances, with some spring mounted to add to the drama by amplifying the crack and splintering effects. By the end of the Middle Ages tourneys were reduced to ritual display, posing little real danger to participants but also teaching them little or nothing of the art of war, which was in any case already bypassing the mounted knight. See also *drill*; *mace*.

Suggested Reading: Juliet Barker, *The Tournament in England, 1100–1400* (1986).

tourney. See *tournaments*.

Towarzysz. Polish: "Comrade." Commanders in the "National Contingent" of the *Polish Army*, recruited among the greater nobles who brought military retinues with them. They dressed extravagantly, wearing tall plumage or even lion and leopard skins. See also *poczet*.

tower-keep. A multi-storied rectangular castle built of stone. It was an advance in defense and comfort over the primitive *motte-and-bailey* fort or even the *keep-and-bailey*. Rather than being built on top of the motte like a simple keep, these much larger structures were built on the scale of the outer bailey.

Tower of London. In addition to its famous history as a royal prison and place of intrigue, treason, betrayal, murder, and execution, the Tower of London served for centuries as the main *armory* for English armies and the *Royal Navy*. To serve the navy, the Tower had a stone quay at which royal warships took aboard powder, shot, bows, crossbows, quarrels, and other military stores. In the late 14th century naval supply obligations were transferred to the "Privy Wardrobe of the Tower." For the army it stockpiled *catapults* and *trebuchets* along with hand-cut stone ammunition; mail and plate armor of all types; halberds, pikes, crossbows, longbows, and masses of arrows loaded in wooden quivers; and later, arquebuses and muskets along with powder and shot. For both the army and navy into the 16th century the only bronze gun foundry in England was located in the Tower. This was because England's rich iron deposits, neatly located close to large forests, encouraged an unusual national reliance on iron cannon and permitted decentralized iron foundries. See also *Wars of the Roses*.

Towton, Battle of (1461). See *Wars of the Roses*.

Toyotomi Castle, Siege of (1614–1615). See *Osaka Castle, Siege of*.

Toyotomi Hideyori (1593–1615). Son of *Toyotomi Hideyoshi*. See also *Osaka Castle, Siege of*.

Toyotomi Hideyoshi (1537–1598). "Taikō" Japanese warlord. Son of a foot soldier in *Oda Nobunaga*'s army, he rose through the ranks based upon toughness and drive. He demonstrated his generalship in 1570 during Nobunaga's invasion of western Honshu. In 1581 he displayed his siegecraft by taking Tottori castle with a novel device: months in advance of the siege he bought up most of the rice in the region, thus speeding starvation of the garrison. When he learned of Nobunaga's death he marched on Kyoto and defeated the treacherous vassal *daimyo* (Akechi Mitsuhide) who had betrayed his master at Yamazaki. This act earned Hideyoshi the loyalty of Nobunaga's army. He fought an inconclusive succession battle with *Tokugawa Ieyasu* at Nagakute (1584). The two warlords then allied to complete the unification of Japan.

Hideyoshi increased the number of *arquebusiers* in his armies, razed the castles of defiant daimyo, and hounded to death all he suspected of contemplating rebellion. Like Nobunaga, he also viciously suppressed *Buddhism*. By the 1580s he commanded the largest armies ever assembled in Japan and campaigned on a truly national scale. With 100,000 men he conquered Shikoku and Etchu in 1585. Two years later he took Kyushu with 200,000 troops. In 1590 he crushed the Hōjō army of 60,000 men with an army of his own numbering nearly 200,000. He reduced garrisons and branch forts and led a three-month siege of Odawara castle, the Hōjō fortress in Sagami province. Having unified the country he sought to pacify it by disarming the population. In 1587 he banned peasants from owning weapons and sent inspectors to seize all swords, spears, bows, and firearms from the non-*samurai* classes. Four years later he banned training of peasants or townsfolk as soldiers ("separation edict"). These measures consolidated the military monopoly of the samurai and thereby bought acquiescence to centralized rule, ultimately with Hideyoshi serving as imperial regent.

Hideyoshi could be magnanimous to defeated daimyo when it suited his political interest, allowing them to relocate to lesser domains but keep their heads and their families and retainers. Yet, he was also capable of great brutality and cruelty akin to Nobunaga's. On numerous occasions he not only killed male prisoners, he impaled their children and crucified their wives and mothers. Among his many victims were one of his heirs, several members of his household, and a number of lifelong companions. When he "forgave" enemies it was for shrewd political reasons. In his last years his rage, paranoia, and cruelty were expressed on a grand canvas. In 1587 Hideyoshi ordered all Christian missionaries to leave Japan, which he affirmed as "land of the gods." Ten years later he ordered mass executions of Japanese Christians (*Kirishitan*), whom he feared would act as a fifth column for foreign influence and conquest.

Hideyoshi planned a great empire to include Indochina, Siam, Taiwan, the Ryukyus, the Philippines, Korea, and indeed, all China: there is some evidence that he hoped to displace the Ming emperor and replace him with the figurehead Japanese emperor, with himself the power behind the thrones of a vast Asian empire. In 1592 he sent a force of 160,000 to invade Korea. His army took poorly fortified Pusan within a day, using superior muskets, better trained musketeers employing *volley fire*, and far more powerful siege cannon than anything the Koreans had ever seen. Three weeks later the Japanese captured Seoul. They took Pyongyang two months after that. Hideyoshi ordered "mopping-up" operations in northern Korea and prepared to invade Manchuria. Instead, he faced intervention by a Ming army advancing from the north. While the Japanese severely damaged this force another Ming army arrived in 1593 while dispersed Koreans waged an effective guerilla campaign. Four years of bloody stalemate ensued. At sea, the Koreans used *turtle ships* to destroy convoys of Japanese junks, which were armed supply ships rather than true warships. On land, Korean guerilla and Ming regular resistance pushed the Japanese back to Seoul. Cut off from Japan by the Korean navy and running out of supplies, Hideyoshi agreed to a truce in 1593: he withdrew to Pusan in exchange for the Ming army departing Korea. In 1597 Hideyoshi re-invaded Korea with a second massive army. The Ming again counter-intervened. More savagery abounded: tens of thousands of Korean and Chinese ears and noses were sent to Kyoto to form a great "victory mound." On land the Japanese were stopped again at Chiksan (1597), south of Seoul; a week later they were defeated at sea, at Myongnyang.

Hideyoshi's major accomplishments were to complete unification of Japan and begin the domestication of daimyo and samurai so that they became the permanent floor of a quiescent Japanese social order under the *Tokugawa shoguns*. On the other hand, the price in lives of his megalomaniacal foreign military adventures was high. The price in lasting Korean and Chinese animosity was higher still.

Suggested Reading: Elizabeth Berry, *Hideyoshi* (1982).

Trabanten. Bohemian mercenaries employed mainly by the Holy Roman Empire until the advent of the *Landsknechte* infantry in 1485. The term was later used about the personal guard of the colonel of a company or regiment.

trace italienne. "Italian traces." Known in Italy as *"alla moderna"* ("modern style"). A key innovation of the 15th–16th-century evolution of fortification techniques was the addition of triangular *bastions* that extended from low broad walls to permit defensive artillery to cover attack lanes and approaches. The "artillery fortress" (historian John Lynn's excellent term) employing trace italienne bastions evolved in stages, all a reaction to improvements in siege artillery. First came the addition of cut-away ports and guns to existing stone fortifications, mostly to provide counterbattery fire against enemy siege engines and cannon. Next came a series of adjustments that lowered the walls ("countersinking") and reinforced them with earthen banks, ditches, and moats; this allowed larger defensive cannon to be mounted on stronger walls or squat towers

> *...the new bastions certainly restored a balance between offense and defense...*

and roundels. Finally, geometric bastions were built or added to maximize the effect of defensive fire. This was done on a grand scale by Italian towns, though the expense was so vast few were completed. The style spread from Italy to nearby city-states such as Mantua, Monferrat, and Geneva, which built single massive works. In the Netherlands, dozens of smaller artillery fortresses provided a layered defense-in-depth that proved unbeatable by the Spanish. Similarly, they supported a system of defense-in-depth in Hungary and Dalmatia that helped stop the advance of powerful Ottoman armies deeper into Europe.

A major debate has taken place among military historians as to whether the new "artillery fortress" constituted a *revolution in military affairs* that resulted in a huge expansion of European armies necessary to overcome the revolutionary effects of the new fortifications (Michael Roberts' thesis). In the 16th century, the new bastions certainly restored a balance between offense and defense that had been broken by siege cannon in the 15th century. This restored balance lasted late into the 18th century. Yet, even this shift to the defense should not be exaggerated: the Ottomans were able to overwhelm "alla moderna" fortifications on several occasions using cannon along with mining and starvation. In addition, trace italienne bastions were hugely expensive: more than one petty ruler went bankrupt and lost his state out of the effort to defend it too well (as Frederick the Great would later warn, "he who defends everything, defends nothing").

The trace italienne traveled overseas along with European expansion and conquest. New model forts were built by the Spanish in the Caribbean, by the Portuguese in Africa and India, and by the Dutch in Southeast Asia. Yet, these were limited applications. In most places outside Europe and the scattered enclaves where Europeans built artillery fortresses overseas to ward off other Europeans, the old styles of fortification sufficed. Since most non-European armies did not have the heavy cannon needed for siege warfare there was usually no need for Europeans to build overseas bastions in the expensive new style. Nor did the trace italienne spread to China, which could easily have afforded and adopted it. Why not? Probably because the usual threat to China in this period was not a modern army with siege capabilities but a host of steppe nomads wholly reliant on cavalry. These nomads could sweep deep into China but were unable to reduce the extant walls of its cities. That changed when *Nurgaci* captured Chinese cannon and Han gunners and incorporated them into the Manchu *banner system*. But by then the Ming had so many other internal enemies and military costs it was too late to fundamentally adapt their system of fortification.

Suggested Reading: Mahhinder Kingra, "The *trace italienne* and the Military Revolution during the Eighty Years' War," *Journal of Military History* (1993); Geoffrey Parker, *The Military Revolution*, 2nd ed. (1996).

train (1). The long tail of baggage carts and people following any army. See also *baggage train*; *Hurenweibel*; *provost*; *Tross*.

train (2). The artillery and related wagons and personnel accompanying an army. See also *artillery train* (1); *pioneers*; *Tross*.

train (3). The tail of a gun carriage.

trained bands. Military advisers to *Elizabeth I* established "trained bands" that built upon the country's *militia* tradition to strengthen domestic forces in the event conflict with Spain led to invasion. The idea was to substitute a well-trained and properly equipped urban militia for the wholly inadequate and ill-equipped amateurs that preceded the trained bands. Nobles and clergy were exempt from trained band obligations since, theoretically, they already contributed through the older feudal levies. During the first year of the *English Civil Wars*, London and other southern trained bands were crucial to survival of the Parliamentary cause. Still, since they mostly did not like to fight far from home they were eventually replaced by the *New Model Army*. In the north and west some trained bands loyal to regional magnates fought for the Royalists. See also *company*; *exact militia*; *Newbury, First Battle of*; *Preston, Campaign of*.

transportation. A penalty of enforced exile in *penal settlements* meted out to common criminals, political dissidents, and rebels by several European states which possessed overseas colonies, notably Portugal, France, and England. The Tudors and Stuarts transported large numbers of forced migrants from Ireland, displaced by the *plantations* of that country. After the battles of *Dunbar* (1650) and *Worcester* (1651), thousands of Scottish prisoners of war were transported to the West Indies as indentured laborers.

Transylvania. See *Hungary*; *Kosovo Polje, Battle of*; *Teutonic Knights, Order of*.

trapper. A thick cloth blanket worn over equine armor.

treasure fleets. See *convoy*.

trebuchet. The traction trebuchet was invented in China during its wars of unification prior to 221 B.C.E. There is controversy over the date at which the technology migrated to Europe, but certainly trebuchets were in wide use there by 1200 C.E. Alternate terms for trebuchets included "martinets," "flying engines" ("engine volants"), and "perrières" ("stone-tossers"). By whatever name, mid-12th-century trebuchets were great stone-throwing engines that used counterweights (a box of stones or slag) rather than simple traction to gain power and increase projectile velocity. By altering the size of the balance different ranges could be located. Once range was established, the second, third, and later shots hit the same spot with high accuracy and destructive effect. Like the largest gunpowder cannon, great trebuchets bore "noms de guerre" and were handed down by name in royal wills. They were used by attackers to hurl heavy stones, including hand-cut stone balls ("pommes") at or over defending walls. Defenders in a siege used trebuchets in a counterbattery role to smash the attacker's trebuchets and kill his artillerymen, or to smash various counter-castles (bastilles) or siege engines that might be brought into range for an assault. Modern tests have shown that a 10-ton counterweight trebuchet of medieval European design could hurl a 300-pound stone ball over 450 feet, achieving much greater impact than either Roman torsion engines or early gunpowder artillery. They also achieved a high rate of fire—recorded in one English siege at over 52 shots per day per trebuchet. Still, they were perfectly useless in field battles.

Trebuchets were expensive siege engines, especially if hurling labor-intensive, cut-stone ammunition. They were also difficult to transport. They were usually dismantled for transport by cart or barge and reassembled at the place of siege. General expense kept numbers down: a maximum of 20 trebuchets were recorded at the greatest sieges of the Middle Ages. The weight of stone ammunition even a few machines expended must have caused prodigious logistical and financial problems and suggests that most stone ammunition may have been quarried and cut by masons near the siege site. As with the much less powerful *catapult*, trebuchets could also hurl disease-ridden animal or human carcases or manure into the defenders' abodes, advancing the general debilitating effects of siege with primitive germ warfare. They were also used to conduct psychological warfare by throwing severed heads and bodies of dead defenders over the walls and, on occasion, live men. And they could hurl incendiaries to burn down a town. The trebuchet was so effective as a siege weapon that it provoked wholesale redesign of castles and other fortified defenses, notably thickening walls and rounding *keeps* and *donjons* to deflect high-impact stones. They remained in use in tandem with the first gunpowder artillery for many decades. In the last quarter of the 14th century, for instance, the French had over a hundred trebuchets in service in various sieges or fixed defenses. In the 1420s new trebuchets were still being ordered for use in the *Hundred Years' War* (1337–1453). Inventories of royal armories in France still showed a number of trebuchets in stock as late as the 1460s. See also *Albigensian Crusade*;

armories; *artillery*; *castles, on land*; *fortification*; *siege warfare*; *Teutonic Knights, Order of*.

Suggested Reading: Donald Hill, "Trebuchets," *Viator*, 4 (1973).

Trent, Council of (1545–1563). See *Council of Trent*.

Trent, Peace of (1501). See *Italian Wars*.

Treuga Dei. "Truce of God." In the 11th century the Catholic Church attempted to go beyond the strictures of the *Pax Dei* to impose limits to permissible violence against additional classes of people by forbidding warfare on certain days of the week: Thursdays, in commemoration of the "Last Supper"; Fridays, in memory of the Crucifixion of Jesus of Nazareth ("The Christ"); Saturday, to remember the day Jesus lay in his tomb; and Sunday, "The Lord's Day." Also, the Treuga Dei banned fighting during the month of Lent which preceded Easter, during Advent, and on Christmas Day and other Feast Days. This helped protect peasants and other food producers, merchants, and travelers from brigands in the guise of soldiers. A number of powerful lay authorities picked up the chalice and acted to enforce these rules within their domains. They did so partly for reasons of piety but also because social order and peace suited their instincts as governors. Ultimately, the Church attempted to effect a ban on killing of any Christian by other Christians, though with minimal effect. The main practical result of the "Truce of God" was not to restrain war but to restrict its practice to a chosen few: the feudal nobility and town militias.

tribute. Treasure and political homage paid to a greater power by a weaker magnate, ruler, or state. Tribute was elicited by raids and paid to gain protection from future raids, as when the Anglo-Saxons paid the "Danegeld" to Viking raiders. When simple raiding failed, more violent and sustained warfare ensued in the form of sieges by land and blockades by sea until the point was well-taken. Wherever relations of *overlordship* existed tribute followed: even in the distant Arctic some Norse enforced tribute payments in reindeer hides from the Lapps. In the absence of the modern idea of sovereign equality of states the surest way to avoid subservience was to establish dominance over someone else. For a time *Crusader* princes of Antioch held small Muslim states in Syria in tribute. At the other end of the scale, very large states might pay tribute, as with Austrian payments to the Ottomans in exchange for part of Hungary. Or tribute might be paid within an empire, as when the Abbasid caliphs demanded boys from their eastern provinces to be raised as military slaves (*mamlūks*), and the later Ottomans took Christian boys to become *Janissaries*. The *taifa states* of Iberia were forced into tributary status to Berber dynasties when the recruitment base of their armies shrank because the supply of north European slave boys, on which they depended to fill mamlūk regiments, dried up with the eastward advance of the *Teutonic Knights* in the Baltic. A number of Muslim taifa states were forced to pay tribute to Christian

Aragon, Castile, and Portugal. The most elaborate tribute system was developed by China. Besides flattering and confirming the prestige of the emperors of the Middle Kingdom, ritual tribute disguised what was really mercantile trade. Why the subterfuge? Because trade was despised by the Confucian scholar-elite, an attitude that greatly hampered development of overseas commercial relations. Since Ming emperors officially regarded Dutch, Portuguese, and English traders as representatives of "tributary nations," diplomatic confusion reigned as well. See also *Assassins*; *Aztec Empire*; *Hungary*; *Mali Empire*; *Murad I*; *Reconquista*; *Songhay*; *Thirteen Years' War*; *Xochiyaoyotl*.

Tridentine Reforms. See *Council of Trent*.

Triebel, Battle of (1647). See *Montecuccoli, Raimundo*.

Trier, bishopric of. One of the eight larger polities within the *Holy Roman Empire*. It had about 400,000 souls at the start of the *Thirty Years' War*. Its bishop was an Imperial Elector. See also *Richelieu, Cardinal Armand Jean du Plessis de*; *Westphalia, Peace of*.

Triple Alliance. See *Aztec Empire*.

Tripoli (Tripolitania). From the 7th century C.E., Tripoli was governed by various Arab and Muslim dynasties. It formed part of *Ifriqiya* in the 13th century and was the northern terminus of the shortest of the trans-Saharan trade routes. It was occupied by Ferdinand I of Aragon (1452–1516) in 1511 then given over to the Knights of St. John, one of the Christian *Military Orders*. They were expelled in 1551 by the Ottomans. By the end of the 16th century Tripoli was fully incorporated as an Ottoman province, along with Tunis and Algiers. See also *Barbary corsairs*; *Tuareg*.

Triumvirate. An anti-Protestant league formed in 1561 by *Anne Montmorency*, *François Guise*, and Jacques d'Albon, Marshal of Saint-André. See also *French Civil Wars*.

Tromp, Maarten van (1598–1653). Dutch admiral. While at sea with his father he was taken prisoner by an English ship and made to serve as a cabin boy for two years. In 1624 he took command of a Dutch frigate in the war against Spain. He rose to admiral and became one of the premier sea captains of the 17th century. In mid-1639 he carried out a raid on the Dunkirk pirates. That October he defeated a huge Spanish invasion fleet off *The Downs* (October 11/21), capturing 13 prize galleons and 57 other ships out of a Spanish convoy of 100 ships. It was an astonishing, decisive, crushing victory that helped decide the outcome of the *Eighty Years' War* (1568–1648). Tromp later fought several important battles in the Anglo-Dutch wars.

Troppau, Battle of (1642). See *Montecuccoli, Raimundo*.

Tross. The *train* following any German army.

trou de loup. "Wolf hole." A conical pit dug to the height of a man or deeper, with a sharpened iron spike embedded at the bottom. The top of the hole was covered with taut cloth or wicker and further camouflaged with dirt. It might be filled with water to facilitate slipping and then drowning of any man impaled on, or wounded by, the spike. Wolf holes were used singly or sometimes in dense fields in front of a defended position.

Troyes, Treaty of (1420). See *Henry V, of England*; *Hundred Years' War*; *safeguard the sea*.

truages. "Truces" in which protection money was extorted from towns or peasants by *routiers* or *Free Companies*. See also *appatis*.

Truce of God. See *Treuga Dei*.

True Pure Land. "Ikkō-ikki" or "single-minded bands." Adherents of Jodo Shinshu, or the True Pure Land sect of Buddhism. Most were warrior monks or peasant farmers. This radical sect was headquartered in the fortress of *Honganji* in Osaka where it produced its own guns and cannon. Locally, the sect was organized into confederacies that spanned central and eastern Japan. During the *Sengoku jidai* the confederacies clashed with local *daimyo*, overturning some. Its adherents seldom gave or asked for quarter so that fights often were unusually bloody and fought to the last man. It became active in opposition to the centralizing conquests of *Oda Nobunaga* after 1570. In 1574 Nobunaga massacred—without regard to age or gender—all adherents of the sect who lived in the Nagashima delta region, perhaps as many as 20,000 souls. Some he starved to death after refusing mercy; others he burned alive. Sporadic fighting with the sect continued for a decade, until the fall of Honganji in 1580.

> *...Nobunaga massacred—without regard to age or gender—all adherents of the sect...*

trunnion. Developed by the French toward the end of the 15th century, this simple device had a major impact on *artillery*. A trunnion was an axle cast together with, and as an integral part of, a gun barrel. It served two key purposes. First, by channeling the force of recoil into the *gun carriage* the gun itself could be rolled back into firing position more easily, with the position marked by blocks placed underneath the front of the carriage wheels. Older guns, without trunnions, had to be manhandled back into position and re-aimed after each shot. Second, with trunnions the gun barrel could be elevated independently, while resting on the gun carriage by using a simple pre-formed step system. Trunnions, and hence the barrel from which they extruded, were fixed to the carriage by bolts and fittings called "capsquares."

Tuareg. A fierce nomadic people who dominated the central portion of the great trans-Saharan trade routes, breeding camels and enslaving sudanese blacks to mine the salt deposits of the central Sahara. They were a complex ethnic mix with a Berber military aristocracy at the top and a black underclass descended from former slaves at the bottom. What made them one people was the great leveling effect of *Islam*, to which most converted. In the 11th century the Tuareg helped establish caravan links from *Mali* and *Songhay* as the southern termini, to Tripoli and Ifriqiya on the Mediterranean coast. A Tuareg *jihad* carried into *al-Andalus* in the form of the Almoravids in the 11th century. In the 15th century they connected the city-states (and leather and cloth manufactures) of the Hausa to North Africa. Timbuktu, capital of the ancient empire of Mali, fell to the Tuareg in 1433 but they lost it to a resurgent Songhay in 1469. Migrating eastward, they established the state of Aïr with a capital at Agades, to which they brought slaves to work salt mines and service the western caravan routes.

Tudor, Mary. See *Mary Tudor*.

Tudors. See *Elizabeth I*; *Henry VIII, of England*; *"King's Two Bodies"*; *Mary Tudor*; *Wars of the Roses*.

tufang. A light *matchlock* firearm in use in India from the 15th century.

Tüfeçis. Ottoman mounted infantry first formed in the 16th century. They wore distinctive red coats and high red hats. They steadily grew in effectiveness and hence military importance to the Ottoman system, reaching a peak of proficiency in the 17th century.

Tula River, Battle of (1372). See *Hongwu Emperor*.

Tumu, Battle of (September I, 1449). In 1449 the Ming emperor Zhu Qizhen (Zhengtong), son of the fierce Xuande emperor, was just 21. Accepting advice from his chief *eunuch*, Wang Zhen, he invaded Mongolia with a huge host several hundred thousand strong and a truly mammoth supply train. Without ever encountering the Mongols the army turned around once it reached the extreme edge of its supplies. Just a few days march from a fortified town, and food and water, its rearguard was ambushed. Another was quickly formed but it too was cut off and wiped out by pursuing Mongols. Then the main body was surrounded. Weak from thirst, hunger, and overlong marches, the Ming Army stood no chance in the battle that followed. Wang Zhen was killed and Emperor Zhu Qizhen captured. As many as 500,000 Chinese may have perished in the Tumu campaign and battle. The Mongol horde then moved toward Beijing, raiding, pillaging, and raping as it passed unimpeded by any Ming army. The eight border garrisons (built by *Hongwu* but later abandoned by *Yongle*) did nothing but tend to themselves. As the Mongols were ill-equipped for a siege, after a week of plundering the outlying districts and countryside around Beijing they left, steppe ponies burdened with booty. In 1450 the Mongols released the boy emperor but in the interim his brother had claimed the throne. The Zhengtong Emperor did not regain power until he mounted a successful coup against his brother in 1457. After a long debate over appropriate strategy toward the Mongols, the Ming court decided to adopt a pure defensive posture and began construction of 700 miles of the *Great Wall*.

Tunis. The state of *Ifriqiya* dominated this area of North Africa from the 13th century. Assaults were made on its coastal cities in 1270 and 1390 by Frankish Crusaders. In the 14th century the Muslim Hafsid dynasty was sustained by Christian Spain when pressured by rival Marind forces. In 1535 *Charles V* commissioned *Andrea Doria* to lead an invasion fleet to capture Tunis. *Barbarossa* was chased off in June and the invasion army landed. After a three-month siege, the city fell and was sacked by Christian marauders for three full days. In 1569 Tunis was occupied by corsairs from neighboring Algiers. After the Ottoman naval defeat at *Lepanto* (1571), the Hafsid dynasty was restored by its Spanish patrons (1571), but within a few years the Hafsids were again deposed as Tunis, Tripoli, and Algiers fell to the Ottomans. See also *Barbary corsairs*.

"tunnage and poundage." A customs duty introduced in England in 1347 to support a fleet raised to besiege Calais during the *Hundred Years' War* (1337–1453). It levied fees on "tuns" of imported wine, and "pounds" of outgoing wool or other goods.

Turcopoles. Christian troops armed and equipped in the manner of lightly armored mounted archers employed by the Seljuks and other Turkic rulers first encountered by the *Crusaders* in the Middle East. The Latin states used Turcopoles as auxiliaries because their *heavy cavalry* had great difficulty coming to grips with the fleet Turkic and Arab mounted archers. They were likely recruited among pilgrims who remained in the Holy Land, from Christian Arabs, and from the offspring of Latin magnates and local Arab women.

Turenne, Henri de (1611–1675). Maréchal de France. Nephew of *Maurits of Nassau*. A Protestant, he was nonetheless a loyal general of *Louis XIII*. He fought in the Rhineland starting with the French intervention in 1635 and was wounded at Saverne. In 1638 he commanded a small army in support of *Bernhard von Sachsen-Weimar*. He might have been dragged down by the involvement of his family in a conspiracy against Louis XIII in 1643, but his loyalty led instead to promotion to field marshal and command of the *Armeé d'Allemagne* after it suffered defeat at *Tüttlingen* (November 24–25, 1643). He and the *Great Condé* (Louis II) joined forces to campaign against *Franz von Mercy* in Germany. Together, they pushed Mercy back from *Freiburg* (1644). The next year Mercy bested Turenne at *Mergentheim*. In 1646 Turenne marched down the Rhine to join *Karl Gustaf Wrangel*. They fought together to victory at *Zusmarshausen* (May 17, 1648). Following the *Thirty Years' War*, Turenne became entangled in the various conspiracies of the Frondes and fled into exile in the Netherlands. He returned to take command of royalist forces and fight against the Spanish and the Great Condé. He fought extensively in Louis XIV's Dutch War, 1672–1678.

Suggested Reading: Jean Bérenger, *Turenne* (1987).

Turkish bow. A Western term for a *composite bow* commonly used by Ottoman troops. About five feet long, it was made of wood, bone, and horn and held together by sinew and various glues. As with every composite bow, each layer of construction added elasticity. In addition, its tips curved forward, which imparted extra energy to iron-tipped arrows when the bow was strung and shot. It had a killing range up to 250 yards. Many weapons historians consider it the best bow ever made prior to modern bows constructed from synthetic materials.

Turks. The Turks first made an impression on world history as military slaves, or *mamlūks*, imported into the Arab empire by the Abbasid *caliphs* and into Iran by various breakaway and regional dynasties. Turkic-speaking slave soldiers soon dominated nearly all Muslim regimes, in several cases taking de facto control and later establishing slave dynasties in India and Egypt. In 960 the Karakhanids, a Turkic frontier people, converted to Islam en masse; others followed as migrants and converts in later centuries, notably the Oghuz Turks and the Kipchak Turks. Among the Oghuz, the sub-group of *Seljuks* (named for the dominant clan) arrived in Bukhara in the 10th century, converted to Islam, and sold military services to various Muslim rulers. One band formed the Ghaznavid dynasty in Iran, but the direct descendants of the Seljuks overthrew the Ghaznavids and overran Iran. In 1055 they conquered Baghdad, the Abbasid capital. Within 25 years all Syria and Palestine fell to the Seljuks, and thereafter they took most of Anatolia from the Byzantine Empire. The Seljuks ruled from Baghdad as "Great Sultans," while keeping the Abbasid caliphs in place as useful figureheads. By the start of the *Crusades*, so uniform was identification of Turkic-speaking converts with Islam and so rapid their rise to political and military dominance of the Middle East, "Turk" and "Muslim" became interchangeable terms in the West.

Under Turkic military leadership the radical *shī'a* regimes of Iran and the shī'a Būyid dynasty in Baghdad were overthrown and replaced by *sunni* rulers. That extended the process of conquest of Anatolia and other Middle Eastern lands first undertaken by the Seljuk Turks. Even the shī'a *Assassins* in Syria were effectively contained by Turkic power, reduced to terrorizing mountain travelers caught alone in passes and valleys. There followed a successful Seljuk assault against the Latin Christian states that had lingered on the Syrian border long after the fall of Jerusalem to *Salāh al-Dīn*. Thus, the Turkish variant of Islam was, from the start, a highly successful and thoroughly militarized culture. Its early ethic was that of holy war and its embodiment was the *ghazi*. This impulse was probably still important into the early 14th century when the Seljuk state was destroyed by Mongol invasions of Iran, Iraq, and Anatolia. This was followed by a new Turkic power that moved into the vacuum left by the collapse of the Seljuks: the *Ottomans*. These were former vassals of the Seljuks who were granted lands close to the Byzantine frontier. Their empire was named for their leader, Osman (or Othman, 1259–1356).

This record of successful conquest and empire-building arose in part from fortunate geography that shaped and reinforced the strengths of Turkic martial culture. During the semi-nomadic phase of their conquests, various Turkic peoples controlled vast herds of steppe ponies from which they supplied their cavalry armies. Next, they were positioned to do maximum damage to the rich trade of the Middle East because they straddled the main trade and caravan routes; this made extortion of tribute a sustainable and lucrative policy. Finally, the lands they conquered were occupied by peoples and governed by states that were constantly at war with one another, which allowed the Ottomans to defeat them in strategic detail, as it were. Turkish dominance was maintained by an ethnic monopoly of military skills in which Turks retained the sword in tribal levies or as military slaves but hired Iranian or Arab scholar-bureaucrats to wield the pen of imperial taxation and administration. The spirit of jihad as a motive to expansion faded as the Ottoman Empire matured, so that by c. 1600 it was more often the case that the sultan or grand vezier made policy for more secular purposes than his Christian counterparts in Europe, who were still engaged in "holy wars" into the mid-17th century. Besides, no sultan after 1362 was actually a "Turk": they were Circassian, Georgian, or Slavic, or some other non-Turkish ethnicity. That fact did not prevent contemporaries, or later historians, from calling the Ottomans "Turks."

> ... *Turks retained the sword* ... *but hired Iranian or Arab scholar-bureaucrats to wield the pen* ...

Turnham Green, Battle of (1642). See *English Civil Wars*.

Turnhout, Battle of (August 22, 1597). One of just two battles fought by *Maurits of Nassau* in 20 years. The speed of his movement to the battlefield caught the Spanish by surprise. The Dutch cavalry drove the Spanish horse from the field and then attacked the Spanish infantry, supported by the main body of Dutch infantry. The Spanish were routed, losing over 3,000 men.

turtle ships. The Koreans built the first "ironclad" ships in 1592 to meet the invasion led by *Toyotomi Hideyoshi*. Commanded by Admiral Yi Sun-Sin, these oared ships had metal rooves to retard fire arrows that were also covered in spikes to prevent boarding. They also sported 14 small cannon, which made them deadly to thin-hulled *junks*. Yi Sun-Sin cut off the Japanese Army from resupply and eventually forced its withdrawal to Japan.

Țuțora, Battle of (1620). See *Cecora, Battle of*.

Tüttlingen, Battle of (November 24–25, 1643). A French army seized Rottweil (November 19, 1643), but lost its able commander, the Compte de Guébriant, who died five days later from wounds incurred in the assault. His lieutenant, the mercenary captain Josias von Rantzau, took the army on to attack Tüttlingen, winter quarters of the Bavarian Army on the Danube. The Bavarians, under *Johann von Werth* and *Franz Mercy*, were reinforced by Imperial troops and moved out to meet the invaders. The Protestant army was thus taken by surprise and bloodied at Tüttlingen. The next day Rantzau tried to counterattack but lost the field again. Rottweil was recaptured by the Imperials on December 2, 1643, as the sole surviving third of the original French army retreated across the Rhine. After Tüttlingen *Turenne* was given command of the Armeé d'Allemagne.

Twelfth-imam shi'ism. See *shī'a Islam*.

Twelve Years' Truce (April 1609–April 1621). A formal cessation of hostilities in the midst of the *Eighty Years' War* between Spain and the Dutch Republic. The first terms for a permanent peace offered by *Philip III* and the *Duke of Lerma* were quite moderate: de jure recognition of Habsburg sovereignty in the Netherlands and some symbolic genuflection towards supremacy of the Catholic Church. *Maurits of Nassau* and *Johan van Old-enbaarneveldt* agreed on little else but they united in opposing such terms for the United Provinces. Spain countered with an offer to concede sovereignty in exchange for the return of rich trade outposts lost to the *Vereenigde Oostindische Compaagnie* (VOC) in the Indies in 1605. A cease-fire was signed in April 1607, but disagreement over the text—widely seen as a humiliation in Spain—and the Dutch naval victory over Spain at *Gibraltar* (April 25, 1607), along with Dutch reluctance to disband the VOC and depart the Indies as they had agreed when it actually came to it, destroyed the last chance for peace. Instead, a truce for 12 years was all that could be arranged. A pause in the fighting was of great importance to Madrid as the 1590s had seen a succession of Spanish defeats at the hands of Maurits, recurrent mutinies in the *Army of Flanders*, and another royal bankruptcy. On the other side, the Dutch feared a Spanish military revival with the end of the Franco-Spanish war at *Vervins* (1598) and a lessening of Spain's conflict with England, both of which freed military resources for the war in the north; and they had in fact fared badly from 1598 to 1606, losing territory to the Spanish and incurring much higher defense costs. Talks were also hurried by Spanish intelligence that *Henri IV* was planning major offensives against Spain in Italy and the Rhineland. In fact, he was assassinated before he could effect either plan but after the Truce was agreed.

The Spanish found the Truce in some ways more costly than the war. With the end of the embargo, Dutch cloth and textile manufactures undermined the wool industry in Castile, while North Sea fish imports undercut

Iberian fisheries. In return for lifting the Spanish embargo the Dutch ended their blockade of Flemish coastal ports, with which Spanish trade resumed. However, the Scheldt was excluded and remained closed throughout by the *Sea Beggars*. Beyond ending the embargoes, the Truce did little else to end the global war at sea. It did not extend to Asia, where Portuguese bases and interests came under ever sharper attack by Dutch privateers released from fighting closer to home. Also excluded was the North Sea and all the waters surrounding the Americas. During the interregnum the Dutch set up forts in Guyana, on the Hudson River, and at Elmina in West Africa (from which they expelled the Portuguese). The Dutch economy continued to grow, the VOC prowled the Indies, and Dutch ships muscled into the rich Baltic and Muscovy trades. Several European states recognized the United Provinces as de jure sovereign, as did Muslim Algiers, Morocco, and the Ottoman Empire. No wonder many thought the Truce a profound mortification of Spain.

As the terminal date approached many in Spain grew eager to resume the fight, not for the old religious reasons but for new economic and geopolitical ones. Recent research suggests that Philip III may even have intended the Truce all along as merely a breathing space to recover from his father's debts and imperial overreach. In the Netherlands, too, there was argument over the wisdom of resuming the war. *Arminians* led by Oldenbaarneveldt, and moderates like *Hugo Grotius*, saw good reason for the United Provinces to seek a more permanent peace, but Maurits and the war party were hot for renewed conflict. Maurits had Oldenbaarneveldt arrested in 1617 and executed the next year. He also imprudently egged on *Friedrich V* to accept the Bohemian crown, hoping to draw Spain into a German war. This full effect of the political division of Holland and the reckless policy of the war party would only be felt at Maurits' death. In the meantime, he intervened with money and 5,000 Dutch troops in the burgeoning revolt in Bohemia and schemed to undermine any renewal of the Truce. The war with Spain thus resumed upon expiration of the Truce in April 1621, and all the blockades and embargos were reinstated. Thereafter, the last three decades of the Eighty Years' War in Flanders and overseas merged with the *Thirty Years' War* (1618–1648) in Germany. See also *Fleurus, Battle of*; *Missio Hollandica*; *Oñate, Treaty of*.

Suggested Reading: Paul C. Allen, *Philip III and the Pax Hispanica 1598–1621: The Failure of Grand Strategy* (2000).

two swords, doctrine of. A fifth-century doctrine of the *Catholic Church* which resonated in the history of feudal and early modern Europe. It was framed by Pope Gelasius I (r.492–496), who held that God gave Man two swords, one secular and the other religious, one for the emperor and the other for the pope. Of these swords the religious was, of course, seen as the higher. With this imaginative metaphor Gelasius became the first pontiff to affirm supremacy of the Church even in secular affairs. This was not immediately of great consequence but it became so during the reign of Pope Gregory "the Great" (540–604, r.590–604), the first pope to claim supremacy over all Christians and all Christendom. A major step was thus taken on the steady march to Christianization of arms and arming of Christians, as well as the centuries-long struggle between papacy and empire over whose writ really ran within the *res publica Christiana*.

Tyndale, William (d.1536). See *printing*.

Tyrone, Earl of (1540–1616). Né Hugh O'Neill. See *Nine Years' War*.

Tyrone's Rebellion. See *Nine Years' War*.

U

Uhlans. See *lancers*.

ujen cooha. See *banner system*.

Ukraine. Most of Ukraine converted to Orthodoxy during the Kievan Rus period, under Byzantine influence. In the 13th century, Ukrainians ("Rusyns") defended Kiev against the Tatar-Mongol "Golden Horde." The metropolitan abandoned Kiev in 1300 and Ukraine's native dynasty was extinguished in 1323, its last princes (from Galicia-Volhynia) possibly dying fighting the Mongols. Ukraine was then loosely attached to Poland under Iurii-Boleslaw. This did not sit well with the *boyars*, who poisoned him in 1340 on charges he favored Catholicism and foreigners. Thus began a new cleavage in Ukrainian history: conflict between Orthodoxy and Catholicism, the former cleaved to by most peasants and the latter the faith of the elite and Ukraine's Polish masters. Casimir III, "The Great" (1310–1370) invaded Galicia in 1340 under an agreement with Hungary to divide Ukraine. For the next 20 years Poland claimed to be the "buffer of Christianity" against Orthodox schismatics and fought Lithuania for control of Galicia and Volhynia. In 1362 Lithuania occupied Kiev, defeated the Golden Horde the next year, and occupied half of Ukraine. That mostly pleased Ukrainians, who were glad to see the back of Mongol rule. In 1452 Volhynia was incorporated as a province of Lithuania, followed by Kiev in 1471. Over the next century Ukraine's nobility was progressively assimilated into Polish-Lithuanian culture and religion, while the peasants toiled loosely untouched by either. The *Union of Lublin* (1569) cemented Ukraine formally to Poland-Lithuania, confirming the main cultural influence on Ukraine as Polish-Catholic.

In the 16th century Muscovy expanded west and south at Polish-Lithuanian expense, under *Ivan IV* (1530–1584) and his successors. Ukrainian *Cossacks*, many former serfs who escaped to join the free bands on the steppe, were enlisted by the Poles in wartime to fight Russians or Ottomans. But they were neglected in peacetime, or worse, treated as little more than rebellious serfs. The first Cossack uprising against the Poles came in 1591. Led by a Ukrainian nobleman, Krystof Kosynsky, it was essentially a rural revolt against privileged, distant, and arbitrary landlords. The Polish-Ukrainian nobility mobilized and crushed the rebels at the Piatka River. A more ambitious rising took place in 1595–1596, with peasants and Cossacks joining to seek a common homeland independent of Poland. However, as the main Cossack army retreated toward Muscovy the cause was betrayed by officers and some wealthy Cossacks, whereupon the Poles massacred the survivors who surrendered.

As Poland embarked on a series of 17th-century wars with Muscovy, the Ottoman Empire, and Sweden, the Cossacks were again called upon by the monarchy as a source of ready recruitment of skilled cavalry. But independent Cossack bands raided the other way, into the Ottoman Crimea. Sultan Othman (Osman) II invaded Ukraine in 1621 to reclaim rebellious Moldavia and punish Cossack raiders. He was beaten decisively by a Polish-Cossack army at *Khotyn* (1621). The Cossacks were restless during the 1620s–1630s. A full-scale and unusually bloody rebellion broke out in 1648: the Khmelnitsky Uprising. It lasted to 1654 and was marked by invasions of Poland by massive Cossack-Tatar armies, several huge cavalry battles, pogroms against Jews, and mutual massacres of prisoners.

Suggested Reading: Paul Magosci, *History of Ukraine* (1996); Orest Subtelny, *Ukraine: A History* (2000).

Ula River, Battle of (1564). See *Northern War, First*.

ulema. See *Islam*.

Ulm, Treaty of (1620). See *Catholic League (Germany)*; *Protestant Union*.

Ulster. An independent kingdom in antiquity, it was also one of four traditional provinces of medieval Ireland that echoed with the history of ancient Celtic kingdoms. An abortive effort at Anglo-Scots colonization was made in northeast Ulster by Thomas Smith in the 1570s. In the 1590s the *Nine Years' War* (1594–1603) began in Ulster, then spread to all Ireland. As a reward for service in the king's wars, and as punishment for Irish Catholic rebellion, *James I* granted Scottish and English Protestants the right to settle in Ulster on land expropriated from defeated Gaelic peasants and *Old Irish* lords. Some 30,000 Scots migrated to Ulster before mid-century. This was the so-called "Plantation of Ulster." Its religious context included a belief that the new colonies would be model societies which would help to civilize a native Gaelic population, judged by Scots and English to be backward in culture and wayward in faith. The Plantation of Ulster was the single most expensive colonial enterprise undertaken from Britain during the 17th century. It did not easily take root. Although it later served as a model of the new "British" nationalism of the Anglo-Scots and of the proper relation of colony to mother country, in fact *New English* military officers were ascendant over both Scots and Irish in Ulster (as they were also in the Dublin *Pale*). Hence, Scots settlers were shunted to marginal land while native Irish were pushed off the land almost entirely and forced to serve as cheap rural labor or in servant classes in the towns. The monarchy was closely involved in the scheme, compelling London merchants to finance fortification of the ports of Derry and Coleraine, for instance. Like the rest of the inhabitants of Ireland, Scots immigrants in Ireland were pulled into the *English Civil Wars* upon the great Irish rebellion of 1641.

uma jirushi. "Horse sign." The elaborate battle standard of a Japanese *daimyo*. Usually large and vertical, some were kitelike, three-dimensional cloth objects that readily identified a Japanese lord and commander on the field of battle.

Umma. See *Islam*.

Uniate Churches. Churches which maintained a distinct Eastern Orthodox liturgy and rite but chose union with the Catholic popes and *Ecumenical Councils* on matters of faith and doctrine, rather than with the new patriarchate set up in Moscow in the late 16th century. Founded in 1596, the Ukrainian church was the largest and oldest. Uniate churches were later established in Armenia, Egypt, Ethiopia, Greece, Lebanon, and Syria.

Unification Wars (1550–1615). During the late Ashikaga period in Japan, the warlord *Oda Nobunaga* overthrew the Ashikaga shogunate in a series of sharp wars in which he effectively deployed firearms and expanded infantry formations to supplant the traditional *samurai* horse archers. This and skillful strategy and daring tactics enabled him to unify about one-third of Japan under his rule. His entrance into Kyoto in 1568 is usually taken as marking the end of the anarchic period called *gekokujō* or *Sengoku jidai*. The wars of national unification in Japan were marked by treachery, assassination, rebellion, and switching loyalties just before (and in several cases during) a battle. Garrisons and samurai might hold for their *daimyo*, or flee or surrender without offering more than token resistance, or seize their commander and hand him over to spare their own lives. After winning an astonishing victory at *Okehazama* (1560) Nobunaga allied with *Tokugawa Ieyasu*. The 1560s were spent consolidating his hold over Honshu. Nobunaga and Ieyasu then defeated their northern enemies decisively at *Anegawa* (1570). Fighting continued as Nobunaga sought unsuccessfully to unify all Japan under his rule. He was betrayed and probably committed ritual suicide (seppuku) in 1582. The great tyrant *Toyotomi Hideyoshi* (1537–1598), after first displacing then allying with Ieyasu, succeeded Nobunaga and is known to history as the second of the great unifiers of Japan. A paranoid brute, Hideyoshi nonetheless consolidated authority over most of central and southern Japan. He then twice invaded Korea with massive armies, only to be stopped by Korean *turtle ships* and guerillas, and by interfering Ming armies from China. When he died chaos returned briefly to Japan along with a war of succession. The fighting continued until Ieyasu imposed a centralized political and military order on all Japan. He was able to complete this task following a decisive victory at *Sekigahara* (1600) and a bloody last stand by Hideyoshi's son at *Osaka Castle* (1615). After that all Europeans save the Dutch were expelled and banned, the *Kirishitan* were massacred or driven underground, and the "Great Tokugawa Peace" settled over Japan for more than 250 years, until the Meiji Restoration. The wars of unification, which were shaped dramatically by the arrival of firearms in Japan in 1543, paralleled centralizing and state-building developments underway in Europe, from Spain to France and Muscovy. See also *castles, on land*; *fortification*; *revolution in military affairs*; *True Pure Land*.

uniforms. Outside Europe, uniform military dress was more common in this period. Boys inducted into the *Janissary Corps*, for instance, dressed in all red, including red caps. Fully trained Janissaries wore an exclusive white felt cap called a "Börk" which distinguished them on the battlefield. The Börk had a wooden spoon attached, in line with nearly all unit symbolism in a corps where even officer ranks and titles expressed a culinary motif rooted in ritual meal sharing. Most uniform cloth was made of wool though officers might add fur trim. The main way to display rank was in the use of belts or sashes of high quality and distinct color. Janissary winter uniforms were sewn in state-run mills in Greece. All Janissaries received a monthly clothing allowance, another for weapons, and still another for horses and grooms. They were therefore expected to dress well. *Serdengeçti* special assault troops decked out their uniforms with fur trim and feathers and unit badges and devices. They replaced the white Börk with a red or white turban to signal their special status as potential warrior-martyrs. Non-Janissaries in Ottoman armies wore a simple red fez. Similarly, red "zami" hats were worn by *mamlūks* who were known by this headgear across the Middle East. Hungarian military costume was directly influenced by contact with the Ottomans, and with Cossacks and Tatars. Hungarian fashions in turn fed back into Central Europe via Polish military contacts, especially in *hussar* units.

During the Middle Ages, European knights and men-at-arms wore a *tabard* over their armor, often decorated with heraldic devices of their king or liege lord. But these were not uniforms strictly speaking. Some infantry, among whom martial egos were less developed, wore uniforms by about 1300. For example, the militia of Tournai dressed in red tunics decorated with a silver castle. Italian city-states dressed their militia uniformly from the late 13th century and towns in Flanders dressed militia in uniforms by the 14th century. English troops fighting in Wales with Edward I wore armbands sporting the Cross of St. George, while at *Falkirk* some English units wore all-white tunics. Among the first military costumes in early modern Europe that approximated a national uniform were those introduced by the *Black Prince*. During the *Hundred Years' War* he dressed his longbowmen alike to prevent their being attacked in error by English regulars, a concern reflecting worry that his English troops might mistake Welsh speakers for foreigners, since the average English soldier heard Welsh and French as similarly odd and suspiciously foreign tongues. Cheshire archers also dressed alike, in identical green-and-white cloth and hats. The Swiss did not wear uniforms. Though in later decades, after they killed thousands of Austrian and Burgundian knights, some covered their poor peasant or town cloth with captured armor. After *Laupen* (1339), most Swiss sewed a cross of white cloth onto their leggings or doublet or painted it onto their weapons. The *Landsknechte* adopted the Swiss fashion of slashed and tattered *Pluderhosen* and huge puffed sleeves, then advanced it to truly ridiculous lengths. They engaged in a cult of outlandish dress that included stuffed or oversized codpieces, different colored hose on each leg, and absurdly tall hats that served as platforms for huge plumes of eagle or ostrich feathers. While this made them as obvious as a punkster on a London railway platform, the intent was to make each Landsknechte look distinct from his neighbor, in other words, the very opposite of the idea of a uniform.

Most Christian armies in the Middle Ages used the cross as an emblem, varying only its color and style. Valois armies usually wore a white cross. *Henry V* forced the people of Normandy to wear the red cross of St. George, which his men-at-arms also wore, but this was a sign of submission not nationhood. *Charles the Rash* put his famous Burgundian *lances* and *compagnies de l'ordonnance* in uniform in the 1470s, numbering each unit and giving it a distinctive pennant, badge, and insignia, and varying styles of crosses. In France, there was some experimentation with uniforms as early as 1340, but an army heavy in noble horse only reluctantly surrendered individual and family insignia in favor of the king's colors, once he adopted some. Scots Archers in French service wore a singular uniform by the 1480s, but the regular French

> *...literal chains of command, hammered out of gold or silver and worn around the neck.*

army did not adopt standard uniforms for another 200 years: *Michel le Tellier* ordered three cuts of uniform cloth in 1647; even then the King's Fusiliers were not dressed in standard costume of common cut and color until 1670. In most armies, officers before 1650 were distinguished not by the splendor of gold braid or burnished insignia of their uniforms but by literal chains of command, hammered out of gold or silver and worn around the neck. After the 1618 coup by *Maurits of Nassau*, Prince of Orange, Dutch troops and *schutterijen* militia wore either the orange of his distant principality or the orange, white, and blue colors of the *Generality* of the United Provinces.

Uniforms caught on earlier in Eastern Europe than in Western Europe. From the 1550s, *Haiduk* musketeers wore uniforms, generally a cloudy blue jacket made from good cloth imported from the Netherlands, with red trousers and black caps and boots. From 1578 the *Polish Army* dressed less valuable "drafted" or "chosen infantry" ("Piechota wybraniecka") in cheap homespun, but also dyed plain blue to match the far finer cloth worn by Haiduks. Even though these uniforms were bought by the men who wore them and thus varied in quality and appearance, they still were advanced as compared to military dress in Western Europe. In contrast to the infantry, because Polish hussars so closely resembled hussars or Cossacks on the other side, they took to wearing white cloths or straw twists in order to recognize each other in battle. Some Polish cavalry were distinguished by the fact that they dyed their horses red, which caused a minor sensation when the *Lisowczyks* fought in France and Germany during the *Thirty Years' War* (1618–1648). In the French Army in the 1560s–1580s only poorly paid and unskilled *pioneers* were put into uniform, not out of kindness but to make desertion harder by men wearing the king's colors, and hence more easily identified when on the run.

In Western Europe it was not until the 17th century that uniforms caught on. The Duke of Neuburg dressed his militia in proper uniforms in 1605, as did the city of Nuremberg from 1619. *Gustavus Adolphus* took his men out of armor to increase their mobility and dressed them in cloth or buff leather uniforms instead. He began with just the royal bodyguard, but ended by setting up depots that contained standardized clothing for all Swedish conscripts, including a light sleeveless tunic, baggy breaches, and wool stockings. Yet, even Swedish regiments still dressed so differently in practice that in battle all Swedish soldiers wore a yellow band around their hats or helmets to declare they were friend not foe. Similarly, Habsburg troops wore red as a token, in the form of a sash or plume or hatband.

Regular uniforms were not adopted by English armies until 1645, during the *English Civil Wars* (1639–1651). This was not done to provide distinctions between the rival armies so much as to address the destitute condition of too many recruits. The cost of these first uniforms was deducted from a soldier's pay. During the course of the Civil Wars the *New Model Army* was issued red coats. Many historians date the English term "Redcoats" from this fact, but others caution that some Royalist regiments also wore red coats. In fact, neither army as a whole dressed in uniform color. As late as 1686, 10 out of 11 English regiments wore red, but the 12th still wore blue. It was more common in the early modern period for armies to wear a common pattern or cut of cloth than it was to sport a common color. Even when standardized clothes were issued they were of such poor quality, or so soon wore out in exposed conditions, that soldiers acquired polyglot replacements on the march through purchase or looting. The idea of a standard uniform and clear national colors was a development that came so late in this period it properly belongs to the next. See also *buff coats*; *cavalry*; *civilians*; *"coat-and-conduct" money*; *eunuchs*; *Tüfeçis*.

Union of Arms. See *Catalonia, Revolt of*; *Olivares, conde-duque de*.

Union of Arras. See *Eighty Years' War*.

Union of Brest (1595). An agreement permitting Orthodox Ukrainians who rejected claims to authority of the new patriarchate in Moscow to instead join Catholics in a *Uniate Church*.

union of crowns. Political union of two or more dynasties through a dynastic marriage that does not unite the kingdoms under a unitary constitution but governs them under separate laws and local traditions. See also *Castile*; *Charles V, Holy Roman Emperor*; *Ferdinand II, of Aragon and Isabella I, of Castile*; *James I and VI*; *Kalmar War*; *Lithuania, Grand Duchy of*; *Poland*; *Reconquista*; *Scotland*; *Union of Kalmar*.

Union of Kalmar (1397). In 1388, Queen Margaret (1353–1412), daughter of Waldemar IV of Denmark and wife of Haakon VI of Norway, was offered the crown of Sweden by that country's nobles, who were greatly displeased with their king, Albert of Mecklenberg. Margaret agreed to the offer and invaded Sweden in order to accept it, taking Albert prisoner. The Union of Kalmar created a *union of crowns* of Denmark, Norway, and Sweden, but stipulated that each retained its domestic laws and traditions. In the 1470s, Christian I of Denmark tried to force Sweden under a more unitary monarchy. He lost to a patriot army that won a decisive victory over the Danes and Norwegians at Brunkeberg (October 10, 1471), thereby preserving Sweden's de facto independence. Sweden's de jure link to the Union of Kalmar was broken by *Gustavus I* in 1523.

Union of Krevo (1385). See *Jagiello dynasty*; *Lithuania, Grand Duchy of*; *Poland*.

Union of Lublin (1569). A constitutional union by which Poland joined with Lithuania in return for acceptance that Ukraine remain attached to Poland. During the *First Northern War* the loss of political authority by the monarchy of Poland-Lithuania to the already powerful nobility accelerated. In 1568 a "Sejm" (assembly of nobles) met at Lublin to forestall a break in the dynastic union between Poland and Lithuania. In 1568 *Sigismund August II* of Poland annexed the Ukrainian territories long claimed by Lithuania. The next year, Poland and Lithuania formed a full constitutional union to replace their old *union of crowns*. While the twinned territories more closely coordinated domestic and foreign policy, they continued to maintain separate armies and legal systems. The Union extended Polish military operations to the eastern border of Lithuania and south into Ukraine, which meant a general reorientation away from Western Europe. While this engaged Poland militarily with the rising powers of Muscovy and Sweden, it disengaged from the other great wars of religion that swept over Central and Western Europe during the 16th–17th centuries. On internal matters religious, the new Union—which was over-whelmingly Catholic—granted toleration to Orthodox nobility.

Union of Utrecht. See *Eighty Years' War*.

United Provinces of the Midi. See *Huguenots*.

United Provinces of the Netherlands. See *Netherlands*.

Uppbåd. See *Swedish Army*.

Urban (n.d.). "Orban." Hungarian master cannoneer and smith. Dissatisfied with his pay in service of the Byzantine emperor, he crossed over and sold his skills to *Muhammad II*. Urban built great bombards using the *hoop-and-stave method* (one of which quickly cracked and broke) and cast many smaller cannon for the sultan. He personally oversaw the Muslim bombardment during the *Siege of Constantinople*. About him little else is known. See also *renegades*.

Urban II. See *Crusades*; *Pax Dei*.

Urban VIII (1568–1644). Warrior pope, 1623–1644. A territorial prince and warlord more than a cleric, Urban even transformed the Vatican Library into an arsenal. He played a key role in disrupting the *Habsburg* hold on northern Italy during the *War of the Mantuan Succession* (1627–1631), securing the Duchy of Urbino to the *Papal States*. He encouraged France to ally with various Protestant princes, all to the end of driving the Spanish out of Italy. Confessional fanatics on the Catholic side suspected that he even subsidized the entry of *Gustavus Adolphus* into the *Thirty Years' War*. True or not, he certainly welcomed the humbling of Habsburg power that Swedish intervention brought about. On the other hand, he vehemently objected to the religious toleration clauses of the *Peace of Prague* (1635). In 1642, he condemned *Jansenism*.

urca. See *hulk*.

Ustí nad Labem, Battle of (1426). An early battle in the *Hussite Wars* (1419–1478). Following the death of the brilliant Hussite general *Jan Žižka* in 1424, the Hussite (or *Taborite*) army was commanded by a former priest, *Procopius the Great*. By this time the Hussite reputation for ferocity, defensive firepower, and tactical skill was such that the papacy and Holy Roman Emperor *Sigismund* had difficulty raising troops willing to face them. An army of about 50,000 Germans was slowly assembled in 1426 and moved to meet the Taborites at Ustí nad Labem on the Elbe in northern Bohemia. Yet again, as at *Kutná Hora* (1422) and *Nêmecký Brod* (1422), the Hussites assembled their *tabor* or wagon fort and hunkered down to hold off all assaults of the Imperial Army. Once more the Imperials charged in the same old way only to dash themselves to pieces, uselessly and bloodily, against the small artillery and arquebus firepower of the lashed-together-wagons of the Hussites. They succumbed when the Hussites countercharged and engaged in a murderous pursuit.

Utraquists. A moderate, predominantly noble faction of the Hussite movement, named for its support of the doctrinal statement in favor of dispensation of the sacrament in both species, or *sub utraque specie*, during the Mass. The two symbols of the rebellion were the peasant goose flag ("hus") and the chalice of the Utraquists. After the Imperial defeat of the *Taborites*, with whom the Utraquists first allied but later split, the *Hussite Wars* broke out again in 1466 when Utraquists rebelled against papal and Imperial authority. A peace was agreed in 1478 that left the Utraquists in Bohemia an essentially national church. After that, liturgical and doctrinal differences between Utraquists and the Roman church were smoothed and reduced to a handful of minor points. Still, a strong tendency to unorthodox belief and independent spirits lingered so that during the *Protestant Reformation* of the 16th century many longtime Utraquists embraced Lutheranism or Calvinism.

Utskrivning. See *Swedish Army*.

Uzbeks. The Uzbeks formed into a people from a confederation of steppe nomads, including *Mongols*, *Turks*, and others. In 1500 an Uzbek army captured Samarkand, lost it soon after to the Timurid chief *Babur*, then retook it in 1501. Starting in 1510 a long frontier war began with the *Safavids* of Iran, to whom the Uzbeks lost the cities of Marv and Herat. In 1512 the Uzbeks took Samarkand for a third time, and held it. They briefly recaptured Herat in 1513 and 1524, lost it, then returned to besiege it in 1528. That year, they lost a field battle to a Safavid relief army that had adopted the wagon-fort tactics of the Ottomans. For much of the rest of the 16th century they remained at war with Iran. They besieged Herat yet again in 1587–1588, taking the city in a final assault. That forced *Abbas I* to sue for peace with the Ottomans so that he could concentrate on military reform as well as turn to fight the Uzbeks. Abbas brought his new army to the Uzbek city of Nishapur in 1598, from whence the garrison fled without offering any resistance. Outside the walls of Uzbek-occupied Herat, Abbas detached a van of 6,000 men and set them as bait to draw out a 12,000-man Uzbek army. Meanwhile, he secretly flanked the overconfident Uzbeks with his cavalry. The ruse worked, the Uzbeks were beaten, and Herat was taken by Abbas. Less successfully, in 1602 Abbas led an army of 50,000 on a weary and fruitless march to Balkh, with the Uzbeks harassing his supplies and attacking his artillery train there and back again. The Uzbeks benefitted from some Ottoman support in their wars with Iran, including shipments of muskets. The Ottoman interest was, of course, to tie down the Safavids along a dangerous second front with the Uzbeks.

Uzkok War (1615–1617). A border war between Venice and Austria broke out in 1615 ("Guerra Arciducale"). The Austrian *Habsburgs* employed wild border mercenaries from a community of Serbian refugees (uzkoks), who were experienced in *piracy* in the Adriatic and Mediterranean. Netherlands troops and ships, and some English ships, along with Savoy and the *Protestant Union* supported Venice. However, the intervention of Spanish troops forced Venice to terms. The Uzkok War may have raised false hopes among Protestants that an international confessional alliance would easily support any anti-Habsburg prince. This may have encouraged Bohemian nobles to rebel against Austria the next year. On the other hand, it also firmed up cooperation between the two branches of the House of Habsburg.

V

vadia. Wages paid by the Capetian monarchs of France, starting in the 13th century, to soldiers not bound to them by ties of *feudal* military obligation. See also *France*; *war finance*.

valet. The lowest rank among *men-at-arms* in a medieval European army. Most were armed retainers attached to a full-fledged ("dubbed") *knight* or served under a *banneret*. See also *page*; *sergeant*; *squire*.

Valois, House of. The Capetian dynasty ruled much of France from its founding by Hugh Capet in 987 until 1328, when the House of Valois, a branch of the Capetians based in the province of Valois, took the throne in the person of *Philip VI* (1293–1350). A Valois monarch governed France from 1328 (Philip VI) to 1589 (*Henri III*), or from before the start of the *Hundred Years' War* (1337–1453) to near the end of the *French Civil Wars* (1562–1629). Having expelled the English from the continent by 1453, the Valois led France in a protracted struggle against the Habsburgs that included the *Italian Wars* (1494–1559). They were succeeded by the *Bourbons* in the *Franco–Spanish War* (1595–1598), the *War of the Mantuan Succession* (1627–1631), and the latter *Thirty Years' War* (1618–1648). The Valois House of Burgundy ruled from 1363 to 1477 (to the death in battle of *Charles the Rash*). See also *Francis I*; *Henri II, of France*; *Medici, Catherine de*.

Valtelline. A strategic alpine valley which could either block or allow troops to move between the Tyrol and Milan and Venice. Its Catholic population was cowed by Protestant occupation and persecution in 1607. In 1618, it was invaded by Protestant troops from the neighboring *Grisons*. With Spain desperate to find an alternative route north from 1620, after France closed Savoy to passage of Spanish troops, Madrid supported Valtelline Catholics in an uprising against The Grisons. The Spanish blocked access to the valley while locals massacred over 600 Protestants, after which Spain garrisoned the Grisons. In 1623 the *League of Lyon* forced Spain to surrender the Valtelline to papal troops. The next year, France occupied the valley. It was returned, by agreement, to papal control in 1626. The last Spanish expedition to use the Valtelline was an army of 12,000 which moved through it en route to *First Nördlingen* in 1634. See also *Monzón, Treaty of*; *Spanish Road*.

vambraces. *Plate armor* covering the lower arms, worn over a *hauberk*. They consisted of articulated gutter-shaped sleeves called the upper and lower "cannons."

van. At sea: the lead squadron of any three squadrons comprising a fleet. On land: the foremost major division of an army; the lead force of a moving army divided into three units. See also *Swiss square*; *vice admiral*.

vanguard. See *van*.

Varna, Battle of (1444). Pope Eugene IV preached a new crusade against the Ottomans who were then advancing through the Balkans and along the Dalmatian coast. *János Hunyadi* took a hodgepodge Christian army, nominally commanded by the kings of Hungary and Poland, to Varna on the Black Sea. He expected to meet Venetian transports and reinforcements. However, the Venetian galleys were unable or unwilling to pass under the guns of Constantinople. A Muslim army came to Varna instead. It quickly routed the Christians with the *Janissary Corps*, a superior and more tactically disciplined force.

Vasa, House of. The ruling house of Sweden. It came to the throne in 1523 when *Gustavus I* broke the *Union of Kalmar* with Denmark and Norway. The dynasty closely allied with great merchants and lesser gentry to face down the landed nobility and Catholic Church. It was bitterly divided by competing claims to the Swedish crown by *Karl IX* and *Sigismund III Vasa* of Poland. See also *Gustavus II Adolphus*.

Vasco da Gama (1469–1524). See *Exploration, Age of*.

Vassy massacre (March 1, 1562). The opening act of violence in what became the *French Civil Wars* (1562–1629), reflecting wide Catholic anger over the call for toleration in the *Edict of Saint-Germain* (January 17, 1562). The *duc de Guise* (François, 1519–1563) stopped to attend Mass at Vassy, a small town inside his domain. A congregation of Protestants was holding a service nearby and Guise went over to lecture them on the errors of their faith. When he was met with a hail of stones his men fired off pistols and arquebuses in reply, then they hacked members of the congregation to death with swords. About 30 died and 100 more were grievously wounded. Catholic Paris rejoiced at the news. The next month Protestant churches met in synod, called for an army of protection to be raised, and gave command of this force to Louis de Bourbon (*Condé*), blood enemy of the Guise family.

vataby. A band of *Cossacks* led into the "wild field" (steppe) by an *otaman*.

Vegetius. See *Art of War*.

Venice. "Queen of the Adriatic." For nearly 800 years Venice was the commercial center of the western Mediterranean, serving also as a conduit of ancient Graeco-Roman learning to Europe. In the fragmented medieval world it was a small military and imperial power in its own right. It was also the only medieval state in Europe to maintain a permanent navy, with which it alternately traded with and warred against the *Byzantine Empire*. During the *Crusades*, rivalry with the Byzantines peaked in 1204 when Venice financed, transported, and successfully redirected the Fourth Crusade from its intended destination of Egypt to instead sack and occupy Constantinople. From the 13th century, the Aegean was the venue of trade wars between Venice and its main commercial and military rival, Genoa, with Venice in control of the Dalmatian coast and Ionian Islands route eastward. The Ottomans began to acquire a permanent navy under *Bayezid I* that competed with Venice from 1390. A century later, under *Bayezid II*, the Ottoman galley fleet overmatched and humiliated the Venetians, ending their domination of the eastern Mediterranean.

In the 14th century, Venice ran the great "Flanders Fleets" to Bruges in cooperation with the *Hanse*, and sent merchants overland into France and as far east as Poland. Venice reached an apex of commercial and secular influence during the *Italian Renaissance*. The shrewd and worldly merchant class which ran the Venetian Republic in the 15th century bequeathed much to the history of diplomacy, navigation, and banking. In response to Milanese and Paduan expansion at the end of the 14th century, and in order to secure grain supplies in the face of Ottoman advances in the Balkans and North Africa, Venice set out to acquire a land empire to its immediate and strategic rear in Italy. It conquered and absorbed Vicenza, Verona, Padua, Friuli, Brescia, and Bergamo between 1404 and 1427. Venice participated in the long war between Milan and Florence from 1423 to 1445. It agreed to the *Peace of Lodi* with Milan in 1454.

Like other Italian city-states Venice was mortally threatened by the overturning of the Italian balance of power by the French invasion of 1494. It became entangled in complex alliance politics and wars during the baleful, prolonged, and destructive *Italian Wars* (1494–1559), sometimes in alliance with France against the popes and sometimes allied with the papacy. Venice was targeted for dismemberment by the *League of Cambrai* and fared badly militarily from 1508 to 1510. The political sands then shifted and by 1515 Venice was allied with France. The last-hour intervention by Venetian cavalry decided the bloody fight at *Marignano* that year, where *Francis I* and Venetian arms ended the infantry dominance of the Swiss. As foreign giants wrestled for control of Italy during the 16th century, Venice shrank from conflict. As Garrett Mattingly put it, "Venice renounced its ambitions and looked simply to its safety." Conflict sought it out, regardless. Surrounded by Austrian and Spanish possessions during the 16th–17th centuries, Venice was the natural, albeit minor, ally of successive anti-Habsburg alliances and wars. See also *Arsenal of Venice*; *Black Death*; *standing army*; *stradiots*.

Suggested Reading: F. Lane, *Venice: A Maritime Republic* (1973); M. E. Mallett and J. R. Hale, *Military Organization of a Renaissance State: Venice, 1400–1617* (1984); Garrett Mattingly, *Renaissance Diplomacy* (1955).

Vereenigde Oostindische Compaagnie (VOC). "Jan Compagnie." Following successful military campaigns in the 1580s–1590s that reopened the riparian trade of northwestern Europe, Dutch overseas trade rapidly expanded. This marked the beginning of global commercial primacy that would last 150 years. From 1595 to 1601, Dutch traders moved aggressively into south India, Java, Sumatra, and the Spice Islands under the auspices of the "Compagnie van Verre" ("Long-Distance Company"), and up to eight other Dutch companies doing trade in the East Indies. The Vereenigde Oostindische Compaagnie (VOC), or Dutch East India Company, was chartered for an initial 21 years by Holland and Zeeland in 1602 to maximize and consolidate these penetrations of Asian markets. Initially, the VOC was far better capitalized than its French or English counterparts, because *Johan van Oldenbaarneveldt* took a lead role in launching the company and the Holland regents and merchants were flush with capital. It was also granted quasi-sovereign rights to build forts and maintain garrisons overseas, to sign treaties with other sovereigns, and to make military alliances. These agreements had to be formally approved by the States General of the United Provinces, but this posed no limitations in practice. Reflecting Dutch republicanism, uniquely among European overseas charter companies the VOC did not rely on nobles as its colonial governors. In 1605 a Dutch fleet forcibly cleared the Portuguese from the Indian Ocean and the VOC seized Portugal's share of the Spice Islands at Amboina. This breakthrough in the Indies became an issue in the talks leading to the *Twelve Years' Truce* (1609–1621). In 1609 the VOC set up shop in Japan, at Hirado. Anglo-Dutch cooperation against the Portuguese and French ended in 1623 when the Dutch judicially murdered ten *East India Company* merchants at Amboina. During the latter *Eighty Years' War* the VOC took numerous overseas entrepôts from Portugal: Pernambuco (1630), Elmina (1637), Luanda (1641–1648), Ceylon (1638–1641), Malacca (1641), and *Deshima* in Japan, from 1641 through most of the era of the *Tokugawa shoguns*. Headquartered at *Batavia*, the VOC concentrated on the more valuable East Indies trades, leaving India to the French and English. By 1650 VOC wealth and naval power helped make the United Provinces the world's greatest trading nation and a foremost world empire.

Suggested Reading: Charles Ralph Boxer, *Jan Compagnie in War and Peace, 1602–1799* (1979); John Wills, *Pepper, Guns, and Parleys: The Dutch East India Company and China, 1622–1681* (1974).

Verneuil, Battle of (August 17, 1424). Following the death of *Henry V* (1422), the French sought to push the English back across the Loire. Joined by 5,000 *Scots Archers*, some 10,000 French assaulted 9,000 English at Verneuil, west of Paris. English longbowmen did their usual deadly work against dismounted Scots and French men-at-arms, killing nearly 7,000 while suffering few casualties themselves. Verneuil was thus very nearly a second *Agincourt* (1415). It added to the weight of defeatism that pervaded France just before *Jeanne d'Arc* aroused the nation to a new fighting spirit, and English weapons complacency and strategic overcommitment snatched defeat from the maw of victory.

verso. A type of small, Iberian *swivel gun*, often with wrought-iron fittings, that loaded from the breech. Similar guns were used on the warships of other nations into the 17th century. They were anti-personnel weapons (man-killers), not *ship-smashers*.

Vervins, Peace of (May 2, 1598). A settlement between *Henri IV* of France and *Philip II* of Spain halting a protracted series of Franco-Spanish wars. Specifically, it ended the *Franco–Spanish War* of 1595–1598. Both sides returned all towns taken since the *Peace of Cateau-Cambrésis* (1559). Now that the French throne was occupied by a Catholic, Philip renounced his claim to it. The peace left the disposition of Saluzzo in abeyance pending arbitration. In 1601 Henri declared war on Savoy to reclaim Saluzzo. He failed, but received the Pont de Grésin. That allowed France to cut the *Spanish Road* whenever it chose, which it did repeatedly during the 1620s and consistently from 1635 during the latter *Thirty Years' War* (1618–1648). The Peace of Vervins also had an impact on Spanish-Dutch negotiations that led to the *Twelve Years' Truce* (1609–1621).

> *Now that the French throne was occupied by a Catholic, Philip renounced his claim to it.*

Vesting Holland. A strategic area serving as a grand redoubt for the Netherlands. It was bordered to the north and west by the North Sea and Zuider Zee, to the east by the Ijssel and broad wetlands, and to the south by multiple parallel rivers. Its low-lying flatlands were easily flooded in defense, and its many canals, rivers, and fortified towns provided highly effective defense in depth against Spanish invasion.

veterans. See *wounds*.

veuglaire. A medium-size medieval cannon.

vice admiral. In the 14th–17th centuries among Atlantic nations, a vice admiral was the second-ranking commander in a fleet, behind the *admiral* but ahead of *rear admiral*. This was also the combat rank of an admiral in command of the *van* of a fleet. In the *Royal Navy*, the title was held by deputies of the *Lord High Admiral*.

victualer. A supply ship carrying foodstuffs.

Vienna, Siege of (September 27–October 15, 1529). The Ottoman defeat of a Hungarian army at *Mohács* on August 29, 1526, opened the road to Vienna before *Suleiman I*. Upon making a secret alliance with France, he moved down it in 1529 with about 80,000 men, sacked Buda en route, then laid siege to Vienna. The city was defended by a *Habsburg* garrison of 24,000, including *Landsknechte* mercenary infantry. Vienna's walls were old (13th century) and too thin, at just six feet, to withstand shelling by the great siege *bombards* Suleiman's men hauled laboriously toward the city. To answer, the Austrians had 72 cannon of various calibers, some of them ancient pieces. These were mounted on tall buildings or hastily built gun platforms to give them clear fields of fire to expected Ottoman positions. Most of the women, children, old men, and other "useless mouths" were evacuated to conserve what supplies there were for the fighting men. Archduke *Ferdinand I* frantically called on his brother, Emperor *Charles V*, to rush to the city's aid. In fact, the siege would end after just 25 days, well before Charles could assemble forces and march them to Vienna in relief, and before starvation could do its work. It has been speculated that the Ottomans and French secretly agreed to a simple show of force before Vienna in order to draw Charles eastward, to relieve military pressure on France. If so, the plan failed: Francis was defeated by Charles and forced to sign the *Treaty of Cambrai* (1529). Moreover, the size of the Ottoman Army and the casualties it took at Vienna belies the suggestion that the Sultan took the field just for show.

The Ottomans burned and pillaged most of the outlying suburbs of the city, adding to destruction the Austrians had done before the siege to open lanes of fire on the anticipated Ottoman trenches and positions. Suleiman could not effect a major breach in the walls of "The Ring" that protected the inner city. This was partly because bad weather slowed the arrival of his great siege guns. In addition, using height to advantage, the Austrians did excellent counter-battery work under the command of Marshal Wilhelm von Roggendorf and Graf Nicholas zu Salm-Reifferscheidt, who ordered the paltry Austrian guns to fire exclusively in a counter-battery role. That put a large number of Suleiman's smaller siege guns and crews out of action, some before they were even brought to bear. The Ottomans also mined extensively but Austrian countermining denied them success: in one case a chamber was prepared and about to be blown but was instead assaulted by Austrian troops and robbed of its casks of black powder before the Ottomans could set off the charge. When smaller breaches were made rubble usually fell outward, impeding attack. And whenever *Serdengeçti* assault commandos rushed a breach they found heavily defended secondary palisades and walls waiting on the other side, along with Austrian cavalry stationed in each of four main squares of the inner city, ready and able to counterattack. Serdengeçti and other Janissaries showed their usual bravery, only to leave many comrades impaled on stalwart Viennese pikes or shot dead at point-blank range. Once the counter-battery work was done, the Austrians disrupted Ottoman assaults by firing their large guns accurately and often into troop assembly areas. As a result, the city was never in imminent danger of falling.

The Ottomans burned everything of value outside the walls (reportedly including their prisoners, though that may be only Christian propaganda) and withdrew. Retreat had been forced on them by a failure of sufficient supply to sustain the Sultan's oversized army that late in the campaign season, a problem aggravated by a huge number of camp followers who accompanied the army to Vienna. In the next few years Vienna's walls, bastions, and defenses were modernized and reinforced in the expectation of more attacks. Some desultory fighting took place along the frontier for two decades before a truce was signed in 1553. In fact, it would be another 154 years before the Ottomans again tried to take Vienna.

Vijayanagar. See *India*.

vintenar. An infantry rank of medieval European officers, roughly equivalent to a modern noncommissioned officer; a man put in charge of a unit of twenty foot soldiers.

Virginia. See *Indian Wars (North America)*.

visor. See *helm*.

vivente rege. "In the lifetime of the king" or "while the king yet lives." In elective monarchies, the royal succession might be decided by a vote before the death of a king. Although this was not required and could still occasion vicious succession struggles, it tended to support more stable transitions of power. See also *Holy Roman Empire*; *Poland*.

Vlachs. See *Militargrenze*.

vlieboot. "Flyboat." A shallow-draft *Sea Beggar* ship with either one or two masts, capable of maneuvering along the shore or up canals where deep-draft Spanish vessels could not pursue.

VOC. See *Vereenigde Oostindische Compaagnie*.

Vögelisegg (Voegelinsegg), Battle of (1403). See *Appenzell Wars*.

voivodes. Levies raised in the wilderness of Wallachia and Moldova by the kings of Hungary. Their quality reflected the vices and virtues of their origins: ill-discipline, but also ferocity and feral cunning.

volley fire. Ancient Romans and Chinese armies used a form of volley fire for various missile troops, but nowhere before the late 16th century was this attempted with guns. Although it is often said that the Dutch reinvented volley fire for muskets based on descriptions of Graeco-Roman javelin tactics, it appears that *Oda Nobunaga* introduced musket volley fire at Muraki Castle in 1554, over 20 years before the first experiments in the Netherlands. Nevertheless, it was the Dutch rather than the Japanese practice that was systematized and spread to other armies, to have lasting influence on developments in world warfare. In 1594 Willem Lodewijk introduced volley fire to the *New Model Army* of the United Provinces. In his system, after the front rank fired the next rank advanced through the front rank, followed by the third rank and the one after that. Lodewijk's more famous cousin, *Maurits of Nassau*, added the *countermarch* in which each successive front rank in a 10-rank line fired in unison before it retired to the rear to reload, allowing the next rank to step forward to fire and retire, and so on. This maintained a steady fire that devastated the older, less gun-heavy *tercios* of the *Army of Flanders*. Reducing the size and depth of Dutch infantry units added flexibility in maneuvers to this advantage in rate of fire. *Gustavus Adolphus* further adapted the volley system, reducing it to just six ranks from 10. He also developed a "double volley," wherein the front three ranks fired at once, front rank prone, second rank kneeling, third rank standing, then countermarched to allow the back three ranks to fire a second double volley. The tactical discipline of these highly trained armies contributed to standardization of *drill* and of weapons such as the "Dutch musket." In striking contrast, the *Janissary Corps* uniquely emphasized individual marksmanship over unit fire. See also *Nagashino, Battle of*; *"skulking way of war"*; *smoothbore*.

Vorhut. "Van." See *Swiss square*; *van*.

votchina/votchiny. See *Muscovy, Grand Duchy of*; *servitor classes*.

vouge. See *bardiche*.

Voynuqs (Voynuks). "Horse soldiers." Ottoman auxiliary cavalry recruited mainly among the Christian populations of the Balkans but including some Muslims. The majority served in the *Militargrenze* as guides or raiders. Voynuqs registered for paid service, which meant they served as an effective reserve that could be called up as need arose. They were not always reliable: more than once they defected to the other side during the *Thirteen Years' War* (1593–1606).

W

waardgelders. Garrison troops in the pay of the Dutch state, as distinct from town militia and the new model mercenary army of *Maurits of Nassau*. In 1617, the "Sharp Resolution" raised waardgelder units in Holland and Utrecht but demanded they swear allegiance to the towns. This threatened civil war between pro- and anti-*Arminian* factions, between *Johan van Oldenbaarneveldt* and the Holland regents on one hand and *Maurits of Nassau* and anti-Holland provinces on the other. Maurits condemned the waardg-elders and had them declared illegal on July 9, 1618. He crushed all opposition in a bloodless coup d'état in July–August 1618, during which the waardgelders were peacefully disbanded. He had Oldenbaarneveldt executed the next year.

Wachmeister. "Master of the watch." The officer charged with ensuring the camp and train of a *Landsknechte* company or regiment was well guarded, and if necessary, also fortified.

waft. A 16th–17th-century English term synonymous with "escort" (of merchant ships). See also *convoy.*

wafter. A warship assigned to escort other ships. See also *convoy; waft.*

Wagenburg. "Wagon fort." An innovation by *Jan Žižka*, first commander of the Hussites. He converted heavy wagons into mobile forts that grew famous with each successive victory in the *Hussite Wars*. This provided the Hussites with a mobile system of fortification that could be set up in minutes even in open country. Moreover, when not in combat the wagons were used as transports for Hussite armies and equipment, as well as for whole families who traveled with their menfolk. This dual-purpose wagon system took full advantage of the relatively flat terrain of Bohemia, giving the Hussites a mobility unique for the time combined with exceptional defensive firepower and technological self-sufficiency: Hussite armies carted mobile ore crushers and forges to make iron on the spot to repair weapons. Hussite wagons were not simple peasant box carts for hauling hay or turnips to market. They were built from heavy timber reinforced with iron, were covered by heavy timber rooves, and could absorb quarrels, arrows, and even musket balls. When lashed together with chains, 10 to 12 wagons formed a Wagenburg (wagon fort) or "vozova hradba" ("mobile fortress"). These served as platforms for Hussite men—and women, who sometimes also bore arms. Defenders stood or knelt inside the wagons firing *arquebuses* ("hand coulverines") and *crossbows* through gun ports cut in the outer facing. Various caliber cannon and more arquebusiers and crossbowmen fired from gaps left between some pairs of wagons to facilitate counterattacks. Other defenders flailed away with iron chains at nearby enemy knights or their mounts: *tabor* forts were especially effective against cavalry.

Counterattacks were mounted through the gaps once an enemy's assault or offensive will was broken by defensive fire. The exceptional defensive capabilities of the Wagenburg were enough to break assaults even by large numbers of attackers, after which the Hussites sallied forth to pursue bewildered, bleeding foes and finish off wounded and stragglers with the usual pitiless ferocity that arises from religious zealotry and class hatred. After battle, Wagenburgs were unlinked and the Hussites moved forward in parallel columns, their women and children safe inside the wagons and further protected by light screens of mounted Hussite scouts guarding the flanks. The tactic of the Wagenburg spread across Europe as the Hussites campaigned in Germany during the 1420s–1430s, but more because success in war always breeds imitation and the Hussites enjoyed unparalleled military success for over a decade. Polish soldiers recognized the worth of the Wagenburg and carried the knowledge north into wars against Sweden and Muscovy. The Hungarians used Wagenburgs in their frontier wars with the Ottomans. In the second half of the 15th century, Imperial troops in Germany adopted the heretic's wagon fort. The *Janissary Corps* also appreciated the worth of mobile forts and used them from the 1440s against Austrians and Hungarians in the west and Safavids to the east. On the march, Janissary Wagenburgs were pulled by mules and carried cases of ammunition inside and slung underneath. The Janissaries used Wagenburgs well into the 18th century, long after they became vulnerable to field artillery. See also *carroccio*; *Fastolf, John*; *German Peasant War*; *Héricourt, Battle of*; *Kutná Hora, Battle of*; *Německý Brod, Battle of*; *Rouvray, Battle of*; *Ustí nad Labem, Battle of*; *Wallenstein, Albrecht von*; *war wagons*.

waist-lames. *Lamellar armor* attached to canvas or cloth and worn over the stomach and hips.

Wakefield, Battle of (1460). See *Wars of the Roses*.

wakō. *Pirates* active in northeast Asia in the 14th–16th centuries. Many were ethnic Chinese who fought alongside Japanese and Koreans; not a few were former merchants reacting to the Xuande emperor's cancellation of overseas trade in 1436. Wakō ravaged the coasts of China, Japan, and Korea, and preyed on the seaborne trade linking Ming China to overseas Chinese communities in Southeast Asia. With Japan politically fragmented and China immersed in civil war, wakō had free rein. Banned from legal trade with China from the 1520s, some Portuguese became pirates, confirming that at its core piracy was large-scale smuggling defended by force of arms. By the mid-16th century the weakness of the Ming allowed wakō fleets to land several thousand armed brigands at once, amphibious pirates who raided deep into China. The wakō even seized semi-permanent coastal bases.

On the other hand, as in England and the Netherlands at that time, piracy and trade were closely linked to seaside communities and the local economy. Like *Drake* or *Hawkyns*, wakō enjoyed local governmental protection and encouragement and the active participation and protection of the shoreside population. The central Ming military response was to attack the pirates in their land bases, not at sea. In retaliation, several thousand pirates landed at three coastal sites in coordinated diversionary raids in 1556, while 10,000 made a main attack on Zhejiang. They looted and burned hundreds of villages. However, the wakō lacked siege equipment or patience or military discipline. After falling out over the spoils they were defeated in detail by the Ming. That forced most wakō south to Fujian and Guangdong provinces. When the Ming ban on overseas voyages and trade was lifted in 1567, many wakō returned to legitimate trade. The problem of the wakō was further eased by Ming naval successes which pushed hard-core pirates out to the Philippines, where Manila was attacked in 1574. Others settled on Taiwan, which served as the main wakō base during the 17th century.

Walcheren, Battle of (1574). See *Eighty Years' War*.

Waldstätte. See *Forest Cantons*; *Swiss Confederacy*.

Wales. See *Edward III*; *England*; *Glyndŵr's Rebellion*; *Hundred Years' War*; *longbow*.

Wallace, William (c.1274–1305). Also "Walays" or "Wallensis." The origins of this Scots patriot and leader in the first years of the *Scottish Wars* are shrouded in speculation and legend. His first confirmed appearance was in 1297, the year after the English sack of Berwick, when he emerged as a brilliant guerilla leader. His first followers were a few dozen men from his own clan. Later, many common Scots and even some nobles rallied to him. At Lanark, his small band burned an English fort and slew the sheriff and garrison in revenge for the judicial murder of Wallace's wife. His father had been killed by the English in an earlier war, and this too nursed his hatred. He led a Scots army to victory over Edward I's men at *Stirling Bridge* (1297). When the English retreated out of Scotland Wallace followed, leading punitive raids through the north country. When he returned to Edinburgh, he was elected by the Scottish nobles "Guardian of Scotland." In 1298 Edward I ("Longshanks") personally invaded Scotland with a huge army of nearly 90,000 men. Wallace and the Scots infantry met Edward at *Falkirk* (1298), where the Scottish noble cavalry abandoned the field leaving the infantry to be mown down by superior Welsh archers using a deadly new weapon, the *longbow*. English swordsmen and Irish infantry finished off the Scots (the Irish did not join Wallace in a warm Celtic embrace, as has been depicted on film).

Wallace went to France and possibly also to Norway and Rome to seek assistance. He was thus absent during the latter part of the Comyn Wars (1297–1304). He reappeared in Scotland in 1304 and resumed his guerrilla campaign, until betrayed and arrested in 1305 and taken to London. He was charged with treason, although he was the one rebel never to have sworn allegiance to England's king. That charge reflected the fact that the English thought of the Scots not as a foreign nation but as unlawful rebels. Wallace was savagely tortured, hanged, drawn, quartered, and beheaded. In accordance with English law for traitors, his head was impaled on a pike for public display and the quarters of his body dispatched as a warning to the four corners of the kingdom: Newscastle, Stirling, Berwick, and Perth. This did not matter for later Scots nationalists, who proclaimed, "He has no tomb. He needed none."

Suggested Reading: James Fergusson, *William Wallace: Guardian of Scotland* (1938); Andrew Fisher, *William Wallace* (2002).

Wallenstein, Albrecht von (1583–1634). Also known as Albrecht von Waldstein. Duke of Friedland and Mecklenburg, Prince of Sagan. He made his name as a mercenary in *Habsburg* service. Although he was a Czech he is remembered by German nationalists as "Der Friedlander." From first to last, in two spectacularly lucrative marriages and in his inspired mercenary commands, Wallenstein was motivated by exceptional ambition for power, titles, and estates. He achieved all three beyond any man of his age, only to lose it all in blood and betrayal. An orphan at 10, he was raised by his uncles and educated by the *Jesuits*, under whose tutelage he nominally adhered to Catholicism. His 1607 marriage gave him great wealth. When his first wife died he married again, gaining even more lands. He first took a command in 1617 when he raised 200 horse to aid Archduke Ferdinand of Austria, later *Ferdinand II*, in a minor dispute with Venice. This led to his appointment as head of the militia of Moravia. When the *Thirty Years' War* broke out, he spurned the entreaties of Bohemian Protestants to join them. Instead, he tried to raise militia from his considerable estates to serve Ferdinand. When this failed he was expelled from Bohemia and forfeited his lands to the rebels.

Wallenstein went to Vienna to offer his services to Ferdinand, now Holy Roman Emperor. He captured a Bohemian *Wagenburg* (a rare military feat) during a skirmish at Rablat, compelling *Count Matthias von Thurn* and the Bohemian army to abandon its assault on Vienna. He then held a key bridge to allow a retreating Imperial army to cross to safety. He played no role, however, at the fight that followed at the *White Mountain* (November 8, 1620), outside Prague. After that decisive defeat of the Bohemian rebels

Wallenstein not only recovered all his estates, he added to them greatly by buying at cut-rate prices the lands of Protestant nobles executed or exiled by Ferdinand. His estates were so extensive Ferdinand designated them the "Principality of Friedland" and made Wallenstein a prince. In 1621 and 1623 he raised armies to block the claims of Bethlen Gabor to the Hungarian throne. For these services he was created "Duke of Friedland" by Ferdinand and given the right to mint coin.

In 1625 Wallenstein was given command of all Imperial armies. At the peak of his power he commanded forces in excess of 100,000 men. To finance this army he devised a system of *contributions* that made his army more effective but so scarred the face of Europe that marauding became irrevocably attached to his reputation, and he became the most hated man in the Empire. Along with *Johan Tilly*, general of the German *Catholic League*, Wallenstein campaigned brilliantly in behalf of Imperial and Catholic authority, although he was himself an agnostic mystic from Bohemia with a penchant for astrology. He governed his lands and appointed officers with broad indifference to religion. That appeared to fanatic Catholics around Ferdinand to be religious tolerance, which for such men was little better than heresy itself. For fanatics of the *Counter-Reformation* indifference to religion was Wallenstein's mortal sin, as it would in time prove his mortal doom. Always, his central ambition was power, wealth, and personal aggrandizement, not occurring advantage to his paymaster in the great confessional and constitutional war. As his ends nonetheless merged with Ferdinand's on most days before 1634, both men were content for Wallenstein to exercise Imperial command with great latitude as to strategy and financing.

> *...marauding became irrevocably attached to his reputation ... the most hated man in the Empire.*

Wallenstein began at *Dessau Bridge* (April 25, 1626) where he bested *Graf von Mansfeld*. Together with Tilly he beat the Danes at *Lutter-am-Barenberg* (August 17/27, 1626). He drove Hungary out of the war in 1627, then linked with Tilly again to push *Christian IV* of Denmark out of Germany in 1628. He next sent Tilly to watch the Dutch frontier while he occupied Brandenburg, Mecklenburg, and Pomerania. He asked for and was given title to the whole of Mecklenburg. In these lands he was tasked to impose the terms of the *Edict of Restitution* (March 28, 1629), which earned him the lasting animosity of Protestant princes. In accord with the new Baltic policy of *Olivares*, Wallenstein invested *Straslund* and began building a Baltic fleet that could contain Denmark and threaten the *Hanse* and Sweden. All that accomplished was permanent alienation of the whole of northern Europe.

As for Vienna, Wallenstein's unquenchable ambition, constant intrigue, military and financial independence, unique ability to raise armies in short order, and irreligious nature, posed a real threat to the interests and policies of the Habsburgs. When Ferdinand tried to send Wallenstein and 50,000 troops to intervene in behalf of Spain in the *War of the Mantuan Succession* (1627–1631), the German princes refused to pay. Instead they demanded a reduction of the

Imperial Army by two-thirds (to 40,000 men) and that Wallenstein be dismissed. Since recent military success made it seem that Ferdinand would have no more need of his Bohemian general, he sacked Wallenstein on August 13, 1630. That weakened Ferdinand just as the threat of launching an Imperial navy into the Baltic, and offers of French gold, provoked *Gustavus Adolphus* to enter the German war.

Wallenstein retired to his estates and waited. He was recalled after the Imperial and Catholic League armies were routed by Gustavus at *First Breitenfeld* (1631). With Vienna threatened, Wallenstein negotiated exceptional terms of pay and command, extracting huge concessions from Ferdinand. He was reinstated in fact in December 1631 and formally confirmed in April 1632. His extraordinary power and ambition, combined with Ferdinand's debilitating political and military weakness, would prove to be Wallenstein's undoing. For the moment, however, his eye was on the great champion of Protestantism descending from the north with a powerful Lutheran army. Blind with ambition, Wallenstein did not appreciate the envy and malice of Catholic nobles to his strategic rear, who were already planning his demise.

To stop Gustavus from marauding over Bavaria and divert him from advancing on Vienna, Wallenstein did an exceptional thing: instead of moving into Bavaria to seek battle he maneuvered against the weaker member of the Swedish alliance, the Saxon Army, then active in Bohemia. That left the road to Vienna open to Gustavus but placed Wallenstein's force behind the Swedes, cutting their lines of communication and supply should they continue south even as he chased the Saxons from continuing their destructive *chevauchée* through Bohemia. After coercing *Maximilian I*, Elector of Bavaria, to join his forces to the Imperial Army, Wallenstein moved farther north into Saxony itself. This forced Gustavus to fall back to the crucial crossroads town of Nuremberg. Instead of fighting, Wallenstein dug in parallel to the Swedish lines, then deployed his superb Austrian and Balkan light horse to harry their foraging parties in a low-level strategy of attrition. Within two weeks Gustavus was provoked into making a rare mistake: an ill-conceived frontal attack that was fairly easily repulsed, and which cost the great Swede more in reputation than in military losses. As Wallenstein put it: "The King has blunted his horns." In a vain effort to lure Wallenstein out of his fortified defenses, Gustavus moved back to Bavaria. In a master stroke of war-of-maneuver, Wallenstein turned north into Saxony, once more checking the southern advance of the Swedish Army by compelling it to follow him northward away from the core Habsburg lands and capital, to waste instead Protestant Saxony. There followed an extraordinary set of marches and countermarches by the two main armies, as well as several smaller and allied forces. The campaign saw a small action at *Alte Feste* (1632) before culminating in the one near-decisive battle of the Thirty Years' War at *Lützen* (1632). Wallenstein was badly beaten by Gustavus: he lost his artillery, baggage train, and thousands of men. But the great Swedish general died of multiple wounds received while leading a cavalry charge into the Imperial flank. This one death nearly counterbalanced thousands of Imperial dead and almost made Lützen an Imperial victory.

Wallenstein rebuilt the Imperial Army in 1632–1633, adopting as many of the Swedish reforms as his troops could absorb, notably returning to a *shock* role for cavalry, thinning infantry ranks, adding lighter field artillery, and filling out the ranks of the *tercios* with more musketeers. While Wallenstein skirmished and maneuvered, he also intrigued with Catholic and Protestant powers alike to hire out his services and army. More crucially, he plotted to forge an alliance that might force Ferdinand to make a peace that took no cognisance of the Emperor's Catholic crusade and personal sense of religious mission. To his later admirers, Wallenstein was readying to end the war by creating a unified and tolerant Germany. Or perhaps he really sought the symbols as well as the substance of power for himself, as emperor? In any case, spies informed Ferdinand of the general's secret talks and he determined to finish Wallenstein for good. Reinforcing the decision was the fact that Spain was readying to enter the German war but would not accept Wallenstein's core demand that he alone have supreme command of all Catholic troops.

In January 1634, Ferdinand secretly removed Wallenstein from office, declared him outlaw and traitor, condemned his hiring of Protestant officers, and ordered his arrest pending a planned judicial murder. Wallenstein learned of the secret orders and fled toward the Protestant lines. He sent word ahead to ask for sanctuary, but was refused. Escorted by a troop of Irish dragoons whose commander, Colonel Butler, was in secret contact with agents from Ferdinand's court, on February 24 Wallenstein's small party reached the fortress of Eger. It was held by two Scottish officers who had served him for years, Colonel Gordon and Major (later Field Marshal), *Walter Leslie*. That night, Butler drew the Scots into the conspiracy. The next evening, after dining with their victims, the dragoons slew Wallenstein's close companions. Butler, Gordon, and Leslie, and a French mercenary captain, Devereux, entered Wallenstein's bedchamber. Devereux struck the first blow with a halberd; the others joined in, hacking Wallenstein to death with their swords. *Ferdinand III* replaced him in nominal command of all Habsburg forces.

Suggested Reading: Golo Mann, *Wallenstein* (1976).

Waller, William (1597–1668). English soldier. He gained military experience under *Graf von Mansfeld* while fighting in Germany. When the *English Civil Wars* broke out Waller accepted a colonel's commission from Parliament. He lost his entire army of 4,500 to *Ralph Hopton* at Roundway Down (July 13, 1643). He recruited another army and destroyed a garrison at Alton (December 13, 1643). The next year he beat Hopton at Cheriton (May 29, 1644). A month later he was beaten by *Charles I* at Cropedy Bridge (June 29, 1644). Waller was active in training the *New Model Army* but later opposed *Oliver Cromwell*'s abuse of the Army to set up a military dictatorship. He spent several years in prison during the Republic.

Wallhof, Battle of (1626). See *Gustavus II Adolphus*.

Walsingham, Sir Francis (c.1530–1590). Secretary of State to *Elizabeth I*. A zealous Protestant, he spent the years of *Mary Tudor*'s reign in prudent exile, returning to serve the young Queen Elizabeth upon Mary's death. His foreign contacts—he had spies in every important court—enabled him to act essentially as head of Elizabethan intelligence. He served as ambassador to France in the 1570s and was in Paris during the *St. Bartholomew's Day Massacres* (1572). His diplomatic experience did not teach him statecraft, however. Where the Queen vacillated to strategic purpose, he lunged ahead with full confessional passion and never understood the subtlety or excellence of her policy. Yet hers was by far the more prudent and successful course. His real value was in keeping the Queen alive in face of over 20 plots to kill her. It was Walsingham, even more than *William Cecil*, who ferreted out the conspiracy that finally persuaded Elizabeth to send *Mary Stuart* to the block. Walsingham also pushed hard, though without success, to alert Elizabeth to the gains Spain derived from its American empire. He hoped to counter those advantages by providing state support to various colonization schemes. In that, at least, he was ahead of the Queen and the county: serious English colonization in North America did not begin until after 1603.

Wanli Emperor (r.1573–1620). Né Zhu Yijun (1563–1620). Ming emperor. His reign was most notable for the "Three Campaigns" he conducted to deal with the old *Mongol* and new *Manchu* threats. The first campaign put down the Yang Yinglong Rebellion, which began in 1587 in southwest China and ended with a slaughter of the rebels in 1600. The second dealt with a minor rebellion in the Ordos region led by a rebel Mongolian officer, Pubei. It ended in a siege of Ningxia, after which Pubei burned himself alive. The third campaign was in Korea, 1592–1598, where Wanli sent Ming armies to block two Japanese invasions ordered by *Toyotomi Hideyoshi*. Domestically, under Wanli there was great ossification of the central government and scholar elite. Endemic corruption and a rigid *Confucianism* was unable to adapt the traditional rural economy to an expanding population. This crisis was aggravated and personified by the progressive isolation and state of unreality of Wanli himself. Once responsible and keen, as he aged Wanli increasingly shirked his duties, retreating into a semi-private and monkish life of study and reflection in the Forbidden City. As he withdrew from effective rule, China's government was left to corrupt advisers and 10,000 palace eunuchs. After Wanli's death Confucian scholars launched the "Donglin" reform movement to try to curb eunuch power, but this effort was violently crushed by the eunuchs from 1624 to 1627.

war at sea. The Ottoman Empire built an impressive *permanent navy* that dominated the eastern Mediterranean by the 15th century while their nominal tributaries, the *Barbary corsairs*, contested for domination of the western Mediterranean with the navies of Venice, Portugal, and Spain. China had an extensive blue-water fleet before 1500 but abandoned the seas by 1536 and thus fell ever further behind Europe in naval technology and capabilities. It was the unique accomplishment of much smaller European societies to construct global maritime empires in the 16th–17th centuries. This was mostly a private activity: the concept of "navy" did not exist in medieval Europe and caught on only slowly in early modern Europe, when the term still referred to the whole shipping complement of a city or country, with just a handful of "the king's ships" added. Only *Henry V* among medieval kings of England had a *Royal Navy*. French kings from the 14th century and Castilian and Portuguese monarchs in the 14th–15th centuries committed real resources to building royal fleets of warships, assembling *maps* and *portolan charts*, and maintaining shipyards and docks. But it is important to remember that prior to the 16th century there was not all that much difference between armed merchants and warships. This meant Atlantic states mostly relied on conversion of private warships to public purposes in time of war, as *privateers* or impressed ships and crews. Mediterranean states were far more advanced in purpose-built warships. For example, the merchants of Venice maintained a sophisticated galley navy for many centuries, as did their main rivals in Genoa.

Battles at sea were few and far between in this period and almost never decisive. They usually occurred when a fleet of privateers or other warships intercepted a convoy of armed merchants and the convoy tried to fight it out or, more often, fought back while it ran and was chased. Even colossal battles with much loss of life such as *Sluys* (1340) and *Lepanto* (1571), which wiped out entire national fleets, proved that victory in battles at sea did not mean victory in wars at sea. Far more important was the role of navies in amphibious warfare. This remained the dominant mode of naval warfare in the Mediterranean (such that some historians even refer to the "Mediterranean system" of amphibious galley warfare). Amphibious operations also dominated war at sea in the British Isles, Caribbean, Black Sea, and other shallow water or coastal war zones. Only toward the very end of the period did long-distance ships appear of hybrid hull design and rigging that were capable of *cruising* for months at a time. Such ships could and did conduct war at transoceanic distances, and even globally. Otherwise, as Jan Glete demonstrated, in this era "warfare at sea, its aims, strategies and tactics, were determined by climate, human endurance, and technology." The idea of "command of the sea" had yet to be conceived, let alone effected in the real world of murderous storms, limited logistics, coastal navigation, and intimidating oceanic horizons. See also *admiralty*; *Almiranta*; *battery*; *battle* (2); *blockade*; *blockship*; *boarding*; *bow(ing)*; *broadside*; *Buckingham, 1st Duke of*; *Calicut, Battle of*; *Capitana*; *capture*; *charter company*; *chase gun(s)*; *Cinque Ports*; *close-fights*; *convoy*; *Diu, Battle of*; *Dover, Battle of*; *The Downs, Battle of*; *Drake, Francis*; *Eighty Years' War*; *Elizabeth I*; *embargo*; *England*; *fireships*; *firing on the roll*; *galley*; *Gibraltar, Battle of*; *Greek fire*; *gun-deck*; *gun tackle*; *Hakata Bay, Battle of (1274)*; *Hakata Bay, Battle of (1281)*; *Hanse*; *haul close*; *haul wind*; *heave to*; *Hormuz*; *Hundred Years' War*; *intelligence*; *Invincible Armada*; *levend/levendat*; *line ahead*; *line astern*; *line of battle*; *muster*; *Navigation Acts*; *Netherlands*; *officer*; *Olivares, conde-duque de*; *Philip II, of Spain*; *piracy*; *Portugal*; *rations*; *Royal Navy*; *royal ships*;

safeguard the sea; *ship-of-the-line*; *ships*; *ship's boys*; *ship-smashers*; *shipyards*; *Sound Tolls*; *"sovereignty of the sea"*; *Spain*; *swivel gun*; *Teutonic Knights, Order of*; *"tunnage and poundage"*; *turtle ships*; *Walcheren, Battle of*; *weather gauge*; *windward*; *Zatoka Swieza, Battle of*.

Suggested Reading: Carlo Cipolla, *Guns, Sails and Empires, 1400–1700* (1965; 1996); Jan Glete, *Navies and Nations* (1993); John Guilmartin, *Gunpowder and Galleys* (2003); John Hattendorf and Richard Unger, eds., *War at Sea in the Middle Ages and Renaissance* (2002); Frank Howard, *Sailing Ships of War 1400–1860* (1979); N.A.M. Roger, *The Safeguard of the Sea: A Naval History of Britain*. Vol. 1 (1997).

War Between the Courts. See *Japan*.

war by diversion. A strategy or policy of indirect attack on an enemy's interests so as to divert him from pursing aggressive policies of invasion and occupation of one's own or an ally's territory. This strategy was largely dictated by the inability of any party to raise armies large enough to dominate a given territory, for instance, Germany during the period of Swedish intervention in the *Thirty Years' War* from 1630 to 1635. See also *Gustavus II Adolphus*; *Wallenstein, Albrecht von*.

war chest. "Kriegskasse." Prior to the development of modern economies and systems of taxation and expenditure, national leaders literally kept chests of gold and other precious metals to finance their wars. This practice contributed to "bullionism" and related mercantilist policies. See also *contributions*; *prisoners of war*.

war cries. See *battle cries*.

war dogs. See *Cortés, Hernán*; *Hunderpanzer*.

war elephants. See *elephants*.

war finance. During the *feudal* period in Europe, military service was generally contracted through a system of vassalage (*servitium debitum*) of *knights* and *men-at-arms*. By the 13th century, however, this system was rarely able to raise a sizeable army. This fact, along with the "commercial revolution" underway in society in general, new taxes and other sources of royal revenue, and *scutage* or commutation of vassal military obligations with money payment, all contributed to a shift to paid military service. Italy, England, and France led the slow but inexorable shift to a wage-based soldiery made possible by a dramatic expansion of population and the return of a money economy, combined with a newly literate clerical class that allowed governments to tap into the new economy. In turn, this new system of war finance led to a progressive increase in the size of armies and

> *...the principle of war finance in Europe was ... "war should pay for itself."*

navies and in expenditure on war, from garrisons to field armies and *galleys* to *galleons*, such that on average 50 percent of public revenues were fed into the maw of war. The costs of war quickly outstripped the new tax systems and sources of monarchical revenue. From the 14th to 17th centuries, with rare exceptions, the principle of war finance in Europe was *bellum se ipse alet* ("war should pay for itself"). In this way, relentlessly bellicose monarchs, warrior aristocracies, and early modern states all sought to export the costs of war to the rural population and cities of their enemies. As payment for military service displaced feudal aristocratic levies with expensive *mercenaries*, the costs of war rose to staggering heights. This placed enormous administrative and tax pressures on governments. Often these costs could only be met by waging war to gain access to new markets, subject populations, and land and tax revenues. In this sense war did not just pay for itself, it begat itself.

Austria and the Holy Roman Empire

In wars along the Austrian frontiers local troops were rewarded by allowing them to take booty as compensation. For larger wars in Italy or with France, the Imperial Diet might provide some troops. Others were raised with revenues from the Habsburg hereditary lands, and Imperial loans were provided by the *Fuggers*. Habsburg finances were more precarious during the *Thirty Years' War* (1618–1648), so much so that *Ferdinand II* essentially relied on private contractors to sustain his war effort in accord with the principle cited above, "bellum se ipse alet." Military entrepreneurs, most importantly *Albrecht von Wallenstein*, raised the men and the money needed to field armies from forced *contributions*. This made Wallenstein effectively independent of Ferdinand. Matters were not helped by the fact that the now bitterly divided German *Estates* refused to vote war taxes for the Empire or to Ferdinand, whom they distrusted. Devolving military obligations to the *Reichskreis* did not solve the problem either, since the Imperial Circles were hobbled by confessionalism and princely rivalries. Much changed after Wallenstein was assassinated in 1634. In the *Peace of Prague* (1635), the Estates agreed to pay regular war taxes in lieu of forced contributions. While this provided for most Imperial garrisons it did nothing to make possible offensive war. Field armies were partly supported by revenue from the Habsburg hereditary lands and continuation of the contribution system on a more limited scale.

China

The Chinese had the most advanced bureaucratic state anywhere in the world in this period and were able to finance their wars through a reasonably efficient general tax system. They used these revenues to pre-stock armories, purchase warhorses from as far away as Tibet, run Imperial breeding stables, stock Imperial granaries, store armor and weapons, finance cannon foundries, and pay their troops. In addition, *Hongwu* set up Ming military colonies astride the *Great Wall*, and elsewhere, that were expected to be self-sustaining through farming, trade, and light manufacture. Over time, independent trade and other economic activity, and distance from the capital, reduced the purely military character and effectiveness of Ming garrison towns while intermarriage with frontier nomads limited their political reliability. That said, Ming China's main military problems were not financial: they were more social, political, technological, and geographical in origin and effect.

England

Under the feudal system military service was determined by a quota (the *servitium debitum*) of knights and other fighting men owed by vassals in fulfillment of their obligation to military service. From the 13th century onward a royal summons of this obligation was never enough to raise an effective army in England. Newer infantry units were formed using increased customs revenues which grew as the monetary economy recovered, and in part with *scutage*. After 1270, a new form of contracted military (and other) service emerged called *indentures for war*. This resulted from the slow degradation of overlordship feudalism in the preceding two centuries. The new system, sometimes called "bastard feudalism," relied on a written contract ("indentures") and money payment for services. This proved highly efficient in raising armies for foreign wars. "Bastard feudalism," however, also permitted the raising of private armies and thus eroded the authority of the English monarchy and the rule of law. During the first phase of the *Hundred Years' War* (1337–1453), *Edward III* had normal revenues on the order of £35–40,000 per annum. But a single *chevauchée* or siege lasting three months might cost £60–70,000, while his naval costs were additionally burdensome. Direct taxes were sometimes raised to pay for foreign wars but only by Edward III and later kings acceding to an unsteady, but still progressive, expansion in the say of the landed and merchant classes over national policy. In a rough sense, English democracy was the bastard child of England's wars, delivered in blood and suffering after several centuries of tormented labor. This trend was accelerated dramatically when Parliament raised taxes on its own authority to make war against the king during the *English Civil Wars*. The costs of the *Royal Navy* were originally paid by shifting the burden to shipowners, largely through failure to compensate them for use of their ships and crew. Then a *"tunnage and poundage"* duty was levied. Finally, naval costs were partly covered by an annual sum called the *Ordinary*. Even with all that, into the early 17th century English naval power was largely in private hands: *pirates* and *privateers* carried the war to the enemy for their own profit and that of investors (who often included the monarch). It was not until the 1640s that John Pym and Parliament created an advanced military finance system of direct taxes and dedicated customs revenue.

France

Feudal forms of military service were used throughout the 13th century, with towns paying for units of infantry that supplemented an unusually large body of knights raised in the old way. Religious houses also had military obligations to the French crown. In the 13th century, the Capetian monarchs began to make use of wages ("vadia") to hire specialized infantry. Some frontier garrisons also served on salary. By the early 14th century wages to knights were being disguised as feudal obligations ("fief de chambre"), as for many decades the old feudal and new wage systems coexisted uneasily. The money system led to a dramatic increase, perhaps as much as fourfold, in the size of French armies in just over 100 years. French kings drew funds from the *taille*, an annual land tax that fell mostly on the peasantry, and the ga-belle, a salt tax that was unevenly applied. In 1555 the *taillon* was expanded from towns to the peasantry in order to pay for the Italian Wars of *Henri II*. The nobility were exempt from most taxation but were pressured to meet the demands of the *arrière-ban* through military service or payments in lieu thereof. Also in 1555, a new system of royal borrowing was set up: the *Grand Parti de Lyon*, which piggybacked on Lyon's four large annual fairs by offering long-term contracts to merchant bankers. This led to royal bankruptcy within just two years, as Henri borrowed far beyond his means. The expanded taillon came to an effective end in 1559 upon the King's death.

The *French Civil Wars* (1562–1629) hence were significantly extended by the fact the monarchy was crippled by debt and a deserved reputation as an untrustworthy borrower. Even in peacetime the army consumed 40 percent of royal revenues. In wartime, a single month's military expenditure might equal three years of peacetime spending. Nor could the crown collect taxes from rebel towns or devastated provinces. *Huguenot* finances were also hand-to-mouth. They relied on donations from the faithful, heavy borrowing, sale of confiscated Catholic benefices and church property, collection and confisca-tion of royal taxes in Huguenot towns and across the Midi, and profits from Rochelais privateering. This fiscal weakness of each side put a premium on fast rather than successful campaigns. Throughout the civil wars, one-half of all royal revenue went to waging war on land, and naval commitments were even more expensive than land warfare.

Fifty years later, under *Cardinal Richelieu*, the French tax system was re-formed and centralized, permitting collections that sustained French armies and those of anti-Habsburg allies such as Sweden. This income was supple-mented by selling bastardized titles and public offices ("droits aliénés") to eager social climbers from the middle classes. The French economy was also larger and more prosperous by the mid-17th century. During the Thirty Years' War, France, like other belligerents, relied on contract mercenaries to raise forced contributions to pay for themselves. However, the areas it oc-cupied were too small to sustain large armies or were already eaten out and plundered. France thus relied more than other large states in the mid-17th century on direct taxes. The spectacular increase in war taxes that resulted in the 1630s and 1640s led to deep resentment that at times threatened France's war effort. Upon victory in 1648 this anger finally exploded into widespread rebellion ("The Frondes").

Italy

The city-states of central and northern Italy pioneered the post-feudal system of wages for military service for citizen militia and in hiring mercenaries. These became known by their contracts, or "condotta," as *condottieri*. Contract mercenaries dominated Italian warfare through the *Italian Renaissance* and continued to be active into the *Italian Wars* (1494–1559), paid from the rich revenues derived from the spice trades and urban commerce. After the French invasion, however, Italian city-states seldom controlled their own military policy or financing.

Mughal Empire

The Mughals ruled a vast and wealthy empire with a military sustained by a mixture of quasi-feudal levies of cavalry and an advanced bureaucracy and taxation system that allowed them to man garrisons, build military roads, and fight protracted campaigns in Central Asia and against the *Marathas* and *Rajputs*. It is worth remembering that India in this period was considered a land of fabulous wealth, which meant in practice that Mughal military and social elites lived high at the price of huge tax burdens borne by a destitute peasantry.

Muscovy

Early Russian military weakness was rooted in its splintered landholding, "udel," or appanage system, which kept each local prince weak. This changed under *Ivan III* in the late 15th century. He introduced *servitor* cavalry, horsemen recruited from a new landholding elite seeded over the countryside in exchange for several months per year of military service. *Ivan IV* set up a servitor palace guard of infantry musketeers, the *strel'sty*, in 1555. They were exempt from the elevated taxation which Muscovites were increasingly forced to pay to support the new military formations. The crisis of the Muscovite service state came during the *Oprichnina* and the *Smutnoe Vremia*, when expansion to the west was blocked so that the state could not fulfill its promises of new land made to servitor soldiers.

Netherlands

The Dutch were the only European nation to raise sufficient taxes at home to pay for their wars, which were fought mainly on their own territory in this period and at sea. That feat is all the more remarkable given that the northern Netherlands was at war with Spain for eight decades. This singular success rested on the most advanced early capitalist (modern) economy in the world. The Dutch also had a sophisticated tax system and a federal governmental structure, disguised as a confederation of provinces, that permitted revenues generated by populous and prosperous core provinces such as Holland to be spent on perimeter defense and fortification of the lesser sisters of the system. The Dutch supplemented tax and customs revenues with lucrative privateering, including occasional interception of lone Spanish treasure ships from the Americas, and once, the whole treasure fleet. Dutch merchants and bankers were so prosperous by the mid-17th century that they made large war loans to other belligerent allies.

Ottoman Empire

In the 14–15th centuries, the Ottomans made heavy use of light cavalry *akincis* paid only in booty. Their *Tatar* allies also survived on booty. During the 16th century, the Ottomans engaged a standing and salaried army as well as a well-developed *magazine* system ("menzil-hane") supported by a special grain tax (*avariz*), innovations centuries ahead of comparable commissariat services in the West. The sultans were also unique in this era in their ability to sustain near-continuous and major land campaigns against the West and Safavid Iran without exceptional tax levies or repeated bankruptcy. Starting in the early 17th century, they levied more often what had been an exceptional military surtax called the *bedel-i nüzul*. The Ottoman military finance system benefitted from the fact that the Empire had lower naval expenses than its rivals (navies were much more expensive than armies). When the Ottomans did fight at sea, as at *Lepanto* (1571), they called upon ships and crews of Barbary vassals to supplement their fleets. This changed in the 17th century as Western navies pulled ahead in ship design, pushing the Ottomans to spend more just to keep pace.

The Ottomans also had to build, and overcome, the new *alla moderna* fortifications. Again, they were unique in controlling fortification costs by utilizing regular troops as military laborers: digging was something few Western soldiers would do without extra pay. Along the frontiers, especially in the *Militargrenze*, costs were kept low by relying on local auxillary troops such as *Voynuqs*, and taking advantage of difficult terrain with minimal fortification. Real money was laid out only for the most vital garrisons, such as at Buda or Mosul or Baghdad. The sultans spent lavishly from taxes on the *Janissary Corps*, but they also kept these troops limited in number. Much of their army remained *sipahis* and *timariot* cavalry paid from land revenues. Military expenditures were made from an Inner Treasury reserve which gathered all revenues from rich provinces such as Egypt, then dispensed funds to an Outer Treasury that paid ongoing expenses in other provinces of the Empire.

Safavid Iran

The Safavids relied initially on traditional feudal cavalry raised by tribe and paid for by local warlords in return for land grants. The creation of a standing army by *Abbas I* changed that. His new cavalry, infantry, and artillery units were paid from royal revenues. As with comparable military reform monarchs in Europe, Abbas was forced to modernize Iran's tax system to concentrate revenue at the center. This entailed loosening the grip of the old religious elite, the *Qizilbash*.

Spain

During the later *Reconquista*, Castile drew upon an exceptional war tax approved by the popes: the *cruzada*. After 1492, the monarchy kept the cruzada in place while drawing revenues also from a dedicated sales tax known as the *alcabala*. After 1500, Spain drew rising amounts of revenue from gold and silver mines in the Americas, though this source went into steep decline in the 17th century as more silver was smuggled into Europe outside of Spain's control. The main problem for Spain was that the monarchs suffered repeated bankruptcy born of too many wars with too many enemies, fought for too little gain over too many decades. Spain's agrarian and ranching economy never produced much surplus revenue to be taxed and the inflow of American silver drove inflation ever higher.

Spain never solved these basic problems but it managed them perhaps better than its repeated bankruptcies make it appear. It did so by floating state loans, with new loans coerced from bankers already overexposed to the king's prior bad debts. And it imposed basic military costs on the areas where its troops were billeted, in Italy and the Netherlands. Spain was able to borrow heavily on capital markets despite its repeated defaults since it controlled much of the territory where Italian and other Mediterranean bankers operated. The threat of a total default on old debt coerced bankers to throw worse money after bad in exchange for some payment of interest (usually, at 5 percent, reduced from original rates as high as 20 percent). Like French kings, Spanish monarchs raised funds through the sale of titles, offices, and monopoly charters for overseas enterprises. Unlike France, Spain squeezed *conversos* for loans tied to promises of eased restrictions on their civic freedoms and extracted vast funds from the sale of properties confiscated from Jews persecuted by the *Inquisition*. Well before the end of the Thirty Years' War, however, most of these sources had dried up. *Olivares* thus tried to extract more taxation from Aragon, Catalonia, and Portugal, but this only provoked serial rebellions and hence created more battlefields on which to spill Spanish blood and treasure.

> Olivares . . . *created more battlefields on which to spill Spanish blood and treasure.*

Sweden

Swedish war finance in the 17th century may almost be reduced to a singular proposition: the Swedes were able to get other belligerents to pay for their armies and wars. France provided over 300,000 thalers per annum, on average, from 1630 to 1648. Forcibly allied German principalities like Brandenburg and Saxony also provided subsidies, while occupied territories in Germany provided vast "contributions." Swedish taxes never paid for more than 5–15 percent of the cost of the German war, which was entered into in good part to make a profit for the impoverished northern kingdom. Sweden also received significant revenue from customs duties leveled on the rich Baltic trade: to that end, the earlier capture of Riga by *Gustavus Adolphus* was a key moment in Swedish martial and imperial history. In the last years of the German war Sweden fell badly into arrears despite these foreign subsidies. Among its essential goals in talks leading to the *Peace of Westphalia* in 1648 was obtaining a huge "indemnity" (20 million thalers) to pay off its veterans, who were mostly non-Swedish mercenaries by then. Sweden finally settled for 5 million thalers and the peace was agreed.

Swiss Confederation

The Swiss cantons initially raised town and rural militia on an unpaid basis for self-defense and joint defense of the Swiss Confederation. As the Swiss emerged as the pre-eminent infantry in Europe over the 14th–15th centuries, they switched to mercenary service. Making war for profit became their hallmark. This fact was captured in the maxim of foreign princes: "Pas d'argent, pas de Suisses" ("no money, no Swiss"). See also *annates*; *appatis*; *bahşiş*; *bullionism*; *carbiniers*; *Crusades*; *esame*; *fusiliers de taille*; *ganimet*; *ishan*; *printing*; *Tenth Penny*; *terakki*; *war chest*; *ziamet*.

Suggested Reading: Richard Bonney, *The King's Debts: Finance and Politics in France, 1589–1661* (1981); J. Collins, *Fiscal Limits of Absolutism* (1988); C. Finkel, *Administration of Warfare: Ottoman Military Campaigns in Hungary, 1593–1606* (1988); P. Hamon, *L'argent du roi* (1994); M. Hart, *In Quest of Funds: Warfare and State Formation in the Netherlands, 1620–50* (1989).

war hammer. A short-hafted weapon with a hammerhead tapering into a spiked tail. It was not widely used, principally because better close-in weapons were readily available. A 13th–14th century war hammer of Swiss origin had some success. In combat the Swiss war hammer was swung as a club, but it could be thrown as need or opportunity arose. In addition to close combat, it served the Swiss as a construction tool in making defensive earthworks and palisades (*Letzinen*) or pitching camp. Polish nobles sometimes carried war hammers, but in general Polish cavalrymen preferred swords. In the 16th century war hammers enjoyed renewed popularity in Europe, but more as affect and decoration than as a real weapon. See also *polearm*.

warhorses. The main association of world historical change with warhorses concerns the impact of the warrior peoples of the steppe on the wider history of the *Oikoumene*. The Central Asian, or Inner Asian, steppe peoples learned horsemanship in their first years (most could ride well by age 5), and learned soon after that to shoot from the saddle with their *composite bows*. Notable among these horse culture migrants were the Magyars. Most famous were the *Mongols*. So dedicated were such warriors to their steppe ponies they were often buried together. Other steppe peoples known generically as *Turks* were as horse savvy and dangerous to settled societies as any Magyar or Mongol. Cavalry power was the basis of the ascendancy of the *Seljuks* and *Ottomans* over older and long-established Muslim and Christian populations of the Middle East and Balkans. Horse soldiers overran much of northern India in the 11th–12th centuries, where Mongol-Turkic skill in mounted archery and use of stirrup and composite bow was unmatched by native Indian horsemen or military technology. Comparable in horsemanship and military skills to the steppe "horse peoples," but settling in the Caucasus and Ukraine later and arising from a different ethnic and social origin, were the *Cossacks*. As skilled in mounted warfare as all these peoples, but emerging from a wholly different desert, were the *Bedouin*.

The warhorses ridden by steppe peoples were stalwart little ponies, fleet of hoof and exclusively grass fed. The absolute food limit imposed by the steppe tended to reduce horse size. In turn, that set a burden limit on the rider, his weapons, and armor. That was normally no great trouble since nomads wore little armor beyond *cuir-bouilli* and had no metal industry. Steppe ponies were far hardier and more numerous than the grain-fed horses of China or Europe. They were capable of long-distance riding while placing fewer demands on their masters for fodder and care. Ming China supplied its cavalry with steeds from four sources: the "tea-horse" trade, in which Chinese tea was exchanged for warhorses raised in Tibet at a rate of some 5,000 per annum, with occasional interruptions of the trade by Mongol raiders; a state breeding program run by the "Court of the Imperial Stud" that produced 3,000 horses per year; private horse markets across rural China that supplied the great bulk of the army's needs, some 25,000 fresh horses per year; and ad hoc purchases of Mongol or other steppe ponies from frontier horse markets for use by border garrisons. Despite all this, Ming cavalry was chronically short of good mounts, a serious military disadvantage when facing Mongol or Manchu equine armies.

Arab warhorses in use in the Middle East, North Africa, and Muslim Iberia were superior breeds to European horses in quality, speed, and endurance. They included fine breeds such as the "Barb" and "Turkmene," the latter of Asian origin and introduced to the Arabs by the Seljuks. The most famous Muslim breed was known simply as the "Arabian." When these fleet stocks reached Spain crossbreeding produced the "Andalusian," a breed prized throughout Europe. Arab stables in Sicily and southern Italy produced the "Apulian" and other crossbreeds that were fast yet adapted easily to heat and distance. Cavalry empires in sub-Saharan Africa such as the *Fulbe, Songhay*, and *Mali* acquired horses from Arab traders and then bred their own. The military limits imposed by the environment on their imperial expansion had to do with the rainforest, which imposed a barrier to African cavalry because it hosted the tsetse fly that bore "sleeping sickness" (African trypanosomiasis) that killed horses. But in the flat and semi-arid sudan and the vast sahel grasslands the horse made its owner master of the battlefield, and hence also of an economy of cowering peasants and monopoly trades in salt, gold, slaves, and other caravan goods.

Equestrian warfare by mounted, armored men is closely associated with the history of Medieval Europe. *Heavy cavalry* began its rise to martial preeminence under the Carolingians in France in the 8th–9th centuries. Thereafter, cavalry rose to predominance not just militarily but as a full horse culture: warhorse and rider were central to *feudalism, chivalry*, and *knighthood*. By the 11th century, heavy horse was overpowering in nearly every European battle. Up to the 15th century, knights of the first rank rode to the fight with at least three types of specialized warhorses. Most important was the "dexterarius," better known as the *destrier* or main battle horse. It was led to combat by hand and ridden only in *tournaments* or on the battlefield. Like the knight, it too was usually clad in cloth and some armor, and decorated with a coat of arms. In the 12th–13th centuries destriers were clad in heavy padded quilts ("trappers"). By the 14th century a destrier wore mail and plate in combination, with a *chanfron* protecting his head and a *peytral* covering his chest (all destriers were stallions). Controversy lingers over the size of medieval chargers. Andrew Ayton, the expert historian of equine warfare, suggests the typical destrier was "of the order of 14 to 15 hands in height—not a large animal by modern standards." That assessment needs this context: people, too, were much smaller on average than today. The overall effect and impression made by a powerful destrier was therefore still that it was a huge battle horse, first in its class and "heavy" by comparison to the normal nags or *hackneys* of town or country life. And like its rider, the appearance of girth and hitting power was enhanced in the charge by its shell of armor and flowing and flapping cloth. The second horse in a knight's stable was a *palfrey*. It carried the knight on the road to battle, thereby keeping the great destrier fresh. Finally, the knight might have one or more pack horses to help his *page* or *squire* carry armor, weapons, and personal comforts. The number of warhorses owned, along with the richness and amount of armor worn, often determined if ordinary soldiers might aspire to gain the status of *men-at-arms*.

Warhorses were carefully bred, highly prized, and very expensive—the equivalent on average of a year's landed income for a knight. This led to systems of reimbursement for warhorses killed or maimed in combat. In Italy this was called "mendum" while in France it was known as "restaur." It normally took up to four years to train a proper cavalry mount. International horse breeding and trading markets arose with annual fairs held in all major theaters of war. The horse market, and related crafts and trade, was a major part of the war economy in England and France during the *Hundred Years' War* (1337–1453). There were large-scale breeding programs and importation from Spain and Lombardy. Breeding programs and the general demand for powerful chargers produced the late medieval "magnus equus," or great warhorse. An earlier English breeding program started by *Edward III* has been described by Andrew Ayton as little short of a "horse-breeding revolution." The breed that resulted was taller than all earlier types (but still less than 18 hands) and sturdy enough to carry the weight of its armor and that of its steel-encased master. However, even equine armor did not suffice when facing potent missile weapons such as the *longbow*. It did much more damage to semi-protected chargers than to the armored knights who rode them. Similarly, horses fared badly when facing new infantry tactics built around the *pike* and *halberd*. The response of Europe's warrior classes to this challenge was to dismount and fight on foot, a tactic pioneered by English knights against the Scots and the French and adopted by the French to fight the English at *Poitiers* (1356). The French were back in the saddle at *Agincourt* (1415) only because they overestimated progress made in equine armor and thought it could resist the longbow; it did not. Milanese knights dismounted to fight the Swiss at *Arbedo* (1422). In eastern Europe, where cavalry warfare survived as the dominant arm into the 17th century, swifter and smaller horses suitable to *hussars* were bred and prized. Poland was famous for such horses, which its kings took great care not to export. In the middle of the 16th century English monarchs also banned the export of cavalry mounts, though this was often evaded in practice by parading the same horse through official countings in different market towns.

Destriers were trained to one purpose: ride without flinching or swerving toward an apparently solid front of other men-at-arms and horses or infantry. The ideal was to pass the front line through with the *couched lance* then put to the sword the remnants of a broken and running formation. This tactic provided the overwhelming *shock* that gave heavy cavalry dominance on the field of battle in Europe for 200 years. Adding to the threatening psychological effect of a charge by heavy horse, the sound of thundering hooves of as many as 2,000 armored warhorses and riders, with lances bent and riding in line with men whooping exhortations and curses, evoked a profound and understandable fear in opposing infantry: a full-throated charge of medieval heavy horse produced the loudest and most terrifying artificial sound heard in the world in that Age. Warhorses charged in this unswerving manner even when facing pikes for the first time at *Courtrai* (1302). If instinct prevailed over training and the lead horses and riders tried to turn aside or hold back at the point of imminent contact, they could not: a turn to the side knocked into other knights in the line while to the rear they were locked in place by a second and even third line of men and horses, pushing blindly forward to mutual impalement on the unmoving, braced pikes. Riders who made it inside the square, still mounted or not, were met by axemen and halberdiers who eagerly hacked hated nobles to death, or sliced a dagger through the visor as a knight floundered in his armor like some ridiculous overturned turtle, or plunged a blade into his unprotected armpit or groin.

> *...medieval heavy horse produced the ... most terrifying artificial sound heard in the world ...*

From such fights men-at-arms and mounts alike learned that enemy infantry no longer divided automatically when knights charged. Cavalry sometimes loosened formation to better pull back from the hedges of planted and braced spears that did not waver. More often, in the early 14th century they came on in the same old way only to die in the new one, on the points of pikes and finishing axe blows. Later, cavalry learned to send in archers and arquebusiers to disorder the enemy pike square so that the cavalry could ride into the gaps with slashing swords or bone-breaking maces. In sum, infantry tactics built around the pike vitiated shock by heavy cavalry and tipped the balance in battle slowly but inexorably toward massed infantry. Cavalry adjusted, but ultimately the combination of new infantry tactics and armor-piercing weapons made the old cavalry shock attack with heavy lance too dangerous and expensive in noble lives. Once that became clear, mounts were no longer chosen for their load-bearing ability but for speed and intelligence, so that they could undertake complex tactics like the *caracole*. Thus, smaller and fleeter horses found their way back to the European battlefield. Among other evidence of the change, the new style of cavalry mounts often missed part of each ear, a consequence of riders slashing at the enemy with sabers wielded on either side of the horse's head and flanks. See also *auxiliaries*; *barded horse*; *booty*; *cog*; *courser*; *dragoons*; *engagements*; *fodder*; *hobelars*; *horse armor*; *jinetes*; *Knights Templar*; *lance* (2); *logistics*; *Propositions*; *rouncey*; *sumpter*.

Suggested Reading: Andrew Ayton, *Knights and Warhorses* (1994); John Clark, *The Medieval Horse and Its Equipment, 1150–1450* (1995); Ann Hyland, *The Medieval Warhorse* (1996); Miklós Jankovich, *They Rode into Europe* (1971); Maurice Keen, ed., *Medieval Warfare* (1999); R. Law, *The Horse in West African History* (1980).

War of Cologne (1583–1588). The first successful effort by the *Counter-Reformation* to reverse the protestantization of German states, in this case the recatholicization of Cologne. It marked a new Catholic militancy. Paradoxically, it also evidenced a sense of urgency among Catholics that they were losing the confessional struggle. *Parma* advanced the Catholic cause simultaneously in Flanders and Brabant.

War of Smolensk (December 1632–June 1634). *Cardinal Richelieu* and *Gustavus Adolphus* sought to build an alliance in eastern Europe to drain away Habsburg troops and resources from Germany. To this end they conspired with the Ottoman sultan, with a Transylvanian prince, and with the *Cossacks*. The plan was to launch coordinated attacks on Poland, Hungary, and Austria. It was far too grand a scheme to work: the sultan was bogged down in another war with Iran and the Cossacks attacked Muscovy instead of Poland. When the Polish throne was vacated in August 1632, Muscovy laid siege to Smolensk. The Swedes intervened in behalf of Muscovy but the death of Gustavus in battle in Germany and superior Polish troops and battlefield tactics forced the Muscovites to withdraw. A peace was agreed at Polyanovka wherein Poland renounced all claim to the Muscovite throne but kept Smolensk.

War of the Breton Succession (1341–1365). A local war over the succession to Brittany fought within the larger *Hundred Years' War* (1337–1453). When the old Duke died without leaving a recognized heir in 1341, France and England clashed over which would put its favored candidate on the throne. The conflict was not settled for over twenty years. Despite the major parties signing the Treaty of Brétigny in 1360, localized fighting continued over the issue until 1364. The next year, in the Treaty of Guérande, France agreed to recognize the English candidate, John de Montfort. Thereafter, the new Duke piloted a neutral course to avoid conflict with either of his giant warring neighbors.

War of the Cities (1454–1466). "Thirteen Years' War." The territorial struggle between the *Teutonic Knights* and the still feudal kingdom of

Poland-Lithuania climaxed in the mid-15th century. Within Prussia economic advances had outstripped political modernization. By mid-century affluent Prussian cities were desperate to escape the economic constrictions imposed on them by the still-feudal economic policies and taxes of the Brethren, and so formed an alliance with the Junkers. This strange alliance was possible because also feeding the rebellion was Junker disgruntlement with the foreign birth of many "Sword Brothers." The leading cities of Prussia (Danzig, Elblag, Torun, Elbing, and Thorn), later joined by 16 other towns, and the Junkers formed the *Preussische Bund* ("Prussian Confederation") in 1440. In 1452 the Bund appealed to Emperor Friedrich III to mediate their grievances with the Brethren. Instead, early the next year Friedrich ordered all Prussians to submit. This forced the Bund to seek help from the Poles. In early 1454, the Bund secretly asked to be incorporated into Poland. *Casimir IV* signaled that he would support the rebels if they made a public request: his interest was to detach Prussia from the Teutons and annex it to Poland-Lithuania. From February 6, the Bund began taking over and destroying lightly garrisoned Teutonic castles. On March 6 a formal agreement was reached between Casimir and the Bund asserting Polish sovereignty over Prussia and declaring war on the Brethren.

Since most of the Teutonic castles in Prussia had fallen to the rebels even before the war officially started, it was widely expected to be a short campaign. In fact, it lasted thirteen years. Cracks in the Teutonic edifice were offset by initial Polish weakness: despite sharing Casimir as joint sovereign, the Lithuanians refused to send troops or finance the war in Prussia. Other Polish troops were tied down by the threat to southern Poland of a possible Ottoman attack. As a result, an undersized Polish army was sent into Prussia. After a desultory and unsuccessful siege of Chojnice by the Prussians, this force engaged in a major battle outside the city. On the field at *Chojnice* (September 18, 1454) the Poles and Prussians were soundly defeated by the Teutonic Knights, aided by a large band (9,000 horse, 6,000 foot) of German mercenaries. Teutonic victory at Chojnice ensured that the war would go on. The rebels seized most of the Order's arsenals and castles in Prussia, but failed in an effort to storm the citadel and Teutonic capital of *Marienburg* (Malbork). The financial weakness of the Order meant that its Grand Master had to promise the mercenaries control of Prussian cities in lieu of wages. Still, the Knights raised small armies from among loyal Brethren outside Prussia and by conscripting their enserfed peasants. While the Prussian towns remained determined to break free of Teutonic overlordship, the larger *Hanse* cities allied with the Knights. Nor did the international situation favor either side: most other powers were preoccupied with their own unsettled internal affairs or other wars, and remained neutral.

The Poles were also forced to hire mercenaries, primarily Czechs and Silesians, greatly straining the royal purse which was light in the best of times. Casimir's repeated call-ups of peasant levies were only agreed to by the Sejm after he made heavy political concessions to the nobility, which started the Polish state down a road that ultimately led to a fatal weakness at the center.

The Poles besieged Lasin in 1455, but again their lack of siegecraft and cavalry-heavy army told against success. As war taxes began to bite into the rebel cities the Teutons enjoyed better luck. Their army was better equipped for siege work, and several towns fell to a combination of internal unrest and external military pressure: Konigsberg surrendered on April 17, 1455, and Knipawa gave in on June 14, 1455. When the Brethren again ran out of money, however, some mercenary captains took Prussian towns for themselves and milked them dry. Several companies also negotiated with the Poles to transfer possession of fortified cities. Now, external powers also intervened: the Holy Roman Empire moved to ban the Bund and the pope threatened to excommunicate any who refused to come to terms with the Teutonic Knights. Denmark declared war on Poland and the Bund but that was largely an empty gesture since Denmark was already engaged in a major naval war with Sweden. Still, this emboldened the Knights, who refused terms to the Poles and rebels. The Poles replied by hiring still more mercenaries from Silesia, more mercenaries from Russia, and even *Tatars* from the Crimea. Fighting resumed, but with both sides suffering internal dissension and bad finances the war settled into a pattern of minor raids and indeterminate sieges.

A Prussian fleet, mostly built in Danzig on orders from Poland, defeated a Teutonic fleet at *Bornholm* (August 1457). As the war lengthened, the fundamental economic weakness of the Brethren was revealed. They were not as rich as in the past and struggled unsuccessfully to meet the payroll of their mercenary troops. In 1457 Bohemian mercenaries garrisoning Marienburg mutinied, sold the fortress to the Poles, and went home. The loss of the Teuton capital should have ended the war but on September 28, 1457, Marienburg was retaken in a surprise assault by the Knights that was abetted by internal treachery which opened its gates before they were forced. In 1458 the Poles invaded Prussia again, employing Tartar auxiliaries, and besieged Marienburg. Yet again the Poles proved incompetent at siege warfare. The campaign collapsed and a cease-fire took effect that lasted nine months, into 1459. The Danes withdrew from the war, an act almost as little noticed as their entry. Pope Pius II tried to mediate peace, hopeful that he could get all sides to join in a new crusade against the Ottomans. The Poles rejected the pope's entreaties and his threats of excommunication (eternal damnation was not what it used to be).

The Knights were briefly resurgent: they defeated the Danzig militia and burned part of the city in July 1460. The fundamental weakness of the Polish recruitment system, based still on feudal levies of peasants and independently minded noble cavalry, became apparent in deep resistance to new enlistment drives. Casimir finally persuaded the nobles to turn the fight over to professionals. That meant raising funds to hire a mercenary army rather than raising peasant levies to be led by amateur noble captains. These harder and more skilled troops crossed into Prussia in 1461. At *Swiecino* (August 17, 1462), the defeat they handed to the Brethren's field army was so sharp that the end of Teuton rule in the eastern Baltic came into sight. Loss of the Brethren's fleet at *Zatoka Swieza* (September 15, 1463) so severely damaged the Order's maritime interests and profits in the eastern Baltic that the Knights could no longer pay for a war being fought mainly by privateers at sea and mercenaries on land. A complete defeat was only averted by the internal divisions of Poland-Lithuania. Negotiations began at Torun but broke down during 1462. Desultory fighting thus continued through 1465. The Poles made small but steady gains, whittling away at the shrinking domain of the Order until they captured Chojnice (September 28, 1466). Pope Paul II mediated the *Second Peace of Torun* (October 19, 1466) in which the Sword Brothers lost half of Prussia outright and accepted Casimir's suzerainty in the rump lands left to them.

War of the Debatable Lands (1532). See *Henry VIII, of England*.

War of the Eight Saints (1375–1378). Fought between Florence and Pope Gregory XI (1370–1378), and named for the eight priors of Florence. It sprang from concern by the Florentine council to prevent expansion of the Papal States being asked by Gregory as the price of an end to the "Avignon Captivity" of the papacy and his return to Rome. Florence sent agents and troops to provoke rebellion inside the Papal States, prompting a swift papal interdict against the city. To pay for the *condottieri* who were waging its war, from 1376 Florence sold church properties, liquidating sacred assets in a way and on a scale not seen before (and not seen again until the mass confiscations of monastery and other church property during the *Protestant Reformation* of the 16th century in England and Germany). This added an anti-Church dimension to what had begun as a territorial conflict, and that turned the opinion of common Florentines against the war. Flagellants appeared in the streets of Florence in protest against cancellation of Church services, culminating in a full-scale rebellion by the "ciompi" (city laborers) in one of the first urban social upheavals in late medieval and early modern Europe. The city's leadership was also divided by the issue of confiscations, and so Florence asked for terms. In the interim Pope Gregory had died, and the papacy lurched into the bitter and enfeebling controversy of the *Great Schism*. As a result, Florence received better terms from Pope Urban VI than its battlefield failures and internal divisions warranted. See also *Hawkwood, John*.

Suggested Reading: David Peterson, "War of the Eight Saints," in William J. Connell, ed., *Society and Individual in Renaissance Florence* (2002).

War of the Mantuan Succession (1627–1631). In December 1627, the Duke of Mantua died, the last male in the main Gonzaga (Gonzague) line. The best claimant to the succession was the Duke of Nevers, who was heavily backed by France. Spain feared that Nevers would give France control of key fortresses that straddled the main road through northern Italy, so they attacked him in Mantua as well as his home principality of Montferrat, which like Mantua was strategically located in Lombardy. In February 1629, a French army crossed into Italy to aid Nevers against the Spanish. As this fighting got under way, the Dutch seized the moment to break the ring of Spanish fortresses that had encircled them since 1604. Led by *Frederik Hendrik*, they overran several key Spanish garrison towns from 1629 to 1632. *Ferdinand II* wanted to send 50,000 Imperial troops to aid Spain in Italy but the German princes balked at the idea of expanding their military obligations to Italy and the Netherlands and refused to pay. Ferdinand managed to send a small army which stormed and sacked Mantua in 1630. A ferocious outbreak of plague in northern Italy in 1631 then crippled both sides. Ferdinand wanted to recall his troops to face the Swedish invasion of Germany, so he agreed to accept Nevers as Duke in exchange for a French promise not to intervene in Germany. *Cardinal Richelieu* rejected the settlement,

> *Ferdinand wanted to recall his troops to face the Swedish invasion of Germany . . .*

however, so that the war in Italy continued even as *Gustavus Adolphus* landed in Pomerania and Richelieu sent him money to fight Ferdinand for control of Germany. Formally, the Mantuan war ended with the Peace of Cherasco in 1631. In fact, a protracted struggle fought initially in the twilight along the Italian frontier continued to 1635, then broke into the open until final victory was achieved by France in 1659 (Peace of the Pyrenees). See also *Maximilian I*; *Regensburg, Treaty of*; *Wallenstein, Albrecht von*.

War of the Schmalkaldic League (1546–1547). See *Schmalkaldic League*.

War of the Sicilian Vespers (1282–1302). The conflict began as a rebellion in Palermo against rule by the Angevin Empire, starting on "vespers" (Easter Monday). Within days, most French in Sicily were butchered by roving mobs. Byzantine Emperor Michael VIII had financed and encouraged leaders of the revolt in secret, hoping to preoccupy the Angevins and forestall any invasion of his own shrunken and vulnerable lands. The Aragonese intervened to press their claim to Sicily. This led to a protracted war between the Angevins and Aragonese over Sicily. Aragon finally won and kept the island under terms of the "Peace of Caltabellota" (1302). The outbreak of peace led the *Catalan Great Company* to shift its operations to the fringes of the Byzantine Empire. Some 140 years later, Sicily was reunited with Naples when the latter was acquired by Alfonso V of Aragon in 1442.

War of the Three Henries (1587–1589). See *French Civil Wars*.

warp. To tow a ship with oared boats or by pulleys and ropes ("warps") along a shoreline or dock.

warrant officer. An army or naval officer who held his rank by virtue of a warrant, rather than a commission; most often a staff officer or functional officer appointed by a regiment's colonel or a ship's captain. Warrant officer rank was most frequently awarded to chaplains and surgeons, but also to some *corporals*, *sergeants*, and most *quartermasters*. See also *purser*.

"Warring States." See *Sengoku jidai*.

Warrington, Battle of (1648). See *Preston, Campaign of*.

warrior monks. See *Aviz*; *Buddhism*; *Crusades*; *Hospitallers*; *Japan*; *Knights of Calatrava*; *Knights of Christ*; *Knights of Our Lady of Montjoie*; *Knights of Santiago*; *Knights Templar*; *Military Orders*; *Negora Temple*; *sōhei*.

warships. See *ships*; *War at Sea*.

Wars of Investiture (1077–1122). See *castles, on land*; *Guelphs and Ghibellines*; *Holy Roman Empire*; *Italy*; *Papal States*.

"Wars of Religion" (in France). See *French Civil Wars*.

Wars of the Roses (1455–1485). An underlying cause was failure of the sustained effort to hold onto English territories in France during the final phase of the *Hundred Years' War* (1337–1453). This was followed by a protracted dynastic dispute between the rival Houses of Lancaster ("Red Rose") and York ("White Rose"), each claiming the throne via descent from *Edward III*. More immediate grievances included the unpopularity of the Lancastrian, Henry VI (1422–1461), and some nobles at his court; the continuing availability to the barony of small private armies; and complex relations with powerful nobles in Ireland and in exile. Ireland itself was valued for its strategic location and as a ready source of cheap troops.

The Wars of the Roses saw sixteen significant battles and dozens of skirmishes and small sieges, none of which were truly decisive. The opening fight came at First St. Albans (May 22, 1455), where Richard of York's 3,000 men defeated 2,500 Lancastrians under Henry VI. There followed four years of uneasy peace. At Blore Heath (September 22, 1459), in Staffordshire, this ended when Yorkist knights under the Earl of Salisbury bested a force of the king's *men-at-arms*. The rebels then hooked up with a larger Yorkist force at Ludford Bridge and moved against Worcester, but fell back when they met a still larger Lancastrian army. At Ludford they spent a cold night waiting on battle, with the Lancastrians drawn up across the river. But too many Yorkist troops deserted during the night and even more fled or switched sides when they saw the enemy in the cold dawn on October 12. The army scattered and the major Yorkist leaders fled abroad, but only to plot a return to power. At Northampton (July 10, 1460), Yorkists defeated the Royal Army when Lord Grey, who was in command of a Lancastrian wing, switched sides in mid-battle. The king was taken prisoner and agreed that the Yorkist claim to the succession should be exercised upon his death. This did not end the fighting: at Wakefield (December 30, 1460) 8,000 Yorkists attacked foolhardily directly into 18,000 waiting Lancastrians only to lose decisively and bloodily. Several leading Yorkists were executed after the battle, signaling that a new seriousness and ruthlessness of purpose and method had entered the conflict, while also clearing the way for a new generation of noble aspirants and rivals to contest for the Plantagenet crown.

At Mortimer's Cross (February 2, 1461), 11,000 Welsh Yorkists led by the future Edward IV routed a force of 8,000 French, Welsh, and Irish mercenaries fighting for the Red Rose. Edward headed to London where he would be crowned two months later. But first he tried to link with a second Yorkist army. At Second St. Albans (February 17, 1461) the rival armies numbered 25,000 each. The Lancastrians attacked before Edward arrived and joined the Yorkist armies. The commander in his absence was the Earl of Warwick (Richard Neville, "The Kingmaker"), who fled at the first hint of danger. Warwick even abandoned his hostage, no less a person than the Lancastrian king, Henry VI, whom he left under a tree! Both sides gathered more forces. At Ferrybridge (March 28, 1461), Edward IV's advance guard was isolated and destroyed, but the main force carried the bridge. The next day, at Towton, the enlarged main armies met in battle. The Yorkist army of 36,000 attacked a Lancastrian force of 40,000 in the midst of a heavy snow storm. Edward used a favorable wind to increase the range of his archers and limit that of the Lancastrians, who were thus enticed to leave their entrenchments and charge the Yorkist lines. The fight lasted many hours, seesawing at the center during one of the bloodiest days ever seen in England. The arrival of reinforcements gave the blood-soaked day to Edward: Henry's infantry broke and ran while hundreds of stranded knights floundered and drowned in the River Cock, pulled under by the weight of their armor.

Towton brought three years of peace to England, though the Lancastrians sought and received aid from Scotland and kept the war going in the north. At Hedgely Moor (April 25, 1464), a small Yorkist army of 5,000 men handed a comparable Lancastrian force another sharp defeat, but the Duke of Somerset evaded capture with some survivors and began to raise new levies. Before they were ready, he was attacked at Hexham (May 15, 1464) and his force annihilated. Somerset was captured and beheaded, the first of many Lancastrian nobles to die on the block on Edward's writ. Henry VI was put in a cell in the *Tower of London*. Harlech Castle in Wales held out against Edward until 1468 but the White Rose was victorious, and champions of the Red Rose mostly dead or in bitter exile. It was only fratricidal quarreling among the Yorkists that kept Lancastrian hope alive. Edward IV's choice of wife, Elizabeth Woodville, and his alliance with *Charles the Rash* of Burgundy displeased even his closest supporters and members of his family. Warwick also resented that the king increasingly appeared to want to rule as well as reign. In early 1469 an uprising against Edward began in Yorkshire stimulated by Warwick, who hoped to replace the king with his brother, George, Duke of Clarence. A major fight took place at Banbury (July 26, 1469), also called "Edgecote Moor," in Northamptonshire when a Yorkist army led by the Earl of Pembroke ran into a rebel army maneuvering to link up with Warwick. After a close fight more rebels arrived and frightened Pembroke's men into fleeing the field. Pembroke was captured the next day and executed.

Edward sent another army to repress a small uprising in Lincolnshire. His men surprised the insurgents at Lose-coat Field (March 12, 1470), so-named because of the number of coats discarded as the rebels took to their heels. Some key Lancastrians were implicated in the rising and forced into exile. Warwick now raised an army in France and crossed to England to force Edward from the throne. Edward fled to Burgundy to raise a mercenary army of his own. In his absence, Henry VI was freed and placed on the throne by Warwick, once again playing the role of the "Kingmaker." The next year Edward landed at Ravenspur with 1,500 Burgundian and German mercenaries, scattered the local defenders (March 14, 1471), and raced for London with Warwick's army close on his heels. Edward seized Henry VI and locked him back in the Tower. Then he turned to meet Warwick at Barnet (April 14, 1471), 12 miles north of London, where the armies fought in a fog-obscured and confused battle. At its end, Warwick was dead and Edward IV held the field and therefore the crown. However, that same day a Lancastrian army raised abroad landed at Weymouth and rallied the western counties to war, raising fresh troops in Wales. At Tewkesbury (May 4, 1471), Edward led an army of 5,000 against 7,000 dug-in Lancastrians. He immediately engaged the enemy, opening with a bombardment from his artillery. The Lancastrians charged the center of Edward's line, mistakenly perceiving a weakness there. The assault was repelled and Edward counterattacked, routing and killing 2,000 of his enemies. This ended the war in Edward's favor.

Upon Edward IV's death in 1483, his 13-year-old son, Edward V, was left vulnerable on the throne. Civil war broke out again after a 12-year hiatus when the Duke of Gloucester deposed the boy king and imprisoned him along with his younger brother, the Duke of York, in the Tower of London. Gloucester claimed the throne as King Richard III and the "little princes" were soon murdered in the Tower. This provided the pretext for Henry Tudor to land at Milford Haven in Wales on August 7, 1485, with an army of 2,000 men. Within days, 3,000 more rallied to his banner. Gloucester moved to meet him with an army of 10,000. Another 6,000 stood on his flanks led by the brothers Stanley. The armies met at Bosworth on August 22, 1485. Each side opened with artillery and archery showers. At a critical moment one of Gloucester's lieutenants, the Earl of Northumberland, fled the field. The Stanleys then turned coats on Gloucester and joined their 6,000 men with Henry Tudor's army. Gloucester (Richard III) died fighting for his crown, which he wore into the battle. A soldier picked it up and handed it to Henry Tudor, who subsequently donned it as Henry VII. The Wars of the Roses were effectively over, even if two years later Yorkist rebels crossed from Ireland with several thousand German mercenaries and Irish *kernes* to be defeated by Henry at East Stoke (June 16, 1647). The English gentry henceforth became the solid foundation of the Tudor monarchy. England was at last severed from its long history of continental entanglement (except for *Calais*), and became more clearly a national kingdom and island realm, increasingly English in its language, culture, and politics. Next would come nationalization of its religion under *Henry VIII* and his daughter, *Elizabeth I*. See also *prickers*; *scourers*.

Suggested Reading: Hubert Cole, *Wars of the Roses* (1973); J. Gillingham, *Wars of the Roses* (1981); Anthony Goodman, *Wars of the Roses* (1981).

Wars of the Three Kingdoms (1639–1651). See *English Civil Wars*.

war wagons. Many late-medieval and early-modern peoples deployed war wagons or some form of portable wooden wall to provide cover in field operations. This was true of the Chinese, Mamlūks, Mughals, Ottomans, Muscovites, and Safavids, all peoples and empires which either frequently fought steppe or desert nomad cavalry or were themselves products of a military culture rooted in mobile horse warfare. On the steppe, cavalry and carts predominated over supply-consuming infantry for logistical reasons: the wagons that carried supplies also doubled as a defensive laager. In Western Europe and Japan, pikes rather than wagons were used to protect infantry archers and musketeers. The Italians had a "war cart" called the *carroccio*, but it served a ceremonial and religious rather than military purpose. In the 14th century, sophis-

> *The Italians had a "war cart" … but it served a ceremonial and religious rather than military purpose.*

ticated military wagon-forts—the Hussite *Wagenburg*—appeared in Bohemia during the *Hussite Wars* (1419–1478), spreading from there to Germany, Hungary, Poland, and elsewhere. The *Janissary Corps* was an avid user of war wagons into the 18th century. See also *arquebus à croc*; *Art of War*; *Chaldiran, Battle of*; *Héricourt, Battle of*; *Khanwa, Battle of*; *mutiny*; *Panipat, Battle of (April 21, 1526)*; *Pinkie Cleugh, Battle of*; *Sarhu, Campaign of*; *tabor*; *Uzbeks*.

wastage. See *casualties*; *desertion*; *disease*; *wounds*.

wasters. "Guastatores." Specialized troops (miners, pioneers) tasked with physical destruction of a enemy's country. This was done as an essential part of the economic warfare of a *chevauchée*, punitive raid, or other scorched earth practice.

weapons. See *Ahlspiess*; *alcancia*; *armories*; *arquebus*; *arquebus à croc* ; *artillery* (and its many cross-references); *atlatl*; *axes*; *balistae*; *bardiche*; *bastard musket*; *bayonet*; *blunderbuss*; *bodkin*; *bolt*; *bombard*; *bombardier*; *bracer*; *bracers*; *brown bill*; *caliver*; *caltrop*; *carbine*; *carreaux*; *cartridges*; *case shot*; *chauve-souris*; *child-mother gun*; *claymore*; *continuous bullet gun*; *corning/corned gunpowder*; *coronal*; *couseque*; *cranequin*; *crossbow*; *crossbow à croc*; *crossbow à jalet*; *cultellus*; *daggers*; *falchion*; *fire*; *fire-lance*; *fireships*; *flintlock*; *garrots*; *gisarmes*; *glaive*; *goedendag*; *Greek fire*; *grenades*; *gunner's rule*; *gunner's quadrant*; *gunpowder weapons*; *hackbut*; *halberd*; *half-pike*; *hanger*; *Holy Water Sprinkler*; *hussars*; *invincible generalissimo*; *Katzbalger*; *Klozbüchse*; *knight*; *kumade*; *lance* (1); *Leonardo da Vinci*; *lochaber axe*; *longbow*; *mace*; *main-gauche*; *masse*; *matchlock*; *military flail*; *military fork*; *miquelet*; *misericord*; *Mordax*;

Morgenstern; muskets; naginata; partisan (1); pennon; pike; pistols; polearm; poleax; pots de fer; quarrel; rawcon; rifled-bore; Schnepper; Schweizerdegen; Schweizerdolch; shells; sling; smoothbore; springald; staff-weapons; swivel gun; swords; tabor; Tartaglia, Niccolò; ten-eyed gun; trou de loup; Turkish bow; verso; volley fire; Wagenburg; war hammer; wheel lock; winged-tiger gun. See also armor; pavisade; shields/shielding; testudo.

Suggested Reading: C. Ashdown, *Armor and Weapons in the Middle Ages* (1925); Bert Hall, *Weapons and Warfare in Renaissance Europe* (1997); S. T. Pope, *Bows and Arrows* (1962); William Reid, *The Lore of Arms: A Concise History of Weaponry* (1984); Eduard Wagner, *European Weapons and Warfare, 1618–1648*, S. Pellar, trans. (1979).

wear. To change course in a ship of sail by tacking one way then another before the wind.

weather (1). The direction from which the wind is blowing, which was critical to handling a ship of sail.

weather (2). To move a ship to *windward* of another ship or point of land.

weather, its effect on military operations. See *Agincourt, Battle of*; *Bedouin*; *China*; *galley*; *Hakata Bay, Battle of* (1274); *Hakata Bay, Battle of* (1281); *India*; *Invincible Armada*; *Lithuania, Grand Duchy of*; *logistics*; *Maurits of Nassau*; *Mongols*; *mutiny*; *Nancy, Battle of*; *Ottoman warfare*; *Pavia, Battle of*; *Sekigahara, Battle of*; *slow match*; *warhorses*; *Wars of the Roses*.

weather gauge. Assuming the *windward* position in relation to another fleet or ship. Running on a following wind was critical in fighting among ships of sail as it permitted the attacker to bear down at speed on the enemy, fire his *broadside* guns, then turn away to reload firing rear-facing *chase guns* as he did so. See also *battle (2)*; *Invincible Armada*.

weatherly. Said of a ship that handled well. That is, a ship which tended to drift very little when *hauled close*.

Weepers. See *Savonarola, Girolamo*.

Weimar Army. The army of the *League of Heilbronn* commanded by *Bernhard von Sachsen-Weimar*.

Wenden, Siege of (1577). See *Ivan IV*.

Werben, Battle of (July 22–28, 1631). After sacking *Magdeburg*, the *Catholic League* general *Johann Tilly* moved north in search of food and forage for his 22,000-man Imperial Army. *Gustavus Adolphus* blocked his way at Werben, at the union of the Rivers Elbe and Havel, with 16,000 entrenched Swedes. Tilly attacked frontally on July 22 but was repulsed with heavy casualties by concentrated musket and cannon fire. He attacked again on July 28 and took the same punishment. Leaving over 6,000 dead on the field, he retreated deep into Saxony to collect reinforcements while Gustavus arranged a new alliance with Saxony then pursued Tilly to Leipzig.

Werth, Johann Count von (c.1595–1652). Known in France as "Jean de Weert." Catholic and *mercenary* cavalry general in the *Thirty Years' War* (1618–1648). He served as a young officer with *Habsburg* forces in Flanders in the 1620s. By 1630 he had secured a colonelship and soon also command of his own regiment in the service of Bavaria. He fought well at *First Nördlingen* (1634), and was rewarded with promotion to Field Marshal. Upon the entry of France into the German war, Werth raided deep into Lorraine in 1635 and even deeper into France the next year, reaching as far as the suburbs of Paris and gaining a lasting reputation in France for terror and destruction. His invasion was pushed back to the borders of France, however, by a large army raised and led by *Cardinal Richelieu*. A year later Werth scourged the Rhine Valley. The next year he snatched defeat from the jaws of victory, and was taken prisoner, at *Rheinfelden*. He was brought to Paris, where he enjoyed the comfortable life of a high-ranking prisoner until 1642. Finally exchanged, he regained a command in the Bavarian Army. The next year he fought at *Tüttlingen*, under *Franz Mercy* and against *Turenne*. He also fought at *Freiburg* (1644) and, again under Mercy, took a major command at *Second Nördlingen* (1645). As the war wound down in 1647, he tried to lead his men out of Bavaria—which was seeking a separate peace—and into Imperial service, but most would not follow him: Werth had not yet had his fill of war, but his men certainly had. When general peace came to Germany and Europe in 1648, Werth retired to vast estates gained from his military service. He died in his bed four years later.

Western Army (England). After founding the unified *New Model Army* in February 1645, Parliament retained two other armies: a Western Army and a Northern Army. These, too, were placed under the overall command of *Thomas Fairfax*.

Western Army (Japan). See *Ōnin War*; *Sekigahara, Battle of*.

Western Association. During the *English Civil Wars*, both Parliament and *Charles I* used this name for opposing regional armies operating in the west of England and in Cornwall and Wales.

West Indies Company (WIC). See *Brazil*; *Eighty Years' War*.

Westphalia, Peace of (1648). A set of discrete Treaties of Westphalia named for the demilitarized cities where they were negotiated and signed: two *Treaties of Münster* and the *Treaty of Osnabrück*. The first Treaty of Münster (January 30, 1648) ended the *Eighty Years' War* between Spain and the Netherlands. The second Treaty of Münster and the Treaty of Osnabrück (both October 24, 1648) framed the general settlement that ended the *Thirty Years' War*, while altering internal constitutional relations of the *Estates* of the Holy Roman Empire to the emperors. The long peace conference at Westphalia did not stop the protracted war between France and Spain which continued to 1659, or the Spanish-Portuguese war which lasted to 1668. But otherwise the agreements reached at Westphalia represented a general and genuine European settlement akin to that achieved at the Congress of Vienna in 1814–1815. It certainly ranks with that settlement in historical importance.

After a preliminary meeting in Frankfurt in January 1643, the first peace envoys arrived in late 1643 to open talks at Münster. Meeting there were representatives of the Holy Roman Empire and France as well as all minor Catholic belligerents and loyal German princes and Estates. Other delegates met in Osnabrück for talks between the Holy Roman Empire and Sweden and all allied Protestant powers and German princes and Estates. All told, 176 diplomats met in Westphalia representing 194 sovereign entities (of which 109 sent their own negotiators while 85 smaller polities shared in other delegations), to frame a general peace to follow three decades of war. They were accompanied by hundreds of lawyers, scribes, and translators. The conference was disrupted for a year by a sharp new war between Denmark and Sweden in which *Ferdinand III* also intervened: *Torstensson's War*. And right through the summer of 1648 campaigning and battles continued in Germany and France. As one tired Catholic delegate put it: "In winter we negotiate, in summer we fight."

Imperial Issues

Delegates returned to Westphalia in 1644. On June 11, 1645, French and Swedish envoys presented their first peace proposals and on September 25 the Empire replied. After much argument it was agreed that 1624 would be the *Normaljahr* for settling religious disputes. While that departed from the exclusively German proposals of the *Peace of Prague* (1635), the Westphalian peace accepted other principles framed at Prague and by the *Imperial Diet* of 1640–1641. However, it permanently broke with the Imperial impositions of the *reservatum ecclesiaticum* (1555) of *Charles V* and the *Edict of Restitution* (1629) of *Ferdinand II*. The major treaties were signed simultaneously on October 24, 1648, and ratified on February 8, 1649. They granted war and treaty-making rights to all princes of the Empire, though in practice such apparent sovereignty was limited by a requirement that such acts be compatible with loyalty to the emperor. In short, the Westphalian settlement of internal affairs of the Empire did not apply the same principles as it did to wider international relations. Instead, it returned to an older tradition of customary law reinforced by *Grotian* principles derived from "natural law." Part of the confusion (mainly among modern political scientists) about princely "sovereignty" as confirmed at Westphalia is that the French text translated "jus territorii et superioritas" as "droit de souverainité." In fact, while the German princes gained real ground vis-à-vis the Emperor, legal sovereignty did not amount to actual or effective sovereignty. All *Reichsritter* (knights) and most *Reichsstädte* (Imperial free cities) were too small to exercise any legal right of sovereignty. Most in fact aligned with the Emperor, seeking his protection against feral predators among neighboring territorial princes. It was more important that on August 29, 1645, Ferdinand III ceded to the Imperial Diet the *jus pacis et belli*, so that German emperors could never again make war or peace without consulting the Diet and princes. The main victors of the war, Sweden and France, were named formal guarantors of the German settlement. That was short of the status as Imperial Estates they had sought but contained an implied right of intervention in Germany. In practice, at least in the short run, both states were too weak and too internally unstable to intervene, and loathe to exercise their legal right.

Territorial Issues

Paris received title to northern Alsace—an ancient Habsburg province—in exchange for 1.2 million Talers. France also took permanent title to the fortified bishoprics of Metz, Toul, and Verdun which it had occupied in fact since the reign of Charles V. Rostock, Wismar, and parts of Bremen, along with most of western Pomerania went to Sweden as imperial fiefs. The Swedes also received an indemnity of 5 million Talers paid by the Empire (they had asked for 20 million). That was a critical issue as Sweden needed to pay off arrears owed to its veterans, most of whom by then were tough non-Swedish mercenaries. The Empire agreed because it was in everyone's interest to demobilize the ruthless armies still eating out parts of Germany and Europe—no one wanted to repeat the 14th-century experience with *Free Companies*. The Count Palatine was restored to his dignities and a new imperial dignity created to replace the one lost by the Palatinate to Bavaria, which was in turn confirmed as seat of an Imperial Elector (raising the *Kurfürsten* of the Empire to eight). Bavaria was granted full control of the Upper Palatinate which it had occupied for 20 years. Brandenburg received the bishoprics of Halberstadt and Minden while the Hohenzollerns were confirmed in possession of eastern Pomerania. Saxony's claim of Lusatia, which dated to 1635, was also confirmed.

The United Provinces and Helvetian Confederation were recognized de jure as independent states, including by Austria and Spain. The French had hoped to acquire the Spanish Netherlands, Franche Comté, and borderlands astride Catalonia and Italy. But the refusal of Spain to accept a universal settlement left these issues open even after a sharp victory for France at *Lens* (August 2, 1648). Knowledge of French plans to expand into Flanders and dominate central Germany helped persuade the Dutch to sign a truce with Spain in 1647 that led to the permanent peace signed at Münster in January 1648. French plans to smash what they saw as Spanish tyranny and hegemony were thus postponed to 1659, even as neighboring states such as the Netherlands began to suspect France as an emerging threat to their hard-won sovereign independence. Also frustrated was *Cardinal Richelieu*'s grand design, which he had provided after his death as written instructions to French envoys attending the peace conference. This had called for a system of collective security in which France displaced Habsburg Spain as hegemon in north Italy and Flanders, and replaced Habsburg Austria as the dominant power in central Germany. No one outside France thought those were desirable ends or likely to maintain the general peace.

Legal Principles

Nor could Sweden impose its will within the southern half of the Empire. Stockholm's demand for religious toleration in the Habsburg hereditary lands and return of exiled Protestants to Austria and Bohemia was rejected. It was in any case far beyond Swedish ability to enforce, even with its troops still in Prague in 1648. The great principle of the *Peace of Augsburg* (1555) of *cuius regio eius religio* ("whosoever controls the territory decides the religion") was abandoned outside the hereditary lands in favor of more general toleration: religious minorities everywhere in the Empire were legally permitted to practice their faith if they had done so in that territory before the Normaljahr of 1624.

The principle of sovereignty permeated the treaties, raising as a new measure of interstate conduct a norm of nonintervention in internal affairs (meaning religious matters). Instead of confessionalism, secularism would dominate a new order in international politics. The pretensions of popes were ignored, including by Catholic princes as jealous of sovereign prerogative as were Protestants. This pragmatism among the Catholic delegates gathered at Osnabrück caused Pope Innocent X to fulminate that all articles affirming tolerance were "null and void, invalid, iniquitous, unjust, condemned, rejected, frivolous, without force or effect, and no one is to observe them, even when they be ratified by oath." No one paid much attention. Rail as the enraged pontiff did, the *Protestant Reformation* and *Counter-Reformation* alike failed to achieve confessional or doctrinal exclusivity in face of a balance of power among secular forces and states. Or, as one Catholic publicist put it in February 1648: "It is lawful by urgent necessity to enter into perpetual peace with heretics."

No more would rituals of the Mass or a public oath of some rabid cleric, or a hard religious doctrine or intemperate and rude tract, shake the affairs of nations in Europe. Instead, the Peace of Westphalia codified rules of an emergent secular order, sanctioning in law and legitimizing a rejection long in the making of the transcendent claims of popes and emperors in favor of the ascendant secularism of monarchs and nation-states. It confirmed that a shift had occurred in the balance of power, from the Habsburgs to France (and to a lesser extent, also Sweden). Even if these processes evolved for many decades after 1648, that date still serves as a useful marker of fundamental change in European and world history, politics, diplomacy, and law. The confessional passions that once roused men to war and atrocity were fading with moral, political, and military exhaustion for all but a few unbending fanatics. In the place of religious wars an age of absolute sovereign claims began. With it, the old pattern of international politics donned new dress: Great Powers still lorded it over weaker nations, but henceforth they did so in the name of secular statecraft, of raisons d'etat and balances of power.

None of that was obvious or even intended at the time. The diplomats gathered in Westphalia had their eyes on closer prizes, from this or that territorial annexation or legal title to compensation to pay the arrears of mutinous troops. Even so their accomplishments were considerable. First, they ended the war. Second, they addressed most of the German constitutional conflicts that brought it about and established a mechanism for resolving future confessional disputes short of violence. Next, they provided the necessary conditions for foreign armies to depart Germany, even if this took several more years. Finally, the Peace of Westphalia was sufficiently just that it was accepted by everyone except the pope, and his dissent was no longer of any consequence in worldly affairs.

...[the pope's] dissent was no longer of any consequence in worldly affairs.

Because the Westphalian treaties became part of the Empire's basic law, and because they were internationally accepted as vital to the new states system, it would be another 200 years before a general European war again erupted out of Germany. If the price for that achievement was delayed German national consolidation and continuing political and military weakness, that too was necessary to avoid another conflagration that had harmed Germans above all others.

Odds and Ends

Westphalia was followed by a conference at Nuremberg that lasted to July 1651. It oversaw payment of wages in arrears to the troops and demobilization of all armies as agreed at Westphalia. This did not always go smoothly: smaller armies were quickly disbanded, but Imperial and French garrisons proved more restless and some mutinied. Sweden, indemnity in hand, withdrew more smoothly at first. But in late 1649, even Swedish troops threatened large-scale mutiny and marauding unless all arrears were paid. On June 26, 1650, Imperial and Swedish delegates agreed to a schedule of troop payments. Even so, Spanish troops remained in the Palatinate to 1653 and Swedish troops stayed in barracks on the Baltic coast of Germany until 1654. It is notable that the two physical and political extremes of Europe—Russia and England—were, during the summer of 1648, the last summer of confessional warfare in Europe, still undergoing purges, revolutions, and civil wars over matters of religious contention. In June, Moscow was wracked by the "Morozov riots," outbursts of rabidly violent piety directed against the boyar retainers of Tsar Alexis. They only frightened him into conducting a bloody purge in the usual Russian style. Meanwhile, the *English Civil Wars* were still raging across the Channel, while the "Republic of Virtue" of *Oliver Cromwell* and his Puritan "soldiers for Christ" still lay in England's future. The affairs of Russia and England were unaffected by the Peace of Westphalia because those states were not involved in the Thirty Years' War (other than England, briefly, in the 1620s). By the end of the century they, too, would put confessional wars behind them and embrace the "Westphalian system." That occurred just in time for all of Europe to engage in still greater wars that got underway between secular Leviathans in the second half of the 17th century. See also *Corpus Catholicorum*; *Corpus Evangelicorum*; *Edict of Nantes*; *étapes*.

Suggested Reading: Ronald Asch, *The Thirty Years' War* (1997); Derek Croxton and Anuschka Tischer, *The Peace of Westphalia: A Historical Dictionary* (2002).

Wexford, Sack of (October 11, 1649). *Oliver Cromwell* marched with 10,000 Puritan veterans from the slaughter at *Drogheda* directly to a second massacre at Wexford. His men stormed the town walls, which were too old and inadequate to resist the new English artillery, on October 11, 1649. Once again they put a mixed English and Irish Catholic population to the sword without pity or mercy.

wheeling. See *drill*.

wheel lock. The expertise of clockmakers was drawn upon to replace the *matchlock* with the first nonmatch firing device. A small steel wheel was wound and locked in place against a piece of pyrite. Powered by a spring, release of the trigger spun the wheel to cause friction and raise sparks from the pyrite that ignited fine powder in the pan, which in turn set off the main charge in the breech that fired the projectile from the gun. This made the wheel lock useful for cavalry: several wheel lock pistols could be wound in advance, carried in holsters or belts or stuck in boot tops, and fired at the enemy before the cavalryman had to withdraw to reload. The main drawback was delicacy of the mechanism and the expense of skilled manufacture, which priced it out of the range of infantry and made it suspect among professional soldiers who wanted reliability above all else in their firearms.

Prototypes appeared as early as 1505 and carbines and pistols used the wheel lock in the field as early as 1515 in Styria and in the 1520s in the Holy Roman Empire. Wheel locks were extensively used across Europe from the mid-16th century. Efforts were made to ban the new wheel lock pistol as an immoral weapon because it was too easily concealed in the absence of a burning match. For the same reason, the new pistol became a favorite weapon of highwaymen. *Maximilian I* banned it in 1517 and the Duke of Ferrara followed suit in 1522, but without much effect. German *Reiter* cavalry switched from lances to wheel lock pistols around 1550 and for a few decades enjoyed some success in battle (though they were never highly respected or reliable). French cavalry was more conservative and cleaved to lances far longer. Polish cavalry remained mainly *hussar* in disposition. The wheel lock never achieved the rate of fire of even the matchlock and was quickly displaced once the *flintlock* musket and pistol became widely available. Bert Hall argues that the wheel lock pistol, more than even muskets, finished knighthood in Europe not by dehorsing knights with missile weapons but by wholly altering cavalry tactics. See also *caracole*; *grenades*; *Gustavus II Adolphus*; *musket*; *pistol*.

Suggested Reading: Bert Hall, *Weapons and Warfare in Renaissance Europe* (1997).

Whiggamore Rising (1648). An uprising led by *Argyll* in southwest Scotland and joined by *David Leslie* and the *Earl of Leven*. They took Edinburgh but lost to Monro at Stirling. Argyll asked *Oliver Cromwell* to cross the Tweed and with his help and presence brokered a compromise peace in the brief Scottish civil war.

white armor. "harnois blanc." Dating from the early-to-mid-15th century, this Italian armor was fully articulated. It derived its name once it became fully exposed as *surcoats* and other cloth coverings were abandoned. White armor was not the same as the "black and white" armor that appeared in the 16th century. That was armor painted black in places for interests of fashion (on land). At sea, the paint provided protection against salt water rusting. See also *Jeanne d'Arc*; *mail*; *plate armor*; *shields/shielding*; *swords*.

White Company. After the *Treaty of Brétigny* (1360) paused fighting in France during the *Hundred Years' War* (1337–1453), mixed *Free Companies* of French and English drifted into Italy. The most famous was the White Company which competed with older *condottieri* Great Companies in the wars of the Italian city-states. It was initially commanded by *John Hawkwood* and was notable for bringing the new English methods of war to Italy: unlike the cavalry-dominated condottieri, men-at-arms in the White Company fought dismounted and protected by large numbers of archers. Following a dispute in 1372, Hawkwood resigned command and returned to Florence while his White Company fought for the pope.

White Hoods. "Capuciati." See *routiers*.

White Mountain, Battle of (November 8, 1620). "Bílá hora." Also known as the "White Hill." After inconclusive skirmishing and missed opportunities during the first two years of the *Thirty Years' War*, a Protestant coalition army that included 5,000 Dutch troops sent by *Maurits of Nassau* assembled to defend the Bohemian crown of *Friedrich V*. It met a much greater Catholic army intent on defending the claims and rights of *Ferdinand II* in the first major battle of the war. The Protestant commander was Count *Mathias von Thurn*, supported by *Christian of Anhalt-Bernburg* and *Graf von Mansfeld*. Against them were ranged 30,000 men of the army of the *Catholic League* under *Johann Tilly*, supported by an Austrian contingent under the French general *Bucquoy*.

Thurn, Christian, and Mansfeld deployed on the slopes of the hill called "Bílá hora" (White Mountain) astride the road to Prague. On their right was a small castle and to the left a narrow brook with marshes to the front. Tilly ignored these minor obstacles and attacked in force straight into the Protestant center. In just two hours, the Protestants were decisively defeated. Tilly then marched on to Prague. Ferdinand and *Maximilian I* of Bavaria thereafter repressed Protestantism in Bohemia with the full rigors of the *Counter-Reformation*. Nobles were executed or exiled, their lands and titles stripped and given in reward to loyal Catholics or sold at cut-rate prices to valued mercenaries (including *Albrecht von Wallenstein*). Catholic and Imperial intolerance in the Czech lands helped spread confessional warfare throughout Germany and beyond, but Bohemia was cemented to the Holy Roman Empire and Czechs forcibly restored to Catholicism. The price was a warning to all Protestants of what they would face should Ferdinand win the larger war. See also *Georg, Johann*; *Protestant Union*; *Ritterstand*.

Wiesloch, Battle of (April 27, 1622). Following the Catholic and Imperial victory at the *White Mountain* (1620), the army of the *Catholic League* moved north under *Johann Tilly* to join Spanish troops from the Netherlands and clear Protestantism from the Palatinate. A mercenary army under *Graf von Mansfeld* and *Bernhard von Sachsen-Weimar* moved to block the planned union of the Catholic armies. Mansfeld briefly checked Tilly at *Mingolsheim* (April 22, 1622). Tilly recovered, then stumbled on Mansfeld's rearguard and drove it back onto his main body. A counterattack drove Tilly back in turn. Mansfeld then made the mistake of digging in. Tilly simply marched around him and linked with a 20,000 man Spanish army. These armies clashed again at *Wimpfen* (May 6, 1622).

William I, of Nassau. See *William the Silent*.

William Louis, of Nassau (1560–1620). Dutch: Willem Lodewijk. See *Maurits of Nassau*; *New Model Army*; *volley fire*.

William the Silent (1533–1584). William I, of Nassau. Prince of Orange; Stadtholder of Holland, Zeeland, and Utrecht. His sobriquet arose from holding his tongue on the most controversial religious matters of the day until finally forced to choose sides. William led one of the major noble factions and "client" patronage systems in the Netherlands. He moved into clear opposition in 1561 when he married Anna of Saxony, niece of the leading Lutheran prince of Germany. Still, William accepted overt rebellion against *Philip II* only with deep reluctance: his consistent hope was to negotiate a compromise religious settlement in which he and other princes would be the arbiters. The definitive break only came, as for so many Dutch nobles, with dispatch of the brutal and politically inept *Duke of Alba* to the Netherlands. Alba's persecutions and juridical murders sent William into exile to avoid arrest. He was convicted in absentia, all his property confiscated, and his 13-year-old son kidnapped and taken to Spain to be raised a Catholic. William retaliated by raising funds and allies, notably the Palatinate and England, for the revolt of the Netherlands that marked the onset of the *Eighty Years' War*. From the start, William made freedom ("Vryheid") the watchword of the revolt, insisting on restored local liberties and even modern individual freedoms of conscience and belief. He insisted on a "Religious Peace," which in practice meant toleration of Protestantism in heavily Catholic towns. After his brother *Louis of Nassau* was defeated at *Jemmingen* in July 1568, William invaded with an army of 25,000 German mercenaries. After several skirmishes, he retreated in the face of Alba's superior generalship and tougher and more disciplined troops. William was not able to return at the head of another large army before 1572. Yet he remained the focus of nationalist aspirations. This was captured in the 1568 Orangist patriotic song the "Wilhelmus."

In exile, William was reduced to making small war across the frontier while the *Sea Beggars* operated in the Channel out of English ports under his *letters of marque*. After the Sea Beggar capture of *Brill* (April 1, 1572) launched the "Great Revolt" of the Netherlands, dozens of towns invited William to established garrisons. He showed his mettle in directing the critical relief of the *Siege of Leiden* (May 26–October 3, 1574). Following the *Spanish Fury* and the *Pacification of Ghent* he tried to radicalize the Catholic south. Although he failed in this effort he was welcomed into Antwerp and Brussels and resided in Brabant from 1577 to 1583, uneasily trying to stay on a middle road in a country where the north-south gap was widening and ultimately unbridgeable. On

William was shot dead on the staircase of his home in Delft by a Catholic fanatic.

May 3, 1579, he accepted the division of the Netherlands and adhered to the Union of Utrecht. He persuaded the States General to invite the *duc d'Anjou* to become the new sovereign, an experiment that ended in disaster. As *Parma* advanced into Brabant, William withdrew to Holland. In 1580 William had been declared outlaw by Philip II; a large reward offer led to many assassination attempts. The final one was successful in May 1584: William was shot dead on the staircase of his home in Delft by a Catholic fanatic.

Suggested Reading: K. Swart, *William the Silent and the Revolt of the Netherlands* (1978).

Wimpfen, Battle of (May 6, 1622). The army of the *Catholic League* under *Johann Tilly* had escaped *Graf von Mansfeld*'s Protestant mercenary army at *Wiesloch* (April 27, 1622), and linked with 20,000 Spanish troops out of the Netherlands. *Christian of Brunswick* failed to link with Mansfeld, as did another Protestant army of 14,000 men under the Margrave of Baden-Durlach. The latter was instead isolated by Tilly's vastly superior army at Wimpfen. Although the German Protestants fought well, a chance explosion of their artillery magazine disrupted the defense. Taking full advantage, Tilly ordered his veteran Catholic troops to charge uphill and overrun the Protestant position, which they did.

Winceby, Battle of (October 11, 1643). *Thomas Fairfax, Oliver Cromwell*, and the *Earl of Manchester* joined forces to defeat a Cavalier force in a small cavalry fight at Winceby, Lincolnshire. Their victory temporarily pushed the Royalists from the eastern counties. Cromwell had a horse shot from under him by enemy *dragoons* but lived. Surviving Royalists were ridden down and dispatched without mercy.

Winchelsea, Battle of (1350). See *Hundred Years' War*.

wind. See *haul close*; *haul wind*; *heave to*; *make sail*; *shorten sail*; *wear*; *weather*; *weather gauge*; *weatherly*; *windward*.

windlass. At sea, a large mechanical device comprised of a drum and handles used for hauling and winding rope or cable. On land, a compact mechanical device employing pulleys and a winding handle used for drawing back the string on a *crossbow*. It was introduced in Europe in the 14th century and greatly increased reloading speed.

windward. The direction from which the wind is blowing at any given moment. Havens and harbors were easier to defend if they lay to windward. This fact enormously advantaged England whose entire east coast was windward of the prevailing Westerlies of the Northern Hemisphere. Similar but less spectacular advantages accrued to Denmark, Scotland, and Sweden. Foes of those countries were highly disadvantaged in naval warfare for the same reason. In the Mediterranean, the wind advantage also lay with the westernmost powers, notably the Christian states in their long naval struggle with the Islamic powers of the eastern Mediterranean. However, this advantage was militated against by the fact that to the end of the 16th century Mediterranean fleets were nearly exclusively comprised of *galleys*. See also *weather gauge*.

winged-tiger gun. A three-barrel Chinese gun that came in heavy (infantry) and lighter (cavalry) versions.

"Winter King." See *Friedrich V*.

Winwick, Battle of (1648). See *Preston, Campaign of*.

witchcraft. In the latter Middle Ages in Europe lay piety increasingly took on folk traditions and beliefs, in good measure stimulated by the *Catholic Church*'s teachings about daemonology, possession, and the active intervention of the occult world in daily affairs of this one. In 1480 the Church responded to this popular movement with persecution of accused witches. It is unlikely very many witches actually existed, but belief that witches conducted secret and satanic sabbaths and dark practices was nearly universal, and often also hysterical. Among the Swiss, the *Black Death* provoked mid-14th-century mobs to murderous rages against Jews and against people accused of witchcraft, usually older, poor, single, or widowed women. In the 16th–17th centuries, "maleficia" trials and mass witch hunts were carried out across Europe. In Würzburg in 1625 and again three years later, great witch hunts and trials led to perhaps 9,000 women (and some men) being burned by the bishop and courts of the *Inquisition*. In Silesia in 1640, at Niesse, it is thought that 1,000 women were burned as condemned witches. *Ferdinand II* actively campaigned to suppress witchcraft in tandem with his crusade against Protestantism.

Suggested Reading: Alan Kors, ed. *Witchcraft in Europe, 400–1700: A Documentary History* (2000); Brian Levack, T*he Witch-Hunt in Early Modern Europe* (1995); Jeffrey Russell, *Witchcraft in the Middle Ages* (1972).

Witkov, Battle of (1420). See *Hussite Wars*.

Wittstock, Battle of (October 4, 1636). After the crushing Swedish defeat at *First Nördlingen* in 1634, Protestant hopes for military victory in Germany waned. Hoping to finish the Protestant cause for once and all, a German army comprised of 35,000 Imperials, Saxons, and smaller allies moved to Brandenburg to try to crush an isolated Swedish-Scottish army of 22,000 men led by Field Marshal *Johann Banér* and *Lennart Torstensson*. Banér moved his main body directly forward while his Scottish troops maneuvered widely and unseen to the flank and rear of the Catholic position. Seeing an inferior force to their front, the Catholics left their works and attacked. They were thus taken by surprise and enfiladed on three sides as the Scots hit them from the side and rear while Banér charged their center. The Imperials and Saxons together lost 11,000 casualties and 8,000 captured to just 5,000 total losses for the Swedes and Scots. The victory delivered much of Brandenburg to Sweden and reversed the psychology of the German war.

wolf holes. See *trou de loup*.

Wolgast, Battle of (September 2, 1628). While *Albrecht von Wallenstein* was unsuccessfully besieging *Straslund*, the militarily inept *Christian IV* invaded Pomerania. Reinforced by Scots mercenaries from Straslund, he occupied Wolgast. Wallenstein broke off his siege and caught Christian unprepared. The Danes were utterly routed by the Imperials, who then occupied Jutland. The victory allowed Wallenstein to send 12,000 troops to aid *Sigismund III* in his war against *Gustavus Adolphus*. A Polish-Imperial army then bested Gustavus at *Stuhm*.

Wolsey, Cardinal Thomas (1471–1530). See *Cromwell, Thomas*; *Henry VIII*.

women. See *Albigensian Crusade*; *baggage train*; *camp followers*; *casting*; *chivalry*; *civilians*; *Cossacks*; *Crusades*; *dévotes*; *Elizabeth I*; *gabions*; *Hurenweibel*; *Hussite Wars*; *Imperial Army*; *Islam*; *"King's Two Bodies"*; *Knights of Calatrava*; *Knox, John*; *La Malinche*; *Mamlūks*; *Margaret of Parma*; *Medici, Catherine de*; *Medici, Marie de*; *Mary Stuart, Queen of Scots*; *Mary Tudor*; *Mongols*; *Naseby, Battle of*; *penal settlements*; *Pequot War*; *Philiphaugh*; *pillaging*; *Rajputs*; *Richelieu, Cardinal Armand Jean du Plessis de*; *Scotland*; *siege warfare*; *"skulking way of war"*; *tabor*; *Tenoctitlán, First Siege of* (1520); *Tenochtitlán, Second Siege of* (1521); *Teutonic Knights, Order of*; *Wagenburg*; *witchcraft*; *wounds*.

Worcester, Battle of (1642). See *English Civil Wars*.

Worcester, Battle of (1651). See *Leslie, David*.

worm. A gunner's device used to clear obstructions such as excess wadding from the barrel of a gun.

Worms, Diet of (1495). See *Maximilian I*.

Worms, Diet of (1521). See *Charles V, Holy Roman Emperor*; *Luther, Martin*; *Netherlands*; *Protestant Reformation*.

wounds. Chinese medicine was well advanced in the medieval period with the Middle East probably second in medical knowledge and Europe a distant third. The *Hospitallers* learned much from Arab medicine and served as a conduit of this knowledge to Europe. The main combat wounds that had to be dealt with everywhere were the usual suspects of slashing and hacking weapons, puncture wounds from quarrels and arrows fired by crossbows and various long and short bows, crushed skulls and broken bones from maces and staff weapons, and burns from incendiaries. Men in closely packed infantry formations like the *tercio* or the *Swiss square* were sometimes crushed to death or suffocated by the combined effect of the push of pike from their own rearward ranks and the close press of the front ranks of the enemy, assuming they avoided being skewered on a three-foot sharpened metal tip at the end of an enemy pike. If the hedge of pikes failed to kill the enemy, *axes, halberds*, and various polearms cleaved off heads and limbs, punctured armor and the vitals of the man inside, and slashed open unprotected bellies and spilled out a man's (or horse's) intestines. There was little that could be done to help men wounded in any of these ways. They were dispatched by the enemy (Japanese *samurai* always took their enemy's head) or crawled off to die. Infantry cut about the head and shoulders by a cavalry saber, or a man or boy whose face was slashed open by a misjudged lance blow, had some chance to survive if blood loss was stanched in time and the wound cleaned so that infection was avoided. However, since the source of infection was not known to be unclean wounds, or at least particles smaller than the naked eye could detect and probing fingers remove, infection and death was highly probable from any serious wound.

With the advent of gunpowder weapons, musket balls caused horrific wounds, shattering bones in limbs or splintering ribs as they tore into the chest to perforate organs and spray bone chips inside the cavity. An arrow or quarrel point penetrated more deeply than a musket ball, but unlike arrow tips, lead musket balls deformed on impact to rip out a larger wound or shattered into micro-shrapnel. All arquebus or musket balls carried powder grains, dirt, and filthy bits of cloth from the injured man into the wound to cause sepsis and usually a lingering and painful death. Gun crews were subject to terrible injuries from burning powder forced under the skin when a cannon misfired or a lighted match or fuse set off a sack or cask of black powder stored near the guns. In 1536, at Milan, a French doctor described one such scene: "Beholding them with pity there came an old soldier who asked me if there was any means of curing them. I told him no. At once he approached them and cut their throats gently."

A wound peculiar to master gunners was the "split thumb." This was incurred by the necessity of placing the thumb over the vent during loading and ramming to prevent premature ignition of the wadding or charge. If there was a premature discharge nonetheless, the explosive gasses passing up the vent sliced through the gunner's thumb like a modern acetylene torch, splitting it in two. Although gunners wore leather "thumbstalls" for protection these did not always suffice. "Serving the vent" in this fashion remained common practice into the 19th century and did not entirely fade from military history until all armies converted to breech-loading guns which did away with the vent. Similarly, certain wounds were peculiar to war at sea where *solid shot* hitting a wooden wall at point-blank range and broadside angle produced huge splinters that exploded inward at high velocity from the inside of the impact point, impaling and terribly wounding men so that they died quickly from loss of blood or slowly from sepsis.

Barber-surgeons were attached to some units in the mid-16th century to treat the wounded. Fifty years later, each regiment in armies following the Dutch system had a surgeon and two assistants. By the mid-17th century adoption of the regimental system in England, two surgeons were assigned per regiment (in theory). Senior officers had access to the best surgeons of the day, which is not saying all that much, but regimental surgeons were unlikely to be at the top of the medical profession. The usual and sometimes the only treatment of a wounded limb by regimental surgeons was amputation. This was not the result of mere incompetence: if a man did not die from lost blood before or during the surgery, to prevent sepsis in a wounded arm or leg spreading to more vital parts amputation was essential; it was also the best way to prevent the deadly curse of gangrene. There was some insight into the role of postsurgical infection, though the practical conclusions drawn were not the happiest. A leading 16th-century German doctor recommended fast amputation with an axe followed by searing the stump with hot pokers and boiling oil. That usually sent the patient into shock, then killed him by promoting infection. The pioneering and deeply humane French surgeon Ambroise Parè instead recommended slow and careful amputation, including tying off severed arteries and most unusually, ordered a regime of rest and follow-up nursing. Whatever the method, no germ theory of infection was known before the late 19th century. This meant surgeons who did not wash their hands or instruments and did not sterilize wounds or incisions almost certainly killed more men by transmitting lethal infections than they saved by surgery.

> *...sometimes the only treatment of a wounded limb by regimental surgeons was amputation.*

Most nursing of wounded men was done by soldiers' wives, mistresses, or camp prostitutes, all of whom were found among *camp followers* and in the *baggage train*. German *Landsknechte* had *Feldarzt* and assistants who performed crude surgeries such as digging out musket balls and bone fragments from wounds and carrying out amputations. Surviving amputees usually turned to begging as the vast majority were left without a soldier's pension. This began to change in England from 1643 when in response to *Leveller* and other *New Model Army* agitation Parliament ordered funds raised to support disabled veterans and soldiers' widows and orphans, though in practice the effort left much wanting. After the English Civil Wars military hospitals were founded (Kilmain in Ireland and Chelsea in England) to care for wounded veterans. On the continent, the scale of destruction and despair of the Thirty Years' War simply overwhelmed similar efforts made earlier in Germany. While most combatant powers did little for men on campaign, Spain and the Netherlands provided medical care for their sick and wounded in highly urban Flanders. The Spanish maintained a 330-bed military hospital in Mechelen and had a pensioners' home for veterans at Hall. Ottoman *Janissaries* were relatively better off than European counterparts. Their *Ortas* kept pensioner homes and cared for surviving wounded and for the families of their dead. Wounded men, Janissary or not, were paid injury money ("merham beha") staggered over five stages according to the severity of the wound. The Janissaries also had a specialized water-bearer corps, the Saka, who doubled as nurses after battle.

For all the suffering and subsequent death caused by wounds, the vast majority of soldiers gave up the ghost to disease, not enemy assault or fire. In addition to the *Black Death* and other plagues, camps full of closely packed soldiers were natural breeding grounds of epidemic diseases. Among these were typhus ("camp fever"), dropsy, dysentery, cholera, deadly influenza viruses, and syphilis. Conditions were much worse aboard warships. See also *hors de combat*; *Jesuits*; *mail*; *springald*.

Wrangel, Karl Gustaf (1613–1676). Swedish general who fought the Danes in 1644. He replaced *Lennart Torstensson* in 1646 and was active in the last two years of the *Thirty Years' War* alongside *Henri de Turenne*. They fought to victory together at *Zusmarshausen* (May 17, 1648) and punished Bavaria for reentering the war. Wrangel fought many later battles against Poland under Karl X and served as regent for Karl XI.

Wu Sangui (1612–1678). See *China*.

Wyatt's Rebellion (1554). A family and Protestant plot to set aside the testament of *Henry VIII* which gave the throne to his Catholic daughter *Mary Tudor*. The conspirators planned to set a naïf, Lady Jane Grey (1537–1554), on the throne in Mary's stead. The coup attempt was foiled and the plotters arrested. Only three executions followed and Mary was soon crowned. However, when she married *Phillip II* the plotters struck again in a more serious rebellion. Mary coolly handled the crisis and put down the revolt. Accused of complicity, probably falsely, the future *Elizabeth I* was imprisoned in the *Tower of London*. The future *Earl of Leicester* was also arrested but was pardoned by Philip. Lady Jane, her husband, and father, and others actually or just thought to be involved in treason were not treated as leniently: many executions followed that earned for the Catholic queen from her Protestant subjects the sobriquet "Bloody Mary." *John Knox* had supported the rebellion and prudently fled to Dieppe upon its failure.

wybraniecka **infantry.** See *Báthory, Stefan*; *Polish Army*.

Wycliffe, John (1320–1384). See *Hus, Jan*; *Lollard Knights*; *Lollards*.

Xanten, Treaty of (1614). See *Jülich-Kleve, Crisis over*.

xebec. A hybrid sail-and-oar warship of the 15th–16th centuries akin to a *galleass*: it had a three-masted rig with lateen sails. Designed as a fast armed merchantman, it was favored by *corsairs*. As long as 130 feet, its sturdy hulls could support up to 40 cannon, though it normally carried fewer than 20. It was used mainly in the Mediterranean, although Sweden and Muscovy also built some of this type of warship.

Xochiyaoyotl. "Flower Wars." Ritual wars among Mesoamericans. They resulted in few immediate deaths because the intention in battle was not conquest but taking living captives for ritual human sacrifice. Alternately, flower wars were occasions for display of overwhelming Aztec might sufficient to coerce an enemy state to surrender as tribute an annual quota of its people to be sacrificed at the Great Temple in Tenochtitlán. If resistance persisted, the Aztec shifted into ruthless combat and imposed the tribute quota anyway.

Xuande Emperor. See *China*; *Tumu, Battle of*; *Zheng He*.

Y

yabusame. The *samurai* art of mounted archery. It emphasized accuracy and precision, the opposite of the volley-firing archery practiced by most infantry.

Yaka. Stateless armed marauders and slavers in eastern and southern Africa. They were roughly comparable to the Mane in West Africa or *Free Companies* in France during the *Hundred Years' War* (1337–1453). See also *Kongo, Kingdom of*; *Ngola*.

yamajiro. "Yamashiro." A squat Japanese mountain fortress common during the *Sengoku jidai* era. They were carved out of canyons and gullies and were usually girded by a wooden palisade and guarded by dry moats and earth ramparts. Some had watchtowers.

Yamazaki, Battle of (1582). See *Toyotomi Hideyoshi*.

Yang Yinglong Rebellion (1587–1600). See *Wanli Emperor*.

yard. A long, horizontal spar secured at its center to any mast on a ship and rigged to bend the sail at top or bottom, thereby spreading canvass before the wind. A "cross-jack" or "crojack" yard (known in French as the "vergue sèche" or "barren yard") did not set canvass of its own. Instead, it spread the foot of a square mizzen topsail. See also *masts*; *sails*.

yardarm. The far tips of a *yard*.

yari. A Japanese infantry spear. It was widely adopted by the 14th century to supplement the *kumade* and *naginata*. The yari was commonly used by *ashigaru*.

yari fusuma. "Spear circle." See also *ashigaru*; *yari*.

Yaya infantry. Early *Beylik* infantry recruited among both Muslim and Christian subjects. The Ottomans also employed Yaya units from the 1330s onward. Some were given land in the Balkans in exchange for military service and provision of local defense.

Yellow Ford, Battle of (1598). See *Nine Years' War*.

Yellow Waters, Battle of (February 1648). At the start of the Khmelnitsky Uprising (1648–1654), 3,000 Polish hussars met about 10,000 rebel *Cossacks* in a freewheeling cavalry battle in Ukraine. The Cossacks repulsed several badly organized attacks by the outnumbered but courageous Poles, then pressed home their own wild assaults. Many Poles died and many nobles were taken prisoner. These were herded to the Crimea and held for ransom.

Yeniçeri Ağasi. "Commander of the *Janissaries*." He was appointed by the sultan, usually from among the top graduates of one of the Palace Schools. He had the power to defy even the orders and wishes of the *Grand Vezir*. His power was limited by two things: a strong-willed sultan and the collective will of the "Divan" (council) of the Janissary Corps. There was also a technical limit to his power: in theory he commanded the corps only when the sultan was also present. Otherwise he was subordinate to whatever favorite the sultan chose to place over him as army commander. The Yeniçeri Ağasi was responsible for policing Constantinople with part of his personal guard. See also *martial music*.

Yeoman of the Guard. See *palace guards*.

Yongle Emperor (1360–1424, r.1402–1424). Né Zhu De. Son of *Hongwu*. He was passed over for the succession in favor of a grandson who was crowned in Nanjing. Zhu De challenged his father's will and after four years of civil war seized the throne. Yongle commissioned the first six spectacular voyages by Admiral *Zheng He* which returned to China foreign goods and ideas along with *tribute* from several southeast Asian kingdoms. Yongle expanded the Forbidden City and was a patron of compilations of *Confucian* learning. But his heart was always in making war. He invaded Tonkin in 1402 and again in 1406. He annexed Tonkin in 1407 but faced protracted guerilla resistance. Three years after his death Ming occupiers were expelled from Tonkin. In 1403 Yongle withdrew from four of the eight northern military colonies set up by Hongwu along the *Great Wall*. He later abandoned the last four colonies. Why? Because with south China pacified, Beijing was secure behind the protection of a huge Ming army in the north and because he wanted to conquer Mongolia, not wage war from his backside in defensive garrisons. He sent a major expedition to split the Oirat Mongols from the Tatars in 1409 but the Tatars used a ruse to lead his army into an ambush and destroyed it. The next year Yongle launched the first of five personally led campaigns against the

Mongols. Although he met and defeated a portion of the enemy's forces in 1420, he also experienced the logistical nightmare of bringing a large Chinese army riding grain-fed horses into the steppe: on the return journey Yongle missed the resupply column and large numbers of his men and horses came close to starvation.

In 1414 Yongle again struck out for Mongolia. After passing over the Tula River he lured the Oirat Mongol horde into a trap and slaughtered thousands with concealed artillery. His troops also used their *divine fire-arrow* guns to some effect. He moved the capital to Beijing in 1421, a shift that required repair of the Grand Canal to facilitate grain shipments to feed an enlarged Imperial city and to supply his northern armies. The main reason he moved the capital was to oversee the conquest of Mongolia he planned and attempted over five major campaigns (two into the Gobi Desert) from 1410 to 1424. In 1422 he marched north on his third Mongolian campaign. He took a monstrous army of 240,000 men supplied from a train of 117,000 heavy wagons and 340,000 donkeys used as pack animals. In preparation for this invasion, he built the Ming supply of cavalry and pack horses during the previous decade to over one million. Not being fools, the Mongols retreated before this vast host. Yongle thus scored only minor tactical successes over groups of Mongol stragglers, while the greater speed and ability of the Mongol hordes to retreat deep into the steppe, taking with them families and herds, denied him a strategic victory. Once he reached the outer limit of his supply chain he was compelled to withdraw, leaving the Mongols undefeated. He returned to Mongolia the next year with 300,000 men. Once again the Mongols simply avoided battle. In part this was a defensive strategy and partly it reflected the fact they were fighting amongst themselves elsewhere. Yongle's final Mongolian campaign took place in 1424. Yet again he failed to find a Mongol army to fight, and on the return journey he died. Although his campaigns failed to conquer Mongolia they probably prevented the Mongol tribes from consolidating into a rival empire that would have presented a serious threat to China's north. See also *Tumu, Battle of*.

Suggested Reading: Shih-shan Henry Tsai, *Perpetual Happiness: The Ming Emperor Yongle* (2001).

Yoruba. By 1400 the Yoruba were organized in a complex city-state system in which Ekiti, Ijebu, Ife, Owu, and Oyo were the main participants. Ife was the oldest Yoruba city and culturally and religiously the most significant. In 1535 the northernmost Yoruba city-state of Oyo was overrun by Nupe and its ruling family forced into a century of exile in Borgu. In the mid-17th century, possibly with aid from Borgu (to whose rulers the Oyo kings were related by dynastic marriage), Oyo fielded a cavalry force which freed the city from Nupe. Oyo went on to conquer other Yoruba cities as well as territory further south, paralleling the rain forest belt where Oyo's cavalry lost its advantage due to the tsetse fly which bore "sleeping sickness" (African trypanosomiasis) that killed the horses.

Z

Zabern, Battle of (May 16–17, 1525). See *German Peasant War*.

zabra. A small (80–100 tons) two- or three-masted Spanish warship. The type was closely related to the *patache*. Most sported lateen sails and were fast ships. They were used in reconnaissance and for carrying messages or supplies between slower hulks and larger warships. The Spanish deployed a full squadron of zabras and pataches as part of the *Invincible Armada*.

zakat. The main Islamic tax, calculated over one lunar year, required of all able Faithful. It was used principally to provide alms to the needy and support more general communal purposes. Payment of the zakat constituted one of the cardinal pillars of the Faith. Its counterpart was the *jizya*, a poll tax on non-Muslims.

Zanzibar. This East African island was home to the *Swahili Arabs* who controlled the East African slave trade with Arabia and India for over 1,000 years. It was ruled by sultans with close ethnic and dynastic ties to Oman. Chinese junks reached Zanzibar in the late 15th century, but in 1536 the Ming abandoned oceanic exploration and trade. That left Portuguese traders and *privateers* from Mombasa (Fort Jesus) to compete with and eventually control the Zanzibar trade in cloves and slaves. A Swahili Arab rebellion occurred in 1632 but within three years the Portuguese regained control.

Zaporozhian Cossacks. See *Cossacks*.

Zaragoza, Treaty of (1529). This treaty extended the settlement of division of the Western Hemisphere laid out in the *Line of Demarcation* (1493) and amended in the Treaty of Tordesillas (1494). Zaragoza applied the principle of the papal line of demarcation between Spain and Portugal in the Atlantic to the Pacific, at 145° east.

zarbzens. Ottoman light field guns. Weighing in at just 125 pounds, they were easily transported by packhorse or camel.

Zatoka Swieza, Battle of (September 15, 1463). This naval victory for the alliance of Poland and the rebel cities of Prussia was a significant turning point during the final phase of *War of the Cities* (1454–1466). A fleet of *privateers* and warships commissioned by the *Teutonic Knights*, comprising forty-four ships in all, was destroyed by thirty warships operating from the rebel cities of Danzig and Elbing. This severely constricted Teutonic maritime trade in the eastern Baltic and undermined the economic basis of the Teutonic war effort.

Zemshchina. See *Ivan IV*; *Oprichnina.*

zemsky sobor. An assembly of Muscovite *Estates.* See *"Time of Troubles."*

zereh bagtar. Armor comprised of a long mail undercoat with four linked plates tied girdle-style around the chest and upper stomach. It was typical of armor used by armies of the *Mughal Empire.*

Zeugherr. The title of a master gunner in the *Swiss Army* from the latter 15th century, when the Swiss acquired artillery by taking hundreds of cannon in battle from *Charles the Rash.* The job of the Zeugherr was maintenance, training of gun crews, and firing cannon in combat. Some also learned to cast guns.

Zheng He (1371–1433). Ming *eunuch* and admiral. A Chinese Muslim sent by the *Yongle Emperor* on six spectacular transoceanic western voyages in 1405, 1407, 1409, 1413, 1417, and 1421. Zheng He explored the coasts of India and Oman and touched the shores of distant Zanzibar. The expeditions were made as much to display Ming military prowess as to seek trade or knowledge of foreign lands. Each voyage averaged 50 large ships, then the biggest by far in the world. Some sported nine masts and had advanced design features such as *sternpost rudders*, watertight bulkheads, and brass cannons. The greatest were 200–300 feet long with many times the cargo capacity of contemporary European vessels. They carried manpower not matched at sea in Europe until the fight at *Lepanto* in 1571 or the sails and guns of the *Invincible Armada* appeared off Gravelines in 1588. Tens of thousands of Ming soldiers, sailors, and marines traveled with Zheng He, who navigated by compass and detailed coastal charts. The 1407 expedition attacked and destroyed a pirate base and fleet on Sumatra. The 1411 fleet intervened in the internal politics of Ceylon (Sri Lanka), kidnapping a local ruler and returning him to China. Zheng He's seventh voyage was commissioned by the Xuande Emperor in 1431 and comprised possibly 300 ships and 35,000 crew and marines. Zheng He died on the journey home in 1433. There is every reason to think that had China continued his explorations *junks* would have skirted the Cape of Good Hope decades before Portuguese *galleons* did, with an enormous impact on world history. Instead, after Zheng He's seventh voyage the Ming fleet never put to sea again. China's lead in nautical exploration and commerce was repressed by Xuande, who forbade oceanic trade and banned new construction of blue-water ships.

Suggested Reading: Louise Levathes, *When China Ruled the Seas: The Treasure Fleet of the Dragon Throne, 1405–1433* (1994; 1996).

ziamet. Ottoman troops at the highest ranks of the *timariots* were rewarded with revenue from a large land assignment, or ziamet, that paid from 20,000 to 100,000 akçes annually. If the soldier promoted was from the *dirlik yememiş* the ziamet replaced the lower revenues (up to 20,000 akçes) of his "timar," or the salary he drew from Imperial tax revenues.

Žižka, Jan (d.1424). One-eyed Taborite fanatic and brilliantly innovative general who invented the Hussite *tabor*. In 1409 he led Tatar, Cossack, Hungarian, and Bohemian mercenaries in the pay of Poland-Lithuania in a campaign against the *Teutonic Knights*, culminating in the extraordinary fight at *Tannenberg* in 1410. His main claim to fame was as the original Hussite commander during the *Hussite Wars*. He won victories at *Kutná Hora* (1422) and *Nêmecký Brod* (1422), both fights where he deployed firearms troops behind the Hussite *Wagenburg*. After his death the Taborites reputedly stretched his skin to make from it a great war drum.

Zsitva Torok, Treaty of (November 1606). Signed by Archduke Matthias in behalf of *Rudolf II*, this treaty codified peace between the Holy Roman Empire and the Ottoman Empire and formally ended the *Thirteen Years' War* (1593–1606). Intended to last 20 years, in fact it kept the peace much longer: it was renewed six times by 1649. In Hungary chronic border warfare continued unaffected by the peace. In Germany, however, the end of the "Long War" in the *Militargrenze* loosened ties of confessionally divided territorial princes to the Emperor, contributing to the divisions that brought on and sustained the *Thirty Years' War*. Zsitva Torok's terms were: the Ottomans received the fortresses of Eger (Eğri) and Esztergom and reacquired "The Principalities" (Transylvania, Moldavia, and Wallachia).

Zuhab Treaty of (May 1639). Also "Qasr-i Shirin." A codification of the restored balance of power between Safavid Iran and the Ottoman Empire. It followed a 16-year war over Iraq that began with defection of the Ottoman garrison in Baghdad in 1623. The Ottomans made its recapture the top priority of their policy, a task in which they were helped by the religious division of traditional Christian enemies in Europe. Zuhab established peace in Iraq to the effective end of the Safavid regime in 1722.

Zuider Zee, Battle of (1573). See *Eighty Years' War*.

Zúñiga y Requesens, Luis (1528–1576). Grand commander of the *Knights of Santiago*. In 1568 he helped *Don Juan of Austria* suppress a *Morisco* revolt in

Granada. Three years later he fought at *Lepanto*. In 1573 he was sent to Flanders to replace the *Duke of Alba*, whose depredations and persecutions left the local population consumed with rage and the Army of Flanders in mutinous mood. Zúñiga failed in a 1574 attempt to crush the Sea Beggars at *Walcheren*. He also failed to complete the *Siege of Leiden*. However, he won a sharp fight at *Mookerheyde*, killing many Flanders nobles. He died in Brussels after less than three years as governor in the Netherlands.

Zusmarshausen, Battle of (May 17, 1648). Having withdrawn from the *Thirty Years' War* earlier in 1647, *Maximilian I* of Bavaria reengaged the fight. This provoked yet another invasion of Bavaria, this time by a French-Swedish army of 30,000 under *Henri de Turenne* and *Karl Gustaf Wrangel*. A Bavarian-Imperial army under the Hessian general Peter Melander (who was killed) and the Habsburg general *Raimundo Montecuccoli* was crushed at Zusmarshausen near Augsburg. While the Austrians fought a rearguard action the Bavarians ran. At the end of the day Montecuccoli had to cut loose from his massive baggage train and camp following and flee. French and Swedish troops then marauded over Bavaria to the end of the war in October.

Zutphen, Battle of (September 22, 1586). After the murder of *William the Silent* and under terms of the *Treaty of Nonsuch*, England dispatched troops to aid the Dutch rebels against Spain. The expedition was commanded by *Elizabeth I*'s court favorite, the *Earl of Leicester*. Two years later Leicester joined *Maurits of Nassau* in laying siege to the Spanish garrison at Zutphen. *Parma* sent a relief column that beat back an attack by Leicester's troops, killed his brother (Philip Sidney) and lifted the siege.

Zutphen, Siege of (1591). See *Maurits of Nassau*.

Zwingli, Huldrych (1484–1531). Swiss reformer. Educated at Basel, he did not let his ordination as a Catholic priest curtail his enthusiasm for womanizing, for which he was infamous. He criticized the *mercenary* trade of his countrymen as early as 1510, but his objections were patriotic rather than moral or religious: he thought serving in foreign wars might be dangerous to Swiss independence. He toyed with moral objections to Swiss killing foreigners for money, but never denounced the mercenary profession or embraced pacifism. In fact, he served as a field chaplain with two Swiss mercenary expeditions during the *Italian Wars* (1494–1559). He saw action in service to the *Holy League* against the French at *Novara* in 1513. Two years later he was in the thick of the fight at *Marignano*, which he commemorated in the poem "The Labyrinth." In the 1520s Zwingli claimed to have called for essential reforms of the Church as early as 1516, a year before *Martin Luther* stunned the Catholic world with his ninety-five theses of protest, but most scholars see this as a post facto assertion produced by their personal rivalry. Indisputably, Zwingli roused Zürich in 1518 to ban peripatetic priests selling indulgences. In 1519, as he recovered from a bout of plague, he clearly parted with Rome on several matters of doctrine and clerical discipline. In 1522 he defended citizens arrested for eating sausages in their homes during Lent, an act of defiance that marked the real beginning of the Reformation in Zürich. The next year he declared his support for clerical marriage. Zwingli mocked the idea of original sin, dismissed the notion that the unbaptised could not be admitted to Heaven, and argued that even pagans could live just and virtuous lives. He also believed firmly in predestination. Yet he remained the most tolerant of the early, major reformers. Many historians depict him as the most socially progressive as well, though that is more arguable.

Zwingli convinced Zürich to abstain from participation in the Swiss Confederation's alliance with France in 1521. In 1523 he so impressed observers by defeating the representative of the Bishop of Constance in theological debate that Zürich adopted the reforms he set out in "sixty-seven theses" (intended to rival Luther's ninety-five). Later that year Zwingli did away with the Mass in Zürich along with all Catholic imagery and statuary, which he condemned as idolatrous. *Iconoclastic* mobs carried the policy through at first, until a more disciplined removal was organized the next year. By 1525 Zwingli broke with the rule of priestly celibacy by marrying. More provocatively, he dispensed the sacrament *sub utraque specie* ("in both kinds"). In 1524 he began a long and bitter quarrel with Luther over the nature of the Mass, with Zwingli rejecting all notions of transubstantiation or consubstantiation. Their argument was unresolved, ending in mutual disdain and a split between the Swiss and German reform movements at a failed conference held at Marburg in 1529. By that time Zwingli's teachings had spread to Bern, across Switzerland, and into southern Germany. Zwingli's teachings and austere religious rule divided the Swiss from each other as well as from Lutherans. When the Anabaptist founder, Conrad Grebel, broke with Zwingli in 1525, he and his family and followers were hounded from the city or put to death for heresy. With Protestant cantons aligned with Zürich, the Catholic Forest Cantons formed an opposing alliance. When Schwyz executed a Protestant preacher in 1529 who dared to speak in a declared neutral zone, a sixteen-day civil war ensued. A more serious civil war broke out in 1531 that included an attack on Zürich. The main clash came at *Kappel* where Zwingli was found among the wounded by Catholic Swiss and killed where he lay. The Catholics then burned his corpse, mixed the ashes with dung, and scattered them. Eighteen years after his death Zwinglians reconciled with Swiss Calvinists (1549) in a union confirmed by the 1566 "Second Helvetic Confession."

Suggested Reading: G. Potter, *Zwingli* (1976); Robert Walton, *Zwingli's Theocracy* (1967).

Chronology of Major Events

1008	Córdoba emirate falls; al-Andalus breaks into *taifa* states.
1027	Church Council proclaims "Truce of God."
1066–1070	Norman conquest of England.
1077–1122	Wars of Investiture.
1085	Capture of Toledo, milestone in Christian *"Reconquista."*
	Capture of Syracuse by Normans; all Sicily conquered by 1091.
1095	First Crusade preached at Clermont.
	"Peace of God" proclaimed.
1099	Crusaders sack Jerusalem.
1104	Venice founds "The Arsenal."
1147–1148	Second Crusade defeated before Damascus.
	Saxon crusade against pagan Slavs east of the Elbe.
1187	Battle of Hattin: Salāh-al-Dīn defeats Crusaders, retakes Jerusalem.
1188–1192	Third Crusade takes Acre.
	Battle of Arsur (1191): Richard I defeats Salāh-al-Dīn.
1204	Fourth Crusade sacks Constantinople, establishes "Latin Kingdom" in Greece.
	French seize Normandy from English.
1209–1229	Albigensian Crusade: Cathars massacred and suppressed in France.
1212	Battle of Las Navas de Tolosa: Aragon defeats the Almohads.
1217–1221	Fifth Crusade.
1228–1229	Emperor Friedrich II secures Jerusalem.

1229	Teutonic Knights crusade against "northern Saracens" of Prussia.
1234	Mongols overthrow Jin Empire.
	Battle of Alamut: Mongols crush the Assassins.
1240	Battle of Jand: Mongols overrun western Iran.
1241	Battle of Liegnitz: Mongols defeat Poles and Teutonic Knights.
1242	Battle of Mohi: Mongols defeat Hungarians.
1260	Battle of Ayn Jālut: Mamlūks defeat Mongols.
1261	Byzantines recapture Constantinople.
1274/1281	Battles of Hakata Bay: two Mongol attempted invasions of Japan fail.
1277–1283	Edward I conquers Wales.
1291	Muslims capture Acre, last "Frankish state" overrun.
	Hospitallers retreat to Cyprus (1291) and Rhodes (1306).
1297–1298	Battle of Stirling Bridge: Scots infantry beat English knights.
	Battle of Falkirk: English knights and Welsh archers defeat Scots.
1302	Battle of Courtrai: Flemish militia defeat French knights.
1314–1315	Battle of Bannockburn: Scottish foot defeat English knights.
	Battle of Morgarten: Swiss infantry defeat Austrian knights.
1334	Buddhist Red Turban Rebellion breaks Mongol hold on China.
1337	Start of Hundred Years' War (to 1453).
1340	Battle of Sluys: greatest naval battle of the medieval period.
1346	Battle of Crécy: English longbowmen and men-at-arms decimate French knights.
1347–1350	"Black Death" first reaches and devastates Europe.
1356	Battle of Poitiers: English infantry again beat French knights; King Jean II captured and held for ransom.
1363–1368	Battle of Lake Boyang: Hongwu defeats Han fleet.
	Hongwu occupies Nanjing; proclaims himself emperor and founds the Ming dynasty.
	Hongwu sets up eight military colonies along the northern border.
1378	"Great Schism" of the West begins; papacy contested and degraded.
1386	Battle of Sempach: Swiss infantry defeats Austrian knights.
1396	Battle of Nicopolis: Sultan Bayezid I defeats Hungarians and French crusaders.
1402–1405	Battle of Ankara: Timur defeats Ottomans, captures Sultan Bayezid I.

	Yongle moves Imperial capital to Beijing.
	Zheng He leaves on first of six transoceanic voyages for Yongle Emperor, 1405–1421.
1410	Battle of Tannenberg: Poles and Lithuanians crush Teutonic Knights.
1415–1417	Battle of Agincourt: English longbowmen and men-at-arms defeat French knights.
	Henry V advances English re-conquest of Normandy.
1419	Hussite Wars begin (to 1478).
1422	Battle of Arbedo: Milanese defeat small Swiss unit.
	Swiss reform and standardize squares, adding more pikemen.
1429–1431	Jeanne d'Arc relieves siege of Orléans, defeats English at Patay (1429).
	Dauphin crowned Charles VII at Rheims (1429).
	Jeanne d'Arc burned at the stake (1431).
	Zheng He makes seventh and final voyage west.
1433–1436	Xuande Emperor dry docks China's blue water fleet.
	Naval exploration prohibited to Chinese.
1444	Battle of Varna: Ottomans defeat Hungarians and Poles.
1449–1450	Battle of Tumu: Zhengtong Emperor loses 500,000 men in campaign against Mongols.
	Mongols attack Beijing.
	Ming renew work on Great Wall, add 700 miles and establish outlying military colonies.
	Battle of Formigny: French defeat English field army, go on to occupy Normandy.
1453	Ottomans besiege and sack Constantinople.
	Battle of Castillon: French victory ends Hundred Years' War.
1454	"War of the Cities" begins in Prussia and Baltic (to 1466).
	Battle of Chojnice: Poland-Lithuania fights Teutonic Knights.
	Peace of Lodi defines balance of power among main city-states in Italy.
	Johannes Gutenberg introduces moveable type at Frankfurt.
1455	"Wars of the Roses" begin (to 1485).
1456	Fortress of Marienburg surrenders to Poles.
	Ottomans capture Athens.
1459–1467	Ottomans conquer Serbia (1459), Morea (1460), Bosnia (1464), and Herzegovina (1467).
1461	Yorkists defeat Lancastrians at Mortimer's Cross and Towton.

1466	"War of the Cities" ends in Prussia.
1467	Ōnin War destroys Kyoto (1467–1477).
	Sengoku jidai era begins in Japan (to 1568).
1469	Ferdinand of Aragon marries Isabella of Castile.
	Niccolò Machiavelli born in Florence (May 3).
1470	Portuguese ships reach Gold Coast (West Africa).
1471	Battle of Tewkesbury: Prince Edward killed.
	Henry VI murdered in the Tower of London.
	Fuggers make first war loan to Habsburgs.
1475	Ottomans invade the Crimea.
1476–1477	Swiss-Burgundian Wars.
	Charles the Rash killed by Swiss.
	Burgundy partitioned by Austria and France.
1480	Ivan III assumes the title "Tsar."
	Inquisition begins in Castile.
1483	Muscovite military expedition to western Siberia.
	Juan II of Portugal declines to finance voyage of exploration by Columbus.
1485	Battle of Bosworth Field: Richard III killed.
	"Wars of the Roses" end.
	Henry Tudor crowned as Henry VII.
1486	Portuguese ships reach Ngola.
	Portuguese explorers reach Kongo.
1487	Bartolomeu Dias navigates Cape of Good Hope.
	Spanish capture Malaga.
1488	Henry VII builds first "Great Ship."
1492	Granada surrenders to Spain, end of "*Reconquista*."
	Ferdinand and Isabella order expulsion of Spanish Jews.
	Columbus makes landfall on Watling Island.
1493	Pope Alexander VI sets "Line of Demarcation."
	Syphilis epidemic in Barcelona.
1494	Treaty of Tordesillas amends "Line of Demarcation" agreement.
	Italian Wars begin (to 1559).
	Leonardo da Vinci publishes *Codex Madrid II*.
1495	Henry VII builds first dry dock at Portsmouth.
	Charles VIII takes Naples.
	Holy League opposes France in Italy.

	Expulsion of Portuguese Jews.
	Soldiers returning from Italy spread syphilis to France.
1496	John Cabot sails in search of northwest passage to Asia.
	Columbus brings tobacco, Caribbean Indians to Europe.
1497	John Cabot claims Newfoundland and Nova Scotia for England.
	Savonarola excommunicated, carries out "bonfire of the vanities" in Florence.
1498	Vasco de Gama reaches India.
	Savonarola burned in Florence.
	Grand Inquisitor Torquemada dies.
1499	Louis XII occupies Milan and Genoa.
	Granadine Moors revolt against Spain.
1500	Charles V born.
	France and Spain agree to partition Naples.
	Amerigo Vespucci discovers mouth of the Amazon.
	Pedro Cabral claims Brazil for Portugal.
1501	Louis XII reinvades Italy.
	Pope Alexander VI orders burnings of books deemed heretical.
1502	Ismail I consolidates Safavid rule in Iran.
1504	Ferdinand of Aragon conquers Naples.
	Treaty of Lyon gives Naples to Spain.
	Treaty of Blois gives Milan to France.
	Isabella of Castile dies.
1505	Ivan III dies.
	First Portuguese factories established in east Africa.
	Portugese muscle into Indian Ocean monopoly trade in cloves and slaves.
1506	Fuggers finance expansion of spice trade.
1508	Portuguese capture Muscat.
	League of Cambrai formed.
1509	Battle of Diu: Portuguese defeat Mamlūk and Gujarati galley fleets.
	Portugal takes full control of Indian Ocean trade routes.
	Henry VIII succeeds Henry VII.
	Battle of Agnadello: French defeat Venetians.
	Persecution of Jews increases inside the Holy Roman Empire.
	Maximilian I orders heretical books burned within the Holy Roman Empire.
1510	Portuguese capture Goa.

1512	Ponce de Leon claims Florida for Spain.
	Battle of Ravenna: French defeated by Holy League.
	Shi'ism established as state religion of Safavid Empire.
1513	Battle of Flodden Field: James IV killed.
	Battle of Novara: French defeated by Swiss.
	"Battle of the Spurs."
	Machiavelli writes *The Prince* (not published until 1532).
1514	Selim I orders a mass slaughter of shi'ia inside the Ottoman Empire.
	Ottoman-Safavid wars begin.
	Battle of Chaldiran: Janissaries and timariots destroy Safavid army.
1515	Louis XII dies: Francis I succeeds as king.
	Battle of Marj Dabiq: Ottomans crush Egyptian Mamlūks.
	Pope Leo X captures Florence.
	Battle of Marignano: French crush Swiss outside Milan.
1516	Battle of al-Raydaniyya: Ottomans defeat Mamlūks, conquer Syria.
	Mary Tudor born.
1517	Egyptian Mamlūks accept Ottoman suzerainty.
	Ottomans take control of the Hejaz.
	Martin Luther registers his protests in Wittenberg.
	John Cabot discovers entrance to Hudson's Bay.
1518	Martin Luther summoned to answer charges of heresy.
1519	Magellan's crew and ship complete circumnavigation of globe, without Magellan.
	Hernán Cortés first hears of existence of Aztec Empire.
	Charles V elevated to Holy Roman Emperor.
	Alonso de Pineda discovers mouth of Mississippi.
	Leonardo da Vinci dies.
1520	Suleiman the Magnificent elevated to Ottoman Emperor.
	"Field of the Cloth of Gold" summit of Henry VIII and Francis I.
	First siege of Tenochtitlán.
	Cortés flees Tenochtitlán.
1521	Ottomans capture Belgrade.
	Martin Luther excommunicated by Pope Leo X.
	Francis I declares war on Charles V.
	Charles V establishes Inquisition in the Netherlands.
	Diet of Worms meets to contend with "Lutheranism."
	Second siege of Tenochtitlán.

	Charles V takes Milan.
	Ming acquire first Portuguese cannon.
1522	Ottomans capture Rhodes after third siege.
	Battle of La Bicocca: Charles V defeats French.
1523	Duke of Bourbon invades France.
	Zürich establishes Zwinglian Protestantism.
1524	French recapture Milan.
1525	Battle of Pavia: Francis I taken prisoner, held in Spain.
	German Peasant War (to 1526).
	Anabaptists burned in Zürich, persecution also begins in Netherlands.
1526	Francis I signs Treaty of Madrid and is released.
	Francis I renounces Treaty of Madrid, Italian Wars resume.
	League of Cognac formed.
	First slave rebellion in New World.
	Battle of Mohács: Ottomans destroy a Hungarian army.
	Mughal Empire founded in India.
1527	Imperial Army runs amok in Rome, pope taken prisoner.
	Medici are expelled from Florence.
	Henry VIII asks pope to annul marriage to Katherine of Aragon.
1529	Treaty of Zaragoza extends "Line of Demarcation" to Pacific.
	Battle of Landriano: French lose at Milan.
	Ottomans besiege Vienna.
	Charles V and pope reconcile, jointly besiege Florence.
	Treaty of Cambrai.
	Henry VIII dismisses Cardinal Wolsey, appoints Thomas More Chancellor of England.
	"Reformation Parliament" called in England.
1530	"Augsburg Confession" published by Luther.
	Ivan IV ("The Terrible") born.
	Cardinal Wolsey dies.
	Schmalkaldic League formed in Germany.
	Florence surrenders to pope.
1531	Battle of Kappel: Zwingli killed in Swiss civil war.
	Lisbon earthquake kills 30,000.
	"Virgin of Guadalupe" said to appear to Mexican child; Indian conversions accelerate.
1532	English Parliament recognizes the ecclesiastical supremacy of Henry VIII.

	Thomas More resigns; Thomas Cromwell elevated in his place.
	War of the Debatable Lands.
1533	Henry VIII marries Anne Boleyn.
	Parliament voids all papal authority in England.
	Elizabeth I born.
	Jean Calvin has vision of a personal mission to reform Church.
	Anabaptists seize control of Münster, 18-month siege begins.
1534	Affair of the Placards in Paris.
	Act of Supremacy establishes Church of England.
	Martin Luther completes German translation of Bible.
1535	Anabaptists burned in Netherlands.
	Thomas More beheaded.
1536	Erasmus dies.
	Francis I invades Savoy.
	Charles V invades Provence from Piedmont.
	Jean Calvin publishes *Institutes of the Christian Religion*.
	Mary and Elizabeth Tudor declared illegitimate by Parliament.
	William Tyndale burned in Brussels.
	Dissolution of smaller monasteries in England.
	Irish Parliament establishes Church of Ireland, under the Crown.
1538	Truce of Nice pauses Franco-Habsburg war.
1539	Francis I and Charles V threaten Henry VIII.
	Ottomans capture Aden.
	Dissolution of greater monasteries in England.
1540	Jean Calvin secures control of Geneva.
	Society of Jesus founded by Ignatius Loyola.
	Francisco Vazquez de Coronado reaches Rio Grande.
1541	Ireland annexed to English Crown.
	Calvinism established in Geneva.
	Ottomans capture Buda, annex central Hungary.
1542	Francis I attacks Luxemburg, Brabant, Navarra.
	Ottoman-French joint fleet sacks Nice.
	Battle of Solway Moss: Scots defeated.
	Mary Stuart born.
1543	Nicholas Copernicus dies.
	Treaty of Greenwich ends Scottish war.

England invades Flanders.

Act of Union fuses Wales to England.

1544	Charles V invades France.
	English occupy Boulogne (to 1550).
1545	Council of Trent convened.
1546	Martin Luther dies.
1547	Henry VIII dies, succeeded by Edward VI.
	Battle of Mühlburg: Charles V defeats Schmalkaldic League.
	Francis I dies, succeeded by Henri II.
	Ivan IV ascends in Muscovy.
1548	*Chambre ardente* tortures accused heretics in France.
1550	Unification Wars begin in Japan.
1551	Edict of Châteaubriant bans Protestantism in France.
1552	Muscovite army takes Kazan.
	Ottomans besiege Eger (Eğri).
1553	Edward VI dies.
	Mary I restores Catholicism in England.
	Henri de Navarre born.
1554	Swedish-Muscovite War begins (to 1557).
	Wyatt's Rebellion.
	Mary I marries Philip II.
1555	Charles V abdicates in Netherlands and Burgundy in favor of Philip II.
	Peace of Amasya ends Ottoman-Safavid war.
	Peace of Augsburg ends religious war in Germany.
1556	Charles V abdicates Iberian crowns to Philip II.
	Muscovites capture Astrakhan.
1557	Spain invades France from Netherlands.
	Battle of St. Quentin: Montmorency and Coligny taken prisoner by Spanish.
1558	First Northern War begins (to 1583).
	Calais retaken by France.
	Mary Stuart marries Francis I.
	Mary Tudor dies.
1559	Treaties of Cateau-Cambrésis: French leave Italy.
	Elizabeth I ascends to throne.
	Henri II killed in jousting accident.

1560	Treaty of Edinburgh: French leave Scotland.
	Scottish Parliament adopts Confession of Faith, bans Catholic Mass.
	Conspiracy of Amboise fails.
	Francis II dies, succeeded by Charles IX.
	Battle of Okehazama: Oda Nobunaga advances unification drive.
1561	Livonian Order secularized, Courland made vassal of Poland.
	Colloquy of Poissy fails.
	Mary Stuart lands in Scotland to claim the crown.
1562	Edict of Saint-German (Toleration).
	Vassy massacre of Huguenots.
	First French Civil War begins.
1563	Nordic Seven Years' War begins (to 1570).
	Peace of Amboise ends First Civil War in France.
	English garrison surrenders Le Havre to French.
1564	Spanish found Manila in Philippines.
	Pope Pius IV affirms Council of Trent's *Professio Fidei*.
	Galileo Galilei born.
	Jean Calvin dies.
1565	Ottoman siege of Malta.
1566	James VI born to Mary Stuart, Queen of Scots.
1567	Mary Stuart abdicates, succeeded by infant James VI.
	Oda Nobunaga enters Kyoto, deposes shogun.
	Second Civil War begins in France.
1568	Edict of Longjumeau ends Second Civil War in France.
	Mary Stuart flees to England.
	Eighty Years' War begins (to 1648).
	Third Civil War begins in France.
1569	Battles of Jarnac and Moncontour: Huguenots defeated; death of Condé.
1570	Reval besieged by Muscovites.
	Peace of Stettin ends Nordic Seven Years' War.
	Peace of St. Germain-en-Laye ends Third Civil War in France.
	Ottoman-Venetian war begins.
	Battle of Anegawa: victory for Oda Nobunaga and Tokugawa Ieyasu.
1571	Ottomans sack Famagusta.
	Battle of Lepanto: Ottoman fleet destroyed by Christian coalition.

1572	Henri de Navarre marries Margaret de Valois.
	St. Bartholomew's Day Massacres.
	Fourth Civil War starts in France.
1573	Peace of La Rochelle ends Fourth Civil War in France.
	Henri Valois elected King of Poland.
	Ottomans conquer Cyprus.
	End of Ottoman-Venetian war.
	England invades Scotland.
	Wan-Li mounts throne in China.
1574	Death of Charles IX; Henri Valois abdicates Polish throne, is crowned Henri III of France.
	Portuguese seed colonies in coastal Angola and Brazil.
	Spanish Inquisition burns its first American victims.
	Oda Nobunaga slaughters True Pure Land Buddhists.
1575	Philip II declares bankruptcy, defaults on Spain's war loans.
	Fifth Civil War begins in France.
	Battle of Nagashino (1575): Oda Nobunaga wins major victory.
1576	Henri de Navarre escapes from Paris, recants his forced conversion to Catholicism.
	Edict of Beaulieu ends Fifth Civil War.
	"Spanish Fury" in Antwerp.
1577	Sixth Civil War begins and ends in France.
1578	Peasant revolts in Dauphiné, Vivarais, and Provence (to 1580).
	Ottoman-Safavid war resumes in Caucasus (to 1590).
1579	Elizabeth I allies with Sea Beggars.
	Union of Arras and Union of Utrecht formally split Netherlands.
1580	Portugal and its empire are annexed to Spain by Philip II.
	Seventh Civil War in France begins.
	Honganji fortress surrenders to Oda Nobunaga.
1581	James VI signs Scottish Confession of Faith.
	Francis Drake captures Spanish treasure ship off Panama.
1582	Gregorian Calendar adopted by most Catholics.
	Oda Nobunaga betrayed and killed; Toyotomi Hideyoshi siezes power, continues Unification Wars.
	First Jesuit mission to China.
	First English colonists settle in Newfoundland.
1583	Albrecht von Wallenstein born.

Chronology of Major Events

1584	Ivan IV dies.
	Boris Godunov becomes regent in Moscow.
	Eighth Civil War begins in France (to 1598).
	Treaty of Joinville: Philip II allies with French Catholic League.
	duc d'Anjou dies; Henri de Navarre becomes presumptive heir to French throne.
	William of Orange assassinated.
	Protestant Plantation of Munster begins.
1585	Francis Drake attacks Vigo and Santo Domingo.
	Treaty of Nonsuch: England allies with United Provinces against Spain.
	Treaty of Nemours: Henri III allies with Catholic League.
	English found colony at Roanoke, Virginia.
1586	Francis Drake attacks Spanish settlement at St. Augustine, Florida.
	English fight Spanish in Netherlands.
	Mary Stuart convicted of treason, names Philip II as heir.
1587	Mary Stuart executed on order of Elizabeth I.
	Phillip II orders "Enterprise of England."
	Francis Drake raids Cadiz, burns Armada warehouses.
	Toyotomi Hideyoshi orders Christian missionaries to leave Japan.
1588	Trained Bands muster at Tilbury.
	Invincible Armada falters in the English Channel.
	Day of the Barricades in Paris.
	Guise assassinated by Henri III.
	Thomas Hobbes born.
1589	Sigismund III deposed in Sweden.
	Abbas I loses Azerbaijan and Georgia to Ottomans.
	Catherine de Medici dies.
	Henri III assassinated; Henri de Navarre succeeds as Henri IV.
	Catholic League launches religious terror in cities.
	Battle of Arques: Henri IV defeats Catholic League.
	Francis Drake attacks Lisbon.
1590	Swedish-Muscovite War begins (to 1595).
	Charles de Bourbon dies.
	Battle of Ivry-la-Bataille: Henri IV defeats Catholic League, besieges Paris.
	Duke of Parma intervenes in France with Spanish army from Netherlands.
	Toyotomi Hideyoshi completes major phase of Unification Wars.

1591   Henri IV excommunicated by Pope Gregory XIV.

Boris Godunov assassinates Tsar Dimitri.

Private warfare breaks out in the *Militargrenze*.

1592   Henri IV besieges Rouen.

Toyotomi Hideyoshi invades Korea.

1593   Thirteen Years' War begins (to 1606).

Henri IV abjures Protestantism.

Peasant revolts in Agenais, Burgundy, Limousin, and Périgord (to 1594).

1594   Henri IV crowned at Chartres; Paris submits to his authority.

Nine Years' War begins in Ireland (to 1603).

1595   End of Swedish-Muscovite War.

Henri IV absolved by Pope Clement VIII, excommunication lifted.

Henri IV declares war on Spain.

Dutch colonies established in East Indies.

English armies finally abandon longbows.

1596   War of Catholic League ends in France.

Elizabeth I orders "pacification of Ireland."

Spanish capture Calais and Cambrai.

English Privy Council raises ship money to pay for Irish war.

1597   Second Spanish Armada fails.

Spanish seize Amiens.

Upper Austria forcibly recatholicized; religious tensions mount in Germany.

England transports convicts and Irish rebels to North American colonies.

Dutch found Batavia as main base of their Asian operations.

Toyotomi Hideyoshi invades Korea for the second time.

Mass executions of Japanese *Kirishitan*.

1598   Edict of Nantes extends toleration to Huguenots.

Eighth Civil War ends in France.

Peace of Vervins: Philip II renounces claim to French crown.

Abbas I moves Iranian capital to Isfahan.

Sigismund III invades Sweden.

Battle of Stegeborg: Swedes defeat Poles.

Fyodor I dies; Boris Godunov elevated to Tsar.

Tyrone defeats English at Béal Atha Buí (Yellow Ford).

Phillip II dies, succeeded by Philip III.

Toyotomi Hideyoshi dies.

Chronology of Major Events

1599	Sigismund III deposed in Sweden.
	Oliver Cromwell born.
	Essex campaigns in Ireland.
1600	Karl IX invades Livonia; Polish-Swedish wars continue intermittently (to 1629).
	Battle of Sekigahara: Tokugawa Ieyasu wins decisive victory, continues Unification Wars.
1601	Spanish land 4,000 troops in Ireland.
	Battle of Kinsale: Tyrone and Spanish defeated.
	East India Company sends out first expedition, to Sumatra.
	Jesuit Matteo Ricci received at Imperial Court in China.
	Nurgaci first organizes Manchu troops into banner system.
1602	Last Spanish in Ireland surrender (January).
	Ottomans defend Buda against Austrian siege.
1603	Tokugawa Ieyasu named shogun.
	Champlain begins six-year expedition to map Canadas.
	Henri IV recalls Jesuits.
	Elizabeth I dies.
	Tyrone surrenders, end of Nine Year's War in Ireland.
	Ottoman-Safavid war over Azerbaijan resumes (to 1612).
1604	Boris Godunov defeats "False Dimitri."
	James VI crowned James I in England.
	"Time of Troubles" in Russia (to 1613).
1605	Battle of Kirkholm: worst defeat in Swedish history.
	Boris Godunov dies.
	Gunpowder Plot foiled.
1606	Thirteen Years' War ends.
	Dutch discover Australia.
	Military brevets of Edict of Nantes renewed.
1607	Jamestown Colony founded in Virginia.
	Flight of the Earls from Ireland.
	Ceasefire in Eighty Years' War (to 1609).
	Donauwörth incident.
1608	Jesuits establish sanctuary for Amazon Indians.
	Protestant Union formed in Germany.
1609	Catholic League formed in Germany.
	Sweden intervenes in Russia.
	Twelve-Year Truce (to April 1621).

VOC ship returns with first tea from China.

Siege of Smolensk (to 1611).

Jülich-Kleve crisis (to 1614).

Polish-Muscovite War (to 1619).

Rudolf II allows freedom of conscience in Bohemia.

Plantation of Ulster begins.

1610 Henri IV assassinated in Paris; regency begins.

Friedrich V succeeds as Elector Palatine.

Swedish troops enter Moscow.

Poland invades Russia.

Battle of Klushino: Russo-Swedish army defeated by Poles.

Poles occupy Moscow, garrison Kremlin (to 1612).

English and Dutch "John Companies" fight in India.

1611 Huguenot assembly at Saumur.

King James Bible printed in England.

War of Kalmar (to 1613).

Karl IX dies; succeeded by Gustavus Adolphus.

1612 Rudolf II dies; Matthias elected Holy Roman Emperor.

Gustavus Adolphus crowned in Sweden.

1613 War of Kalmar ends.

Friedrich V marries Elizabeth Stuart.

German princes ally with United Provinces.

Michael Romanov acclaimed Tsar.

Bethlen Gabor elevated to Prince.

Elector of Brandenburg converts to Calvinism.

Virginian colonists attack Port Royal in New France.

Renewed fighting in the *Militargrenze*.

1614 Revolt against regency in France led by Condé.

Louis XIII attains majority.

Aachen recatholicized.

Jülich-Kleve crisis resolved.

1615 Dutch seize Moluccas from Portuguese.

English fleet defeats Portuguese off Bombay (Mumbai).

Galileo Galilei interrogated by Roman Inquisition.

Lutherans riot in Brandenburg.

Sea Beggars raid Spanish Main.

Tokugawa Ieyasu defeats Toyotomi Hideyori at Osaka Castle.

End of Unification Wars in Japan; start of the long "Tokugawa Peace."

1616	Cardinal Richelieu appointed Minister of War to Louis XIII.
1617	Peace of Stolbova ends Russo-Swedish war.
	Louis XIII dismisses his mother as regent, assumes power (to 1643).
	Catholic League dissolved in Germany.
	Evangelical Union renewed to 1621.
	Ferdinand of Styria recognized as king-designate of Bohemia.
	Sweden invades Livonia, makes peace with Poland (to 1621).
	First African slaves shipped to Jamestown, Virginia.
1618	Truce of Tolsburg ends Polish-Swedish War (to 1621).
	Prussia annexed by Brandenburg.
	William of Orange dies, succeeded by Maurits of Nassau.
	Defenestration of Prague begins Bohemian rebellion.
	Thirty Years' War begins with skirmishes in Bohemia and Lower Austria.
	Oldenbaarneveldt and Hugo Grotius arrested by Maurits of Nassau.
1619	Truce of Deulino: Muscovy cedes Smolensk to Poland.
	Emperor Matthias dies.
	Bohemians besiege Vienna.
	Oldenbaarneveldt executed.
	Bohemians depose Ferdinand of Styria, elect Friedrich V.
	Ferdinand of Styria elected as Holy Roman Emperor Ferdinand II.
	Bethlen Gabor conquers Hungary.
	Poland invades Transylvania.
	Battle of Sarhu: Ming Army devastated by Manchus.
1620	Battle of the White Mountain: Bohemian Protestants crushed.
	Friedrich V flees Bohemia for the Palatinate.
	Battle of Jassy: Ottomans defeat Poles.
	Bavaria occupies Upper Austria (to 1628).
	Spínola invades Palatinate; Friedrich V flees to Netherlands.
	Louis XIII invades Béarn; Habsburgs occupy Valtelline.
	Edict of Restitution restores Catholicism in Béarn.
	Huguenot assembly in La Rochelle.
	Mayflower Pilgrims land at Plymouth Rock.
1621	Friedrich V declared outlaw by the Empire.
	Louis XIII renews war with Huguenots.
	Philip III dies, succeeded by Philip IV.
	Twelve-Years' Truce ends, Eighty Years' War resumes (to 1648).
	Protestant Union dissolved.
	Truce of Tolsburg expires, Polish-Swedish war resumes.

Gustavus Adolphus captures Riga.

Battle of Chocim: Poles fight Ottomans and Tatars.

Bavaria occupies Upper Palatinate (to 1623).

1622	Pope Gregory XV founds *Congregatio de Propaganda Fidei*.

Spínola captures Jülich.

Battle of Wiesloch: Tilly defeated by Mansfeld and Baden.

Battle of Wimpfen: Tilly defeats Baden.

Battle of Höchst: Tilly defeats Brunswick.

Friedrich V dismisses Mansfeld and Brunswick.

Olivares appointed chief minister to Philip IV.

1623 Battle of Stadtlohn: Tilly defeats Brunswick.

Electorate transferred from Palatinate to Bavaria.

EIC founds first factory in India.

First commercial treaty between United Provinces and Iran.

Pope Urban VIII elected (to 1644).

Ottoman garrison in Baghdad defects to Abbas I.

1624 Mansfeld disbands mercenary army.

Spínola besieges Breda.

Dutch found New Amsterdam on Manhattan Island.

Cardinal Richelieu admitted to Privy Council; named first minister of France.

Mansfeld's veterans sail for Netherlands.

1625 James I dies, Charles I succeeds in the Three Kingdoms.

Maurits of Nassau dies.

Army of Flanders occupies Breda (to 1637).

Wallenstein raises mercenary army for Ferdinand II.

First Ottoman siege of Baghdad fails.

Tilly invades Lower Saxony.

Anglo-Dutch raid on Cadiz.

Hague Alliance formed.

1626 Royalists take Ile de Ré.

Gustavus Adolphus campaigns in Royal Prussia (to 1629).

Battle of Dessau Bridge: Wallenstein defeats Mansfeld.

Upper Austria revolts against Habsburgs.

Battle of Lutter-am-Barenberg: Tilly defeats Danes.

Battle of Mewe: Poles lose to Swedes.

Peace of La Rochelle.

French colony set up in Senegal.

Charles I declares war on France.

1627   Philip IV of Spain declares bankruptcy.

                  Wallenstein conquers Pomerania and Holstein.

                  France and Spain declare war on England.

                  Buckingham attacks French on Ile de Ré, repulsed with heavy losses.

                  Siege of La Rochelle begins.

                  Battle of Dirshau: Gustavus Adolphus is wounded.

                  Battle of Oliwa: naval battle off Danzig.

                  Wallenstein invades Silesia.

                  Tilly defeats Protestants in Brunswick.

                  War of the Mantuan Succession starts (to 1631).

1628   Imperial troops overrun Jutland.

                  Wallenstein besieges Straslund.

                  Battle of Wolgast: Wallenstein defeats Danes.

                  La Rochelle capitulates.

                  Dutch conquer Java and Moluccas.

                  Sea Beggars capture Spanish silver treasure fleet.

1629   Louis XIII intervenes in Mantuan War.

                  Imperials counter-invade Italy.

                  Ferdinand II issues Edict of Restitution.

                  Dutch capture s'Hertogenbosch.

                  Peace of Susa ends Anglo-French war.

                  Peace of Alais ends Wars of Religion in France.

                  Battle of Stuhm: Gustavus Adolphus loses to Poles.

                  Peace of Lübeck: Denmark leaves German war.

                  Truce of Altmark ends Polish-Swedish wars (to 1635).

                  Bethlen Gabor dies, succeeded by George Rákóczi.

1630   Dutch occupy Pernambuco, Brazil (to 1654).

                  Gustavus Adolphus lands in Peenemünde.

                  French occupy Savoy.

                  Imperials take Mantua.

                  Outbreak of plague in Italy, to 1631.

                  Magdeburg defies Empire (to May 1631).

                  Wallenstein dismissed by Ferdinand II.

                  Peace of Madrid ends Anglo-Spanish war.

                  Second Ottoman siege of Baghdad fails.

1631   Magdeburg sacked by Tilly and Pappenheim.

                  Swedes take Frankfurt-on-Oder.

                  Swedish–Brandenburg alliance formed.

                  Sweden allies with Saxony, Bremen, Hesse-Kassel.

Battle of First Breitenfeld: Gustavus Adolphus defeats Tilly.

Saxons take Prague (to 1632).

Basque revolt (to 1634).

Swedes take Mainz (to 1636).

Wallenstein recalled by Ferdinand II, raises new army.

Insurrections against Ottomans in Egypt, Lebanon, Yemen.

1632   Battle of Rain: Tilly mortally wounded, dies at Ingolstadt.

Gustavus Adolphus occupies Bavaria.

Sigismund III dies.

Siege of Alte Feste.

English found first factory in Africa.

Portuguese expelled from Bengal.

Russians establish fur-trading post at Yakutsk.

Dutch capture Venlo, Roermond, Maastricht.

Wallenstein captures Leipzig.

Battle of Lützen: Gustavus Adolphus killed.

War of Smolensk begins.

1633   Franco–Swedish alliance renewed.

Heilbronn League formed (to 1635).

Swedish Army mutinies.

Ottomans invade Poland.

French invade Lorraine.

Wallenstein conquers Silesia.

Battle of Steinau: Wallenstein defeats Swedes.

East India Company gains toehold in Bengal.

Galileo Galilei tried by Roman Inquisition.

1634   Wallenstein dismissed by Ferdinand II, flees, is murdered on Ferdinand's order.

English Catholic refugees found colony in Maryland.

Brandenburg breaks alliance with Sweden, over Pomerania.

France increases subsidy to Netherlands.

Charles I raises first instalment of ship money, without consulting Parliament.

War of Smolensk ends.

Saxons invade Bohemia.

Battle of Nördlingen: Swedes lose to Imperials.

France occupies part of Alsace.

Heilbronn League allies with France.

Preliminaries of Pirna point way to religious peace in Germany.

Chronology of Major Events

1635	Franco–Dutch alliance renewed.
	Spain occupies Trier.
	France occupies Valtelline (to 1637).
	Franco–Swedish alliance fortified.
	France declares war on Spain.
	Peace of Prague in Germany.
	Truce of Stuhmsdorf extends Truce of Altmark for 26 years.
	Dutch establish base on Formosa.
	Louis XIII hires Bernhard von Sachsen-Weimar.
1636	Sweden surrenders Mainz.
	Ferdinand II declares war on France.
	Treaty of Wismar formally allies Sweden with France.
	Army of Flanders invades France.
	Imperial Army invades Burgundy.
	Croquant revolt.
	Regensburg Diet.
	Battle of Wittstock: Swedes defeat Imperials.
	Dutch establish colony on Ceylon.
	Ferdinand III elected king of the Romans.
1637	Swedes retreat to Torgau.
	Ferdinand II dies, succeeded by Ferdinand III.
	Revolt in Valtelline and Spanish occupation.
	Swedish Army withdraws to Pomerania.
	Christianity prohibited in Japan; Kirishitan slaughtered, move underground.
	Dutch expel Portuguese from Gold Coast.
	English trade with China begins, at Canton.
	France intervenes in Catalonia.
	Breda falls to United Provinces.
1638	Battle of Rheinfelden: Bernhard von Sachsen-Weimar defeats Johann von Werth.
	France and Sweden renew alliance.
	English fortify factories in Africa.
	Louis XIV born.
	Third Ottoman siege of Baghdad takes city.
	Bernhard von Sachsen-Weimar captures Breisach.
1639	Battle of Chemnitz: Saxons defeated by Swedes.
	Sweden invades Bohemia.
	First Bishops' War begins.

Bernhard von Sachsen-Weimar dies; France seizes army and lands.

Ottoman conquest of Iraq.

Battle of The Downs: Sea Beggars destroy Spanish fleet, block reinforcements.

Revolt in Normandy.

1640   Revolt in Catalonia (to 1652).

France occupies part of Alsace.

Georg Wilhelm dies; Friedrich Wilhelm succeeds in Brandenburg.

Massacre of Protestants in Ulster.

Revolt of Portugal (to 1668).

1641   Catalans accept French protectorate.

Banér dies.

Swedish Army mutinies.

Netherlands and Portugal sign anti-Spanish alliance.

France and Sweden deepen alliance, to end of war (1648).

Dutch occupy Angola (to 1648).

1642   Brunswick departs the German war.

First English Civil War begins.

Swedes occupy Saxony, invade Moravia.

French found fortified settlement at Montréal, New France.

Battle of Edgehill: Parliament defeated by Cavaliers.

Second Breitenfeld: Imperials beaten by Swedes.

1643   Olivares loses power.

Sweden invades Denmark, starting Torstensson's War (to 1645).

Battle of Rocroi: the Great Condé defeats Army of Flanders.

Louis XIII dies; Louis XIV, age five, succeeds.

Peace talks begin at Münster and Osnabrück (to 1648).

Tüttlingen: Armeé d'Allemagne defeated by Bavarian-Imperial army.

1644   Battle of Marston Moor: Roundheads and Scots defeat Cavaliers.

Battle of Freiburg: Franz von Mercy defeated by the Great Condé and Turenne.

French occupy rest of Alsace.

Pope Urban VIII dies, succeeded by Innocent X.

Manchus overthrow Ming dynasty, establish Qing Empire.

1645   Battle of Jankov: Imperials defeated by Swedes.

Battle of Mergentheim: Franz von Mercy defeats Turenne.

French take 10 towns in Spanish Netherlands.

Crete besieged by Ottomans (to 1669).

New Model Army funded by Parliament.

Battle of Naseby: Charles I defeated by Fairfax and Cromwell.

Michael Romanov dies.

Peace of Brömsebro ends Torstensson's War.

Battle of Allerheim: Bavarian-Imperial army defeated by French and Hessians.

Westphalian delegates meet in full session for first time.

Saxony and Sweden make separate peace.

1646 Dutch diplomats arrive in Münster.

Charles I surrenders to Scots; end of First English Civil War.

France and the Holy Roman Empire agree to provisional peace.

French retake Dunkirk.

1647 Spain and the Netherlands agree to truce.

France and Bavaria agree to truce.

Charles I sold to Parliament by Scots.

Revolt of Sicily.

Revolt of Naples.

Spain declares another bankruptcy.

1648 First Treaty of Münster ends Eighty Years' War.

Second English Civil War begins.

The Frondes begin in France.

Cossacks revolt in Ukraine (to 1654).

Battle of Zusmarshausen: Bavarians defeated by French.

Battle of Batoh: Polish Quarter Army defeated by Cossacks.

Sweden and the Empire agree to preliminary peace.

Battle of Lens: Spanish defeated by French.

Treaty of Osnabrück and Second Treaty of Münster end Thirty Years' War.

1649 Bavaria evacuated by French and Swedes.

Charles I tried for treason, executed.

Cromwell in Ireland.

Imperial cities accept toleration.

1650 Congress of Nuremberg sets demobilization schedule for troop withdrawals from Germany.

Military settlement of Thirty Years' War completed.

SELECTED BIBLIOGRAPHY

Contemporary Sources and Published Documents

d'Albuquerque, Alfonso. *Commentaries of the Great Alfonso d'Albuquerque*, Walter Birch, trans. (1877).

Andrews, Kenneth, ed. *English Privateering Voyages to the West Indies, 1588–1595: Documents* (1986).

Babur. *The Babur-nama in English*, Susannah Beveridge, trans. (1921).

Balbi, F. *The Siege of Malta*, E. Bradford, trans. (1965).

Barbao, Nicolò. *The Diary of the Siege of Constantinople, 1453*, J. R. Melville Jones, trans. (1969).

Barret, Robert. *Theorike and Practike of Moderne Warres* (1598).

Beneke, G. *Germany in the Thirty Years' War* (1978).

Bingham, John. *The Tacktics of Aelien* (1616).

Bourne, William. *The Arte of Shooting in Great Ordnance* (1587).

Champlain, Samuel. *The Voyages of Samuel de Champlain*, C. Pomeroy, trans. (1880).

Cortés, Hernán. *Letters from Mexico* (1971).

Cromwell, Oliver. *The Writings and Speeches of Oliver Cromwell*, 4 vols., W. Abbot, ed. (1937).

De Fuentez, P. *The Conquistadores: First-Person Accounts of the Conquest of Mexico* (1963).

Díaz del Castillo, B. *The True History of the Conquest of Mexico*, 5 vols. (1908–1916).

du Bellay, Martin. *Discipline Militaire* (1548).

Du Praissac, Lord. *A Short Method for the Easie Resolving of any Militarie Question Propounded*, John Cruso, trans. (1639).

Evans, John, ed. *The Works of Sir Roger Williams* (1972).

Fallon, Robert, ed. *The Christian Soldier: Religious Tracts Published for Soldiers on Both Sides during and after the English Civil Wars, 1642–1648* (2003).

Fletcher, Giles. *Of the Russe Commonwealth*, Richard Pipes, ed. (1966).

Gheyn, Jacob de. *Exercise of Armies for Calivres, Muskettes, and Pikes* (1607), J. Kist, trans. (1971).

Giraud, J. *Documents pour servir à l'histoire de l'armement au moyen âge et à la Renaissance*, 2 vols. (1895; 1899).

Hale, J. R., ed. *Certain Discourses Military, by Sir John Smythe* (1590).

Selected Bibliography

Henning, S. *Soloman Henning's Chronicle of Courland and Livonia*, V. Zeps, ed. (1992).

Hogan, E., ed. *A History of the War in Ireland, 1641–1652*, 3 vols. (1879–1880).

Jones, J., trans. *The Siege of Constantinople, 1453: Seven Contemporary Accounts* (1972).

Kors, Alan, ed. *Witchcraft in Europe, 400–1700: A Documentary History* (2000).

Limm, Peter, ed. *The Thirty Years' War* (1984).

Lostal, Pierre de. *Le soldat françois* (1604).

Macauly, G. C., ed. *The Chronicles of Jean Froissart* (1904).

Machiavelli, Niccolò. *The Art of War*, Ellis Farnesworth, trans. (1965; 2003).

———. *The Prince* (1532).

Markham, Francis. *Five Decades of Epistles of Warre* (1622).

Markham, Gervase. *The Last Fight of the Revenge* (1598).

———. *The Souldiers Accidence* (1625).

———. *The Souldiers Exercise in Three Bookes* (1639; 1964).

———. *The Souldiers Grammar* (1627).

Massa, I. *A Short History of the Beginnings and Origins of These Present Wars in Muscovy, to the Year 1610*, G. E. Orchard, trans. (1982).

Monk, George. *Observations Upon Military and Political Affairs* (1671).

Monro, Robert. *Robert Munro, His Expedition with the Worthy Scots Regiment* (1637).

Pasek, J. C. *Memoirs of the Polish Baroque*, C. S. Leach, trans. (1976).

Potter, David. *The French Wars of Religion: Selected Documents* (1997).

Rich, Barnabe. *Farewell to Military Profession, 1581* (1959).

———. *The Pathway to Military Practice* (1587; 1969).

Richelieu, Armand de. *Les Papiers de Richelieu*, Vol. 1, *Section politique extérieure*, P. Gillon, ed. (1982).

———. *Lettres, Instructions, diplomatique et papiers d'etat du Cardinal de Richelieu*, 8 vols. (1853–1877).

Roberts, Keith, ed. *Military Discipline for the Young Artilleryman, by William Barrife* (1661; 1988).

Smythe, John. *Instructions, Observations, and Orders Mylitarie* (1598).

Soman, A., ed. *The Massacre of St. Bartholomew: Reappraisals and Documents* (1974).

Staden, H. *The Land and Government of Muscovy: A 16th Century Account*, T. Esper, trans. (1967).

Stegmann, Andre, ed. *Edits des guerres de religion* (1979).

Tincey, John, ed. *The Young Horseman, or Honest Plain-dealing Cavalier, by John Vernon* (1644; 1993).

Usherwood, Stephen, ed. *The Great Enterprise: History of the Spanish Armada* (1978).

Vauciennes, L. de. *Mémoires de ce qui c'est passé en Suède trés de dépêhes de Chanut*, 2 vols. (1677).

Ward, Robert. *Animadversions of Warre* (1639).

Williams, Roger. *A Briefe Discourse of Warre* (1590).

Young, Peter, ed. *Militarie Instructions for the Cavall'rie, by John Cruso* (1632; 1972).

Young, Peter et al., eds. *The Civil War* (1968).

Zarain. *A Relation of the Late Siege and Taking of the City of Babylon [Baghdad] by the Turks* (1639).

Zólkiewski, S. *Expedition to Moscow*, M. W. Stephen, trans. (1959).

Journals

American Historical Review

Archeological Journal

Archivum Ottomanicum
English Historical Review
European History Quarterly
European Studies Review
French Historical Studies
French History
Gladius
Historical Journal
History Today
International History Review
Islamic Quarterly
Journal of Arms and Armour Society
Journal of Asian Civilizations
Journal of Asian History
Journal of Ecclesiastical History
Journal of European Studies
Journal of Medieval History
Journal of Medieval Military History
Journal of Military History
Journal of Modern History
Journal of World History
The Mariner's Mirror
Military Affairs
Military History Quarterly
Modern Asian Studies
Past and Present
Proceedings of the Huguenot Society of London
Renaissance Studies
Revue d'histoire moderne et contemporaine
Revue du nord
Revue historique
Russian History
Scandinavian Journal of History
Scottish Historical Review
Sixteenth Century Journal
Studies in Medieval and Renaissance History
Technology and Culture
Turcica
Viator
War and Society
War in History
World History Bulletin

General Histories

Cambridge History of Africa, Vol. 3, Roland Oliver, ed. (1977).
Cambridge History of China, Vol. 7, *Ming Dynasty* (1988).
Cambridge History of Early Inner Asia, Denis Sinor, ed. (1990).
Cambridge History of India (1922).

Selected Bibliography

Cambridge History of Iran, Vol. 6, *Timurid and Safavid Periods* (1986).

Cambridge History of Islam, 2 vols. (1970). P. M. Holt, Ann K. S. Lambton, and Bernard Lewis, eds.

Cambridge History of Japan, Vol. 4, *Early Modern Japan* (1991). John W. Hall et al., gen. eds.

New Cambridge History of India, Vol. 1, *The Portuguese in India* (1987). Gordon Johnson, gen. ed.

Oxford History of Britain, rev. ed., Kenneth O. Morgan, ed. (2001).

Oxford History of Christianity, John McManners, ed. (1993).

Oxford History of India, 4th ed., Percival Spear, ed. (1981).

Oxford History of Islam, John Esposito, ed. (1999).

Oxford History of Italy, George Holmes, ed. (1997).

Oxford History of Medieval Europe, George Holmes, ed. (1992).

Oxford History of the British Empire, Vol. 1, W. Roger Lewis, ed. (1998).

Oxford History of the Crusades, Jonathan Riley-Smith, ed. (1999).

Selected Secondary Works

Battles

Books

Ayton, Andrew, and Philip Preston. *The Battle of Crécy, 1346* (2005).

Creasy, Edward. *Fifteen Decisive Battles of the World: Marathon to Waterloo* (1851; 1992).

Davis, Paul. *100 Decisive Battles: Ancient Times to the Present* (1999).

Eggenberger, David. *An Encyclopedia of Battles, 1479 B.C. to the Present* (1985).

Fuller, J.F.C. *A Military History of the Western World*, Vols. 1 and 2 (1954; 1955).

Guthrie, William. *Battles of the Thirty Years War* (2002).

Keegan, John. *The Face of Battle* (1976).

Koustam, Angus. *Pavia 1525: Climax of the Italian Wars* (1996).

Liddell Hart, Basil. *Great Captains Unveiled* (1927; 1996).

Lynn, John A. *Battle* (2003).

Mackenzie, W. M. *The Battle of Bannockburn* (1913).

McCoy, G. *Irish Battles* (1990).

Morgan, Hiram. *The Battle of Kinsale* (2004).

Pratt, Fletcher. *Battles that Changed the History* (1956).

Wailly, Henri de. *Crécy, 1346: Anatomy of a Battle* (1987).

Whistler, Catherine. *The Battle of Pavia* (2003).

Woolrych, Austin. *Battles of the English Civil War* (1991).

War and Society: Africa

Article

Law, R. "Horses, Firearms, and Political Power in Pre-colonial West Africa," *Past and Present* (1976).

Books

Ajayi, J.F.A., and Michael Crowder, eds. *History of West Africa*, 2 vols. (1974).

Black, Jeremy. *War and the World: Military Power and the Fate of Continents, 1450–2000* (2002).

Bovill, E. W. *The Caravans of the Old Sahara* (1933).
——. *The Golden Trade of the Moors*, new ed. (1968).
Choueiri, Youssef M. *Arab Nationalism: A History* (2000).
Conrad, David. *The Songhay Empire* (1998).
Cook, Weston. *The Hundred Years' War for Morocco: Gunpowder and the Military Revolution in the Early Modern Muslim World* (1994).
Daaku, K. Y. *Trade and Politics on the Gold Coast, 1600–1720* (1970).
Davis, D. *The Problem of Slavery in Western Culture* (1966).
Earle, Peter. *The Corsairs of Malta and Barbary* (1970).
Hassan, Y. F. *The Arabs and the Sudan* (1967).
Hess, A. *The Forgotten Frontier: A History of the 16th Century Ibero-African Frontier* (1978).
Klein, Herbert. *The Atlantic Slave Trade* (1999).
Last, Murray. *The Sokoto Caliphate* (1967).
Law, R. *The Horse in West African History* (1980).
Lovejoy, Paul. *Transformations in Slavery* (1983).
Nasr, J. Abun. *A History of the Maghreb* (1971).
Newbury, C. W. *The Western Slave Coast and its Rulers* (1961).
Northrup, David. *The Atlantic Slave Trade* (1994).
Oliver, Roland, and Anthony Atmore. *Medieval Africa 1250–1800* (2001).
Oliver, Roland, and J. D. Fage. *A Short History of Africa* (1962; 1995).
Petry, Carl. *Protectors or Praetorians? The Last Mamluk Sultans and Egypt's Waning as a Great Power* (1994).
Phillip, Thomas, and Ulrich Haarmaan, eds. *The Mamluks in Egyptian Politics and Society* (1998).
Phillipson, David. *Ancient Ethiopia* (1998).
Pipes, Daniel. *Slave Soldiers and Islam: Genesis of a Military System* (1981).
Popper, William. *Egypt and Syria under the Circassian Sultans, 1382–1468*, 2 vols. (1955–1957).
Ryder, Allan. *Benin and the Europeans, 1485–1897* (1969).
Sellassie, Sergew. *Ancient and Medieval Ethiopia* (1972).
Smith, Robert. *Warfare & Diplomacy in Pre-Colonial West Africa* (1989).
Thornton, John K. *Africa and Africans in the Making of the Atlantic World, 1400–1680* (1998).
——. *Kingdom of the Kongo: Civil War and Transition, 1641–1718* (1983).
——. *Warfare in Atlantic Africa, 1500–1800* (1999).
Vansina, Jan. *Kingdoms of the Savannah* (1966).

War and Society: The Americas

Articles and Chapters

Clendinnen, Inga. "Fierce and Unnatural Cruelty: Cortés and the Conquest of Mexico," in Stephen Greenblatt, ed., *New World Encounters* (1993).
Eccles, W. J. "The History of New France According to Francis Parkman," *William and Mary Quarterly*, 18/2 (1961).
Hirsch, A. "The Collision of Military Cultures in 17th Century New England," *Journal of American History*, 74 (1997/1998).
Raudzens, G. "Why Did Amerindian Defenses Fail?" *War in History*, 3/2 (1996).
Richter, D. "War and Culture: The Iroquois Experience," *William and Mary Quarterly*, 40 (1983).

Selected Bibliography

Books

Axtel, J. *Beyond 1492* (1992).

Beck, Roger B. *Christian Missionaries and European Expansion, 1450 to the Present* (1999).

Beeching, Jack. *An Open Path: Christian Missionaries, 1515–1914* (1980).

Black, Jeremy. *War and the World: Military Power and the Fate of Continents, 1450–2000* (2002).

Boxer, Charles Ralph. *The Dutch in Brazil* (1957; 1973).

———. *Four Centuries of Portuguese Expansion* (1961).

———. *The Portuguese Seaborne Empire* (1969).

Bradford, Burns E. *A History of Brazil* (1970).

———. *Latin America: A Concise Interpretive History*, 6th ed. (1994).

Brading, D. A. *The First America: The Spanish Monarchy, Creole Patriots, and the Liberal State, 1492–1867* (1991).

Bradley, Peter. *The Lure of Peru: Maritime Intrusion into the South Sea, 1598–1701* (1989).

Brundage, B. *A Rain of Darts: The Mexican Aztecs* (1972).

Carman, Philip. *Lost Paradise: The Jesuit Republic in South America* (1976).

Clendinnen, Inga. *The Aztecs* (1991).

Conrad, Geoffrey, and Arthur Demarest. *Religion and Empire: The Dynamics of Aztec and Inca Expansionism* (1984).

Cook, Noble. *Born to Die: Disease and New World Conquest, 1492–1650* (1998).

Davidson, Miles H. *Columbus Then and Now* (1997).

Davies, Nigel. *The Aztec Empire* (1987).

Diamond, Jared. *Guns, Germs and Steel* (1997).

Eccles, W. J. *The Canadian Frontier, 1534–1760* (1969).

———. *The French in North America, 1500–1783* (1998).

Ferling, J. *A Wilderness of Miseries: War and Warriors in Early America* (1980).

Fernández-Armesto, Felipe. *Columbus* (1991).

Fisher, John. *Economic Aspects of Spanish Imperialism in America* (1997).

Hassig, Ross. *Aztec Warfare* (1988).

———. *Mexico and the Spanish Conquest* (1995).

Hemming, John. *Red Gold: The Conquest of the Brazilian Indians* (1978).

Hoffman, P. *The Spanish Crown and Defense of the Caribbean, 1535–1585* (1980).

Hulme, Peter. *Colonial Encounters: Europe and the Caribbean, 1492–1797* (1986).

Jennings, F. *The Ambiguous Iroquois Empire* (1984).

———. *The Invasion of America: Indians, Colonialism, and the Cant of Conquest* (1975).

Kicza, John, ed. *The Indian in Latin American History* (1993).

Leon-Portilla, M. *Broken Spears: The Aztec Account of the Conquest of Mexico* (1966).

Lockhart, J. *We People Here: Nahuatl Accounts of the Conquest of Mexico* (1993).

Lunenfeld, Martin. *1492: Discovery, Invasion, Encounter* (1991).

Malone, Patrick. *The Skulking Way of War: Technology and Tactics among the New England Indians* (1991).

Naylor, R. T. *Canada in the European Age, 1453–1919* (1988).

Patterson, Thomas C. *The Inca Empire* (1991).

Phillips, William, and Carla Rahn. *The Worlds of Christopher Columbus* (1992).

Quinn, Frederick. *The French Overseas Empire* (2000).

Richter, D. *The Ordeal of the Longhouse: Peoples of the Iroquois League in the Era of European Colonization* (1992).

Salisbury, N. *Manitou and Providence* (1982).

Starkey, A. *European and Native American Warfare* (1998).

Steele, Ian. *Warpaths: Invasions of North America* (1994).

Thomas, Hugh. *Conquest: Montezuma, Cortés, and the Fall of Old Mexico* (1994).

Townsend, Richard. *The Aztecs* (1990; 2000).

Trigger, B. *The Children of Aataentsic: History of the Huron Peoples to 1660*, 2 vols. (1976).

Vaughan, A. *The New England Frontier: Puritans and Indians, 1620–1675* (1965).

Watts, David. *The West Indies* (1987).

Webb, Stephen. *Governors General: The English Army and the Definition of Empire, 1569–1681* (1979).

Weber, D. *The Spanish Frontier in North America* (1992).

Wood, Michael. *The Conquistadors* (2001).

War and Society: Ottoman Empire and Asia

Articles and Chapters

Agoston, Gábor. "Gunpowder for the Sultan's Army," *Turcica*, 23 (1993).

———. "Ottoman Artillery and European Military Technology in the 15th–17th Centuries," *Acta Orientalia Acadediae Scientiarum Hungaricae*, 47 (1994).

Brown, Delmer. "The Impact of Firearms on Japanese Warfare, 1543–1598," *Far Eastern Quarterly*, 7 (1948).

Collins, L. "Military Organization and Tactics of the Crimean Tatars, 16th–17th Centuries," in V. J. Parry and M. Yapp, eds., *War, Technology, and Society in the Middle East* (1975).

Cook, Theodore. "The Mongol Invasion," *Military History Quarterly*, 11/2 (1998).

Dryer, Edward. "The Military Origins of Ming China," in *Cambridge History of China*, Vol. 7 (1988).

Fall, Bernard. "2000 Years of War in Vietnam," *Horizon* (1967).

Finkel, C. "The Costs of Ottoman Warfare and Defense," *Byzantinische Forschungen*, 16 (1991).

Gommens, J. "The Silent Frontier of South Asia, 1100–1800," *Journal of World History*, 9 (1998).

Goodrich, L. C., and Chia-Sheng. "Early Development of Firearms in China," *Isis*, 35 (1944).

Grant, Jonathan. "Rethinking the Ottoman 'Decline': Military Technology Diffusion in the Ottoman Empire, 15th–18th Centuries," *Journal of World History*, 10 (1999).

Guilmartin, John. "Ideology and Conflict: The Wars of the Ottoman Empire, 1453–1606," *Journal of Interdisciplinary History*, 18 (1988).

Heesterman, Jan. "The Hindu Frontier," *Itinerario*, 13 (1989).

———. "Warrior, Peasant, and Brahmin," *Modern Asian Studies*, 29 (1995).

Hess, A. "The Ottoman Conquest of Egypt," *International Journal of Middle East Studies*, 4 (1973).

Huang, Yi-Long. "Military Expenditures in 16th Century Ming China," *Oriens Extremus*, 17 (1970).

Inalcik, H. "Military and Fiscal Transformation in the Ottoman Empire, 1600–1700," *Archivum Ottomanicum*, 6 (1980).

———. "Ottoman Methods of Conquest," *Studia Islamica*, 2 (1954).

Iqtidar, Alam. "The Coming of Gunpowder to the Islamic World and North India," *Journal of Asian History*, 30 (1996).

———. "Early Use of Cannon and Musket in India, 1442–1526," *Journal of the Economic and Social History of the Orient*, 24 (1981).

———. "Origin and Development of Gunpowder Technology in India, 1250–1500," *Indian Historical Review*, 4 (1977).

Kaldy-Nagy, G. "The Holy War (Jihad) in the First Centuries of the Ottoman Empire," *Harvard Ukrainian Studies*, 3–4 (1979–1980).

Lal, K. "Striking Power of the Army of the Sultanate," *Journal of Indian History*, 55 (1977).

Latham, J. "The Archers of the Middle East," *Iran*, 8 (1970).

Lockhart, Lawrence. "The Persian Army in the Safavid Period," *Der Islam*, 34 (1959).

Morillo, David. "Guns and Government: A Comparative Study of Europe and Japan," *Journal of World History* (1995).

Murphey, Rhoads. "Horsebreeding in Eurasia," *Central and Inner Asian Studies*, 4 (1990).

———. "Ottoman Resurgence in the 17th Century Mediterranean," *Mediterranean Historical Review*, 8 (1993).

———. "An Ottoman View from the Top," *Turcica*, 28 (1996).

Nadvi, S. "The Use of Cannon in Muslim India," *Islamic Culture*, 12 (1938).

Nicolle, David. "The Impact of the European Couched Lance on Muslim Military Tradition," *Journal of Arms and Armour Society*, 10 (1980).

Patterson, W. P. "Archers of Islam," *Journal of Economic and Social History of the Orient*, 9 (1966).

———. "Archery in Moghul India," *Islamic Quarterly*, 16 (1972).

Serruys, Henry. "The Mongols in China: 1400–1450," *Monumenta Serica*, 27 (1968).

———. "The Mongols in China during the Hongwu Period, 1368–1398," *Melanges Chinois et Bouddhiques*, 11 (1959).

Smith, John Masson. "Ayn Jālūt: Mamluk Success or Mongol Failure?" *Harvard Journal of Asiatic Studies*, 44 (1984).

———. "Nomads on Ponies vs. Slaves on Horses," *Journal of American Oriental Society*, 118 (1998).

Sugar, P. "A Near-Perfect Military Society: The Ottoman Empire," in L. Farrar, ed., *War* (1978).

Thompson, William. "The Military Superiority Thesis and the Ascendancy of Western Eurasia in the World System," *Journal of World History*, 10 (1999).

Van de Ven, Hans. "Military Mobilization in 17th and 18th Century China, Russia, and Mongolia," *Modern Asian Studies*, 30 (1996).

Waldron, Arthur. "Chinese Strategy from the 14th to the 17th Centuries," in William Murray et al., eds., *Making of Strategy: Rulers, States, and War* (1994).

Yar Khan, Muhammad. "Use of Artillery during the Sultanate Period," *Islamic Culture*, 35 (1961).

Zaman, M. "Use of Artillery in Mughal Warfare," *Islamic Culture*, 57 (1983).

Books

Adshead, S.A.M. *Central Asia in World History* (1994).

Alam, Muzaffar, and Sanjay Subrahmanyan. *The Mughal State, 1526–1750* (1998).

Allsen, Thomas. *Mongol Imperialism* (1987).

Amitai-Preiss, Reuven. *Mongols and Mamluks* (1995).

Amitai-Preiss, Reuven, and David Morgan, eds. *The Mongol Empire and its Legacy* (1999).

Arjomand, Said. *The Shadow of God and the Hidden Imam* (1984).

Ayalon, David. *Eunuchs, Caliphs and Sultans* (1999).

———. *Gunpowder and Firearms in the Mamluk Kingdom* (1956).

———. *Islam and the Abode of War: Military Slaves and Islamic Adversaries* (1994).

———. *Mamlūks and Naval Power: The Struggle Between Islam and Christian Europe* (1965).

———. *Outsiders in the Lands of Islam: Mamluks, Mongols, and Eunuchs* (1988).

Babinger, F. *Mehmed the Conqueror and His Time*, Ralph Manheim, trans. (1978).

Barfield, Thomas. *The Perilous Frontier: Nomadic Empires and China* (1989).

Basham, A. L. *The Origins and Development of Classical Hinduism* (1989).

———. *The Wonder That Was India* (1963).

Beasley, W. G. *The Japanese Experience: A Short History of Japan* (2000).

———. *The Rise of Modern Japan*, 2nd ed. (1995).

Beckwith, Christopher. *The Tibetan Empire in Central Asia* (1987).

Berry, Elizabeth. *The Culture of Civil War in Kyoto* (1992).

———. *Hideyoshi* (1982).

Bhakari, S. *Indian Warfare: Strategy and Tactics in the Early-Medieval Period* (1981).

Black, Jeremy. *War and the World: Military Power and the Fate of Continents, 1450–2000* (2002).

Bomati, Yves, and Houchang Nahavandi. *Shah Abbas, Empereur de Perse, 1587–1629* (1998).

Boxer, Charles Ralph. *The Dutch Seaborne Empire* (1965).

———, ed. *Portuguese Commerce and Conquest in Southern Asia, 1500–1750* (1985).

———. *The Portuguese Seaborne Empire, 1415–1825* (1969).

———, ed. *South China in the 16th Century* (1953).

Calmard, Jean, ed. *Etudes Safavides* (1993).

Canfield, Robert. *Turko-Persia in Historical Perspective* (1991).

Chan, A. *The Glory and Fall of the Ming Dynasty* (1982).

Chaudhuri, K. *Asia before Europe* (1990).

Clot, André. *Suleiman the Magnificent: The Man, His Life, His Epoch* (1992).

Cosomo, Nicola. *Warfare in Inner Asian History, 500–1800* (2002).

Crone, Patricia. *Slaves on Horses: The Evolution of Islamic Polity* (1980).

Crossley, Pamela. *The Manchus* (1997).

Dávid, Géza, and Pál Fodor, eds. *Hungarian-Ottoman Military and Diplomatic Relations in the Age of Süleyman the Magnificent* (1994).

Davidson, Roderic H. *Turkey: A Short History*, 3rd ed. (1998).

De Bary, William T., ed. *The Buddhist Tradition in India, China, and Japan* (1972).

———. *The Trouble with Confucianism* (1991).

de Silva, Chandra. *Sri Lanka: A History*, 2nd rev. ed. (1997).

Digby, Simon. *Warhorse and Elephant in the Delhi Sultanate* (1971).

Djévad, Ahmed. *Etat Militaire Ottoman*, Vol. 1: *Les Corps des Janissaires* (1882).

Eaton, Richard. *The Rise of Islam and the Bengal Frontier, 1204–1760* (1993).

Eber, Irene. *Confucianism* (1986).

Elison, George, and B. Smith. *Warlords, Artists, and Commoners: Japan in the 16th Century* (1981).

Esin, E. *The Age of Sultan Süleyman the Magnificent* (1987).

Farris, William. *Heavenly Warriors: The Evolution of Japan's Military, 500–1300* (1992).

Fodor, Pál, and Géza Dávid, eds. *Ottomans, Hungarians, and Habsburgs in Central Europe: The Military Confines in the Era of Ottoman Conquest* (2000).

Fowler, Jeaneane. *Hinduism: Beliefs and Practices* (1997).

Friday, Karl. *Hired Swords: The Rise of Private Warfare in Early Japan* (1992).

Gabrielli, F. *Muhammad and the Conquests of Islam* (1968).

Gascoigne, Bamber. *The Great Moghuls* (1971).

Gernet, Jaques. *China and the Christian Impact* (1985).

Glamann, Kristof. *The Dutch-Asiatic Trade* (1958).

Goodwin, Godfrey. *The Janissaries* (1995).

Goodwin, Jason. *Lords of the Horizons: A History of the Ottoman Empire* (1999).

Grew, Raymond. *Food in Global History* (1999).

Grewal, J. S. *The Sikhs of the Punjab*, rev. ed. (1998).

Groot, A. *The Ottoman Empire and the Dutch Republic, 1610–1630* (1978).

Haider, Syed. *Islamic Arms and Armour of Muslim India* (1991).

Halecki, O. *The Borderlands of Western Civilization* (1952).

Hall, J. et al., eds. *Japan before Tokugawa* (1981).

Hallissey, Robert. *The Rajput Rebellion Against Aurangzeb* (1977).

Har-el, Shai. *The Struggle for Domination in the Middle East: The Ottoman-Mamluk War, 1485–1491* (1995).

Hartog, Leo de. *Ghengis Khan, Conqueror of the World* (1989).

Henthorn, William. *Korea: The Mongol Invasions* (1963).

Hillenbrand, Carole. *The Crusades: Islamic Perspectives* (2000).

Hinago, Motoo. *Japanese Castles* (1986).

Hodgson, Marshall. *The Classical Age of Islam* (1974).

——. *The Expansion of Islam* (1974).

——. *Gunpowder Empires and Modern Times* (1974).

——. *Rethinking World History* (1993).

——. *The Venture of Islam*, 3 vols. (1958–1961).

Holt, P. M. *The Age of the Crusades* (1986).

——. *Egypt and the Fertile Crescent, 1516–1922* (1966).

Hourani, Albert. *A History of the Arab Peoples* (1997).

Hucker, Charles. *China's Imperial Past* (1975).

Ikegami, Eiko. *The Taming of the Samurai* (1995).

Imber, Colin. *The Ottoman Empire, 1300–1650* (2002).

Inalcik, H. *The Ottoman Empire: The Classical Age, 1300–1600* (1973).

——. *The Ottoman Empire: Conquest, Organization and Economy* (1978).

——. *Süleyman the Second and His Times* (1993).

Irvine, W. *The Army of the Indian Mughals* (1903).

Jackson, Peter. *The Delhi Sultanate: Political and Military History* (1999).

Jagchid, Sechin, and Luc Kwanten. *Imperial Nomads: A History of Central Asia, 500–1500* (1979).

Jagchid, Sechin, and V. J. Symons. *Peace, War, and Trade Along the Great Wall* (1989).

Jankovich, Miklós. *They Rode into Europe* (1971).

Johnson, James T., and John Kelsey. *Cross, Crescent and Sword* (1990).

Kaeppelin, P. *La Compagnie des Indes Orientales* (1908).

Kafadar, Cemal. *Between Two Worlds: Construction of the Ottoman State* (1995).

Karsh, Efraim. *Empires of the Sand* (1999).

Keay, John. *India: A History* (2000).

Kennedy, Hugh. *The Armies of the Caliphs* (2001).

——. *The Prophet and the Age of the Caliphates* (1986).

Kiernan, Frank, and John Fairbanks. *Chinese Ways in Warfare* (1974).

Kolff, Dirk. *Naukar, Rajput, and Sepoy* (1990).

Koprulu, Mehmet. *The Seljuks of Anatolia*, Gary Leiser, trans. (1992).

Kortepeter, C. M. *Ottoman Imperialism during the Reformation* (1992).

Kunt, Metin, and Christine Woodhead, eds. *Suleyman the Magnificent and His Age* (1995).

Lamers, Jeroen. *Japonius Tyrannus: The Japanese Warlord Oda Nobunaga Reconsidered* (2000).

Langlois, J., ed. *China under Mongol Rule* (1981).

Lawson, Philip. *The East India Company* (1993).

Lewis, Bernard. *Arabs in History* (1966).

———. *The Assassins: A Radical Sect in Islam* (1967; 2002).

———. *The Middle East* (1995).

———. *The Muslim Discovery of Europe* (1982).

Liu, Xinru. *Ancient India and Ancient China: Trade and Religious Exchanges* (1994).

Lyons, M. C., and D. Jackson. *Saladin: Politics of the Holy War* (1982).

Maalouf, Amin. *The Crusades Through Arab Eyes* (1984).

Manz, Beatrice. *The Rise and Rule of Tamerlane* (1999).

Matar, Nabil. *Turks, Moors, and Englishmen in the Age of Discovery* (1999).

McCarthy, Justin. *The Ottoman Turks* (1997).

McLeod, W. H. *Sikhism* (1997).

McMullen, N. *Buddhism and the State in 16th Century Japan* (1984).

McNeill, William H. *The Age of Gunpowder Empires, 1450–1800* (1999).

———. *Europe's Steppe Frontier, 1500–1800* (1964).

———. *Plagues and Peoples* (1977; 1998).

Melville, Charles, ed. *Safavid Persia* (1996).

Monshi, Eskandar Beg. *The History of Shah Abbas the Great*, Roger Savory, trans. (1978).

Morgan, David. *Medieval Persia, 1040–1797* (1988).

———. *The Mongols* (1993).

Mote, Frederick. *Imperial China, 900–1800* (2000).

Muldoon, James. *Empire and Order: The Concept of Empire, 800–1800* (1999).

Murphey, Rhoads. *Ottoman Warfare, 1500–1700* (1999).

Murphy, P., ed. *Holy War* (1976).

Nakane, Chie, and Shinzabur Oishi, eds. *Tokugawa Japan* (1990).

Nicolle, David. *The Janissaries* (1995).

Nouzille, J. *Histoire de Frontières: l'Autriche et l'empire Ottoman* (1991).

Olmstead, A. T. *History of the Persian Empire*, 2nd ed. (1969).

Ostrowski, Donald. *Muscovy and the Mongols* (1998).

Pagden, Anthony. *Lords of All the World* (1995).

Paludan, Ann. *Chronicle of the Chinese Emperors* (1998).

Parry, V., and M. Yapp. *War, Technology and Society in the Middle East* (1975).

Parry, V. J. *A History of the Ottoman Empire to 1730* (1976).

Parsons, James. *The Peasant Rebellions of the Late Ming Dynasty* (1970).

Pearson, M. N. *Port Cities and Intruders: The Swahili Coast, India, and Portugal in the Early Modern Era* (1998).

———. *The Portuguese in India* (1987).

Perrin, Noel. *Giving Up the Gun: Japan's Reversion to the Sword, 1543–1879* (1979).

Selected Bibliography

Pomeranz, Kenneth. *The Great Divergence: Europe, China, and the Making of the Modern World Economy* (2000).

Ratchnevsky, Paul. *Ghengis Khan: His Life and Legacy* (1992).

Raychaudhuri, T. *Jan Company in Coromandel, 1605–1690* (1962).

Richards, John. *The Mughal Empire* (1993).

Roberts, J.A.G. *A Concise History of China* (1999).

Robinson, David. *Bandits, Eunuchs, and the Son of Heaven* (2001).

Robinson, R. H. *The Buddhist Religion*, 3rd ed. (1982).

Rossabi, Morris. *China and Inner Asia From 1368* (1975).

———. *Khubilai Khan* (1988).

Sansom, George. *A History of Japan, 1334–1615* (1961).

Sarkar, J. *The Art of War in Medieval India* (1984).

———. *Military History of India* (1970).

Savory, Roger. *Iran under the Safavids* (1980).

Saxena, R. *The Army of the Rajputs* (1989).

Sen, S. *The Military System of the Marathas* (1928).

Shaw, Stanford, and E. K. Shaw. *History of the Ottoman Empire and Modern Turkey*, Vol. 1 (1977).

Sinor, Denis. *Studies in Medieval Inner Asia* (1997).

So Kwan-wai. *Japanese Piracy in Ming China during the 16th Century* (1975).

Souchek, Svat. *A History of Inner Asia* (2000).

Spence, Jonathan. *The Search for Modern China* (1990).

Spence, Jonathan, and John Wills. *From Ming to Ch'ing* (1979).

Spruyt, J., and J. B. Robertson. *History of Indonesia*, rev. ed. (1973).

Srivastava, A. L. *The Mughal Empire, 1526–1803*, 6th ed. (1971).

Stein, Burton. *A History of India* (1998).

Stiles, A. *The Ottoman Empire, 1450–1700* (1989).

Stresusand, Douglas. *The Formation of the Mughal Empire* (1999).

Stripling, George. *The Ottoman Turks and the Arabs, 1511–1574* (1942; 1977).

Struve, Lynn. *The Southern Ming, 1644–1662* (1984).

Subrahmanyan, Sanjay. *The Portuguese Empire in Asia, 1500–1700* (1993).

Toby, R. *State and Diplomacy in Early Modern Japan* (1984).

Tong, James. *Disorder Under Heaven: Collective Violence in the Ming Dynasty* (1991).

Totman, Conrad. *Early Modern Japan* (1993).

———. *Tokugawa Ieyasu: Shogun* (1983).

Tsai, Shih-shan Henry. *Perpetual Happiness: The Ming Emperor Yongle* (2001).

Turnbull, Stephen. *The Samurai: A Military History* (1977).

———. *Samurai Warfare* (1996).

———. *War in Japan, 1467–1645* (2002).

Van de Ven, Hans, ed. *Warfare in Chinese History* (2000).

Varley, H. *The Ōnin War* (1994).

———. *Warriors of Japan* (1994).

Waldron, Arthur. *The Great Wall of China: From History to Myth* (1990).

Watts, Sheldon. *Epidemics and History* (1998).

Weber, H. *La Compagnie Française des Indes* (1904).

Weissmann, Nahoum. *Les Janissaires: Étude de l'Organisation Militaire des Ottomans* (1938).

Wheatcroft, Andrew. *The Ottomans* (1993).

Wink, A. *The Making of the Indo-Islamic World*, 2 vols. (1997).

Wolpert, Stanley. *A New History of India*, 6th ed. (2000).

War and Society: The Baltic

Articles and Chapters

Agren, K. "Rise and Decline of an Aristocracy: The Swedish Social and Political Elite in the 17th Century," *Scandinavia Journal of History*, 1 (1976).

Alberg, A. "The Swedish Army from Lutzen to Narva," in M. Roberts, ed., *Sweden's Age of Greatness, 1632–1718* (1973).

Böhme, K-R. "Building a Baltic Empire: Aspects of Swedish Expansion, 1550–1660," in G. Rystad et al., eds., *In Quest of Trade and Security: The Baltic in Power Politics, 1500–1990* (1994).

Jespersen, K.J.V. "Absolute Monarchy in Denmark," *Scandinavian Journal of History*, 12 (1987).

———. "The Rise and Fall of the Danish Nobility, 1600–1800," in H. M. Scott, ed., *The European Nobilities in the 17th and 18th Centuries* (1995).

Lind, G. "Military and Absolutism: The Army Officers of Denmark-Norway as a Social Group and Political Factor, 1660–1848," *Scandinavian Journal of History*, 12 (1987).

Lindegren, Jan. "The Swedish 'Military State,' 1560–1720," *Scandinavian Journal of History*, 10 (1985).

Lockhart, P. D. "Denmark and the Empire: A Reassessment of the Foreign Policy of King Christian IV, 1596–1648," *Scandinavian Studies*, 62 (1992).

Roberts, Michael. "Gustav Adolf and the Art of War," in Michael Roberts, *Essays in Swedish History* (1967).

———. "The Military Revolution, 1560–1660," in Michael Roberts, *Essays in Swedish History* (1967).

———. "Queen Christiana and the General Crisis of the 17th Century," in Michael Roberts, *Essays in Swedish History* (1967).

Troebst, S. "Debating the Mercantile Background to Early Modern Swedish Empire-Building," *European History Quarterly*, 24 (1994).

Viirankoski, P. "The Impact of Military Service on Finnish Rural Society in the 17th Century," *Turun Historiallinen Arkisto*, 38 (1982).

Books

Ahnlund, Nils. *Gustavus Adolphus the Great* (1940).

Andersson, Ingvar. *A History of Sweden* (1975).

Brondsted, J. B. *The Vikings* (1965).

Burleigh, M. *Prussian Society and the German Order, 1410–1466* (1984).

Carsten, F. L. *The Origins of Prussia* (1954).

Christiansen, E. *The Northern Crusades: The Baltic and the Catholic Frontier, 1100–1525* (1980).

Dodge, Theodore. *Gustavus Adolphus* (1895).

Dollinger, P. *The German Hansa* (1964; 1970).

Dow, J. *Ruthven's Army in Sweden and Estonia* (1965).

Fitzhugh, W. W., and E. I. Ward, eds. *The Vikings* (2000).

Foote, P., and D. M. Wilson. *The Viking Achievement* (1970).

Friedrich, K. *The Other Prussia: Poland, Prussia and Liberty, 1559–1772* (2000).

Frost, Robert. *The Northern Wars, 1558–1721* (2000).

Grell, Ole. *The Scandinavian Reformation* (1995).

Grosjean, Alexis. *An Unofficial Alliance: Scotland and Sweden, 1569–1654* (2003).

Hill, C. E. *The Danish Sound Dues and the Command of the Baltic* (1926; 1955).

Johannesson, K. *The Renaissance of the Goths in 16th Century Sweden* (1991).

Jones, Gwyn. *A History of the Vikings* (1968; 2001).

Kirby, D. *Northern Europe in the Early Modern Period: The Baltic World, 1492–1772* (1990).

Kirchner, W. *The Rise of the Baltic Question* (1954).

Koch, H. W. *A History of Prussia* (1978).

Lisk, J. *The Struggle for Supremacy in the Baltic, 1600–1725* (1967).

Lockhart, Paul. *Denmark in the Thirty Years' War, 1618–1648* (1996).

Oakley, S. *War and Peace in the Baltic, 1560–1790* (1992).

Ringmar, E. *Identity, Interest and Action: Sweden's Intervention in the Thirty Years' War* (1996).

Roberts, Michael. *Early Vasas: A History of Sweden, 1523–1611* (1968).

———. *Essays in Swedish History* (1967).

———. *Gustavus Adolphus* (1992).

———. *Gustavus Adolphus and the Rise of Sweden* (1973).

———. *Sweden as a Great Power, 1611–1697* (1968).

———, ed. *Sweden's Age of Greatness, 1632–1718* (1973).

———. *Swedish Diplomats at Cromwell's Court* (1988).

———. *The Swedish Imperial Experience, 1560–1718* (1979).

Roesdahl, Else. *The Vikings*, 2nd ed. (trans. 1998).

Rystad, G. et al., eds. *In Quest of Trade and Security: The Baltic in Power Politics, 1500–1990* (1994).

Sawyer, P. H. *The Age of the Vikings* (1972).

Stiles, A. *Sweden and the Baltic, 1523–1721* (1992).

War and Society: Eastern Europe and Muscovy

Articles and Chapters

Alef, G. "Muscovite Military Reforms in the Second Half of the 15th Century," *Forschungen zur Osteuropäschen Geschichte*, 18 (1973).

Crummey, R. "The Fate of the Boyar Clans, 1565–1613," *Forschungen zur Osteuropäschen Geschichte*, 38 (1986).

Davies, B. "Village into Garrison: The Militarized Peasant Communities of Southern Muscovy," *Russian Review*, 51 (1992).

Frost, R. I. "The Nobility of Poland-Lithuania, 1569–1795," in H. M. Scott, ed., *The European Nobilities in the 17th and 18th Centuries* (1995).

———. "Poland-Lithuania and the Thirty Years' War," in K. Bussmann and H. Schilling, eds., *War and Peace in Europe, 1618–1648* (1998).

Loewe, K. "Military Service in Early 16th Century Lithuania," *Slavic Review*, 30 (1971).

Paul, Michael. "The Military Revolution in Russia, 1550–1682," *Journal of Military History*, 68/1 (2004).

Poe, M. "Consequences of the Military Revolution in Muscovy," *Comparative Studies in Society and History*, 38 (1996).

Shaw, Dennis. "Southern Frontiers of Muscovy, 1550–1700," in James Bater and R. French, eds., *Studies in Russian Historical Geography* (1983).

Skrynnikov, R. G. "The Civil War in Russia at the Beginning of the 17th Century (1603–1607)," in L. Hughes, ed., *New Perspectives on Muscovite History* (1993).

Smith, D. L. "Muscovite Logistics, 1462–1598," *Slavonic and East European Studies Review*, 71 (1993).

Sysyn, F. "The Problem of Nobilities in the Ukrainian Past: The Polish Period, 1569–1648," in L. Rudnitsky, ed., *Rethinking Ukrainian History* (1981).

Books

Alef, Gustave. *Ruklers and Nobles in 15th Century Muscovy* (1983).

Bak, J. M., and R. Király, eds. *From Hunyadi to Rakocki: War and Society in Late Medieval and Early Modern Hungary* (1982).

Bartos, F. *The Hussite Revolution* (1986).

Brzezinski, R. *Polish Armies, 1559–1696*, 2 vols. (1987).

Bushkovitch, Paul. *Religion and Society in Russia: The 16th and 17th Centuries* (1992).

Crummey, Robert. *Aristocrats and Servitors: The Boyar Elite in Russia, 1613–1689* (1983).

———. *The Formation of Muscovy, 1304–1613* (1987).

Davies, Norman. *God's Playground: A History of Poland*, Vol. 1 (1981).

Fedorowicz, J. K., ed. *A Republic of Nobles: Studies in Polish History to 1864* (1982).

Finkel, C. *The Administration of Warfare: Ottoman Military Campaigns in Hungary, 1593–1606* (1988).

Friedrich, K. *The Other Prussia: Poland, Prussia and Liberty, 1559–1772* (2000).

Graham, Hugh F. *Ivan the Terrible* (1981).

Grey, Ian. *Ivan III and the Unification of Russia* (1964).

Halperin, Charles. *Russia and the Golden Horde* (1987).

Hellie, R. *Enserfment and Military Change in Muscovy* (1971).

Heyman, F. G. *Jan Zizka and the Hussite Revolution* (1955).

Hughes, Lindsay, ed. *New Perspectives on Muscovite History* (1993).

Kaminsky, Howard. *A History of the Hussite Revolution* (1967).

Keep, J. L. *Soldiers of the Tsar: Army and Society in Russia, 1462–1874* (1985).

Koch, H. W. *A History of Prussia* (1978).

Kollmann, N. S. *Kingship and Politics: The Making of the Muscovite Political System, 1345–1547* (1996).

Lieven, Dominic. *Empire: The Russian Empire and its Rivals* (2001).

Lincoln, W. Bruce. *The Conquest of a Continent: Siberia and the Russians* (1994).

Magosci, Paul. *A History of Ukraine* (1996).

Perjés, Géza. *The Fall of the Medieval Kingdom of Hungary: Mohács 1526–Buda 1541*, Mario Fenyó, trans. (1977; 1989).

Péter, K. et al., eds. *A History of Hungary* (1990).

Posnic, Roger, ed. *Histoire militaire de la Pologne* (1970).

Reddaway, W. et al., eds. *Cambridge History of Poland*, Vol. 1: *From the Origins to Sobieski* (1950).

Riasanovsky, Nicholas. *A History of Russia* (1984).

Rothenberg, G. *The Austrian Military Border in Croatia, 1522–1747* (1960).

Rudnitsky, L., ed. *Rethinking Ukrainian History* (1981).

Skrynnikov, R. G. *Boris Gudonov*, Hugh Graham, trans. (1982).

———. *Ivan the Terrible*, Hugh Graham, trans. (1981).

———. *The Time of Troubles*, Hugh Graham, trans. (1988).

Stavrianos, Leften. *The Balkans Since 1453* (1958).

Stevens, C. B. *Soldiers on the Steppe: Army Reform and Social Change in Early Modern Russia* (1995).

Subtelny, Orest. *Ukraine: A History* (2004).

Sugar, Peter. *Southeastern Europe under Ottoman Rule, 1354–1804* (1977).

Troyat, Henri. *Ivan the Terrible* (1984).

War and Society: Western Europe and the Mediterranean

Articles and Chapters

Allmand, C. T. "War and Profit in the Late Middle Ages," *History Today*, 15 (1965).

Antonucci, Michael. "Siege Without Reprieve," *Military History* (April 1992).

Baraude, Henri. "Le Siège d'Orleans et Jeanne d'Arc," in *Revue des questions historiques*, 80 (1906) and 81 (1907).

Benecke, G. "The Problem of Death and Destruction in Germany during the Thirty Years' War," *European Studies Review*, 2 (1972).

Benedict, Philip. "The Saint Bartholomew's Day Massacre in the Provinces," *Historical Journal* (1978).

Bossy, John. "The Counter-Reformation and the People of Catholic Europe," *Past and Present*, 47 (1970).

Brightwell, P. "Spain and Bohemia: The Decision to Intervene, 1619," *European Studies Review*, 12 (1982).

———. "Spanish Origins of the Thirty Years' War," *European Studies Review*, 9 (1979).

Brown, S. "The Mercenary and His Master," *History*, 74 (1989).

Carr, A. "Welshmen and the Hundred Years' War," *Welsh History Review*, 4 (1968).

Cogswell, T. "Foreign Policy and Parliament: The Case of La Rochelle, 1625–26," *English Historical Review*, 99 (1984).

Cowdery, H. E. "The Peace and the Truce of God," *Past and Present*, 46 (1970).

Curry, Anne. "English Armies in the Fifteenth Century," in A. Curry and M. Hughes, eds., *Armies and Fortifications in the Hundred Years War* (1994).

Davis, Natalie. "Rites of Violence: Religious Riots in 16th Century France," *Past and Present*, 59 (1973).

Dickson, G. "The Flagellants of 1260 and the Crusades," *Journal of Modern History*, 15 (1989).

Diefendorf, Barbara. "Prologue to a Massacre: Popular Unrest in Paris, 1557–1572," *American Historical Review*, 90 (1985).

Donagan, B. "Halcyon Days and the Literature of War: England's Military Education before 1642," *Past and Present*, 147 (1995).

Dukes, P. "The Leslie Family in the Swedish Period of the Thirty Years' War," *European Studies Review*, 12 (1982).

Eltis, David. "Towns and Defence in Later Medieval Germany," *Nottingham Medieval Studies* (1989).

Finó, J-F. "Les armées françaises lors de la guerre de cent ans," *Gladius*, 13 (1977).

Flynn, D. "Fiscal Crisis and the Decline of Spain," *Journal of Economic History*, 42 (1982).

Gaupp, F. "The Condottieri John Hawkwood," *History*, 23 (1938–1939).

Gentile, I. "Why Men Fought in the English Civil Wars, 1639–1651," *History Teacher*, 26 (1993).

Gilbert, F. "Machiavelli and the Renaissance of the Art of War," in E. M. Earle, ed., *Makers of Modern Strategy* (1952).

Grayson, J. "The Civic Militia in the County of Holland," *BMGN*, 95 (1981).

Greengrass, Mark. "The Later Wars of Religion in the French Midi," in P. Clark, ed., *The European Crisis of the 1590s* (1985).

Griffiths, G. "Saint Bartholomew Reappraised," *Journal of Modern History* (1976).

Hale, J. R. "War and Public Opinion in the 15th and 16th Centuries," *Past and Present*, 21 (1962).

Harari, Yuval. "Strategy and Supply in 14th Century Western European Invasion Campaigns," *Journal of Military History*, 64 (2000).

Hayden, J. "Continuity in the France of Henri IV and Louis XIII: French Foreign Policy, 1598–1615," *Journal of Modern History*, 45 (1973).

Hendrix, S. "Luther's Impact on the 16th Century," *Sixteenth Century Journal*, 16 (1985).

Henry, L. "The Earl of Essex and Ireland, 1599," *Bulletin of the Institute of Historical Research*, 32 (1959).

————. "The Earl of Essex as Strategist and Military Organizer (1596–97)," *English Historical Review*, 68 (1953).

Holt, Mack. "Putting Religion Back into the 'Wars of Religion,'" *French Historical Studies*, 18 (1993).

Israel, J. I. "Central European Jewry during the Thirty Years' War," *Central European History*, 16 (1993).

Jensen, D. "French Diplomacy and the Wars of Religion," *Sixteenth Century Journal*, 5 (1974).

Kamen, Henry. "The Decline of Spain: A Historical Myth?" *Past and Present*, 81 (1978).

————. "Economic Consequences of the Thirty Years' War," *Past and Present*, 39 (1968).

Kettering, Sharon. "Cleintage during the Wars of Religion," *Sixteenth Century Journal*, 20 (1989).

Kiernan, V. "Foreign Mercenaries and Absolute Monarchy," *Past and Present*, 11 (1957).

Kingdom, Robert. "Calvinism and Resistance Theory, 1550–1580," in *Cambridge History of Political Thought, 1450–1700* (1991).

Koenigsberger, H. "Orange, Granville, and Philip II," *BMGN*, 99 (1984).

Love, Ronald. "All the King's Horsemen: The Equestrian Army of Henry IV, 1585–1598," *Sixteenth Century Journal*, 22 (1991).

Lynn, John A. "How War Fed War: The Tax of Violence and Contributions during the *Grand Siècle*," *Journal of Modern History*, 65 (1993).

————. "Recalculating French Army Growth during the *Grand Siècle*, 1610–1715," in Clifford Rogers, ed., *The Military Revolution Debate* (1995).

————. "Tactical Evolution in the French Army, 1560–1660," *French Historical Studies*, 14 (1985).

Malcolm, J. "All the King's Men," *Irish Historical Studies*, 22 (1979).

Nicolle, David. "Medieval Warfare," *Journal of Military History*, 63 (1999).

Nusbacher, E. "Civil Supply in the Civil War," *English Historical Review* (2000).

Ogilvie, S. "Germany and the 17th Century Crisis," *Historical Journal*, 35 (1992).

Parker, Geoffrey. "The Making of Strategy in Habsburg Spain: Philip II's 'Bid for Mastery,'" in William Murray et al., eds., *The Making of Strategy: Rulers, States, and War* (1994).

————. "Soldiers of the Thirty Years' War," in K. Repgen, ed., *Krieg und Politik, 1618–1648* (1983).

Parrott, D. "Causes of the Franco-Spanish War of 1635–59," in J. Black, ed., *Origins of War in Early Modern Europe* (1987).

———. "Richelieu, the *Grands*, and the French Army," in Joseph Bergin and Laurence Brockliss, eds., *Richelieu and His Age* (1992).

———. "Strategy and Tactics in the Thirty Years' War," in Clifford Rogers, ed., *The Military Revolution Debate* (1995).

Peterson, David. "War of the Eight Saints," in William J. Connell, ed., *Society and Individual in Renaissance Florence* (2002).

Potter, D. "The International Mercenary Market in the 16th Century," *English Historical Review* (1996).

———. "Kingship in the Wars of Religion," *European History Quarterly*, 25 (1995).

Rabb, T. K. "The Effect of the Thirty Years' War on the German Economy," *Journal of Modern History*, 34 (1962).

Redlich, Fritz. "Contributions in the Thirty Years' War," *Economic History Review*, 12 (1959–1960).

Reinhard, W. "Reformation, Counter-Reformation, and the Early Modern State," *Catholic History Review*, 75 (1989).

Rogers, Clifford. "By Fire and Sword," in Clifford Rogers and Mark Grimsley, eds., *Civilians in the Path of War* (2002).

———. "Edward III and the Dialectics of Strategy, 1327–1360," *Transactions of the Royal Historical Society* (1994).

———. "Military Revolutions of the Hundred Years' War," *Journal of Military History*, 57 (1993).

———. "The Offensive/Defensive in Medieval Strategy, From Crecy to Mohacs," *Acta of the XXIInd Colloquium of the International Commission of Military History* (1997).

———. "The Scottish Invasion of 1346," *Northern History*, 34 (1998).

Salmon, J.H.M. "The Paris Sixteen," in J.H.M. Salmon, *Renaissance and Revolt* (1987).

Scot, Tom. "The Peasants' War," *Historical Journal*, 22 (1979).

Slutter, E. "Dutch-Spanish Rivalry in the Caribbean Area, 1594–1609," *Hispanic American Historical Review*, 28 (1948).

Stevenson, D. "Financing the Cause of the Covenanters, 1638–51," *Scottish Historical Review* (1972).

Storrs, C., and H. M. Scott. "The Military Revolution and the European Nobility, 1600–1800," *War in History*, 3 (1996).

Stradling, R. "Olivares and the Origins of the Franco-Spanish War, 1627–1635," *English Historical Review*, 101 (1986).

Sutherland, N. "Origins of the Thirty Years' War and the Structure of European Politics," *English Historical Review*, 107 (1992).

———. "Queen Elizabeth and the Conspiracy of Amboise," *English Historical Review*, 81 (1966).

Theibault, J. "The Rhetoric of Death and Destruction in the Thirty Years' War," *Social History*, 27 (1993).

Turchetti, Marco. "Concorde ou tolerance? de 1562 à 1598," *Revue historique*, 274 (1985).

———. "Religious Concord and Political Tolerance in 16th Century France," *Sixteenth Century Journal*, 22 (1991).

Venard, Marc. "Arrètez le massacre!" *Revue d'histoire moderne et contemporaine*, 39 (1992).

Verbruggen, J. "La tactic militaire des armées de chevaliers," *Revue du nord*, 29 (1947).

Weber, H. "'Un Bonne Paix': Richelieu's Foreign Policy and the Peace of Christendom," in J. Bergin and L. Brockliss, eds., *Richelieu and His Age* (1992).

Whaley, D. P. "Condotte and Condottieri in the 13th Century," *Proceedings of the British Academy*, 61 (1975).

Wijn, H. "Military Force and Warfare, 1610–1648," in *The New Cambridge Modern History*, Vol. 4 (1970).

Wood, James. "The Royal Army during the Early Wars of Religion in France, 1559–1576," in Mack Holt, ed., *Society and Institutions in Early Modern France* (1991).

Wright, Nicholas. "Ransoms of Non-combatants during the Hundred Years' War," *Journal of Medieval History*, 17 (1991).

Books

Allen, Paul C. *Philip III and the Pax Hispanica, 1598–1621: The Failure of Grand Strategy* (2000).

Allmand, Christopher. *Henry V* (1992).

———. *The Hundred Years' War* (1988).

Anderson, Alison. *On the Verge of War: International Relations and the Jülich-Kleve Succession Crises, 1609–1614* (1999).

Anderson, M. *War and Society in Europe of the Old Regime, 1620–1789* (1988).

André, Louis. *Michel le Tellier et l'organisation de l'armée monarchique* (1906; 1980).

Angold, Michael. *The Byzantine Empire, 1025–1204* (1997).

Arnold, Thomas F. *The Renaissance at War* (2001).

Asch, Ronald. *The Thirty Years' War* (1997).

Ashley, M. *The English Civil War* (1980).

Ashton, Robert. *The Counter-Revolution: The Second Civil War and its Origins, 1646–1648* (1994).

———, ed. *James I* (1969).

Ashton, T., ed. *Crisis in Europe, 1550–1660* (1965).

Ashworth, William. *A Short History of the World Economy* (1987).

Aveling, John. *The Jesuits* (1982).

Ayton, Andrew. *Knights and Warhorses* (1994).

Baird, Henry Martyn. *The Huguenots and Henry of Navarre* (1886; 1970).

Bak, Janos, ed. *The German Peasant War of 1525* (1976).

Barber, M. *The New Knighthood* (1994).

———. *The Trial of the Templars* (1978).

Barber, Richard. *Edward, Prince of Wales and Aquitaine* (1978).

———. *The Knight and Chivalry* (1970).

Barbier, Pierre. *La France féodale, 987–1515* (1974).

Barker, Juliet. *The Tournament in England, 1100–1400* (1986).

Barker, Thomas M. *Army, Aristocracy, Monarchy* (1982).

———. *Double Eagle and Crescent* (1967).

———. *The Military Intellectual and Battle* (1975).

Barkey, K. *Bandits and Bureaucrats* (1994).

Barratt, John. *Cavaliers: The Royalist Army at War* (2000).

———. *The Great Siege of Chester* (2003).

Barrie-Curien, Viviane, ed. *Guerre et Pouvoir en Europe au XVIIe Siècle* (1991).

Barrow, G. *Feudal Britain* (1956).

Bartlett, Thomas, and Keith Jeffrey, eds. *A Military History of Ireland* (1996).

Bartusis, Humfrey. *The Late Byzantine Army, 1204–1453* (1992).

Basin, Thomas. *Histoire de Charles VII*, 2 vols. (1933–1944).

Baugert, W. V. *A History of the Society of Jesus* (1972).

Selected Bibliography

Baumgartner, Frederick. *Henri II: King of France, 1547–1559* (1988).

———. *Radical Reactionaries* (1975).

Beaumont, R. *War, Chaos and History* (1994).

Beeler, John. *Warfare in England, 1066–1189* (1966).

———. *Warfare in Feudal Europe, 730–1200* (1971).

Beer, G. *The Origins of the British Colonial System, 1578–1660* (1959).

Benecke, Gerhard, ed. *Germany in the Thirty Years' War* (1979).

Benedict, Philip. *Rouen during the Wars of Religion* (1981).

Benedict, Philip et al., eds. *Reformation, Revolt, and Civil War in France and the Netherlands, 1555–1585* (1999).

Bennett, M. *Civil Wars in Britain and Ireland, 1638–1651* (1997).

Bérenger, Jean. *Turenne* (1987).

Bergin, J. *Cardinal Richelieu, Power, and the Pursuit of Wealth* (1985).

———. *The Rise of Richelieu* (1991).

Bergin, J., and Laurence Brockliss, eds. *Richelieu and His Age* (1992).

Bertram, Henry, ed. and trans. *Political Testament of Cardinal Richelieu* (1961).

Best, Geoffrey. *Humanity in Warfare* (1983).

Bireley, Robert. *Counter-Reformation Prince* (1990).

———. *The Jesuits and the Thirty Years' War* (2003).

———. *Religion and Politics in the Age of the Counter-Reformation* (1981).

Black, J. B. *Oxford History of England: The Reign of Elizabeth, 1558–1603* (1994).

Black, Jeremy. *A History of the British Isles* (2000).

———. *A Military Revolution? Military Change and European Society, 1550–1800* (1991).

———, ed. *War in the Early Modern World, 1450–1815* (1999).

Bloch, Marc. *Feudal Society*, L. Manyon, trans. (1964).

Bonney, Richard. *European Dynastic States, 1494–1660* (1991).

———. *The King's Debts: Finance and Politics in France, 1589–1661* (1981).

———. *Political Change in France Under Richelieu and Mazarin, 1624–1661* (1978).

Bossy, John. *Christianity in the West, 1400–1700* (1985).

Boucher, Jacqueline. *La cour de Henri III* (1986).

Bourgeon, J-L. *L'assassinat de Coligny* (1992).

Bouwsma, William. *John Calvin* (1988).

Bradford, E. *The Great Siege* (1961).

Brady, Thomas. *The Protestant Reformation in German History* (1998).

Brake, W. *Regents and Rebels* (1989).

Brecé, Yves-Marie. *A History of Peasant Revolts*, Amanda Whitmore, trans. (1991).

Brenner, Robert. *Merchants and Revolution* (1993).

Brewer, Paul. *Warfare in the Renaissance World* (1999).

Brotton, Jerry. *The Renaissance Bazaar* (2002).

Brown, R. *Castles, Conquest, and Charters* (1989).

Browning, Robert. *The Byzantine Empire* (1992).

Bryce, James. *The Holy Roman Empire* (1892; 1978).

Buisseret, David. *Henry IV* (1984).

———, ed. *Monarchs, Ministers, and Maps* (1992).

Bullough, D. *The Age of Charlemagne* (1966).

Bumke, Joachim. *The Concept of Knighthood in the Middle Ages* (trans. 1982).

Burkhardt, Carl Jacob. *Richelieu and His Age*, 3 vols. (1967).

Burkhardt, Jacob. *The Civilization of the Renaissance in Italy* (1995).

Burman, Edward. *The Templars* (1986; 1990).

Burne, Alfred H. *The Agincourt War* (1956; 1999).

———. *The Crécy War* (1955; 1999).

Bussmann, K., and H. Schilling, eds. *War and Peace in Europe, 1618–1648* (1998).

Cachia, P. *A History of Islamic Spain* (1965).

Cahill, T. *How the Irish Saved Civilization* (1995).

Cameron, Keith, ed. *From Valois to Bourbon* (1989).

———. *Henri III, a Maligned or Malignant King?* (1978).

Canny, Nicholas. *Elizabethan Conquest of Ireland* (1976).

———. *Europeans on the Move, 1500–1800* (1994).

———. *Kingdom and Colony* (1988).

———. *Making Ireland British: 1580–1650* (2001).

Carlin, Norah. *Causes of the English Civil War* (1999).

Carlton, Charles. *Going to the Wars: The Experience of the English Civil Wars, 1638–1651* (1992).

Carmona, M. *Richelieu, L'Ambition et le pouvoir* (1983).

Carpenter, Stanley. *Military Leadership in the British Civil Wars, 1642–1651* (2005).

Carr, Raymond, ed. *Spain* (2000).

Carrol, S. *Noble Power during the French Wars of Religion* (1998).

Carter, C. H., ed. *From the Renaissance to the Counter-Reformation* (1965).

Castries, duc de. *The Lives of the Kings and Queens of France*, Anne Dobell, trans. (1997).

Casway, Jerrold. *Owen Roe O'Neill and the Struggle for Catholic Ireland* (1984).

Cazaux, Yves. *Henri IV ou la grande victoire* (1977).

Chadwick, Owen, series ed. *Pelican History of the Church*, 6 vols. (1970–).

———. *The Popes and European Revolution* (1981).

———. *The Reformation* (1972).

Chatellier, Louis. *The Europe of the Devout*, John Birrell, trans. (1989).

Chibnall, Marjorie. *The Normans* (2001).

Chickering, H., and T. Seiler, eds. *The Study of Chivalry* (1989).

Chidester, David. *Christianity* (2000).

Childs, John. *Warfare in the 17th Century* (2001).

Church, W. *Richelieu and Reason of State* (1972).

Cipolla, Carlo. *An Economic History of World Population*, 7th ed. (1978).

Clark, George. *War and Society in the 17th Century* (1958; 1985).

Clark, Peter, ed. *The European Crisis of the 1590s* (1985).

Clarke, Adrian. *The Old English in Ireland, 1625–42* (1966).

Clasen, C-P. *Anabaptism* (1972).

Cloulas, I. *Catherine de Medici* (1979).

———. *Henri II* (1985).

Cogswell, T. *The Blessed Revolution: English Politics and the Coming of War, 1621–1624* (1989).

Cole, Hubert. *The Wars of the Roses* (1973).

Collins, J. *The Fiscal Limits of Absolutism* (1988).

Collinson, Patrick. *Elizabethan Puritan Movement* (1967).

———. *Religion of Protestants: The Church in English Society, 1559–1625* (1982).

Connell, William, ed. *Society and Individual in Renaissance Florence* (2002).

Contamine, Philippe. *Guerre, état et société à la fin du moyen âge* (1972).

———, ed. *Histoire militaire de la France: tom 1, Des origines à 1715* (1992).

———. *War in the Middle Ages*, Michael Jones, trans. (1984; 1990).

Selected Bibliography

Corfis, A., and Michael Wolfe, eds. *The Medieval City under Siege* (1995).

Corvisier, Andre. *Armies and Societies in Europe, 1494–1789* (1979).

Cowen, I. *The Scottish Reformation* (1978).

Crew, P. M. *Calvinist Preaching and Iconoclasm in the Netherlands, 1544–1569* (1978).

Crouzet, Denis. *La nuit de la Saint-Barthélemy* (1994).

———. *Les guerriers de Dieu: la violence au temps des troubles de religion*, 2 vols. (1990).

Croxton, Derek, and Anuschka Tischer. *The Peace of Westphalia: A Historical Dictionary* (2002).

Cruikshank, G. *Elizabeth's Army* (1966).

———. *Henry VIII and the Invasion of France* (1990).

Curry, Anne. *The Hundred Years' War, 1337–1453* (2003).

Curtin, Philip. *The World and the West* (2000).

Cust, Edward. *Lives of the Warriors of the Civil Wars of France and England* (1867; 1972).

———. *Lives of the Warriors of the Thirty Years' War* (1865; 1972).

Cust, R., and Ann Hughes, eds. *The English Civil War* (1997).

Dame, Frederick William. *A History of Switzerland* (2001).

Davidson, N. S. *The Counter-Reformation* (1987).

Davies, D. W. *Elizabethans Errant* (1967).

Davies, Norman. *The Isles: A History* (2000).

Davis, Natalie. *Society and Culture in Early Modern France* (1975).

De Gaury, Gerald. *The Grand Captain: Gonzalo de Córdoba* (1955).

Delbrück, Hans. *History of the Art of War*, Vol. 4, *Dawn of Modern Warfare*, Walter Renfroe, trans. (1920; 1990).

Delumeau, Jean. *Catholicism Between Luther and Voltaire*, J. Moiser, trans. (1977).

Dembkowski, H. E. *The Union of Lublin: Polish Federalism in the Golden Age* (1982).

Denieul-Cormier, Anne. *Wise and Foolish Kings: The First House of Valois 1328–1498* (1980).

De Vries, Jan. *The Economy of Europe in an Age of Crisis, 1600–1750* (1976).

De Vries, Jan, and Ad Van Der Woude. *The First Modern Economy* (1997).

DeVries, Kelly. *Joan of Arc: A Military Leader* (2003).

Dickens, A. *The English Reformation* (1964).

Diefendorf, Barbara. *Beneath the Cross: Catholics and Huguenots in 16th Century Paris* (1991).

Diffy, B., and G. Winius. *Foundations of the Portuguese Empire* (1977).

Douglas, David C. *The Norman Achievement, 1050–1100* (1969).

Duby, G. *The Chivalrous Society* (1978).

Duke, A. *Reformation and Revolt in the Low Countries* (1990).

Dunn, R. *The Age of Religious Wars, 1559–1689* (1970).

Éditions, G. *La merveilluese histoire de l'armée Française* (1947).

Edwards, Peter. *Dealing in Death: The Arms Trade and the British Civil Wars, 1638–1652* (2000).

Elliott, J. H. *The Count-Duke of Olivares: The Statesman in an Age of Decline* (1986).

———. *Europe Divided, 1559–1598* (1969).

———, ed. *The Hispanic World, Civilization, and Empire: Europe and the Americas* (1991).

———. *Imperial Spain, 1469–1716* (1964; 1970).

———. *The Revolt of the Catalans* (1963).

———. *Richelieu and Olivares* (1984).

———. *Spain and Its World, 1500–1700* (1989).

Elton, G. *Reformation Europe* (1963).

Estèbe, Janine. *Tocsin pour un massacre: La saison des Saint-Barthélemy* (1968).

Evans, R. W. *The Making of the Habsburg Monarchy, 1550–1700* (1979).

———. *Rudolf II and His World* (1973).

Falls, Cyril. *Elizabeth's Irish Wars* (1950).

Favier, J. *La Guerre de Cent Ans* (1980).

Fergusson, James. *William Wallace: Guardian of Scotland* (1938).

Fernandez-Armesto, F. *Ferdinand and Isabella* (1975).

Firth, Charles. *Cromwell's Army* (1912; 1992).

Fisher, Andrew. *William Wallace* (2002).

Fissel, Mark. *The Bishops' Wars: Charles I's Campaigns Against Scotland, 1638–1640* (1994).

———. *English Warfare, 1511–1642* (2001).

———, ed. *War and Government in Britain: 1598–1650* (1991).

Forey, A. *Military Orders from the 12th to the Early 14th Centuries* (1992).

Foster, R. F. *Modern Ireland, 1600–1972* (1989).

Fowler, K. A. *The Age of Plantagenet and Valois* (1967).

———, ed. *The Hundred Years' War* (1971).

———. *Medieval Mercenaries: "The Great Companies,"* Vol. 1 (2001).

France, John. *Western Warfare in the Age of the Crusades* (1999).

Fraser, Antonia. *Mary, Queen of Scots* (1969).

Friedrichs, C. *Urban Society in an Age of War: Nördlingen, 1580–1720* (1979).

Fulaine, Jean-Charles. *Le duc Charles IV de Lorraine et son armée: 1624–1675* (1997).

Fuller, W. C. *Strategy and Power in Russia, 1600–1914* (1992).

Gail, M. *The Three Popes* (1969).

Gajecky, G., and A. Baran. *Cossacks in the Thirty Years' War*, 2 vols. (1969).

Gallagher, P., ed. *God's Obvious Design* (1988).

Garrison, Janine. *L'Edit de Nantes et sa révocation* (1985).

———. *Protestants du Midi, 1559–1598* (1980).

Gash, G. *Renaissance Armies* (1975; 1982).

Gay, Peter, and R. K. Webb. *Modern Europe* (1973).

Gelder, H. *The Two Reformations of the 16th Century* (1961).

Gelderen, Martin van. *Political Thought of the Dutch Revolt, 1555–1590* (1992).

Gentles, Ian. *The New Model Army in England, Ireland, and Scotland, 1645–1653* (1992).

Geyl, Peter. *The Netherlands in the 17th Century*, 2 vols. (1961).

———. *Orange and Stuart*, Arnold Pomerans, trans. (1939; 1969).

———. *The Revolt of the Netherlands, 1555–1609* (1980).

Gibbon, Edward. *The Decline and Fall of the Roman Empire*, abridged by D. M. Low (1960).

Gies, Frances. *Joan of Arc: The Legend and the Reality* (1981).

Gille, Betrand. *Engineers of the Renaissance* (1966).

Gillingham, J. *The Wars of the Roses* (1981).

Glénisson, J., ed. *Jeanne d'Arc, une èpoque, un rayonnment* (1982).

Glete, Jan. *War and the State in Early Modern Europe* (2002).

Glick, Thomas. *Islamic and Christian Spain in the Early Middle Ages*, 2nd ed. (2005).

Goodman, Anthony. *The Wars of the Roses* (1981).

Gordon, M. *Joan of Arc* (2000).

Gravett, Christopher. *Medieval Siege Warfare* (1990).

Green, David. *The Battle of Poitiers, 1356* (2002).

Greengrass, Mark. *Conquest and Coalescence* (1991).

———. *France in the Age of Henry IV* (1995).

———. *The French Reformation* (1987).

Griffin, Margaret. *Regulating Religion and Morality in the King's Armies, 1639–1646* (2004).

Gruber von Arni, Eric. *Justice to the Maimed Soldier* (2001).

Guillemin, H. *Joan, Maid of Orleans* (1973).

Gush, George. *Renaissance Armies, 1480–1650* (1975; 1982).

Gutmann, M. *War and Rural Life in the Early Modern Low Countries* (1980).

Guy, John. *Queen of Scots* (2004).

———, ed. *The Reign of Elizabeth I* (1995).

———. *Tudor England* (1988).

Haigh, C., ed. *The English Reformation Revised* (1987).

———, ed. *The Reign of Elizabeth I* (1984).

Haldon, John. *Byzantium* (2000).

Hale, John R. *Machiavelli and Renaissance Italy* (1960).

———. *Renaissance War Studies* (1983).

———. *War and Society in Renaissance Europe, 1450–1620* (1986).

Hale, John R. et al. *Europe in the Late Middle Ages* (1965).

Hall, Bert. *Weapons and Warfare in Renaissance Europe* (1997).

Hamilton, B. *The Medieval Inquisition* (1981).

Hammer, Paul. *Elizabeth's Wars* (2003).

Hamon, P. *L'argent du roi* (1994).

Harper-Bill, D., ed. *The Ideals and Practice of Knighthood* (1986).

Hart, M. *In Quest of Funds: Warfare and State Formation in the Netherlands, 1620–50* (1989).

———. *The Making of a Bourgeois State: War, Politics, and Finance during the Dutch Revolt* (1993).

Harvey, L. *Islamic Spain, 1250–1500* (1990).

Head, T., and R. Landes, eds. *The Peace of God* (1992).

Heer, Friedrich. *The Holy Roman Empire* (1968).

Heller, H. *Iron and Blood: Civil Wars in 16th Century France* (1991).

Henry, Gráinne. *The Irish Military Community in Spanish Flanders, 1586–1621* (1992).

Herlihy, D., ed. *The History of Feudalism* (1970).

Herzstein, R. E., ed. *The Holy Roman Empire in the Middle Ages* (1966).

Hewitt, H. *The Black Prince's Expedition of 1355–1357* (1958).

———. *The Organization of War under Edward III, 1338–1362* (1966).

Hillgarth, J. *The Spanish Kingdoms, 1250–1516*, 2 vols. (1978).

Hollister, C. W. *The Military Organization of Norman England* (1965).

Holt, Mack. *The Duke of Anjou and the Politique Struggle during the Wars of Religion* (1986).

———. *The French Wars of Religion, 1562–1629* (1995).

Howard, Michael. *War in European History* (1976).

Hsia, R. *Society and Religion in Münster, 1535–1618* (1984).

Hsia, R. P., ed. *The German People and the Reformation* (1988).

Hughes, Anne. *Causes of the English Civil War* (1998).

Hussey, J. M. *The Orthodox Church in the Byzantine Empire* (1986).

Hutchinson, H. *Henry V* (1967).

Hutton, Ronald. *The British Republic, 1649–1660* (2000).

———. *The Royalist War Effort, 1642–1646* (1999).

Ingrao, Charles. *The Habsburg Monarchy, 1618–1848* (1994).

Israel, Jonathon. *The Dutch Republic: Its Rise, Greatness and Fall, 1477–1806* (1995).

———. *The Dutch Republic and the Hispanic World, 1606–1661* (1982).

Jedin, H. *A History of the Council of Trent*, 2 vols. (1957; 1961).

Johnson, James. *Ideology, Reason, and the Limitation of War* (1975).

Johnson, James Turner. *Just War Tradition and the Restraint of War* (1981).

Johnson, Paul. *The Life & Times of Edward III* (1973).

Kamen, Henry. *Imperial Spain* (1983).

———. *Philip of Spain* (1997).

———. *Phoenix and the Flame: Catalonia and the Counter-Reformation* (1993).

———. *The Spanish Inquisition: A Historical Revision* (rev. ed. 1998).

Kann, R. *The History of the Habsburg Empire, 1526–1918* (1974).

Keen, Maurice. *The Laws of War in the Late Middle Ages* (1965).

———, ed. *Medieval Warfare* (1999).

Kelly, John. *The Great Mortality: An Intimate History of the Black Death* (2005).

Kennedy, Hugh. *Muslim Spain and Portugal* (1996).

King, E. *The Knights Hospitaller in the Holy Land* (1931).

Kingdon, Robert. *Geneva and the Coming of the Wars of Religion in France, 1555–1563* (1956).

Kitson, Frank. *Old Ironsides: Military Biography of Oliver Cromwell* (2004).

Knecht, Robert. *Catherine de Medici* (1998).

———. *Francis I* (1982).

———. *The French Civil Wars, 1562–1598* (2000).

———. *The French Wars of Religion, 1562–1598* (1996).

———. *Renaissance Warrior and Patron: The Reign of Francis I* (1994).

———. *The Rise and Fall of Renaissance France, 1483–1610* (2001).

Koch, H. W. *Medieval Warfare* (1978).

———. *The Rise of Modern Warfare, 1618–1815* (1982).

Labarge, Margaret. *Gasgony: England's First Colony, 1204–1453* (1980).

———. *Henry V: The Cautious Conqueror* (1975).

Lacroix, Paul. *Military and Religious Life in the Middle Ages and Renaissance* (1874).

Lambert, Malcolm. *Medieval Heresy* (2002).

Lamont, William. *Godly Rule: Politics and Religion, 1603–1660* (1969).

Langer, H. *The Thirty Years' War* (1980).

La Patourel, John. *The Norman Empire* (1976).

Lenihan, Pádraig. *Confederate Catholics at War, 1641–1648* (2000).

———, ed. *Conquest and Resistance: War in Seventeenth-Century Ireland* (2001).

Lenman, Bruce. *England's Colonial Wars, 1550–1688* (2001).

Lennon, Colm. *Sixteenth Century Ireland: The Incomplete Conquest* (1994).

Le Patourel, John. *The Norman Empire* (1976).

Levack, Brian. *The Witch-Hunt in Early Modern Europe* (1995).

Levene, M., and P. Roberts, eds. *The Massacre in History* (1999).

Lewis, Archibald. *Nomads and Crusaders* (1988).

Lewis, P. S., ed. *The Recovery of France in the 15th Century* (1972).

Limm, P. *The Thirty Years' War* (1984).

Lindsay, Jack. *The Normans and Their World* (1974).

Livermore, H. *A New History of Portugal*, 2nd ed. (1976).

Livet, Georges. *La Guerre de trente ans* (1972).

———. *Les guerres de religion, 1559–1598* (1962).

Selected Bibliography

Lloyd, Howell. *The Rouen Campaign, 1590–1592: Politics, Warfare, and the Early Modern State* (1973).

Lomax, L. *The Reconquest of Spain* (1978).

Lynch, J. *The Hispanic World in Crisis and Change, 1598–1700* (1992).

———. *Spain Under the Habsburgs*, 2 vols. (1981).

Lynn, John A. *A Giant of the Grand Siècle: The French Army, 1610–1715* (1997).

MacCaffrey, Wallace. *Elizabeth I, War and Politics, 1588–1603* (1983).

———. *Queen Elizabeth and the Making of Policy, 1572–1588* (1981).

MacHardy, Karin. *War, Religion and Court Patronage in Habsburg Austria* (2003).

MacInnes, Allan. *Charles I and the Making of the Covenanting Movement, 1625–1641* (1991).

Mackay, A. *Spain in the Middle Ages* (1977).

Madden, T. *A Concise History of the Crusades* (1999).

Maland, D. *Europe at War, 1600–1650* (1980).

Mallett, M. E. *Mercenaries and Their Masters: Warfare in Renaissance Italy* (1974).

Mallett, M. E., and J. R. Hale. *Military Organization of a Renaissance State: Venice, 1400–1617* (1984).

Maltby, William. *Alba* (1983).

———. *The Reign of Charles V* (2002).

Mann, Golo. *Wallenstein* (1976).

Mariejol, J-H. *La Réforme, la Ligue, l'Édit de Nantes* (1983).

Marius, Richard. *Martin Luther* (1999).

Marwick, Arthur. *War and Social Change* (1974).

Mason, Roger, ed. *Scots and Britons* (1994).

Matmatey, V. S. *The Rise of the Habsburg Empire, 1526–1815* (1978).

Matthias, P. *The First Industrial Nation* (1969).

Mattingly, Garrett. *Renaissance Diplomacy* (1955).

Mayer, Hans. *The Crusades* (trans. and rev. ed. 1988).

McCavitt, John. *The Flight of the Earls* (2004).

McGuire, B., ed. *War and Peace in the Middle Ages* (1987).

McGurk, John. *The Elizabethan Conquest of Ireland* (1997).

McNeill, John. *The History and Character of Calvinism* (1954).

Méthivier, Hubert. *La Fronde* (1984).

Miller, Douglas, and Gerry Embleton. *The Swiss at War, 1300–1500* (1979).

Miller, E. *War in the North* (1960).

Monod, Paul. *The Power of Kings: Monarchy and Religion in Europe, 1589–1715* (1999).

Monter, William. *Calvin's Geneva* (1967).

Moody, T. et al., eds. *A New History of Ireland*, Vol. 3, *Early Modern Ireland, 1534–1691* (1976).

Moote, Lloyd. *Louis XIII* (1989).

Morrill, John. *Oliver Cromwell and the English Revolution* (1990).

———, ed. *Reactions to the English Civil War, 1642–1649* (1983).

Morris, J. *The Welsh Wars of Edward I* (1901).

Munk, T. *17th Century Europe* (1990).

Murray, J. L. *History of Switzerland* (1985).

Murray, W. et al., eds. *The Making of Strategy: Rulers, States, and War* (1994).

Nalle, Sarah. *God in La Mancha, 1500–1650* (1992).

Neale, J. E. *The Age of Catherine de Medici* (1943).

Neillands, Robin. *The Hundred Years' War* (1990; 2001).

Newark, P. *Medieval Warfare* (1979).

Newhall, R. *The English Conquest of Normandy, 1416–1424* (1924).

Nicholson, Helen. *The Knights Hospitaller* (2001).

Nicholson, Ranald. *Edward III and the Scots: Formative Years of a Military Career, 1327–1335* (1965).

Nischan, B. *Prince, People, and Confession: The Second Reformation in Brandenburg* (1994).

Oberman, Heiko. *Luther: Man Between God and the Devil* (1989).

Oblonsky, D. *The Byzantine Commonwealth* (1971).

Okey, Robin. *The Habsburg Monarchy* (2000).

O'Malley, John W., ed. *Catholicism in Early Modern Europe* (1988).

———, ed. *The Jesuits* (1999).

Oman, Charles. *A History of the Art of War in the Middle Ages* (1924; 1976).

———. *A History of the Art of War in the 16th Century* (1937; 1987).

O'Shea, Stephen. *Perfect Heresy: The Revolutionary Life and Death of the Medieval Cathars* (2000).

O'Siochru, M. *Confederate Ireland* (1999).

Ottway-Ruthven, A. *A History of Medieval Ireland* (1968).

Ozment, Steven. *The Age of Reform, 1250–1550* (1980).

Packe, Michael. *King Edward III* (1984).

Pagès, G. *La Guerre de trente ans* (1949).

Paraskevas, J., and F. Reinstein. *The Eastern Orthodox Church* (1969).

Paret, Peter, ed. *Makers of Modern Strategy: From Machiavelli to the Nuclear Age* (1986).

Parker, David. *La Rochelle and the French Monarchy* (1980).

———. *The Making of French Absolutism, 1450–1660* (1983).

Parker, Geoffrey. *The Army of Flanders and the Spanish Road, 1567–1659* (1972).

———. *The Dutch Revolt* (1977; 1985).

———. *Empire, War and Faith in Early Modern Europe* (2002).

———. *Europe in Crisis, 1598–1648* (1980; 2001).

———. *The General Crisis of the 17th Century* (1978).

———. *The Grand Strategy of Philip II* (1998).

———. *Spain and the Netherlands, 1559–1659* (1977).

———, ed. *The Thirty Years' War* (1987).

Parker, Geoffrey, and Angela Parker. *European Soldiers, 1550–1650* (1977).

Parrott, David. *Richelieu's Army: War, Government, and Society in France, 1624–1642* (2001).

Pernot, Michel. *Les guerres de religion en France, 1559–1598* (1987).

Perrie, M. *Pretenders and Popular Monarchism in Early Modern Russia* (1995).

Perroy, Édouard. *The Hundred Years' War* (1951).

Phillips, Carla. *Six Galleons for the King of Spain: Imperial Defense in the 17th Century* (1986).

Phillips, Gervase. *The Anglo-Scots Wars, 1513–1550* (1999).

Phillips, Henry. *The Church and Culture in 17th Century France* (1997).

Pincus, Steven. *Protestantism and Patriotism* (1996).

Pirenne, Henri. *Medieval Cities* (1925).

———. *Muhammad and Charlemagne* (1939).

Polisensky, J. *The Thirty Years' War* (1971).

———. *Tragic Triangle: The Netherlands, Spain and Bohemia, 1617–1621* (1991).

———. *War and Society in Europe, 1618–1648* (1978).

Potter, D. *A History of France, 1460–1560* (1995).

———. *War and Government in the French Provinces* (1993).

Potter, G. *Zwingli* (1976).

Powers, James. *A Society Organized for War: The Iberian Militias, 1000–1284* (1988).

Powicke, Michael. *Military Obligation in Medieval England* (1962).

Prestwich, Meena, ed. *International Calvinism, 1541–1715* (1985).

Prestwich, Michael. *Armies and Warfare in the Middle Ages: The English Experience* (1996).

———. *The Three Edwards: War and the State in England, 1272–1377* (1980).

Price, J. *Holland and the Dutch Republic in the 17th Century* (1994).

Rabb, T., ed. *The Thirty Years' War* (1971).

Rady, Martyn. *Emperor Charles V* (1988; 1995).

Ranum, Orest. *The Fronde: A French Revolution, 1648–1652* (1993).

Read, Piers. *The Templars* (2000).

Redlich, F. *De Praeda Militari: Looting and Booty, 1500–1815* (1956).

———. *The German Military Enterpriser and His Workforce, 13th–17th Centuries*, 2 vols. (1964–1965).

Reeve, L. *Charles I and the Road to Personal Rule* (1989).

Reid, Stuart. *All the King's Armies: A Military History of the English Civil War* (1998).

Ridley, Jasper. *John Knox* (1968).

Riley-Smith, Jonathon. *The Crusades* (1990).

———. *A History of the Crusades* (2000).

———. *The Hospitallers: History of the Order of St. John* (1999).

Robinson, I. H. *Henry IV of Germany, 1056–1106* (1999).

Rodger, N.A.M. *The Safeguard of the Sea: A Naval History of Britain*, Vol. 1 (1997).

Rodríguez-Salgado, M. *The Changing Face of Europe* (1988).

Roelker, Nancy. *One King, One Faith* (1996).

Rogers, Clifford. *War Cruel and Sharp: English Strategy Under Edward III, 1327–1360* (2000).

Rogers, P. *Fifth Monarchy Men* (1966).

Rosen, S. *Societies and Military Power* (1996).

Rowen, Herbert, ed. *The Low Countries in Early Modern Times* (1972).

———. *The Princes of Orange* (1988).

Rowse, A. L. *The Elizabethan Renaissance* (2000).

———. *The England of Elizabeth* (1950; 1978).

———. *The Expansion of Elizabethan England* (1955).

Runciman, Steven. *The Fall of Constantinople* (1903; 1968).

———. *A History of the Crusades*, 3 vols. (1951–1954).

———. *The Medieval Manichee* (1947; 1961).

Russell, Conrad. *Causes of the English Civil War* (1990).

———. *The Fall of the British Monarchies, 1637–1641* (1991).

Russell, F. H. *Just War in the Middle Ages* (1975).

Russell, Jeffrey. *Witchcraft in the Middle Ages* (1972).

Russell, Peter. *Prince Henry "the Navigator"* (2000).

Ryder, I. *An English Army for Ireland* (1987).

Salmon, J.H.M. *Renaissance and Revolt* (1987).

———. *Society in Crisis: France in the 16th Century* (1975).

Saul, Nigel. *Knights and Esquires* (1981).

Sauzet, Robert, ed. *Henri III et sons temps* (1992).

Schama, Simon. *A History of Britain* (2000).

Schilling, H. *Religion, Political Culture and the Emergence of Early Modern Society* (1992).

Schlight, J. *Monarchies and Mercenaries* (1968).

Scott, H. M., ed. *European Nobilities in the 17th and 18th Centuries* (1995).

Scribner, R., and G. Benecke. *The German Peasant War, 1525* (1979).

Seaver, Paul. *Sir Walter Raleigh* (2004).

Setton, Kenneth, ed. *A History of the Crusades*, 7 vols. (1955–1990).

———. *Venice, Austria, and the Turks in the 17th Century* (1991).

Seward, Desmond. *The Hundred Years' War* (1978).

———. *Monks of War: The Military Religious Orders* (1972; 1995).

———. *Prince of the Renaissance: The Golden Life of Francis I* (1973).

Shannon, Albert C. *The Medieval Inquisition* (1991).

Sharpe, Kevin. *The Personal Rule of Charles I* (1992).

Shearer, David. *Private Armies and Military Intervention* (1998).

Shimizu, J. *Conflict of Loyalties: Politics and Religion in the Career of Gaspard de Coligny* (1970).

Siméon, L. *Histoire de Bertrand du Guesclin et de son époque* (1867).

Simpson, Leslie. *Encomienda in New Spain* (1966).

Sire, H. *The Knights of Malta* (1994).

Smail, R. *Crusading Warfare, 1097–1193* (1956).

Smith, Denis. *A History of Sicily, 800–1713* (1968).

Smith, H. M. *Henry VIII and the Reformation* (1948).

Smith, J. H. *The Great Schism* (1970).

Solt, Leo. *Saints in Arms: Puritanism and Democracy in Cromwell's Army* (1959).

Starkey, D. *The Reign of Henry VIII* (1986).

Steen, C. *A Chronicle of Conflict: Tournai, 1559–1567* (1985).

Steinberg, S. H. *The "Thirty Years' War" and the Conflict for European Hegemony, 1600–1660* (1966).

Stevenson, David. *Scottish Covenanters and Irish Confederates* (1981).

———. *The Scottish Revolution, 1637–1644* (1973).

Stone, L. *Causes of the English Revolution* (1972).

Strachan, Hew. *European Armies and the Conduct of War* (1983).

Stradling, R. *The Armada of Flanders: Spanish Maritime Strategy and the European War, 1568–1668* (1992).

———. *Europe and the Decline of Spain* (1981).

———. *Philip IV and the Government of Spain, 1621–1665* (1988).

———. *Spanish Monarchy and Irish Mercenaries: The Wild Geese in Spain, 1618–1668* (1994).

Strayer, Joseph. *Feudalism* (1979).

Strickland, M. *War and Chivalry* (1996).

Stroud, Philip. *The Siege of Colchester, 1648* (2003).

Sugden, John. *Sir Francis Drake* (1992).

Sumption, Jonathon. *The Albigensian Crusade* (1978).

———. *The Hundred Years' War* (1990; 1999).

Sutherland, N. M. *Catherine de Medici and the Ancien Régime* (1968).

———. *The Huguenot Struggle for Recognition* (1980).

———. *The Massacre of St. Bartholomew and the European Conflict, 1559–1572* (1973).

———. *Princes, Power, and Religion, 1547–1589* (1984).

Swart, K. *William the Silent and the Revolt of the Netherlands* (1978).

Tallett, Frank. *War and Society in Early Modern Europe, 1495–1715* (1992).

Tapié, Victor-Louis. *France in the Age of Louis XIII and Richelieu*, D. Lockie, trans. (1975).

———. *La politique de la France et le début de la guerre de trente ans* (1934).

Taylor, A.J.P. *The Habsburg Monarchy* (1948).

Taylor, F. L. *The Art of War in Italy: 1494 to 1529* (1921).

Templeman, Geoffrey. *Edward III and the Beginnings of the Hundred Years' War, 1337–1453* (1952).

Thompson, I. A. *War and Government in Habsburg Spain, 1560–1620* (1976).

Thompson, J. A. *Popes and Princes, 1417–1517* (1980).

Thompson, J. W. *Feudal Germany*, 2 vols. (1927; 1962).

———. *The Wars of Religion in France, 1559–1576* (1909; 1958).

Tracy, James. *Emperor Charles V, Impresario of War* (2002).

———. *Europe's Reformations, 1450–1650: Doctrine, Politics, and Community*, 2nd ed. (2002).

———. *Holland under Habsburg Rule, 1506–1566* (1990).

———, ed. *Luther and the Modern State in Germany* (1986).

———, ed. *The Political Economy of Merchant Empires* (1991).

———, ed. *Religion and the Early Modern State* (2004).

Trease, G. *Condottieri, Soldiers of Fortune* (1970).

Trevelyan, G. M. *England in the Age of Wycliffe* (1904; 1975).

———. *The English Revolution* (1967).

Trevor-Roper, Hugh. *Catholics, Anglicans, Puritans* (1987).

Trim, D., ed. *The Chivalric Ethos and the Development of Military Professionalism* (2003).

Tuchman, Barbara W. *A Distant Mirror: The Calamitous 14th Century* (1978).

Tyler, Royall. *Emperor Charles the Fifth* (1956).

Underdown, David. *Revel, Riot, and Rebellion* (1985).

Vale, Juliet. *Edward III and Chivalry* (1983).

Vale, Malcolm. *Charles VII* (1974).

———. *English Gascony, 1399–1453* (1970).

———. *War and Chivalry* (1981).

Van der Hoevan, Marco, ed. *Exercise of Arms: Warfare in the Netherlands, 1568–1648* (1997).

Vaughan, Richard. *Charles the Bold* (1973).

———. *John the Fearless* (1966).

———. *Philip the Bold* (1962).

———. *Philip the Good* (1970).

———. *Valois Burgundy* (1975).

Verbruggen, J. F. *The Art of Warfare in Western Europe during the Middle Ages* (1977).

Verheyden, A. *Anabaptism in Flanders, 1530–1650* (1961).

Villalon, Andrew, and Donald Kagay, eds. *Crusaders, Condottieri, and Cannon* (2003).

Wagner, Eduard. *European Weapons and Warfare, 1618–1648*, S. Pellar, trans. (1979).

Walton, Robert. *Zwingli's Theocracy* (1967).

Wanklyn, Malcolm, and Frank Jones. *A Military History of the English Civil War, 1642–1646* (2004).

Wedgewood, C. V. *The King's Peace, 1637–1641* (1955).

———. *The King's War, 1641–1647* (1958).

———. *Montrose* (1952).

———. *The Thirty Years' War* (1938).

Wernham, R. B. *After the Armada: Elizabethan England and the Struggle for Mastery in Western Europe, 1588–1595* (1988).

———. *Before the Armada: The Growth of English Foreign Policy, 1485–1588* (1966).

———. *The Making of Elizabethan Foreign Policy, 1588–1603* (1980).

———. *The Return of the Armadas: The Last Years of the Elizabethan War Against Spain, 1595–1603* (1994).

Wheatcroft, Andrew. *The Habsburgs* (1996).

Wheeler, Bonnie, and Charles Wood, eds. *Fresh Verdicts on Joan of Arc* (1996).

Wheeler, James. *Cromwell in Ireland* (1999).

———. *Irish and British Wars, 1637–1654* (2002).

Whitehead, A. *Gaspard de Coligny, Admiral of France* (1904).

Wilson, Charles. *The Dutch Republic* (1969).

———. *Queen Elizabeth and the Revolt of the Netherlands* (1970).

Wilson, D. *The King and the Gentleman: Charles Stuart and Oliver Cromwell* (1999).

———. *King James VI and I* (1967, revised).

Wilson, J. *Fairfax: General of Parliament's Forces* (1999).

Wilson, Peter. *The Holy Roman Empire, 1495–1806* (1999).

Wise, T. *Medieval Warfare* (1976).

Wolfe, Martin. *The Conversion of Henri IV* (1993).

———. *The Fiscal System of Renaissance France* (1972).

Wood, James. *The Army of the King* (1996).

Woolrych, Austin. *From Commonwealth to Protectorate* (1982).

———. *Soldiers and Statesmen: The General Council of the Army and its Debates, 1647–1648* (1987).

Worthington, David. *The Scots in Habsburg Service, 1618–1648* (2004).

Wright, A. D. *The Counter-Reformation* (1982).

Wright, N.A.R. *Knights and Peasants: The Hundred Years' War in the French Countryside* (1998).

Zeller, G. *La Guerre de Trente Ans et les relations internationales* (1948).

Ziegler, Philip. *The Black Death* (1969).

War at Sea

Articles and Chapters

Adam, P. "Conclusions sur les développements des techniques nautiques médiévales," *Revue d'histoire éonomique et sociale*, 54 (1976).

Anderson, R. "Operations of the English Fleet," *English Historical Review*, 31 (1916).

Ayalon, D. "The Mamlūks and Naval Power," *Proceedings of the Israel Academy of Sciences and Humanities*, Vol. 1 (1965).

Dames, M. "The Portuguese and the Turks in the Indian Ocean in the 16th Century," *Journal of the Royal Asiatic Society* (1921).

Deny, J., and L. Laroche. "L'expédition en Provence de l'armée de mer du Sultan Süleyman, 1543–1544," *Turcica*, 1 (1968).

Glasgow, Tom. "The Shape of the Ships that Defeated the Spanish Armada," *The Mariner's Mirror*, 49 (1963).

Hamblin, William. "The Fatamid Navy during the Crusades," *American Neptune*, 46 (1986).

Hess, A. "The Evolution of the Ottoman Seaborne Empire in the Age of Oceanic Discoveries, 1453–1525," *American Historical Review*, 75 (1970).

Howard, Frank. "Early Ship Guns, Part I: Built-up Breech-Loaders," *The Mariner's Mirror*, 72 (1986).

———. "Early Ship Guns, Part II: Swivels," *The Mariner's Mirror*, 73 (1987).

Imber, Colin. "The Navy of Süleyman the Magnificent," *Archivum Ottomanicum*, 6 (1980).

———. "The Reconstruction of the Ottoman Fleet after the Battle of Lepanto," *Studies in Ottoman History and Law* (1996).

Lo, Jung-pang. "The Decline of the Early Ming Navy," *Oriens Extremus*, 5 (1958).

Marshall, P. "Western Arms in Maritime Asia," *Modern Asian Studies*, 14 (1980).

Ohlmeyer, J. "The Dunkirk of Ireland: Wexford Privateers during the 1640s," *Journal of the Wexford Historical Society*, 10 (1989).

———. "Irish Privateers during the Civil War, 1642–1649," *The Mariner's Mirror*, 76 (1990).

Parker, Geoffrey. "The *Dreadnought* Revolution of Tudor England," *The Mariner's Mirror*, 82 (1996).

Rodger, N.A.M. "The Development of Broadside Gunnery, 1450–1650," *The Mariner's Mirror*, 82 (1996).

Tinniswood, J. T. "English Galleys, 1272–1377," *The Mariner's Mirror*, 35 (1949).

Unger, Richard. "Dutch Ship Design in the 15th and 16th Centuries," *Viator*, 4 (1973).

———. "Warships and Cargo Ships in Medieval Europe," *Technology and Culture*, 22 (1981).

Books

Adams, Simon. *The Armada Campaign of 1588* (1988).

Ahrweiler, H. *Byzance et la mer* (1966).

Anderson, R. C. *Naval Wars in the Baltic, 1522–1850* (1919; 1969).

———. *Naval Wars in the Levant, 1559–1853* (1952; 2005).

Anderson, R. C., and Romola Anderson. *Oared Fighting Ships From Classical Times to the Age of Steam* (1962; 1976).

———. *A Short History of the Sailing Ship* (1926; 2003).

Andrews, Kenneth. *Drake's Voyages* (1968; 1970).

———. *Elizabethan Privateering* (1964).

———. *Ships, Money, and Politics: Seafaring and Naval Enterprise in the Reign of Charles I* (1991).

———. *The Spanish Caribbean: Trade and Plunder, 1530–1630* (1978).

———. *Trade, Plunder, and Settlement: Maritime Enterprise and the Genesis of the British Empire, 1480–1630* (1984).

Andrews, Kenneth et al., eds. *Westward Enterprise: English Activities in Ireland, the Atlantic, and America, 1480–1650* (1979).

Barendse, R. *The Arabian Seas* (2002).

Baumber, M. *General at Sea* (1989).

Belabre, F. *Rhodes of the Knights* (1908).

Bernard, Jacques. *Navires et Gens de Mer à Bordeaux*, 3 vols. (1968).

Boxer, Charles Ralph. *Jan Compagnie in War and Peace, 1602–1799* (1979).

Bracewell, C. *The Uskoks of Senj: Piracy, Banditry, and Holy War in the 16th Century Adriatic* (1992).

Braudel, Fernand. *The Mediterranean and the Mediterranean World in the Age of Philip II*, 2 vols., Siân Reynolds, trans. (1966; 1995).

Bruihn, J. *The Dutch Navy of the 17th and 18th Centuries* (1993).

Brummett, Palmira. *Ottoman Seapower and Levantine Diplomacy in the Age of Discovery* (1994).

Cipolla, Carlo. *Guns, Sails, and Empires, 1400–1700* (1965; 1996).

Friel, I. *The Good Ship* (1995).

Fulton, T. *The Sovereignty of the Sea* (1911).

Gaea, M. *The German Knights of Malta* (1986).

Glete, Jan. *Navies and Nations* (1993).

―――. *Warfare at Sea, 1500–1650* (2000).

Goodman, D. *Spanish Naval Power, 1589–1665: Reconstruction and Defeat* (1996).

Gray, Colin. *The Leverage of Sea Power* (1992).

Guilmartin, John F. *Gunpowder and Galleys* (1974; 2003).

Hale, John R. *The Age of Exploration* (1974).

Harding, Richard. *The Evolution of the Sailing Navy, 1509–1815* (1995).

Hattendorf, John, and Richard Unger, eds. *War at Sea in the Middle Ages and Renaissance* (2002).

Hebb, D. *Piracy and the English Government, 1616–1642* (1994).

Heckscher, Eli. *Mercantilism* (1965).

Heers, Jacques. *The Barbary Corsairs* (2003).

Hill, J. R., ed. *Oxford Illustrated History of the Royal Navy* (1995).

Horden, Peregrine, and Nicholas Purcell. *The Corrupting Sea: A Study of Mediterranean History* (2000).

Howard, Frank. *Sailing Ships of War 1400–1860* (1979).

Howarth, David. *The Voyage of the Armada: The Spanish Story* (1981).

Hutchinson, G. *Medieval Ships and Shipping* (1994).

Israel, Jonathon. *Conflicts of Empires: Spain, the Low Countries, and the Struggle for World Supremacy, 1585–1713* (1997).

―――. *Dutch Primacy in World Trade* (1989).

―――. *Empires and Entrepots* (1990).

Kelsey, Harry. *Sir Francis Drake: The Queen's Pirate* (1998).

―――. *Sir John Hawkins: Queen Elizabeth's Slave Trader* (2002).

Kendall, C. *Private Men-of-War* (1931).

Konstam, Angus, and Angus McBride. *Elizabethan Sea Dogs, 1560–1605* (2000).

Lane, F. *Venetian Ships and Shipbuilders of the Renaissance* (1934).

―――. *Venice: A Maritime Republic* (1973).

Lev, Yakov, ed. *War and Society in the Eastern Mediterranean, 7th–15th Centuries* (1997).

Levathes, Louise. *When China Ruled the Seas: The Treasure Fleet of the Dragon Throne, 1405–1433* (1994; 1996).

Lewis, Archibald. *Naval Power in the Mediterranean, 500–1500* (1951).

Lewis, Michael. *Armada Guns* (1961).

Loades, David. *The Tudor Navy* (1992).

Love, R., ed. *Changing Interpretations and New Sources in Naval History* (1980).

Lydon, James G. *Pirates, Privateers, and Profits* (1970).

Mallett, M. E. *Florentine Galleys in the 15th Century* (1967).

Martin, Colin, and Geoffrey Parker. *The Spanish Armada* (1988).

McDermott, James. *Sir Martin Frobisher: Elizabethan Privateer* (2001).

Mollat, M. *Europe and the Sea* (1993).

Morrison, J., ed. *The Age of the Galley* (2003).

O'Connel, Daniel. *The Influence of Law on Sea Power* (1975).

Padfield, P. *Guns at Sea* (1973).

Parry, J. H. *Trade and Dominion* (1971).

Peers, Douglas, ed. *Warfare and Empires: Contact and Conflict Between European and Non-European Military and Maritime Forces and Cultures* (1997).

Selected Bibliography

Potter, E. *Sea Power* (1981).

Powell, J. *The Navy in the English Civil War* (1962).

Quinn, David, and A. Ryan. *England's Sea Empire, 1550–1642* (1983).

Reynolds, Clark. *Command of the Sea* (1974).

——. *Navies in History* (1998).

Rodgers, William. *Naval Warfare Under Oars, 4th–16th Centuries* (1940).

Rodríguez-Salgado, M., ed. *England, Spain, and the Gran Armada, 1585–1604* (1990).

Rose, Susan. *Medieval Naval Warfare, 1000–1500* (2002).

Scammel, G. V. *The First Imperial Age: European Overseas Expansion, 1400–1715* (1989; 1992).

——. *World Encompassed: The First European Maritime Empires, 800–1650* (1981).

Senior, C. *A Nation of Pirates* (1976).

Tenenti, Alberto. *Piracy and the Decline of Venice, 1580–1615* (1961).

Unger, Richard. *Cogs, Caravels, and Galleons* (1994).

——. *The Ship in the Medieval Economy* (1980).

Walton, Timothy. *Spanish Treasure Fleets* (1994).

Williams, Neville. *The Sea Dogs: Privateers, Plunder and Piracy in the Elizabethan Age* (1975).

Wills, John. *Pepper, Guns, and Parleys: The Dutch East India Company and China, 1622–1681* (1974).

Withey, L. *Voyages of Discovery: Captain Cook and the Exploration of the Pacific* (1989).

Weapons, Fortification, and Military Technology

Articles and Chapters

Bachrach, Bernard. "Charles Martel, Mounted Shock Combat, the Stirrup, and Feudalism," *Studies in Medieval and Renaissance History*, 7 (1970).

Bruhn de Hoffmeyer, Ada. "From Medieval Sword to Renaissance Rapier," *Gladius*, 2 (1963).

Buttin, François. "La lance et l'arrêt de cuirasse," *Archaeologia*, 99 (1965).

Clephan, R. "Ordnance of the 14th and 15th Centuries," *Archeological Journal*, 68 (1911).

Contamine, Philippe. "Les fortifications urbaines en France à la fin du Moyen Âge," *Revue historique*, 260 (1978).

Cook, Weston. "Cannon Conquest of Nasrid Spain," *Journal of Military History*, 57 (1993).

De Vries, Kelly. "Military-Surgical Practice and the Advent of Gunpowder Weaponry," *Canadian Bulletin of Medical History*, 7 (1990).

Dubled, H. "L'artillerie royale Française à l'époque de Charles VII et au début du règne de Louis XI: Les frères Bureau," *Memorial de l'artillerie Française*, 50 (1976).

Esper, Thomas. "Military Self-sufficiency and Weapons Technology in Muscovite Russia," *Slavic Review*, 28 (1969).

——. "Replacement of the Longbow by Firearms in the English Army," *Technology and Culture*, 6 (1965).

——. "A 16th Century Anti-Russian Arms Embargo," *Jahrbücher für Geschichte Osteuropas*, 15 (1967).

Finó, J-F. "L'artillerie en France à la fin du moyen âge," *Gladius*, 12 (1974).

——. "Le Feu et ses Usages Militaires," *Gladius*, 9 (1970).

——. "Machines de jet médiévales," *Gladius*, 10 (1972).

Foley, Vernard et al. "The Crossbow," *Scientific American* (April 1981).

Hale, J. R. "The Development of the Bastion, 1440–1534," in J. R. Hale, ed., *Europe in the Late Middle Ages* (1965).

———. "Gunpowder and the Renaissance," in C. Carter, ed., *From the Renaissance to the Reformation* (1965).

———. "War and Public Opinion in the 15th and 16th Centuries," *Past and Present*, 21 (1962).

Harbinson, Michael. "The Longbow as a Close Quarter Weapon in the 15th Century," *Hobilar* (1995).

Hess, A. "Firearms and the Decline of Ibn Kaldun's Military Elite," *Archivum Ottomanicum*, 4 (1972).

Hill, Donald. "Trebuchets," *Viator*, 4 (1973).

Hope-Taylor, Brian. "Norman Castles," *Scientific American* (March 1958).

Iqtidar, Alam. "The Origin and Development of Gunpowder Technology in India, 1250–1500," *Indian Historical Review*, 4 (1977).

Kenyon, John. "Early Artillery Fortifications in England and Wales," *Archeological Journal* (1981).

Kingra, Mahhinder. "The *trace italienne* and the Military Revolution during the Eighty Years' War," *Journal of Military History* (1993).

Lane, Frederic. "The Crossbow in the Nautical Revolution of the Middle Ages," *Explorations in Economic History*, 7 (1969–1970).

Larsen, Henrietta. "The Armor Business in the Middle Ages," *Business History Review*, 14 (1940).

McGuffe, T. "The Longbow as a Decisive Weapon," *History Today*, 5 (1955).

Rogers, Clifford. "The Efficacy of the Medieval Longbow," *War in History*, 5/2 (1998).

Smith, Robert D. "Artillery and the Hundred Years' War: Myth and Interpretation," in A. Curry and M. Hughes, eds., *Armies and Fortifications in the Hundred Years' War* (1994).

Stone, John. "Technology, Society, and the Infantry Revolution of the 14th Century," *Journal of Military History*, 68/2 (2004).

Tout, T. "Firearms in England in the 14th Century," *English Historical Review*, 26 (1911).

Vogt, John. "Saint Barbara's Legions: Portuguese Artillery in the Struggle for Morocco, 1415–1578," *Military Affairs*, 41 (1977).

Williams, Alan. "The Manufacture of Mail in Medieval Europe," *Gladius*, 13 (1980).

Books

Alm, Joat. *European Crossbows* (1994).

Anderson, W. *Castles of the Middle Ages* (1970).

Ashdown, C. *Armor and Weapons in the Middle Ages* (1925).

Baumgartner, Frederick. *From Spear to Flintlock* (1991).

Blair, Claude. *European Armor* (1958).

———. *European Armour, 1066–1700* (1958).

Bradbury, Jim. *The Medieval Archer* (1985).

———. *The Medieval Siege* (1992).

Brassey's Book of Body Armor (2000).

Brown, M. *Firearms in Colonial America, 1492–1792* (1980).

Bruhn de Hoffmeyer, Ada. *Arms and Armor in Spain* (1972).

Buchanan, Brenda J. *Gunpowder: The History of an International Technology* (1996).

Carman, W. *A History of Firearms* (1955).

Chatelain, A. *Architecture militaire mèdièvale* (1970).

Clark, John. *The Medieval Horse and Its Equipment, 1150–1450* (1995).

Crosby, Alfred. *Throwing Fire: Projectile Technology Through History* (2002).

Curry, Anne, and M. Hughes, eds. *Arms, Armies and Fortifications in the Hundred Years' War* (1999).

Davis, R. *The Medieval Warhorse* (1989).

DeVries, Kelly. *Guns and Men in Medieval Europe, 1200–1500* (2002).

———. *Infantry Warfare in the Early 14th Century* (1996).

———. *Medieval Military Technology* (1992).

Downing, Brian. *The Military Revolution and Political Change* (1992).

Duffy, C. *Siege Warfare: The Fortress in the Early Modern World, 1494–1660* (1979).

Duffy, M. *The Military Revolution and the State, 1500–1800* (1980).

Elgood, Robert, ed. *Islamic Arms and Armour* (1979).

Ellis, John. *Cavalry: The History of Mounted Warfare* (2002).

Eltis, David. *The Military Revolution in 16th Century Europe* (1995).

Finó, J-F. *Fortresses de la France médiévale* (1970).

Fuller, J.F.C. *Armaments and History* (1946).

Hale, John R. *Renaissance Fortification* (1977).

Hardy, R. *The Longbow: A Social and Military History* (1976).

Harley, J., and D. Woodward, eds. *A History of Cartography* (1992).

al-Hassan, A., and D. Hill. *Islamic Technology* (1986).

Hayward, J. F. *European Armour* (1951; 1965).

Headrich, D. *Tools of Empire* (1981).

Heath, E. *Archery: A Military History* (1980).

———. *Bow versus Gun* (1973).

Held, Robert. *The Age of Firearms* (1957; 1970).

Hime, H. W. *The Origin of Artillery* (1915; 1945).

Hogg, O. *Artillery: Its Origins, Heyday, and Decline* (1970).

———. *English Artillery: 1336–1716* (1963).

Hoppen, A. *The Fortification of Malta by the Order of St. John, 1530–1798* (1979).

Hyland, Ann. *The Medieval Warhorse* (1996).

Kenyon, John. *Medieval Fortifications* (1991).

Kishlansky, Mark. *The Rise of the New Model Army* (1979).

Klopsteg, Paul. *Turkish Archery and the Composite Bow* (1934; 1947).

Knox, MacGregor, and Williamson Murray, eds. *The Dynamics of Military Revolution, 1300–2050* (2001).

Latham, J., and W. Paterson. *Saracen Archery* (1970).

Lombarès, Michel. *Histoire de l'artillerie Française* (1984).

Lugs, Jaroslav. *Firearms Past and Present* (1973).

Lynn, John A. *Feeding Mars* (1995).

———, ed. *Tools of War: Instruments, Ideas, and Institutions of Warfare, 1445–1871* (1990).

McNeill, William H. *The Pursuit of Power: Technology, Armed Force and Society Since A.D. 1000* (1982).

Moykr, Joel. *Twenty-Five Centuries of Technological Change* (1990).

Needham, J. et al. *Military Technology* (1986).

Needham, Joseph. *Science and Civilization in China*, Vol. 5/Part 7: *The Gunpowder Epoch* (1986).

Nicolle, David. *Arms and Armor of the Crusading Era, 1050–1350* (1988).

———, ed. *Companion to Medieval Arms and Armour* (2002).

Norris, John. *Artillery: A History* (2000).

Oakeshott, R. Ewart. *European Weapons and Armor* (1980).

———. *A Knight and His Armour* (1961).

———. *A Knight and His Weapons* (1964).

———. *Records of the Medieval Sword* (1991).

———. *The Sword in the Age of Chivalry* (1964).

O'Connell, Robert L. *Of Arms and Men* (1989).

O'Neil, B. H. *Castles and Cannon* (1960).

Parker, Geoffrey. *The Military Revolution*, 2nd ed. (1996).

Partington, J. R. *A History of Greek Fire and Gunpowder* (1960).

Patrick, John Merton. *Artillery and Warfare during the Thirteenth and Fourteenth Centuries* (1961).

Payne-Gallwey, Ralph. *The Crossbow* (1958).

Pepper, Simon, and Nicholas Adams. *Firearms & Fortifications* (1986).

Pope, S. T. *Bows and Arrows* (1962).

Preston, Richard et al. *Men in Arms* (1962).

Pringle, D. *The Red Tower* (1986).

Pryor, J. H. *Geography, Technology, and War* (1988).

Reid, William. *The Lore of Arms: A Concise History of Weaponry* (1984).

Reyerson, E., and F. Powe, eds. *The Medieval Castle* (1984).

Ritter, R. *L'architecture militaire mèdiévale* (1974).

Roberts, Keith. *The Matchlock Musketeer, 1588–1688* (2002).

Rodgers, R. *Siege Warfare in the 12th Century* (1992).

Rogers, Clifford, ed. *The Military Revolution Debate* (1995).

Rogers, Hugh. *Artillery Through the Ages* (1971).

Russell, H. *Oriental Armour* (1967).

Thompson, A. *Military Architecture in Medieval England* (1912).

Thompson, M. W. *The Decline of the Castle* (1987).

Toy, Sidney. *A History of Fortification* (1955).

van Creveld, Martin. *Command in War* (1985).

———. *Supplying War* (1977).

———. *Technology and War* (1989).

White, Lynn. *Medieval Technology and Social Change* (1962).

Web Sites of Special Interest

General

All Empires.com	http://www.allempires.com
BBC Wars and Conflicts	http://www.bbc.co.uk/history/war/launch_gms_bfacademy.shtml
ehistory.com	http://www.ehistory.com/index.cfm
Historical Journals	http://www.deremilitari.org/link/newlinks6.htm
Historical Journals Online	http://www2.tntech.edu/history/journals.html
History Journals Guide	http://www.history-journals.de
History Learning Site	http://www.historylearningsite.co.uk
History of Warfare	http://www.zum.de/whkmla/military/warindex.html
International History Review	http://www.sfu.ca/ihr
Journal of Military History	http://www.smh-hq.org/jmh
Military History Magazine	http://www.historynet.com/mh
Military History Online	http://www.militaryhistoryonline.com
Modern History Sourcebook	http://www.fordham.edu/halsall/mod/modsbook.html

Selected Bibliography

On War.com	http://www.onwar.com
Society for Military History	http://www.smh-hq.org
War and Society	http://www.deremilitari.org/RESOURCES/ ARTICLES/warandsociety.htm

Wars by Region

Arab and Ottoman warfare	http://www.zum.de/whkmla/military/asmin/ milxottomananatolia.html
	http://www2.let.uu.nl/Solis/anpt/ejos/EJOS-1.html
Chinese warfare	http://www.sonshi.com
	http://www.usc.edu/isd/archives/arc/libraries/ eastasian/china/toqing.html
Crusades	http://crusades.boisestate.edu
	http://www.callisto.si.usherb.ca/~croisade/ Byzance.htm
	http://www.cathares.org
	http://www.crusades.dk
	http://www.deremilitari.org/NEWS/ crusadesjournal.htm
	http://www.unf.edu/classes/crusades/ crusadesbibliography.htm
	http://xenophongroup.com/montjoie/albigens.htm
	http://xenophongroup.com/montjoie/crusade2.htm
Early Modern Baltic States	http://66.188.129.72:5980/History/ PreModernEurope/index.htm
Eighty Years' War	http://www.nnp.org/project/historical.html
English Civil Wars	http://easyweb.easynet.co.uk/~crossby/ECW
	http://www.bbc.co.uk/history/war/englishcivilwar/ index.shtml
	http://www.british-civil-wars.co.uk/index.htm
	http://www.kingorparliament.com
	http://www.open2.net/civilwar/index.html
French Civil Wars	http://www.lepg.org/wars.htm
Hundred Years' War	http://www.hyw.com/books/history/1_Help_C.htm
	http://xenophongroup.com/montjoie/hyw_fp.htm
Hussite Wars	http://archiv.radio.cz/history_96/history05.html
Indian warfare	http://www.mewarindia.com/history/ indexhissyn.html
Japanese warfare	http://www.samurai-archives.com/index.html
Medieval warfare	http://www.cc.jyu.fi/~mirator/ukmira.html
	http://www.chronique.com
	http://www.cusd.claremont.edu/~ccandy/his/ medmil.html
	http://www.deremilitari.org
	http://www.deremilitari.org/JMMH/jmmh.htm
	http://www.harnois.fr/hm
	http://www.humnet.ucla.edu/cmrs/Publications/ Pub_default.htm
	http://www.mtp.dk/periodicals/classica/index.htm

	http://www.revistamirabilia.com
	http://www.secretsofthenormaninvasion.com
	http://xenophongroup.com/montjoie/oriflam.htm
Mongols	http://www.friesian.com/mongol.htm#crimea
Polish warfare	http://www.allempires.com/empires/polish_lit_full/polish_lit1.htm#7
	http://www.jasinski.co.uk/wojna/index.htm
Reconquista	http://www.deremilitari.org
Safavid Empire	http://www.ucalgary.ca/applied_history/tutor/islam/empires
Swiss warfare	http://www.geschichte-schweiz.ch/alte-eidgenossenschaft-1291.html
Thirty Years' War	http://www.bodley.ox.ac.uk/dept/readerserv/history/thirty.htm
	http://www.historylearningsite.co.uk/thirty_years_war.htm
	http://www.lwl.org/LWL/Kultur/Westfaelischer_Friede
	http://www.uni-potsdam.de/u/geschichte/mdk
	http://www.zum.de/whkmla/military/17cen/xxxywar.html
Wars of the Roses	http://www.bbc.co.uk/history/timelines/england/lmid_wars_roses.shtml
	http://www.warsoftheroses.com

Weapons

Early firearms	http://www.geocities.com/Yosemite/Campground/8551
	http://xenophongroup.com/montjoie/gp_wpns.htm
Fortifications	http://pages.ca.inter.net/~ttoyooka/oshiro
	http://www.castles-of-britain.com
	http://www.castlesontheweb.com/search/Medieval_Studies
	http://www.castlewales.com/home.html
	http://www.deremilitari.org/RESOURCES/ARTICLES/bachrach1.htm
Medieval arms and armor	http://netsword.com
	http://www.chronique.com/Library/Armour/armour.htm
	http://www.maney.co.uk/search?fwaction=show&fwid=464
	http://www.vikingsword.com
Non-gunpowder artillery	http://members.iinet.net.au/~rmine/seemore.html
	http://www.cathares.org/mma-trebuchet.html
	http://www.pbs.org/wgbh/nova/lostempires/trebuchet
	http://xenophongroup.com/montjoie/ngp_arty.htm

Index

Index

Index

Index

Index

Index

Index

Index

Index

Index

Index

Index

Index

Index

Index

Index

Index

About the Author

CATHAL J. NOLAN is Executive Director of Boston University's International History Institute, and Associate Professor of History. He is the author of the multiple award-winning *The Greenwood Encyclopedia of International Relations* (Greenwood, 2002) and the award-winning *Notable U.S. Ambassadors since 1775: A Biographical Dictionary* (Greenwood, 1997). Dr. Nolan has also authored, co-authored, or edited many books, including *Ethics and Statecraft: The Moral Dimension of International Affairs* (Praeger, 2004); *Power and Responsibility in World Affairs: Reformation versus Transformation* (Praeger, 2004); *NATO for a New Century: Atlanticism and European Security* (with Carl Hodge, Praeger, 2002); and *Principled Democracy: Security and Rights in U.S. Foreign Policy* (Praeger, 1993).